COST AND MANAGEMENT ACCOUNTING 7TH EDITION
AN INTRODUCTION

2.2014

COLIN DRURY

COST AND MANAGEMENT ACCOUNTING

AN INTRODUCTION

SEVENTH EDITION

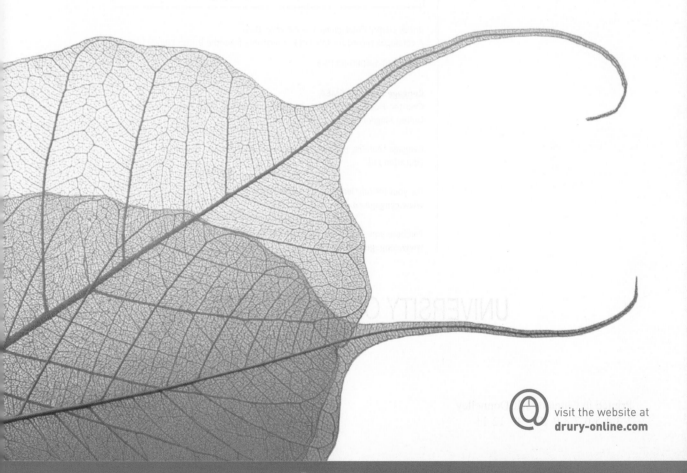

visit the website at
drury-online.com

SOUTH-WESTERN
CENGAGE Learning

Australia • Brazil • Japan • Korea • Mexico • Singapore • Spain • United Kingdom • United States

SOUTH-WESTERN
CENGAGE Learning

Cost and Management Accounting
An Introduction
Seventh edition
Colin Drury

Publishing Director: Linden Harris

Publisher: Brendan George

Editorial Assistant: Helen Green

Content project Editor: Lucy Arthy

Production Controller: Eyvett Davis

Marketing Manager: Amanda Cheung

Typesetter: Integra, India

Cover design: Adam Renvoize

For product information and technology assistance, contact
emea.info@cengage.com.
For permission to use material from this text or product,
and for permission queries,
email **emea.permissions@cengage.com.**

British Library Cataloguing-in-Publication Data
A catalogue record for this book is available from the British Library.

ISBN: 978-1-4080-3213-8

Cengage Learning EMEA
Cheriton House, North Way, Andover, Hampshire, SP10 5BE
United Kingdom

Cengage Learning products are represented in Canada by Nelson Education Ltd.

For your lifelong learning solutions, visit
www.cengage.co.uk

Purchase your next print book, e-book or e-chapter at
www.cengagebrain.co.uk

Printed in China by RR Donnelley
2 3 4 5 6 7 8 9 10 – 13 12 11

BRIEF CONTENTS

CONTENTS

PART 2 COST ACCUMULATION FOR INVENTORY VALUATION AND PROFIT MEASUREMENT 45

PART 3 INFORMATION FOR DECISION-MAKING

9 COST–VOLUME–PROFIT ANALYSIS

10 COST ESTIMATION AND COST BEHAVIOUR

11 MEASURING RELEVANT COSTS AND REVENUES FOR DECISION-MAKING

PREFACE AND ACKNOWLEDGEMENTS

The aim of the seventh edition of this book is to provide an introduction to the theory and practice of cost and management accounting. A cost accounting system is concerned with accumulating costs for inventory valuation to meet external financial accounting and internal monthly or quarterly profit measurement requirements. A management accounting system accumulates, classifies, summarizes and reports information that will assist employees within an organization in their decision-making, planning, control and performance measurement activities. This book is concerned with both cost and management accounting, with similar emphasis being placed on both systems.

Intended primarily for students who are pursuing a one-year cost and management accounting course, the book is ideal for those approaching this subject for the first time. The more advanced topics contained in the final stages of the cost and management accounting syllabuses of the professional accountancy bodies and final year degree courses are not included. These topics are included in the author's successful *Management and Cost Accounting,* the seventh edition of which is also published by Cengage Learning EMEA.

Feedback from instructors in a large number of universities indicated that they had found the content, structure and presentation of *Management and Cost Accounting* extremely satisfactory and most appropriate for students pursuing a two-year management accounting course at an advanced professional or degree level. They also indicated that there was a need for a book (based on *Management and Cost Accounting)* tailored to meet the requirements of a one-year introductory course in cost and management accounting. Many lecturers, in particular those running introductory courses, felt there was a need for an introductory text which covered the required ground in an academically sound manner and which was also appropriate for students on non-advanced courses. This book is aimed specifically at students who are pursuing a one-year non-advanced cost and management accountancy course and is particularly suitable for the following courses:

- Foundation/introductory professional accountancy (e.g. Chartered Association of Certified Accountants, Chartered Institute of Management Accountants and one-year college foundation courses).
- Association of Accounting Technicians.
- Higher National Certificate and Diploma in Business and Finance.
- A first-level course for undergraduate accounting and finance or business students.

An introductory course in financial accounting is not a prerequisite, although many students will have undertaken such a course. The flexibility provided by modular courses can result in introductory classes consisting of a group of students not studying management accounting beyond an intermediate level and a further group continuing their studies beyond the intermediate level. *Cost and Management Accounting: An Introduction* is appropriate for the former group and *Management and Cost Accounting* can be adopted by the latter. Because much of the content and assessment material in *Cost and Management Accounting: An Introduction* has been extracted from *Management and Cost Accounting,* lecturers can assign identical reading and assessment and also recommend two separate books that are geared to the specific requirements of the students.

STRUCTURE AND PLAN OF THE BOOK

In writing this book I have adopted the same structure as that in *Management and Cost Accounting.* The major theme is that different financial information is required for different purposes. The framework is based on the principle that there are three ways of constructing accounting information. The first is cost accounting with its emphasis on producing product costs for allocating costs between cost of goods sold and inventories to meet external and internal financial accounting inventory valuation and profit measurement requirements. The second is the notion of decision-relevant costs with the emphasis on providing information to help managers to make good decisions. The third is responsibility accounting and performance measurement which focuses on both financial and non-financial information, in particular the assignment of costs and revenues to responsibility centres.

This book has 15 chapters divided into four parts. Part 1 consists of two chapters and provides an introduction to cost and management accounting and a framework for studying the remaining chapters. The following three parts reflect the three different ways of constructing accounting information. Part 2 consists of six chapters and is entitled 'Cost Accumulation for Inventory Valuation and Profit Measurement'. This section focuses mainly on assigning costs to products to separate the costs incurred during a period between costs of goods sold and the closing inventory valuation for internal and external profit measurement. The extent to which product costs accumulated for inventory valuation and profit measurement should be adjusted for meeting decision-making, cost control and performance measurement requirements is also considered briefly. Part 3 consists of four chapters and is entitled 'Information for Decision-making'. Here the focus is on measuring and identifying those costs which are relevant for different types of decisions. The title of Part 4 is 'Information for Planning, Control and Performance Measurement'. It consists of three chapters and concentrates on the process of translating goals and objectives into specific activities and the resources that are required, via the short-term (budgeting) and long-term planning processes, to achieve the goals and objectives. In addition, the management control systems that organizations use are described and the role that management accounting control systems play within the overall control process is examined. The emphasis here is on the accounting process as a means of providing information to help managers control the activities for which they are responsible.

In devising a framework around the three methods of constructing financial information there is a risk that the student will not appreciate that the three categories use many common elements, that they overlap, and that they constitute a single overall management accounting system, rather than three independent systems. I have taken steps to minimize this risk in each section by emphasizing why financial information for one purpose should or should not be adjusted for another purpose. In short, each section of the book is not presented in isolation and an integrative approach has been taken.

MAJOR CHANGES IN THE CONTENT OF THE SEVENTH EDITION

Feedback from a lecturers' survey from users of the sixth edition indicated that many students found cost and management accounting to be a complex subject and there was a need for a simplified and more accessible text. The major objective in writing the seventh edition has therefore been to produce a less complex and more accessible text. This objective created the need to thoroughly review the entire content of the sixth edition and to rewrite, simplify and improve the presentation of much of the existing material. Most of the chapters have been rewritten. The end result has been the most extensive rewrite of the text since the book was first published.

Feedback from the lecturers' survey indicated that some of the more advanced and complex topics in the sixth edition were not included in their teaching programmes whereas a minority of respondents indicated that the same topics were included in their teaching programmes. In order to meet the different requirements of lecturers, some of the advanced and more complex topics from the sixth edition have been transferred from the text to learning notes that can be accessed by students and lecturers on the companion website. Examples of topics that are now incorporated as learning notes within the seventh edition include the application of linear programming to management accounting, decision-making under conditions of risk and uncertainty and responsibility accounting in profit and investment centres. All learning notes are appropriately referenced within the text. For example, at appropriate points within specific chapters the reader's attention is drawn to the fact that, for a particular topic, more complex issues exist and that a discussion of these issues can be found by referring to a specific learning note on the open access website.

The feedback relating to the structure and content of the previous editions has been extremely favourable and therefore only minor changes have been made to the existing structure, while incorporating the extensive changes that have been made to the content of the new edition. The sixth edition included the application of linear programming to management accounting (Chapter 12), decision-making under conditions of risk and uncertainty (Chapter 14) and a chapter on capital investment appraisal (Chapter 15). In response to feedback from lecturers and examination of the syllabuses of the professional management accounting bodies, these chapters have been deleted from the seventh edition and the content relating to chapters 12 and 14 (sixth edition) can now be accessed on the open access dedicated website. No other changes have been made to the structure of the text.

Finally, much of the assessment material has been extensively changed and new assessment material added. In addition, many 'Real World Views' that provide examples of the practical application of management accounting have been replaced by more recent examples that provide better illustrations of the practical applications. Questions have been added to the 'Real World Views' to encourage readers to think about the issues involved.

Case studies

Over 20 case studies are available on the dedicated website for this book. A list of these case studies is provided in a separate section immediately following the final chapter. Both lecturers and students can download these case studies from the open access section of the website. Teaching notes for the case studies can be downloaded only by lecturers from the password-protected lecturers' section of the website. The cases generally cover the content of several chapters and contain questions to which there is no ideal answer. They are intended to encourage independent thought and initiative and to relate and apply your understanding of the content of this book in more uncertain situations. They are also intended to develop your critical thinking and analytical skills.

International focus

The book has now become an established text in many different countries throughout the world. Because of this a more international focus has been adopted. A major feature is the presentation of boxed exhibits of surveys and practical applications of management accounting in companies in many different countries, particularly the European mainland. To simplify the presentation, however, the UK pound monetary unit has mostly been used throughout the book. Most of the assessment material has incorporated questions set by the UK professional accountancy bodies. These questions are, however, appropriate for worldwide use.

Assessment material

Throughout this book simple illustrations have been provided. You can check your understanding of each chapter by answering the review questions. Each question is followed by page numbers within parentheses that indicate where in the text the answers to specific questions can be found. More complex review problems are also set at the end of each chapter to enable students to pursue certain topics in more depth. Fully worked solutions to the review problems are provided in a separate section at the end of the book.

This book is part of an integrated educational package. A *Students' Manual* that includes additional review problems and accompanying answers is available to download from the accompanying website. Additional review problems and case studies are available for students and lecturers to access on the accompanying website www.drury-online.com. Solutions to the review problems and case study teaching notes are only available to lecturers on the lecturer's password-protected section of the website.

Also available for adopting lecturers to download from the companion website is an Examview® testbank, offering over 1000 questions tailored to the content of the book, for use in classroom assessment.

In recognition of the increasing need for the integration of IT teaching into the curriculum, this book is accompanied by an online *Spreadsheet Applications Manual,* which has been written by Dr Alicia Gazely. This explains basic spreadsheet techniques and then builds up ten spreadsheet models which illustrate, and allow students to explore, examples in the main text. The spreadsheets, guidance notes and online access are available to teachers on adoption. Further details of this package are given in the section covering the dedicated website below.

SUPPLEMENTARY MATERIAL

Dedicated website

The dedicated website can be found at www.drury-online.com. The lecturer section is password-protected and the password is available free to lecturers who confirm their adoption of the seventh edition. Lecturers should complete the registration form on the website to apply for their password, which will then be sent to them by e-mail. The following range of material is available:

For students and lecturers (open access):

Learning notes

The learning notes relate to either specific topics that may be only applicable to the curriculum for a minority of the readers, or a discussion of topics where more complex issues are involved that not all readers may wish to pursue. All learning notes are appropriately cross-referenced within the text to the website. For example, at appropriate points within specific chapters the reader's attention is drawn to the fact that, for a particular topic, more complex issues exist and that a discussion of these issues can be found by referring to a specific learning note on the student resources section of the website.

Case studies

Internationally focused case studies. (Teaching notes to accompany the cases are available in the password-protected lecturer area of the website.)

Examview® interactive self-test questions

(compiled by Wayne Fiddler of Huddersfield University)

Interactive multiple choice questions to accompany each chapter. The student takes the test online to check their grasp of the key points in each chapter. Detailed feedback is provided for each question if the student chooses the wrong answer.

PowerPoint™ slides

PowerPoint presentations to accompany each chapter.

Guide to Excel

(written by Steve Rickaby)

A PDF guide to Microsoft Excel giving you all the information you need to train yourself in basic Excel skills.

Links to accounting and finance sites on the web

Including links to the main accounting firms, accounting magazines and journals, and careers and job search pages.

Definitions of accounting and finance terms

A handy introduction to accounting and finance techniques, disciplines and concepts

Students' manual and extra review problems

The *students' manual* is now provided free from the site in PDF (Portable Document Format), the *students' manual* contains further questions for students which are accompanied by the supporting answers.

Extra review problems are also provided and solutions to these appear in the *instructor's manual* on the lecturer's password-protected section of the website.

For lecturers only (password protected)

ExamView®

This testbank and test generator provides a huge amount of different types of questions, allowing lecturers to create online, paper and local area network (LAN) tests.

Instructor's manual

Available to download free from the site in PDF (Portable Document Format), the manual includes answers to the extra review problems on the open access website.

Teaching notes to the case studies

To accompany the case studies available in the student area of the website.

Spreadsheet exercises

(compiled and designed by Alicia Gazely of Nottingham Trent University)

Created in Excel to accompany the self assessment exercises in the book, the exercises can be saved by the lecturer to their own directories and distributed to students as each topic is covered. Each exercise explains a basic spreadsheet technique which illustrates, and allows the student to explore, examples in the main text.

PowerPoint^{TM} slides

PowerPoint presentations to accompany each chapter.

Overhead transparencies

Available to download as pdf files.

ACKNOWLEDGEMENTS

I am indebted to many individuals for their ideas and assistance in preparing this and previous editions of the book.

Rona O'Brien, Sheffield Hallam University

Jonathan Rooks, South Bank University

Pieter Koortzen, Polytechnic of Namibia

John MacKenzie, Napier University

Lau Siok Hwa, Multimedia University, Malaysia

Chong Chin Wei, Multimedia University, Malaysia

Mark Pilkington, University of Westminster

Darren Duxbury, Leeds University

Norwood Whittle, University College Northampton

Elaine Shellard, University of Glamorgan

Professor M B Adams, Swansea University

Kirsten Wallace, University of Glasgow

A Abofaid, Manchester Metropolitan University

Cathy Knowles, Oxford Brookes University

George Arthur Qua-Enoo, University of Johannesburg

Venus Leung, Lingnan University

Iris Kwok, University of Hong Kong

Shirley Venzke, Vaal University of Technology

I am also indebted to Stephen Wellings and Helen Green at Cengage Learning for their valuable publishing advice, support and assistance; and to all of the staff at Cengage Learning who have worked on the book. My appreciation goes also to the Chartered Institute of Management Accountants, the Chartered Association of Certified Accountants, the Institute of Chartered Accountants in England and Wales, and the Association of Accounting Technicians for permission to reproduce examination questions. Questions from the Chartered Institute of Management Accountants' examinations are designated CIMA; questions from the Chartered Association of Certified Accountants are designated ACCA; questions from the Institute of Chartered Accountants in England and Wales are designated ICAEW; and questions from the Association of Accounting Technicians are designated AAT. The answers at the end of this book and in the accompanying teachers' and students' guides to this book are my own and are in no way the approved solutions of the above professional bodies. Finally, and most importantly, I would like to thank my wife, Bronwen, for converting the original manuscript of the earlier editions into final typewritten form and for her continued help and support throughout the seven editions of this book.

WALK THROUGH TOUR

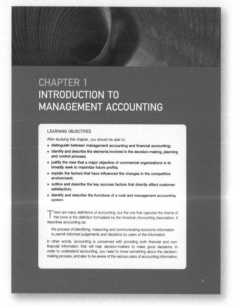

Learning objectives Listed at the start of each chapter, highlighting the core coverage that you should acquire after studying each chapter.

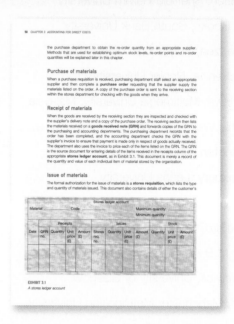

Exhibits Illustrations of accounting techniques and information are presented throughout the text.

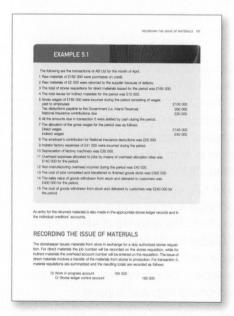

Examples Worked accounting examples are shown throughout the text.

Key terms and concepts Highlighted throughout the text where they first appear alerting the student to the core concepts and techniques.

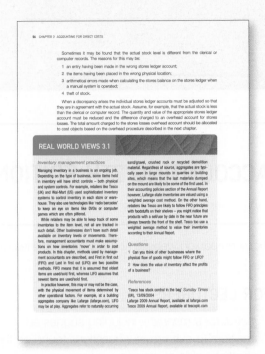

Real world views Real world cases are provided throughout the text, they help to demonstrate the theory in practice and practical application of accounting in real companies internationally.

Key examination points Important examination tips are presented at the end of each chapter. They show the main concepts to be learnt from the chapter when studying for your examinations.

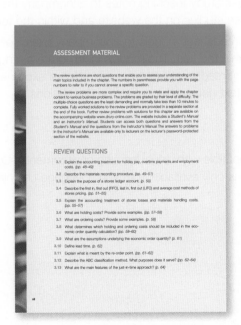

Review questions Review questions allow revision of the main issues and concepts learnt within the chapter. Page numbers next to the questions show where the answers can be found.

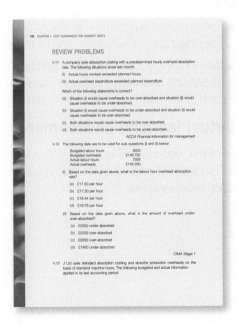

Review problems Review problems allow you to relate and apply the chapter content to various business problems. Fully worked solutions are found in the back of the text.

ABOUT THE WEBSITE

A companion website accompanies

COST AND MANAGEMENT ACCOUNTING 7TH EDITION
COLIN DRURY

Visit the *Cost and Management Accounting*, 7th edition companion website at www.drury-online.com to find further teaching and learning material including:

FOR STUDENTS

- Learning notes for more complex and advanced topics
- Downloadable PowerPoint slides
- Multiple-choice self-test questions for each chapter
- Case studies with accompanying questions
- Related weblinks
- Extra review questions – answers are provided on the lecturer's side of the site
- *Student's manual* – including additional questions and accompanying answers, now available free to download from the website

FOR LECTURERS

- *Instructor's manual* – including suggested answers to extra review questions found on the student's side of the site
- ExamView® testbank and test generator software
- Downloadable PowerPoint slides
- Case study teaching notes to accompany the case studies on the website and within the text
- Spreadsheet models to accompany exercises within the text. The models incorporate a range of spreadsheet techniques which are explained in text notes adjacent to the calculations

Virtual learning environment

All of the web material is available in a format that is compatible with virtual learning environments such as Blackboard and WebCT. This version of the product is only available from your Cengage Learning sales representative.

PART 1
INTRODUCTION TO MANAGEMENT AND COST ACCOUNTING

1   Introduction to management accounting

2   An introduction to cost terms and concepts

The objective of this section is to provide an introduction to cost and management accounting. In Chapter 1 we define accounting and distinguish between financial, management and cost accounting. This is followed by an examination of the role of management accounting in providing information to managers for decision-making, planning, control and performance measurement. We also consider the important changes that are taking place in the business environment. As you progress through the book you will learn how these changes are influencing management accounting systems. In Chapter 2 the basic cost terms and concepts that are used in the cost and management accounting literature are described.

CHAPTER 1
INTRODUCTION TO
MANAGEMENT ACCOUNTING

LEARNING OBJECTIVES

After studying this chapter, you should be able to:

- distinguish between management accounting and financial accounting;
- identify and describe the elements involved in the decision-making, planning and control process;
- justify the view that a major objective of commercial organizations is to broadly seek to maximize future profits;
- explain the factors that have influenced the changes in the competitive environment;
- outline and describe the key success factors that directly affect customer satisfaction;
- identify and describe the functions of a cost and management accounting system.

There are many definitions of accounting, but the one that captures the theme of this book is the definition formulated by the American Accounting Association. It describes accounting as:

the process of identifying, measuring and communicating economic information to permit informed judgements and decisions by users of the information.

In other words, accounting is concerned with providing both financial and non-financial information that will help decision-makers to make good decisions. In order to understand accounting, you need to know something about the decision-making process, and also to be aware of the various users of accounting information.

During the past two decades many organizations in both the manufacturing and service sectors have faced dramatic changes in their business environment. Deregulation and extensive competition from overseas companies in domestic markets has resulted in a situation where most companies now operate in a highly competitive global market. At the same time there has been a significant reduction in product life cycles arising from technological innovations and the need to meet increasingly discriminating customer demands. To succeed in today's highly competitive environment, companies have made customer satisfaction an overriding priority. They have also adopted new management approaches and manufacturing companies have changed their manufacturing systems and invested in new technologies. These changes have had a significant influence on management accounting systems.

The aim of this first chapter is to give you the background knowledge that will enable you to achieve a more meaningful insight into the issues and problems of cost and management accounting that are discussed in the book. We begin by looking at the users of accounting information and identifying their requirements. This is followed by a description of the decision-making process and the changing business environment. Finally, the different functions of management accounting are described.

THE USERS OF ACCOUNTING INFORMATION

Accounting is a language that communicates economic information to people who have an interest in an organization. These people fall into several groups (e.g. managers, shareholders and potential investors, employees, creditors and the government) and each of these groups has its own requirements for information:

- Managers require information that will assist them in their decision-making and control activities; for example, information is needed on the estimated selling prices, costs, demand, competitive position and profitability of various products/services that are provided by the organization.

- Shareholders require information on the value of their investment and the income that is derived from their shareholding.

- Employees require information on the ability of the firm to meet wage demands and avoid redundancies.

- Creditors and the providers of loan capital require information on a firm's ability to meet its financial obligations.

- Government agencies such as the Central Statistical Office collect accounting information and require such information as the details of sales activity, profits, investments, stocks, dividends paid, the proportion of profits absorbed by taxation and so on. In addition, HM Revenue & Customs needs information on the amount of profits that are subject to taxation. All this information is important for determining policies to manage the economy.

The need to provide accounting information is not confined to business organizations. Individuals sometimes have to provide information about their own financial situation; for example, if you want to take out a mortgage or a personal loan, you may be asked for details of your private financial affairs. Non-profit-making organizations such as churches, charitable organizations, clubs and government units such as local authorities, also require accounting information for decision-making, and for reporting the results of their activities. For example, a tennis club will require information on the cost of undertaking its various activities so that a decision can be made as to the amount of the annual subscription that it will charge to its members. Similarly, municipal authorities need information on the costs of undertaking specific activities so that decisions can be made as to which activities will be undertaken and the resources that must be raised to finance them.

As you can see, there are many different users of accounting information who require information for decision-making. The objective of accounting is to provide sufficient information to meet the needs of the various users at the lowest possible cost. Obviously, the benefit derived from using an information system for decision-making must be greater than the cost of operating the system.

The users of accounting information can be divided into two categories:

1 internal users within the organization;
2 external users such as shareholders, creditors and regulatory agencies, outside the organization.

It is possible to distinguish between two branches of accounting, which reflect the internal and external users of accounting information. **Management accounting** is concerned with the provision of information to people within the organization to help them make better decisions and improve the efficiency and effectiveness of existing operations, whereas **financial accounting** is concerned with the provision of information to external parties outside the organization. Thus, management accounting could be called internal reporting and financial accounting could be called external reporting. This book concentrates on management accounting.

DIFFERENCES BETWEEN MANAGEMENT ACCOUNTING AND FINANCIAL ACCOUNTING

The major differences between these two branches of accounting are:

- *Legal requirements.* There is a statutory requirement for public limited companies to produce annual financial accounts regardless of whether or not management regards this information as useful. Management accounting, by contrast, is entirely optional and information should be produced only if it is considered that the benefits it offers management exceed the cost of collecting it.

- *Focus on individual parts or segments of the business.* Financial accounting reports describe the whole of the business, whereas management accounting focuses on small parts of the organization; for example the cost and profitability of products, services, departments, customers and activities.

- *Generally accepted accounting principles.* Financial accounting statements must be prepared to conform with the legal requirements and the generally accepted accounting principles established by the regulatory bodies such as the Financial Accounting Standards Board (FASB) in the USA, the Accounting Standards Board (ASB) in the UK and the International Accounting Standards Board. These requirements are essential to ensure uniformity and consistency, which make intercompany and historical comparisons possible. Financial accounting data should be verifiable and objective. In contrast, management accountants are not required to adhere to generally accepted accounting principles when providing managerial information for internal purposes. Instead, the focus is on serving management's needs and providing information that is useful to managers when they are carrying out their decision-making, planning and control functions.

- *Time dimension.* Financial accounting reports what has happened in the past in an organization, whereas management accounting is concerned with *future* information as well as past information. Decisions are concerned with *future* events and management, therefore, requires details of expected *future* costs and revenues.

- *Report frequency.* A detailed set of financial accounts is published annually and less detailed accounts are published semi-annually. Management usually requires information more quickly than this if it is to act on it. Consequently management accounting reports on various activities may be prepared at daily, weekly or monthly intervals.

THE DECISION-MAKING PROCESS

Information produced by management accountants must be judged in the light of its ultimate effect on the outcome of decisions. It is therefore important to have an understanding of the *decision-making process.*

Figure 1.1 presents a diagram of the decision-making, planning and control process. The first four stages represent the decision-making or planning process. The final two stages represent the **control process**, which is the process of measuring and correcting actual performance to ensure that the alternatives that are chosen and the plans for implementing them are carried out. We will now examine the stages in more detail.

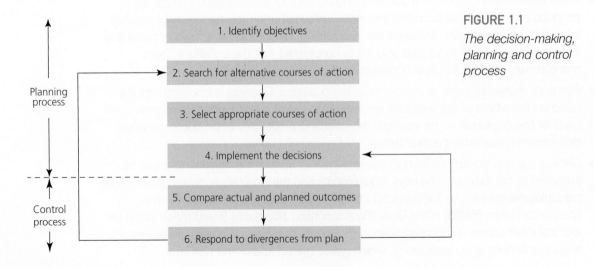

FIGURE 1.1

The decision-making, planning and control process

Identifying objectives

Before good decisions can be made there must be some guiding aim or direction that will enable the decision-makers to assess the desirability of choosing one course of action over another. Hence, the first stage in the decision-making process should be to specify the company's goals or organizational objectives.

This is an area where there is considerable controversy. Economic theory normally assumes that firms seek to maximize profits for the owners of the firm or, more precisely, the maximization of shareholders' wealth. Some writers (e.g. Simon, 1959) believe that many managers are content to find a plan that provides satisfactory profits rather than to maximize profits. Clearly it is too simplistic to say that the only objective of a business firm is to maximize profits. Some managers seek to establish a power base and build an empire. Another common goal is security, and the removal of uncertainty regarding the future may override the pure profit motive. Organizations may also pursue more specific objectives, such as producing high quality products or being the market leader within a particular market segment. Nevertheless, the view adopted in this book is that, broadly, firms seek to maximize future profits. There are two reasons for us to concentrate on this objective:

1 It is unlikely that any other objective is as widely applicable in measuring the ability of the organization to survive in the future.
2 It is unlikely that maximizing future profits can be realized in practice, but by establishing the principles necessary to achieve this objective you will learn how to increase profits.

The search for alternative courses of action

The second stage in the decision-making model is a search for a range of possible courses of action (or **strategies**) that might enable the objectives to be achieved. If the management of a company concentrates entirely on its present product range and markets, and market shares and profits are allowed to decline, there is a danger that the company will be unable to survive in the future. If the business is to survive, management must identify potential opportunities and threats in the current environment and take specific steps now so that the organization will not be taken by surprise by future developments. In particular, the company should consider one or more of the following courses of action:

1 developing *new* products for sale in *existing* markets;
2 developing *new* products for *new* markets;
3 developing *new* markets for *existing* products.

The search for alternative courses of action involves the acquisition of information concerning future opportunities and environments; it is the most difficult and important stage of the decision-making process.

Select appropriate alternative courses of action

In order for managers to make an informed choice of action, data about the different alternatives must be gathered. For example, managers might ask to see projected figures on:

- the potential growth rates of the alternative activities under consideration;
- the market share the company is likely to achieve;
- projected profits for each alternative activity.

The alternatives should be evaluated to identify which course of action best satisfies the objectives of an organization. The selection of the most advantageous alternative is central to the whole decision-making process and the provision of information that facilitates this choice is one of the major functions of management accounting. We shall return to this subject in Chapters 9–12.

Implementation of the decisions

Once the course of action has been selected, it should be implemented as part of the budgeting and long-term planning process. The **budget** is a financial plan for implementing the decisions that management has made. The budgets for all of the various decisions a company takes are expressed in terms of cash inflows and outflows, and sales revenues and expenses. These budgets are merged together into a single unifying statement of the organization's expectations for future periods. This statement is known as a *master budget* and consists of budgeted profit and cash flow statements. The budgeting process communicates to everyone in the organization the part that they are expected to play in implementing management's decisions. We shall examine the budgeting process in Chapter 13.

Comparing actual and planned outcomes and responding to divergencies from plan

The final stages in the process outlined in Figure 1.1 involve comparing actual and planned outcomes and responding to divergencies from plan. The managerial function of **control** consists of the measurement, reporting and subsequent correction of performance in an attempt to ensure that the firm's objectives and plans are achieved.

To monitor performance, the accountant produces **performance reports** and presents them to the managers who are responsible for implementing the various decisions. These reports compare actual outcomes (actual costs and revenues) with planned outcomes (budgeted costs and revenues) and should be issued at regular intervals. Performance reports provide feedback information and should highlight those activities that do not conform to plans, so that managers can devote their scarce time to focusing mainly on these items. This process represents the application of **management by exception**. Effective control requires that corrective action is taken so that actual outcomes conform to planned outcomes. Alternatively, the plans may require modification if the comparisons indicate that the plans are no longer attainable.

The process of taking corrective action, or modifying the plans if the comparisons indicate that actual outcomes do not conform to planned outcomes, is indicated by the arrowed lines in Figure 1.1 linking stages 6 and 4 and 6 and 2. These arrowed lines represent 'feedback loops'. They signify that the process is dynamic and stress the interdependencies between the various stages in the process. The feedback loop between stages 6 and 2 indicates that the plans should be regularly reviewed, and if they are no longer attainable then alternative courses of action must be considered for achieving the organization's objectives. The second loop stresses the corrective action taken so that actual outcomes conform to planned outcomes. Chapters 13–15 focus on the planning and control process.

CHANGING COMPETITIVE ENVIRONMENT

Prior to the 1990s many organizations in Western countries operated in a protected competitive environment. Barriers of communication and geographical distance, and sometimes protected markets, limited the ability of overseas companies to compete in domestic markets. There was little incentive for firms to maximize efficiency and improve management practices, or to minimize costs, as cost increases could often be passed on to customers. During the 1990s, however, organizations began to encounter severe competition from overseas competitors that offered high-quality products at low prices. By establishing global networks for acquiring raw materials and distributing goods overseas, competitors were able to gain access to domestic markets throughout the world. Nowadays, organizations have to compete against the best companies in the world.

Before the 1990s many service organizations, such as those operating in the airlines, utilities and financial service industries, were either government-owned monopolies or operated in a highly regulated, protected and non-competitive environment. These organizations were not subject to any great pressure to improve the quality and efficiency of their operations or to improve profitability by eliminating services or products that were making losses. Prices were set to cover operating costs and provide a predetermined return on capital. Hence cost increases could often be absorbed by increasing the prices of the services. Little attention was therefore given to developing cost systems that accurately measured the costs and profitability of individual services.

Privatization of government-controlled companies and deregulation in the 1980s and 1990s completely changed the competitive environment in which service companies operated. Pricing and competitive restrictions were virtually eliminated. Deregulation, intensive competition and an expanding product range created the need for service organizations to focus on cost management and develop management accounting information systems that enabled them to understand their cost base and determine the sources of profitability for their products, customers and markets. One of the major features of the business environment in recent decades has been the growth in the service sector and the growth of management accounting within service organizations.

FOCUS ON CUSTOMER SATISFACTION AND NEW MANAGEMENT APPROACHES

In order to survive in today's competitive environment, companies have had to become more customer-driven and make customer satisfaction an overriding priority. Customers are demanding ever-improving levels of service in cost, quality, reliability, delivery, and the choice of innovative new products. These are the key success factors on which organizations must concentrate.

Cost efficiency

Keeping costs low and being cost efficient provides an organization with a strong competitive advantage. Increased competition has also made decision errors (due to poor cost information) potentially hazardous to an organization. Many companies have become aware of the need to improve their cost systems so that they can produce more accurate cost information to determine the cost of their products and services, monitor trends in costs over time, pinpoint loss-making activities and analyze profits by products, sales outlets, customers and markets.

Quality

In addition to demanding low costs, customers are demanding high quality products and services. Most companies are responding to this by focusing on **total quality management (TQM)**. TQM is a term used to describe a situation where *all* business functions are involved in a process of continuous quality improvement that focuses on delivering products or services of consistently high quality in a timely fashion. The emphasis on TQM has created fresh demands on the management accounting function to measure and evaluate the quality of products and services and the activities that produce them.

Time as a competitive weapon

Organizations are also seeking to increase customer satisfaction by providing a speedier response to customer requests, ensuring 100 per cent on-time delivery and reducing the time taken to develop and bring new products to market. For these reasons management accounting systems now place more emphasis on time-based measures, such as **cycle time**. This is the length of time from start to completion of a product or service. It consists of the sum of processing time, move time, wait time and inspection time. Only processing time adds value to the product, and the remaining activities are **non-value added activities** in the sense that they can be reduced or eliminated without altering the product's service potential to the customer. Organizations are therefore focusing on minimizing cycle time by reducing the time spent on such activities. The management accounting system has an important role to play in this process by identifying and reporting on the time devoted to value added and non-value added activities. Cycle time measures have also become important for service organizations. For example, the time taken to process mortgage loan applications by financial organizations can be considerable, involving substantial non-value added waiting time. Reducing the time taken to process applications enhances customer satisfaction and creates the potential for increasing sales revenue.

Innovation and continuous improvement

To be successful companies must develop a steady stream of innovative new products and services and have the capability to adapt to changing customer requirements. Management accounting information systems have begun to report performance measures relating to innovation. Examples include:

- the total launch time for new products/services;
- an assessment of the key characteristics of new products relative to those of competitors;
- feedback on customer satisfaction with the new features and characteristics of newly introduced products and the number of new products launched.

Organizations are also attempting to achieve customer satisfaction by adopting a philosophy of **continuous improvement**. Traditionally, organizations have sought to study activities and establish standard operating procedures. Management accountants developed systems and measurements that compared actual results with predetermined standards. This process created a climate whereby the predetermined standards represented a target to be achieved and maintained. In today's competitive environment, companies must adopt a philosophy of continuous improvement, an ongoing process that involves a continuous search to reduce costs, eliminate waste, and improve the quality and performance of activities that increase customer value or satisfaction. Management accounting supports continuous improvement by identifying opportunities for change and then reporting on the progress of the methods that have been implemented.

Social responsibility and corporate ethics

In addition to the four key success factors already described, companies are also focusing on social responsibility and corporate ethics to enhance customer satisfaction. It is no longer enough for a company simply to comply with legal requirements; many customers and company stakeholders expect managers to be more proactive in terms of social responsibility, safety and environmental issues and corporate ethics. In response, many companies are now introducing mechanisms for measuring, reporting and monitoring their environmental costs and activities. A code of ethics has also become an essential part of corporate culture.

Professional accounting organizations also play an important role in promoting a high standard of ethical behaviour by their members. Both of the professional bodies representing management accountants, in the UK (Chartered Institute of Management Accountants) and in the USA (Institute of Management Accountants), have issued a code of ethical guidelines for their members and established mechanisms for monitoring and enforcing professional ethics. The guidelines are concerned with ensuring that accountants follow fundamental principles relating to:

- integrity (not being a party to any falsification);
- objectivity (not being biased or prejudiced);
- confidentiality and professional competence and due care (maintaining the skills required to ensure a competent professional service).

THE IMPACT OF INFORMATION TECHNOLOGY

During the past decade the use of information technology (IT) to support business activities has increased dramatically and the development of electronic business communication technologies known as e-business, e-commerce or internet commerce have had a major impact. For example, consumers who have access to the internet are able to compare the relative merits of different products and are more discerning in their purchases. E-commerce (such as bar coding) has allowed considerable cost savings to be made by streamlining business processes and has generated extra revenues from the adept use of online sales facilities (such as ticketless airline bookings and internet banking). The proficient use of e-commerce has given many companies a competitive advantage.

REAL WORLD VIEWS 1.1

A look at a key feature of easyJet's business

As one of the pioneers in the low cost airline market, easyJet bases its business on a number of principles:

- Minimize distribution costs by using the internet to take bookings. About 90 per cent of all easyJet tickets are sold via the Web. This makes the company one of Europe's largest internet retailers.

- Maximize efficient use of assets, by increasing turnaround time at airports.

- A 'simple-service model' means the end of free on-board catering.

- Ticketless travel, where passengers receive an e-mail confirming their booking, cuts the cost of issuing, distributing and processing tickets.

- Intensive use of IT in administration and management, aiming to run a paperless office.

Discussion point

How can the management accounting function provide information to support a low-cost strategy?

Source: Easyjet Website (www.easyjet.com)

One advanced IT application that has had a considerable impact on business information systems is **enterprise resource planning systems (ERPS)**. An ERPS comprises a set of integrated software applications modules that aim to control all information flows within a company. Users can use their personal computers (PCs) to access the organization's database and follow developments almost as they happen. Using real time data enables managers to analyze information quickly and thus continually improve the efficiencies of processes.

The introduction of ERPS has the potential to have a significant impact on the work of management accountants. In particular, it substantially reduces routine information gathering and the processing of information. Instead of managers asking management accountants for information, they can access the system to derive the information they require directly and do their own analyses. This has freed accountants to adopt the role of advisers and internal consultants to the business. Management accountants have now become more involved in interpreting the information generated from the ERPS and providing business support for managers.

INTERNATIONAL CONVERGENCE OF MANAGEMENT ACCOUNTING PRACTICES

This book has become an established text in many different countries. Its widespread use supports the premise that management accounting practices generally do not differ across national borders. Granlund and Lukka (1998) argue that there is a strong current tendency towards global homogenization of management accounting practices within the industrialized world.

Granlund and Lukka distinguish between management accounting practices at the macro and micro levels. The macro level relates to concepts and techniques; in other words, it relates mainly to the content of this book. In contrast, the micro level is concerned with the behavioural patterns relating to how management accounting information is actually used. At the macro level Granlund and Lukka suggest that the convergence of management accounting practices in different countries has occurred because of intensified global competition, developments in information technology, the increasing tendency of transnational companies to standardize their practices, the global consultancy industry and the use of globally applied textbooks and teaching.

At the micro level, Granlund and Lukka acknowledge that differences in national and corporate culture can result in management accounting information being used in different ways across countries. For example, there is evidence to suggest that the rigor with which accounting information is employed to evaluate managerial performance evaluation is linked to the culture of the country in which it used.

FUNCTIONS OF MANAGEMENT ACCOUNTING

A cost and management accounting system should generate information to meet the following requirements. It should:

1 allocate costs between cost of goods sold and inventories for internal and external profit reporting;
2 provide relevant information to help managers make better decisions;
3 provide information for planning, control, performance measurement and continuous improvement.

Financial accounting rules require that we match costs with revenues to calculate profit. Consequently any unsold finished goods stock or partly completed stock (work in progress) will *not* be included in the cost of goods sold, which is matched against sales revenue during a given period. In an organization that produces a wide range of different products it will be necessary, for stock (inventory) valuation purposes, to charge the costs to each individual product. The total value of the stocks of completed products and work in progress, plus any unused raw materials, forms the basis for determining the inventory valuation to be deducted from the current period's costs when calculating profit. This total is also the basis for determining the stock valuation for inclusion in the balance sheet. Costs are therefore traced to each individual job or product for financial accounting requirements in order to allocate the costs incurred during a period between cost of goods sold and inventories. This information is required for meeting *external* financial accounting requirements, but most organizations also produce *internal* profit reports at monthly intervals. Thus product costs are also required for periodic internal profit reporting. Many service organizations, however, do not carry any stocks and product costs are therefore not required by these organizations for valuing inventories.

The second requirement of a cost and management accounting system is to provide relevant financial information to managers to help them make better decisions. Information is required relating to the profitability of various segments of the business such as products, services, customers and distribution channels in order to ensure that only profitable activities are undertaken. Information is also required for making resource allocation and product/service mix and discontinuation decisions. In some situations information extracted from the costing system also plays a crucial role in determining selling prices, particularly in markets where customized products and services that do not have readily available market prices are provided.

Management accounting systems should also provide information for planning, control, performance measurement and continuous improvement. Planning involves translating goals and objectives into the specific activities and resources that are required to achieve them. Companies develop both long-term and short-term plans and the management accounting function plays a critical role in this process. Short-term plans, in the form of the budgeting process, are prepared in more detail than the longer-term plans and are one of the mechanisms used by managers as a basis for control and performance evaluation. The **control process** involves the setting of targets or standards (often derived from the budgeting process) against which actual results are measured. The management accountant's role is to provide managers with feedback information in the form of periodic reports, suitably analyzed, to enable them to determine if operations for which they are responsible are proceeding according to plan and identify those activities where corrective action is necessary. In particular, the management accounting function should provide economic feedback to managers to assist them in controlling costs and improving the efficiency and effectiveness of operations.

It is appropriate at this point to distinguish between cost accounting and management accounting. **Cost accounting** is concerned with cost accumulation for inventory valuation to meet the requirements of external reporting and internal profit measurement, whereas management accounting relates to the provision of appropriate information for decision-making, planning, control and performance evaluation. However, a study of the literature reveals that the distinction between cost accounting and management accounting is not clear cut and the two terms are often used synonymously. In this book no further attempt will be made to distinguish between them.

You should now be aware that a management accounting system serves multiple purposes. The emphasis throughout this book is that costs must be assembled in different ways for different purposes. Most organizations record cost information in a single database, with costs appropriately coded and classified so that relevant information can be extracted to meet the requirements of different users. We shall examine this topic in the next chapter.

SUMMARY OF THE CONTENTS OF THIS BOOK

This book is divided into four parts. Part One consists of two chapters and provides an introduction to management and cost accounting and a framework for studying the remaining chapters. Part Two consists of six chapters and is entitled 'Cost Accumulation for Inventory Valuation and Profit Measurement'. This section focuses mainly on cost accounting. It is concerned with assigning costs to products in order to separate costs incurred during a period between costs of goods sold and the closing inventory valuation. The extent to which product costs accumulated for inventory valuation and profit measurement should be adjusted for meeting decision-making, cost control and performance measurement requirements is also briefly considered. Part Three consists of four chapters and is entitled 'Information for Decision-making'. Here the focus is on measuring and identifying those costs which are relevant for different types of decisions.

The title of Part Four is 'Information for Planning, Control and Performance Measurement'. It consists of three chapters and concentrates on the process of translating goals and objectives into specific activities and the resources that are required, via the short-term (budgeting) and long-term planning processes, to achieve the goals and objectives. In addition, the management control systems that organizations use are described and the role that management accounting control systems play within the overall control process is examined. The emphasis here is on the accounting process as a means of providing information to help managers control the activities for which they are responsible.

SUMMARY

The following items relate to the learning objectives listed at the beginning of the chapter.

- **Distinguish between management accounting and financial accounting.**
  Management accounting differs from financial accounting in several ways. Management accounting is concerned with the provision of information to internal users to help them make better decisions and improve the efficiency and effectiveness of operations. Financial accounting is concerned with the provision of information to external parties outside the organization. Unlike financial accounting there is no statutory requirement for management accounting to produce financial statements or follow externally imposed rules. Furthermore, management accounting provides information relating to different parts of the business whereas financial accounting reports focus on the whole business. Management accounting also tends to be more future oriented and reports are often published on a daily basis, whereas financial accounting reports are published semi-annually.

- **Identify and describe the elements involved in the decision-making, planning and control process.** The following elements are involved in the decision-making, planning and control process: (a) identify the objectives that will guide the business; (b) search for a range of possible courses of action that might enable the objectives to be achieved; (c) select appropriate alternative courses of action that will enable the objectives to be achieved; (d) implement the decisions as part of the planning and budgeting process; (e) compare actual and planned outcomes; and (f) respond to divergencies from plan by taking corrective action so that actual outcomes conform to planned outcomes or modify the plans if the comparisons indicate that the plans are no longer attainable.

- **Justify the view that a major objective of commercial organizations is to broadly seek to maximize future profits.** The reasons for identifying maximizing future profits as a major objective are: (a) it is unlikely that any other objective is as widely applicable in measuring the ability of the organization to survive in the future; and (b) although it is unlikely that maximizing future profits can be realized in practice it is still important to establish the principles necessary to achieve this objective.

- **Explain the factors that have influenced the changes in the competitive environment.** The factors influencing the change in the competitive environment are (a) globalization of world trade; (b) privatization of government-controlled companies and deregulation in various industries; (c) changing customer tastes that demand ever-improving levels of service in cost, quality, reliability, delivery and the choice of new products; and (d) the emergence of e-business.

- **Outline and describe the key success factors that directly affect customer satisfaction.** The key success factors are cost efficiency, quality, time and innovation and continuous improvement. Keeping costs low and being cost efficient provides an organization with a strong competitive advantage. Customers also demand high quality products and services and this has resulted in companies making quality a key competitive variable. Organizations are also seeking to increase customer satisfaction by providing a speedier response to customer requests, ensuring 100 per cent on-time delivery and reducing the time taken to bring new products to the market. To be successful companies must be innovative and develop a steady stream of new products and services and have the capability to rapidly adapt to changing customer requirements.

- **Identify and describe the functions of a cost and management accounting system.** A cost and management accounting system should generate information to meet the following requirements: (a) allocate costs between cost of goods sold and inventories for internal and external profit reporting and inventory valuation; (b) provide relevant information to help managers make better decisions; and (c) provide information for planning, control and performance measurement.

KEY TERMS AND CONCEPTS

Budget a financial plan for implementing management decisions.

Continuous improvement an ongoing search to reduce costs, eliminate waste, and improve the quality and performance of activities that increase customer value or satisfaction.

Control a managerial function that consists of the measurement, reporting and subsequent correction of performance in order to achieve the organization's objectives.

Control process the process of setting targets or standards against which actual results are measured.

Cost accounting accounting concerned with cost accumulation for inventory valuation to meet the requirements of external reporting and internal profit measurement.

Cycle time the length of time from start to completion of a product or service and is the sum of processing time, move time, wait time and inspection time.

Enterprise resource planning system (ERPS) a set of integrated software applications modules that aim to control all information flows within a company.

Financial accounting accounting concerned with the provision of information to parties that are external to the organization.

Management accounting accounting concerned with the provision of information to people within the organization to aid decision-making and improve the efficiency and effectiveness of existing operations.

Management by exception a situation where management attention is focused on areas where outcomes do not meet targets.

Non-value added activities activities that can be reduced or eliminated without altering the product's service potential to the customer.

Performance reports regular reports to management that compare actual outcomes with planned outcomes.

Strategies courses of action designed to ensure that objectives are achieved.

Total quality management (TQM) a situation where all business functions in a continuous search for improvement in the delivery of quality products in a timely fashion.

KEY EXAMINATION POINTS

Chapter 1 has provided an introduction to the scope of management accounting. It is unlikely that examination questions will be set that refer to the content of an introductory chapter. However, questions are sometimes set requiring you to outline how a costing system can assist the management of an organization. Note that the examiner may not distinguish between cost accounting and management accounting. Cost accounting is often used to also embrace management accounting. Your discussion of a cost accounting system should therefore include a description (with illustrations) of how the system provides information for decision-making, planning and control. Make sure that you draw off your experience from the whole of a first-year course and not just this introductory chapter.

ASSESSMENT MATERIAL

The review questions are short questions that enable you to assess your understanding of the main topics included in the chapter. The numbers in parentheses provide you with the page numbers to refer to if you cannot answer a specific question.

The remaining chapters also contain review problems. These are more complex and require you to relate and apply the chapter content to various business problems. Fully worked solutions to the review problems are provided in a separate section at the end of the book.

The website also includes over 20 case study problems. A list of these cases is provided on pages 427–30. The Electronic Boards case is a case study that is relevant to the introductory stages of a management accounting course.

REVIEW QUESTIONS

1.1 Identify and describe the different users of accounting information. *(pp. 6–7)*

1.2 Describe the differences between management accounting and financial accounting. *(pp. 7–8)*

1.3 Explain each of the elements of the decision-making, planning and control process. *(p. 10)*

1.4 Describe what is meant by management by exception. *(p. 10)*

1.5 Explain how the competitive environment that businesses face has changed over the past decades and discuss how this has had an impact on management accounting *(p. 11)*

1.6 Describe each of the key success factors that companies should concentrate on to achieve customer satisfaction. *(pp. 11–13)*

1.7 Explain why firms are beginning to concentrate on social responsibility and corporate ethics. *(p. 13)*

1.8 Describe the different functions of management accounting. *(pp. 15–16)*

1.9 Describe enterprise resource planning systems and their impact on management accountants. *(pp. 13–14)*

1.10 Explain why management accounting practices tend not to differ across countries *(pp. 14–15)*

CHAPTER 2
AN INTRODUCTION TO COST TERMS AND CONCEPTS

LEARNING OBJECTIVES

After studying this chapter, you should be able to:

- explain why it is necessary to understand the meaning of different cost terms;
- define and illustrate a cost object;
- explain the meaning of each of the key terms or concepts highlighted in bold in this chapter;
- explain why in the short term some costs and revenues are not relevant for decision-making;
- describe the three purposes for which cost information is required.

In Chapter 1 we discussed how accounting information systems measure costs which are used for different purposes – such as profit measurement and inventory valuation, decision-making, performance measurement and control. Different types of costs are used in different situations, and a large terminology has arisen to describe them. Examples include variable cost, fixed cost, opportunity cost and sunk cost. The aim of this chapter is to provide you with an understanding of the basic cost terms and concepts that are used in the management accounting literature.

COST OBJECTS

A **cost object** is any activity for which a separate measurement of costs is desired. In other words, if the users of accounting information want to know the cost of something, this something is called a cost object. Examples of cost objects include the cost of a product, the cost of rendering a service to a bank customer or hospital patient, the cost of operating a particular department or sales territory, or indeed anything for which one wants to measure the cost of resources used.

We shall see that the cost collection system typically accounts for costs in two broad stages:

1 It accumulates costs by classifying them into certain categories such as by type of expense (e.g. direct labour, direct materials and indirect costs) or by cost behaviour (such as fixed and variable costs).

2 It then assigns these costs to cost objects.

In this chapter we shall focus on the following cost terms and concepts:

- direct and indirect costs;
- period and product costs;
- cost behaviour in relation to volume of activity;
- relevant and irrelevant costs;
- avoidable and unavoidable costs;
- sunk costs;
- opportunity costs;
- incremental and marginal costs.

DIRECT AND INDIRECT COSTS

Costs that are assigned to cost objects can be divided into two broad categories – direct and indirect costs. Both categories can be further divided into direct and indirect materials and direct and indirect labour costs.

Direct materials

Direct material costs represent those material costs that can be specifically and exclusively identified with a particular cost object. Where the cost object is a product or service, physical observation can be used to measure the quantity consumed by each individual product or service and the cost of direct materials can be directly charged to them. In other words, direct materials become part of a physical product or are used in providing a service. For example, wood used in the manufacture of different types of furniture can be directly identified with each specific type of furniture such as chairs, tables and bookcases.

Direct labour

Direct labour costs are those labour costs that can be specifically and exclusively identified with a particular cost object. Physical observation can be used to measure the quantity of labour used to produce a specific product or provide a service. The direct labour cost in producing a product includes the cost of converting the raw materials into a product, such as the costs of the machine operatives engaged in the production process in the manufacture of televisions. The direct labour cost used to provide a service includes the labour costs in providing a service that can be specifically identified with an individual client or with a specific instance of service.

Indirect costs

Indirect costs cannot be identified specifically and exclusively with a given cost object. They consist of indirect labour, materials and expenses. Where products are the cost object the wages of all employees whose time cannot be identified with a specific product represent indirect labour costs. Examples include the labour cost of staff employed in the maintenance and repair of production equipment and staff employed in the stores department. The cost of materials used to repair machinery cannot be identified with a specific product and can therefore be classified as indirect material costs. Examples of indirect expenses, where products or the provision of a service are the cost objectives, include lighting and heating expenses and property taxes. These costs cannot be specifically identified with a particular product or service.

The term **'overheads'** is widely used instead of indirect costs. In a manufacturing organization overhead costs are categorized as either manufacturing, administration and marketing (or selling) overheads. Manufacturing overheads include all the costs of manufacturing apart from direct labour and material costs. Administrative overheads consist of all costs associated with the general administration of the organization that cannot be assigned to either manufacturing, marketing and distribution overheads. Examples of administrative overheads include top-executive salaries, general accounting, secretarial and research and development costs. Those costs that are necessary to market and distribute a product or service are categorized as marketing (selling) costs, also known as order-getting and order-filling costs. Examples of marketing costs include advertising, sales personnel salaries/commissions, warehousing and delivery transportation costs.

Figure 2.1 illustrates the various classifications of manufacturing and non-manufacturing costs. You will see from this figure that two further classifications of manufacturing costs are sometimes used. **Prime cost** consists of all direct manufacturing costs (i.e. it is the sum of direct material and direct labour costs). **Conversion cost** is the sum of direct labour and manufacturing overhead costs. It represents the cost of converting raw materials into finished products.

Distinguishing between direct and indirect costs

Sometimes, direct costs are treated as indirect because it is not cost effective to trace costs directly to the cost object. For example, the nails used to manufacture a particular desk can be identified specifically with the desk, but, because the cost is likely to be insignificant, the expense of tracing such items does not justify the possible benefits from calculating more accurate product costs.

The distinction between direct and indirect costs also depends on the cost object. A cost can be treated as direct for one cost object but indirect in respect of another. For example, if

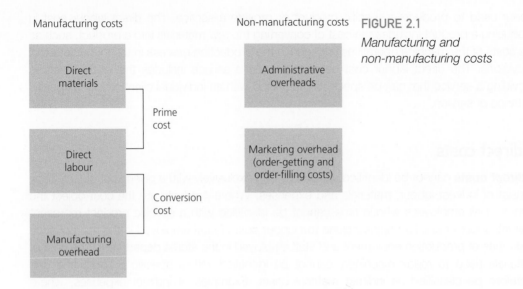

FIGURE 2.1

Manufacturing and non-manufacturing costs

the cost object is the cost of using different distribution channels, then the rental of warehouses and the salaries of storekeepers will be regarded as direct for each distribution channel. If, on the other hand, the cost object is the product, both the warehouse rental and the salaries of the storekeepers will be an indirect cost because these costs cannot be specifically identified with the product.

Assigning direct and indirect costs to cost objects

Direct costs can be traced easily and accurately to a cost object. For example, where products are the cost object, direct materials and labour used can be physically identified with the different products that an organization produces. It is a relatively simple process to establish an information technology system that records the quantity and cost of direct labour and material resources used to produce specific products.

In contrast, indirect costs cannot be traced to cost objects. Instead, an estimate must be made of the resources consumed by cost objects using **cost allocations**. A cost allocation is the process of assigning costs when a direct measure does not exist for the quantity of resources consumed by a particular cost object. Cost allocations involve the use of surrogate rather than direct measures. For example, consider an activity such as receiving incoming materials. Assuming that the cost of receiving materials is strongly influenced by the number of receipts then costs can be allocated to products (i.e. the cost object) based on the number of material receipts each product requires. If 20 per cent of the total number of receipts for a period were required for a particular product then 20 per cent of the total costs of receiving incoming materials would be allocated to that product. If that product was discontinued, and not replaced, we would expect action to be taken to reduce the resources required for receiving materials by 20 per cent.

In this example the surrogate allocation measure is assumed to be a significant determinant of the cost of receiving incoming materials. The process of assigning indirect costs (overheads) and the accuracy of such assignments will be discussed in Chapter 4 but at this stage you should note that only direct costs can be accurately assigned to cost objects. Therefore, the more direct costs that can be traced to a cost object, the more accurate is the cost assignment.

PERIOD AND PRODUCT COSTS

For profit measurement and inventory/stock valuation (i.e. the valuation of completed unsold products and partly completed products or services) purposes it is necessary to classify costs as either product costs or period costs. **Product costs** are those costs that are identified with goods purchased or produced for resale. In a manufacturing organization they are costs that the accountant attaches to the product and that are included in the inventory valuation for finished goods, or for partly completed goods (work in progress), until they are sold; they are then recorded as expenses and matched against sales for calculating profit. **Period costs** are those costs that are not included in the inventory valuation and as a result are treated as expenses in the period in which they are incurred. *Hence no attempt is made to attach period costs to products for inventory valuation purposes.*

In a manufacturing organization all manufacturing costs are regarded as product costs and non-manufacturing costs are regarded as period costs. Companies operating in the merchandizing sector, such as retailing or wholesaling organizations, purchase goods for resale without changing their basic form. The cost of the goods purchased is regarded as a product cost and all other costs, such as administration and selling and distribution expenses, are considered to be period costs. The treatment of period and product costs for a manufacturing organization is illustrated in Figure 2.2. You will see that both product and period costs are eventually classified as expenses. The major difference is the point in time at which they are so classified.

There are two reasons why non-manufacturing costs are treated as period costs and not included in the inventory valuation. First, inventories are assets (unsold production) and assets represent resources that have been acquired and that are expected to contribute to future revenue. Manufacturing costs incurred in making a product can be expected to generate future revenues to cover the cost of production. There is no guarantee, however, that non-

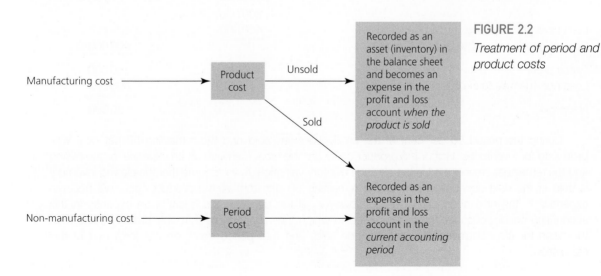

FIGURE 2.2

Treatment of period and product costs

manufacturing costs will generate future revenue, because they do not represent value added to any specific product. Therefore, they are not included in the inventory valuation. Second, many non-manufacturing costs (e.g. distribution costs) are not incurred when the product is being stored. Hence it is inappropriate to include such costs within the inventory valuation.

An illustration of the accounting treatment of period and product costs for income (profit) measurement purposes is presented in Example 2.1.

EXAMPLE 2.1

The Laurs company produces 100 000 identical units of a product during period 1. The costs for the period are as follows:

	(£)	(£)
Manufacturing costs:		
Direct labour	400 000	
Direct materials	200 000	
Manufacturing overheads	200 000	800 000
Non-manufacturing costs		300 000

During period 1, the company sold 50 000 units for £750 000, and the remaining 50 000 units were unsold at the end of the period. There was no opening stock at the start of the period. The profit and loss account for period 1 will be as follows:

	(£)	(£)
Sales (50 000)		750 000
Manufacturing costs *(product costs):*		
Direct labour	400 000	
Direct materials	200 000	
Manufacturing overheads	200 000	
	800 000	
Less closing stock (50% or 50 000 units)	400 000	
Cost of goods sold (50% or 50 000 units)		400 000
Gross profit		350 000
Less non-manufacturing costs *(period costs)*		300 000
Net profit		50 000

During the period 50 per cent of the production was sold and the remaining 50 per cent was produced for inventories. Half of the product costs are therefore identified as an expense for the period and the remainder are included in the closing inventory valuation. If we assume that the closing inventory is sold in the next accounting period, the remaining 50 per cent of the product costs will become expenses in the next accounting period. However, all the period costs became an expense in this accounting period, because this is the period to which they relate. Note that only product costs form the basis for the calculation of cost of goods sold, and that period costs do not form part of this calculation.

COST BEHAVIOUR

A knowledge of how costs and revenues will vary with different levels of activity (or volume) is essential for decision-making. Managers might require information in order to answer questions such as these:

1 How will costs and revenues change if activity is increased (or decreased) by 15 per cent?

2 What will be the impact on profits if we reduce selling price by 10 per cent based on the estimate that this will increase sales volume by 15 per cent?

3 How do the cost and revenues change for a university if the number of students is increased by 5 per cent?

4 How do costs and revenues of a hotel change if a room and meals are provided for two guests for a three-day stay?

5 How many tickets must be sold for a concert in order to break-even?

Activity or volume may be measured in terms of units of production or sales, hours worked, miles travelled, patients seen, students enrolled or any other appropriate measure of the activity of an organization.

The terms 'variable', 'fixed', 'semi-variable' and 'semi-fixed' have been traditionally used in the management accounting literature to describe how a cost reacts to changes in activity. **Variable costs** vary in direct proportion to the volume of activity; that is, doubling the level of activity will double the *total* variable cost. Consequently, *total* variable costs are linear and unit variable cost is constant. Examples of variable costs in a manufacturing organization include direct materials, energy to operate the machines and sales commissions. Examples of variable costs in a merchandizing company, such as a supermarket, include the purchase costs of all items that are sold. In a hospital, variable costs include the cost of drugs and meals which may be assumed to fluctuate with the number of patient days.

Consider the example of a bicycle manufacturer that purchases component parts. Assume that the cost of purchasing two wheels for a particular bicycle is £10 per bicycle. Figure 2.3(a) illustrates the concept of variable costs in graphic form. You can see that as the number of units of output of bicycles increases or decreases, the *total* variable cost of wheels increases and decreases proportionately. Look at Figure 2.3(b). This diagram shows that variable cost

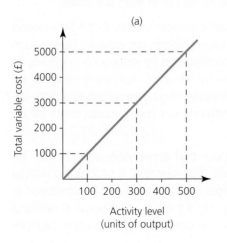

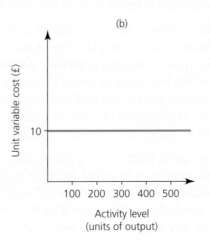

FIGURE 2.3
Variable costs: (a) total; (b) unit

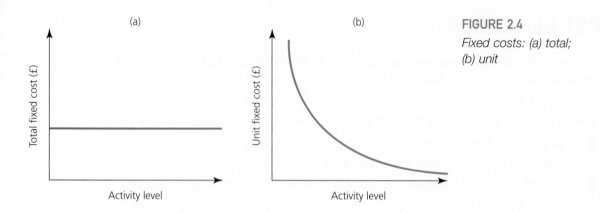

FIGURE 2.4
*Fixed costs: (a) total;
(b) unit*

per *unit* of output is constant even though total variable cost increases/decreases proportionately with changes in activity.

Fixed costs remain constant over wide ranges of activity for a specified time period. They are not affected by changes in activity. Examples of fixed costs include depreciation of equipment, property taxes, insurance costs, supervisory salaries and leasing charges for cars used by the sales force. Figure 2.4 illustrates how *total* fixed costs and fixed cost per *unit* of activity react with changes in activity.

You will see from this diagram that *total* fixed costs are constant for all units of activity whereas *unit* fixed costs decrease proportionally with the level of activity. For example, if the total of the fixed costs is £5000 for a month the fixed costs per *unit* of activity will be as follows:

Units produced	Fixed cost per unit (£)
1	5000
10	500
100	50
1000	5

Because unit fixed costs are not constant per unit they must be interpreted with caution. For decision-making, it is better to work with total fixed costs rather than unit costs.

The distinction between fixed and variable costs must be made relative to the time period under consideration. Over a period of several years, virtually all costs are variable. During such a long period of time, contraction in demand will be accompanied by reductions in virtually all categories of costs. For example, senior managers can be released, machinery need not be replaced and even buildings and land can be sold. Similarly, large expansions in activity will eventually cause all categories of costs to increase. Within shorter time periods, costs will be fixed or variable in relation to changes in activity.

Spending on some fixed costs, such as direct labour and supervisory salaries, can be adjusted in the short term to reflect changes in activity. For example, if production activity declines significantly then direct workers and supervisors might continue to be employed in the hope that the decline in demand will be temporary; but if there is no upsurge in demand then staff might eventually be made redundant. If, on the other hand, production capacity

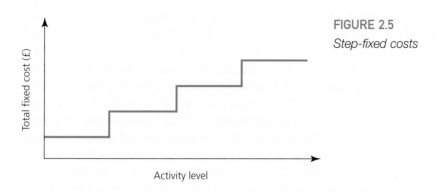

FIGURE 2.5
Step-fixed costs

expands to some critical level, additional workers might be employed, but the process of recruiting such workers may take several months. Thus, within a short-term period, such as one year, labour costs can change in response to changes in demand in a manner similar to that depicted in Figure 2.5. Costs that behave in this manner are described as **semi-fixed** or **step-fixed costs**. The distinguishing feature of step-fixed costs is that within a given time period they are fixed within specified activity levels, but they eventually are subject to step increases or decreases by a constant amount at various critical activity levels.

Our discussion so far has assumed a one-year time period. If we consider a shorter time period, such as one month, the step-fixed costs described in the previous paragraph will not occur, because it takes several months to respond to changes in activity and alter spending levels. Over very short-term periods such as one month, spending on direct labour and supervisory salaries will be fixed in relation to changes in activity.

Even though fixed costs are normally assumed to remain unchanged in response to changes in the level of activity in the short term, they may change in response to other factors. For example, if price levels increase then some fixed costs such as management salaries will increase.

Before concluding our discussion of cost behaviour in relation to volume of activity, we must consider **semi-variable costs** (also known as **mixed costs**). These include both a fixed and a variable component. If you refer to your telephone account for your land line you will probably find that it consists of a fixed component (the line rental) plus a variable component (the number of telephone calls made multiplied by the cost per call). Similarly, the office photocopying costs may consist of a fixed rental charge for the photocopiers plus a variable cost (the cost of the paper multiplied by the number of photocopies).

RELEVANT AND IRRELEVANT COSTS AND REVENUES

For decision-making, costs and revenues can be classified according to whether they are relevant to a particular decision. **Relevant costs and revenues** are those *future* costs and revenues that will be changed by a decision, whereas **irrelevant costs and revenues** are those that will not be affected by the decision. For example, if you are faced with a choice of making a journey using your own car or by public transport, the car tax and insurance costs are irrelevant, since they will remain the same whether or not you use your car for this journey. However, petrol costs for the car will differ depending on which alternative is chosen, and this cost will be relevant for decision-making.

Let us now consider a further illustration of the classification of relevant and irrelevant costs. A company purchased raw materials for £100 per unit and then found that it was impossible to use them in future production or to sell them in their current state. A former customer is prepared to purchase a product that will require the use of all these materials, but he is not prepared to pay more than £250 per unit. The additional costs of converting these materials into the required product are £200. Should the company accept the order for £250? It might appear that the cost of the order is £300, consisting of £100 material cost and £200 conversion cost, but this is incorrect because the £100 material cost will remain the same whether the order is accepted or rejected. The material cost is therefore irrelevant for the decision. If the order is accepted the conversion costs will change by £200, and this conversion cost is a relevant cost. If we compare the revenue of £250 with the relevant cost for the order of £200, it means that the order should be accepted, assuming of course that no higher-priced orders can be obtained elsewhere. The following calculation shows that this is the correct decision.

	Do not accept order (£)	Accept order (£)
Materials	100	100
Conversion costs	—	200
Revenue	—	(250)
Net costs	100	50

The net costs of the company are £50 less; in other words, the company is £50 better off as a result of accepting the order. This agrees with the £50 advantage which was suggested by the relevant cost method.

In this illustration the sales revenue was relevant to the decision because future revenue changed depending on which alternative was selected. However, in some circumstances sales revenue may also be irrelevant for decision-making. Consider a situation where a company can meet its sales demand by purchasing either machine A or machine B. The output of both machines is identical, but the operating costs and purchase costs of the machines are different. In this situation the sales revenue will remain unchanged irrespective of which machine is purchased (assuming of course that the quality of output is identical for both machines). Consequently, sales revenue is irrelevant for this decision; the relevant items are the operating costs and the cost of the machines. We have now established an important principle regarding the classification of cost and revenues for decision-making; namely, that in the short-term not all costs and revenues are relevant for decision-making.

AVOIDABLE AND UNAVOIDABLE COSTS

Sometimes the terms **avoidable** and **unavoidable costs** are used instead of relevant and irrelevant cost. Avoidable costs are those costs that may be saved by not adopting a given alternative, whereas unavoidable costs cannot be saved. Only avoidable costs are relevant for decision-making purposes. In the example that we used to illustrate relevant and irrelevant costs, the material costs of £100 are unavoidable and irrelevant, but the conversion costs of £200 are avoidable and hence relevant. The decision rule is to accept those alternatives that generate revenues in excess of the avoidable costs.

SUNK COSTS

These costs are the cost of resources already acquired where the total will be unaffected by the choice between various alternatives. They are costs that have been created by a decision made in the past and that cannot be changed by any decision that will be made in the future. The expenditure of £100 on materials that were no longer required, referred to in the preceding section, is an example of a **sunk cost**. Similarly, the written down values of assets

REAL WORLD VIEWS 2.1

Cost structures in the airline sector

Many low-cost carriers like easyJet and Ryanair regularly offer flights to customers at a very low price or even free. They continue to do this even during depressed economic times. Both continue to make good profits, with easyJet posting pre-tax profits of £54m in 2009, Ryanair €251m. More traditional carriers like Lufthansa and British Airways reported less positive results, with losses of €229m and £401m respectively. Why do low-cost carriers do better, even if they give away free seats from time to time? One reason is their cost structures.

You might be thinking surely there is a cost of providing a seat to a passenger, so how can one be given away for free? To answer this, we need to consider the nature of costs at low-cost carriers. Most costs are fixed in nature. First, the aircraft cost (of about $75m USD for a Boeing 737) is fixed. Second, the salaries of the pilot, first officer and cabin crew are also fixed. Third, maintenance costs would also be considered as a fixed cost. And what about the fuel cost? This is also treated as a fixed cost, since it is incurred once the aircraft flies. Thus, if one additional passenger flies with a low-cost carrier, the variable cost associated with this passenger is zero and hence tickets could be given for free.

Traditional carriers like Lufthansa and British Airways have similar costs to the low-cost carriers – fuel, fleet purchase, maintenance and salaries, etc. These costs too are likely to be fixed. The difference is that these costs are most likely at a higher level than low cost carriers. For example, low cost carriers typically use one model of aircraft which reduces

maintenance costs and adds buying leverage. Salaries too are likely to be higher. Traditional airlines may have some variable costs too, e.g. passenger meals. Thus with overall higher costs, it is more difficult to reduce ticket prices or offer free seats. Of course, low-cost carriers do not give away all seats for free. They do, however, have sophisticated yield management systems to maximize the revenues from flights. This might mean that some customers pay a high price while others go free. Overall, they try to ensure all fixed costs are covered on every flight.

Questions

1 Do you agree that the variable cost associated with a passenger can be zero? Can this be said for both low-cost and traditional carriers?

2 What options do more traditional carriers have to improve their fixed cost base?

References

EasyJet 2009 Annual Report, available at: http://2009annualreport.easyjet.com/
Ryanair 2009 Annual Report, available at: http://www.ryanair.com/en/investor/download/2009
Lufthansa 2009 Annual Report, available at: http://reports.lufthansa.com/2009
British Airways 2009 Annual Report, available at: http://www.britishairways.com/cms/global/microsites/ba_reports0809/financial/income.html
2008 737 Range price list, available at: http://www.boeing.com/commercial/prices/

previously purchased are sunk costs. For example, if equipment was purchased four years ago for £100 000 with an expected life of five years and nil scrap value then the written down value will be £20 000 if straight line depreciation is used. This written down value will have to be written off, no matter what possible alternative future action might be chosen. If the equipment was scrapped, the £20 000 would be written off; if the equipment was used for productive purposes, the £20 000 would still have to be written off. This cost cannot be changed by any future decision and is therefore classified as a sunk cost.

Sunk costs are irrelevant for decision-making, but not all irrelevant costs are sunk costs. For example, two alternative production methods may involve identical direct material expenditure. The direct material cost is irrelevant because it will remain the same whichever alternative is chosen, but the material cost is not a sunk cost since it will be incurred in the future.

OPPORTUNITY COSTS

An **opportunity cost** is a cost that measures the opportunity that is lost or sacrificed when the choice of one course of action requires that an alternative course of action is given up. Consider the situation where a student is contemplating taking a gap year overseas after completing their studies. Assume that the student has an offer of a job upon completion of their studies. The lost salary is an opportunity cost of choosing the gap year that must be taken into account when considering the financial implications of the decision. For a further illustration of an opportunity cost you should now look at Example 2.2.

Opportunity costs cannot normally be recorded in the accounting system since they do not involve cash outlays. They also only apply to the use of scarce resources. Where resources are not scarce, no sacrifice exists from using these resources. In Example 2.2 if machine X was operating at 80 per cent of its potential capacity and the decision to accept the contract would not have resulted in reduced production of product A there would have been no loss of revenue, and the opportunity cost would be zero.

Opportunity costs are of vital importance for decision-making. If no alternative use of resources exists then the opportunity cost is zero, but if resources have an alternative use, and are scarce, then an opportunity cost does exist.

EXAMPLE 2.2

A company has an opportunity to obtain a contract for the production of a special component. This component will require 100 hours of processing on machine X. Machine X is working at full capacity on the production of product A, and the only way in which the contract can be fulfilled is by reducing the output of product A. This will result in a lost profit contribution of £200. The contract will also result in *additional* variable costs of £1000.

If the company takes on the contract, it will sacrifice a profit contribution of £200 from the lost output of product A. This represents an opportunity cost, and should be included as part of the cost when negotiating for the contract. The contract price should at least cover the additional costs of £1000 plus the £200 opportunity cost to ensure that the company will be better off in the short term by accepting the contract.

INCREMENTAL AND MARGINAL COSTS

Incremental costs, which are also called **differential costs**, are the difference between the costs of each alternative action that is being considered. For example, a university is evaluating the financial implications of increasing student numbers by 20 per cent. The two alternatives are:

1 no increase in the number of students;

2 a 20 per cent increase in the number of students.

If alternative 2 is chosen, the university will have to increase its budget for full-time lecturers on permanent contracts by £150 000 per annum. It will also need to employ additional part-time lecturers at a cost of £15 000 (300 hours at £50 per hour) per annum. The differential cost between the two alternatives is £165 000.

Incremental costs can include both fixed and variable costs. In the example above, the full-time staff represent a fixed cost and the part-time staff represent a variable cost. You will also meet the concept of incremental, or differential, revenues. These are the difference in revenues resulting from each alternative.

If you have studied economics you may have noticed that incremental costs and revenues are similar in principle to the concept of **marginal cost** and **marginal revenue**. The main difference is that marginal cost/revenue represents the additional cost/revenue of one extra unit of output whereas incremental cost/revenue represents the additional cost/revenue resulting from a group of additional units of output. Business decisions normally entail identifying the change in costs and revenues arising from comparing two alternative courses of action and where this involves a change in activity it is likely that this will involve multiple, rather than single units of activity.

THE COST AND MANAGEMENT ACCOUNTING INFORMATION SYSTEM

In the previous chapter we noted that a cost and management accounting information system should generate information to meet the following requirements:

1 to allocate costs between cost of goods sold and inventories for internal and external profit measurement and inventory valuation;

2 to provide relevant information to help managers make better decisions;

3 to provide information for planning, control and performance measurement.

Modern information technology allows a business to maintain a database with costs appropriately coded and classified, so that relevant cost information can be extracted to meet each of the above requirements. A suitable coding system enables costs to be accumulated by the required *cost objects* (such as products or services, departments, responsibility centres, distribution channels, etc.) and also to be classified by appropriate *categories of expenses* (e.g. direct materials, direct labour and overheads) and also by cost behaviour (i.e. fixed and variable costs). In practice, direct material costs will be accumulated by each individual type of material, direct labour costs by different grades of labour and overhead costs by different categories of indirect expenses (e.g. rent, depreciation, supervision, etc.).

For *inventory valuation* in a manufacturing organization, the costs of all partly completed products (i.e. work in progress) and unsold finished products can be extracted from the database to ascertain the total cost assigned to inventories. The cost of goods sold that is deducted from sales revenues to compute the profit for the period can also be extracted by summing the manufacturing costs of all those products that have been sold during the period. We shall consider this process in more detail in Chapters 4 and 5.

Future costs, rather than past costs, are required for *decision-making*. Therefore costs extracted from the database should be adjusted for anticipated price changes. Where a company sells many products or services their profitability should be monitored at regular intervals so that potentially unprofitable products can be highlighted for a more detailed study of their future viability. This information is extracted from the database with costs reported by categories of expenses and divided into their fixed and variable elements. In Chapter 11 we shall focus in more detail on product/segmented profitability analysis.

For *cost control and performance measurement* costs and revenues must be traced to the individuals who are responsible for incurring them. This system is known as **responsibility accounting**. Responsibility accounting involves the creation of responsibility centres. A **responsibility centre** is an organization unit or part of a business for whose performance a manager is held accountable. At this stage it may be easier for you to consider responsibility centres as being equivalent to separate departments within an organization. Responsibility accounting enables accountability for financial results and outcomes to be allocated to individuals (typically heads of departments) throughout the organization. Performance reports are produced at regular intervals for each responsibility centre. The reports are generated by extracting costs from the database analyzed by responsibility centres and categories of expenses. Actual costs for each item of expense listed on the performance report should be compared with budgeted costs so that those costs that do not conform to plan can be pinpointed and investigated. We shall examine responsibility accounting in more detail in Chapter 14.

SUMMARY

The following items relate to the learning objectives listed at the beginning of the chapter.

- **Explain why it is necessary to understand the meaning of different cost terms.** The term 'cost' has multiple meanings and different types of costs are used in different situations. A knowledge of cost and management accounting depends on a clear understanding of the terminology it uses.

- **Define and illustrate a cost object.** A cost object is any activity for which a separate measurement of cost is required. In other words managers often want to know the cost of something and the 'thing' that they want to know the cost of is a cost object. Examples of cost objects include the cost of a new product, the cost of operating a sales outlet and the cost of operating a specific machine.

- **Explain the meaning of each of the key terms listed at the end of this chapter.** You should check your understanding of each of the terms or concepts highlighted in bold.

- **Explain why in the short term some costs and revenues are not relevant for decision-making.** In the short term some costs and revenues may remain unchanged for all alternatives under consideration. For example, if you wish to determine the costs of driving to work in your own car or using public transport, the cost of the road fund taxation licence and insurance will remain the same for both alternatives, assuming that you intend to keep your car for leisure purposes. Therefore, the costs of these items are not relevant for assisting you in your decision to travel to work by public transport or using your own car. Costs that remain unchanged for all alternatives under consideration are not relevant for decision-making.

- **Describe the three purposes for which cost information is required.** A cost and management accounting system should generate information to meet the following requirements:

  (a) to allocate costs between cost of goods sold and inventories for internal and external profit reporting and inventory valuation;

  (b) to provide relevant information to help managers make better decisions;

  (c) to provide information for planning, control and performance measurement.

  A database should be maintained with costs appropriately coded or classified, so that relevant information can be extracted for meeting each of the above requirements.

KEY TERMS AND CONCEPTS

Avoidable costs costs that may be saved by not adopting a given alternative.

Conversion cost the sum of direct labour and manufacturing overhead costs; it is the cost of converting raw materials into finished products.

Cost allocation the process of assigning costs to cost objects where a direct measure of the resources consumed by these cost objects does not exist.

Cost object any activity for which a separate measurement of costs is desired.

Direct labour costs labour costs that can be specifically and exclusively identified with a particular cost object.

Direct material costs material costs that can be specifically and exclusively identified with a particular cost object.

Fixed costs costs that remain constant for a specified time period and which are not affected by the volume of activity.

Incremental costs or **differential costs** the difference between the costs of each alternative action under consideration.

Indirect costs costs that cannot be identified specifically and exclusively with a given cost object.

Irrelevant costs and revenues future costs and revenues that will not be affected by a decision.

Marginal cost and **marginal revenue** economic terms used to describe the additional cost/revenue of one extra unit of output.

Opportunity cost costs that measure the opportunity that is sacrificed when the choice of one course of action requires that an alternative is given up.

Overheads another term for indirect costs.

Period costs costs that are not included in the inventory valuation of goods and which are treated as expenses for the period in which they are incurred.

Prime cost all direct manufacturing costs.

Product costs costs that are identified with goods purchased or produced for resale and which are attached to products and included in the inventory valuation of goods.

Relevant costs and revenues future costs and revenues that will be changed by a decision.

Responsibility accounting accounting that involves tracing costs and revenues to responsibility centres.

Responsibility centre a unit or department within an organization for whose performance a manager is held responsible.

Semi-fixed costs or **step-fixed costs** costs that remain fixed within specified activity levels for a given amount of time but which eventually increase or decrease by a constant amount at critical activity levels.

Semi-variable costs or **mixed costs** costs that contain both a fixed and a variable component.

Sunk costs costs that have been incurred by a decision made in the past and that cannot be changed by any decision that will be made in the future.

Unavoidable costs costs that cannot be saved, whether or not an alternative is adopted.

Variable costs costs which vary in direct proportion to the volume of activity.

KEY EXAMINATION POINTS

First year management accounting course examinations frequently involve short essay questions requiring you to describe various cost terms or to discuss the concept that different costs are required for different purposes (see Review problems 2.22–2.27 for examples). It is therefore important that you understand all of the cost terms that have been described in this chapter. In particular, you should be able to explain the context within which a cost term is normally used. For example, a cost such as wages paid to casual labourers will be classified as indirect for inventory valuation purposes but as a direct charge to a responsibility centre or department for cost control purposes. A common error is for students to produce a very short answer, but you must be prepared to expand your answer and to include various situations within which the use of a cost term is appropriate. Always make sure your answer includes illustrations of cost terms. Multiple choice questions are also often set on topics included in this chapter. Review problems 2.16–2.21 are typical examples of such questions. You should now attempt these and compare your answers with the solutions.

ASSESSMENT MATERIAL

The review questions are short questions that enable you to assess your understanding of the main topics included in the chapter. The numbers in parentheses provide you with the page numbers to refer to if you cannot answer a specific question.

The review problems are more complex and require you to relate and apply the chapter content to various business problems. The problems are graded by their level of difficulty. The multiple-choice questions are the least demanding and normally take less than 10 minutes to complete. Fully worked solutions to the review problems are provided in a separate section at the end of the book. Further review problems with solutions for this chapter are available on the accompanying website www.drury-online.com. The website includes a *Student's Manual* and an *Instructor's Manual*. Students can access both questions and answers from the *Student's Manual* and the questions from the *Instructor's Manual*. The answers to problems in the *Instructor's Manual* are available only to lecturers on the lecturer's password-protected section of the website.

The website also includes over 20 case study problems. A list of these cases is provided on pages 427–30. The Electronic Boards case is a case study that is relevant to the introductory stages of a management accounting course.

REVIEW QUESTIONS

2.1 Define the meaning of the term 'cost object' and provide three examples of cost objects. *(p. 22)*

2.2 Distinguish between a direct and an indirect cost. *(p. 22)*

2.3 Describe how a given direct cost item can be both a direct and an indirect cost. *(p. 23)*

2.4 Provide examples of each of the following: (a) direct labour, (b) indirect labour, (c) direct materials, (d) indirect materials, and (e) indirect expenses. *(pp. 22–23)*

2.5 Explain the meaning of the terms: (a) prime cost, (b) overheads, and (c) cost allocations. *(pp. 23–24)*

2.6 Distinguish between product costs and period costs. *(pp. 25–26)*

2.7 Provide examples of decisions that require knowledge of how costs and revenues vary with different levels of activity. *(p. 27)*

2.8 Explain the meaning of each of the following terms: (a) variable costs, (b) fixed costs, (c) semi-fixed costs, and (d) semi-variable costs. Provide examples of costs for each of the four categories. *(pp. 27–29)*

2.9 Distinguish between relevant (avoidable) and irrelevant (unavoidable) costs and provide examples of each type of cost. *(pp. 29–30)*

2.10 Explain the meaning of the term 'sunk cost'. *(pp. 31–32)*

2.11 Distinguish between incremental and marginal costs. *(p. 33)*

2.12   What is an opportunity cost? Give some examples. *(p. 32)*

2.13   Explain responsibility accounting. *(p. 34)*

REVIEW PROBLEMS

2.14   Classify each of the following as being usually fixed (F), variable (V), semi-fixed (SF) or semi-variable (SV):

    (a)   direct labour;

    (b)   depreciation of machinery;

    (c)   factory rental;

    (d)   supplies and other indirect materials;

    (e)   advertising;

    (f)   maintenance of machinery;

    (g)   factory manager's salary;

    (h)   supervisory personnel;

    (i)   royalty payments.

2.15   Which of the following costs are likely to be controllable by the head of the production department?

    (a)   price paid for materials;

    (b)   charge for floor space;

    (c)   raw materials used;

    (d)   electricity used for machinery;

    (e)   machinery depreciation;

    (f)   direct labour;

    (g)   insurance on machinery;

    (h)   share of cost of industrial relations department.

2.16   Which of the following should be classified as indirect labour?

    (a)   machine operators in a factory producing furniture;

    (b)   lawyers in a legal firm;

    (c)   maintenance workers in a power generation organization;

    (d)   lorry drivers in a road haulage company.

ACCA Financial Information for Management

2.17   Which ONE of the following costs could NOT be classified as a production overhead cost in a food processing company?

    (a)   The cost of renting the factory building.

    (b)   The salary of the factory manager.

(c) The depreciation of equipment located in the materials store.

(d) The cost of ingredients.

CIMA Management Accounting Fundamentals

2.18 The following data relate to two output levels of a department:

Machine hours	17 000	18 500
Overheads	£246 500	£251 750

The variable overhead rate per hour is £3.50. The amount of fixed overheads is:

(a) £5 250

(b) £59 500

(c) £187 000

(d) 246 500   *CIMA Stage 1*

2.19 Prime cost is:

(a) all costs incurred in manufacturing a product;

(b) the total of direct costs;

(c) the material cost of a product;

(d) the cost of operating a department.   *CIMA Stage 1*

2.20 A direct cost is a cost which:

(a) is incurred as a direct consequence of a decision;

(b) can be economically identified with the item being costed;

(c) cannot be economically identified with the item being costed;

(d) is immediately controllable;

(e) is the responsibility of the board of directors.   *CIMA Stage 2*

2.21 Fixed costs are conventionally deemed to be:

(a) constant per unit of output;

(b) constant in total when production volume changes;

(c) outside the control of management;

(d) those unaffected by inflation.   *CIMA Stage 1*

2.22 Prepare a report for the Managing Director of your company explaining how costs may be classified by their behaviour, with particular reference to the effects both on total and on unit costs. Your report should:

(i) say why it is necessary to classify costs by their behaviour, and

(ii) be illustrated by sketch graphs within the body of the report.   *(15 marks)*
                                                   CIMA Stage 1

2.23 Describe three different methods of cost classification and explain the utility of each method. *(11 marks)*
ACCA Level 1

2.24 Cost classifications used in costing include:

(i)   period costs

(ii)   product costs

(iii) variable costs

(iv)   opportunity costs

Required:
Explain each of these classifications, with examples of the types of costs that may be included. *(17 marks)*
ACCA Level 1

2.25 (a) Describe the role of the cost accountant in a manufacturing organization. *(8 marks)*

(b) Explain whether you agree with each of the following statements:

(i)   'All direct costs are variable.'

(ii)   'Variable costs are controllable and fixed costs are not.'

(iii) 'Sunk costs are irrelevant when providing decision-making information.'

(9 marks)
ACCA Level 1

2.26 *Opportunity cost* and *sunk cost* are among the concepts of cost commonly discussed. You are required:

(i)   to define these terms precisely; *(4 marks)*

(ii)   to suggest for each of them situations in which the concept might be applied; *(4 marks)*

(iii) to assess briefly the significance of each of the concepts. *(4 marks)*
ICAEW Management Accounting

2.27 Distinguish between, and provide an illustration of:

(i)   'avoidable' and 'unavoidable' costs;

(ii)   'cost centres' and 'cost units'.
(8 marks)
ACCA Foundation

2.28 A manufacturing company has four types of cost (identified as T1, T2, T3 and T4). The total cost for each type at two different production levels is:

Cost type	Total cost for 125 units £	Total cost for 180 units £
T1	1000	1250
T2	1750	2520
T3	2475	2826
T4	3225	4644

Which cost types would be classified as being semi-variable?

(a) T1

(b) T2

(c) T3

(d) T4

ACCA Financial Information for Management

2.29 Cost behaviour

Data	(£)
Cost of motor car	5500
Trade-in price after 2 years or 60 000 miles is expected to be	1500
Maintenance – 6-monthly service costing	60
Spares/replacement parts, per 1000 miles	20
Vehicle licence, per annum	80
Insurance, per annum	150
Tyre replacements after 25 000 miles, four at £37.50 each	150
Petrol, per gallon	1.90
Average mileage from one gallon is 25 miles.	

(a) From the above data you are required:

   (i) to prepare a schedule to be presented to management showing for the mileages of 5000, 10 000, 15 000 and 30 000 miles per annum:

   (1) total variable cost

   (2) total fixed cost

   (3) total cost

   (4) variable cost per mile (in pence to nearest penny)

   (5) fixed cost per mile (in pence to nearest penny)

   (6) total cost per mile (in pence to nearest penny)

If, in classifying the costs, you consider that some can be treated as either variable or fixed, state the assumption(s) on which your answer is based together with brief supporting reason(s).

   (ii) On graph paper plot the information given in your answer to (i) above for the costs listed against (1), (2), (3) and (6).

   (iii) Read off from your graph(s) in (ii) and state the approximate total costs applicable to 18 000 miles and 25 000 miles and the total cost per mile at these two mileages.

(b) 'The more miles you travel, the cheaper it becomes.' Comment briefly on this statement.

(25 marks)

CIMA Cost Accounting

2.30 Sunk and opportunity costs for decision-making

Mrs Johnston has taken out a lease on a shop for a down payment of £5000. Additionally, the rent under the lease amounts to £5000 per annum. If the lease is cancelled, the initial payment of £5000 is forfeit. Mrs Johnston plans to use the shop for the sale of clothing, and has estimated operations for the next 12 months as follows:

	(£)	(£)
Sales	115 000	
Less Value-added tax (VAT)	15 000	
Sales Less VAT		100 000
Cost of goods sold	50 000	
Wages and wage related costs	12 000	
Rent including the down payment	10 000	
Rates, heating, lighting and insurance	13 000	
Audit, legal and general expenses	2000	
		87 000
Net profit before tax		13 000

In the figures no provision has been made for the cost of Mrs Johnston but it is estimated that one half of her time will be devoted to the business. She is undecided whether to continue with her plans, because she knows that she can sublet the shop to a friend for a monthly rent of £550 if she does not use the shop herself.

You are required to:

(a) (i) explain and identify the 'sunk' and 'opportunity' costs in the situation depicted above;

 (ii) state what decision Mrs Johnston should make according to the information given, supporting your conclusion with a financial statement;

(11 marks)

(b) explain the meaning and use of 'notional' (or 'imputed') costs and quote *two* supporting examples. *(4 marks)*

CIMA Foundation Cost Accounting

PART 2
COST ACCUMULATION FOR INVENTORY VALUATION AND PROFIT MEASUREMENT

This section focuses mainly on assigning costs to products in order to separate costs incurred during a period between costs of goods sold and the closing inventory valuation. The extent to which product costs accumulated for inventory valuation and profit measurement should be adjusted for meeting decision-making, cost control and performance measurement requirements is also briefly considered.

Chapter 3 is concerned with the recording procedures for direct labour and materials. It also examines the materials control procedure and methods of establishing optimal stock levels. Chapter 4 aims to provide you with an understanding of how costs are assigned to cost objects. In particular the chapter focuses on the assignment of indirect costs using traditional costing systems. In Chapter 5 the emphasis is on the accounting entries necessary to record transactions within a job costing system. The issues relating to a cost accumulation procedure for a process costing system are described in Chapter 6. This is a system that is applicable to industries that produce many units of the same product during a particular period. In Chapter 7 the problems associated with calculating product costs in those industries that produce joint and by-products are discussed. The final chapter in this section is concerned with the alternative accounting methods of assigning fixed manufacturing overheads to products and their implications for profitmmeasurement and inventory valuation.

CHAPTER 3
ACCOUNTING FOR DIRECT COSTS

LEARNING OBJECTIVES

After studying this chapter, you should be able to:

- describe the materials recording procedure;
- explain the accounting treatment of holiday pay, overtime premiums, employment costs, stores losses and delivery and materials handling costs;
- distinguish between first in, first out (FIFO), last in, first out (LIFO) and average cost methods of stores pricing;
- justify which costs are relevant and should be included in the calculation of the economic order quantity (EOQ);
- calculate the EOQ using the tabulation and formula methods;
- describe the ABC classification method;
- outline the main features of a just-in-time approach.

The assignment of direct labour and materials to cost objects merely involves the implementation of suitable clerical/computer procedures to identify the quantity and prices of the resources consumed. By contrast, indirect labour and material costs are classified as overheads and the costs are assigned to overhead accounts and then allocated to cost objects using the cost allocation procedures described in the next chapter.

The emphasis throughout this chapter is on how labour and materials' costs that have already been incurred should be accumulated for allocating costs between cost of goods sold and inventories for internal and external profit reporting purposes. For decision-making, the emphasis is on using future costs rather than past costs, so the accumulation of past costs is generally not relevant. For example, many companies obtain customers' orders by submitting bids or quotations, which, if accepted, become the agreed selling prices. The assignment of actual costs incurred may provide useful feedback information on the accuracy of the bids, and help to improve the accuracy of future bids, but past costs are normally not directly used for decision-making. Exceptions do exist, however, such as garages that charge for repairs on the basis of actual costs incurred.

An understanding of the process of accounting for labour and materials requires a knowledge of the appropriate recording procedures and documentation. To simplify the presentation, and help you understand the recording procedures, manual clerical procedures are described. You should note, however, that in most organizations the recording procedure is computerized. Nevertheless, the basic principles described in this chapter still apply.

ACCOUNTING TREATMENT OF VARIOUS LABOUR COST ITEMS

Holiday pay received by employees whose labour cost is normally regarded as direct should be charged to activities by means of an inflated hourly rate. For example, if the employee is normally paid £12 per hour for a 40-hour week and is entitled to six weeks annual holiday he or she will receive a total of £2880 holiday pay (six weeks at £480 per week). During the rest of the year, the employee will work 1840 hours (46 weeks at 40 hours per week). Dividing £2880 by 1840 hours gives an addition of approximately £1.57 per hour to the employee's hourly wage rate to ensure that the holiday pay is recovered. The advantage of this approach is that holiday pay is treated as a direct labour cost.

Overtime premiums and shift-work premiums are included as part of overheads. If overtime premiums are charged directly to products/services or customers' orders undertaken during the overtime or night-shift period, they will bear higher costs than those produced during a regular working week. Overtime and night-shift work is usually necessitated by a generally high level of activity, not by specific products or customers. It is therefore inappropriate to record activities undertaken during overtime or night hours as being more costly than their counterparts undertaken during the normal working day. If, however, the overtime or shift premiums are a direct result of a customer's urgent request for the completion of the order and not due to the general pressure of work, then the overtime or shift premiums should be charged directly to the customer. It is important that overtime and shift premiums are also analyzed by departments for cost control purposes.

Consider a situation where an employee is paid time and a half for weekly hours worked in excess of 40 hours. Assume that the employee works for 50 hours and that the 10 hours of overtime were spent on a particular activity. The hourly wage rate is £12. The employee's weekly wage will be calculated as follows:

Normal time rate wage: 50 hours at £12	£600
Overtime premium (1/2 × 10 hours at £12)	£60
	£660

The normal time rate wage will be allocated to the activities on which the employee was engaged during the period, but if the overtime was a result of demand exceeding productive capacity, it would be unreasonable to charge the overtime premium to the particular activity merely because it was scheduled to be produced during the overtime period. In such circumstances it would be preferable to charge the overtime premium to the appropriate overhead account, the total of which would be apportioned to all activities worked on during the period.

In addition to the wage and salary payments to employees, the employer will incur a number of other **employment costs**. These include the employer's share of National Insurance contributions and pension fund contributions. Some firms record employment costs as overheads, but it is preferable to calculate an average hourly rate for employment costs and add this to the hourly wage rate paid to the employees. For example, the employer may be responsible for employment costs of £60 per week for an operative who is paid £12 per hour for a 40-hour week. Here we can establish that the employment costs are £1.50 per hour and this cost can be added to the hourly wage rate of £12 per hour, giving a total rate of £13.50 per hour. This approach is conceptually preferable to the alternative of charging the £60 to an overhead account, since employment costs are a fundamental part of acquiring labour services.

MATERIALS RECORDING PROCEDURE

According to a survey by Drury and Tayles (2000) of 176 UK organizations, the cost of direct materials represented the dominant costs in manufacturing organizations, averaging 51 per cent of total costs for the responding organizations within the manufacturing sector. The accounting and control of materials is therefore of vital importance in manufacturing organizations. In the remainder of this chapter the mechanisms for recording and controlling materials are explained. Because of the importance to the manufacturing sector the focus is mainly on manufacturing organizations but the materials recording procedure that is described is also applicable to non-manufacturing organizations. The materials recording procedure involves the following stages:

- storage of materials;
- purchase of materials;
- receipt of materials;
- issue of materials;
- assigning the cost of materials to cost objects.

We will describe the clerical procedures for each of the above stages, although in most organizations the recording procedure is computerized using barcoding and other forms of on-line information recording. The source documents that are described and illustrated are likely to exist only in the form of computer records.

Storage of materials

In a manufacturing organization the stores department is responsible for ensuring that optimal stock levels are maintained for each item of material in stock. Thus, to control the quantity of stocks held, adequate records must be maintained for each stores item. When items of materials have reached their re-order point a **purchase requisition** is initiated requesting the purchase department to obtain the re-order quantity from an appropriate supplier. Methods that are used for establishing optimum stock levels, re-order points and re-order quantities will be explained later in this chapter.

Purchase of materials

When a purchase requisition is received, purchasing department staff select an appropriate supplier and then complete a **purchase order** requesting that the supplier supply the materials listed on the order. A copy of the purchase order is sent to the receiving section within the stores department for checking with the goods when they arrive.

Receipt of materials

When the goods are received by the receiving section they are inspected and checked with the supplier's delivery note and a copy of the purchase order. The receiving section then lists the materials received on a **goods received note (GRN)** and forwards copies of the GRN to the purchasing and accounting departments. The purchasing department records that the order has been completed, and the accounting department checks the GRN with the supplier's invoice to ensure that payment is made only in respect of goods actually received. The department also uses the invoice to price each of the items listed on the GRN. The GRN is the source document for entering details of the items received in the receipts column of the appropriate **stores ledger account**, as in Exhibit 3.1. This document is merely a record of the quantity and value of each individual item of material stored by the organization.

Issue of materials

The formal authorization for the issue of materials is a **stores requisition**, which lists the type and quantity of materials issued. This document also contains details of either the customer's

Stores ledger account											
Material: . ... Code:					Maximum quantity: .... Minimum quantity:						
	Receipts				Issues				Stock		
Date	GRN no.	Quantity	Unit price (£)	Amount (£)	Stores req. no.	Quantity	Unit price (£)	Amount (£)	Quantity	Unit price (£)	Amount (£)

EXHIBIT 3.1

A stores ledger account

EXHIBIT 3.2

A stores requisition

Stores requisition				No.		
Material required for:						
(Product code or overhead account)						
Department:						
				Date:		
[Quantity]	Description	Code no.	Weight	Rate	£	[Notes]
Departmental Head						

order number, product/service code or overhead account for which the materials are required. Exhibit 3.2 provides an illustration of a typical stores requisition. Each of the items listed on the materials requisition are priced from the information recorded in the receipts column of the appropriate stores ledger account. The information for each of the items listed on the stores requisition is then recorded in the issues column of the appropriate stores ledger account and a balance of the quantity and value is calculated for each item of material.

Assigning the cost of materials to cost objects

The total cost of the items of material listed on the stores requisition is assigned to the appropriate customer's account number, overhead account or product or service code. The details on the material requisition thus represent the source information for assigning the cost of the materials to the appropriate cost object. Thus the accounting entries required for an issue of materials involve:

1 Reducing the value of raw materials stocks by recording the values issued in the issues column of the appropriate stores ledger account.

2 Assigning the cost of the issues to the appropriate customer's order number, product/ service code or overhead account.

PRICING THE ISSUES OF MATERIALS

It may be difficult to associate costs with a specific issue of materials. This is because the same type of material may have been purchased at several different prices. Actual cost can take on several different values, and some method of pricing material issues must be selected. Consider the situation presented in Example 3.1.

There are three alternative methods that you might consider for calculating the cost of materials issued to job Z which will impact on both the cost of sales and the inventory valuation that is incorporated in the April monthly profit statement and balance sheet.

EXAMPLE 3.1

On 5 March Nordic purchased 5000 units of materials at £1 each. A further 5000 units were purchased on 30 March at £1.20 each. During April, 5000 units were issued to job Z. No further issues were made during April and you are now preparing the monthly accounts for April.

First, you could assume that the first item received was the first item to be issued, that is **first in, first out (FIFO)**. In the example the 5000 units issued to job Z would be priced at £1 and the closing inventory would be valued at £6000 (5000 units at £1.20 per unit).

Second, you could assume that the last item to be received was the first item to be issued, that is, **last in, first out (LIFO)**. Here a material cost of £6000 (5000 units at £1.20 per unit) would be recorded against the cost of job Z and the closing inventory would be valued at £5000 (5000 units at £1 per unit).

Third, you could issue the items at the average cost of the materials in stock (i.e. £1.10 per unit). With an average cost system the job cost would be recorded at £5500 and the closing inventory would also be valued at £5500. The following is a summary of the three different materials pricing methods relating to Example 3.1:

	Cost of sales (i.e. charge to job Z) £	Closing inventory £	Total costs £
First in, first out (FIFO)	5000 (5000 × £1)	6000 (5000 × £1.20)	11 000
Last in, first out (LIFO)	6000 (5000 × £1.20)	5000 (5000 × £1)	11 000
Average cost	5500 (5000 × £1.10)	5500 (5000 × £1.10)	11 000

FIFO appears to be the most logical method in the sense that it makes the same assumption as the physical flow of materials through an organization. During periods of inflation, the earliest materials that have the lowest purchase price will be issued first. This assumption leads to a lower cost of sales calculation, and therefore a higher profit than would be obtained by using either of the other methods. Note also that the closing inventory will be at the latest, and therefore higher, prices. With the LIFO method the latest and higher prices are assigned to the cost of sales and therefore lower profits will be reported, compared with using either FIFO or average cost. The value of the closing inventory will be at the earliest, and therefore lower, prices. Under the average cost method, the cost of sales and the closing inventory will fall somewhere between the values recorded for the FIFO and LIFO methods.

LIFO is not an acceptable method of pricing for taxation purposes in the UK and if it is used, the accounts must be adjusted for tax. The UK Statement of Standard Accounting Practice (SSAP9) and the International Accounting Standard (IAS2) on inventory valuation state that LIFO does not bear a reasonable relationship to actual costs obtained during the period, and imply that this method is inappropriate for external reporting. In view of these comments, the FIFO or the average cost method should be used for external financial accounting purposes. Instead of using FIFO or average cost for inventory valuation and profit measurement many organizations maintain their inventories at standard prices using a standard costing system, which considerably simplifies pricing material issues. We shall look at standard costing in detail in Chapter 15.

The above discussion relates to pricing the issue of materials for internal and external profit measurement and inventory valuation. Remember that, for decision-making the focus is on future costs, rather than the allocation of past costs, and therefore the choice of method of pricing materials is not normally an issue.

In practice, pricing stores issues is not likely to be as simple as the situation presented in Example 3.1. You should now refer to Example 3.2, which presents a more complex situation, and then examine each of the entries in stores ledger accounts for the three different pricing methods that are presented in Exhibit 3.3. Do remember, however, that in practice computer programs exist for pricing stores issues by the chosen method so it is most unlikely that the process will be carried out manually.

You should note in Exhibit 3.3 that with the FIFO method the issue of 1240 units on 15 September is at three different purchase prices. This is because 1400 units out of the earliest purchase of 2000 units have already been issued. The remaining 600 units are therefore the first items to be issued out of the 1240 units on 15 September. The next earliest purchase of 520 units is now issued, leaving a balance of 120 units to be issued from the purchase of 5 August. The closing stock consists of the final purchase for the period of 1000 units plus 40 units from the 22 August purchase that have not yet been issued.

Now refer to the LIFO method in Exhibit 3.3 and look at the issue of 480 units on 14 October. This issue includes the 160 units at the 5 August purchase price of £11.50 because all of the units from the latest purchase on 22 August have previously been issued, together with 640 units from the next latest purchase of 5 August. Only 160 units from the 5 August purchase are available for issue. The balance of 320 units issued is at £10 as all the previous later purchases have already been issued. Hence LIFO does not always ensure that the issues are at the latest purchase price. The closing stock consists of 240 units at the latest purchase price of £11 plus 800 units at the earliest purchase price of £10.

EXAMPLE 3.2

The purchase and issue of a raw material by the Midshire Water Authority for a five-month period were as follows:

1 July	Received	2000 units at £10 per unit
9 July	Received	520 units at £10.50 per unit
18 July	Issued	1400 units
5 August	Received	800 units at £11.50 per unit
22 August	Received	600 units at £12.50 per unit
15 September	Issued	1240 units
14 October	Issued	480 units
8 November	Received	1000 units at £11 per unit
24 November	Issued	760 units

There was no opening stock of the raw material. You are required to prepare the stores ledger accounts when issues are priced, respectively, according to the FIFO, LIFO and average cost methods. Please refer to Exhibit 3.3 for the answer.

EXHIBIT 3.3

Pricing stores issues for the Midshire Water Authority

Stores ledger account – **FIFO method**

Material: .... Code: .... Maximum quantity: ....
Minimum quantity: ....

Date	GRN no.	Quantity	Unit price (£)	Amount (£)	Quantity	Unit price (£)	Amount (£)	Quantity	Unit price (£)	Amount (£)
		Receipts			Issues			Stock		
July 1		2000	10.00	20 000				2000		20 000
9		520	10.50	5 460				2520		25 460
18					1400	10.00	14 000	1120		11 460
Aug 5		800	11.50	9 200				1920		20 660
Aug 22		600	12.50	7 500				2520		28 160
Sept 15					600	10.00				
					520	10.50				
					120	1240	11.50	12 840	1280	15 320
Oct 14						480	11.50	5520	800	9800
Nov 8		1000	11.00	11 000	200		11.50		1800	20 800
Nov 24					560	760	12.50	9300	1040	11 500

The closing stock represents:

40 units at £12.50 per unit =	£500
1000 units at £11.00 per unit =	£11 000
	£11 500

Stores ledger account – **LIFO method**

Material: .... Code: .... Maximum quantity: ....
Minimum quantity: ....

Date	GRN no.	Quantity	Unit price (£)	Amount (£)	Quantity	Unit price (£)	Amount (£)	Quantity	Unit price (£)	Amount (£)
		Receipts			Issues			Stock		
July 1		2000	10.00	20 000				2000		20 000
9		520	10.50	5 460				2520		25 460
18					520	10.50				
					880	1400	10.00	14 260	1120	11 200
Aug 5		800	11.50	9 200				1920		20 400
Aug 22		600	12.50	7 500				2520		27 900
Sept 15					600	12.50				
					640	1240	11.50	14 860	1280	13 040
Oct 14					160		11.50			
					320	480	10.00	5040	800	8000
Nov 8		1000	11.00	11 000				1800		19 000
Nov 24						760	11.00	8360	1040	10 640

The closing stock represents:

800 units at £10.00 per unit =	£ 8000
240 units at £11.00 per unit =	£ 2640
	£10 640

Stores ledger account – **average-cost method**

Material: .... Code: .... Maximum quantity: ....
Minimum quantity: ....

Date	Receipts				Issues				Stock		
	GRN no.	Quantity	Unit price (£)	Amount (£)	Stores req.	Quantity	Unit price (£)	Amount (£)	Quantity	Unit price (£)	Amount (£)
July 1		2000	10.00	20 000					2000	10.00	20 000
9		520	10.50	5 460					2520	10.1032	25 460
18						1400	10.1032	14 144	1120		11 316
Aug 5		800	11.50	9 200					1920	10.6854	20 516
Aug 22		600	12.50	7 500					2520	11.1175	28 016
Sept 15						1240	11.1175	13 785	1280		14 231
Oct 14						480	11.1175	5 536	800		8 895
Nov 8		1000	11.00	11 000					1800	11.0528	19 895
Nov 24						760	11.0528	8 400	1040		11 495

$$9\ \text{July} = \frac{£25\,460}{2520\ \text{units}} = £10.1032$$

$$22\ \text{August} = \frac{£28\,016}{2520\ \text{units}} = £11.1175$$

Finally, with the average cost method shown in the third section of Exhibit 3.3 you should note that each of the items are issued at the average cost per unit. This is calculated by dividing the total value of the material in stock by the total quantity in stock after each new purchase. An illustration of the average unit cost calculations for the 9 July and 22 August purchases is shown in the third section of Exhibit 3.3. An important point to note with the average cost method is that each item is issued at the latest average price and this average price changes only when a new purchase is received.

ISSUES RELATING TO ACCOUNTING FOR MATERIALS

In this section we examine three issues that relate to accounting for materials. They relate to the treatment of:

1 stores losses;

2 materials delivery costs; and

3 materials handling costs.

Treatment of stores losses

To achieve accurate profit measurement, the clerical or computer record in respect of each item of materials in stock must be in agreement with the actual stock held. This means that the actual stock must be physically counted and compared with the clerical or computer record. For this to be done effectively, there must be either a **complete periodic stockcount** or some form of continuous stocktaking. In a complete stockcount, all the stores items are counted at one point in time, which can disrupt production. Continuous stocktaking involves a sample of stores items being counted regularly on, say, a daily basis, and is less disruptive.

Sometimes it may be found that the actual stock level is different from the clerical or computer records. The reasons for this may be:

1 an entry having been made in the wrong stores ledger account;

2 the items having been placed in the wrong physical location;

3 arithmetical errors made when calculating the stores balance on the stores ledger when a manual system is operated;

4 theft of stock.

When a discrepancy arises the individual stores ledger accounts must be adjusted so that they are in agreement with the actual stock. Assume, for example, that the actual stock is less than the clerical or computer record. The quantity and value of the appropriate stores ledger account must be reduced and the difference charged to an overhead account for stores losses. The total amount charged to the stores losses overhead account should be allocated to cost objects based on the overhead procedure described in the next chapter.

REAL WORLD VIEWS 3.1

Inventory management practices

Managing inventory in a business is an ongoing job. Depending on the type of business, some items held in inventory will have strict controls – both physical and system controls. For example, retailers like Tesco (UK) and Wal-Mart (US) used sophisticated inventory systems to control inventory in each store or warehouse. They also use technologies like 'radio barcodes' to keep an eye on items like DVDs or computer games which are often pilfered.

While retailers may be able to keep track of some inventories to the item level, not all are tracked in such detail. Other businesses don't have such detail available on inventory levels or movements. Therefore, management accountants must make assumptions on how inventories 'move' in order to cost products. In this chapter, methods used by management accountants are described, and First in first out (FIFO) and Last in first out (LIFO) are two possible methods. FIFO means that it is assumed that oldest items are used/sold first, whereas LIFO assumes that newest items are used/sold first.

In practice however, this may or may not be the case, with the physical movement of items determined by other operational factors. For example, at a building aggregates company like Lafarge (lafarge.com), LIFO may be at play. Aggregates refer to naturally occurring sand/gravel, crushed rock or recycled demolition material. Regardless of source, aggregates are typically seen in large mounds in quarries or building sites, which means that the last materials dumped on the mound are likely to be some of the first used. In their accounting policies section of the Annual Report however, Lafarge state inventories are valued using a weighted average cost method. On the other hand, retailers like Tesco are likely to follow FIFO principles with foodstuffs on their shelves – you might notice that products with a sell/use by date in the near future are always towards the front of the shelf. Tesco too use a weighted average method to value their inventories according to their Annual Report.

Questions

1 Can you think of other businesses where the physical flow of goods might follow FIFO or LIFO?

2 How does the value of inventory affect the profits of a business?

References

'Tesco has stock control in the bag' Sunday Times (UK), 13/09/2004

Lafarge 2009 Annual Report, available at lafarge.com

Tesco 2009 Annual Report, available at tescoplc.com

Treatment of materials delivery costs

Ideally, delivery charges made by suppliers should be included as part of the purchase price of the materials so that these costs can be charged as direct costs. Wherever possible, materials should be charged directly to cost objects rather than being grouped as indirect costs and apportioned to cost objects. The delivery charge will normally be shown separately on the invoice for the consignment of materials delivered. When the invoice is for one kind of material only, there is no problem in accounting for the materials and the resulting total entered as a receipt for the appropriate item of material. However, when the delivery charge refers to several different types of material, the charge must be apportioned to each type of material delivered. The apportionment could be made according to either the value or the weight of the materials. Alternatively, the clerical work could be simplified by charging delivery costs to an overhead account and apportioning these costs as part of the overhead procedure described in the next chapter.

Treatment of materials handling costs

The term **materials handling costs** refers to the expenses involved in receiving, storing, issuing and handling materials. Various approaches can be used to account for them, involving charging the costs to a materials handling overhead account and allocating these costs to cost objects. We will examine how this is done in the next chapter. However, you should be aware that some companies establish a separate **materials handling rate**.

Consider, for example, a situation where the materials handling costs for a period were £1 million and the direct materials issued during the period were valued at £5 million. In this situation the materials handling cost could be allocated to cost objects (i.e. products, services or customers) at a materials handling rate of 20 per cent of the cost of direct materials issued (£1 million/£5 million).

QUANTITATIVE MODELS FOR THE PLANNING AND CONTROL OF STOCKS

Investment in stocks represents a major asset of most industrial and commercial organizations, and it is essential that stocks be managed efficiently so that these investments do not become unnecessarily large. A firm should determine its optimum level of investment in stocks – and, to do this, two conflicting requirements must be met. First, it must ensure that stocks are sufficient to meet the requirements of production and sales; and, second, it must avoid holding surplus stocks that are unnecessary and risk becoming obsolescent. The optimal stock level lies somewhere between these two extremes. We will now consider how economic order quantities and the levels at which stocks should be replenished can be derived.

RELEVANT COSTS FOR QUANTITATIVE MODELS UNDER CONDITIONS OF CERTAINTY

The relevant costs that should be considered when determining optimal stock levels consist of holding costs and ordering costs.

Holding costs usually consist of the following:

1 opportunity cost of investment in stocks;

2 incremental insurance costs;

3 incremental warehouse and storage costs;

4 incremental material handling costs;

5 cost of obsolescence and deterioration of stocks.

The relevant holding costs for use in quantitative models should include only those items that will vary with the levels of stocks. Costs that will not be affected by changes in stock levels are not relevant costs. For example, in the case of warehousing and storage, salaries of storekeepers, depreciation of equipment and fixed rental of equipment and buildings are often irrelevant because they are unaffected by changes in stock levels.

There is an opportunity cost of holding stocks. This is the return that is lost by investing in stocks rather than some alternative investment. The opportunity cost should be applied only to those costs that vary with the number of units purchased. The relevant holding costs for other items such as material handling, obsolescence and deterioration are difficult to estimate, but we shall see that these costs are unlikely to be critical to the investment decision. Normally, holding costs are expressed as a percentage rate per pound of average investment.

Ordering costs usually consist of the clerical costs of preparing purchase orders, receiving deliveries and paying invoices. Ordering costs that are common to all stock decisions are not relevant, and only the incremental costs of placing an order are used in formulating the quantitative models.

The costs of acquiring stocks through buying or manufacturing are not a relevant cost to be included in the quantitative models, since the acquisition costs remain unchanged, irrespective of the order size or stock levels, unless quantity discounts are available. (For a discussion of how quantity discounts should be incorporated you should refer to Drury, 2008; ch.24.) For example, it does not matter in terms of acquisition cost whether total annual requirements of 1000 units at £10 each are purchased in one 1000-unit batch, ten 100-unit batches or one hundred 10-unit batches; the acquisition cost of £10 000 will remain unchanged. The acquisition cost is not therefore a relevant cost, but the ordering and holding costs will change in relation to the order size, and these will be relevant for decision-making models.

DETERMINING THE ECONOMIC ORDER QUANTITY

If more units are ordered at one time, fewer orders will be required per year. This will mean a reduction in the ordering costs. However, when fewer orders are placed, larger average stocks must be maintained, which leads to an increase in holding costs. The problem is therefore one of trading off the costs of carrying large stocks against the costs of placing more orders. The optimum order size is the order quantity that will result in the total amount of the ordering and holding costs being minimized. This optimum order size is known as the **economic order quantity (EOQ)**; it can be determined by tabulating the total costs for various order quantities, by a graphical presentation or by using a formula. All three methods are illustrated using the information given in Example 3.3.

EXAMPLE 3.3

A company purchases a raw material from an outside supplier at a cost of £9 per unit. The total annual demand for this product is 40 000 units, and the following additional information is available.

	(£)	(£)
Required annual return on investment in stocks (10% × £9)	0.90	
Other holding costs per unit	0.10	
Holding costs per unit		1.00
Cost per purchase order:		
Clerical costs, stationery, postage, telephone etc.		2.00

You are required to determine the optimal order quantity.

Order quantity	100	200	300	400	500	600	800	10 000
Average stock in units[a]	50	100	150	200	250	300	400	5 000
Number of purchase orders[b]	400	200	133	100	80	67	50	4
Annual holding costs[c]	£50	£100	£150	£200	£250	£300	£400	£5 000
Annual ordering cost	£800	£400	£266	£200	£160	£134	£100	£8
Total relevant cost	£850	£500	£416	£400	£410	£434	£500	£5 008

EXHIBIT 3.4
Relevant costs for various order quantities

[a]If there are no stocks when the order is received and the units received are used at a constant rate, the average stock will be one-half of the quantity ordered. Even if a minimum safety stock is held, the average stock relevant to the decision will still be one-half of the quantity ordered, because the minimum stock will remain unchanged for each alternative order quantity.
[b]The number of purchase orders is ascertained by dividing the total annual demand of 40 000 units by the order quantity.
[c]The annual holding cost is ascertained by multiplying the average stock by the holding cost of £1 per unit.

Tabulation method

It is apparent from Example 3.3 that a company can choose to purchase small batches (e.g. 100 units) at frequent intervals or large batches (e.g. 10 000 units) at infrequent intervals. The annual relevant costs for various order quantities are set out in Exhibit 3.4. You will see that the economic order quantity is 400 units. This is the point at which the total annual relevant costs are at a minimum.

Graphical method

The information tabulated in Exhibit 3.4 is presented in graphical form in Figure 3.1 for every order size up to 800 units. The vertical axis represents the relevant annual costs for the investment in stocks, and the horizontal axis can be used to represent either the various order quantities or the average stock levels; two scales are actually shown on the horizontal axis so

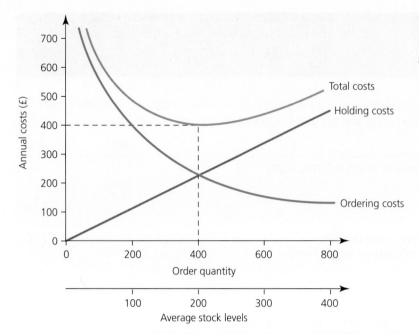

FIGURE 3.1

Economic order quantity graph

that both items can be incorporated. You will see from the graph that as the average stock level or the order quantity increases, the holding cost also increases. Alternatively, the ordering costs decline as stock levels and order quantities are increased. The total cost line represents the summation of both the holding and the ordering costs.

Note that the total cost line is at a minimum for an order quantity of 400 units and occurs at the point where the ordering cost and holding cost curves intersect. In other words, the economic order quantity is found at the point where the holding costs equal the ordering costs. It is also interesting to note from the graph (see also Exhibit 3.4) that the total relevant costs are not particularly sensitive to changes in the order quantity. For example, if you refer to Exhibit 3.4 you will see that a 25 per cent change in the order quantity from 400 units to either 300 or 500 units leads to an increase in annual costs from £400 to £410 or £416, an increase of 2.5 per cent or 4 per cent. Alternatively, an increase of 50 per cent in the order quantity from 400 units to 600 units leads to an increase in annual costs from £400 to £434 or 8.5 per cent.

Formula method

The economic order quantity can be found by applying a formula that incorporates the basic relationships between holding and ordering costs and order quantities. These relationships can be stated as follows: the number of orders for a period is the total demand for that item of stock for the period (denoted by D) divided by the quantity ordered in units (denoted by Q). The total ordering cost is obtained by multiplying the number of orders for a period by the ordering cost per order (denoted by O), and is given by the formula:

$$\frac{\text{total demand for period}}{\text{quantity ordered}} \times \text{ordering cost per order} = \frac{DO}{Q}$$

Assuming that holding costs are constant per unit, the total holding cost for a period will be equal to the average stock for the period, which is represented by the quantity ordered divided by two *(Q/2),* multiplied by the holding cost per unit (denoted by H); it is therefore given by

$$\frac{\text{quantity ordered}}{2} \times \text{holding cost per unit} = \frac{QH}{2}$$

The total relevant cost (TC) for any order quantity can now be expressed as

$$TC = \frac{DO}{Q} + \frac{QH}{2}$$

We can determine a minimum for this total cost function by differentiating the above formula with respect to Q and setting the derivative equal to zero.[1] We then get the economic order quantity Q:

$$Q = \sqrt{\left(\frac{2DO}{H}\right)}$$

or

$$Q = \sqrt{\left(\frac{2 \times \text{total demand for period} \times \text{cost per order}}{\text{holding cost per unit}}\right)}$$

If we apply this formula to Example 3.3, we have:

$$Q = \sqrt{\left(\frac{2 \times 40\,000 \times 2}{1}\right)} = 400 \text{ units}$$

ASSUMPTIONS OF THE EOQ FORMULA

The calculations obtained by using the EOQ model should be interpreted with care, since the model is based on a number of important assumptions. One of these is that the holding cost per unit will be constant. While this assumption might be correct for items such as the funds invested in stocks, other costs might increase on a step basis as stock levels increase. For example, additional storekeepers might be hired as stock levels reach certain levels. Alternatively, if stocks decline, it may be that casual stores labour may be released once stocks fall to a certain critical level.

Another assumption that we made in calculating the total holding cost is that the average balance in stock was equal to one-half of the order quantity. If a constant amount of stock is not used per day, this assumption will be violated; there is a distinct possibility that seasonal and cyclical factors will produce an uneven usage over time. Despite the fact that much of the data used in the model represents rough approximations, calculation of the EOQ is still likely to be useful. If you examine Figure 3.1, you will see that the total cost curve tends to flatten out, so that total cost may not be significantly affected if some of the underlying assumptions are violated or if there are minor variations in the cost of predictions.

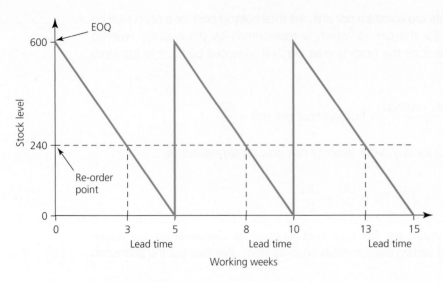

FIGURE 3.2

Fluctuations in stock levels under conditions of certainty

DETERMINING WHEN TO PLACE THE ORDER

To determine the point at which the order should be placed to obtain additional stocks (i.e. the **re-order point**), we must ascertain the time that will elapse between placing the order and the actual delivery of the stocks. This time period is referred to as the **lead time**. In a world of certainty the re-order point will be the number of days/weeks lead time multiplied by the daily/weekly usage during the period. For materials, components and supplies the re-order point is the point in time when the purchase requisition is initiated and the order is sent to the supplier. For the finished goods stock of a manufacturer, the re-order point is the level of finished goods stock at which the production order should be issued.

If we assume that an annual usage of a raw material is 6000 units and the weekly usage is constant then if there are 50 working weeks in a year, the weekly usage will be 120 units. If the lead time is two weeks, the order should be placed when stocks fall to 240 units. The economic order quantity can indicate how frequently the stocks should be purchased. For example, if the EOQ is 600 then, with an annual demand of 6000 units, ten orders will be placed every five weeks. However, with a lead time of two weeks, the firm will place an order three weeks after the first delivery when the stock will have fallen to 240 units (600 units EOQ less three weeks usage at 120 units per week). The order will then be repeated at five-weekly intervals. The EOQ model can therefore under certain circumstances be used to indicate when to replenish stocks and the amount to replenish. This process is illustrated in Figure 3.2.

CONTROL OF STOCKS THROUGH CLASSIFICATION

In large firms it is quite possible for tens of thousands of different items to be stored. It is clearly impossible to apply the techniques outlined in this chapter to all of these items. It is therefore essential that stocks be classified into categories of importance so that a firm can apply the most elaborate procedures of controlling stocks only to the most important items. The commonest procedure is known as the **ABC classification method**. This is illustrated in Exhibit 3.5.

The ABC method requires that an estimate be made of the total purchase cost for each item of stock for the period. The sales forecast is used for estimating the quantities of each

EXHIBIT 3.5

*ABC Classification
of stocks*

Stage 1. For each item in stock multiply the estimated usage for a period by the estimated unit price to obtain the total purchase cost:

Item	Estimated usage	Unit price (£)	Total purchase cost (£)
1	60 000	1.00	60 000
2	20 000	0.05	1 000
3	1 000	0.10	100
4	10 000	0.02	200
5	100 000	0.01	1 000
6	80 000	2.00	160 000

(This list is continued until all items in stock are included.)

Stage 2. Group all the above items in descending order of purchase price and then divide into class A (top 10%), class B (next 20%) and then Class C (bottom 70%). The analysis might be as follows:

	Number of items in stock		Total cost	
	No	%	Amount (£)	%
Class A	1 000	10	730 000	73
Class B	2 000	20	190 000	19
Class C	7 000	70	80 000	8
	10 000	100	1 000 000	100

item of stock to be purchased during the period. Each item is then grouped in decreasing order of annual purchase cost. The top 10 per cent of items in stock in terms of annual purchase cost are categorized as A items, the next 20 per cent as B items and the final 70 per cent as C items. If we assume there are 10 000 stock items then the top 1000 items in terms of annual purchase costs will be classified as A items, and so on. In practice, it will be unnecessary to estimate the value of many of the 7000 C items, since their annual purchase cost will be so small it will be obvious that they will fall into the C category.

You will see from Exhibit 3.5 that 10 per cent of all stock items (i.e. the A items) represents 73 per cent of the total cost; 20 per cent of the items (B items) represent 19 per cent of the total cost; and 70 per cent of the items (C items) represent 8 per cent of the total cost. It follows that the greatest degree of control should be exerted over the A items, which account for the high investment costs, and it is the A category items that are most appropriate for the application of the quantitative techniques discussed in this chapter. For these items an attempt should be made to maintain low safety stocks consistent with avoiding high stockout costs. Larger orders and safety stocks are likely to be a feature of the C-category items. Normally, re-order points for these items will be determined on a subjective basis rather than using quantitative methods, the objective being to minimize the expense in controlling these items. The control of B-category items is likely to be based on quantitative methods, but they are unlikely to be as sophisticated as for the A-category items.

The percentage value of total cost for the A B and C categories in Exhibit 3.5 is typical of most manufacturing companies. In practice, it is normal for between 10 and 15 per cent of the items in stock to account for between 70 and 80 per cent of the total value of purchases. At the other extreme, between 70 and 80 per cent of the items in stock account for approximately 10 per cent of the total value. The control of stock levels is eased considerably it if is concentrated on that small proportion of stock items that account for most of the total cost.

JUST-IN-TIME SYSTEMS

The success of Japanese firms in international markets in the 1980s generated interest among many Western companies. The implementation of just-in-time production methods was considered to be one of the major factors contributing to this success. A **just-in-time (JIT)** approach aims to eliminate **non-value-added activities**. A non-value-added activity is defined as an activity where there is an opportunity for cost reduction without reducing the customer's perceived usefulness of a product or service. Examples include the costs of setting-up equipment involving adjusting the equipment settings to retool for a new product or the cost of setting-up and negotiating purchase orders. Longer set-up times make the production of small batches of output or the purchase of a small number of units uneconomic. However, the production and purchase of large batches leads to the creation of high inventory levels. The JIT philosophy is to reduce and eventually eliminate set-up times. For example, by investing in advanced manufacturing technologies some machine settings can be adjusted automatically instead of manually. By significantly reducing set-up times, smaller production batches and the purchase of smaller batch sizes become economical.

In recent years many companies have developed strategic supply partnerships involving JIT purchasing arrangements whereby the materials are only delivered immediately before they are used. By arranging with suppliers for more frequent deliveries, stocks can be cut to a minimum. Considerable savings in material handling expenses can be obtained by requiring suppliers to inspect materials before their delivery and guaranteeing their quality. This improved service is obtained by giving more business to fewer suppliers and placing longer-term purchasing orders. A critical component of JIT purchasing is that strong relationships are established with suppliers.

The proponents of JIT approach claim that by giving more business to a few high quality suppliers and placing long-term purchasing orders results in a dramatic decline in ordering costs. They also claim that holding costs, in terms of maintaining stock levels, have been seriously underestimated in the past. How will a reduction in the ordering cost and an increase in the holding cost per unit affect the EOQ? If you refer back to the EOQ formula you will see that a decrease in the ordering cost reduces the numerator and the increase in the carrying cost increases the denominator so that the EOQ declines. Therefore under JIT purchasing EOQ supports more frequent purchases of lower quantities.

MATERIALS REQUIREMENT PLANNING

In this chapter we have focused on the determination of re-order points and order quantities (i.e. the EOQ) in non-complex production environments. The approaches described can also be extended to more complex manufacturing environments using a system called materials requirement planning (MRP). This topic tends to be covered on more advanced courses and may not form part of your course curriculum. If your curriculum requires an understanding of MRP you will find that this topic is covered in Learning Note 3.1 on the open access website (see Preface for details).

SUMMARY

The following items relate to the learning objectives listed at the beginning of the chapter.

- **Describe the materials recording procedure.** When the materials are received the quantities and values are recorded in a separate stores ledger account for each item of material. The issues of materials are recorded on a stores requisition, which contains details of the job number product code or overhead account for which the materials are required. The information on the stores requisition is then recorded in the issues column of the appropriate stores ledger account and after each issue a balance of the quantity and value for each of the specific items of materials is calculated. The cost of each item of material listed on the stores requisition is assigned to the appropriate job number, product or overhead account. In practice this clerical process is likely to be computerized.

- **Explain the accounting treatment of holiday pay, overtime premiums, employment costs, stores losses and delivery and material handling costs.** You should check your understanding of the accounting treatment for these items by referring to the appropriate pages for these items within the chapter.

- **Distinguish between first in, first out (FIFO), last in, first out (LIFO) and average cost methods of stores pricing.** Because the same type of materials may have been purchased at several different prices actual cost can take on different values. Therefore an assumption must be made when pricing the materials used. FIFO assumes that the first item that was received in stock was the first item issued so the earlier purchase prices are used. LIFO assumes that the last item to be received is the first item to be issued resulting in the later purchase prices being used. The average cost method assumes that materials are issued at the average cost of materials in stock.

- **Justify which costs are relevant and should be included in the calculation of the economic order quantity (EOQ).** The relevant costs that should be considered when determining the EOQ consist of holding costs and ordering costs. The relevant holding costs should include only those items that will vary with the levels of stocks. Examples include the opportunity cost in terms of the return that is lost from the capital tied up in stocks and incremental insurance, materials handling, and warehousing and storage costs. Ordering costs usually consist of the incremental clerical costs of preparing a purchase order, receiving deliveries and paying invoices. The purchase price is not normally a relevant cost since the cost per unit will be the same, irrespective of the order size. Note that special techniques can be applied to incorporate quantity discounts.

- **Calculate the EOQ using the tabulation and formula methods.** The tabulation method merely involves listing the ordering and holding costs for each potential order quantity over a selected period. The order costs are computed by multiplying the number of orders by the incremental cost per order. To compute the holding costs the average stock level is multiplied by the holding cost per unit. Assuming constant usage, average stock levels are derived by dividing the potential order quantities by 2. The computation of the EOQ using both methods was illustrated using Example 3.3.

- **Describe the ABC classification method.** The ABC method classifies stocks into categories of importance so that the most elaborate procedures of controlling stocks can be applied to the most important items. The ABC classification method requires that an estimate be made of the total purchase cost for each item in stock for a period. Each item is then grouped in decreasing order in terms of their purchase cost for the period. The top 10 per cent of items in stock in terms of the purchase cost for the period are classified as 'A' items. The next 20 per cent as 'B' items and the final 70 per cent as 'C' items. It is generally found that the 'A' items can account for over 70 per cent of the total purchase cost for a period. The most sophisticated procedures for planning and controlling stocks are applied to the 'A' items.

- **Outline the main features of a just-in-time approach.** A just-in-time (JIT) approach aims to eliminate non-value-added activities (e.g. set-up times). By significantly reducing set-up times, smaller production batches and the purchase of smaller batch sizes become economical. Many companies have developed strategic supply partnerships involving JIT purchasing arrangements whereby the delivery of materials immediately precedes their use. By arranging with suppliers for more frequent deliveries, stocks can be cut to a minimum and ordering costs substantially reduced. The overall impact of adopting this approach is that the EOQ declines.

Note

1. The steps are as follows:

$$TC = \frac{DO}{Q} + \frac{QH}{2}$$

$$\frac{dTC}{dQ} = \frac{-DO}{Q^2} + \frac{H}{2}$$

$$\frac{dtC}{dQ} = 0 : \frac{H}{2} - \frac{DO}{Q^2} = 0$$

$$HQ^2 = 2DO = 0$$

$$Q^2 = \frac{2DO}{H}$$

$$\text{Therefore } Q = \sqrt{\left(\frac{2DO}{H}\right)}$$

KEY TERMS AND CONCEPTS

ABC classification method classifies stocks into categories of importance so that the most elaborate procedures of controlling stocks can be applied to the most important items.

Complete periodic stockcount the process of physically counting all items of stock and comparing them with the records.

Economic order quantity (EOQ) the optimum size of order, where the total amount of ordering and holding costs are minimized.

Employment costs the costs to the company of employing staff; they include wages or salary and employer's contributions to National Insurance and pension funds.

First in, first out (FIFO) a system of issuing items in the order in which they were received.

Goods received note (GRN) a document prepared by the receiving section of the stores department when goods are delivered and forwarded to the purchasing and accounting departments.

Holding costs the costs to the company of holding stocks; they include opportunity costs, incremental insurance, warehousing, storage and handling costs and the cost of obsolescence and deterioration.

Just-in-time (JIT) an approach that aims to reduce and eventually eliminate non-value-added activities such as set-up times and to cut stocks to a minimum.

Last in, first out (LIFO) a system of issuing items in the reverse order to when they were received.

Lead time is the time that elapses between the re-order point and delivery.

Material handling costs the expenses involved in receiving, storing, issuing and handling materials.

Materials handling rate the percentage rate at which some companies assign handling costs to cost objects.

Non-value-added activities activities that add nothing to the customer's perception of the usefulness of a product or service and provide an opportunity for cost reduction.

Ordering costs the clerical costs of preparing purchase orders, receiving deliveries and paying invoices.

Purchase order a document sent by the purchasing department to a supplier requesting that items listed are supplied.

Purchase requisition a document issued by the stores department of a manufacturing organization to the purchase department, requesting that stocks of an item are re-ordered.

Re-order point is the point at which an order is actually placed.

Stores ledger account a record of the quantity and value of each item of material stored by the organization.

Stores requisition a document that lists the type and quantity of any item issued by the stores department.

KEY EXAMINATION POINTS

Typical examination questions relating to the content of this chapter include questions on incentive schemes, stores pricing and computations of the economic order, maximum, minimum and re-order quantities. Question 3.30 is an example of a question relating to incentive schemes. Questions on stores pricing often require you to calculate the amount charged to products/production, to determine the stock valuation and discuss arguments for and against using each method. Question SM3.7 in the Students' Manual on the website is concerned with most aspects covered in this chapter relating to the computation of the economic order quantity and is typical of the type of examination questions set on this topic. A common mistake that students make in computing the EOQ is to unitize fixed holding and ordering costs. The EOQ should be calculated using only variable costs. Also note that the purchase cost of materials should not be included in EOQ calculations. When the purchase cost per unit varies with the quantity ordered you should prepare a schedule of relevant costs for different order quantities. For an illustration of this approach, see Exhibit 3.4 in this chapter. Sometimes examination questions (see questions 3.22 and SM3.6c in the Students' Manual on the website) require you to calculate maximum, minimum and re-order levels. You should use the following formulae:

Re-order level = Maximum usage × maximum lead time
Minimum stock level = Re-order level – average usage during average lead time
Maximum stock level = Re-order level + EOQ – minimum usage for the minimum lead time

ASSESSMENT MATERIAL

The review questions are short questions that enable you to assess your understanding of the main topics included in the chapter. The numbers in parentheses provide you with the page numbers to refer to if you cannot answer a specific question.

The review problems are more complex and require you to relate and apply the chapter content to various business problems. The problems are graded by their level of difficulty. The multiple-choice questions are the least demanding and normally take less than 10 minutes to complete. Fully worked solutions to the review problems are provided in a separate section at the end of the book. Further review problems with solutions for this chapter are available on the accompanying website www.drury-online.com. The website includes a *Student's Manual* and an *Instructor's Manual.* Students can access both questions and answers from the *Student's Manual* and the questions from the Instructor's Manual The answers to problems in the *Instructor's Manual* are available only to lecturers on the lecturer's password-protected section of the website.

REVIEW QUESTIONS

3.1 Explain the accounting treatment for holiday pay, overtime payments and employment costs. *(pp. 48–49)*

3.2 Describe the materials recording procedure. *(pp. 49–51)*

3.3 Explain the purpose of a stores ledger account. *(p. 50)*

3.4 Describe the first in, first out (FIFO), last in, first out (LIFO) and average cost methods of stores pricing. *(pp. 51–55)*

3.5 Explain the accounting treatment of stores losses and materials handling costs. *(pp. 55–57)*

3.6 What are holding costs? Provide some examples. *(p. 58)*

3.7 What are ordering costs? Provide some examples. *(p. 58)*

3.8 What determines which holding and ordering costs should be included in the economic order quantity calculation? *(p. 58)*

3.9 What are the assumptions underlying the economic order quantity? *(p. 61)*

3.10 Define lead time. *(p. 62)*

3.11 Explain what is meant by the re-order point. *(p. 62)*

3.12 Describe the ABC classification method. What purposes does it serve? *(pp. 62–64)*

3.13 What are the main features of the just-in-time approach? *(p. 64)*

REVIEW PROBLEMS

3.14 A machine operator is paid $10.20 per hour and has a normal working week of 35 hours. Overtime is paid at the basic rate plus 50 per cent. If in week 7, the machine operator worked 42 hours, the overtime premium paid to the operator would be:

(a) $28.20

(c) $71.40

(b) $35.70

(d) $107.10

CIMA Management Accounting Fundamentals

3.15 An advertising agency uses a job costing system to calculate the cost of client contracts. Contract A42 is one of several contracts undertaken in the last accounting period. Costs associated with the contract consist of:

Direct materials	$5 500
Direct expenses	$14 500

Design staff worked 1020 hours on contract A42, of which 120 hours were overtime. One third of these overtime hours were worked at the request of the client who wanted the contract to be completed quickly. Overtime is paid at a premium of 25 per cent of the basic wage of $24.00 per hour. The prime cost of contract A42 is:

(a) $41 600

(c) $44 720

(b) $44 480

(d) $45 200

CIMA Management Accounting Fundamentals

3.16 The effect of using the last in, first out (LIFO) method of stock valuation rather than first, in, first out (FIFO) method in a period of rising prices is:

(a) to report lower profits and a lower value of closing stock

(b) to report higher profits and a higher value of closing stock

(c) to report lower profits and a higher value of closing stock

(d) to report higher profits and a lower value of closing stock

CIMA Management Accounting Fundamentals

3.17 An organization's stock records show the following transactions for a specific item during last month:

Date	Receipts units	Issues units
4th		50
13th	200	
20th		50
27th		50

The stock at the beginning of last month consisted of 100 units valued at £6700. The receipts last month cost £62 per unit.

The value of the closing stock for last month has been calculated twice – once using a FIFO valuation and once using a LIFO valuation.

Which of the following statements about the valuation of closing stock for last month is correct?

(a) The FIFO valuation is higher than the LIFO valuation by £250;

(b) The LIFO valuation is higher than the FIFO valuation by £250;

(c) The FIFO valuation is higher than the LIFO valuation by £500;

(d) The LIFO valuation is higher than the FIFO valuation by £500.

ACCA Financial Information for Management

3.18 An organization's records for last month show the following in respect of one stores item:

Date	Receipt units	Issues units	Stock units
1st			200
5th		100	100
7th	400		500
19th		190	310
27th		170	140

Last month's opening stock was valued at a total of £2900 and the receipts during the month were purchased at a cost of £17.50 per unit.

The organization uses the weighted average method of valuation and calculates a new weighted average after each stores receipt.

What was the total value of the issues last month?

(a) £7360   (c) £7590

(b) £7534   (d) £7774.

ACCA Financial Information for Management

3.19 The following data relate to material J for last month:

			£
Opening stock	300 kg	valued at	3300
Purchases:			
4th	400 kg	for	4800
18th	500 kg	for	6500
Issues:			
13th	600 kg		
25th	300 kg		

Using the LIFO valuation method, what was the value of the closing stock for last month?

(a) £3300

(c) £3700

(b) £3500

(d) £3900

ACCA Financial Information for Management

3.20 E Ltd's stock purchases during a recent week were as follows:

Day	Price per unit ($)	Units purchased
1	1.45	55
2	1.60	80
3	1.75	120
4	1.80	75
5	1.90	130

There was no stock at the beginning of the week. 420 units were issued to production during the week. The company updates its stock records after every transaction.

(a) Using a first in, first out (FIFO) method of costing stock issues, the value of closing stock would be:

A $58.00

C $72.00

B $70.00

D $76.00

(b) If E Ltd changes to the weighted average method of stock valuation, the effect on closing stock value and on profit compared with the FIFO method will be:

A Higher closing stock value and higher gross profit

B Lower closing stock value and higher gross profit

C Lower closing stock value and lower gross profit

D Higher closing stock value and lower gross profit

CIMA Management Accounting Fundamentals

3.21 W plc uses the economic order quantity (EOQ) as part of its materials control policy. The objective of the EOQ is to ensure that:

(a) the company never runs out of stock except in exceptional circumstances

(b) the cost of being out of stock is minimized

(c) the combined cost of ordering and holding stock is minimized

(d) stock is purchased from suppliers are the cheapest price

CIMA Management Accounting Fundamentals

3.22 A domestic appliance retailer with multiple outlets stocks a popular toaster known as the Autocrisp 2000, for which the following information is available:

Average sales	75 per day
Maximum sales	95 per day
Minimum sales	50 per day
Lead time	12–18 days
Re-order quantity	1750

(i) Based on the data above, at what level of stocks would a replenishment order be issued?

(a) 1050   (c) 1710

(b) 1330   (d) 1750

(ii) Based on the data above, what is the maximum level of stocks possible?

(a) 1750   (c) 3460

(b) 2860   (d) 5210

CIMA Stage 1

3.23 A manufacturing company uses 25 000 components at an even rate during a year. Each order placed with the supplier of the components is for 2000 components, which is the economic order quantity. The company holds a buffer inventory of 500 components. The annual cost of holding one component in inventory is $2. What is the total annual cost of holding inventory of the component?

(a) $2000   (c) $3000

(b) $2500   (d) $4000

ACCA F2 Management Accounting

3.24 The purchase price of a stock item is £25 per unit. In each three-month period the usage of the item is 20 000 units. The annual holding costs associated with one unit equate to 6 per cent of its purchase price. The cost of placing an order for the item is £20. What is the economic order quantity (EOQ) for the stock item to the nearest whole unit?

(a) 730   (c) 1461

(b) 894   (d) 1633

ACCA Financial Information for Management

3.25 A company determines its order quantity for a raw material using the EOQ model. What would be the effects on the EOQ and on the total annual stockholding cost of a decrease in the cost of placing an order for the raw material?

	EOQ	Total annual stockholding cost
A	Increase	No effect
B	Decrease	No effect
C	Increase	Increase
D	Decrease	Decrease

ACCA Financial Information for Management

3.26 Data relating to one particular stores item are as follows:

Average daily issues	70 units
Maximum daily issues	90 units
Minimum daily issues	50 units
Lead time for the replenishment of stock	11 to 17 days
Re-order quantity	2000
Re-order level	1800

What is the maximum stock level (in units) for this stores item?

(a) 2950   (c) 3250

(b) 3100   (d) 3800

ACCA Financial Information for Management

3.27 Calculation of number of orders and holding costs

N Ltd's Chief Executive believes the company is holding excessive stocks and has asked the Management Accountant to carry out an investigation. Information on the two stock items is given below:

Stock item	Purchase price $ per unit	Administration cost $ per order	Demand units	Holding cost per year % of purchase price
G	200	80	15 000 per year	13.33
H	25	28	2800 per year	8.00

The company's stock ordering policy is based on the economic order quantity (EOQ). Required:

(a) Determine the number of orders per year that the company will place for item G

(3 marks)

(b) Determine the annual holding cost of the stock of item H

(3 marks)

CIMA Management Accounting Fundamentals

3.28 EOQ and the impact of quantity discounts

Point Ltd uses the economic order quantity (EOQ) model to establish the re-order quantity for raw material Y. The company holds no buffer stock. Information relating to raw material Y as follows:

Annual usage	48 000 units
Purchase price	£80 per unit
Ordering costs	£120 per order
Annual holding costs	10% of the purchase price

Required:

(a) Calculate:

(i) the EOQ for raw material Y, and

(ii) the total annual cost for purchasing, ordering and holding stocks of raw material Y.

The supplier has offered Point Ltd a discount of 1 per cent on the purchase price if each order placed is for 2000 units.

(b) Calculate the total annual saving to Point Ltd of accepting this offer.

(c) List FOUR examples of holding costs.

ACCA Financial Information for Management

3.29 Calculation of the EOQ and re-order level
Jane plc purchases its requirements for component RB at a price of £80 per unit. Its annual usage of component RB is 8760 units. The annual holding cost of one unit of component RB is 5 per cent of its purchase price and the cost of placing an order is £12.50.

Required:

(a) Calculate the economic order quantity (to the nearest unit) for component RB.

(b) Assuming that usage of component RB is constant throughout the year (365 days) and that the lead time from placing an order to its receipt is 21 days, calculate the stock level (in units) at which an order should be placed.

(c)

(i) Explain the terms 'stockout' and 'buffer (also known as safety) stocks'.
(ii) Briefly describe the circumstances in which Jane plc should consider a buffer stock of component RB.

ACCA Financial Information for Management

3.30 Effect of an incentive scheme on company profits
You have been approached for your advice on the proposed introduction of an incentive scheme for the direct operatives in the final production department of a factory producing one standard product. This department, the Finishing Shop, employs 30 direct operatives, all of whom are paid £8 per hour for a basic 40-hour week, with a guaranteed wage of £320 per week. When necessary, overtime is worked up to a maximum of 15 hours per week per operative and is paid at time rate plus one-half. It is the opinion of the personnel manager that no more direct operatives could be recruited for this department.

An analysis of recent production returns from the Finishing Shop indicates that the current average output is approximately 6 units of the standard product per productive man-hour. The work study manager has conducted an appraisal of the working methods in the Finishing Shop and suggests that it would be reasonable to expect operatives to process 8 units of the product per man-hour and that a piecework scheme be introduced in which the direct operatives are paid £1.40 for each unit processed. It is anticipated that, when necessary, operatives would continue to work overtime up to the previous specified limit, although as the operatives would be on piecework no premium would be paid.

Next year's budgeted production for the factory varies from a minimum of 7000 units per week to a maximum of 12 000 units per week, with the most frequent budgeted weekly output being 9600 units. The expected selling price of the product next year is £11 per unit and the budgeted variable production cost of the incomplete product passed into the Finishing Shop amounts to £8 per unit. Variable production overheads in the Finishing Shop, excluding the overtime premium of the direct operatives, are budgeted to be £0.48 per direct labour hour worked, and it is considered that variable overheads do vary directly with productive hours worked. Direct material costs are not incurred by the Finishing Shop. The fixed overheads incurred by the factory amount in total to £9000 per week.

Stocks of work in progress and finished goods are not carried.

Required:

(i) Calculate the effect on the company's budgeted weekly profits of the proposed incentive scheme in the Finishing Shop. (Calculation should be to the nearest £.)

(15 marks)

(ii) Explain the reasons for the changes in the weekly budgeted profits caused by the proposed incentive scheme.

(7 marks)
ACCA Level 1

CHAPTER 4
COST ASSIGNMENT FOR INDIRECT COSTS

LEARNING OBJECTIVES

After studying this chapter, you should be able to:

- distinguish between cause-and-effect and arbitrary cost allocations;
- explain why different cost information is required for different purposes;
- describe how cost systems differ in terms of their level of sophistication;
- understand the factors influencing the choice of an optimal cost system;
- explain why departmental overhead rates should be used in preference to a single blanket overhead rate;
- construct an overhead analysis sheet and calculate cost centre allocation rates;
- justify why budgeted overhead rates should be used in preference to actual overhead rates;
- calculate and explain the accounting treatment of the under- over-recovery of overheads.

In Chapters 1 and 2 we discussed how companies need cost and management accounting systems to perform a number of different functions. In this chapter we are going to concentrate on two of these functions: (i) allocating costs between cost of goods sold and inventories for internal and external profit reporting, and (ii) providing relevant decision-making information for distinguishing between profitable and unprofitable activities.

In order to perform these functions a cost accumulation system is required that assigns costs to cost objects. The aim of this chapter is to provide you with an understanding of how costs are accumulated and assigned to cost objects. You should remember from Chapter 2 that a cost object is anything for which a separate measurement of cost is desired. Typical cost objects include products, services, customers and locations. In this chapter we shall either use the term cost object as a generic term or assume that products are the cost object. However, the cost assignment principles we explain here can be applied to all cost objects.

We begin by explaining how the cost assignment process differs for direct and indirect costs.

ASSIGNMENT OF DIRECT AND INDIRECT COSTS

Costs that are assigned to cost objects can be divided into two categories – direct costs and indirect costs. Sometimes the term overheads is used instead of indirect costs. Direct costs can be accurately traced to cost objects because they can be specifically and exclusively traced to a particular cost object whereas indirect costs cannot. Where a cost can be directly assigned to a cost object the term **cost tracing** is used. In contrast, indirect costs cannot be traced directly to a cost object because they are usually common to several cost objects. Indirect costs are therefore assigned to cost objects using cost allocations.

Cost allocations involve the use of surrogate rather than direct measures. For example, consider an activity such as receiving incoming materials. Assuming that the cost of receiving materials is strongly influenced by the number of receipts then costs can be allocated to products (i.e. the cost object) based on the number of material receipts each product requires. The basis that is used to allocate costs to cost objects (i.e. the number of material receipts in our example) is called an **allocation base** or **cost driver**. If 20 per cent of the total number of receipts for a period were required for a particular product then 20 per cent of the total costs of receiving incoming materials would be allocated to that product. Assuming that the product was discontinued, and not replaced, we would expect action to be taken to reduce the resources required for receiving materials by 20 per cent.

Where allocation bases are significant determinants of the costs, as in the illustration above, we describe them as **cause-and-effect allocations**. Where a cost allocation base is used that is not a significant determinant of its cost the term **arbitrary allocation** is used. An example of an arbitrary allocation would be if direct labour hours were used as the base to allocate the costs of materials receiving. If a labour-intensive product required a large proportion of direct labour hours (say 30 per cent) but few material receipts, it would be allocated with a large proportion of the costs of material receiving. The allocation would be an inaccurate assignment of the resources consumed by the product. Furthermore, if the product were discontinued, and not replaced, the cost of the material receiving activity would not decline by 30 per cent because the allocation base is not a significant determinant of the costs of the materials receiving activity. Arbitrary allocations are therefore likely to result in inaccurate allocations of indirect costs to cost objects.

Figure 4.1 provides a summary of the cost assignment process. Two types of systems can be used to assign indirect costs to cost objects. They are **traditional costing systems** and **activity-based-costing (ABC) systems**. Traditional costing systems were developed in the early 1900s and are still widely used today. They rely extensively on arbitrary cost allocations. ABC systems only emerged in the late 1980s. One of the major aims of ABC systems is to use only cause-and-effect cost allocations. Both cost systems adopt identical approaches to

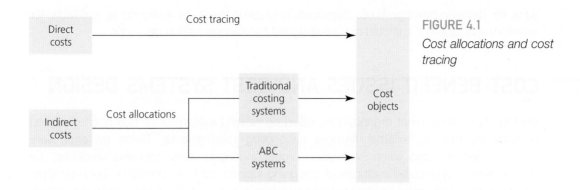

FIGURE 4.1
Cost allocations and cost tracing

assigning direct costs to cost objects. In this chapter we shall concentrate on traditional costing systems and ABC systems will be examined in Chapter 12.

DIFFERENT COSTS FOR DIFFERENT PURPOSES

Earlier in this chapter it was pointed out that manufacturing organizations assign costs to products for two purposes: first, for internal profit measurement and external financial accounting requirements in order to allocate the manufacturing costs incurred during a period between cost of goods sold and inventories; second, to provide useful information for managerial decision-making requirements. In order to meet financial accounting requirements, it may not be necessary to accurately assign costs to *individual* products. Consider a situation where a firm produces 1000 different products and the costs incurred during a period are £10 million. A well-designed product costing system should accurately analyze the £10 million costs incurred between cost of sales and inventories. Let us assume the true figures are £7 million and £3 million. Approximate but inaccurate *individual* product costs may provide a reasonable approximation of how much of the £10 million should be attributed to cost of sales and inventories. Some product costs may be overstated and others may be understated, but this would not matter for financial accounting purposes as long as the *total* of the individual product costs assigned to cost of sales and inventories was approximately £7 million and £3 million.

For decision-making purposes, however, more accurate product costs are required. By more accurately measuring the resources consumed by products, or other cost objects, a firm can distinguish between profitable and unprofitable activities. If the cost system does not capture the consumption of resources by products sufficiently accurately, the reported product costs will be distorted, and there is a danger that managers may drop profitable products or continue production of unprofitable products.

Different cost information is required for different purposes. For meeting external financial accounting requirements, financial accounting regulations and legal requirements in most countries require that inventories should be valued at manufacturing cost. Therefore only manufacturing costs are assigned to products for meeting external financial accounting requirements. For decision-making purposes, non-manufacturing costs must be taken into account and assigned to products. As we have discussed, not all costs are relevant for decision-making. For example, depreciation of plant and machinery will not be affected by a decision to discontinue a product. Such costs were described in Chapter 2 as irrelevant and sunk for decision-making. Thus, depreciation of plant must be assigned to products for inventory valuation but it should not be assigned for discontinuation decisions.

COST-BENEFIT ISSUES AND COST SYSTEMS DESIGN

Until the late 1980s most organizations relied on costing systems that had been designed primarily for meeting external financial accounting requirements. These systems were designed decades ago when information processing costs were high and precluded the use of more sophisticated methods of assigning indirect costs to products. Such systems are still widely used today. They rely extensively on arbitrary cost allocations which may not be sufficiently accurate for meeting decision-making requirements.

In the late 1980s ABC systems were promoted as a mechanism for more accurately assigning indirect costs to cost objects. Surveys in many countries suggest that between 20 and 30 per cent of the surveyed organizations currently use ABC systems. The majority of organizations, therefore, continue to operate traditional systems. Both traditional and ABC systems vary in their level of sophistication but, as a general rule, traditional systems tend to be simplistic whereas ABC systems tend to be more sophisticated. What determines the chosen level of sophistication of a costing system? The answer is that the choice should be made on costs versus benefits criteria. Simplistic systems are inexpensive to operate, but they are likely to result in inaccurate cost assignments and the reporting of inaccurate costs, which can cause managers to make dangerous mistakes. The end result may be a high cost of errors. Conversely, sophisticated systems are more expensive to operate but they minimize the cost of errors.

Figure 4.2 illustrates the above points with costing systems ranging from simplistic to sophisticated. In practice, cost systems in most organizations are not located at either of these extreme points but are positioned somewhere within the range shown in Figure 4.2.

The optimal cost system for an organization can be influenced by several factors. For example, the optimal costing system will be located towards the extreme left for an organization whose indirect costs are a low percentage of total costs and which also has a fairly standardized product range, all consuming organizational resources in similar proportions. In these circumstances simplistic systems may not result in the reporting of inaccurate costs. In contrast, the optimal costing system for organizations with a high proportion of indirect costs, whose products consume organizational resources in different proportions, will be located towards the extreme right. More sophisticated costing systems are required to capture the diversity of consumption of organizational resources and accurately assign the high level of indirect costs to different cost objects.

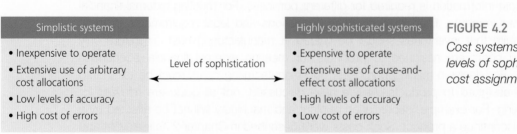

FIGURE 4.2

Cost systems – varying levels of sophistication for cost assignment

PLANT-WIDE (BLANKET) OVERHEAD RATES

The most simplistic traditional costing system assigns indirect costs (overheads) to cost objects using a single overhead rate for the organization as a whole, known as **blanket overhead rate** or **plant-wide rate**. Such a costing system would be located at the extreme left of the level of sophistication shown in Figure 4.2. Let us assume that the total manufacturing overheads for the manufacturing plant of Arcadia are £9 million and that the company has selected direct labour hours as the allocation base for assigning overheads to products. Assuming that the total number of direct labour hours are 600 000 for the period, the plant-wide overhead rate for Arcadia is £15 per direct labour hour (£9 million/600 000 direct labour hours). This calculation consists of two stages. First, overheads are accumulated in one single plant-wide pool for a period. Second, a plant-wide rate is computed by dividing the total amount of overheads accumulated (£9 million) by the selected allocation base (600 000 direct labour hours). The overhead costs are assigned to products by multiplying the plant-wide rate by the units of the selected allocation base (direct labour hours) used by each product.

Assume now that Arcadia is considering establishing separate overheads for each of its three production departments. Further investigations reveal that the products made by the company require different operations and some products do not pass through all three departments. These investigations also indicate that the £9 million total manufacturing overheads and 600 000 direct labour hours can be analyzed as follows:

	Department A	Department B	Department C	Total
Overheads	£2 000 000	£6 000 000	£1 000 000	£9 000 000
Direct labour hours	200 000	200 000	200 000	600 000
Overhead rate per direct labour hour	£10	£30	£5	£15

Now consider a situation where product Z requires 20 direct labour hours in department C but does not pass through departments A and B. If a plant-wide overhead rate is used then overheads of £300 (20 hours at £15 per hour) will be allocated to product Z. On the other hand, if a departmental overhead rate is used, only £100 (20 hours at £5 per hour) would be allocated to product Z. Which method should be used? The logical answer must be to establish separate departmental overhead rates, since product Z only consumes overheads in department C. If the plant-wide overhead rate were applied, all the factory overhead rates would be averaged out and product Z would be indirectly allocated with some of the overheads of department B. This would not be satisfactory, since product Z does not consume any of the resources and this department incurs a large amount of the overhead expenditure.

Where some departments are more 'overhead-intensive' than others, products spending more time in these departments should be assigned more overhead costs than those spending less time. Departmental rates capture these possible effects but plant-wide rates do not, because of the averaging process. We can conclude that a plant-wide rate will generally result in the reporting of inaccurate product costs and can only be justified when all products consume departmental overheads in approximately the same proportions. In the above illustration each department accounts for one-third of the total direct labour hours. If all products spend approximately one-third of their time in each department, a plant-wide overhead rate can safely be used. Consider a situation where product X spends one hour in each department and product Y spends five hours in each department. Overheads of £45 and

£225 respectively would be allocated to products X and Y using either a plant-wide rate (3 hours at £15 and 15 hours at £15) or separate departmental overhead rates. However, if a diverse product range is produced with products spending different proportions of time in each department, separate departmental overhead rates should be established. Research evidence indicates that less than 5 per cent of the surveyed organizations use a single plant-wide overhead rate. In Scandinavia 5 per cent of the Finnish companies (Lukka and Granlund, 1996), one Norwegian company (Bjornenak, 1997b) and none of the Swedish companies sampled (Ask *et al.,* 1996) used a single plant-wide rate. Zero usage of plant-wide rates was also reported from a survey of Greek companies (Ballas and Venieris, 1996). In a more recent study of UK organizations Al-Omiri and Drury (2007) reported that a plant-wide rate was used by 4 per cent of surveyed organizations.

THE TWO-STAGE ALLOCATION PROCESS

It is apparent from the previous section that separate departmental overhead rates should normally be established. To establish departmental overhead rates, the two-stage allocation process is used. This process applies to assigning costs to other cost objects, besides products, and is applicable to all organizations that assign indirect costs to cost objects. The approach applies to both traditional and ABC systems.

The two-stage allocation process is illustrated in Figure 4.3. You can see that in the first stage overheads are assigned to cost centres (also called cost pools). The terms **cost centres** or **cost pools** are used to describe a location to which overhead costs are initially assigned. Normally cost centres consist of departments, but in some cases they consist of smaller segments such as separate work centres within a department. In the second stage the costs accumulated in the cost centres are allocated to cost objects using selected allocation bases. (You should remember from our discussion earlier that allocation bases are also called cost drivers.) Traditional costing systems tend to use a small number of second stage allocation bases, typically direct labour hours or machine hours. In other words, traditional systems assume that direct labour or machine hours have a significant influence in the long term on the level of overhead expenditure. Other allocation bases used to a lesser

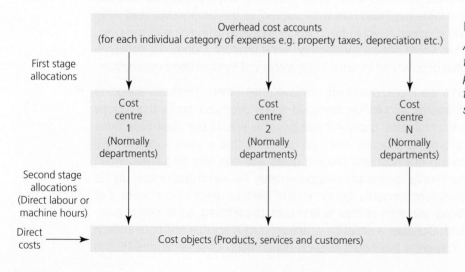

FIGURE 4.3

An illustration of the two-stage allocation process for a traditional costing system

extent by traditional systems are direct labour cost, direct materials cost and units of output. These methods are described and illustrated in Learning Note 4.1 on the dedicated open access website (see Preface for details).

How many cost centres should a firm establish? If only a small number are established it is likely that activities within a cost centre will not be homogeneous and, as a consequence, activity resource consumption will not be accurately measured. In most situations, increasing the number of cost centres increases the accuracy of measuring the indirect costs consumed by cost objects. The choice of the number of cost centres should be based on cost-benefit criteria using the principles described on page 80. Exhibit 4.1 (first section) shows the number of cost centres and second stage cost allocation bases reported by Drury and Tayles (2005) in a survey of 170 UK organizations. It can be seen that 35 per cent of the organizations used less than 11 cost centres whereas 36 per cent used more than 20 cost centres. In terms of the number of different types of second stage cost drivers/allocation bases, 59 per cent of the responding organizations used less than four.

A survey of 170 companies by Drury and Tayles (2005) reported the following details in terms of the number of cost centres and number of different types of second stage allocation bases/cost drivers used:

Number of cost centres	Number of different types of cost drivers
14% used less than 6 cost centres	34% used 1 cost driver
21% used 6–10 cost centres	25% used 2 cost drivers
29% used 11–20 cost centres	31% used 3–10 cost drivers
36% used more than 20 cost centres	10% used more than 10 cost drivers

The percentages below indicate how frequently different cost allocation bases/cost drivers are used. Note that the reported percentages exceed 100 per cent because many companies used more than one allocation base.

	Norway[a]	Holland[b]	Ireland[c]	Australia[d]	Japan	UK	UK[e]
Direct labour hours/cost	65%	20%	52%	57%	57%	68%	73%
Machine hours	29	9	19	19	12	49	26
Direct material costs	26	6	10	12	11	30	19
Units of output	40	30	28	20	16	42	31
Prime cost				1	21		
Other	23	35	9				
ABC cost drivers						9	7

Notes
[a] Bjornenak (1997b)
[b] Boons et al. (1994)
[c] Clarke (1995)
[d] Blayney and Yokoyama (1991)
[e] Drury et al. (1993) – The first column relates to the responses for automated and the second to non-automated production centres

EXHIBIT 4.1
Surveys of practice

AN ILLUSTRATION OF THE TWO-STAGE PROCESS FOR A TRADITIONAL COSTING SYSTEM

We shall now use Example 4.1 to provide a more detailed illustration of the two-stage allocation process for a traditional costing system. To keep the illustration manageable it is assumed that the company has only five cost centres – machine departments X and Y, an assembly department, and materials handling and general factory support cost centres. The illustration focuses on manufacturing costs but we shall look at non-manufacturing costs later in the chapter. Applying the two-stage allocation process requires the following four steps:

1 assigning all manufacturing overheads to production and service cost centres;
2 reallocating the costs assigned to service cost centres to production cost centres;
3 computing separate overhead rates for each production cost centre;
4 assigning cost centre overheads to products or other chosen cost objects.

Steps 1 and 2 comprise stage one and steps 3 and 4 relate to the second stage of the two-stage allocation process. Let us now consider each of these steps in detail.

Step 1 – Assigning all manufacturing overheads to production and service cost centres

Using the information given in Example 4.1 our initial objective is to assign all manufacturing overheads to production and service cost centres. This requires the preparation of an overhead analysis sheet, which is shown in Exhibit 4.2. In most organizations it will exist only in computer form.

If you look at Example 4.1 you will see that the indirect labour and indirect material costs have been directly traced to cost centres. Although these items cannot be directly assigned to products they can be directly assigned to the cost centres. In other words, they are indirect costs when products are the cost objects and direct costs when cost centres are the cost object. Therefore they are traced directly to the cost centres shown in the overhead analysis sheet in Exhibit 4.2. The remaining costs shown in Example 4.1 cannot be traced directly to the cost centres and must be allocated to the cost centre using appropriate allocation bases. The term 'first stage allocation bases' is used to describe allocations at this point. The following list summarizes commonly used first stage allocation bases:

Cost	Basis of allocation
Property taxes, lighting and heating	Area
Employee-related expenditure:	
works management, works canteen, payroll office	Number of employees
Depreciation and insurance of plant and machinery	Value of items of plant and machinery

Applying the allocation bases to the data given in respect of the Enterprise Company in Example 4.1 it is assumed that property taxes, lighting and heating, and insurance of buildings are related to the total floor area of the buildings, and the benefit obtained by each cost centre can therefore be ascertained according to the proportion of floor area which it occupies. The total floor area of the factory shown in Example 4.1 is 50 000 square metres; machine centre

EXAMPLE 4.1

The annual overhead costs for the Enterprise Company which has three production centres (two machine centres and one assembly centre) and two service centres (materials procurement and general factory support) are as follows:

		(£)	(£)
Indirect wages and supervision			
Machine centres:	X	1 000 000	
	Y	1 000 000	
Assembly		1 500 000	
Materials procurement		1 100 000	
General factory support		1 480 000	6 080 000
Indirect materials			
Machine centres:	X	500 000	
	Y	805 000	
Assembly		105 000	
Materials procurement		0	
General factory support		10 000	1 420 000
Lighting and heating		500 000	
Property taxes		1 000 000	
Insurance of machinery		150 000	
Depreciation of machinery		1 500 000	
Insurance of buildings		250 000	
Salaries of works management		800 000	4 200 000
			11 700 000

The following information is also available:

		Book value of machinery (£)	Area occupied (sq. metres)	Number of employees	Direct labour hours	Machine hours
Machine shop:	X	8 000 000	10 000	300	1 000 000	2 000 000
	Y	5 000 000	5 000	200	1 000 000	1 000 000
Assembly		1 000 000	15 000	300	2 000 000	
Stores		500 000	15 000	100		
Maintenance		500 000	5 000	100		
		15 000 000	50 000	1000		

Details of total materials issues (i.e. direct and indirect materials) to the production centres are as follows:

	£
Machine shop X	4 000 000
Machine shop Y	3 000 000
Assembly	1 000 000
	8 000 000

To allocate the overheads listed above to the production and service centres we must prepare an overhead analysis sheet, as shown in Exhibit 4.2.

Item of expenditure	Basis of allocation	Total (£)	Production centres			Service centres	
			Machine centre X (£)	Machine centre Y (£)	Assembly (£)	Material procurement (£)	General factory support (£)
Indirect wage and supervision	Direct	6 080 000	1 000 000	1 000 000	1 500 000	1 100 000	1 480 000
Indirect materials	Direct	1 420 000	500 000	805 000	105 000	150 000	10 000
Lighting and heating	Area	500 000	100 000	50 000	150 000	150 000	50 000
Property taxes	Area	1 000 000	200 000	100 000	300 000	300 000	100 000
Insurance of machinery	Book value of machinery	150 000	80 000	50 000	10 000	5 000	5 000
Depreciation of machinery	Book value of machinery	1 500 000	800 000	500 000	100 000	50 000	50 000
Insurance of buildings	Area	250 000	50 000	25 000	75 000	75 000	25 000
Salaries of works management	Number of employees	800 000	240 000	160 000	240 000	80 000	80 000
	Step 1 of stage 1	11 700 000	2 970 000	2 690 000	2 480 000	1 760 000	1 800 000
Reallocation of service centre costs							
Materials procurement	Value of materials issued		880 000	660 000	220 000	1 760 000	
General factory support	Direct labour hours		450 000	450 000	900 000		1 800 000
	Step 2 of stage 1	11 700 000	4 300 000	3 800 000	3 600 000	—	—
Machine hours and direct labour hours			2 000 000	1 000 000	2 000 000		
Machine hour overhead rate	Step 3 (stage 2)		£2.15	£3.80			
Direct labour hour overhead rate	Step 3 (stage 2)				£1.80		

EXHIBIT 4.2

Overhead analysis sheet

X occupies 20 per cent of this and machine centre Y a further 10 per cent. Therefore, if you refer to the overhead analysis sheet in Exhibit 4.2 you will see that 20 per cent of property taxes, lighting and heating and insurance of buildings are allocated to machine centre X, and 10 per cent are allocated to machine centre Y.

The insurance premium paid and depreciation of machinery are generally regarded as being related to the book value of the machinery. Because the book value of machinery for machine centre X is 8/15 of the total book value and machine centre Y is 5/15 of the total book value then 8/15 and 5/15 of the insurance and depreciation of machinery is allocated to machine centres X and Y.

It is assumed that the amount of time that works management devotes to each cost centre is related to the number of employees in each centre; since 30 per cent of the total employees are employed in machine centre X, 30 per cent of the salaries of works management will be allocated to this centre.

If you now look at the overhead analysis sheet shown in Exhibit 4.2, you will see in the row labelled 'step 1 of stage 1' shown in the second column that all manufacturing overheads for the Enterprise Company have been assigned to the three production and two service cost centres.

Step 2 – Reallocating the costs assigned to service cost centres to production cost centres

The next step is to reallocate the costs that have been assigned to service cost centres to production cost centres. **Service departments** (i.e. service cost centres) are those departments that exist to provide services of various kinds to other units within the organization. They are sometimes called **support departments**. The Enterprise Company has two service centres. They are materials procurement and general factory support which includes activities such as production scheduling and machine maintenance. These service centres render essential services that support the production process, but they do not deal directly with the products. Therefore, it is not possible to allocate service centre costs to products passing through these centres. To assign costs to products traditional costing systems reallocate service centre costs to production centres that actually work on the product. The method that is chosen to allocate service centre costs to production centres should be related to the benefits that the production centres derive from the service rendered.

We shall assume that the value of materials issued (shown in Example 4.1) provides a suitable approximation of the benefit that each of the production centres receives from materials procurement. Therefore, 50 per cent of the value of materials is issued to machine centre X, resulting in 50 per cent of the total costs of materials procurement being allocated to this centre. If you refer to Exhibit 4.2 you will see that £880 000 (50 per cent of material procurement costs of £1 760 000) has been reallocated to machine centre X. It is also assumed that direct labour hours provides an approximation of the benefits received by the production centres from general factory support. Since machine centre X consumes 25 per cent of the direct labour hours £450 000 (25 per cent of the total costs of £1 800 000 assigned to general factory support) has been reallocated to machine centre X. You will see in the row labelled 'step 2 of stage 1' shown in the second column in Exhibit 4.2 that all manufacturing costs have now been assigned to the three production centres. This completes the first stage of the two-stage allocation process.

REAL WORLD VIEWS 4.1

SOURCE: BREALEY, J. A. (2006), THE CALCULATION OF PRODUCT COSTS AND THEIR USE IN DECISION-MAKING IN THE BRITISH MANUFACTURING INDUSTRY, PHD DISSERTATION, UNIVERSITY OF HUDDERSFIELD.

Views on the treatment of manufacturing overheads

A questionnaire survey by Brealey (2006) reported the following results in respect of UK manufacturing companies:

	N	%
Blanket (plant-wide rates)	31	13
Production department rates	150	63
Activity-based costing rates	8	4
Variable costing rates (i.e. overheads not assigned to products)	45	19
Other	3	1
	237	100

Nine of the 31 respondents who used a blanket rate were interviewed to ascertain the reasons for using such a rate. Five interviewees were happy with the product costs derived from using this rate and four acknowledged its limitations. The following is a response from one of the respondents that argued that the improved accuracy of the product costs derived from replacing a blanket overhead rate with a departmental rate could not be justified on cost-benefit criteria:

The added value … for breaking [the overhead] down any further would be minimal … I think if I go down any further within separate areas in the manufacturing operations to split down production, purchasing and quality departments, I don't think it would make much difference to the blanket overhead rate that we've got.

One of the four interviewees who acknowledged the limitations of blanket overhead rates argued that it was reasonable to use a blanket rate because overheads were a small proportion of total costs. The second interviewee argued that the rate was used because it was simple to calculate and the third cited a lack of resources. The final interviewee intended to change from a blanket rate to multiple departmental rates. Forty of the respondents who used separate production department rates were interviewed. Reasons cited for using these rates included: the factory was divided into different production processes; cost centres use different resources in different proportions; and the fact that the factory was organized so that each production department was responsible for a product group. One respondent justified the use of separate overhead rates throughout the factory as follows:

We actually have manufacturing cells which are cost centres in their own right, so it's best if we have a cost centre which is trying to recover those costs against what it's manufacturing. So rather than saying we have lots of manufacturing cells but only one cost centre, it seems more straightforward to say here's a cell of cost which manufactures and fills something and does some sort of service. It's easier to allocate the costs so that a particular cost centre can recover the costs of that cost centre and certainly you can see overall whether it's over or under recovering.

Five interviews were conducted with units that only assigned variable costs to products. They justified this approach on the grounds that fixed overheads would remain unchanged irrespective of the decisions that were made so they were irrelevant for decision-making.

Discussion point

1 What are the major limitations of a blanket overhead rate?

Step 3 – Computing separate overhead rates for each production cost centre

The second stage of the two-stage process is to allocate the overheads of each production centre to products passing through that centre. The most frequently used allocation bases in traditional costing systems are based on the amount of time products spend in each production centre – normally direct labour hours and machine hours. In respect of non-machine centres, direct labour hours is the most frequently used allocation base. This implies that the overheads incurred by a production centre are closely related to direct labour hours worked. In the case of machine centres a machine hour overhead rate is preferable since most of the overheads (e.g. depreciation) are likely to be more closely related to machine hours. We shall assume that the Enterprise Company uses a *machine hour rate* for the machine production centres and a *direct labour hour rate* for the assembly centre. The overhead rates are calculated by applying the following formula:

$$\frac{\text{cost centre overheads}}{\text{cost centre direct labour hours or machine hours}}$$

The calculations using the information given in Example 4.1 are as follows:

$$\text{Machine centre X} = \frac{£4\,300\,000}{2\,000\,000 \ \text{machine hours}} = £2.15 \text{ per machine hour}$$

$$\text{Machine centre Y} = \frac{£3\,800\,000}{1\,000\,000 \ \text{machine hours}} = £3.80 \text{ per machine hour}$$

$$\text{Assembly department} = \frac{£3\,600\,000}{2\,000\,000 \ \text{direct labour hours}} = £1.80 \text{ per direct labour hour}$$

Step 4 – Assigning cost centre overheads to products or other chosen cost objects

The final step is to allocate the overheads to products passing through the production centres. Therefore, if a product spends 10 hours in machine cost centre A overheads of £21.50 (10 × £2.15) will be allocated to the product. We shall compute the manufacturing costs of two products. Product A is a low sales volume product with direct costs of £100. It is manufactured in batches of 100 units and each unit requires 5 hours in machine centre A, 10 hours in machine centre B and 10 hours in the assembly centre. Product B is a high sales volume product thus enabling it to be manufactured in larger batches. It is manufactured in batches of 200 units and each unit requires 10 hours in machine centre A, 20 hours in machine centre B and 20 hours in the assembly centre. Direct costs of £200 have been assigned to product B. The calculations of the manufacturing costs assigned to the products are as follows:

Product A	£
Direct costs (100 units × £100)	10 000
Overhead allocations	
Machine centre A (100 units × 5 machine hours × £2.15)	1 075
Machine centre B (100 units × 10 machine hours × £3.80)	3 800
Assembly (100 units × 10 direct labour hours × £1.80)	1 800
Total cost	16 675

Cost per unit (£16 675/100 units) = £166.75

Product B	£
Direct costs (200 units × £200)	40 000
Overhead allocations	
Machine centre A (200 units × 10 machine hours × £2.15)	4 300
Machine centre B (200 units × 20 machine hours × £3.80)	15 200
Assembly (200 units × 20 direct labour hours × £1.80)	7 200
Total cost	66 700

Cost per unit (£66 700/200 units) = £333.50

The overhead allocation procedure is more complicated where service cost centres serve each other. In Example 4.1 it was assumed that neither materials procurement nor general factory support provide any services for each other. An understanding of situations where service cost centres do serve each other is not necessary for a general understanding of the overhead procedure, and the problem of service centre reciprocal cost allocations is therefore dealt with in Appendix 4.1.

EXTRACTING RELEVANT COSTS FOR DECISION-MAKING

The cost computations relating to the Enterprise Company for products A and B represent the costs that should be generated for meeting stock valuation and profit measurement requirements. For decision-making, non-manufacturing costs should also be taken into account. In addition, some of the costs that have been assigned to the products may not be relevant for certain decisions. For example, if you look at the overhead analysis sheet in Exhibit 4.2 you will see that property taxes, depreciation of machinery and insurance of buildings and machinery have been assigned to cost centres, and thus included in the costs assigned to products. If these costs are unaffected by a decision to discontinue a product they should not be assigned to products when undertaking product discontinuation reviews. However, if cost information is used to determine selling prices these costs may need to be assigned to products. It is therefore necessary to ensure that the costs incorporated in the overhead analysis are suitably coded so that different overhead rates can be extracted for different combinations of costs and relevant cost information can be extracted from the database for meeting different requirements. For an illustration of this approach you should refer to the answer to Review problem 4.20 shown at the end of this chapter.

BUDGETED OVERHEAD RATES

Our discussion in this chapter has assumed that the *actual* overheads for an accounting period have been allocated to the products. However, the use of actual figures can be problematic. This is because the product cost calculations have to be delayed until the end of the accounting period, since the overhead rate calculations cannot be obtained before this date. However, information on product costs is required more quickly if it is to be used for monthly profit calculations and inventory valuations or as a basis for setting selling prices. One may argue that the timing problem can be resolved by calculating actual overhead rates at more frequent intervals, say on a monthly basis, but the difficulty here is that a large amount of overhead expenditure is fixed in the short term whereas activity will vary from month to month, giving large fluctuations in the overhead rates.

Consider Example 4.2. The monthly overhead rates of £2 and £5 per hour are not representative of typical, normal production conditions. Management has committed itself to a specific level of fixed costs in the light of foreseeable needs for beyond one month. Thus, where production fluctuates, monthly overhead rates may be volatile. Furthermore, some costs such as repairs, maintenance and heating are not incurred evenly throughout the year. Therefore, if monthly overhead rates are used, these costs will not be allocated fairly to units of output. For example, heating costs would be charged only to winter production so that products produced in winter would be more expensive than those produced in summer.

An average, annualized rate based on the relationship of total annual overhead to total annual activity is more representative of typical relationships between total costs and volume than a monthly rate. What is required is a normal product cost based on average long-term production rather than an actual product cost, which is affected by month-to-month fluctuations in production volume. Taking these factors into consideration, it is preferable to establish a **budgeted overhead rate** based on annual *estimated* overhead expenditure and activity.

EXAMPLE 4.2

The fixed overheads for Euro are £24 million per annum, and monthly production varies from 400 000 to 1 000 000 direct labour hours. The monthly overhead rate for fixed overhead will therefore fluctuate as follows:

Monthly overhead	£2 000 000	£2 000 000
Monthly production	400 000 hours	1 000 000 hours
Monthly overhead rate	£5 per hour	£2 per hour

Overhead expenditure that is fixed in the short term remains constant each month, but monthly production fluctuates because of holiday periods and seasonal variations in demand. Consequently the overhead rate varies from £2 to £5 per hour. It would be unreasonable for a product worked on in one month to be allocated overheads at a rate of £5 per hour and an identical product worked on in another month allocated at a rate of only £2 per hour.

UNDER- AND OVER-RECOVERY OF OVERHEADS

The effect of calculating overhead rates based on budgeted annual overhead expenditure and activity is that it will be most unlikely that the overhead allocated to products manufactured during the period will be the same as the actual overhead incurred. Consider a situation where the estimated annual fixed overheads are £2 000 000 and the estimated annual activity is 1 000 000 direct labour hours. The estimated fixed overhead rate will be £2 per hour. Assume that actual overheads are £2 000 000 and are therefore identical with the estimate, but that actual activity is 900 000 direct labour hours instead of the estimated 1 000 000 hours. In this situation only £1 800 000 will be charged to production. This calculation is based on 900 000 direct labour hours at £2 per hour, giving an under-recovery of overheads of £200 000.

Consider an alternative situation where the actual overheads are £1 950 000 instead of the estimated £2 000 000, and actual activity is 1 000 000 direct labour hours, which is identical to the original estimate. In this situation 1 000 000 direct labour hours at £2 per hour will be charged to production, giving an over-recovery of £50 000. This example illustrates that there will be an **under- or over-recovery of overheads** whenever actual activity or overhead expenditure is different from the budgeted overheads and activity used to estimate the budgeted overhead rate.

Accounting regulations in most countries recommend that the under- or over-recovery of overheads should be regarded as a period cost adjustment. For example, the UK Statement of Standard Accounting Practice on Stocks and Work in Progress (SSAP 9) and the International Accounting Standard on Inventories (IAS2) recommend that the allocation of overheads in the valuation of inventories and work in progress needs to be based on the company's normal level of activity and that any under- or over-recovery should be written off in the current year. This procedure is illustrated in Figure 4.4. Note that any under- or over-recovery of overhead is not allocated to products. Also note that the under-recovery is recorded as an expense in the current accounting period whereas an over-recovery is recorded as a reduction in the expenses for the period. Finally, you should note that our discussion here is concerned with how to treat any under- or over-recovery for the purpose of financial accounting and its impact on inventory valuation and profit measurement.

NON-MANUFACTURING OVERHEADS

For financial accounting purposes, only manufacturing costs are allocated to products. Non-manufacturing overheads are regarded as period costs and are disposed of in exactly the

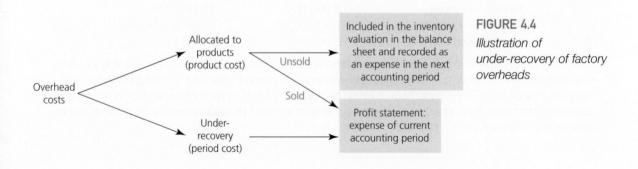

FIGURE 4.4

Illustration of under-recovery of factory overheads

EXAMPLE 4.3

The estimated non-manufacturing overhead and manufacturing costs of a company for the year ending 31 December are £500 000 and £1 million respectively. The non-manufacturing overhead absorption rate is calculated as follows:

$$\frac{\text{estimated non-manufacturing overhead}}{\text{estimated manufacturing cost}}$$

In percentage terms each product will be allocated with non-manufacturing overheads at a rate of 50 per cent of its total manufacturing cost.

same way as the under- or over-recovery of manufacturing overheads outlined in Figure 4.4. However, for decision-making non-manufacturing costs should be assigned to products. For example, in many organizations it is not uncommon for selling prices to be based on estimates of total cost or even actual cost. Housing contractors and garages often charge for their services by adding a percentage profit margin to actual cost.

Some non-manufacturing costs may be a direct cost of the product. Delivery costs, salesmen's salaries and travelling expenses may be directly identifiable with the product, but it is likely that many non-manufacturing overheads cannot be allocated directly to specific products. On what basis should we allocate non-manufacturing overheads? The problem is that cause-and-effect allocation bases often cannot be established for non-manufacturing overheads. Therefore traditional systems tend to use arbitrary, rather than cause-and-effect allocation bases, to allocate non-manufacturing overheads to products. The most widely used approach is to allocate non-manufacturing overheads on the ability of the products to bear such costs. This approach can be implemented by allocating non-manufacturing costs to products on the basis of their manufacturing costs. This procedure is illustrated in Example 4.3.

SUMMARY

The following items relate to the learning objectives listed at the beginning of the chapter.

- **Distinguish between cause-and-effect and arbitrary allocations.** Allocation bases which are significant determinants of costs that are being allocated are described as cause-and-effect allocations whereas arbitrary allocations refer to allocation bases that are not the significant determinants of the costs. To accurately measure the cost of resources used by cost objects cause-and-effect allocations should be used.

- **Explain why different cost information is required for different purposes.** Manufacturing organizations assign costs to products for two purposes: first for external (financial accounting) profit measurement and inventory valuation purposes in order to allocate manufacturing costs incurred during a period to cost of goods sold and inventories; second to provide useful information for managerial decision-making requirements. Financial accounting regulations specify that only manufacturing costs should be assigned to products for meeting inventory and profit measurement requirements. Both manufacturing and non-manufacturing costs, however, may be relevant for decision-making. In addition, not all costs that are assigned to products for inventory valuation and profit measurement are relevant for decision-making. For example, costs that will not be affected by a decision (e.g. depreciation) are normally not relevant for decision-making.

- **Describe how cost systems differ in terms of their level of sophistication.** Cost systems range from simplistic to sophisticated. Simplistic systems are inexpensive to operate, involve extensive use of arbitrary allocations, have a high likelihood of reporting inaccurate product costs and generally result in a high cost of errors. Sophisticated costing systems are more expensive to operate, rely more extensively on cause-and-effect allocations, generally report more accurate product costs and have a low cost of errors. Further distinguishing features are that simplistic costing systems have a small number of first-stage cost centres/pools and use a single second-stage cost driver. In contrast, sophisticated costing systems use many first-stage cost centres/pools and many different types of second-stage drivers.

- **Understand the factors influencing the choice of an optimal costing system.** The optimal costing system is different for different organizations and should be determined on a costs versus benefits basis. Simplistic costing systems are appropriate in organizations whose indirect costs are a low percentage of total costs and which also have a fairly standardized product range, all consuming organizational resources in similar proportions. Under these circumstances simplistic costing systems may report costs that are sufficiently accurate for decision-making purposes. Conversely, organizations with a high proportion of indirect costs, whose products consume organizational resources in different proportions are likely to require sophisticated costing systems. Relying on sophisticated costing systems under these circumstances is likely to result in the additional benefits from reporting more accurate costs exceeding the costs of operating more sophisticated systems.

- **Explain why departmental overhead rates should be used in preference to a single blanket overhead rate.** A blanket (also known as plant-wide) overhead rate establishes a single overhead rate for the organization as a whole, whereas departmental rates involve indirect costs being accumulated by different departments and a separate overhead rate being established for each department. A blanket overhead rate can only be justified when all products or services consume departmental overheads in approximately the same proportions. Such circumstances are unlikely to be applicable to most organizations resulting in blanket overheads generally reporting inaccurate product/service costs.

- **Construct an overhead analysis sheet and calculate cost centre allocation rates.** Cost centre overhead allocation rates are established and assigned to cost objects using the two-stage allocation overhead procedure. In the first stage, an overhead analysis sheet is used to (a) allocate overheads to production and service centres or departments and (b) to reallocate the total service department overheads to production departments. The second stage involves (a) the calculation of appropriate departmental overhead rates and (b) the allocation of overheads to products passing through each department. These steps were illustrated using data presented in Example 4.1.

- **Justify why budgeted overhead rates should be used in preference to actual overhead rates.** Because the uses of actual overhead rates causes a delay in the calculation of product or service costs, and the establishment of monthly rates results in fluctuations in the overhead rates throughout the year, it is recommended that annual budgeted overhead rates should be used.

- **Calculate and explain the treatment of the under- over-recovery of overheads.** The use of annual budgeted overhead rates gives an under- or over-recovery of overheads whenever actual overhead expenditure or activity is different from budget. Any under- or over-recovery is generally regarded as a period cost adjustment and written off to the profit and loss statement and thus not allocated to products.

- **Additional learning objective presented in Appendix 4.1.** The appendix to this chapter includes the following additional learning objective: to be able to reallocate service department costs to production departments when service departments provide services for other service departments as well as production departments. This topic tends to be included in the syllabus requirements of the examinations set by professional accountancy bodies but may not be part of the course curriculum for other courses. You can omit Appendix 4.1 if this topic is not part of your course curriculum.

APPENDIX 4.1: INTER-SERVICE DEPARTMENT REALLOCATION

Service departments may provide services for other service departments as well as for production departments. For example, a personnel department provides services for other service departments such as the power generating plant, maintenance department and stores. The power generating department also provides heat and light for other service departments, including the personnel department, and so on. When such interactions occur, the allocation process can become complicated. Difficulties arise because each service department begins to accumulate charges from other service departments from which it receives services, and these must be reallocated back to the user department. Once it has begun, this allocation and reallocation process can continue for a long time before a solution is found. The problem is illustrated in Example 4A.1. We shall use the example to illustrate four different methods of allocating the service department costs:

1 repeated distribution method;
2 simultaneous equation method;
3 specified order of closing method;
4 direct allocation method.

1. Repeated distribution method

Where this method is adopted, the service department costs are repeatedly allocated in the specified percentages until the figures become too small to be significant. You can see from line 2 of Exhibit 4A.1 that the overheads of service department 1 are allocated according to the prescribed percentages. As a result, some of the overheads of service department 1 are transferred to service department 2. In line 3 the overheads of service department 2 are allocated, which means that service department 1 receives some further costs. The costs of service department 1 are again allocated, and service department 2 receives some further costs. This process continues until line 7, by which time the costs have become so small that any further detailed apportionments are unnecessary. As a result, the total overheads in line 8 of £152 040 are allocated to production departments only.

EXAMPLE 4A.1

A company has three production departments and two service departments. The overhead analysis sheet provides the following totals of the overheads analyzed to production and service departments:

		(£)
Production department	X	48 000
	Y	42 000
	Z	30 000
Service department	1	14 040
	2	18 000
		152 040

The expenses of the service departments are apportioned as follows:

	Production departments			Service departments	
	X	Y	Z	1	2
Service department 1	20%	40%	30%	–	10%
Service department 2	40%	20%	20%	20%	–

Line	Production department			Service departments		Total
	X	Y	Z	1	2	
1 Allocation as per overhead analysis	48 000	42 000	30 000	14 040	18 000	152 040
2 Allocation of service department 1	2 808 (20%)	5 616 (40%)	4 212 (30%)	(14 040)	$\frac{1\,404}{19\,404}$ (10%)	
3 Allocation of service department 2	7 762 (40%)	3 881 (20%)	3 880 (20%)	3 881 (20%)	(19 404)	
4 Allocation of service department 1	776 (20%)	1 552 (40%)	1 165 (30%)	(3 881)	388 (10%)	
5 Allocation of service department 2	154 (40%)	78 (20%)	78 (20%)	78 (20%)	(388)	
6 Allocation of service department 1	16 (20%)	31 (40%)	23 (30%)	(78)	8 (10%)	
7 Allocation of service department 2	4 (40%)	2 (20%)	2 (20%)	–	(8)	
8 Total overheads	59 520	53 160	39 360	–	–	152 040

EXHIBIT 4A.1

Repeated distribution method

2. Simultaneous equation method

When this method is used simultaneous equations are initially established as follows: Let

$$x = \text{total overhead of service department 1}$$
$$y = \text{total overhead of service department 2}$$

The total overhead transferred into service departments 1 and 2 can be expressed as

$$x = 14\,040 + 0.2y$$
$$y = 18\,000 + 0.1x$$

Rearranging the above equations:

$$x - 0.2y = 14\,040 \qquad\qquad (1)$$
$$-0.1x + y = 18\,000 \qquad\qquad (2)$$

We can now multiply equation (1) by 5 and equation (2) by 1, giving

$$5x - y = 70\,200$$
$$-0.1x + y = 18\,000$$

Adding the above equations together we have

$$4.9x = 88\,200$$

Therefore
$$x = 18\,000\,(= 88\,200/4.9)$$

Substituting this value for x in equation (1), we have

$$18\,000 - 0.2y = 14\,040$$

Therefore
$$-0.2y = -3\,960$$

Therefore
$$y = 19\,800$$

We now apportion the values for x and y to the production departments in the agreed percentages.

Line		X	Y	Z	Total
1	Allocation as per overhead analysis	48 000	42 000	30 000	120 000
2	Allocation of service department 1	3 600 (20%)	7 200 (40%)	5 400 (30%)	16 200
3	Allocation of service department 2	7 920 (40%)	3 960 (20%)	3 960 (20%)	15 840
4		59 520	53 160	39 360	152 040

You will see from line 2 that the value for X (service department 1) of £18 000 is allocated in the specified percentages. Similarly, in line 3 the value for Y (service department 2) of £19 800 is apportioned in the specified percentages. As a result the totals in line 4 are in agreement with the totals in line 8 of the repeated distribution method (Exhibit 4A.1).

Line	Production departments			Service departments		Total
	X	Y	Z	1	2	
1 Allocation as per overhead analysis	48 000	42 000	30 000	14 040	18 000	152 040
2 Allocate service department 2	7200 (40%)	3600 (20%)	3600 (20%)	3600 (20%)	(18 000)	
3 Allocate service department 1	3 920 (2/9)	7 840 (4/9)	5 880 (3/9)	(17 640)	—	
4	59 120	53 440	39 480	—	—	152 040

EXHIBIT 4A.2
Specified order of closing method

3. Specified order of closing

If this method is used the service departments' overheads are allocated to the production departments in a certain order. The service department that does the largest proportion of work for other service departments is closed first; the service department that does the second largest proportion of work for other service departments is closed second; and so on. Return charges are not made to service departments whose costs have previously been allocated. Let us now apply this method to the information contained in Example 4A.1. The results are given in Exhibit 4A.2.

The costs of service department 2 are allocated first (line 2) because 20 per cent of its work is related to service department 1, whereas only 10 per cent of the work of service department 1 is related to service department 2. In line 3 we allocate the costs of service department 1, but the return charges are not made to department 2. This means that the proportions allocated have changed as 10 per cent of the costs of service department 1 have not been allocated to service department 2. Therefore 20 per cent out of a 90 per cent total or 2/9 of the costs of service department 1 are allocated to department X.

You will see that the totals allocated in line 4 do not agree with the totals allocated under the repeated distribution or simultaneous equation methods. This is because the specified order of closing method sacrifices accuracy for clerical convenience. However, if this method provides a close approximation to an alternative accurate calculation then there are strong arguments for its use.

4. Direct allocation method

This method is illustrated in Exhibit 4A.3. It ignores inter-service department service realloca-tions. Therefore, service department costs are reallocated only to production departments. This means that the proportions allocated have changed as 10 per cent of the costs of service

| | Production departments | | | Service departments | | |
Line	X	Y	Z	1	2	Total
1 Allocation as per overhead analysis	48 000	42 000	30 000	14 040	18 000	152 040
2 Allocate service department 1	3 120 (2/9)	6 240 (4/9)	4 680 (3/9)	(14 040)		
3 Allocate service department 2	9 000 (4/8)	4 500 (2/8)	4 500 (2/8)	—	(18 000)	
4	60 120	52 740	39 180	—	—	152 040

EXHIBIT 4A.3

Direct allocation method

department 1 have not been allocated to service department 2. Therefore 20 per cent out of a 90 per cent total, or 2/9 of the costs of service department 1, are allocated to department X, 4/9 are allocated to department Y and 3/9 are allocated to department Z. Similarly the proportions allocated for service department 2 have changed with 4/8 (40 per cent out of 80 per cent) of the costs of service department 2 being allocated to department X, 2/8 to department Y and 2/8 to department Z. The only justification for using the direct allocation method is its simplicity. The method is recommended when inter-service reallocations are relatively insignificant.

KEY TERMS AND CONCEPTS

Activity-based-costing (ABC) systems costing systems that use only cause-and-effect cost allocations to assign indirect costs to cost objects.

Allocation base or **cost driver** the basis that is used to allocate costs to cost objects.

Arbitrary allocation a cost allocation where the base is not a significant determinant of costs.

Blanket overhead rate, or **plant-wide overhead rate** overhead rate that assigns indirect costs to cost objects using a *single* overhead rate for the whole organization.

Budgeted overhead rate an overhead rate based on dividing annual estimated overhead expenditure by the budgeted activity.

Cause-and-effect allocation a cost allocation where the base is a significant determinant of costs.

Cost allocation the process of assigning costs to a cost object where direct measures do not exist and surrogate measures must be used instead.

Cost centre, or **cost pool** a location (e.g. departments or work centres) to which overhead costs are initially assigned.

Cost tracing the process of assigning a direct cost to a cost object.

Service departments, or **support departments** departments that exist that provide services to the other departments within the organization.

Traditional costing systems costing systems that rely on arbitrary cost allocations to assign indirect costs to cost objects.

Under- or **over-recovery of overheads** a situation that occurs whenever actual activity or overhead expenditure differs from the budgeted overheads and activity used to estimate the budgeted overhead rate.

KEY EXAMINATION POINTS

A typical question (e.g. Review problem 4.17) will require you to analyze overheads by departments and calculate appropriate overhead allocation rates. These questions may require a large number of calculations, and it is possible that you will make calculation errors. Do make sure that your answer is clearly presented, since marks tend to be allocated according to whether you have adopted the correct method. You are recommended to present your answer in a format similar to Exhibit 4.2. For a traditional costing system you should normally recommend a direct labour hour rate if a department is non-mechanized and a machine hour rate if machine hours are the dominant activity. You should only recommend the direct wages percentage method (see Learning Note 4.1 on the companion website) when the rates within a non-mechanized department are uniform.

Where a question requires you to present information for decision-making, do not include apportioned fixed overheads in the calculations. Remember the total manufacturing costs should be calculated for stock valuation, but incremental costs should be calculated for decision-making purposes (see answer to Review problem 4.20).

Finally, ensure that you can calculate under- or over-recoveries of overheads. To check your understanding of this topic you should refer to the solution to Review problem 4.18.

ASSESSMENT MATERIAL

The review questions are short questions that enable you to assess your understanding of the main topics included in the chapter. The numbers in parentheses provide you with the page numbers to refer to if you cannot answer a specific question.

The review problems are more complex and require you to relate and apply the chapter content to various business problems. The problems are graded by their level of difficulty. The multiple-choice questions are the least demanding and normally take less than 10 minutes to complete. Fully worked solutions to the review problems are provided in a separate section at the end of the book. Further review problems with solutions for this chapter are available on the accompanying website www.drury-online.com. The website includes a *Student's Manual* and an *Instructor's Manual.* Students can access both questions and answers from the *Student's Manual* and the questions from the Instructor's Manual. The answers to problems in the *Instructor's Manual* are available only to lecturers on the lecturer's password-protected section of the website.

The website also includes over 20 case study problems. A list of these cases is provided on pages 427-30. Oak City is a case study that is relevant to the content of this chapter.

REVIEW QUESTIONS

4.1 Why are indirect costs not directly traced to cost objects in the same way as direct costs? *(p. 78)*

4.2 Define cost tracing, cost allocation, allocation base and cost driver. *(p. 78)*

4.3 Distinguish between arbitrary and cause-and-effect allocations. *(p. 78)*

4.4 Explain how cost information differs for profit measurement/inventory valuation requirements compared with decision-making requirements. *(p. 79)*

4.5 Explain why cost systems should differ in terms of their level of sophistication. *(p. 80)*

4.6 Why are separate departmental or cost centre overhead rates preferred to a plant-wide (blanket) overhead rate? *(pp. 81–82)*

4.7 Describe the two-stage overhead allocation procedure. *(pp. 82–83)*

4.8 Why are some overhead costs sometimes not relevant for decision-making purposes? *(p. 90)*

4.9 Why are budgeted overhead rates preferred to actual overhead rates? *(p. 91)*

4.10 Give two reasons for the under- or over-recovery of overheads at the end of the accounting period. *(pp. 91–92)*

REVIEW PROBLEMS

4.11   A company uses absorption costing with a predetermined hourly overhead absorption rate. The following situations arose last month:

(i)   Actual hours worked exceeded planned hours.

(ii)   Actual overhead expenditure exceeded planned expenditure.

Which of the following statements is correct?

(a)   Situation (i) would cause overheads to be over-absorbed and situation (ii) would cause overheads to be under-absorbed.

(b)   Situation (i) would cause overheads to be under-absorbed and situation (ii) would cause overheads to be over-absorbed.

(c)   Both situations would cause overheads to be over-absorbed.

(d)   Both situations would cause overheads to be under-absorbed.

ACCA Financial Information for Management

4.12   The following data are to be used for sub-questions (i) and (ii) below:

Budgeted labour hours	8500
Budgeted overheads	£148 750
Actual labour hours	7928
Actual overheads	£146 200

(i)   Based on the data given above, what is the labour hour overhead absorption rate?

(a)   £17.50 per hour

(b)   £17.20 per hour

(c)   £18.44 per hour

(d)   £18.76 per hour

(ii)   Based on the data given above, what is the amount of overhead under-over-absorbed?

(a)   £2550 under-absorbed

(b)   £2529 over-absorbed

(c)   £2550 over-absorbed

(d)   £7460 under-absorbed

CIMA Stage 1

4.13   J Ltd uses standard absorption costing and absorbs production overheads on the basis of standard machine hours. The following budgeted and actual information applied in its last accounting period:

	Budget	Actual
Production overhead	$180 000	$178 080
Machine hours	50 000	48 260
Units produced	40 000	38 760

At the end of the period, production overhead will be reported as:

A   under-absorbed by $4344

B   under-absorbed by $3660

C   over-absorbed by $4344

D   over-absorbed by $3660

CIMA – Management Accounting Fundamentals

4.14   The management accountant's report shows that fixed production overheads were over-absorbed in the last accounting period. The combination that is certain to lead to this situation is:

	Production activity	and	Fixed overhead expenditure
A	lower than budget	and	higher than budget
B	higher than budget	and	higher than budget
C	As budgeted	and	as budgeted
D	higher than budget	and	lower than budget

CIMA – Management Accounting Fundamentals

4.15   An engineering firm operates a job costing system. Production overhead is absorbed at the rate of $8.50 per machine hour. In order to allow for non-production overhead costs and profit, a mark up of 60 per cent of prime cost is added to the production cost when preparing price estimates.

The estimated requirements of job number 808 are as follows:

Direct materials	$10 650
Direct labour	$3260
Machine hours	140

The estimated price notified to the customer for job number 808 will be:

(a)   A $22 256

(b)   B $22 851

(c)   C $23 446

(d)   D $24 160

CIMA – Management Accounting Fundamentals

4.16   A factory consists of two production cost centres (G and H) and two service cost centres (J and K). The total overhead allocated and apportioned to each cost centre are as follows:

G	H	J	K
£40 000	£50 000	£30 000	£18 000

The work done by the service cost centres can be represented as follows:

	G	H	J	K
Percentage of service cost centre J to	30%	70%	–	–
Percentage of service cost centre K to	50%	40%	10%	–

The company apportions service cost centre costs to production cost centres using a method that fully recognizes any work done by one service cost centre for another. What are the total overheads for production cost centre G after the reapportionment of all service cost centre costs?

(a)   £58 000

(b)   £58 540

(c)   £59 000

(d)   £59 540

ACCA – Financial information for management

4.17 Overhead analysis and calculation of product costs

A furniture-making business manufactures quality furniture to customers' orders. It has three production departments and two service departments. Budgeted overhead costs for the coming year are as follows:

	Total (£)
Rent and rates	12 800
Machine insurance	6000
Telephone charges	3200
Depreciation	18 000
Production supervisor's salaries	24 000
Heating, lighting	6400
	70 400

The three production departments – A, B and C, and the two service departments – X and Y, are housed in the new premises, the details of which, together with other statistics and information, are given below.

	Departments				
	A	B	C	X	Y
Floor area occupied (sq. metres)	3000	1800	600	600	400
Machine value (£000)	24	10	8	4	2
Direct labour hrs budgeted	3200	1800	1000		
Allocated overheads:					
Specific to each department (£000)	2.8	1.7	1.2	0.8	0.6
Service department X's costs apportioned	50%	25%	25%		
Service department Y's costs apportioned	20%	30%	50%		

Required:

(a) Prepare a statement showing the overhead cost budgeted for each department, showing the basis of apportionment used. Also calculate suitable overhead absorption rates.

(9 marks)

(b) Two pieces of furniture are to be manufactured for customers. Direct costs are as follows:

	Job 123	Job 124
Direct material	£154	£108
Direct labour	20 hours Dept A	16 hours Dept A
	12 hours Dept B	10 hours Dept B
	10 hours Dept C	14 hours Dept C

Calculate the total costs of each job.

(5 marks)

(c) If the firm quotes prices to customers that reflect a required profit of 25 per cent on selling price, calculate the quoted selling price for each job.

(2 marks)

(d) If material costs are a significant part of total costs in a manufacturing company, describe a system of material control that might be used in order to effectively control costs, paying particular attention to the stock control aspect.

(9 marks)

AAT Stage 3 Cost Accounting and Budgeting

4.18 Various overhead absorption rates and under- over-recovery

The following data relate to a manufacturing department for a period:

	Budget data (£)	Actual data (£)
Direct material cost	100 000	150 000
Direct labour cost	250 000	275 000
Production overhead	250 000	350 000
Direct labour hours	50 000 hours	55 000 hours

Job ZX was one of the jobs worked on during the period. Direct material costing £7000 and direct labour (800 hours) costing £4000 were incurred.

Required:

(i) Calculate the production overhead absorption rate predetermined for the period based on:

(a) percentage of direct material cost;

(b) direct labour hours.

(3 marks)

(ii) Calculate the production overhead cost to be charged to Job ZX based on the rates calculated in answer to (i) above.

(2 marks)

(iii)   Assume that the direct labour hour rate of absorption is used. Calculate the under- or over-absorption of production overheads for the period and state an appropriate treatment in the accounts.

(4 marks)

(iv)   Comment briefly on the relative merits of the two methods of overhead absorption used in (i) above.   *(6 marks)*

AAT Cost Accounting and Budgeting

4.19   Calculation of product overhead costs

Bookdon Public Limited Company manufactures three products in two production departments, a machine shop and a fitting section; it also has two service departments, a canteen and a machine maintenance section. Shown below are next year's budgeted production data and manufacturing costs for the company.

	Product X	Product Y	Product Z
Production	4200 units	6900 units	1700 units
Prime cost:			
Direct materials	£11 per unit	£14 per unit	£17 per unit
Direct labour:			
Machine shop	£6 per unit	£4 per unit	£2 per unit
Fitting section	£12 per unit	£3 per unit	£21 per unit
Machine hours per unit	6 hours per unit	3 hours per unit	4 hours per unit

	Machine shop	Fitting section	Canteen	Machine maintenance section	Total
Budgeted overheads (£):					
Allocated overheads	27 660	19 470	16 600	26 650	90 380
Rent, rates, heat and light					17 000
Depreciation and insurance of equipment					25 000
Additional data:					
Gross book value of equipment (£)	150 000	75 000	30 000	45 000	
Number of employees	18	14	4	4	
Floor space occupied (square metres)	3600	1400	1000	800	

It has been estimated that approximately 70 per cent of the machine maintenance section's costs are incurred servicing the machine shop and the remainder incurred servicing the fitting section.

Required:

(a)   (i)   Calculate the following budgeted overhead absorption rates:
A machine hour rate for the machine shop. A rate expressed as a percentage of direct wages for the fitting section. All workings and assumptions should be clearly shown.

(12 marks)

(ii)   Calculate the budgeted manufacturing overhead cost per unit of product X.

(b) The production director of Bookdon PLC has suggested that 'as the actual overheads incurred and units produced are usually different from the budgeted and as a consequence profits of each month end are distorted by over- under-absorbed overheads, it would be more accurate to calculate the actual overhead cost per unit each month end by dividing the total number of all units actually produced during the month into the actual overheads incurred'.

Critically examine the production director's suggestion.

(8 marks)
ACCA Level 1 Costing

4.20 Make or buy decision

Shown below is next year's budget for the forming and finishing departments of Tooton Ltd. The departments manufacture three different types of component, which are incorporated into the output of the firm's finished products.

	Component		
	A	**B**	**C**
Production (units)	14 000	10 000	6000
Prime cost (£ per unit):			
Direct materials			
Forming dept	8	7	9
Direct labour			
Forming dept	6	9	12
Finishing dept	10	15	8
	24	31	29
Manufacturing times (hours per unit):			
Machining			
Forming dept	4	3	2
Direct labour			
Forming dept	2	3	4
Finishing dept	3	10	2

	Forming department (£)	**Finishing department (£)**
Variable overheads	200 900	115 500
Fixed overheads	401 800	231 000
	£602 700	£346 500
Machine time required and available	98 000 hours	–
Labour hours required and available	82 000 hours	154 000 hours

The forming department is mechanized and employs only one grade of labour, the finishing department employs several grades of labour with differing hourly rates of pay.

Required:

(a) Calculate suitable overhead absorption rates for the forming and finishing departments for next year and include a brief explanation for your choice of rates.

(6 marks)

(b) Another firm has offered to supply next year's budgeted quantities of the above components at the following prices:

Component A   £30   Component B   £65
Component C   £60

Advise management whether it would be more economical to purchase any of the above components from the outside supplier. You must show your workings and, considering cost criteria only, clearly state any assumptions made or any aspects that may require further investigation.

(8 marks)

(c) Critically consider the purpose of calculating production overheads absorption rates.

(8 marks)
(Total 22 marks)
ACCA Foundation Costing

4.21 Reapportionment of service department costs

Phoebe Ltd manufactures many different products which pass through two production cost centres (P1 and P2). There are also two service cost centres (S1 and S2) in the factory. The following information has been extracted from the budget for the coming year:

	P1	P2	S1	S2
Allocated and apportioned production overheads	£477 550	£404 250	£132 000	£96 000
Number of employees	30	65	10	15
Total machine hours	68 000	11 400		
Total direct labour hours	4000	14 000		

Service cost centre S1 costs are reapportioned to all other cost centres based on the number of employees. Service cost centre S2 only does work for P1 and P2 and its costs are reapportioned to these centres in the ratio 5:3 respectively.

Required:

(a) Calculate:

   (i) the machine hour absorption rate for cost centre P1, and

   (ii) the direct labour hour absorption rate for cost centre P2.

(b) Explain the difference between production overheads that have been 'allocated' and those which have been 'apportioned' to cost centres. Explain why some manufacturing companies are able to allocate electric power costs to production cost centres, whereas others can only apportion them.

ACCA Financial information for management

CHAPTER 5
ACCOUNTING ENTRIES FOR A JOB COSTING SYSTEM

LEARNING OBJECTIVES

After studying this chapter, you should be able to:

- record the accounting entries for an integrated and interlocking accounting system;
- distinguish between an integrated and an interlocking accounting system;
- explain the distinguishing features of contract costing;
- prepare contract accounts and calculate the profit attributable to each contract.

This chapter is concerned with the accounting entries necessary to record transactions within a job costing system. A **job costing system** is required in organizations where each 'job', or unit or batch of output of a product or service is unique. This creates the need for the cost of each unit to be calculated separately. In the next chapter we shall consider an alternative system called **process costing** that is applied to situations where masses of identical units are produced and it is unnecessary to assign costs to individual units of output. In practice these two costing systems represent extreme ends of a continuum. The output of many organizations requires a combination of the elements of both job costing and process costing.

The accounting system on which we shall concentrate our attention is one in which the cost and financial accounts are combined in one set of accounts; this is known as an **integrated cost accounting system**. An alternative system, where the cost and financial accounts are maintained independently, is known as an **interlocking cost accounting system**. The integrated cost accounting system is generally considered to be preferable to the interlocking system, since the latter involves a duplication of accounting entries.

CONTROL ACCOUNTS

The recording system is based on a system of control accounts. A **control account** is a summary account, where entries are made from totals of transactions for a period. For example, the balance in the stores ledger control account will be supported by a voluminous file of stores ledger accounts, which will add up to agree with the total in the stores ledger control account. Assuming 1000 items of materials were received for a period that totalled £200 000, an entry of the total of £200 000 would be recorded on the debit (receipts side) of the stores ledger *control* account. This will be supported by 1000 separate entries in each of the individual stores ledger accounts. The total of all these *individual* entries will add up to £200 000. A system of control accounts enables one to check the accuracy of the various accounting entries. The file of all the individual accounts (for example the individual stores ledger accounts) supporting the total control account is called the subsidiary ledger.

We shall now examine the accounting entries necessary to record the transaction outlined in Example 5.1. A manual system is described so that the accounting entries can be followed, but these accounts are now normally maintained on a computer. You will find a summary of the accounting entries set out in Exhibit 5.1, where each transaction is prefixed by a number to give a clearer understanding of the necessary entries relating to it. In addition, the appropriate journal entry is shown for each transaction together with a supporting explanation.

RECORDING THE PURCHASE OF RAW MATERIALS

The entry to record the purchase of materials in transaction 1 is:

Dr Stores ledger control account	182 000	
Cr Creditors control account		182 000

This accounting entry reflects the fact that the company has incurred a short-term liability to acquire a current asset consisting of raw material stock. Each purchase is also entered in the receipts column of an individual stores ledger account for the quantity received, a unit price and amount. In addition, a separate credit entry is made in each individual creditor's account. Note that the entries in the control accounts form part of the system of double entry, whereas the separate entries in the individual accounts are detailed subsidiary records, which do not form part of the double entry system.

The entry for transaction 2 for materials returned to suppliers is:

Dr Creditors control account	2000	
Cr Stores ledger control account		2000

EXAMPLE 5.1

The following are the transactions of AB Ltd for the month of April.

1 Raw materials of £182 000 were purchases on credit.

2 Raw materials of £2 000 were returned to the supplier because of defects.

3 The total of stores requisitions for direct materials issued for the period was £165 000.

4 The total issues for indirect materials for the period was £10 000.

5 Gross wages of £185 000 were incurred during the period consisting of wages

paid to employees	£105 000
Tax deductions payable to the Government (i.e. Inland Revenue)	£60 000
National Insurance contributions due	£20 000

6 All the amounts due in transaction 5 were settled by cash during the period.

7 The allocation of the gross wages for the period was as follows:

Direct wages	£145 000
Indirect wages	£40 000

8 The employer's contribution for National Insurance deductions was £25 000.

9 Indirect factory expenses of £41 000 were incurred during the period.

10 Depreciation of factory machinery was £30 000.

11 Overhead expenses allocated to jobs by means of overhead allocation rates was £140 000 for the period.

12 Non-manufacturing overhead incurred during the period was £40 000.

13 The cost of jobs completed and transferred to finished goods stock was £300 000.

14 The sales value of goods withdrawn from stock and delivered to customers was £400 000 for the period.

15 The cost of goods withdrawn from stock and delivered to customers was £240 000 for the period.

An entry for the returned materials is also made in the appropriate stores ledger records and in the individual creditors' accounts.

RECORDING THE ISSUE OF MATERIALS

The storekeeper issues materials from store in exchange for a duly authorized stores requisition. For direct materials the job number will be recorded on the stores requisition, while for indirect materials the overhead account number will be entered on the requisition. The issue of direct materials involves a transfer of the materials from stores to production. For transaction 3, material requisitions are summarized and the resulting totals are recorded as follows:

```
        Dr Work in progress account        165 000
            Cr Stores ledger control account              165 000
```

EXHIBIT 5.1

Summary of accounting transactions for AB Ltd

Stores ledger control account

1. Creditors a/c	182 000	2. Creditors a/c	2 000
		3. Work in progress a/c	165 000
		4. Factory overhead a/c	10 000
		Balance c/d	5 000
	182 000		182 000
Balance b/d	5 000		

Factory overhead control account

4. Stores ledger a/c	10 000	11. Work in progress a/c	140 000
7. Wages control a/c	40 000	Balance – under recovery	
8. National Insurance		transferred to costing	
contributions a/c	25 000	P&L a/c	6 000
9. Expense creditors a/c	41 000		
10. Provision for			
depreciation a/c	30 000		
	146 000		146 000

Non-manufacturing overhead control account

12. Expense creditor a/c	40 000	Transferred to costing	
		P&L a/c	40 000

Creditors account

2. Stores ledger a/c	2 000	1. Stores ledger a/c	182 000

Wages accrued account

6. Cash/bank	105 000	5. Wages control a/c	105 000

Tax payable account

6. Cash/bank	60 000	5. Wages control a/c	60 000

National Insurance contributions account

6. Cash/bank	20 000	5. Wage control a/c	20 000
8. Cash/bank	25 000	8. Factory overhead a/c	25 000
	45 000		45 000

Expense creditors account

		9. Factory overhead a/c	41 000
		12. Non-manufacturing	
		overhead	40 000

Work in progress control account

3. Stores ledger a/c	165 000	13. Finished goods	
7. Wages control a/c	145 000	stock a/c	300 000
11. Factory overhead a/c	140 000	Balance c/d	150 000
	450000		450000
Balanced b/d	150 000		

Finished goods stock account

13. Work in progress a/c	300 000	15. Cost of sales a/c	240 000
		Balance c/d	60 000
	300000		300000
Balance b/d	60 000		

Cost of sales account

15. Finished goods stock a/c	240 000	Transferred to costing P&L a/c	240 000

Provision for depreciation account

		10. Factory overhead	30 000

Wages control account

5. Wages accrued a/c	105 000	7. Work in progress a/c	145 000
5. Tax payable a/c	60 000	7. Factory overhead a/c	40 000
5. National Insurance a/c	20000		
	185000		185000

Sales account

Transferred to costing P&L	400 000	14. Debtors	400000

Debtors account

14. Sales a/c	400 000		

Costing profit and loss account

Sales a/c		400000
Less cost of sales a/c		204000
Gross profit		160000
Less under recovery of factory overhead	6 000	
Non-manufacturing overhead	40000	46000
Net profit		114000

This accounting entry reflects the fact that raw material stock is being converted into work in progress (WIP) stock. In addition to these entries in the control accounts, the individual jobs will be charged with the cost of the material issued so that job costs can be calculated. Each issue is also entered in the issues column on the appropriate stores ledger record.

The entry for transaction 4 for the issue of indirect materials is:

Dr Factory overhead control account   10 000
    Cr Stores ledger control account   10 000

In addition to the entry in the factory overhead account, the cost of material issued is entered in the individual overhead accounts. These separate overhead accounts normally consist of individual indirect material accounts for each responsibility centre. Periodically, the totals of each responsibility centre account for indirect materials are entered in performance reports for comparison with the budgeted indirect material cost.

After transactions 1–4 have been recorded, the stores ledger control account would look like this:

Stores ledger control account

1. Creditors a/c	182 000	2. Creditors a/c	2 000
		3. Work in progress a/c	165 000
		4. Factory overhead a/c	10 000
		Balance c/d	5 000
	182 000		182 000
Balance b/d	5 000		

ACCOUNTING PROCEDURE FOR LABOUR COSTS

Accounting for labour costs can be divided into the following two distinct phases:

1 Computations of the gross pay for each employee and calculation of payments to be made to employees, government, pension funds, etc. (**payroll accounting**).

2 Allocation of labour costs to jobs, overhead accounts and capital accounts (**labour cost accounting**).

An employee's gross pay is computed from information on the employee's personal record, and attendance or production records. A separate record is kept for each employee, showing their employment history with the company, current rate of pay and authorized deductions such as National Insurance, pension plans, savings plans, union dues and so on. The gross wages are calculated from these documents, and an entry is then made in the payroll for each employee, showing the gross pay, tax deductions and other authorized deductions. The gross pay less the deductions gives the net pay, and this is the amount of cash paid to each employee.

The payroll gives details of the total amount of cash due to employees and the amounts due to the government (i.e. Inland Revenue), pension funds and savings funds, etc. To keep the illustration simple at this stage, transaction 5 includes only deductions in respect of taxes and National Insurance. The accounting entries for transaction 5 are:

```
Dr Wages control account                          185 000
    Cr Tax payable account                                    60 000
    Cr National Insurance contributions account               20 000
    Cr Wages accrued account                                 105 000
```

The credit entries in transaction 5 will be cleared by a payment of cash. The payment of wages will involve an immediate cash payment, but some slight delay may occur with the payment of tax and National Insurance since the final date for payment of these items is normally a few weeks after the payment of wages. The entries for the cash payments for these items (transaction 6) are:

```
Dr Tax payable account                          60 000
Dr National Insurance contributions account     20 000
Dr Wages accrued account                       105 000
    Cr Cash/bank                                            185 000
```

Note that the credit entries for transaction 5 merely represent the recording of amounts due for future payments. The wages control account, however, represents the gross wages for the period, and it is the amount in this account that must be allocated to the job, overhead and capital accounts. Transaction 7 gives details of the allocation of the gross wages. The accounting entries are:

```
Dr Work in progress control account         145 000
Dr Factory overhead control account          40 000
    Cr Wages control account                             185 000
```

In addition to the total entry in the work in progress control account, the labour cost will be charged to the individual job accounts. Similarly, the total entry in the factory overhead control account will be supported by an entry in each individual overhead account for the indirect labour cost incurred.

Transaction 8 represents the employer's contribution for National Insurance payments. (The National Insurance deductions in transaction 5 represent the employees' contributions where the company acts merely as an agent, paying these contributions on behalf of the employee). The employer is also responsible for making a contribution in respect of each employee. To keep the accounting entries simple here, the employer's contributions will be charged to the factory overhead account. The accounting entry for transaction 8 is therefore:

```
Dr Factory overhead control account             25 000
    Cr National Insurance contributions account            25 000
```

The National Insurance contributions account will be closed with the following entry when the cash payment is made:

```
Dr National Insurance contributions account     25 000
    Cr Cash/bank                                           25 000
```

After recording these transactions, the wages control account would look like this:

Wages control account

5. Wages accrued a/c	105 000	7. Work in progress a/c	145 000
5. Tax payable a/c	60 000	7. Factory overhead a/c	40 000
5. National Insurance a/c	20 000		
	185 000		185 000

ACCOUNTING PROCEDURE FOR MANUFACTURING OVERHEADS

Accounting for manufacturing overheads involves entering details of the actual amount of manufacturing overhead incurred on the debit side of the factory overhead control account. The total amount of overheads charged to production is recorded on the credit side of this account. In the previous chapter we established that manufacturing overheads are charged to production using budgeted overhead rates. It is most unlikely, however, that the actual amount of overhead incurred, which is recorded on the debit side of the account, will be in agreement with the amount of overhead allocated to jobs, which is recorded on the credit side of the account. The difference represents the under- or over-recovery of factory overheads, which is transferred to the profit and loss account, in accordance with the requirements of the UK Statement of Standard Accounting Practice (SSAP9) and the International Accounting Standard (IAS9) on inventory valuation.

Transaction 9 represents various indirect expenses that have been incurred, such as property taxes and lighting and heating, that will eventually have to be paid in cash. Transaction 10 includes other indirect expenses that do not involve a cash commitment. For simplicity we are assuming that depreciation of factory machinery is the only item that falls into this category. The accounting entries for transactions 9 and 10 are

Dr Factory overhead control account	71 000	
Cr Expense creditors control account		41 000
Cr Provision of depreciation account		30 000

In addition, subsidiary entries, not forming part of the double entry system, will be made in individual overhead accounts. These accounts will be headed by the title of the cost centre followed by the object of expenditure. For example, it may be possible to assign indirect materials directly to specific cost centres, and separate records can then be kept of the indirect materials charge for each centre. It will not, however, be possible to allocate property taxes, lighting and heating directly to cost centres, and entries should be made in individual overhead accounts for these items. These expenses should, however, be apportioned to cost centres (using the procedures described in Chapter 4) to compute product costs for meeting stock valuation requirements.

Transaction 11 refers to the total overheads that have been charged to jobs using the estimated overhead absorption rates. The accounting entry in the control accounts for allocating overheads to jobs is:

Dr Work in progress control account	140 000	
Cr Factory overhead control account		140 000

In addition to this entry, the individual jobs are charged so that job costs can be calculated. When these entries have been made the factory overhead control account would look like this:

Factory overhead control account

4.	Stores ledger control a/c	10 000	11.	Work in progress	
7.	Wages control a/c	40 000		control a/c	140 000
8.	Employer's National	25 000		Balance – Under-recovery of	6 000
	Insurance contributions a/c			overhead transferred to costing	
				profit and loss a/c	
9.	Expense creditors a/c	41 000			
10.	Provision for depreciation a/c	30 000			
		146 000			146 000

The debit side of this account indicates that £146 000 overhead has been incurred, but examination of the credit side indicates that only £140 000 has been allocated to jobs via overhead allocation rates. The balance of £6000 represents an under-recovery of factory overhead, which is regarded as a period cost to be charged to the costing profit and loss account in the current accounting period. The reasons for this were explained in the previous chapter.

NON-MANUFACTURING OVERHEADS

You will have noted in the previous chapter that non-manufacturing overhead costs are regarded as period costs and not product costs, and non-manufacturing overheads are not therefore charged to the work in progress control account. The accounting entry for transaction 12 is:

> Dr Non-manufacturing overheads account   40 000
>   Cr Expense creditors account   40 000

At the end of the period the non-manufacturing overheads will be transferred to the profit and loss account as a period cost by means of the following accounting entry:

> Dr Profit and loss account   40 000
>   Cr Non-manufacturing overheads account   40 000

In practice, separate control accounts are maintained for administrative, marketing and financial overheads, but, to simplify this example, all the non-manufacturing overheads are included in one control account. In addition, subsidiary records will be kept that analyze the total non-manufacturing overheads by individual accounts, for example office stationery account, sales person's travelling expenses account, etc.

ACCOUNTING PROCEDURES FOR JOBS COMPLETED AND PRODUCTS SOLD

When jobs have been completed, they are transferred from the factory floor to the finished goods store. The total of the job accounts for the completed jobs for the period is recorded as a transfer from the work in progress control account to the finished goods stock account. The accounting entry for transaction 13 is:

Dr Finished goods stock account	300 000	
Cr Work in progress control account		300 000

When the goods are removed from the finished goods stock and delivered to the customers, the revenue is recognized. It is a fundamental principle of financial accounting that only costs associated with earning the revenue are included as expenses. The cost of those goods that have been delivered to customers must therefore be matched against the revenue due from delivery of the goods so that the gross profit can be calculated. Any goods that have not been delivered to customers will be included as part of the finished stock valuation. The accounting entries to reflect these transactions are:

Transaction 14		
Dr Debtors control account	400 000	
Cr Sales account		400 000
Transaction 15		
Dr Cost of sales account	240 000	
Cr Finished goods stock account		240 000

COSTING PROFIT AND LOSS ACCOUNT

At frequent intervals management may wish to ascertain the profit to date for the particular period. The accounting procedure outlined in this chapter provides a database from which a costing profit and loss account may easily be prepared. The costing profit and loss account for AB Ltd based on the information given in Example 5.1 is set out in Exhibit 5.1 shown on page 113. Alternatively, management may prefer the profit statement to be presented in a format similar to that which is necessary for external reporting. Such information can easily be extracted from the subsidiary records.

INTERLOCKING ACCOUNTING

With an *interlocking cost accounting system* the cost and financial accounts are maintained independently of each other, and no attempt is made in the cost accounts to keep a separate record of the financial accounting transactions, such as entries in the various creditors, debtors and capital accounts. To maintain the double entry records, an account must be maintained in the cost accounts to record the corresponding entry that, in an integrated accounting system, would normally be made in one of the financial accounts (creditors, debtors accounts, etc.). This account is called a cost control or general ledger adjustment account.

Using an interlocking accounting system to record the transactions listed in Example 5.1, the entries in the creditors, wages accrued, taxation payable, National Insurance contributions, expense creditors, provision for depreciation and debtors accounts would be replaced by the entries shown below in the cost control account. Note that the entries in the remaining accounts will be unchanged.

Cost control account

2. Stores ledger control a/c	2 000	1. Stores ledger control a/c	182 000
14. Sales a/c	400 000	5. Wages control a/c	185 000
Balance c/d	215 000	8. Factory overhead control a/c	25 000
		9. Expense creditors a/c	41 000
		12. Non-manufacturing overhead a/c	40 000
		10. Factory overhead a/c	30 000
		Profit and loss a/c (profit for period)	114 000
	617 000		617 000
		Balance b/d	215 000

For a detailed answer to an interlocking accounts question you should refer to the solution to Review problem 5.17. Sometimes examination questions are set that require you to reconcile the profit that has been calculated in the cost accounts with the profits calculated in the financial accounts. In practice, most firms use an integrated accounting system, and hence there is no need to reconcile a separate set of cost and financial accounts. The reconciliation of cost and financial accounts is not therefore dealt with in this book. For an explanation of the reconciliation procedure you should refer to the solution to Review problem 5.19.

CONTRACT COSTING

Contract costing is a system of job costing that is applied to relatively large cost units, which normally take a considerable length of time to complete. Building and construction, civil engineering and shipbuilding are examples of industries where large contract work is undertaken, and where contract costing is appropriate.

A contract account is maintained for each contract. All the direct costs of the contract are debited to the specific contract and overheads are apportioned in the manner prescribed in Chapter 4. The contract price is credited to the contract account, and each contract account therefore becomes a small profit and loss account.

Because of the length of time taken to complete a large contract, it is necessary to determine the profit to be attributed to each accounting period. Financial accounting normally recognizes revenue when the goods are delivered, but such an approach is inappropriate for long-term contracts, since profits on large contracts would not be reported until they were completed. The profit and loss account would not reflect a fair view of the profitability of the company during the year but would show only the results of contracts that had been completed before the year end. To overcome this problem, it is preferable to take credit for profit while contracts are in progress.

The UK Statement of Standard Accounting Practice on Stocks and Work in Progress (SSAP9) provides the following guidance on the attributable profit to be taken up for a particular period:

Where the business carries out long-term contracts and it is considered that their outcome can be assessed with reasonable certainty before their conclusion, the attributable profit should be calculated on a prudent basis and included in the accounts for the period under review. The profit taken up needs to reflect the proportion of the work carried out at the accounting date and to take into account any known inequalities of profitability in the various stages of a contract. The procedure to recognize profit is to include an appropriate proportion of total contract value as turnover in the profit and loss account as the contract activity progresses. The costs incurred in reaching that stage of completion are matched with this turnover, resulting in the reporting of results that can be attributed to the proportion of work completed.

Where the outcome of long-term contracts cannot be assessed with reasonable certainty before the conclusion of the contract, no profit should be reflected in the profit and loss account in respect of those contracts although, in such circumstances, if no loss is expected it may be appropriate to show as turnover a proportion of the total contract value using a zero estimate of profit.

If it is expected that there will be a loss on a contract as a whole, all of the loss should be recognized as soon as it is foreseen (in accordance with the prudence concept).

EXAMPLE 5.2

A construction company is currently undertaking three separate contracts and information relating to these contracts for the previous year, together with relevant data, are shown below:

	Contract A (£000)	Contract B (£000)	Contract C (£000)
Contract price	1760	1485	2420
Balances b/fwd at beginning of year:			
Material on site	—	20	30
Written-down value of plant and machinery	—	77	374
Wages accrued	—	5	10
Transactions during previous year:			
Profit previously transferred to profit and loss a/c	—	—	35
Cost of work certified (cost of sales)	—	418	814
Transactions during current year:			
Materials delivered to sites	88	220	396
Wages paid	45	100	220
Salaries and other costs	15	40	50
Written-down value of plant issued to sites	190	35	—
Head office expenses apportioned during the year	10	20	50
Balances c/fwd at the end of year:			
Material on site	20	—	—
Written-down value of plant and machinery	150	20	230
Wages accrued	5	10	15
Value of work certified at end of year	200	860	2100
Cost of work not certified at end of year	—	—	55

The agreed retention rate is 10 per cent of the value of work certified by the contractee's architects. Contract C is scheduled for handing over to the contractee in the near future, and the site engineer estimates that the extra costs required to complete the contract, in addition to those tabulated above, will total £305 000. This amount includes an allowance for plant depreciation, construction services and for contingencies.

You are required to prepare a cost account for each of the three contracts and recommend how much profit or loss should be taken up for the year.

Let us now prepare some contract accounts and determine the attributable profit to be taken up for an accounting period. Consider Example 5.2.

Before we compile the accounts, some of the terms used in Example 5.2 require an explanation. A customer is likely to be required under the terms of the contract to make **progress payments** to the contractor throughout the course of the work. The amount of the payments will be based on the sales value of the work carried out, as assessed by the architect or surveyor in the **architect's certificate**. The amount of the progress payment will consist of:

1 the sales value of work carried out and certified by the architect; less

2 a retention; less

3 the payments made to date.

So if the architect's certificates assess the value of work carried out to be £300 000 and if the retention is 10 per cent, and if £230 000 has already been paid in progress payments, the current payment will be:

£300 000 – £30 000 retention – £230 000 previous payment = £40 000

There is frequently a contract clause which entitles the customer to withhold payment of **retention money** for a proportion of the value of work certified for a specified period after the end of the contract. During this period, the contractor must make good all contractual defects and the customer will then release the retention money.

Let us now prepare the cost accounts from the information contained in Example 5.2 for contracts A, B and C:

Contract accounts

	A (£000)	B (£000)	C (£000)		A (£000)	B (£000)	C (£000)
				Wages accrued b/fwd		5	10
Materials on site b/fwd		20	30	Materials on site c/fwd	20		
Plant on site b/fwd		77	374	Plant on site c/fwd	150	20	230
Materials control a/c	88	220	396				
Wages control a/c	45	100	220	Cost of work not certified c/fwd			55
Salaries	15	40	50				
Plant control a/c	190	35					
Apportionment of head office expenses	10	20	50	Cost of sales – current period (balance) c/fwd	183	497	840
Wages accrued c/fwd	5	10	15				
	353	522	1135		353	522	1135
Cost of sales b/fwd	183	497	840	Attributable sales revenue (current period)[a]	183	442	1122
Profit taken this period			282	Loss taken		55	
	183	497	1122		183	497	1122
				Wages accrued b/fwd	5	10	15
Cost of work not certified b/fwd			55				
Materials on site b/fwd	20						
Plant on site b/fwd	150	20	230				

[a] Profit taken plus cost of sales for the current period or cost of sales less loss to date.

You will see that the contract accounts are divided into three sections. The objective of the first section is to determine the costs that should be included in the cost of sales for the purposes of calculating the profit taken up for the period. The balance shown in the first section of the contract accounts represents the *cost of sales* (also known as *cost of work certified*) attributable to each of the contracts.

You should note that unexpired costs such as the cost of work not certified and the written-down balance of the plant at the end of the period are carried forward to the third section of the contract accounts. This section represents the unexpired costs of the current period which will become an expired cost in future periods. The third section of the account should therefore be regarded as a future cost section.

In the second section of the contract accounts the period cost of sales is compared with the sales revenue that is estimated to be attributable to the contracts. The sales revenues attributable to the contracts for each period are estimated by adding the attributable profit taken up for the current period to the cost of sales for the current period (or cost of sales less the loss where a contract is currently running at a loss). The profits/losses on the three contracts to date are calculated by deducting the cost of sales (consisting of the sum of the cost of sales for the current and previous periods) from the value of work certified:

	(£000)	
Contract A	17	(£200–£183)
Contract B	(55)	(£860–£915)
Contract C	446	(£2100–£1654)

However, these profits/(losses) do not necessarily represent the profits/(losses) taken up on the contracts. According to SSAP9, the concept of prudence should be applied when determining the profits/(losses) taken up on contracts. You are recommended to adopt the following guidelines:

1 If the contract is in its early stages, no profit should be taken. Profit should only be taken when the outcome of the contract can be assessed with reasonable certainty. You will see from Example 5.2 that the contract price for Contract A is £1 760 000, but the value of work certified is only £200 000. The contract is therefore approximately one-eighth complete, and it is unlikely that the outcome of the contract can be foreseen with reasonable certainty. Despite the fact that the profit to date is £17 000, it is recommended that no profit be taken.

2 If a loss is incurred, the prudence concept should be applied, and the total loss should be recognized in the period in which it is incurred. Consequently, the loss of £55 000 on Contract B is recognized in the current accounting period. Where further additional future losses are anticipated, all of the loss should be recognized as soon as it is foreseen and added to the cost of sales. In addition, the foreseeable loss should be shown in the balance sheet under the heading 'Provision/accrual for foreseeable losses'.

3 If the contract is nearing completion, the size of the eventual profit can be foreseen with reasonable certainty, and there is less need to be excessively prudent in determining the amount of profit to be recorded in the profit and loss account. With regard to Contract C, the value of work certified is approximately 87 per cent of the contract price, and the anticipated profit is calculated as follows:

	(£000)
Cost of work certified (cost of sales to date = 814 + 840)	1654
Cost of work not certified	55
Estimated costs to complete	305
Estimated cost of contract	2014
Contract price	2420
Anticipated profit	406

The profit taken is calculated using the following formula:

$$\text{cash received to date} \frac{(0.90 \times £2100)}{\text{contract price } (£2420)}$$

$$\times \text{ estimated profit from the contract } (£406) = £317\,000$$

You should note that other more prudent approaches are sometimes used to determine the profit earned to date. The profit for the current period consists of the profit to date (£317 000) less the profit of £35 000 previously transferred to the profit and loss account. The profit taken to the profit and loss account for the current period is therefore £282 000.

4 Where substantial costs have been incurred on a contract, and it is not nearing completion (say it is in the region of 35–85 per cent complete), the following formula is often used to determine the attributable profit to date:

$$\text{profit taken} = 2/3 \times \text{notional profit} \times \frac{\text{cash received}}{\text{value of work certified}}$$

This formula is one of several approaches that can be used to apply the prudence concept. Estimates of anticipated profit are likely to be inaccurate when contracts are not near to completion. To overcome this problem, **notional profit** should be used instead of anticipated profit. Notional profit is the value of work certified to date less the cost of work certified (that is, cost of sales) to date less a provision for any anticipated unforeseen eventualities.

Note than for Contract C £35 000 profit was recognized in the previous period and cost of sales of £814 000 was recorded. Therefore, attributable sales revenue of £849 000 (£814 000 + £35 000) would have been recorded in the contract account for *the previous* period. For Contract B, no profits were recognized in the *previous period* and attributable sales for the period will thus be identical to the cost of sales (£418 000). Contract A commenced in the current period and so no transactions will have been recorded in the previous period. The debit side of the debtors accounts will be as follows:

	Contract A **(£000)**	**Contract B** **(£000)**	**Contract C** **(£000)**
Previous period – attributable sales	—	418	849
Current period – attributable sales	183	442	1122
Total to date	183	860	1971

WORK IN PROGRESS VALUATION AND AMOUNTS RECOVERABLE ON CONTRACTS

The UK Statement of Standard Accounting Practice on Stocks on Work in Progress (SSAP9) requires that the proportion of the total contract value appropriate to the stage of completion reached at balance sheet date be recognized as sales revenue. The costs relating to that completed work are included in the cost of sales. Any further costs that are attributable to the contract but which have not been included in the cost of sales are included at cost in the balance sheet and separately disclosed as 'Long-term contract balances' under the balance sheet heading 'Stocks'.

The associated balance sheet item for the contract value that is recorded as sales is debtors. The debtors balance is calculated by deducting progress payments received on account from the amount recognized as sales. This balance is included as a separate item within debtors and described as 'Amounts recoverable on contracts'. The balance sheet entries for Example 5.2 are as follows:

	Contract A (£000)	Contract B (£000)	Contract C (£000)	
Stocks:				
Total costs incurred to date	183	860	1709	(814 + 840 + 55)
Included in cost of sales	183	860	1654	
Included in long-term contract balances	0	0	55	
Debtors				
Cumulative sales turnover	183	860	1971	
Less cumulative progress payments	180	774	1890	
Amounts recoverable on contracts	3	86	81	

For Contract B, the total costs incurred to date are £915 000 (£418 000 + £497 000) but £55 000 of these costs have been recognized as a loss in the current period, so that the cumulative cost of sales to be matched against cumulative sales is £860 000 (£915 000 – £55 000). Note also that the cumulative progress payments are 90 per cent of the value of work certified and that the loss on Contract B has been charged to the current period. Other balance sheet entries will include the following:

	(£000)
Materials on site	20
Plant on site	400
Accruals	30

SUMMARY

The following items relate to the learning objectives listed at the beginning of the chapter.

- **Record the accounting entries for an integrated and interlocking accounting system.** A summary of the accounting entries for an integrated accounting system, where all purchases and expenses are settled in cash, is shown diagrammatically in Figure 5.1.

Flow of accounting entries in an integrated accounting system

- **Distinguish between an integrated and an interlocking cost accounting system.** With an integrated costing accounting system, the cost and financial accounts are combined in one set of accounts whereas the cost and financial accounts are maintained independently with an interlocking accounting system. An integrated accounting system is recommended since it avoids the duplication of accounting entries.

- **Explain the distinguishing features of contract costing.** Contract costing is a system of job costing that is applied to relatively large cost units, which normally take a considerable time to complete (normally in excess of one year). It is applied in the building and construction, civil engineering and shipbuilding industries. Where contract costing is not applied, sales revenues are normally recognized for determining profits when the goods are received or the service has been completed. With a contract costing system sales revenues are attributed to the contract based on the proportion of work carried out to date.

- **Prepare contract accounts and calculate the profit attributable to each contract.** A contract account is maintained for each contract. Each contract account represents a separate profit and loss account. Typically, contract accounts consist of three sections. The objective of the first section is to determine the costs that should be included in the cost of sales attributable to the contract. In the second section the period cost of sales is compared with the sales revenue that is estimated to be attributable to the contracts so that the profit can be derived. The third section represents the unexpired costs of the current period that will become expenses in future periods. The preparation of contract accounts and the calculation of attributable profit were illustrated using the data presented in Example 5.2.

KEY TERMS AND CONCEPTS

Architect's certificate an assessment of the sales value of work carried out so far in a construction contract and can trigger progress payments.

Contract costing a system of job costing that is applied to large cost units that take a considerable length of time to complete.

Control account a summary account in which entries are made from totals of transactions for a period.

Integrated cost accounting system a system that combines cost and financial accounts in one set of accounts.

Interlocking cost accounting system a system that maintains cost and financial accounts separately.

Job costing system a system used when each unit or batch of output is unique and must be costed separately.

Labour cost accounting accounting involving the allocation of labour costs to jobs, overhead accounts and capital accounts.

Notional profit the value of work certified to date, less the cost of work certified, less a provision for unforeseen eventualities.

Payroll accounting accounting involving the computation of gross pay and the payments to be made to employees, government, pension funds, etc.

Process costing system a system used where masses of identical units of output are produced and it is unnecessary to assign costs to individual units.

Progress payments fees paid by the customer to the contractor throughout the course of the work.

Retention money a payment that is withheld for a specified time after the end of a contract, until any contractual defects have been made good.

KEY EXAMINATION POINTS

Examination questions set by the professional accountancy examination bodies require the preparation of accounts for both interlocking and integrated accounting systems (see answers to Review problems 5.17 and 5.18 for examples). You may also be required to reconcile the cost and financial accounts. For an illustration of a reconciliation see the answer to Review problem 5.19). However, the reconciliation of cost and financial accounts is a topic that tends to be examined only on rare occasions.

Students often experience difficulty in recommending the amount of profit to be taken during a period for long-term contracts. Make sure you are familiar with the four recommendations listed on pages 122–23 and that you can apply these recommendations to Review problems 5.20 and SM5.3 and 5.4 in the Student's Manual that can be accessed on the accompanying website.

ASSESSMENT MATERIAL

The review questions are short questions that enable you to assess your understanding of the main topics included in the chapter. The numbers in parentheses provide you with the page numbers to refer to if you cannot answer a specific question.

The review problems are more complex and require you to relate and apply the chapter content to various business problems. The problems are graded by their level of difficulty. The multiple-choice questions are the least demanding and normally take less than 10 minutes to complete. Fully worked solutions to the review problems are provided in a separate section at the end of the book. Further review problems with solutions for this chapter are available on the accompanying website www.drury-online.com. The website includes a *Student's Manual* and an *Instructor's Manual.* Students can access both questions and answers from the *Student's Manual* and the questions from the *Instructor's Manual* The answers to problems in the *Instructor's Manual* are available only to lecturers on the lecturer's password-protected section of the website.

REVIEW QUESTIONS

5.1 Distinguish between an integrated and interlocking accounting system. *(p. 110)*

5.2 Explain the purpose of control accounts. *(p. 110)*

5.3 List the accounting entries for the purchase of issues of direct and indirect materials. *(pp. 110–14)*

5.4 List the accounting entries for the payment and the allocation of gross wages. *(pp. 114–15)*

5.5 List the accounting entries for the payment and the allocation of overheads. *(pp. 116–17)*

5.6 Explain the major features of contract costing. *(pp. 119–20)*

5.7 Define progress payments, architect's certificates, retention money, cost of work certified and notional profit. *(pp. 121–23)*

5.8 Describe the four guidelines that should be used to determine the amount of profit that should be taken for a contract during a specific period. *(pp. 122–23)*

REVIEW PROBLEMS

5.9 A company operates an integrated cost and financial accounting system. The accounting entries for the return of unused direct materials from production would be:

   (a) DR Work-in-progress account;   CR Stores control account.

   (b) DR Stores control account;   CR Work-in-progress account.

   (c) DR Stores control account;   CR Finished goods account.

   (d) DR Cost of sales account;   CR Work-in-progress account.

CIMA Stage 1

5.10 At the end of a period, in an integrated cost and financial accounting system, the accounting entries for overhead over-absorbed would be:

(a) DR Profit and loss account   CR Work-in-progress control account

(b) DR Profit and loss account   CR Overhead control account

(c) DR Work-in-progress control   CR Overhead control account

(d) DR Overhead control account   CR Profit and loss account

CIMA Stage 1

5.11 In an interlocking accounting system, the profit shown in the financial accounts was £79 252 but the cost accounts showed £74 294 profit. The following stock valuations were the only differences between the two sets of accounts:

Stock valuations	Cost accounts	Financial accounts
Opening stock	£10 116	£9 217
Closing stock	£24 053	X

What was the value of X?

(a) £18 196

(b) £23 154

(c) £24 952

(d) £28 112

CIMA Stage 1

5.12 The following data have been taken from the books of CB plc, which uses a non-integrated accounting system:

	Financial accounts £	Cost accounts £
Opening stock of materials	5000	6400
Closing stock of materials	4000	5200
Opening stock of finished goods	9800	9600
Closing stock of finished goods	7900	7600

The effect of these stock valuation differences on the profit reported by the financial and cost accounting ledgers is that:

(a) the financial accounting profit is £300 greater than the cost accounting profit

(b) the financial accounting profit is £2100 greater than the cost accounting profit

(c) the cost accounting profit is £300 greater than the financial accounting profit

(d) the cost accounting profit is £900 greater than the financial accounting profit

(e) the cost accounting profit is £2100 greater than the financial accounting profit

CIMA Stage 2

5.13 The profit shown in the financial accounts was £158 500 but the cost accounts showed a different figure. The following stock valuations were used:

Stock valuations	Cost accounts	Financial accounts
	(£)	(£)
Opening stock	35 260	41 735
Closing stock	68 490	57 336

What was the profit in the cost accounts?

(a) £163 179

(b) £140 871

(c) £176 129

(d) £153 821

CIMA Stage 1

5.14 A construction company has the following data concerning one of its contracts:

Contract price	£2 000 000
Value certified	£1 300 000
Cash received	£1 200 000
Costs incurred	£1 050 000
Cost of work certified	£1 000 000

The profit (to the nearest £1000) to be attributed to the contract is:

(a) £250 000

(b) £277 000

(c) £300 000

(d) £950 000

(e) £1 000 000

CIMA Stage 2

5.15 The following statements relate to long-term contracts:

(i) Levels of completion of the contract can be estimated using either costs to date or work certified to date.

(ii) Any anticipated losses should be taken as soon as they are expected.

(iii) If the contract is half complete it is expected that half the expected profit will always be taken.

Which of the above are correct?

(a) (i) and (ii) only

(b) (i) and (iii) only

(c) (ii) and (iii) only

(d) (i), (ii) and (iii)

5.16 The following could relate to contract costing:

(i)   Work is for a period of long duration.

(ii) Progress payments are amounts paid for the contract throughout the course of the contract.

(iii) Architects' certificates are provided to establish the amount of work certified.

Which of the above are correct?

(a)   (i) and (ii) only

(b)   (i) and (iii) only

(c)   (ii) and (iii) only

(d)   (i), (ii) and (iii)

5.17   Interlocking accounts

CD Ltd, a company engaged in the manufacture of specialist marine engines, operates a historic job cost accounting system that is not integrated with the financial accounts. At the beginning of May the opening balances in the cost ledger were as follows:

	(£)
Stores ledger control account	85 400
Work in progress control account	167 350
Finished goods control account	49 250
Cost ledger control account	302 000

During the month, the following transactions took place:

	(£)
Materials:	
Purchases	42 700
Issues to production	63 400
to general maintenance	1450
to construction of manufacturing equipment	7650
Factory wages:	
Total gross wages paid	124 000

£12 500 of the above gross wages was incurred on the construction of manufacturing equipment, £35 750 was indirect wages and the balance was direct.

Production overheads: the actual amount incurred, excluding items shown above, was £152 350; £30 000 was absorbed by the manufacturing equipment under construction and under-absorbed overhead written off at the end of the month amounted to £7550.

Royalty payments: one of the engines produced is manufactured under licence. £2150 is the amount that will be paid to the inventor for the month's production of that particular engine.

Selling overheads: £22 000.

Sales: £410 000.

The company's gross profit margin is 25 per cent on factory cost.

At the end of May stocks of work in progress had increased by £12 000. The manufacturing equipment under construction was completed within the month, and transferred out of the cost ledger at the end of the month.

Required:

Prepare the relevant control accounts, costing profit and loss account, and any other accounts you consider necessary to record the above transactions in the cost ledger for May.

(22 marks)
ACCA Foundation Costing

5.18 **Integrated accounts**
In the absence of the accountant you have been asked to prepare a month's cost accounts for a company which operates a batch costing system fully integrated with the financial accounts. The cost clerk has provided you with the following information, which he thinks is relevant:

	(£)
Balances at beginning of month:	
Stores ledger control account	24 175
Work in progress control account	19 210
Finished goods control account	34 164
Prepayments of production overheads	
brought forward from previous month	2100

	(£)
Transactions during the month:	
Materials purchased	76 150
Materials issued: to production	26 350
for factory maintenance	3280
Materials transferred between batches	1450

	Direct workers (£)	Indirect workers (£)
Total wages paid:		
Net	17 646	3342
Employees deductions	4364	890
Direct wages charged to batches from work tickets	15 236	
Recorded non-productive time of direct workers	5230	
Direct wages incurred on production of capital		
equipment, for use in the factory	2670	
Selling and distribution overheads incurred	5240	
Other production overheads incurred	12 200	
Sales	75 400	
Cost of finished goods sold	59 830	
Cost of goods completed and transferred into finished		
goods store during the month	62 130	
Physical stock value of work in progress at end of month	24 360	

The production overhead absorption rate is 150 per cent of direct wages, and it is the policy of the company to include a share of production overheads in the cost of capital equipment constructed in the factory.

Required:

(a) Prepare the following accounts for the month:
        stores ledger control account;
        wages control account;
        work in progress control account;
        finished goods control account;
        production overhead control account;
        profit/loss account.

(12 marks)

(b) Identify any aspects of the accounts which you consider should be investigated.
(4 marks)

(c) Explain why it is necessary to value a company's stocks at the end of each period and also why, in a manufacturing company, expense items such as factory rent, wages of direct operatives, power costs, etc. are included in the value of work in progress and finished goods stocks.

(6 marks)
(Total 22 marks)
ACCA Level 1 Costing

5.19 Reconciliation of cost and financial accounts

K Limited operates separate cost accounting and financial accounting systems. The following manufacturing and trading statement has been prepared from the financial accounts for the *quarter* ended 31 March:

	(£)	(£)
Raw materials:		
Opening stock	48 800	
Purchases	108 000	
	156 800	
Closing stock	52 000	
Raw materials consumed		104 800
Direct wages		40 200
Production overhead		60 900
Production cost incurred		205 900
Work in progress:		
Opening stock	64 000	
Closing stock	58 000	6000
Cost of goods produced		211 900
Sales		440 000
Finishing goods:		
Opening stock	120 000	
Cost of goods produced	211 900	
	331 900	
Closing stock	121 900	
Cost of goods sold		210 000
Gross profit		230 000

From the cost accounts, the following information has been extracted:

Control account balances at 1 January	(£)
Raw material stores	49 500
Work in progress	60 100
Finished goods	115 400

Transactions for the quarter:	(£)
Raw materials issued	104 800
Cost of goods produced	222 500
Cost of goods sold	212 100
Loss of materials damaged by flood (insurance claim pending)	2400

A notional rent of £4000 *per month* has been charged in the cost accounts. Production overhead was absorbed at the rate of 185 per cent of direct wages.

You are required to:

(a) prepare the following control accounts in the cost ledger:
raw materials stores;
work in process;
finished goods;
production overhead;

(10 marks)

(b) prepare a statement reconciling the gross profits as per the cost accounts and the financial accounts;

(11 marks)

(c) comment on the possible accounting treatment(s) of the under- or over-absorption of production overhead, assuming that the financial year of the company is 1 January to 31 December.

(4 marks)
(Total 25 marks)
CIMA Cost Accounting

5.20 **Contract costing**

HR Construction plc makes up its accounts to 31 March each year. The following details have been extracted in relation to two of its contracts:

	Contract A	Contract B
Commencement date	**1 April 2009**	**1 December 2009**
Target completion date	**31 May 2010**	**30 June 2010**
Retention %	**4**	**3**
	£000	**£000**
Contract price	2000	550
Materials sent to site	700	150
Materials returned to stores	80	30
Plant sent to site	1000	150
Materials transferred	(40)	40
Materials on site 31 March 2010	75	15
Plant hire charges	200	30
Labour cost incurred	300	270
Central overhead cost	75	18
Direct expenses incurred	25	4
Value certified	1500	500
Cost of work not certified	160	20
Cash received from client	1440	460
Estimated cost of completion	135	110

Depreciation is charged on plant using the straight line method at the rate of 12 per cent per annum.

Required:

(a) Prepare contract accounts, in columnar format, for EACH of the contracts A and B, showing clearly the amounts to be transferred to profit and loss in respect of each contract.

(20 marks)

(b) Show balance sheet extracts in respect of EACH contract for fixed assets, debtors and work in progress.

(4 marks)

(c) Distinguish between job, batch and contract costing. Explain clearly the reasons why these methods are different.

(6 marks)
(Total 30 marks)
CIMA Stage 2

CHAPTER 6
PROCESS COSTING

LEARNING OBJECTIVES

After studying this chapter you should be able to:

- **explain when process costing systems are appropriate;**
- **explain the accounting treatment of normal and abnormal losses;**
- **prepare process, normal loss, abnormal loss and abnormal gain accounts when there is no ending work in progress;**
- **explain and calculate equivalent units;**
- **compute the value of closing work in progress and completed production using the weighted average and first in, first out methods of valuing work in progress.**

A process costing system is used in industries where masses of similar products or services are produced. Products are produced in the same manner and consume the same amount of direct costs and overheads. It is therefore unnecessary to assign costs to individual units of output. Instead, the average cost per unit of output is calculated by dividing the total costs assigned to a product or service for a period by the number of units of output for that period. Industries where process costing is widely used include chemical processing, oil refining, food processing and brewing.

In this chapter we will examine the cost accumulation procedure that is required for inventory valuation and profit measurement for a process costing system. We begin with a description of the flow of production and costs in a process costing environment. We shall then look in detail at the cost accumulation system. Three different scenarios will be presented. First, all output is fully complete. Second, ending work in progress exists, but no beginning work in progress, and some of the units started during the period are incomplete at the end of the period. Our third scenario is the existence of both beginning and ending work in progress of uncompleted units. One of the most complex areas in process costing is accounting for losses when units within the process are both fully and partially complete. Because some courses omit this topic it will be discussed in Appendix 6.1.

FLOW OF PRODUCTION AND COSTS IN A PROCESS COSTING SYSTEM

The flow of production and costs in a process costing system is illustrated in Exhibit 6.1. The major differences between process and job costing are also highlighted. You will see that production moves from one process (or department) to the next until final completion occurs. Each production process performs some part of the total operation and transfers its completed production to the next process, where it becomes the input for further processing. The completed production of the last process is transferred to the finished goods inventory.

The cost accumulation procedure follows this production flow. Control accounts are established for each process (or department) and direct and indirect costs are assigned to each process. A process costing system is easier to operate than a job costing system because the detailed work of allocating costs to many individual cost units is unnecessary. Also, many of the costs that are indirect in a job costing system may be regarded as direct in a process costing system. For example, supervision and depreciation that is confined to one process would be treated as part of the direct costs of that process, since these costs are directly attributable to the cost object (i.e. the department or process). By contrast, such costs are normally regarded as indirect in a job costing system because they are not directly attributable to a specific job.

As production moves from process to process costs are transferred with it. For example, in Exhibit 6.1 the costs of process A would be transferred to process B; process B costs would then be added to this cost and the resulting total cost transferred to process C; process C costs would then added to this cost. Therefore the cost becomes cumulative as production proceeds. The cost per unit of the completed product thus consists of the total cost accumulated in process C for the period divided by the output for that period.

PROCESS COSTING WHEN ALL OUTPUT IS FULLY COMPLETE

Throughout this section it is assumed that all output within each process is fully complete. We shall examine the following six cases:

1 no losses within a process;
2 normal losses with no scrap value;
3 abnormal losses with no scrap value;
4 normal losses with a scrap value;
5 abnormal losses with a scrap value;
6 abnormal gains with a scrap value.

You should now look at Example 6.1. The information it contains will be used to illustrate the accounting entries. To simplify the presentation it is assumed that the product is produced within a single process.

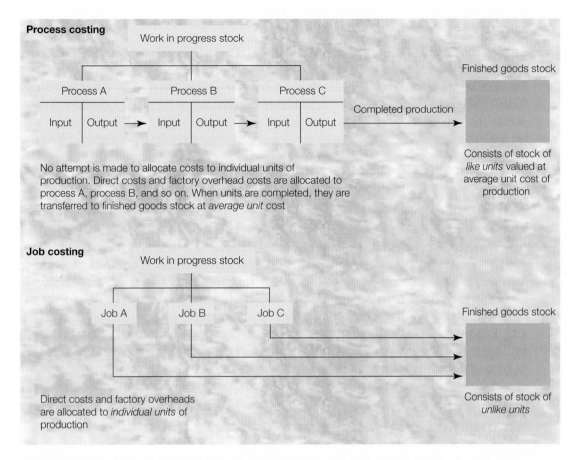

EXHIBIT 6.1

A comparison of job and process costing

EXAMPLE 6.1

Dartmouth Company produces a liquid fertilizer within a single production process. During the month of May the input into the process was 12 000 litres at a cost of £120 000. There were no opening or closing inventories and all output was fully complete. We shall prepare the process account and calculate the cost per litre of output for the single process for each of the six cases listed below:

Case	Input (litres)	Output (litres)	Normal loss (litres)	Abnormal loss (litres)	Abnormal gain (litres)	Scrap value of spoilt output (£ per litre)
1	12 000	12 000	0	0	0	0
2	12 000	10 000	2000 (1/6)	0	0	0
3	12 000	9 000	2000 (1/6)	1 000	0	0
4	12 000	10 000	2000 (1/6)	0	0	5
5	12 000	9 000	2000 (1/6)	1 000	0	5
6	12 000	11 000	2000 (1/6)	0	1 000	5

No losses within the process

To calculate the cost per unit (i.e. litre) of output for case 1 in Example 6.1 we merely divide the total cost incurred for the period of £120 000 by the output for the period (12 000 litres). The cost per unit of output is £10. In practice the cost per unit is analyzed by the different cost categories such as direct materials and **conversion cost** which consists of the sum of direct labour and overhead costs.

Normal losses in process with no scrap value

Certain losses are inherent to the production process. For example, liquids may evaporate, part of the cloth required to make a suit may be lost and losses occur in cutting wood to make furniture. These losses occur under efficient operating conditions and are unavoidable. They are referred to as **normal or uncontrollable losses** and are absorbed by the good production. Where normal losses apply the cost per unit of output is calculated by dividing the costs incurred for a period by the *expected* output from the actual input for that period. In case 2 in Example 6.1 the normal loss is one sixth of the input. Therefore, for an input of 12 000 litres the expected output is 10 000 litres so that the cost per unit of output is £12 (£120 000/10 000 litres). When actual output is equal to expected output there is neither an abnormal loss nor gain. Compared with case 1 the unit cost has increased by £2 per unit because the cost of the normal loss has been absorbed by the good production. Our objective is to calculate the cost of normal production under normal efficient operating conditions.

Abnormal losses in process with no scrap value

There may be some losses that are not expected to occur under efficient operating conditions, caused for example by the improper mixing of ingredients, the use of inferior materials and the incorrect cutting of cloth. These losses are not an inherent part of the production process, and are referred to as **abnormal or controllable losses**. Because they are not an inherent part of the production process and arise from inefficiencies they are not included in the process costs. Instead, they are removed from the appropriate process account and reported separately as an abnormal loss. The abnormal loss is treated as a period cost and written off in the profit statement at the end of the accounting period. This ensures that abnormal losses are not incorporated in any inventory valuations.

For case 3 in Example 6.1 the expected output is 10 000 litres but the actual output was 9000 litres, resulting in an abnormal loss of 1000 litres. Our objective is the same as that for normal losses. We need to calculate the cost per litre of the *expected* output (i.e. normal production), which is:

$$\frac{\text{input cost}(£120\ 000)}{\text{expected output }(10\ 000\text{ litres})} = £12$$

Note that the unit cost is the same for an output of 10 000 or 9000 litres since our objective is to calculate the cost per unit of normal output. The distribution of the input costs is as follows:

	(£)
Completed production transferred to the next process (or finished goods inventory) 9000 litres at £12	108 000
Abnormal loss: 1000 litres at £12	12 000
	120 000

The abnormal loss is valued at the cost per unit of normal production. Abnormal losses can only be controlled in the future by establishing the cause of the abnormal loss and taking appropriate remedial action. The entries in the process account will look like this:

Process account

	Litres	Unit cost (£)	(£)		Litres	Unit cost (£)	(£)
Input cost	12 000	10	120 000	Normal loss	2 000	—	—
				Output to finished goods inventory	9 000	12	108 000
				Abnormal loss	1 000	12	12 000
			120 000				120 000

REAL WORLD VIEWS 6.1

Producing a world-famous whiskey

Bushmills Irish Whiskey, a world renowned brand of Diageo plc, is distilled in County Antrim in Northern Ireland. The Old Bushmills distillery has been in operation since 1608 and currently markets five distinct whiskeys under the Bushmills brand.

Whiskey production is essentially a five part process. The basic raw materials are barley and natural water. The first process, malting, allows barley corns to germinate for four days. An enzyme called diastase is formed inside each grain, which converts the starch in the grain to sugar. The corns are then dried in an oven.

The second process, mashing, takes the dried barley and grinds it into a flour called 'grist'. Hot water is added to the grist to produce a sugary liquid called 'wort'. The wort is now ready to be transformed into alcohol by fermentation.

The third process, fermentation, is a simple natural process which occurs when yeast and sugar are mixed. The wort is pumped into a large vessel, where yeast is added. Fermentation is allowed to proceed for two days. The resultant liquid, called the 'wash' is now ready for transfer to the still house for distillation, the fourth process.

Distillation involves heating the wash gradually in a large copper kettle called the pot still. As alcohol has a lower boiling point than water, the alcohol vapours condense first, run off and cool down to a liquid. Two further distillations are performed to ensure purity. The resulting liquid, called spirit, is a clear liquid with a high alcohol content.

The final step, maturation, sees the spirit placed in seasoned oak casks for a number of years ranging from three to 21 years. The casks tend to be former American bourbon or Spanish sherry casks. The spirit acquires its colour and flavour from the casks. Once matured for the required period, the whiskies are bottled in the bottling plant at Bushmills, typically in 750ml bottles.

Discussion points

1 Why is job costing not appropriate to a process such as whiskey production?

2 Do you think losses of spirit might occur during the maturation process?

Process accounts represent work in progress (WIP) accounts. Input costs are debited to the process account and the output from the process is entered on the credit side. You will see from the process account that no entry is made in the account for the normal loss (except for an entry made in the units column). The transfer to the finished goods inventory (or the next process) is at the cost of normal production. The abnormal loss is removed from the process costs and reported separately as a loss in the abnormal loss account. This draws the attention of management to those losses that may be controllable. At the end of the accounting period the abnormal loss account is written off in the profit statement as a period cost. The inventory valuation will not therefore include any abnormal expenses. The overall effect is that the abnormal losses are correctly allocated to the period in which they arise and are not carried forward as a future expense in the closing inventory valuation.

Normal losses in process with a scrap value

In case 4 actual output is equal to the expected output of 10 000 litres so there is neither an abnormal gain nor loss. All of the units lost represent a normal loss in process. However, the units lost now have a scrap value of £5 per litre. The sales value of the spoiled units should be offset against the costs of the appropriate process where the loss occurred. Therefore the sales value of the normal loss is credited to the process account and a corresponding debit entry will be made in the cash or accounts receivable (debtors) account. The calculation of the cost per unit of output is as follows:

$$\frac{\text{Input cost less scrap value of normal loss}}{\text{Expected output}} = \frac{£120\,000 - (2000 \times £5)}{10\,000 \text{ litres}} = £11$$

Compared with cases 2 and 3 the cost per unit has declined from £12 per litre to £11 per litre to reflect the fact that the normal spoilage has a scrap value which has been offset against the process costs.

The entries in the process account will look like this:

Process account

	Litres	Unit cost (£)	(£)		Litres	Unit cost (£)	(£)
Input cost	12 000	10	120 000	Normal loss	2 000	—	10 000
				Output to finished goods inventory	10 000	11	110 000
			120 000				120 000

Note that the scrap value of the normal loss is credited against the normal loss entry in the process account.

Abnormal losses in process with a scrap value

In case 5 expected output is 10 000 litres for an input of 12 000 litres and actual output is 9000 litres, resulting in a normal loss of 2000 litres and an abnormal loss of 1000 litres. The lost units have a scrap value of £5 per litre. Since our objective is to calculate the cost per unit for the expected (normal) output, only the scrap value of the normal loss of 2000 litres should be deducted in ascertaining the cost per unit. Therefore the cost per unit calculation is the same as that for case 4 (i.e. £11). The sales value of the additional 1000 litres lost represents revenue of an abnormal nature and should not be used to reduce the process unit cost. This revenue is offset against the cost of the abnormal loss which is of interest to management. The net cost incurred in the process is £105 000 (£120 000 input cost less 3000 litres lost with a scrap value of £5 per litre), and the distribution of this cost is:

	(£)	(£)
Completed production transferred to the next process (or finished goods inventory) (9000 litres at £11 per litre)		99 000
Abnormal loss:		
1000 litres at £11 per litre	11 000	
Less scrap value (1000 litres at £5)	5000	6000
		105 000

The entries in the process account will be as follows:

Process account

	Litres	Unit cost (£)	(£)		Litres	Unit cost (£)	(£)
Input cost	12 000	10	120 000	Normal loss	2 000	—	10 000
				Output to finished			
				goods inventory	9 000	11	99 000
				normal loss	1 000	11	11 000
			120 000				120 000

Abnormal loss account

	(£)		(£)
Process account	11 000	Cash sale for units scrapped	5000
		Balance transferred to profit statement	6000
	11 000		11 000

Abnormal gains with a scrap value

On occasions the actual loss in process may be less than expected, in which case an **abnormal gain** occurs (see case 6 in Example 6.1). As in the previous cases it is necessary with case 6 to begin by calculating the cost per unit of normal output. For normal output our assumptions are the same as those for cases 4 and 5 (i.e. a normal loss of 1/6 and a scrap value of £5 per litre) so the cost per unit of output is the same (i.e. £11 per litre). The calculation is as follows:

$$\frac{\text{Input cost less scrap value of normal loss}}{\text{Expected output}} = \frac{\text{£120 000} - (2000 \times \text{£5})}{10\,000 \text{ litres}} = \text{£11}$$

The net cost incurred in the process is £115 000 (£120 000 input cost less 1000 litres spoilt with a sales value of £5 per litre), and the distribution of this cost is as follows:

	(£)
Transferred to finished goods inventory (11 000 litres at £11 per litre)	121 000
Less: abnormal gain (1000 litres at £11 per litre)	11 000
lost sales of spoiled units (1000 litres at £5 per litre)	5 000 6 000
	115 000

Note that the cost per unit is based on the normal production cost per unit and is not affected by the fact that an abnormal gain occurred or that sales of the spoiled units with a sales value of £5000 did not materialize. As before, our objective is to produce a cost per unit based on normal operating efficiency.

The accounting entries are as follows:

Process account

	Litres	Unit cost (£)	(£)		Litres	Unit cost (£)	(£)
Input cost	12 000	10	120 000	Normal loss	2 000	—	10 000
Abnormal gain	1 000	11	11 000	Output to finished			
				goods inventory	11 000	11	121 000
			131 000				131 000

Abnormal gain account

	(£)		(£)
Normal loss account	5 000	Process account	11 000
Profit and loss statement (Balance)	6 000		
	11 000		11 000

Income due from normal losses

	(£)		(£)
Process account	10 000	Abnormal gain account	5 000
		Cash from spoiled units (1000 litres at £5)	5 000
	10 000		10 000

You will see that the abnormal gain has been removed from the process account and that it is valued at the cost per unit of normal production (£11). However, as 1000 litres were gained, there was a loss of sales revenue of £5000, and this lost revenue is offset against the abnormal gain. The net gain is therefore £6000, and this is the amount that should be credited to the profit statement.

The process account is credited with the expected sales revenue from the normal loss (2000 litres at £5), since the objective is to record in the process account normal net costs of production. Because the normal loss of 2000 litres does not occur, the company will not obtain the sales value of £10 000 from the expected lost output. This problem is resolved by making a corresponding debit entry in a normal loss account, which represents the amount due from the sale proceeds from the expected normal loss. The amount due (£10 000) is then reduced by £5000 to reflect the fact that only 1000 litres were lost. This is achieved by crediting the normal loss account (income due) and debiting the abnormal gain account with £5000, so that the balance of the normal loss account shows the actual amount of cash received for the income due from the spoiled units (i.e. £5000, which consists of 1000 litres at £5 per litre).

PROCESS COSTING WITH ENDING WORK IN PROGRESS PARTIALLY COMPLETE

So far we have assumed that all output within a process is fully complete. We shall now consider situations where output started during a period is partially complete at the end of the period. In other words, ending work in progress exists within a process. In this situation, unit costs cannot be computed by simply dividing the total costs for a period by the output for that period. For example, if 8000 units were started and completed during a period and another 2000 units were partly completed then these two items cannot be added together to ascertain their unit cost. We must convert the work in progress into finished equivalents (also referred to as **equivalent production**) so that the unit cost can be obtained.

To do this we must estimate the percentage degree of completion of the work in progress and multiply this by the number of units in progress at the end of the accounting period. If the 2000 partly completed units were 50 per cent complete, we could express this as an equivalent production of 1000 fully completed units. This would then be added to the completed production of 8000 units to give a total equivalent production of 9000 units. The cost per unit would then be calculated in the normal way. For example, if the costs for the period were £180 000 then the cost per unit completed would be £20 (£180 000/9000 units) and the distribution of this cost would be as follows:

	(£)
Completed units transferred to the next process (8000 units at £20)	160 000
Work in progress (1000 equivalent units at £20)	20 000
	180 000

Elements of costs with different degrees of completion

A complication that may arise is that, in any given stock of work in progress, not all of the elements that make up the total cost may have reached the same degree of completion. For example, materials may be added at the start of the process, and are thus fully complete, whereas labour and manufacturing overhead (i.e. the conversion costs) may be added uniformly throughout the process. Hence, the ending work in progress may consist of materials that are 100 per cent complete and conversion costs that are only partially complete. Where this situation arises, separate equivalent production calculations must be made for each element of cost.

The following statement shows the calculation of the cost per unit for process A in Example 6.2:

Calculation of cost per unit for process A

Cost element	Total cost (£)	Completed units	WIP equivalent units	Total equivalent units	Cost per unit (£)
Materials	210 000	10 000	4 000	14 000	15.00
Conversion cost	144 000	10 000	2 000	12 000	12.00
	354 000				27.00

	(£)	(£)
Value of work in progress:		
Materials (4000 units at £15)	60 000	
Conversion cost (2000 units at £12)	24 000	84 000
Completed units (10 000 units at £27)		270 000
		354 000

The process account will look like this:

Process A account

Materials	210 000	Completed units transferred to process B	270 000
Conversion cost	144 000	Closing WIP c/fwd	84 000
	354 000		354 000
Opening WIP b/fwd	84 000		

You will see from the above statement that details are collected relating to the equivalent production for completed units and work in progress by materials and conversion costs. This information is required to calculate the cost per unit of equivalent production for each element of cost. As materials are issued at the start of the process any partly completed units in ending work in progress must be fully complete as far as materials are concerned. Therefore an entry of 4000 units is made in the work in progress equivalent units column. Regarding conversion cost, the 4000 units in progress are only 50 per cent complete and therefore the entry in the work in progress column for this element of cost is 2000 units. To compute the value of work in progress, the unit costs are multiplied separately by the materials and conversion cost work in progress equivalent production figures. Only one calculation is required to ascertain the value of completed production. This is obtained by multiplying the total cost per unit of £27 by the completed production. Note that the cost of the output of £354 000 in the above statement is in agreement with the cost of input of £354 000.

Previous process cost

As production continues, the output of one process becomes the input of the next process. The next process will carry out additional conversion work, and may add further materials. It is important to distinguish between these different cost items and this is achieved by labelling the transferred cost from the previous process '**previous process cost**'. Note that this element of cost will always be fully complete as far as closing work in progress is concerned.

EXAMPLE 6.2

The Fontenbleau Company manufactures a product that passes through two processes. The following information relates to the two processes:

	Process A	Process B
Opening work in progress	—	—
Units introduced into the process	14 000	10 000
Units completed and transferred to the next process or finished goods inventory	10 000	9 000
Closing work in progress	4 000	1 000
Costs of production transferred from process A[a]		£270 000
Material costs added	£210 000	£108 000
Conversion costs	£144 000	£171 000

Materials are added at the start of process A and at the end of process B and conversion costs are added uniformly throughout both processes. The closing work in progress is estimated to be 50 per cent complete for both processes.

Note

[a]This information is derived from the preparation of process A accounts.

Let us now calculate the unit costs and the value of work in progress and completed production for process B in Example 6.2. To do this we prepare a statement similar to the one we prepared for process A.

Calculation of cost per unit for process B

Cost element	Total cost (£)	Completed units	WIP equivalent units	Total equivalent units	Cost per unit (£)
Previous process cost	270 000	9 000	1000	10 000	27.00
Materials	108 000	9 000	—	9 000	12.00
Conversion cost	171 000	9 000	500	9 500	18.00
	549 000				57.00

	(£)	(£)
Value of work in progress:		
Previous process cost (1000 units at £27)	27 000	
Materials	—	
Conversion cost (500 units at £18)	9 000	36 000
Completed units (9000 units at £57)		513 000
		549 000

Process B account

Previous process cost	270 000	Completed production transferred to	
Materials	108 000	finished stock	513 000
Conversions cost	171 000	Closing work in progress c/fwd	36 000
	549 000		549 000
Opening WIP b/fwd	36 000		

You will see that the previous process cost is treated as a separate process cost, and, since this element of cost will not be added to in process B, the closing work in progress must be fully complete as far as previous process cost is concerned. Note that, after the first process, materials may be issued at different stages of production. In process B materials are not issued until the end of the process, and the closing work in progress will not have reached this point; the equivalent production for the closing work in progress will therefore be zero for materials.

Normally, material costs are introduced at one stage in the process and not uniformly throughout the process. If the work in progress has passed the point at which the materials are added then the materials will be 100 per cent complete. If this point has not been reached then the equivalent production for materials will be zero.

BEGINNING AND ENDING WORK IN PROGRESS OF UNCOMPLETED UNITS

When opening stocks of work in progress exist, an assumption must be made regarding the allocation of this opening stock to the current accounting period to determine the unit cost for the period. Two alternative assumptions are possible.

- First, one may assume that opening work in progress is inextricably merged with the units introduced in the current period and can no longer be identified separately – the **weighted average method**.

- Second, one may assume that the opening work in progress is the first group of units to be processed and completed during the current month – the **first in, first out method**.

We now compare these methods using the information contained in Example 6.3.

For more complex problems it is always a good idea to start by calculating the number of units completed during the period. The calculations are as follows:

	Process X	Process Y
Opening work in progress	6 000	2 000
Units introduced during period	16 000	18 000
Total input for period	22 000	20 000
Less closing work in progress	4 000	8 000
Balance – completed production	18 000	12 000

EXAMPLE 6.3

The Baltic Company has two processes, X and Y. Material is introduced at the start of process X, and additional material is added to process Y when the process is 70 per cent complete. Conversion costs are applied uniformly throughout both processes. The completed units of process X are immediately transferred to process Y, and the completed production of process Y is transferred to finished goods stock. Data for the period include the following:

	Process X	Process Y
Opening work in progress	6000 units 60% converted, consisting of materials £72 000 and conversion cost £45 900	2000 units 80% converted, consisting of previous process cost of £91 800, materials £12 000 and conversion costs £38 400
Units started during the period	16 000 units	18 000 units
Closing work in progress	4000 units 3/4 complete	8000 units 1/2 complete
Material costs added during the period	£192 000	£60 000
Conversion costs added during the period	£225 000	£259 200

Weighted average method

The calculation of the unit cost for process X using the weighted average method is as follows:

Process X – weighted average method

Cost element	Opening WIP (£)	Current cost (£)	Total cost (£)	Completed units	WIP equiv. units	Total equiv. units	Cost per unit (£)
Materials	72 000	192 000	264 000	18 000	4000	22 000	12.00
Conversion cost	45 900	225 000	270 900	18 000	3000	21 000	12.90
	117 900		534 900				24.90

	(£)	(£)
Work in progress:		
Materials (4000 units at £12)	48 000	
Conversion (3000 units at £12.90)	38 700	86 700
Completed units (18 000 units at £24.90)		448 200
		534 900

Process X account

Opening work in progress b/fwd	117 900	Completed production	
Materials	192 000	transferred to process Y	448 200
Conversion cost	225 000	Closing work in progress c/fwd	86 700
	534 900		534 900
Opening work in progress b/fwd	86 700		

You can see from the statement of unit cost calculations that the opening work in progress is assumed to be completed in the current period. The current period's costs will include the cost of finishing off the opening work in progress, and the cost of the work in progress will be included in the total cost figure. The completed units will include the 6000 units in progress that will have been completed during the period. The statement therefore includes all the costs of the opening work in progress and the resulting units, fully completed. In other words, we have assumed that the opening work in progress is intermingled with the production of the current period to form one homogeneous batch of production. The equivalent number of units for this batch of production is divided into the costs of the current period, plus the value of the opening work in progress, to calculate the cost per unit.

Let us now calculate the unit cost for process Y using the weighted average method. From the calculation of the unit costs shown below you can see the previous process cost is fully complete as far as the closing work in progress is concerned. Note that materials are added when the process is 70 per cent complete, but the closing work in progress is only 50 per cent complete. At the stage in question no materials will have been added to the closing work in progress, and the equivalent production will be zero. As with process X, it is necessary to add the opening work in progress cost to the current cost. The equivalent production of

Process Y – Weighted average method

Cost element	Opening WIP value (£)	Current period cost (£)	Total cost (£)	Completed units	WIP equiv. units	Total equiv. units	Cost per unit (£)
Previous process cost	91 800	448 200	540 000	12 000	8000	20 000	27.00
	12 000	60 000	72 000	12 000	—	12 000	6.00
Materials							
Conversion cost	38 400	259 200	297 600	12 000	4000	16 000	18.60
	142 200		909 600				51.60

	(£)	(£)
Value of work in progress:		
Previous process cost (8000 units at £27)	216 000	
Materials	—	
Conversion cost (4000 units at £18.60)	74 400	290 400
Completed units (12 000 units at £51.60)		619 200
		909 600

Process Y account

Opening work in progress	142 200	Completed production	
Transferred from process X	448 200	transferred to finished stock	619 200
Materials	60 000	Closing work in progress c/fwd	290 400
Conversion cost	259 200		
	909 600		909 600
Opening work in progress b/fwd	290 400		

opening work in progress is ignored since this is included as being fully complete in the completed units column. Note also that the completed production cost of process X is included in the current cost column for 'the previous process cost' in the unit cost calculation for process Y.

First in first out (FIFO) method

Many courses focus only on the weighted average method of process costing. You should therefore check your course curriculum to ascertain whether or not you need to read this section relating to the FIFO method. The FIFO method of process costing assumes that the opening work in progress is the first group of units to be processed and completed during the current period. The opening work in progress is charged separately to completed production, and the cost per unit is based only on the *current period* costs and production for the current period. The closing work in progress is assumed to come from the new units started during the period. Let us now use Example 6.3 to illustrate the FIFO method for process X and Y.

Process X – FIFO method

Cost element	Current period costs (£)	Completed units less opening WIP equiv. units	Closing WIP equiv. units	Current total equiv. units	Cost per unit (£)
Materials	192 000	12 000 (18 000 − 6000)	4000	16 000	12.00
Conversion cost	225 000	14 400 (18 000 − 3600)	3000	17 400	12.93
	417 000				24.93

		(£)	(£)
Completed production:			
Opening WIP		117 900	
Materials (12 000 units at £12)		144 000	
Conversion cost (14 400 units at £12.93)		186 207	448 107
Closing WIP:			
Materials (4000 units at £12)		48 000	
Conversion cost (3000 units at £12.93)		38 793	86 793
			534 900

From this calculation you can see that the average cost per unit is based on current period costs divided by the current total equivalent units for the period. The latter figure excludes the equivalent production for opening work in progress since this was performed in the previous period. Note that the closing work in progress is multiplied by the current period average cost per unit. The closing work in progress includes only the current costs and does not include any of the opening work in progress, which is carried forward from the previous period. The objective is to ensure that the opening work in progress is kept separate and is identified as part of the cost of the completed production. The opening work in progress of £117 900 is not therefore included in the unit cost calculations, but is added directly to the completed production.

Let us now calculate the units costs for process Y:

Process Y – FIFO method

Cost element	Current costs (£)	Completed units less opening WIP equiv. units	Closing WIP equiv. units	Current total equiv. units	Cost per unit (£)
Previous process cost	448 107	10 000 (12 000 – 2000)	8000	18 000	24.8948
Materials	60 000	10 000 (12 000 – 2000)	—	10 000	6.0
Conversion cost	259 200	10 400 (12 000 – 1600)	4000	14 400	18.0
	767 307				48.8948

	(£)	(£)
Cost of completed production:		
Opening WIP	142 200	
Previous process cost (10 000 units at £24.8948)	248 948	
Materials (10 000 units at £6)	60 000	
Conversion cost (10 400 units at £18)	187 200	638 348
Cost of closing work in progress:		
Previous process cost (8000 units at £24.8948)	199 159	
Materials	—	
Conversion cost (4000 units at £18)	72 000	271 159
		909 507

Note that in this calculation the *opening* work in progress is 80 per cent completed, and that the materials are added when the process is 70 per cent complete. Hence, materials will be fully complete. Remember also that previous process cost is always 100 per cent complete. Therefore in the third column of the above statement 2000 units opening work in progress is deducted for these two elements of cost from the 12 000 units of completed production. Conversion cost will be 80 per cent complete so 1600 equivalent units are deducted from the completed production. Our objective in the third column is to extract the equivalent completed units that were derived from the units started during the current period. You should also note that the previous process cost of £448 107 represents the cost of completed production of process X, which has been transferred to process Y.

The closing work in progress valuations and the charges to completed production are fairly similar for both methods. The difference in the calculations between FIFO and the weighted average method is likely to be insignificant where the quantity of inventories and the input prices do not fluctuate significantly from month to month. Both methods are acceptable for product costing.

PARTIALLY COMPLETED OUTPUT AND LOSSES IN PROCESS

Earlier in this chapter we looked at how to deal with losses in process when all of the output in a process was fully complete. We also need to look at the treatment of losses when all of the output is not fully complete. When this situation occurs the computations can become complex. Accounting for losses when all of the output is not fully complete does not form part of the curriculum for many courses. However, some professional management accounting courses do require you to have a knowledge of this topic. Because of these different requirements this topic is dealt with in Appendix 6.1. You should therefore check the requirements of your curriculum to ascertain whether you can omit Appendix 6.1.

BATCH/OPERATING COSTING

It is not always possible to classify cost accumulation systems into job costing and process costing systems. Where manufactured goods have some common characteristics and also some individual characteristics, the cost accumulation system may be a combination of both the job costing and process costing systems. For example, the production of footwear, clothing and furniture often involves the production of batches, which are variations of a single design and require a sequence of standardized operations. Let us consider a company that makes kitchen units. Each unit may have the same basic frame, and require the same operation, but the remaining operations may differ: some frames may require sinks, others may require to be fitted with work tops; different types of doors may be fitted to each unit, some may be low-quality doors while others may be of a higher quality. The cost of a kitchen unit will therefore consist of the basic frame plus the conversion costs of the appropriate operations. The principles of the cost accumulation system are illustrated in Exhibit 6.2.

The cost of each product consists of the cost of operation 1 plus a combination of the conversion costs for operations 2–5. The cost per unit produced for a particular operation consists of the average unit cost of each batch produced for each operation. It may well be that some products may be subject to a final operation that is unique to the product. The production cost will then consist of the average cost of a combination of operations 1–5 plus the specific cost of the final unique operation. The cost of the final operation will be traced specifically to the product using a job costing system. The final product cost therefore consists of a combination of process costing techniques and job costing techniques. This system of costing is referred to as **operation costing** or **batch costing**.

Product	Operations 1	2	3	4	5	Product cost
A	✔	✔	✔			A = cost of operations 1, 2, 3
B	✔			✔	✔	B = cost of operations 1, 4, 5
C	✔	✔		✔		C = cost of operations 1, 2, 4
D	✔		✔		✔	D = cost of operations 1, 3, 5
E	✔	✔			✔	E = cost of operations 1, 2, 5

EXHIBIT 6.2

A batch costing system

SUMMARY

The following items relate to the learning objectives listed at the beginning of the chapter.

- **Explain when process costing systems are appropriate.** A process costing system is appropriate in those situations where masses of identical units or batches are produced thus making it unnecessary to assign costs to individual or batches of output. Instead, the average cost per unit or batch of output is calculated by dividing the total costs assigned to a product or service for the period by the number of units or batches of output for that period. Industries using process costing systems include chemicals, textiles and oil refining.

- **Explain the accounting treatment of normal and abnormal losses.** Normal losses are inherent in the production process and cannot be eliminated: their cost should be borne by the good production. This is achieved by dividing the costs incurred for a period by the expected output rather than the actual output. Abnormal losses are avoidable, and the cost of these losses should not be assigned to products but recorded separately as an abnormal loss and written off as a period cost in the profit statement. Scrap sales (if any) that result from the losses should be allocated to the appropriate process account (for normal losses) and the abnormal loss account (for abnormal losses).

- **Prepare process, normal loss, abnormal loss and abnormal gain accounts when there is no ending work in progress.** The cost accumulation procedure follows the production flow. Control accounts are established for each process (or department) and costs are assigned (debited) to each process. Abnormal losses are credited to the process where they were incurred and debited to an abnormal loss account. Scrap sales arising from normal losses are credited to the process account and any sales of scrap arising from abnormal losses are credited to the abnormal losses account. The accounting entries were illustrated using Example 6.1.

- **Explain and calculate equivalent units.** Where stocks of work in progress are in existence, it is necessary in order to create homogeneous units of output to convert the work in progress into finished equivalent units of output. To do this we must estimate the percentage degree of completion of the work in progress and multiply this by the number of units in progress at the end of the accounting period. For example, if there are 5000 completed units estimated to be 40 per cent complete this represents an equivalent production of 2000 completed units.

- **Compute the value of closing work in progress and completed production using the weighted average method and first in, first out methods of valuing work in progress.** There are two alternative methods of allocating opening work in progress costs to production: the weighted average and first in, first out methods. If the weighted average method is used, both the units and the value of opening work in progress are merged with the current period costs and production to calculate the average cost per unit. Using the first in, first out method, the opening work in progress is assumed to be the first group of units to be processed and completed during the current period. The opening work in progress is therefore assigned separately to completed production and the cost per unit is based only on current costs and production for the period. The closing work in progress is assumed to come from the new units that have been started during the period.

- **Additional learning objectives specified in Appendix 6.1.** The appendix to this chapter includes one additional objective: to compute the value of normal and abnormal losses when there is ending work in progress. Because accounting for losses when all of the output is not fully complete is a complex topic that does not form part of the curriculum for many first level courses, this topic is dealt with in Appendix 6.1. You should check your course curriculum to ascertain if you need to read Appendix 6.1.

APPENDIX 6.1: LOSSES IN PROCESS AND PARTIALLY COMPLETED UNITS

Normal losses

Losses can occur at different stages within a process. Where losses are assumed to occur at the final stage of completion only units that have reached this stage should be allocated with the cost of the loss. Therefore none of the cost should be allocated to closing work in progress (WIP), since they represent incomplete units. Consider Example 6A.1.

The cost per unit is calculated as follows:

Element of cost	Total cost (£)	Completed units	Normal loss	WIP equiv. units	Total equiv. units	Cost per unit (£)
Materials	5000	600	100	300	1000	5.0
Conversion cost	3400	600	100	150	850	4.0
	8400					9.0

	(£)	(£)
Value of work in progress:		
Materials (300 units at £5)	1500	
Conversion cost (150 units at £4)	600	2100
Completed units (600 units at £9)	5400	
Normal loss (100 units at £9)	900	6300
		8400

EXAMPLE 6A.1

A department with no opening work in progress introduces 1000 units into the process; 600 are completed, 300 are half-completed and 100 units are lost (all normal). *Losses occur upon completion.* Material costs are £5000 (all introduced at the start of the process) and conversion costs are £3400.

You can see from the unit cost calculation that an additional column is added for the equivalent units of normal loss. Note also that the cost of the normal loss is added to the cost of completed production, since it is detected at the final sage of completion. The closing WIP has not reached this stage, and therefore does not bear any of the loss. The cost per unit completed after the allocation of the normal loss is £10.50 (£6 300/600 units).

Most examination questions, however, are normally based on the assumption that you will adopt a more simplistic alternative method known as the short-cut method. With this method no entry is made in the unit cost statement for normal losses. The calculations adopting the short-cut method are as follows:

	Total cost (£)	Completed units	WIP equiv. units	Total equiv. units	Cost per unit (£)	WIP (£)
Materials	5000	600	300	900	5.5555	1666.65
Conversion cost	3400	600	150	750	4.5333	680.00
					10.0888	2346.65
			Completed units (600 × £10.0888)			6053.3
						8400.00

With the short cut method the costs allocated to WIP and completed units differs from the allocations based on assigning all of the cost of the normal loss to completed production. This is because the short cut method allocates the cost of the normal loss to both closing WIP and completed units based on the ratio of WIP and completed units equivalent production. The short-cut method is only theoretically correct where losses occur at an earlier stage in the production process and the WIP has reached this stage. In these circumstances it is appropriate to allocate the cost of the normal loss between WIP and completed units. Let us now assume for Example 6A.1 that the loss is detected when the process has reached the 50 per cent stage of completion. In our revised example the WIP has been processed beyond the point where the loss occurs (the 50 per cent stage of completion) so it is appropriate to allocate a share of the cost of normal loss to WIP. The revised cost per unit, if the short cut method is not adopted, is as follows:

Element of cost	Total cost (£)	Completed units	Normal loss	WIP equiv. units	Total equiv. units	Cost per unit
Materials	5000	600	100	300	1000	5.00
Conversion cost	3400	600	50	150	800	4.25
	8400					9.25

The 100 lost units will not be processed any further once the loss is detected at the 50 per cent completion stage. Therefore 50 units equivalent production (100 units × 50 per cent) is entered in the normal loss column for conversion cost equivalent production. Note that materials are introduced at the start of the process and are fully complete when the loss is detected. The cost of the normal loss is:

	£
Materials (100 × £5)	500.00
Conversion cost (50 × £4.25)	212.50
	712.50

How should we allocate the normal loss between completed production and work in progress? Several different approaches are advocated, but the most common approach is to apportion the normal loss in the ratio of completed units and WIP equivalent units as follows:

		WIP	
Completed units	**(£)**		**(£)**
Materials 600/900 × £500	333.33	300/900 × £500	166.67
Conversion cost 600/750 × £212.50	170.00	150/750 × £212.50	42.50
	503.33		209.17

The cost of completed units and WIP is:

	(£)	**(£)**
Completed units:		
(600 × £9.25)	5550.00	
Share of normal loss	503.33	6053.33
WIP:		
Materials (300 × £5)	1500.00	
Conversion cost (150 × £4.25)	637.50	
Share of normal loss	209.17	2346.67
		8400.00

The costs allocated to completed unit and WIP are now identical to the costs that have been allocated with the short-cut method. For the revised circumstances where the WIP has reached the stage where the losses are assumed to occur the short-cut method is theoretically correct. However, even when circumstances exist where the short cut method is not theoretically correct (i.e. WIP has not reached the stage where losses are assumed to occur) examination questions are normally based on the assumption that you will adopt this method because of its simplicity.

Abnormal losses

Where abnormal losses occur the normal unit cost statement using the short-cut method should be prepared (i.e. without a column for normal losses) but with an additional column for abnormal loss equivalent units. Consider the information presented in Example 6A.2. You can see from this example that losses are detected when production has reached the 50 per cent stage of completion and that WIP has been processed beyond this point. Therefore it is appropriate to use the short cut method.

EXAMPLE 6A.2

A department with no opening work in progress introduced 1000 units into the process; 600 are completed, 250 are 60 per cent complete, and 150 units are lost consisting of 100 units normal loss and 50 units of abnormal loss. Losses are detected *when production is 50 per cent complete*. Material costs are £8000 (all introduced at the start of the process), conversion costs are £2900 and previous process cost is £10 000.

The unit cost calculations are as follows:

Element of cost	Total cost (£)	Completed units	Abnormal loss	WIP equiv. units	Total equiv. units	Cost per unit (£)
Previous process cost	10 000	600	50	250	900	11.111
Materials	8 000	600	50	250	900	8.888
Conversion cost	2 900	600	25	150	775	3.742
	20 900					23.741

From this calculation you can see that materials and the previous process cost are 100 per cent complete when the loss is discovered. However, spoilt units will not be processed any further once the loss is detected, and the lost units will be 50 per cent complete in respect of conversion costs.

The costs are accounted for as follows:

	£	£
Value of work in progress:		
Previous process cost (250 units at £11.111)	2 777	
Materials (250 units at £8.888)	2 222	
Conversion cost (150 units at £3.742)	561	5 560
Completed units:		
600 units at £23.741		14 246
Abnormal loss:		
Previous process cost (50 units at £11.111)	556	
Materials (50 units at £8.888)	444	
Conversion cost (25 units at £3.742)	94	1 094
		20 900

KEY TERMS AND CONCEPTS

Abnormal gain gain that occurs when the level of a normal loss is less than expected.

Abnormal losses, or **controllable losses** losses that are not inherent to the production process and which are not

expected to occur under efficient operating conditions.

Conversion cost the sum of direct labour and overhead costs.

Equivalent production the term used when work in progress is converted into finished equivalents.

First in, first out method a method of calculating process unit costs that assumes that the opening work in progress is the first group of units to be processed and completed during the current period. The opening work in progress is charged separately to completed production, and the cost per unit is based only on current period costs and production for the current period.

Normal losses, or **uncontrollable losses** unavoidable losses that are inherent to the production process and can be expected to occur in efficient operating conditions.

Operation costing, or **batch costing** that makes use of a combination of job costing and process costing techniques.

Previous process cost the cost that is transferred from the previous process and is always fully complete in respect of closing WIP.

Weighted average method a method of calculating process unit costs that assumes that opening work in progress is inextricably merged with the units produced in the current period and can no longer be identified separately.

KEY EXAMINATION POINTS

Process costing questions require many calculations and there is a possibility that you will make calculation errors. Make sure that your answer is clearly presented so that the examiner can ascertain whether or not you are using correct methods to calculate the cost per unit. Questions can generally be classified by three categories. First, all output is fully complete and the problem of equivalent production does not arise (see Review problems 6.11 and 6.12). Second, work in progress (WIP) output is partially complete and there are no losses in process. Third, losses in process apply when WIP is partially complete. Because of its simplicity you should adopt the short cut method for questions involving losses in process and equivalent production. You should, however, point out that the short cut method is not theoretically correct if losses are assumed to occur at the end of the process. Examination questions generally assume that you will adopt the short cut method.

ASSESSMENT MATERIAL

The review questions are short questions that enable you to assess your understanding of the main topics included in the chapter. The numbers in parentheses provide you with the page numbers to refer to if you cannot answer a specific question.

The review problems are more complex and require you to relate and apply the chapter content to various business problems. The problems are graded by their level of difficulty. The multiple-choice questions are the least demanding and normally take less than 10 minutes to complete. Fully worked solutions to the review problems are provided in a separate section at the end of the book. Further review problems with solutions for this chapter are available on the accompanying website www.drury-online.com. The website includes a *Student's Manual* and an *Instructor's Manual.* Students can access both questions and answers from the *Student's Manual* and the questions from the *Instructor's Manual* The answers to problems in the *Instructor's Manual* are available only to lecturers on the lecturer's password-protected section of the website.

REVIEW QUESTIONS

6.1 Describe the differences between process costing and job costing. *(pp. 135–36)*

6.2 Provide examples of industries that use process costing. *(p. 135)*

6.3 Why is cost accumulation easier with a process costing system compared with a job costing system? *(p. 136)*

6.4 Distinguish between normal and abnormal losses and explain how their accounting treatment differs. *(pp. 137–38)*

6.5 What are equivalent units? Why are they needed with a process costing system? *(p. 143)*

6.6 Why is it necessary to treat 'previous process cost' as a separate element of cost in a process costing system? *(p. 144)*

6.7 How is the equivalent unit cost calculation affected when materials are added at the beginning or at a later stage of the process rather than uniformly throughout the process? *(p. 146)*

6.8 Describe how the weighted average and FIFO methods differ in assigning costs to units completed and closing work in progress. *(pp. 146–50)*

6.9 Under what conditions will the weighted average and FIFO methods give similar results? *(p. 150)*

6.10 Explain the distinguishing features of a batch/operating costing system. *(p. 151)*

REVIEW PROBLEMS

6.11   A company uses process costing to value its output and all materials are input at the start of the process. The following information relates to the process for one month:

Input	3000 units
Opening stock	400 units
Losses	10% of input is expected to be lost
Closing stock	200 units

How many good units were output from the process if actual losses were 400 units?

(a)   2800 units

(b)   2900 units

(c)   3000 units

(d)   3200 units

ACCA Financial Information for Management

6.12   A company uses process costing to value its output. The following was recorded for the period:

Input materials	2000 units at £4.50 per unit
Conversion costs	£13 340
Normal loss	5% of input valued at £3 per unit
Actual loss	150 units

There were no opening or closing stocks.

What was the valuation of one unit of output to one decimal place?

(a)   £11.8

(b)   £11.6

(c)   £11.2

(d)   £11.0

ACCA Financial Information for Management

6.13   KL Processing Limited has identified that an abnormal gain of 160 litres occurred in its refining process last week. Normal losses are expected and have a scrap value of £2.00 per litre. All losses are 100 per cent complete as to material cost and 75 per cent complete as to conversion costs.

The company uses the weighted average method of valuation and last week's output was valued using the following costs per equivalent unit:

Materials	£9.40
Conversion costs	£11.20

The effect on the profit and loss account of last week's abnormal gain is:

(a)   Debit £2528

(b)   Debit £2828

(c)   Credit £2528

(d)   Credit £2848

(e)   Credit £3168

CIMA Stage 2

6.14   The following details relate to the main process of W Limited, a chemical manufacturer:

Opening work in progress	2000 litres, fully complete as to materials and 40% complete as to conversion
Material input	24 000 litres
Normal loss is 10% of input	
Output to process 2	19 500 litres
Closing work in progress	3000 litres, fully complete as to materials and 45% complete as to conversion

The number of equivalent units to be included in W Limited's calculation of the cost per equivalent unit using a FIFO basis of valuation are:

	Materials	Conversion
A	19 400	18 950
B	20 500	20 050
C	21 600	21 150
D	23 600	20 750
E	23 600	21 950

CIMA Stage 2

6.15   Process B had no opening stock. 13 500 units of raw material were transferred in at £4.50 per unit. Additional material at £1.25 per unit was added in process. Labour and overheads were £6.25 per completed unit and £2.50 per unit incomplete.

If 11 750 completed units were transferred out, what was the closing stock in process B?

(a)   £77 625.00

(b)   £14 437.50

(c)   £141 000.00

(d)   £21 000.00

CIMA Stage 1

6.16   Information relating to two processes (F and G) was as follows:

Process	Normal loss as % of input	Input litres	Output litres
F	8	65 000	58 900
G	5	37 500	35 700

For each process, was there an abnormal loss or an abnormal gain?

Process F	Process G
(a) Abnormal gain	Abnormal gain
(b) Abnormal gain	Abnormal loss
(c) Abnormal loss	Abnormal gain
(d) Abnormal loss	Abnormal loss

ACCA Financial Information for Management

6.17 The following details relate to the main process of Z Limited, a paint manufacturer:

Opening work in process	2400 litres	fully complete as to materials and 30% complete as to conversion
Material input	58 000 litres	
Normal loss is 5% of input		
Output to next process	52 500 litres	
Closing work in process	3000 litres	fully complete as to materials and 50% complete as to conversion

All losses occur at the end of the process.

The numbers of equivalent units to be included in Z Limited's calculation of the cost per equivalent unit, using a *weighted average basis* of valuation, are:

	Materials	Conversion
A	53 100	51 600
B	55 500	54 000
C	55 500	53 300
D	57 500	56 000
E	57 500	55 300

CIMA Stage 2

6.18 The following information is required for sub-questions (a) to (c).

The incomplete process account relating to period 4 for a company which manufactures paper is shown below:

Process account

	Units	$		Units	$
Material	4000	16 000	Finished goods	2750	
Labour		8125	Normal loss	400	700
Production overhead		3498	Work in progress	700	

There was no opening work in process (WIP). Closing WIP, consisting of 700 units, was complete as shown:

Material	100%
Labour	50%
Production overhead	40%

Losses are recognized at the end of the production process and are sold for $1.75 per unit.

(a) Given the outcome of the process, which ONE of the following accounting entries is needed to complete the double entry to the process account?

	Debit	Credit
A	Abnormal Loss account	Process account
B	Process account	Abnormal Loss account
C	Abnormal Gain account	Process account
D	Process account	Abnormal Gain account

(b) The value of the closing WIP was:

A $3868

B $4158

C $4678

D $5288

(c) The total value of the units transferred to finished goods was:

A $21052.50

B $21587.50

C $22122.50

D $22 656.50

CIMA – Management Accounting Fundamentals

6.19 A company operates a process costing system using the first-in-first-out (FIFO) method of valuation. No losses occur in the process. All materials are input at the commencement of the process. Conversion costs are incurred evenly throughout the process.

The following data relate to last period:

	Units	Degree of completion
Opening work in progress	2000	60%
Total number of units completed	14 000	
Closing work in progress	3000	30%
Costs arising:		
Materials		51 000
Conversion		193 170

(a) What was the total number of units input during last period?

A   12 000

B   13 000

C   15 000

D   17 000

(b) What was the value of the closing work in progress for last period?

A   £21 330

B   £21 690

C   £22 530

D   £22 980

ACCA Financial Information for Management

6.20   A company operates a process costing system using the first-in-first-out (FIFO) system of valuation. No losses occur in the process. The following data relate to last month:

	Units
Opening work-in-progress	200 with a total value of £1530
Input to the process	1000
Completed production	1040

Last month the cost per equivalent unit of production was £20 and the degree of completion of the work-in-progress was 40% throughout the month.

(a)   What was the value (at cost) of last month's closing work-in-progress?

A   £1224

B   £1280

C   £1836

D   £1920

(b)   What was the cost of the 1040 units completed last month?

A   £19 200

B   £19 930

C   £20 730

D   £20 800

ACCA Financial Information for Management

6.21   **Weighted average method with losses**

CW Ltd makes one product in a single process. The details of the process for period 2 were as follows:

There were 800 units of opening work in progress valued as follows:

Material	£98 000
Labour	£46 000
Production overheads	£7600

During the period 1800 units were added to the process and the following costs were incurred:

Material	£387 800
Labour	£276 320
Production overheads	£149 280

There were 500 units of closing work in progress, which were 100 per cent complete for material, 90 per cent complete for labour and 40 per cent complete for production overheads. A normal loss equal to 10 per cent of new material input during the period was expected. The actual loss amounted to 180 units. Each unit of loss was sold for £10 per unit.

CW Ltd uses weighted average costing.

Calculate the cost of the output for the period.

(4 marks)
CMA P1 Management Accounting: Performance Evaluation

6.22   Equivalent production with losses (FIFO method)
Partlet Ltd makes a product that passes through two manufacturing processes. A normal loss equal to 8 per cent of the raw material input occurs in Process I but no loss occurs in Process II. Losses have no realizable value. All the raw material required to make the product is input at the start of Process I. The output from Process I each month is input into Process II in the same month. Work in progress occurs in Process II only. Information for last month for each process is as follows:

Process I
Raw material input	50 000 litres at a cost of £365 000
Conversion costs	£256 000
Output to Process II	47 000 litres

Process II
Opening work-in-progress	5000 litres (40% complete for conversion costs) valued at £80 000
Conversion costs	£392 000
Closing work in progress	2000 litres (50% complete for conversion costs)

Required:

(a) Prepare the Process I account for last month.

(5 marks)

(b) Calculate in respect of Process II for last month:
   (i) The value of the completed output; and
   (ii) The value of closing work in progress.

(5 marks)

(c) If the losses in Process I were toxic and the company incurred costs in safely disposing of them, state how the disposal costs associated with the normal loss would have been recorded in the Process I account. No calculations are required.

(2 marks)
ACCA Financial Information for Management

6.23   Equivalent production with losses (FIFO method)
Adam, the management accountant of Mark Limited, has on file the costs per equivalent unit for the company's process for the last month but the input costs and quantities appear to have been mislaid.

Information that is available to Adam for last month is as follows:

Opening work in progress	100 units, 30% complete
Closing work in progress	200 units, 40% complete
Normal loss	10% of input valued at £2 per unit
Output	1250 units

The losses were as expected and Adam has a record of there being 150 units scrapped during the month. All materials are input at the start of the process. The cost per equivalent unit for materials was £2.60 and for conversion costs was £1.50.

Mark Limited uses the FIFO method of stock valuation in its process account.

Required:

(a) Calculate the units input into the process.

(2 marks)

(b) Calculate the equivalent units for materials and conversion costs.

(4 marks)

(c) Using your answer from (b) calculate the input costs.

(4 marks)

6.24 **Equivalent production and losses in process**
A concentrated liquid fertilizer is manufactured by passing chemicals through two consecutive processes. Stores record cards for the chemical ingredients used exclusively by the first process show the following data for May:

Opening stock	4000 litres	£10 800
Closing stock	8000 litres	£24 200
Receipts into store	20 000 litres	£61 000

Other process data for May is tabulated below:

	Process 1	Process 2
Direct labour	£4880	£6000
Direct expenses	£4270	—
Overhead absorption rates	250% of direct labour	100% of direct labour
Output	8000 litres	7500 litres
Opening stock of work in process	—	—
Closing stock of work in process	5600 litres	—
Normal yield	85% of input	90% of input
Scrap value of loss	—	—

In process 1 the closing stock of work in process has just passed through inspection, which is at the stage where materials and conversion costs are 100 per cent and 75 per cent completed respectively.

In process 2 inspection is the final operation.

Required:

(a) Prepare the relevant accounts to show the results of the processes for May and present a detailed working paper showing your calculations and any assumptions in arriving at the data shown in those accounts.

(18 marks)

(b) If supplies of the required chemicals are severely restricted and all production can be sold immediately, briefly explain how you would calculate the total loss to the company if, at the beginning of June, 100 litres of the correct mix of chemicals were spilt on issue to process 1.

(4 marks)
ACCA Foundation Costing

6.25 Equivalent production with losses (FIFO method)

Yeoman Ltd uses process costing and the FIFO method of valuation. The following information for last month relates to Process G, where all the material is added at the beginning of the process:

Opening work-in-progress:	2000 litres (30 per cent complete in respect of conversion costs) valued in total at £24 600 (£16 500 for direct materials; £8 100 for conversion).
Costs incurred:	Direct materials £99 600 for 12 500 litres of input Conversion £155 250
Normal loss:	8% of input in the period. All losses, which are incurred evenly throughout the process, can be sold for £3 per litre.
Actual output:	10 000 litres were transferred from Process G to the finished goods warehouse.
Closing work-in-progress:	3 000 litres (45 per cent complete in respect of conversion costs).

Required:

(a) Prepare the Process G Account for last month in £ and litres.

(10 marks)

(b) Identify TWO types of organization where it would be appropriate to use service (operation) costing. For each one suggest a suitable unit cost measure.

(2 marks)
ACCA Financial Information for Management

CHAPTER 7
JOINT AND BY-PRODUCT COSTING

LEARNING OBJECTIVES

After studying this chapter, you should be able to:

- distinguish between joint products and by-products;
- explain and identify the split-off point in a joint-cost situation;
- explain the alternative methods of allocating joint costs to products;
- discuss the arguments for and against each of the methods of allocating joint costs to products;
- present relevant financial information for a decision as to whether a product should be sold at a particular stage or further processed;
- describe the accounting treatment of by-products.

Some production processes result in more than one product. These may be separate substances that are extracted from the same raw material, or different quality grades of the same product. Depending on their relative value, these products are known as joint products or by-products, and are treated differently for accounting purposes.

By definition, a joint product only becomes identifiable as a separate product at a specific stage in the production process. Before this point, all the joint products go through the same treatment together and incur joint costs. The main issue that we shall be considering in this chapter is how these joint costs should be allocated to the various joint products. There is more than one way in which this can be done, and the different methods have significant implications for the calculation of profit and the valuation of inventory.

JOINT PRODUCTS AND BY-PRODUCTS

Joint products and by-products arise in situations where the production of one product makes inevitable the production of other products. For example, the extraction of petroleum from crude oil also produces kerosene and paraffin.

We can distinguish between joint products and by-products by looking at their relative sales value. When a group of individual products is produced simultaneously and each product has a significant relative sales value, the outputs are usually called **joint products**. Products that only have a minor sales value when compared with the joint products are called **by-products**.

As their name implies, by-products are those products that result incidentally from the main joint products. By-products may have a considerable absolute value, but the crucial classification test is that the sales value is small when compared with the values of the joint products. Joint products are crucial to the commercial viability of an organization, whereas by-products are incidental. In other words, by-products do not usually influence the decision as to whether or not to produce the main product, and they normally have little effect on the prices set for the main (joint) products. Examples of industries that produce both joint and by-products include chemicals, oil refining, mining, flour milling and gas manufacturing.

A distinguishing feature of the production of joint and by-products is that the products are not identifiable as different individual products until a specific point in the production process is reached, known as the **split-off point**. All products may separate at one time, or different products may emerge at intervals. Before the split-off point, costs cannot be traced to particular products. For example, it is not possible to determine what part of the cost of processing a barrel of crude oil should be allocated to petrol, kerosene or paraffin. After the split-off point, joint products may be sold or subjected to further processing. In the latter case, any **further processing costs** can be traced to the specific products involved.

Figure 7.1 illustrates a simplified production process for joint and by-products. In this example, joint products A and B and by-product C all emerge at the same split-off point. Before this point, they share the same raw materials, labour and overhead costs. After the split-off point, further processing costs are added to the joint products before sale, and these costs can be specifically allocated to them. In this example, by-product C is sold at the split-off point without further processing, although sometimes by-products may be further processed after the split-off point before they are sold on the outside market.

Later in this chapter we will examine the accounting treatment of by-products. First, we will concentrate our attention on the allocation of joint costs to joint products.

METHODS OF ALLOCATING JOINT COSTS

If all the production for a particular period is sold, the problem of allocating joint costs to products for inventory valuation and profit measurement does not arise. Inventory valuations are not necessary, and the calculation of profit merely requires the deduction of total cost from total sales. However, if some stock remains unsold, inventories will exist at the end of the period and it is necessary to allocate costs to particular products. There is more than one method of making this allocation and, as you will see, the choice of method can have significant implications

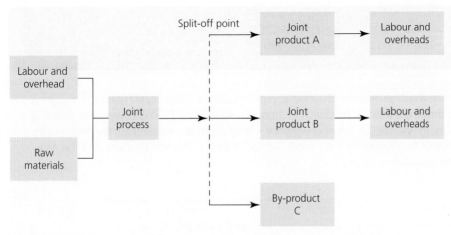

FIGURE 7.1

Production process for joint and by-products

for the calculation of profit and the valuation of inventories. This area will involve the accountant in making subjective decisions which can be among the most difficult to defend. All one can do is to attempt to choose an allocation method that seems to provide a rational and reasonable method of cost distribution. The most frequently used methods that are used to allocate joint costs up to split-off point can be divided into the following two categories:

1 Methods based on physical measures such as weight, volume, etc.
2 Methods based on allocating joint costs relative to the market values of the products.

We shall now look at four methods that are used for allocating joint costs using the information given in Example 7.1. Products X, Y and Z all become finished products at the split-off point. We must decide how much of the £600 000 joint costs should be allocated to each individual product. The £600 000 cannot be specifically identified with any of the individual products, since the products themselves were not separated before the split-off point, but some method must be used to split the £600 000 among the products X, Y and Z so that inventories can be valued and the profit for the period calculated.

Physical measures method

Using the **physical measures method**, we simply allocate the joint cost in proportion to volume. Each product is assumed to receive similar benefits from the joint cost, and is therefore charged with its proportionate share of the total cost. The cost allocations using this method are as follows:

Product	Units produced	Proportion to total	Joint costs allocated (£)	Cost per unit (£)
X	40 000	$1/3$	200 000	5
Y	20 000	$1/6$	100 000	5
Z	60 000	$1/2$	300 000	5
	120 000		600 000	

Note that this method assumes that the cost per unit is the same for each of the products. To calculate the cost per unit, we simply divide the total cost by the number of units:

cost per unit $= £5$ (£600 000/120 000)

EXAMPLE 7.1

During the month of July the Van Nostrand Company processes a basic raw material through a manufacturing process that yields three products – products X, Y and Z. There were no opening inventories and the products are sold at the split-off point without further processing. We shall initially assume that all of the output is sold during the period. Details of the production process and the sales revenues are given in the following diagram.

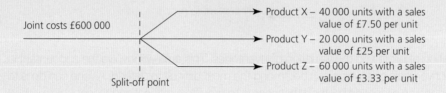

Thus the joint cost allocations are:

$$\text{Product X} : 40\,000 \times £5 = £200\,000$$
$$\text{Product Y} : 20\,000 \times £5 = £100\,000$$
$$\text{Product Z} : 60\,000 \times £5 = £300\,000$$

Where market prices of the joint products differ, the assumption of identical costs per unit for each joint product will result in some products showing high profits while others may show losses. This can give misleading profit calculations. Let us look at the product profit calculations using the information given in Example 7.1:

Product	Sales revenue (£)	Total cost (£)	Profit (loss) (£)	Profit/sales (%)
X	300 000	200 000	100 000	33⅓
Y	500 000	100 000	400 000	80
Z	200 000	300 000	(100 000)	(50)
	1 000 000	600 000	400 000	40

You will see from these figures that the allocation of the joint costs bears no relationship to the revenue-producing power of the individual products. Product Z is allocated with the largest share of the joint costs but has the lowest total sales revenue; product Y is allocated with the lowest share of the joint costs but has the highest total sales revenue. This illustrates a significant problem with the physical measures method.

A further problem is that the joint products must be measurable by the same unit of measurement. Sometimes, the products emerging from the joint process consist of solids, liquids and gases, and it can be difficult to find a common base to measure them. The main advantage of using the physical measures method is simplicity, but this is outweighed by its many disadvantages.

Sales value at split-off point method

When the **sales value at split-off point method** is used, joint costs are allocated to joint products in proportion to the estimated sales value of production. A product with higher sales value will be allocated a higher proportion of the joint costs. To a certain extent, this method could better be described as a means of apportioning profits or losses according to sales value, rather than a method for allocating costs. Using the information in Example 7.1, the allocations under the sales value method would be as follows:

Product	Units produced	Sales value (£)	Proportion of sales value to total (%)	Joint costs allocated (£)
X	40 000	300 000	30	180 000
Y	20 000	500 000	50	300 000
Z	60 000	200 000	20	120 000
		1 000 000		600 000

The revised product profit calculations would be as follows:

Product	Sales revenue	Total cost (£)	Profit (loss) (£)	Profit/sales (%)
X	300 000	180 000	120 000	40
Y	500 000	300 000	200 000	40
Z	200 000	120 000	80 000	40
	1 000 000	600 000	400 000	

The sales value method ensures that joint costs are allocated based on a product's ability to absorb the joint costs but it can itself be criticized because it is based on the assumption that sales revenue determines prior costs. This can result in an unprofitable product with low sales revenue being allocated with a small share of joint cost, thus mistakenly giving the impression that it is generating profits.

Net realizable value method

In Example 7.1 we have assumed that all products are sold at the split-off point and that no additional costs are incurred beyond that point. In practice, it is likely that joint products will each require further processing after the split-off point, and market values may not exist for the products before this processing has taken place. To estimate the sales value at the split-off point, it is therefore necessary to use the estimated sales value at the point of sale and work backwards. This method is called the **net realizable value method**. The net realizable value at split-off point can be estimated by deducting the further processing costs from the sales revenues. This approach is illustrated with the data given in Example 7.2 which is the same as Example 7.1 except that further processing costs beyond split-off point are now assumed to exist. You should now refer to Example 7.2.

REAL WORLD VIEWS 7.1

Joint product costing in the semiconductor industry

In the semiconductor industry, the production of memory chips may be viewed as a joint processing situation because the output consists of different quality chips from a common production run. The manufacturing operation is composed of three phases: fabrication, assembly and a 'stress test'. The first and second steps are mandatory. The third is optional and necessary to produce memory with a longer life expectancy. Of the three cases, only fabrication represents a joint production process; assembly and stress testing are separable steps.

The input to the fabrication phase is raw silicon wafers, which are first photolithographed and then baked at high temperatures. Each wafer will yield multiple chips of identical design. Upon completion of the fabrication process, the finished wafer is tested to identify usable and unusable chips. The test also classifies usable chips according to density (the number of good memory bits) and speed (the time required to access those bits).

The input to the assembly process is usable chips, which are encapsulated in ceramic and wired for use on a memory board. The encapsulation process varies according to the number of chips, which constitute a finished module. Modules of a given density may be composed of one all-good chip or multiple partially good chips. The finished modules are subjected to a non-destructive functional test to identify defective output.

If an extended life expectancy is not required, the good modules are not processed any further. A small sample of the good modules is subjected to the destructive reliability test before the finished product is considered saleable. This destructive reliability test is a traditional quality control step designed to establish the 'time-to-failure' distribution of the output. The profile of this distribution will depend, in part, upon whether the modules were subjected to the optional stress test.

If a longer life expectancy is desired, the modules are stressed before being tested for reliability. This optional step exposes the modules to extreme conditions and those that survive are labelled extended-life modules. The proportion of the modules selected to undergo the stress test is under management control and can be varied with market conditions. The final output of the process differs in quality according to a variety of dimensions. These include number of chips per module, speed, life expectancy and temperature tolerance.

Discussion point

● Which costs are relevant for determining whether an extended life expectancy is required for the good models?

SOURCE: ADAPTED FROM CATS-BARIL, W.L. ET AL. (1986) JOINT PRODUCT COSTING IN THE SEMICONDUCTOR INDUSTRY, MANAGEMENT ACCOUNTING (USA), PP. 28-35.

The calculation of the net realizable value and the allocation of joint costs using this method is as follows:

Product	Sales value (£)	Costs beyond split-off point (£)	Estimated net realizable value at split-off point (£)	Proportion to total (%)	Joint costs allocated (£)	Profit (£)	Gross profit (%)
X	300 000	80 000	220 000	27.5	165 000	55 000	18.33
Y	500 000	100 000	400 000	50.0	300 000	100 000	20.00
Z	200 000	20 000	180 000	22.5	135 000	45 000	22.50
	1 000 000	200 000	800 000		600 000	200 000	20.00

Note that the joint costs are now allocated in proportion to each product's net realizable value at split-off point.

EXAMPLE 7.2

Assume the same situation as Example 7.1 except that further processing costs now apply. Details of the production process and sales revenues are given in the following diagram:

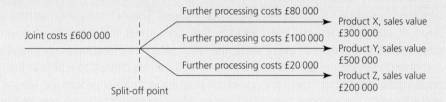

Constant gross profit percentage method

When joint products are subject to further processing after split-off point and the net realizable method is used, the gross profit percentages are different for each product. In the above illustration they are 18.33 per cent for product X, 20 per cent for Y and 22.5 per cent for Z. It could be argued that, since the three products arise from a single productive process, they should earn identical gross profit percentages. The **constant gross profit percentage method** allocates joint costs so that the overall gross profit percentage is identical for each individual product.

From the information contained in Example 7.2 the joint costs would be allocated in such a way that the resulting gross profit percentage for each of the three products is equal to the overall gross profit percentage of 20 per cent. Note that the gross profit percentage is calculated by deducting the *total* costs of the three products (£800 000) from the total sales (£1 000 000) and expressing the profit (£200 000) as a percentage of sales. The calculations are as follows:

	Product X (£)	Product Y (£)	Product Z (£)	Total (£)
Sales value	300 000	500 000	200 000	1 000 000
Gross profit (20%)	60 000	100 000	40 000	200 000
Cost of goods sold	240 000	400 000	160 000	800 000
Less separable further processing costs	80 000	100 000	20 000	200 000
Allocated joint costs	160 000	300 000	140 000	600 000

You can see that the required gross profit percentage of 20 per cent is computed for each product. The additional further processing costs for each product are then deducted, and the balance represents the allocated joint costs.

The constant gross profit percentage method assumes that there is a uniform relationship between cost and sales value for each individual product. However, this assumption is questionable, since we do not observe identical gross profit percentages for individual products in multi-product companies that do not involve joint costs.

Comparison of methods

What factors should be considered in selecting the most appropriate method of allocating joint costs? The cause-and-effect criterion, described in Chapter 4, cannot be used because there is no cause-and-effect relationship between the *individual* products and the incurrence of joint costs. Joint costs are caused by all products and not by individual products.

Where cause-and-effect relationships cannot be established, allocations should be based on the benefits received criterion. If benefits received cannot be measured, costs should be allocated based on the principle of equity or fairness. The net realizable method and the sales value at split-off point are the methods that best meet the benefits received criterion. If sales values at the split-off point exist, the latter also has the added advantage of simplicity. A problem with the net realizable method is that it can be difficult to estimate the net realizable value in industries where there are numerous subsequent further processing stages and multiple split-off points. As we have discussed, similar measurement problems can also apply with the physical measures method. A summary of the advantages and disadvantages of each allocation method is presented in Exhibit 7.1.

What methods do companies actually use? Little empirical evidence exists apart from a UK survey undertaken many years ago by Slater and Wootton (1984). Their survey findings are presented in Exhibit 7.2.

You will see that a physical measures method is most widely used, despite its disadvantages. In practice, firms are likely to use a method where the output from the joint process can be measured without too much difficulty. In some organizations it is extremely difficult to establish a common output measure and to overcome this problem Slater and Wootton reported that they valued inventories at their estimated net realizable value, minus a normal profit margin.

Method	Advantages	Disadvantages
Physical measurement	Simple to operate where there is a common unit of measurement	• Can distort profit reporting and inventory valuation • Can be difficult to find a common unit of measurement
Sales value at split-off point	Provides more realistic inventory valuations	• Assumes that sales value determines prior costs • Assumes that a sales value at split-off point can be determined
Net realizable value	Takes further processing costs into account Simple to apply if there is only one split-off point	Can be difficult to calculate for a complex process with many split-off points
Constant gross profit percentage	Appropriate only if a constant gross profit for each joint product is a logical assumption	Only appropriate if a constant gross profit for each product makes sense

EXHIBIT 7.1

Advantages and disadvantages of the different allocation methods

A survey of UK chemical and oil refining companies by Slater and Wootton (1984) reported the following methods of allocating joint costs:

	%
Physical measures method	76
Sales value method	5
Negotiated basis	19
Other	14

Note

The percentages add up to more than 100% because some companies used more than one method.

The analysis by industry indicated that the following methods were used:

Type of company	Predominant cost allocation method used
Petrochemicals	Sales value at split-off point or estimated net realizable method
Coal processing	Physical measures method
Coal chemicals	Physical measures method
Oil refining	No allocation of joint costs

EXHIBIT 7.2

Surveys of company practice

IRRELEVANCE OF JOINT COST ALLOCATIONS FOR DECISION-MAKING

So far, we have concentrated on the allocation of joint costs for the purposes of inventory valuation and profit measurement. Joint product costs that have been computed for inventory valuation are normally inappropriate for decision-making. You will remember from Chapter 2 that for decision-making, only relevant costs should be used and that these represent the incremental costs relating to a decision. Costs that will be unaffected by a decision are classed as irrelevant. Joint-cost allocations are thus irrelevant for decision-making. Consider the information presented in Example 7.3, which shows the additional revenue and costs involved in converting product M into product Z.

A joint cost of £1 000 000 will be incurred irrespective of which decision is taken, and is not relevant for this decision. The information which is required for the decision is a comparison of the additional costs with the additional revenues from converting product Y into product Z. The following information should therefore be provided:

Additional revenue and costs from converting product Y into product Z	(£)
Additional revenues (50 000 × £2)	100 000
Additional conversion costs	60 000
Additional profit from conversion	40 000

EXAMPLE 7.3

The Adriatic Company incurs joint product costs of £1 000 000 for the production of two joint products, X and Y. Both products can be sold at split-off point. However, if additional costs of £60 000 are incurred on product Y then it can be converted into product Z and sold for £10 per unit. The joint costs and the sales revenue at split-off point are illustrated in the following diagram:

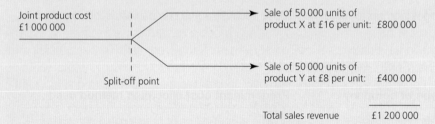

You are requested to advise management whether or not product Y should be converted in product Z.

The proof that profits will increase by £40 000 if conversion takes place is as follows:

	Convert to product Z (£)	Do not convert (£)
Sales	1 300 000	1 200 000
Total costs	1 060 000	1 000 000
Profits	240 000	200 000

The general rule is that it will be profitable to extend the processing of a joint product as long as the additional revenues exceed the additional costs.

ACCOUNTING FOR BY-PRODUCTS

By-products are products that have a minor sales value and that emerge incidentally from the production of the major product. As the major objective of the company is to produce the joint products, it can justifiably be argued that the joint costs should be allocated only to the joint products and that the by-products should not be allocated with any portion of the joint cost that are incurred before the split-off point. Any further costs that are incurred in producing by-products after the split-off point can justifiably be charged to the by-product, since such costs are incurred for the benefit of the by-product only.

By-product revenues or by-product net revenues (the sales revenue of the by-product less the additional further processing costs after the split-off point) should be deducted from the cost of the joint products or the main product from which it emerges. Consider Example 7.4.

None of the joint costs shown in Example 7.4 is allocated to the by-product but the further processing costs of £5000 (5000 kg × £1) are charged to the by-product. The net revenues

EXAMPLE 7.4

The Neopolitan Company operates a manufacturing process which produces joint products A and B and by-product C. The joint costs of the manufacturing process are £3 020 000, incurred in the manufacture of:

Product A	30 000 kg
Product B	50 000 kg
Product C	5 000 kg

By-product C requires further processing at a cost of £1 per kg, after which it can be sold at £5 per kg.

from the by-product of £20 000 (sales revenue of £25 000 less further processing costs of £5000) are deducted from the costs of the joint process (£3 020 000). Thus joint costs of £3 000 000 will be allocated to joint products A and B using one of the allocation methods described in this chapter. The accounting entries for the by-product will be as follows:

Dr By-product stock (5000 × £4)	20 000	
Cr Joint process WIP account		20 000

With the net revenue due from the production of the by-product:

Dr By-product stock	5000	
Cr Cash		5000

REAL WORLD VIEWS 7.2

Environmentally friendly products from paper-mill sludge

Each year, the paper and pulp industry produces millions of tons of sludge in the production of paper. This sludge is typically disposed of in landfill sites or incinerated. Both disposal methods are costly and environmentally undesirable. However, some firms are now transforming undesirable by-products into commercially viable consumer and industrial products.

One such firm is Kadant Grantek Inc, based in Wisconsin, USA. Kadant Grantek process paper mill sludge from local paper mills at a rate of approximately 250 tons per day. The sludge is dried and granulated to make a number of products – an agricultural seed carrier called Biodac, an industrial absorbent called Gran-sorb and a cat litter called PaPurr. The process is clean, releasing only steam into the atmosphere. No waste or further by-products are produced.

Kadant Grantek collect the paper mill sludge free of charge from the paper mills. The paper mills in turn do not incur landfill or incineration costs and can portray a greener image. A win–win situation for both parties.

Discussion point

- Assuming paper mills decide to sell their sludge for a small fee, how might they account for the revenue generated?

With the separable manufacturing costs incurred:

Dr Cash	25 000	
Cr By-product stock		25 000

With the value of by-products sales for the period.

SUMMARY

The following items relate to the learning objectives listed at the beginning of the chapter.

- **Distinguish between joint products and by-products.** Both joint products and by-products arise from a joint production process whereby they are not separately identifiable until after they have emerged from this joint process. Joint products have relatively high sales value while by-products have a low sales value compared with the sales value of a joint product. Joint products are also crucial to the commercial viability of an organization, whereas by-products are incidental.

- **Explain and identify the split-off point in a joint cost situation.** The split-off point is the point in the process when products become separately identifiable.

- **Explain the alternative methods of allocating joint costs to products.** Four different methods of allocating joint costs to products were described – physical measures, sales value at split-off point, net realizable value and gross profit percentage methods. The physical measures method simply allocates joint costs to individual products in proportion to their production volumes. The sales value at split-off point method allocates joint costs to individual products based on their sales value at split-off point. If market prices of products at the split-off point do not exist, the sales value can be estimated using the net realizable method. Here, the net realizable values of the joint products at split-off point are estimated by deducting the further processing costs from the sales value at the point of sale. The gross profit percentage method allocates joint costs so that the overall gross profit percentage is identical for each product.

- **Discuss the arguments for and against each of the methods of allocating joint costs to products.** Cost should be allocated based on cause-and-effect relationships. Such relationships cannot be observed with joint products. When this situation occurs it is recommended that joint costs should be allocated based on the benefits received criterion. The advantage of the physical measures method is its simplicity but it suffers from the disadvantage that it can lead to a situation where the recorded joint cost inventory valuation for a product is in excess of its net realizable value. The sales value at split-off point suffers from the disadvantage that sales values for many joint products do not exist at the split-off point. The gross profit percentage method assumes that there is a uniform relationship between cost and sales value for each product. However, such a relationship is questionable since identical gross profit percentages for individual products in multi-product companies that do not have joint costs are not observed. Both the sales value at split-off point and the net realizable value methods most closely meet the benefits received criterion but the latter is likely to be the preferred method if sales values at the split-off point do not exist.

- **Present relevant financial information for a decision as to whether a product should be sold at a particular stage or further processed.** The joint costs allocated to products are irrelevant for decisions relating to further processing. Such decisions should be based on a comparison of the incremental costs with the incremental revenues arising from further processing. The presentation of relevant financial information for further processing decisions was illustrated using the data presented in Example 7.3.

- **Describe the accounting treatment of by-products.** By-product net revenues should be deducted from the cost of the joint production process prior to allocating these costs to the individual joint products. The accounting treatment of by-products was illustrated with the data presented in Example 7.4.

KEY TERMS AND CONCEPTS

By-products products that are incidental to the production of joint products and have a low relative sales value.

Constant gross profit percentage method a method that allocates joint costs so that the overall gross profit percentage is the same for each product.

Further processing costs costs incurred by a joint product or by-product after the split-off point and can be traced to the product involved.

Joint products products that have a high relative sales value and are crucial to the commercial viability of the organization.

Net realizable value method the method that allocates joint costs on the basis of net realizable value at the split-off point, which is calculated by deducting further processing costs from sales revenues.

Physical measures method a method that allocates joint costs in proportion to volume.

Sales value at split-off point method a method that allocates joint costs in proportion to the estimated sales value of production.

Split-off point the point in a production process at which a joint product or by-product separates from the other products.

KEY EXAMINATION POINTS

It is necessary to apportion joint costs to joint products for inventory valuation and profit measurement purposes. Remember that the costs calculated for inventory valuation purposes should not be used for decision-making purposes. Examination questions normally require joint product cost calculations and the presentation of information as to whether a product should be sold at split-off point or further processed (see the answers to Review problems 7.15–7.17). A common mistake with the latter requirement is to include joint cost apportionments. You should compare incremental revenues with incremental costs and indicate that, in the short term, joint costs are not relevant to the decision to sell at the split-off point or process further.

ASSESSMENT MATERIAL

The review questions are short questions that enable you to assess your understanding of the main topics included in the chapter. The numbers in parentheses provide you with the page numbers to refer to if you cannot answer a specific question.

The review problems are more complex and require you to relate and apply the chapter content to various business problems. The problems are graded by their level of difficulty. The multiple-choice questions are the least demanding and normally take less than 10 minutes to complete. Fully worked solutions to the review problems are provided in a separate section at the end of the book. Further review problems with solutions for this chapter are available on the accompanying website www.drury-online.com. The website includes a *Student's Manual* and an *Instructor's Manual.* Students can access both questions and answers from the *Student's Manual* and the questions from the *Instructor's Manual*. The answers to problems in the *Instructor's Manual* are available only to lecturers on the lecturer's password-protected section of the website.

REVIEW QUESTIONS

7.1 Define joint costs, split-off point and further processing costs. *(p. 168)*

7.2 Distinguish between joint products and by-products. *(p. 168)*

7.3 Provide examples of industries that produce both joint products and by-products. *(p. 168)*

7.4 Explain why it is necessary to allocate joint costs to products. *(pp. 168–69)*

7.5 Describe the four different methods of allocating joint costs to products. *(pp. 169–73)*

7.6 Why is the physical measure method considered to be an unsatisfactory joint-cost allocation method? *(p. 170)*

7.7 Explain the factors that should influence the choice of method when allocating joint costs to products. *(p. 174)*

7.8 Explain the financial information that should be included in a decision as to whether a product should be sold at the split-off point or further processed. *(pp. 175–76)*

7.9 Describe the accounting treatment of by-products. *(pp. 176–77)*

REVIEW PROBLEMS

7.10 A company simultaneously produces three products (X, Y and Z) from a single process. X and Y are processed further before they can be sold; Z is a by-product that is sold immediately for $6 per unit without incurring any further costs. The sales prices of X and Y after further processing are $50 per unit and $60 per unit respectively. Data for October are as follows:

	$
Joint production costs that produced 2500 units of X, 3500 units of Y and 3000 units of Z	140 000
Further processing costs for 2500 units of X	24 000
Further processing costs for 3500 units of Y	46 000

Joint costs are apportioned using the final sales value method.

Calculate the total cost of the production of X for October.

CIMA P1 Management Accounting: Performance Evaluation

7.11 In a process where there are no work-in-progress stocks, two joint products (J and K) are created. Information (in units) relating to last month is as follows:

Product	Sales	Opening stock of finished goods	Closing stock of finished goods
J	6000	100	300
K	4000	400	200

Joint production costs last month were £110,000 and these were apportioned to the joint products based on the number of units produced.

What were the joint production costs apportioned to product J for last month?

(a) £63 800

(b) £64 000

(c) £66 000

(d) £68 200

ACCA Financial Information for Management

7.12 Two products (W and X) are created from a joint process. Both products can be sold immediately after spilt-off. There are no opening inventories or work-in-progress. The following information is available for last period:

Total joint production costs $776 160

Product	Production units	Sales units	Selling price per unit
W	12 000	10 000	$10
X	10 000	8000	$12

Using the sales value method of apportioning joint production costs, what was the value of the closing inventory of product X for last period?

(a) $68 992

(b) $70 560

(c) $76 032

(d) £77 616

ACCA F2 Management Accounting

7.13 The output of a process consists of two joint products, Jointpro A and Jointpro B, and a by-product. Jointpro B could go through a further process in order to increase its sales value. To assist management in making the decision whether to carry out further processing, which ONE of the following is relevant?

(a) The share of the total processing cost which has been allocated to Jointpro B.

(b) The sales value of Jointpro A and the by-product.

(c) The physical quantities of all three products at separation point.

(d) The cost of further processing Jointpro B and the increase in sales value that will result.

CIMA – Management Accounting Fundamentals

7.14 At the end of manufacturing in Process I, product K can be sold for £10 per litre. Alternatively, product K could be further processed into product KK in process II at an additional cost of £1 per litre input into this process. Process II is an existing process with spare capacity in which a loss of 10 per cent of the input volume occurs. At the end of the further process, product KK could be sold for £12 per litre. Which of the following statements is correct in respect of 9000 litres of product K?

(a) Further processing into product KK would increase profits by £9000.

(b) Further processing into product KK would increase profits by £8100.

(c) Further processing into product KK would decrease profits by £900.

(d) Further processing into product KK would decrease profits by £1800.

ACCA Financial Information for Management

7.15 Joint cost apportionment and decisions on further processing
A process costing £200 000 produces 3 products – A, B and C. Output details are as follows:

Product A	6000 litres
Product B	10 000 litres
Product C	20 000 tonnes

Each product may be sold at the completion of the process as follows:

	Sales value at the end of the first process
Product A	£10 per litre
Product B	£4 per litre
Product C	£10 per tonne

Alternatively, further processing of each individual product can be undertaken to produce an enhanced product thus:

	Subsequent processing costs	Sales value after final process
Enhanced Product A	£14 per litre	£20 per litre
Enhanced Product B	£2 per litre	£8 per litre
Enhanced Product C	£6 per tonne	£16 per tonne

Required:

(a) Explain the following terms:

   (i)   normal process loss;

   (ii) joint product;

   (iii) by-product;

   and state the appropriate costing treatments for normal process loss and for by-products.

   (10 marks)

(b) Calculate the apportionment of joint process costs to products A, B and C above.

   (8 marks)

(c) Explain whether the initial process should be undertaken and which, if any, of the enhanced products should be produced.

   (7 marks)
   AAT

7.16 Process costing and a decision on further processing

Corcoran Ltd operated several manufacturing processes. In process G, joint products (P1 and P2) are created in the ratio 5:3 by volume from the raw materials input. In this process a normal loss of 5 per cent of the raw material input is expected. Losses have a realizable value of £5 per litre. The company holds no work-in-progress. The joint costs are apportioned to the joint products using the physical measure basis.

The following information relates to process G for last month:

Raw materials input	60 000 litres (at a cost of £381 000)
Abnormal gain	1000 litres
Other costs incurred:	
Direct labour	£180 000
Direct expenses	£54 000
Production overheads	110% of direct labour cost

(a) Prepare the process G account for last month in which both the output volumes and values for each of the joint products are shown separately.

   (7 marks)

The company can sell product P1 for £20 per litre at the end of process G. It is considering a proposal to further process P1 in process H in order to create product PP1. Process H has sufficient spare capacity to do this work. The further processing in process H would cost £4 per litre input from process G. In process H there would be a normal loss in volume of 10 per cent of the input to that process. This loss has no realizable value. Product PP1 could then be sold for £26 per litre.

(b) Determine, based on financial considerations only, whether product P1 should be further processed to create product PP1.

   (3 marks)

(c)   In the context of process G in Corcoran Ltd, explain the difference between 'direct expenses' and 'production overheads'.

(2 marks)
(12 marks)
ACCA Financial Information for Management

7.17   Process costing and a decision on further processing

Luiz Ltd operates several manufacturing processes in which stocks of work-in-progress are never held. In process K, joint products (P1 and P2) are created in the ratio 2:1 by volume from the raw materials input. In this process a normal loss of 4 per cent of the raw materials input is expected. Losses have a realizable value of £5 per litre. The joint costs of the process are apportioned to the joint products using the sales value basis. At the end of process K, P1 and P2 can be sold for £25 and £40 per litre respectively.

The following information relates to process K for last month:

Raw material input	90 000 litres at a total cost of £450 000
Actual loss incurred	4800 litres
Conversion costs incurred	£216 000

Required:

(a)   Prepare the process K account for last month in which both the output volumes and values for each joint product are shown separately.

(7 marks)

The company could further process product P1 in process L to create product XP1 at an incremental cost of £3 per litre input. Process L is an existing process with spare capacity. In process L a normal loss of 8 per cent of input is incurred which has no value. Product XP1 could be sold for £30 per litre.

Required:

(b)   Based on financial considerations only, determine, with supporting calculations, whether product P1 should be further processed in process L to create product XP1.

(3 marks)
(10 marks)
ACCA Financial Information for Management

CHAPTER 8
INCOME EFFECTS OF ALTERNATIVE COST ACCUMULATION SYSTEMS

LEARNING OBJECTIVES

After studying this chapter, you should be able to:

● explain the differences between an absorption costing and a variable costing system;

● prepare profit statements based on a variable costing and absorption costing system;

● explain the difference in profits between variable and absorption costing profit calculations;

● explain the arguments for and against variable and absorption costing.

In the previous chapters we looked at the procedures necessary to ascertain product or job costs for inventory valuation to meet the requirements of external reporting. The approach that we adopted was to allocate all manufacturing cost to products, and to value unsold stocks at their total cost of manufacture. Non-manufacturing costs were not allocated to the products but were charged directly to the profit statement and excluded from the inventory valuation. A costing system based on these principles is known as an **absorption** or **full costing system**.

In this chapter we are going to look at an alternative costing system known as **variable costing, marginal costing** or **direct costing**. Under this system, only variable manufacturing costs are assigned to products and included in the inventory valuation. Fixed manufacturing costs are not allocated to the product, but are considered as period costs and charged directly to the profit statement. With both systems, non-manufacturing costs are treated as period costs. The difference between the systems lies in whether or not manufacturing fixed overhead should be regarded as a period cost or a product cost. An illustration of the contrasting treatment of fixed manufacturing overhead for both absorption and variable costing systems is shown in Exhibit 8.1. You should note that here direct labour is assumed to be a variable cost. Generally direct labour is not a short term variable cost that varies in direct proportion to the volume of activity. It is a step fixed cost (see Chapter 2) that varies in the longer term. In other words, it is a longer term variable cost. Because of this, variable costing systems generally assume that direct labour is a variable cost.

EXTERNAL AND INTERNAL REPORTING

There are arguments for and against the use of variable costing for inventory valuation for the purpose of external reporting. One important requirement for external reporting is consistency. It would be unacceptable if companies changed their methods of inventory valuation from year-to-year and inter-company comparison would be difficult if some companies valued their stocks on an absorption cost basis while others did so on a variable cost basis. Furthermore, the users of external accounting reports need the reassurance that the published financial statements have been prepared in accordance with generally accepted standards of good accounting practice. Therefore. there is a strong case for the acceptance of one method of stock valuation for external reporting. In the UK a *Statement of Standard Accounting Practice on Stocks and Work in Progress* was published by the Accounting Standards Committee (SSAP 9). This states:

In order to match costs and revenue, cost of stocks and work in progress should comprise that expenditure which has been incurred in the normal course of business in bringing the product or service to its present location and condition. Such costs will include all related production overheads, even though these may accrue on a time basis.

The effect of this statement in SSAP 9 was to require absorption costing for external reporting and for non-manufacturing costs to be treated as period costs. The International Accounting Standard on Inventories (IAS 2) also requires that companies in other countries adopt absorption costing.

In spite of the fact that absorption costing is required for external reporting, the variable costing versus absorption costing debate is still of considerable importance for internal reporting. Management normally require profit statements at monthly or quarterly intervals, and will demand separate profit statements for each major product group or segment of the business. This information is particularly useful in evaluating the performance of divisional managers. Management must therefore decide whether absorption costing or variable costing provides the more meaningful information in assessing the economic and managerial performance of the different segments of the business.

Before discussing the arguments for and against absorption and variable costing, let us look at an illustration of both methods using Example 8.1. To keep things simple we shall assume that the company in this example produces only one product using a single overhead rate for the company

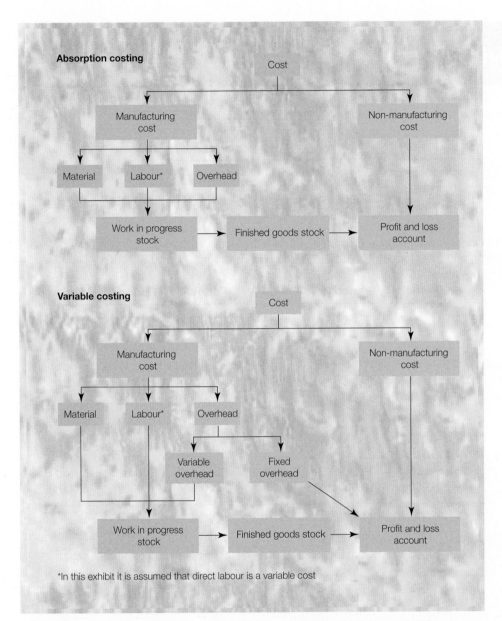

EXHIBIT 8.1
Absorption and variable costing systems

*In this exhibit it is assumed that direct labour is a variable cost

as a whole, with units of output being used as the allocation base. These assumptions are very simplistic but the same general principles can be applied in more complex product settings.

VARIABLE COSTING

The variable costing profit statements are shown in Exhibit 8.2. You will see that when a system of variable costing is used, the product cost is £6 per unit, and includes variable costs only. In period 1 production is 150 000 units at a variable cost of £6 per unit. The total fixed costs are then added separately to produce a total manufacturing cost of £1 200 000. Note that the fixed costs of £300 000 are assigned to the period in which they are incurred.

EXAMPLE 8.1

The following information is available for periods 1–6 for the Hoque Company:

	(£)
Unit selling price	10
Unit variable cost	6
Fixed costs per each period	300 000

The company produces only one product. Budgeted activity is expected to average 150 000 units per period, and production and sales for each period are as follows:

	Period 1	Period 2	Period 3	Period 4	Period 5	Period 6
Units sold (000s)	150	120	180	150	140	160
Units produced (000s)	150	150	150	150	170	140

There were no opening stocks at the start of period 1, and the actual manufacturing fixed overhead incurred was £300 000 per period. We shall also assume that non-manufacturing overheads are £100 000 per period.

	Period 1 (£000s)	Period 2 (£000s)	Period 3 (£000s)	Period 4 (£000s)	Period 5 (£000s)	Period 6 (£000s)
Opening stock	—	—	180	—	—	180
Production cost	900	900	900	900	1020	840
Closing stock	—	(180)	—	—	(180)	(60)
Cost of sales	900	720	1080	900	840	960
Fixed costs	300	300	300	300	300	300
Total costs	1200	1020	1380	1200	1140	1260
Sales	1500	1200	1800	1500	1400	1600
Gross profit	300	180	420	300	260	340
Less non-manufacturing costs	100	100	100	100	100	100
Net profit	200	80	320	200	160	240

EXHIBIT 8.2

Variable costing statements

In period 2, 150 000 units are produced but only 120 000 are sold. Therefore 30 000 units remain in stock at the end of the period. In order to match costs with revenues, the sales of 120 000 units should be matched with costs for 120 000. As 150 000 units were produced, we need to value the 30 000 units in stock and deduct this sum from the production cost. Using the variable costing system, the 30 000 units in stock are valued at £6 per unit. A closing inventory of £180 000 will then be deducted from the production costs, giving a cost of sales figure of £720 000. Note that the closing inventory valuation does not include any fixed overheads.

The 30 000 units of closing inventory in period 2 becomes the opening inventory for period 3 and therefore an expense for this period. The production cost for the 150 000 units made in period 3 is added to this opening inventory valuation. The overall effect is that costs for 180 000 units are matched against sales for 180 000 units. The profits for periods 4–6 are calculated in the same way.

ABSORPTION COSTING

Let us now consider in Exhibit 8.3 the profit calculations when closing stocks are valued on an absorption costing basis. With the absorption costing method, a share of the fixed production overheads are allocated to individual products and are included in their production cost. Fixed overheads are assigned to products by establishing overhead absorption rates as described in Chapter 4. To establish the overhead rate we must divide the fixed overheads of £300 000 for the period by an appropriate denominator level. Most companies use an annual budgeted activity measure of the overhead allocation base as the denominator level. Our allocation base in Example 8.1 is units of output and we shall assume that the annual budgeted output is 1 800 000 units giving an average for each monthly period of 150 000 units. Therefore, the budgeted fixed overhead rate is £2 per unit (£300 000/150 000 units). The product cost now consists of a variable cost (£6) plus a fixed manufacturing cost (£2), making a total of £8 per unit. Hence, the production cost for period 1 is £1 200 000 (150 000 units at £8).

Now compare the absorption costing statement (Exhibit 8.3) with the variable costing statement (Exhibit 8.2) for period 1. With absorption costing, the fixed cost is included in the production cost figure, whereas with variable costing only the variable cost is included. With variable costing, the fixed cost is allocated separately as a lump sum and is not included in the cost of sales figure. Note also that the closing inventory of 30 000 units for period 2 is valued at £8 per unit in the absorption costing statement, whereas the closing inventory is valued at only £6 in the variable costing statement.

	Period 1 (£000s)	Period 2 (£000s)	Period 3 (£000s)	Period 4 (£000s)	Period 5 (£000s)	Period 6 (£000s)
Opening stock	—	—	240	—	—	240
Production cost	1200	1200	1200	1200	1360	1120
Closing stock	—	(240)	—	—	(240)	(80)
Cost of sales	1200	960	1440	1200	1120	1280
Adjustments for under/(over) recovery of overhead	—	—	—	—	(40)	20
Total costs	1200	960	1440	1200	1080	1300
Sales	1500	1200	1800	1500	1400	1600
Gross profit	300	240	360	300	320	300
Less non-manufacturing costs	100	100	100	100	100	100
Net profit	200	140	260	200	220	200

EXHIBIT 8.3

Absorption costing statements

In calculating profits, the matching principle that has been applied in the absorption costing statement is the same as that described for variable costing. However, complications arise in periods 5 and 6; in period 5, 170 000 units were produced, so the production cost of £1 360 000 includes fixed overheads of £340 000 (170 000 units at £2). The total fixed overheads incurred for the period are only £300 000, so £40 000 too much has been allocated. This over recovery of fixed overhead is recorded as a **period cost adjustment**. (A full explanation of under- and over-recoveries of overheads and the reasons for period cost adjustments was presented in Chapter 4; if you are unsure of this concept, please refer back now to the section headed 'Under- and over-recovery of overheads'.) Note also that the under- or over-recovery of fixed overheads is also called **volume variance**.

In period 6, 140 000 units were produced at a cost of £1 120 000, which included only £280 000 (140 000 units at £2) for fixed overheads. As a result, there is an under recovery of £20 000, which is written off as a period cost. You can see that an under or over recovery of fixed overhead occurs whenever actual production differs from the budged average level of activity of 150 000 units, since the calculation of the fixed overhead rate of £2 per unit was based on the assumption that actual production would be 150 000 units per period. Note that both variable and absorption costing systems do not assign non-manufacturing costs to products for stock valuation.

VARIABLE COSTING AND ABSORPTION COSTING: A COMPARISON OF THEIR IMPACT ON PROFIT

A comparison of the variable costing and absorption costing statements produced from the information contained in Example 8.1 reveals the following differences in profit calculations:

(a)   The profits calculated under the absorption costing and variable costing systems are identical for periods 1 and 4.
(b)   The absorption costing profits are higher than the variable costing profits in periods 2 and 5.
(c)   The variable costing profits are higher than the absorption costing profits in periods 3 and 6.

Let us now consider each of these in a little more detail.

Production equals sales

In periods 1 and 4 the profits are the same for both methods of costing; in both periods production is equal to sales, and inventories will neither increase nor decrease. Therefore, if opening inventories exist, the same amount of fixed overhead will be carried forward as an expense to be included in the current period in the opening inventory valuation as will be deducted in the closing inventory valuation from the production cost figure. The overall effect is that, with an absorption costing system, the only fixed overhead that will be included as an expense for the period will be the amount of fixed overhead that is incurred for the period. Thus, whenever sales are equal to production the profits will be the same for both the absorption costing and variable costing systems.

Production exceeds sales

In periods 2 and 5 the absorption costing system produces higher profits; in both periods production exceeds sales. Profits are higher for absorption costing when production is in excess of sales, because inventories are increasing. A greater amount of fixed overheads in the closing inventory is being deducted from the expenses of the period than is being brought forward in the opening inventory for the period. For example, in period 2 the opening inventory is zero and no fixed overheads are brought forward from the previous period. However, a closing inventory of 30 000 units means that £60 000 fixed overhead has to be deducted from the production cost for the period. In other words, only £240 000 is being allocated for fixed overhead with the absorption costing system, whereas the variable costing system allocates the £300 000 fixed overhead incurred for the period. The effect of this is that profits are £60 000 greater with the absorption costing system. As a general rule, if production is in excess of sales, the absorption costing system will show a higher profit than the variable costing system.

Sales exceed production

In periods 3 and 6 the variable costing system produces higher profits; in both periods sales exceed production. When this situation occurs, inventories decline and a greater amount of fixed overheads will need to be brought forward as an expense in the opening inventory than is being deducted in the closing inventory adjustment. With the absorption costing system, in period 6, 30 000 units of opening inventory are brought forward, so that fixed costs of £60 000 are included in the inventory valuation. However, a closing inventory of 10 000 units requires a deduction of £20 000 fixed overheads from the production costs. The overall effect is that an additional £40 000 fixed overheads is included as an expense within the stock movements, and a total of £340 000 fixed overheads is allocated for the period. In contrast, the variable costing system would allocate fixed overheads for the period of only £300 000. As a result, profits are £40 000 greater with the variable costing system. As a general rule, if sales are in excess of production, the variable costing system will show a higher profit than the absorption costing system.

Impact of sales fluctuations

The profit calculations for an absorption costing system can produce some strange results. For example, in period 6 the sales volume has increased but profits have declined, in spite of the fact that both the selling price and the cost structure have remained unchanged. A manager whose performance is being judged in period 6 is likely to have little confidence in an accounting system that produces this information. The opposite occurs in period 5, when the sales volume declines but profit increases. The situations in periods 5 and 6 arise because the under- or over-recovery of fixed overhead is treated as a period cost, and such adjustments can at times give a misleading picture of profits.

In contrast, the variable costing profit calculations show that when sales volume increases profit also increases. Alternatively, when sales volume decreases, profit also decreases. These relationships continue as long as the selling price and cost structure remain unchanged. Looking again at the variable costing profit calculations, you will note that profit declines in period 5 when the sales volume declines, and increases in period 6 when the sales volume also increases. The reasons for these changes are that, with a system of variable costing, profit is a function of sales volume only, when the selling price and cost structure remain unchanged. However, with absorption costing, profit is a function of both sales volume and production volume.

A MATHEMATICAL MODEL OF THE PROFIT FUNCTIONS

In this section simple mathematical formulae are used to calculate the profits reported by variable and absorption costing systems. You may omit this section if you do not wish to use mathematical formulae. Formula (8.1) shows the profit function for an absorption costing system when unit costs remain unchanged throughout the period (you can refer to Appendix 8.1 for an explanation of how this formula has been derived).

$$OPBT_{AC} = (ucm - ufmc)Q_s + (ufmc \times Q_p) - FC \qquad (8.1)$$

where

ucm	= Contribution margin per unit (i.e. selling price per unit – variable cost per unit)
ufmc	= Predetermined fixed manufacturing overhead per unit of output
Q_p	= Number of units produced
Q_s	= Number of units sold
FC	= Total fixed costs (manufacturing and non-manufacturing)
$OPBT_{AC}$	= Operating profit before taxes for the period (Absorption costing)
$OPBT_{VC}$	= Operating profit before taxes for the period (Variable costing)

Applying formula 8.1 to the data given in Example 8.1 gives the following profit function:

$$(£4 - £2)Q_s + (£2 \times Q_p) - £400\,000 = £2Q_s + £2Q_p - £400\,000$$

Applying the above profit function to periods 4–6 we get:

$$Period\ 4 = £2(150\,000) + £2(150\,000) - £400\,000 = £200\,000$$
$$Period\ 5 = £2(140\,000) + £2(170\,000) - £400\,000 = £220\,000$$
$$Period\ 6 = £2(160\,000) + £2(140\,000) - £400\,000 = £200\,000$$

When production equals sales identical profits with an absorption and variable costing system are reported. Therefore formula 8.1 converts to the following variable costing profit function if we let $Q_s = Q_p$:

$$Variable\ costing\ operating\ profit = ucm \cdot Q_s - FC \qquad (8.2)$$

Using the data given in Example 8.1 the profit function is:

$$£4Q_s - £400\,000$$

Applying the above profit function to periods 4–6 we get:

$$Period\ 4 = £4(150\,000) - £400\,000 = £200\,000$$
$$Period\ 5 = £4(140\,000) - £400\,000 = £160\,000$$
$$Period\ 6 = £4(160\,000) - £400\,000 = £240\,000$$

The difference between the reported operating profits for an absorption costing and a variable costing system can be derived by deducting formulae 8.2 from 8.1 giving:

$$\text{ufmc}(Q_p - Q_s) \tag{8.3}$$

If you look closely at the above term you will see that it represents the inventory change (in units) multiplied by the fixed manufacturing overhead rate. Applying formula 8.3 to period 5 the inventory change $(Q_p - Q_s)$ is 30 000 units (positive) so that absorption costing profits exceed variable costing profits by £60 000 (30 000 units at £2 overhead rate). For an explanation of how formulae (8.1) and (8.2) are derived you should refer to Appendix 8.1.

SOME ARGUMENTS IN SUPPORT OF VARIABLE COSTING

Variable costing provides more useful information for decision-making

The separation of fixed and variable costs helps to provide relevant information about costs for making decisions. Relevant costs are required for a variety of short-term decisions, for example whether to make a component internally or to purchase externally, as well as problems relating to product-mix. These decisions will be discussed in Chapter 10. In addition, the estimation of costs for different levels of activities requires that costs be split into their fixed and variable elements. Supporters of variable costing contend that the projection of future costs and revenues for different activity levels, and the use of relevant cost decision-making techniques, are possible only if a variable costing system is adopted. There is no reason, however, why an absorption costing system cannot be used for profit measurement and inventory valuation and costs can be analyzed into their fixed and variable elements for decision-making. The advantage of variable costing is that the analysis of variable and fixed costs is highlighted while such an analysis is not a required feature of an absorption costing system.

Variable costing removes from profit the effect of inventory changes

We have seen that, with variable costing, profit is a function of sales volume, whereas, with absorption costing, profit is a function of both sales and production. We have also learned, using absorption costing principles, that it is possible for profit to decline when sales volumes increase. Where stock levels are likely to fluctuate significantly, profits may be distorted when they are calculated on an absorption costing basis, since the stock changes will significantly affect the amount of fixed overheads allocated to an accounting period.

Fluctuating stock levels are less likely to occur when one measures profits on an annual basis, but on a monthly or quarterly basis, seasonal variations in sales may cause significant fluctuations. As profits are likely to be distorted by an absorption costing system, there are strong arguments for using variable costing methods when profits are measured at frequent intervals and stock levels fluctuate from month to month.. Because frequent profit statements are presented only for management, the argument for variable costing is stronger for management accounting. A survey by Drury and Tayles (2006) relating to 187 UK companies reported that 84 per cent of the companies prepared profit statements at monthly or quarterly intervals. Financial accounts are presented for public release annually or at half-yearly intervals; because significant changes in stock levels are less likely on an annual basis, the argument for the use of variable costing in financial accounting is not as strong.

A further argument for using variable costing for internal reporting is that the internal profit statements may be used as a basis for measuring managerial performance and absorption costing provides opportunities for unscrupulous managers to manipulate the figures. For example, it would be possible for a manager to deliberately defer some of the fixed overhead allocation by unnecessarily increasing stocks over successive periods.

However, there is a limit to how long managers can continue to increase stocks, and eventually the situation will arise when it is necessary to reduce them, and the deferred fixed overheads will eventually be allocated to the periods when the inventories are reduced. Senior management can also implement control performance measures to guard against such behaviour. Nevertheless, there is likely to remain some scope for distorting profits in the short term.

REAL WORLD VIEWS 8.1

Tools and techniques used by management accountants

The Chartered Institute of Management Accountants (CIMA) in London undertake regular surveys of the tools and techniques used by management accountants in practice. As a discipline, management accounting is of course free to use whatever techniques fit the job and is not bound by regulations.

A global CIMA survey in summer 2009 of almost 500 management accountants provides a good snapshot of the tools and techniques used. One portion of the survey reports on the operational tools used, which includes how the respondent organizations cost products and services. Variable (or marginal) costing is a technique which focuses on just variable costs when calculating the cost of a product or service. Fixed costs are not attributed to unit costs. Instead, fixed costs are treated as a total figure in any profit statements prepared for management use. The CIMA survey reports that close to 40 per cent of respondents use variable costing as a tool to cost their products or services. Its use was quite evenly spread among all firms, from small to very large organizations.

An alternative to variable costing is of course the traditional absorption costing approach which allo-cates overheads and other fixed costs to the product or service cost. This technique remains extremely popular, with approximately 75 per cent of respondents indicating use of overhead allocation of some form. CIMA also report that, on average, an organization uses 4 of the 14 techniques included in the survey. The number of techniques increases with the size of the organization. This means that an organization might use both variable and absorption costing as part of its repertoire on management accounting techniques.

Questions

1 When might calculating profits using variable costing techniques be more useful to managers?

2 What effect would the use of variable costing have on product/services costs compared to allocating fixed costs? What effect would this have on profit?

References

'Management accounting tools for today and tomorrow', CIMA London, available at cimaglobal.com/ma

Variable costing avoids fixed overheads being capitalized in unsaleable stocks

In a period when sales demand decreases, a company can end up with surplus stocks on hand. With an absorption costing system, only a portion of the fixed overheads incurred during the period will be allocated as an expense because the remainder of the fixed overhead will be included in the valuation of the surplus stocks. If these surplus stocks cannot be disposed of, the profit calculation for the current period will be misleading, since fixed overheads will have been deferred to later accounting periods. However, there may be some delay before management concludes that the stocks cannot be sold without a very large reduction in the selling price. In the meantime, the stocks will be over-valued and the overall effect may be that the current period's profits will be overstated.

SOME ARGUMENTS IN SUPPORT OF ABSORPTION COSTING

Absorption costing does not understate the importance of fixed costs

Some people argue that decisions based on a variable costing system may concentrate only on sales revenues and variable costs and ignore the fact that fixed costs must be met in the long run. For example, if a pricing decision is based on variable costs only, then sales revenue may be insufficient to cover all the costs. It is also argued that the use of an absorption costing system, by allocating fixed costs to a product, ensures that fixed costs will be covered. In fact, these arguments are incorrect. Absorption costing will not ensure that fixed costs will be recovered if actual sales volume is less than the estimate used to calculate the fixed overhead rate. For example, consider a situation where fixed costs are £100 000 and an estimated normal activity of 10 000 units is used to calculate the overhead rate. Fixed costs are recovered at £10 per unit. Assume that variable cost is £5 per unit and selling price is set at £20 (total cost plus one-third). If actual sales volume is 5000 units then total sales revenue will be £100 000 and total costs will be £125 000. Total costs therefore exceed total sales revenue. The argument that a variable costing system will cause managers to ignore fixed costs is based on the assumption that such managers are not very bright! A failure to consider fixed costs is due to faulty management and not to a faulty accounting system. Furthermore, using variable costing for inventory valuation and profit measurement still enables full cost information to be extracted for pricing decisions.

Absorption costing avoids fictitious losses being reported

In a business that relies on seasonal sales and in which production is built up outside the sales season to meet demand, the full amount of fixed overheads incurred will be charged, in a variable costing system, against sales. However, in those periods where production is being built up for sales in a later season, sales revenue will be low but fixed costs will be recorded as an expense. The result is that losses will be reported during out-of-season periods, and large profits will be reported in the periods when the goods are sold.

By contrast, in an absorption costing system fixed overheads will be deferred and included in the closing inventory valuation, and will be recorded as an expense only in the period in which the goods are sold. Losses are therefore unlikely to be reported in the periods when stocks are being built up. In these circumstances absorption costing appears to provide the more logical profit calculation.

Fixed overheads are essential for production

The proponents of absorption costing argue that the production of goods is not possible if fixed manufacturing costs are not incurred. Consequently, fixed manufacturing overheads should be allocated to units produced and included in the inventory valuation.

Consistency with external reporting

Top management may prefer their internal profit reporting systems to be consistent with the external financial accounting absorption costing systems so that they will be congruent with the measures used by financial markets to appraise overall company performance. In a pilot study of six UK companies Hopper et al. (1992) observed that senior managers are primarily interested in financial accounting information because it is perceived as having a major influence on how financial markets evaluate companies and their management. If top management believe that financial accounting information does influence share prices then they are likely to use the same rules and procedures for both internal and external profit measurement and inventory valuation so that managers will focus on the same measures as those used by financial markets. The fact that managerial rewards are often linked to external financial measures provides a further motivation to ensure that internal accounting systems do not conflict with external financial accounting reporting requirements.

SUMMARY

The following items relate to the learning objectives listed at the beginning of the chapter.

- **Explain the differences between an absorption costing and a variable costing system.** With an absorption costing system, fixed manufacturing overheads are allocated to the products and these are included in the inventory valuations. With a variable costing system, only variable manufacturing costs are assigned to the product; fixed manufacturing costs are regarded as period costs and written off as a lump sum to the profit and loss account. Both variable and absorption costing systems treat non-manufacturing overheads as period costs.

- **Prepare profit statements based on a variable costing and absorption costing system.** With a variable costing system manufacturing fixed costs are added to the variable manufacturing cost of sales to determine total manufacturing costs to be deducted from sales revenues. Manufacturing fixed costs are assigned to products with an absorption costing system. Therefore, manufacturing cost of sales is valued at full cost (manufacturing variable costs plus manufacturing fixed costs). With an absorption costing system fixed manufacturing costs are unitized by dividing the total manufacturing costs by estimated output. If actual output differs from estimated output an under- or over-recovery of overheads arises. This is recorded as a period cost adjustment in the current accounting period.

- **Explain the difference in profits between variable and absorption costing profit calculations.** When production exceeds sales, absorption costing systems report higher profits. Variable costing systems yield higher profits when sales exceed production. Nevertheless, total profits over the life of the business will be the same for both systems. Differences arise merely in the profits attributed to each accounting period.

- **Explain the arguments for and against variable and absorption costing.** The proponents of variable costing claim that it enables more useful information to be presented for decision-making but such claims are questionable since similar relevant cost information can easily be extracted from an absorption costing system. The major advantage of variable costing is that profit is reflected as a function of sales, whereas, with an absorption costing system, profit is a function of both sales and production. It is possible with absorption costing, when all other factors remain unchanged, for sales to increase and profit to decline. In contrast, with a variable costing system, when sales increase, profits also increase. A further advantage of variable costing is that fixed overheads are not capitalized in unsaleable stocks. The arguments that have been made supporting absorption costing include: (a) absorption costing does not understate the importance of fixed costs; (b) absorption costing avoids the possibility of fictitious losses being reported; (c) fixed manufacturing overheads are essential to production and therefore should be incorporated in the product costs, and (d) internal profit measurement should be consistent with absorption costing profit measurement that is used for external reporting requirements.

APPENDIX 8.1: DERIVATION OF THE PROFIT FUNCTION FOR AN ABSORPTION COSTING SYSTEM

Using the notation listed in Exhibit 8A.1 the variable costing profit function can be expressed in equation form as follows:

$$
\begin{aligned}
\text{OPBT}_{VC} &= \text{Sales} - \text{Variable manufacturing costs of goods sold} \\
&\quad - \text{non-manufacturing variable costs} - \text{All fixed costs} \\
&= usp \cdot Q_s - uvmc \cdot Q_s - uvnmc \cdot Q_s - FC \qquad (8.A1) \\
&= ucm \cdot Q_s - FC \text{ (Note that the term contribution margin is used to} \\
&\quad \text{describe unit selling price less unit variable cost)}
\end{aligned}
$$

The distinguishable feature between absorption costing and variable costing relates to the timing of the recognition of fixed manufacturing overheads (FC_m) as an expense. Variable and absorption costing reported profits will differ by the amount of fixed manufacturing overheads that are included in the change in opening and closing inventories. This is equivalent to the difference between production and sales volumes multiplied by the manufacturing fixed overhead absorption rate.

ucm = Contribution margin per unit (i.e. selling price per unit – variable cost per unit)
usp = Selling price per unit
uvmc = Variable manufacturing cost per unit
uvnmc = Variable non-manufacturing cost per unit
ufmc = Predetermined fixed manufacturing overhead per unit of output
Q_p = Number of units produced
Q_s = Number of units sold
FC = Total fixed costs (manufacturing and non-manufacturing)
$OPBT_{AC}$ = Operating profit before taxes for the period (Absorption costing)
$OPBT_{VC}$ = Operating profit before taxes for the period (Variable costing)

EXHIBIT 8A.1
Summary of notation used

We can therefore use equation (8.A1) as the basis for establishing the equation for the absorption costing profit function:

$$OPBT_{AC} = ucm \cdot Q_s - FC + (Q_p - Q_s)ufmc$$
$$= ucm \cdot Q_s - FC + (Q_p \times ufmc) - (Q_s \times ufmc)$$
$$= (ucm - ufmc)Q_s + (ufmc \times Q_p) - FC$$

KEY TERMS AND CONCEPTS

Absorption costing system, or **full costing system** a costing system that allocates all manufacturing costs, including fixed manufacturing costs, to products and values unsold stocks at their total cost of manufacture.

Period cost adjustment the record of under- and over-recovery of fixed overheads at the end of a period.

Variable costing system, or **marginal costing system** or **direct costing system** a costing system that assigns only variable manufacturing costs, not fixed manufacturing costs, to products and includes them in the inventory valuation.

Volume variance another term used to refer to the under- or over-recovery of fixed overheads.

KEY EXAMINATION POINTS

A common mistake is for students to calculate *actual* overhead rates when preparing absorption costing profit statements. Normal or budgeted activity should be used to calculate overhead absorption rates, and this rate should be used to calculate the production overhead cost for all periods given in the question. Do not calculate different actual overhead rates for each accounting period.

Remember not to include non-manufacturing overheads in the inventory valuations for both variable and absorption costing. Also note that variable selling overheads will vary with sales and not production. Another common mistake is not to include an adjustment for under- or over-recovery of fixed overheads when actual production deviates from the normal or budgeted production. You should note that under- or over-recovery of overhead arises only with fixed overheads and when an absorption costing system is used.

The review questions are short questions that enable you to assess your understanding of the main topics included in the chapter. The numbers in parentheses provide you with the page numbers to refer to if you cannot answer a specific question.

The review problems are more complex and require you to relate and apply the chapter content to various business problems. The problems are graded by their level of difficulty. The multiple-choice questions are the least demanding and normally take less than 10 minutes to complete. Fully worked solutions to the review problems are provided in a separate section at the end of the book. Further review problems with solutions for this chapter are available on the accompanying website www.drury-online.com. The website includes a *Student's Manual* and an *Instructor's Manual*. Students can access both questions and answers from the *Student's Manual* and the questions from the *Instructor's Manual*. The answers to problems in the *Instructor's Manual* are available only to lecturers on the lecturer's password-protected section of the website.

REVIEW QUESTIONS

8.1 Distinguish between variable costing and absorption costing. *(pp. 185–86)*

8.2 How are non-manufacturing fixed costs treated under absorption and variable costing systems? *(p. 186)*

8.3 Describe the circumstances when variable and absorption costing systems will report identical profits. *(p. 190)*

8.4 Under what circumstances will absorption costing report higher profits than variable costing? *(p. 191)*

8.5 Under what circumstances will variable costing report higher profits than absorption costing? *(p. 191)*

8.6 What arguments can be advanced in favour of variable costing? *(pp. 193–95)*

8.7 What arguments can be advanced in favour of absorption costing? *(pp. 195–96)*

8.8 Explain how absorption costing can encourage managers to engage in behaviour that is harmful to the organization. *(p. 194)*

REVIEW PROBLEMS

8.9 WTD Ltd produces a single product. The management currently uses marginal costing but is considering using absorption costing in the future.

The budgeted fixed production overheads for the period are £500 000. The budgeted output for the period is 2000 units. There were 800 units of opening inventory at the beginning of the period and 500 units of closing inventory at the end of the period.

If absorption costing principles were applied, the profit for the period compared to the marginal costing profit would be:

(a) £75 000 higher

(b) £75 000 lower

(c) £125 000 higher

(d) £125 000 lower

(2 marks)

CIMA P1 Management Accounting: Performance Evaluation

8.10 The following information relates to a manufacturing company for next period:

	Units		£
Production	14 000	Fixed production costs	63 000
Sales	12 000	Fixed selling costs	12 000

Using the absorption costing the profit for next period has been calculated as £36 000. What would the profit for next period be using marginal costing?

(a) £25 000

(b) £27 000

(c) £45 000

(d) £47 000

ACCA Financial Information for Management

8.11 Last month a manufacturing company's profit was $2000, calculated using absorption costing principles. If marginal costing principles had been used, a loss of $3000 would have occurred. The company's fixed production cost is $2 per unit. Sales last month were 10 000 units.

What was last month's production (in units)?

(a) 7500

(b) 9500

(c) 10 500

(d) 12 500

ACCA Financial Information for Management

8.12 A company which uses marginal costing has a profit of £37 500 for a period. Opening stock was 100 units and closing stock was 350 units.

The fixed production overhead absorption rate is £4 per unit.

What is the profit under absorption costing?

(a) £35 700

(b) £36 500

(c) £38 500

(d) £39 300

ACCA Financial Information for Management

8.13 A newly formed company has drawn up the following budgets for its first two accounting periods:

	Period 1	Period 2
Sales units	9500	10 300
Production units (equivalent to normal capacity)	10 000	10 000

The following budgeted information applies to both periods:

	$
Selling price per unit	6.40
Variable cost per unit	3.60
Fixed production overhead per period	15 000

(a) In period 1, the budgeted profit will be

    (i) the same under both absorption costing and marginal costing.

    (ii) $750 higher under marginal costing.

    (iii) $750 higher under absorption costing.

    (iv) $1400 higher under absorption costing.

(b) In period 2, everything was as budgeted, except for the fixed production overhead, which was $15 700.
The reported profit, using absorption costing in period 2, would be

    (i) $12 300

    (ii) $12 690

    (iii) $13 140

    (iv) $13 840

CIMA – Management Accounting Fundamentals

8.14 In a period, opening stocks were 12 600 units and closing stocks 14 100 units. The profit based on marginal costing was £50 400 and profit using absorption costing was £60 150. The fixed overhead absorption rate per unit (to the nearest penny) is:

(a) £4.00

(b) £4.27

(c) £4.77

(d) £6.50

CIMA Stage 1 Cost Accounting

8.15 **Adjustment of variable costing profits to absorption costing**
Pinafore Ltd manufactures and sells a single product. The budgeted profit statement for this month, which has been prepared using marginal costing principles, is as follows:

		£000	£000
Sales (24 000 units)			864
Less	Variable production cost of sales:		
	Opening stock (3000 units)	69	
	Production (22 000 units)	506	
	Closing stock (1000 units)	(23)	
			(552)
			312
Less	Variable selling cost		(60)
	Contribution		252
Less	Fixed overhead costs:		
	Production	125	
	Selling and administration	40	
			(165)
Net profit			87

The normal monthly level of production is 25 000 units and stocks are valued at standard cost.

Required:

(a) Prepare in full a budgeted profit statement for this month using absorption costing principles. Assume that fixed production overhead costs are absorbed using the normal level of activity.

(6 marks)

(b) Prepare a statement that reconciles the net profit calculated in (a) with the net profit using marginal costing.

(2 marks)

(c) Which of the two costing principles (absorption or marginal) is more relevant for short-run decision-making, and why?

(2 marks)
(10 marks)

ACCA Financial Information for Management

8.16 **Preparation of variable and absorption costing statements and an explanation of the differences in profits**

Bittern Ltd manufactures and sells a single product at a unit selling price of £25. In constant-price-level terms its cost structure is as follows:

Variable costs:
Production materials	£10 per unit produced
Distribution	£1 per unit sold

Semi-variable costs:
Labour	£5000 per annum, plus £2 per unit produced

Fixed costs:
Overheads	£5000 per annum

For several years Bittern has operated a system of variable costing for management accounting purposes. It has been decided to review the system and to compare it for management accounting purposes with an absorption costing system.

As part of the review, you have been asked to prepare estimates of Bittern's profits in constant-price-level terms over a three-year period in three different hypothetical situations, and to compare the two types of system generally for management accounting purposes.

(a) In each of the following three sets of hypothetical circumstances, calculate Bittern's profit in each of years t_1, t_2 and t_3, and also in total over the three year period t_1 to t_3, using first a variable costing system and then a full-cost absorption costing system with fixed cost recovery based on a normal production level of 1000 units per annum:

(i) Stable unit levels of production, sales and inventory

	t_1	t_2	t_3
Opening stock	100	100	100
Production	1000	1000	1000
Sales	1000	1000	1000
Closing stock	100	100	100

(5 marks)

(ii) Stable unit level of sales, but fluctuating unit levels of production and inventory

	t_1	t_2	t_3
Opening stock	100	600	400
Production	1500	800	700
Sales	1000	1000	1000
Closing stock	600	400	100

(5 marks)
ICAEW Management Accounting

(iii) Stable unit level of production, but fluctuating unit levels of sales and inventory

	t_1	t_2	t_3
Opening stock	100	600	400
Production	1000	1000	1000
Sales	500	1200	1300
Closing stock	600	400	100

(5 marks)

(Note that all the data in (i)–(iii) are volumes, not values.)

(b) Write a short comparative evaluation of variable and absorption costing systems for management accounting purposes, paying particular attention to profit measurement, and using your answer to (a) to illustrate your arguments if you wish.

(10 marks)
ICAEW Management Accounting

PART 3
INFORMATION FOR DECISION-MAKING

9   Cost–volume–profit analysis

10 Cost estimation and cost behaviour

11 Measuring relevant costs and revenues for decision-making

12 Activity-based costing

The objective of Part 3, which contains four chapters, is to consider how to provide managers with the financial information they need to make good decisions. Chapters 9–12 are concerned mainly with short-term decisions based on the environment of today, and the physical, human and financial resources that are currently available to a firm. Although short-term decisions are determined to a considerable extent by the quality of the firm's long-term decisions, it is important to understand the difference between them. Long-term decisions cannot easily be reversed whereas short-term decisions can often be changed. The actions that follow short-term decisions are frequently repeated, and it is possible for different actions to be taken in the future. For example, the setting of a particular selling price or product mix can often be changed fairly quickly. With regard to long-term decisions, such as capital investment, which might involve the purchase of new plant and machinery, it is not easy to change such decisions in the short term. Resources may only be available for major investments in plant and machinery at lengthy intervals.

Chapters 9–12 concentrate mainly on how accounting information can be applied to different forms of short-term decisions. Chapter 9 focuses on what will happen to the financial results if a specific level of activity or volume fluctuates. This information is required for making optimal short-term output decisions. Chapter 10 examines how cost behaviour patterns can be determined for cost–volume–profit analysis and decision-making and Chapter 11 examines the approaches that should be used to establish the relevant costs and revenues for a range of non-routine short-term and long-term decisions. Chapter 12 focuses on an alternative approach, known as activity-based costing, used for measuring resources consumed by cost objectives.

Long-term capital investment decisions are normally covered in advanced management accounting courses. If you wish to study capital investment decisions you should refer to Drury (2008) *Management and Cost Accounting*, Chapter 13.

CHAPTER 9
COST–VOLUME–PROFIT ANALYSIS

LEARNING OBJECTIVES

After studying this chapter you should be able to:

- justify the use of linear cost and revenue functions;
- apply the numerical approach to answer questions similar to those listed in Example 9.1;
- construct break-even, contribution and profit–volume graphs;
- apply cost–volume–profit analysis in a multi-product setting;
- identify and explain the assumptions on which cost–volume–profit analysis is based.

You will remember from the first chapter that the decision-making process involves selecting from a range of possible courses of action. Before they make their choice, managers need to compare the likely effects of the options they are considering. This chapter looks at one technique that allows them to consider the consequences of particular courses of action. It provides answers to questions such as:

- How many units must be sold to break-even?
- What would be the effect on profits if we reduce our selling price and sell more units?
- What sales volume is required to meet the additional fixed charges arising from an advertising campaign?
- Should we pay our sales people on the basis of a salary only, or on the basis of a commission only, or by a combination of the two?

These and other questions can be answered using cost–volume–profit (CVP) analysis.

CVP analysis examines the relationship between changes in activity (i.e. output) and changes in total sales revenue, costs and net profit. It allows us to predict what will happen to the financial results if a specified level of activity or volume fluctuates. This information is vital to management, since one of the most important variables influencing total sales revenue, total costs and profits is output or volume. Knowledge of this relationship enables management to identify critical output levels, such as the level at which neither a profit nor a loss will occur (i.e. the **break-even point**).

CVP analysis is based on the relationship between volume and sales revenue, costs and profit in the *short run*. This is normally a period of one year, or less, a time in which the output of a firm is likely to be restricted to that available from the current operating capacity. In the short run some inputs can be increased, but others cannot. For example, additional supplies of materials and unskilled labour may be obtained at short notice, but operating capacity cannot be significantly changed. For example, it is not possible for a hospital to expand its facilities in the short run in order to increase the number of beds. Similarly, a hotel cannot increase the number of rooms in the short run to increase the number of guests. It is also important to remember that most of the costs and prices of a firm's products or services will already have been predetermined over a short-run period, and the major area of uncertainty will be sales volume. Short-run profitability will, therefore, be most sensitive to sales volume. CVP analysis thus highlights the effects of changes in sales volume on the level of profits in the short run.

The term 'volume' is used within CVP analysis but this has multiple meanings. Different measures can be used to represent the term. For example, sales revenue is a generic term that can be used by most organizations. However, units of output, or activity, tend to be the most widely used terms. This raises the question of what constitutes a unit of output or activity. For a manufacturing organization, such as a car manufacturer, determining units of output is straightforward. It is the number of cars produced. For a computer manufacturer it is the number of computers produced. Service organizations face a more difficult choice. Hotels may define units as the number of guest nights, leisure centres may use the number of visitors as a measure of output/activity and airlines might use the number of passenger miles.

CURVILINEAR CVP RELATIONSHIPS

A diagram showing CVP behaviour is presented in Figure 9.1. You will see that the total revenue and total cost lines are curvilinear. The total revenue line (OE) initially resembles a straight line but then begins to rise less steeply and eventually starts to decline. This arises because the firm is only able to sell increasing quantities of output by reducing the selling price per unit; thus the total revenue line does not increase proportionately with output. To increase the quantity of sales, it is necessary to reduce the unit selling price, which results in the total revenue line rising less steeply, and eventually beginning to decline. The decline occurs because the adverse effect of price reductions outweighs the benefits of increased sales volume.

The total cost line (AD) illustrates cost behaviour in a manufacturing firm but similar cost behaviour also applies in non-manufacturing firms. Between points A and B, total costs rise steeply at first as the firm operates at the lower levels of the volume range. This reflects the

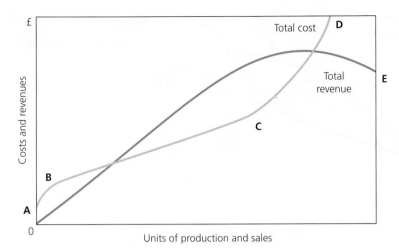

FIGURE 9.1

Curvilinear CVP relationships

difficulties of efficiently using manufacturing facilities designed for much larger volume levels. Between points B and C, the total cost line begins to level out and rise less steeply because the firm is now able to operate its manufacturing facilities within the efficient operating range and can take advantage of economies of scale (e.g. specialization of labour and smooth production schedules). Economists describe this situation as **increasing returns to scale**. In the upper portion of the volume range the total cost line between points C and D rises more steeply as the cost per unit increases. This is because manufacturing facilities are being operated beyond their capacity. Bottlenecks develop, production schedules become more complex and equipment breakdowns begin to occur. The overall effect is that the cost per unit of output increases and causes the total cost line to rise steeply. Economists describe this situation as **decreasing returns to scale**.

It is also clear from Figure 9.1 that the shape of the total revenue line is such that it crosses the total cost line at two points. In other words, there are two output levels at which the total costs are equal to the total revenues; or, more simply, there are two break-even points.

LINEAR CVP RELATIONSHIPS

In Figure 9.2 the total cost line XY and the total revenue line OV assume that variable cost and selling price are constant per unit of output. This results in a linear relationship (i.e. a straight line) for total revenue and total cost as output/volume changes. If you look at these two lines you will see that a linear relationship results in only one break-even point. You can also see that the profit area (i.e. the difference between the total revenue line OV and the total cost line XY) widens as volume increases. For comparative purposes the curvilinear relationships shown in Figure 9.1 are also reproduced in Figure 9.2 (with line AD and line OE showing, respectively, curvilinear total cost and total revenue relationships).

Management accounting assumes linear CVP relationships when applying CVP analysis to short-run business problems. Curvilinear relationships appear to be more realistic of cost and revenue behaviour, so how can we justify CVP analysis based on the assumption of linear relationships? The answers are provided in the following sections.

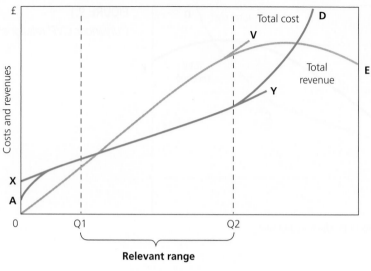

FIGURE 9.2

Linear CVP relationships

Relevant range

Linear relationships are not intended to provide an accurate representation of total cost and total revenue throughout all ranges of output. The objective is to represent the behaviour of total cost and revenue over the range of output at which a firm expects to be operating within a short-term planning horizon. This range of output is represented by the output range between points Q1 and Q2 in Figure 9.2. The term **relevant range** is used to refer to the output range at which the firm expects to be operating within a short-term planning horizon. This relevant range also broadly represents the output levels that the firm has had experience of operating in the past and for which cost information is available.

It is clear from Figure 9.2 that, between points Q1 and Q2, the cost and revenue relationships are more or less linear. It would be unwise, however, to make this assumption for output levels outside the relevant range. CVP analysis should therefore only be applied within the relevant range. If the relevant range changes, different fixed and variable costs and selling prices must be used.

Fixed cost function

Figure 9.2 indicates that at zero output level fixed costs equivalent to 0X would be incurred. This fixed cost level of 0X is assumed to be applicable to activity level Q1 to Q2, shown in Figure 9.3. If there were to be a prolonged economic recession then output might fall below Q1, and this could result in redundancies and shutdowns. Therefore fixed costs may be reduced to 0B if there is a prolonged and a significant decline in sales demand. Alternatively, additional fixed costs will be incurred if long-term sales volume is expected to be greater than Q2. Over a longer-term time horizon, the fixed cost line will consist of a series of step functions as shown in Figure 9.3. However, since within its short term planning horizon the firm expects to be operating between output levels Q1 and Q2 (i.e. the relevant range), it will be committed, in the short term, to fixed costs of 0X. Thus the fixed cost of 0X shown in Figures 9.2 and 9.3 represent the fixed costs that would be incurred only for the relevant range.

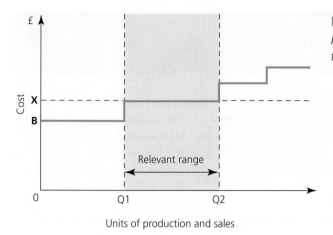

FIGURE 9.3
Fixed costs applicable within the relevant range

Total revenue function

Linear CVP relationships assume that selling price is constant over the relevant range of output, and therefore the total revenue line is a straight line. This is a realistic assumption in those firms that operate in industries where selling prices tend to be fixed in the short term. Beyond the relevant range, increases in output may only be possible by offering substantial reductions in price. As it is not the intention of firms to operate outside the relevant range it is appropriate to assume constant selling prices.

A NUMERICAL APPROACH TO COST–VOLUME–PROFIT ANALYSIS

As an alternative to using diagrams for CVP analysis we can also use a numerical approach. Diagrams are useful for presenting the outcomes in a more visual form to non-accounting managers, but the numerical approach is often a quicker and more flexible method for producing the appropriate information. Indeed, it is possible to express CVP relationships in a simple mathematical equation format so that they can form an input for computer financial models. To keep things simple we shall avoid mathematical formulae and use a simple numerical approach.

In the previous sections we pointed out that CVP analysis is based on the assumption that selling price and variable cost are constant per unit of output. In contrast, you will remember from Chapter 2 that over a short-run period fixed costs are a constant total amount whereas unit cost changes with output levels. As a result, profit per unit also changes with volume. For example, if fixed costs are £10 000 for a period and output is 10 000 units, the fixed cost will be £1 per unit. Alternatively, if output is 5000 units, the fixed cost will be £2 per unit. Profit per unit will not therefore be constant over varying output levels and it is incorrect to unitize fixed costs for CVP decisions.

Instead of using profit per unit we shall use contribution margins to apply the numerical approach. **Contribution margin** is equal to sales revenue minus variable expenses. Because the variable cost per unit and the selling price per unit are assumed to be constant the contribution margin per unit is also assumed to be constant. We will use Example 9.1 to illustrate the application of the numerical approach to CVP analysis.

EXAMPLE 9.1

Lee Enterprises operates in the leisure and entertainment industry and one of its activities is to promote concerts at locations throughout the world. The company is examining the viability of a concert in Singapore. Estimated fixed costs are £60 000. These include the fees paid to performers, the hire of the venue and advertising costs. Variable costs consist of the cost of a pre-packed buffet that will be provided by a firm of caterers at a price which is currently being negotiated, but it is likely to be in the region of £10 per ticket sold. The proposed price for the sale of a ticket is £20. The management of Lee have requested the following information:

1   The number of tickets that must be sold to break even (that is, the point at which there is neither a profit nor loss).
2   How many tickets must be sold to earn £30 000 target profit?
3   What profit would result if 8000 tickets were sold?
4   What selling price would have to be charged to give a profit of £30 000 on sales of 8000 tickets, fixed costs of £60 000 and variable costs of £10 per ticket?
5   How many additional tickets must be sold to cover the extra cost of television advertising of £8000?

Example 9.1 calculations

1 Break-even point in units (i.e. number of tickets sold)

You will see from Example 9.1 that each ticket sold generates a contribution of £10 (£20 selling price – £10 variable cost), which is available to cover fixed costs and, after they are covered, to contribute to profit. When we have obtained sufficient total contribution to cover fixed costs, the break-even point is achieved, and so

$$\text{Break-even point in units} = \frac{\text{Fixed costs (£60 000)}}{\text{Contribution per unit (£10)}}$$

$$= 6000 \text{ tickets}$$

2 Units to be sold to obtain a £30 000 profit

To achieve a profit of any size we must first obtain sufficient contribution to cover the fixed costs (i.e. the break-even point). If the total contribution is not sufficient to cover the fixed costs then a loss will occur. Once a sufficient total contribution has been achieved any excess contribution represents profit. Thus, to determine the total contribution to obtain a target profit we simply add the target profit to the fixed costs and divide by the contribution per unit, so that:

$$\text{Units sold for the target profit} = \frac{\text{Fixed costs (£60 000)} + \text{Target profit (£30 000)}}{\text{Contribution per unit (£10)}}$$

$$= 9000 \text{ tickets}$$

3 Profit from the sale of 8000 tickets

The total contribution from the sale of 8000 tickets is £80 000 (8000 × £10). To ascertain the profit we deduct the fixed costs of £60 000, giving a net profit of £20 000. Let us now assume that we wish to ascertain the impact on profit if a further 1000 tickets are sold so that sales volume increases from 8000 to 9000 tickets. Assuming that fixed costs remain unchanged, the impact on a firm's profits resulting from a change in the number of units sold can be determined by multiplying the unit contribution margin by the change in units sold. Therefore the increase in profits will be £10 000 (1000 units times a unit contribution margin of £10).

4 Selling price to be charged to show a profit of £30 000 on sales of 8000 tickets

First we must determine the total required revenue to obtain a profit of £30 000. This is £170 000, which is derived from the sum of the fixed costs (£60 000), variable costs (8000 × £10) and the target profit (£30 000). Dividing the required sales revenues of £170 000 by the sales volume (8000 tickets) gives a selling price of £21.25.

5 Additional sales volume to meet £8000 additional fixed advertisement charges

The contribution per unit is £10 and fixed costs will increase by £8000. Therefore an extra 800 tickets must be sold to cover the additional fixed costs of £8000.

REAL WORLD VIEWS 9.1

Starting a business

For any person starting a business, determining whether the business is a profitable venture or otherwise is often problematic. However, the business idea should be a financially sound idea to be valuable.

Quite often, the first point of contact for a fledgling entrepreneur is a bank, business association or government agency. For the typical start-up business, it is more important to ensure that ongoing operating costs are covered by sales revenue in the short to medium term. It would of course be the intention to make a profit in the medium to long term.

The United States Small Business Administration (SBA)[1] was set up in 1953. It provides advice and finance to small business. Over 20 million US businesses have benefited from SBA loans, advice and counselling. One basic tool recommended by the SBA is break-even analysis. Break-even means a business makes neither profit nor loss. If a start up business can identify its costs and revenues it can establish the level of sales required to at least break-even. If the level of break-even sales cannot be achieved the business idea may not be sound financially.

In order to identify the break-even point, a business must be able to identify its fixed and variable costs. Fixed costs must be paid regardless of sales volume. Therefore the sales revenue less the variable costs must be enough to cover the fixed costs. The calculation of the break-even point requires no more than simple arithmetic – providing a simple tool for the entrepreneur to make a quick decision to abandon or revise the business plan.

Discussion points

1 Are fixed and variable costs always readily identifiable?

2 In what other business scenarios might break-even calculations prove useful?

[1]http://www.sba.gov

THE PROFIT–VOLUME RATIO

The **profit–volume ratio** (also known as the **contribution margin ratio**) is the contribution divided by sales. It represents the proportion of each £1 of sales available to cover fixed costs and provide for profit. In Example 9.1 the contribution is £10 per unit and the selling price is £20 per unit; the profit–volume ratio is 0.5. This means that for each £1 sale a contribution of £0.50 is earned. Because we assume that selling price and contribution per unit are constant, the profit–volume ratio is also assumed to be constant. This means that the profit–volume ratio can be computed using either unit figures or total figures. Given an estimate of total sales revenue, it is possible to use the profit–volume ratio to estimate total contribution. For example, if total sales revenue is estimated to be £200 000, the total contribution will be £100 000 (£200 000 × 0.5). To calculate the profit, we deduct fixed costs of £60 000; thus a profit of £40 000 will be obtained from total sales revenue of £200 000.

This computation can be expressed in equation form:

$$\text{Profit} = (\text{Sales revenue} \times \text{PV ratio}) - \text{Fixed costs}$$

We can rearrange this equation:

$$\text{Profit} + \text{Fixed costs} = \text{Sales revenue} \times \text{PV ratio}$$

Therefore the break-even sales revenue (where profit = 0) = Fixed costs/PV ratio.

If we apply this approach to Example 9.1, the break-even sales revenue is £120 000 (£60 000 fixed costs/0.5 PV ratio).

RELEVANT RANGE

It is vital to remember that CVP analysis can only be used for decisions that result in outcomes within the relevant range. Outside this range the unit selling price and the variable cost are no longer deemed to be constant per unit, and any results obtained from the formulae that fall outside the relevant range will be incorrect. The concept of the relevant range is more appropriate for production settings but it can apply within non-production settings. Returning to Lee Enterprises in Example 9.1, we shall now assume that the caterers' charges will be higher per ticket if ticket sales are below 4000 but lower if sales exceed 12 000 tickets. Thus, the £10 variable cost relates only to a sales volume within a range of 4000 to 12 000 tickets. Outside this range other costs apply. In other words, we will assume that the relevant range is a sales volume of 4000 to 12 000 tickets and outside this range the results of our CVP analysis do not apply.

MARGIN OF SAFETY

The **margin of safety** indicates by how much sales may decrease before a loss occurs. Using Example 9.1, where unit selling price and variable cost were £20 and £10 respectively and fixed costs were £60 000, we noted that the break-even point was 6000 tickets or £120 000 sales value. If sales are expected to be 8000 tickets or £160 000, the margin of safety will be 2000 tickets or £40 000. Alternatively, we can express the margin of safety in a percentage form based on the following ratio:

$$\text{Percentage margin of safety} = \frac{\text{Expected sales} - \text{Break-even sales}}{\text{Expected sales}}$$

$$= \frac{£160\ 000 - £120\ 000}{£160\ 000} = 25\%$$

CONSTRUCTING THE BREAK-EVEN CHART

Managers may obtain a clearer understanding of CVP behaviour if the information is presented in graphical format. Using the data in Example 9.1 we can construct the **break-even chart** for Lee Enterprises (Figure 9.4). Note that activity/output is plotted on the horizontal axis and monetary amounts for total costs, total revenues and total profits (or loss) are recorded on the vertical axis. In constructing the graph, the fixed costs are plotted as a single horizontal line at the £60 000 level. Variable costs at the rate of £10 per unit of volume are added to the fixed costs to enable the total cost line to be plotted. Two points are required to insert the total cost line. At zero sales volume total cost will be equal to the fixed costs of £60 000. At 12 000 units sales volume total costs will be £180 000 consisting of £120 000 variable costs plus £60 000 fixed costs. The total revenue line is plotted at the rate of £20 per unit of volume. At zero output total sales are zero and at 12 000 units total sales revenue is £240 000. The total revenues for these two points are plotted on the graph and a straight line is drawn that joins these points. The constraints of the relevant range consisting of two vertical lines are then added to the graph; beyond these lines we have little assurance that the CVP relationships are valid.

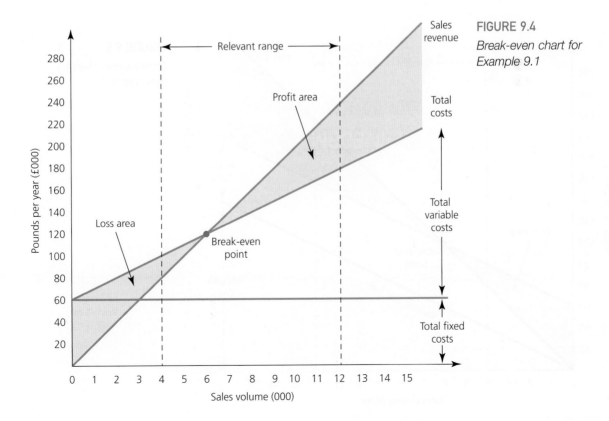

FIGURE 9.4

Break-even chart for Example 9.1

The point at which the total sales revenue line cuts the total cost line is the point where the concert makes neither a profit nor a loss. This is the break-even point and is 6000 tickets or £120 000 total sales revenue. The distance between the total sales revenue line and the total cost line at a volume below the break-even point represents losses that will occur for sales levels below 6000 tickets. Similarly, if the company operates at a sales volume above the break-even point, the difference between the total revenue and the total cost lines represents the profit that results.

ALTERNATIVE PRESENTATION OF COST–VOLUME–PROFIT ANALYSIS

Contribution graph

In Figure 9.4 the fixed cost line is drawn parallel to the horizontal axis, and the variable cost is the difference between the total cost line and the fixed cost line. An alternative to Figure 9.4 for the data contained in Example 9.1 is illustrated in Figure 9.5. This alternative presentation is called a **contribution graph**. In Figure 9.5 the variable cost line is drawn first at £10 per unit of volume. The fixed costs are represented by the difference between the total cost line and the variable cost line. Because fixed costs are assumed to be a constant sum throughout the entire output range, a constant sum of £60 000 for fixed costs is added to the variable cost line, which results in the total cost line being drawn parallel to the variable cost line. The advantage of this form of presentation is that it emphasizes the total contribution, which is represented by the difference between the total sales revenue line and the total variable cost line.

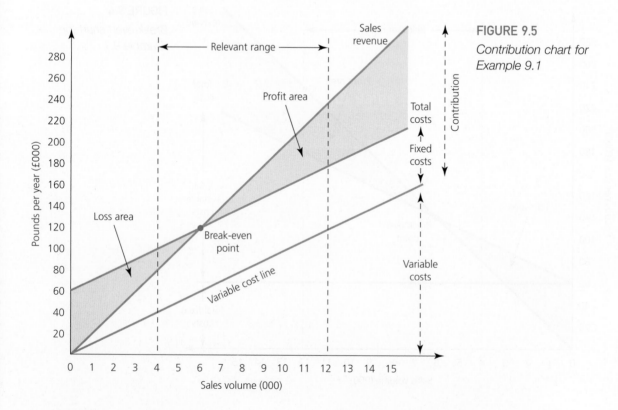

FIGURE 9.5

Contribution chart for Example 9.1

REAL WORLD VIEWS 9.2

A joint venture or not – iron ore mining in Western Australia

Rio Tinto (riotinto.com) is a leading global mining company, with turnover in excess of $40 billion in 2009, realizing a pre-tax profit of $7.8 billion. It has listings on both the London and Australian stock exchanges. The company has operations on all five continents, but 90 per cent of its operations are in Australia, North America and Europe.

Rio Tinto outputs approximately 300 million tonnes of iron ore (the main raw material for steel) per annum. Like any mining company, seeking new sources of ore/minerals is an ongoing task. Finding deposits of iron ore for example is only the start. Costs of bringing an ore deposit to an active working mine are high. When a mine finally is active, the resulting profits are to a large extent determined by the market price of the output. Iron ore prices, like any other commodity, fluctuate according to supply and demand. Thus whether or not a mining project is profitable, or breaks even, is dependent on the price the output can be sold at, as costs of development and extraction are by and large stable.

In June 2009, Rio Tinto announced a joint-venture with Australian mining company BHP-Billiton (bhpbilliton. com) to manage both companies iron ore assets in West Australia. The savings from the venture were estimated at $10 billion for each company. These savings arise from combining adjacent mining operations and more efficient use of ports and transportation. The only snag was that BHP Billiton pay $5.8 billion to equalize the venture as Rio Tinto had a greater share of the underlying iron ore resources in the venture.

Both Rio Tinto and BHP-Billiton based the venture on iron ore prices as of June 2009. However, the spot price of iron ore almost doubled from June 2009 – March 2010, meaning that the agreed equalization payment of $5.8 billion might need review. If the savings of $10 billion were to be exceeded by a higher equalization payment, the deal would be a poor one for BHP-Billiton. According to the *Wall Street Journal* (March 25, 2010), the joint-venture deal while publicly still on, was starting to look a bit shaky.

Discussion points

1 Do you think companies like Rio Tinto and BHP Billiton can do anything about the costs of extracting ore, or increase output volumes, in order to break-even or increase profitability in the case of falling ore prices?

2 Would a mining company know what market price they need to obtain to cover all mining development and extraction costs?

References

Rio Tinto press release, June 5 2009 http://www. riotinto.com/media/5157_18100.asp

'Rio Tinto-BHP Iron-Ore JV Is Losing Luster' – *Wall Street Journal*, 25 March 2010, http://online.wsj.com/article/SB100014240527487033125045751413 43839076992.html?mod=WSJ_latestheadlines.

Annual Report 2009 available at riotinto.com/annualreport2009.

Profit–volume graph

Neither the break-even nor the contribution graphs highlight the profit or loss at different volume levels. To ascertain the profit or loss figures from a break-even graph, it is necessary to determine the difference between the total cost and total revenue lines. The **profit–volume graph** is a more convenient method of showing the impact of

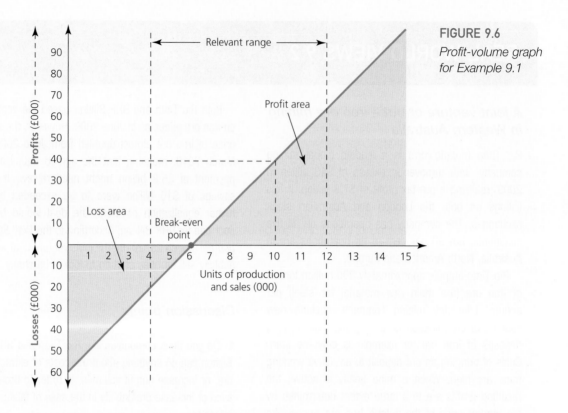

FIGURE 9.6

Profit-volume graph for Example 9.1

changes in volume on profit. Such a graph is illustrated in Figure 9.6. The horizontal axis represents the various levels of sales volume, and the profits and losses for the period are recorded on the vertical scale. You will see from Figure 9.6 that profits or losses are plotted for each of the various sales levels, and these points are connected by a profit line. Two points are required to plot the profit line. When units sold are zero a loss equal to the amount of fixed costs (£60 000) will be reported. At the break-even point (zero profits) sales volume is 6000 units. This is plotted at the point where the profit line intersects the horizontal line at a sales volume of 6000 tickets. The profit line is drawn between the two points. With each unit sold, a contribution of £10 is obtained towards the fixed costs, and the break-even point is at 6000 tickets, when the total contribution exactly equals the total of the fixed costs. With each additional unit sold beyond 6000 tickets, a surplus of £10 per ticket is obtained. If 10 000 tickets are sold, the profit will be £40 000 (4000 tickets at £10 contribution). You can see this relationship between sales and profit at 10 000 tickets from the dotted lines in Figure 9.6.

MULTI-PRODUCT COST–VOLUME–PROFIT ANALYSIS

Our analysis so far has assumed a single-product setting. However, most firms produce and sell many products or services. In this section we shall consider how we can adapt CVP analysis to a multi-product setting. Consider the situation described in Example 9.2. You will see that the company sells two products so that there are two unit contribution margins. If all of the fixed costs are directly attributable to products (i.e. there are no common fixed costs), we can apply the same approach as that used for a single product. We simply apply the analysis separately to each product as follows:

Deluxe washing machine break – even point
= Direct fixed costs (£90 000)/Unit contribution (£150)
= 600 units
Standard washing machine break – even point
= Direct fixed costs (£27 000)/Unit contribution (£90)
= 300 units

However, the situation described in Example 9.2 is more complicated than this. There are some common fixed costs that must be taken into account. Selling 600 deluxe and 300 standard washing machines will generate a contribution that only covers direct fixed costs; the common fixed costs will not be covered. A loss equal to the common fixed costs will be reported. The break-even point for the firm as a whole has not been ascertained.

You might think that the break-even point for the firm as a whole can be derived if we allocate the common fixed costs to each individual product. However, this approach is

EXAMPLE 9.2

The Super Bright Company sells two types of washing machines – a deluxe model and a standard model. The financial controller has prepared the following information based on the sales forecast for the period:

	Deluxe machine 1200 (£)	Standard machine 600 (£)	Total (£)
Sales volume (units)			
Unit selling price	300	200	
Unit variable cost	150	110	
Unit contribution	150	90	
Total sales revenues	360 000	120 000	480 000
Less: Total variable cost	180 000	66 000	246 000
Contribution to direct and common fixed costs[a]	180 000	54 000	234 000
Less: Direct avoidable fixed costs	90 000	27 000	117 000
Contribution to common fixed costs[a]	90 000	27 000	117 000
Less common (indirect) fixed costs			39 000
Operating profit			78 000

The common fixed costs relate to the costs of common facilities and can only be avoided if neither of the products is sold. The managing director is concerned that sales may be less than forecast and has requested information relating to the break-even point for the activities for the period.

Note

[a]Contribution was defined earlier in this chapter as sales less variable costs. Where fixed costs are divided into direct and common (indirect) fixed costs it is possible to identify two separate contribution categories. The first is described as contribution to direct and common fixed costs and this is identical to the conventional definition, being equivalent to sales less variable costs. The second is after a further deduction of direct fixed costs and is described as 'Contribution to common or indirect fixed costs'.

inappropriate because the allocation will be arbitrary. The common fixed costs cannot be specifically identified with either of the products since they can only be avoided if *both* products are not sold. The solution to our problem is to convert the sales volume measure of the individual products into standard batches of products based on the planned sales mix. You will from see from Example 9.2 that Super Bright plans to sell 1200 deluxe and 600 standard machines giving a sales mix of 1200:600. Reducing this sales mix to the smallest whole number gives a mix of 2:1. In other words, for the sale of every two deluxe machines one standard machine is expected to be sold. We therefore define our standard batch of products as comprising two deluxe and one standard machine giving a contribution of £390 per batch (two deluxe machines at a contribution of £150 per unit sold plus one standard machine at a contribution of £90).

The break-even point in standard batches can be calculated by using the same break-even equation that we used for a single product, so that:

$$\text{Break-even number of batches} \quad = \quad \frac{\text{Total fixed costs (£156 000)}}{\text{Contribution margin per batch (£390)}}$$

$$= \quad 400 \text{ batches}$$

The sales mix used to define a standard batch (2:1) can now be used to convert the break-even point (measured in standard batches) into a break-even point expressed in terms of the required combination of individual products sold. Thus, 800 de-luxe machines (2 × 400) and 400 (1 × 400) standard machines must be sold to break even. The following profit statement verifies this outcome:

Units sold	Deluxe machine 800 (£)	Standard machine 400 (£)	Total (£)
Unit contribution margin	150	90	
Contribution to direct and common fixed costs	120 000	36 000	156 000
Less: Direct fixed costs	90 000	27 000	117 000
Contribution to common fixed costs	30 000	9 000	39 000
Less: Common fixed costs			39 000
Operating profit			0

Let us now assume that the actual sales volume for the period was 1200 units, the same total volume as the break-even volume, but consisting of a sales mix of 600 units of each machine. Thus, the actual sales mix is 1:1 compared with a planned sales mix of 2:1. The total contribution to direct and common fixed costs will be £144 000 ([£150 × 600 for de-luxe] + [£90 × 600 for standard]) and a loss of £12 000 (£144 000 contribution – £156 000 total fixed costs) will occur. It should now be apparent to you that *the break-even point (or the sales volumes required to achieve a target profit) is not a unique number: it varies depending upon the composition of the sales mix*. Because the actual sales mix differs from the planned sales mix, the sales mix used to define a standard batch has changed from 2:1 to 1:1 and the contribution per batch changes from £390 to £240 ([1 × £150] + [1 × £90]). This means that the revised break-even point will be 650 batches (£156 000 total fixed costs/£240 contribution per batch), which converts to a sales volume of 650 units of each machine based on a 1:1 sales mix. Generally, an increase in the proportion of sales of higher contribution margin products will decrease the break-even point whereas increases in sales of the lower margin products will increase the break-even point.

COST–VOLUME–PROFIT ANALYSIS ASSUMPTIONS

It is essential that anyone preparing or interpreting CVP information is aware of the underlying assumptions on which the information has been prepared. If these assumptions are not recognized, or the analysis is modified, errors may result and incorrect conclusions may be drawn from the analysis. We shall now consider these important assumptions. They are as follows:

1 All other variables remain constant.
2 A single product or constant sales mix.
3 Total costs and total revenue are linear functions of output.
4 Profits are calculated on a variable costing basis.
5 Costs can be accurately divided into their fixed and variable elements.
6 The analysis applies only to the relevant range.
7 The analysis applies only to a short-term time horizon.

1 All other variables remain constant

It has been assumed that all variables other than the particular one under consideration have remained constant throughout the analysis. In other words, it is assumed that volume is the only factor that will cause costs and revenues to change. However, changes in other variables such as production efficiency, sales mix and price levels can have an important influence on sales revenue and costs. If significant changes in these other variables occur, the CVP analysis presentation will be incorrect.

2 Single product or constant sales mix

CVP analysis assumes that either a single product is sold or, if a range of products is sold, that sales will be in accordance with a predetermined sales mix. When a predetermined sales mix is used, it can be depicted in the CVP analysis by measuring sales volume using standard batch sizes based on a planned sales mix. As we have discussed, any CVP analysis must be interpreted carefully if the initial product mix assumptions do not hold.

3 Total costs and total revenue are linear functions of output

The analysis assumes that unit variable cost and selling price are constant. This assumption is only likely to be valid within the relevant range of production described earlier in this chapter.

4 Profits are calculated on a variable costing basis

The analysis assumes that the fixed costs incurred during the period are charged as an expense for that period. Therefore, variable-costing profit calculations are assumed. If absorption-costing profit calculations are used, it is necessary to assume that production is equal to sales for the analysis to predict absorption costing profits. For the application of CVP analysis with an absorption costing system you should refer to Drury (2008, Ch. 8).

5 Cost can be accurately divided into their fixed and variable elements

CVP analysis assumes that costs can be accurately analyzed into their fixed and variable elements. In practice, the separation of semi-variable costs into their fixed and variable elements is extremely difficult. Nevertheless, a reasonably accurate analysis is necessary if CVP analysis is to provide relevant information for decision-making.

6 Analysis applies only to the relevant range

Earlier in this chapter we noted that CVP analysis is appropriate only for decisions taken within the relevant production range, and that it is incorrect to project cost and revenue figures beyond the relevant range.

7 Analysis applies only to a short-term time horizon

CVP analysis is based on the relationship between volume and sales revenue, costs and profit in the short run, typically a period of one year, in which the output of a firm is likely to be restricted to that available from the current operating capacity. During this period significant changes cannot be made to selling prices and fixed and variable costs. CVP analysis thus examines the effects of changes in sales volume on the level of profits in the short run. It is inappropriate to extend the analysis to long-term decision-making.

THE IMPACT OF INFORMATION TECHNOLOGY

The output from a CVP model is only as good as the input. The analysis will include assumptions about sales mix, production efficiency, price levels, total fixed costs, variable costs and selling price per unit. In practice, estimates regarding these variables will be subject to varying degrees of uncertainty.

Sensitivity analysis is one approach for coping with changes in the values of the variables. Sensitivity analysis focuses on how a result will be changed if the original estimates or the underlying assumptions change. With regard to CVP analysis, sensitivity analysis answers questions such as the following:

1 What will the profit be if the sales mix changes from that originally predicted?
2 What will the profit be if fixed costs increase by 10 per cent and variable costs decline by 5 per cent?

Developments in information technology have enabled management accountants to build CVP computerized models. Managers can now consider alternative plans by keying the information into a computer, which can quickly show changes both graphically and numerically. Thus, managers can study various combinations of changes in selling prices, fixed costs, variable costs and product mix, and can react quickly without waiting for formal reports from the management accountant.

SUMMARY

The following items relate to the learning objectives listed at the beginning of the chapter.

- **Justify the use of linear cost and revenue functions**. Within the relevant range it is generally assumed that cost and revenue functions are approximately linear. Outside the relevant range linearity is unlikely to apply. Care is therefore required in interpreting CVP relationships outside the relevant range.

- **Apply the numerical approach to answer questions similar to those listed in Example 9.1**. In Example 9.1, the break-even point was derived by dividing fixed costs by the contribution per unit. To ascertain the number of units sold to achieve a target profit the sum of the fixed costs and the target profit is divided by the contribution per unit.

- **Construct break-even, contribution and profit–volume graphs**. Managers may obtain a clearer understanding of CVP behaviour if the information is presented in graphical format. With the break-even chart the fixed costs are plotted as a single horizontal line. The total cost line is plotted by adding variable costs to fixed costs. The reverse situation applies with a contribution graph. The variable costs are plotted first and the fixed costs are added to variable costs to plot the total cost line. Because fixed costs are assumed to be a constant sum throughout the output range, the total cost line is drawn parallel to the variable cost line. The break-even and contribution graphs do not highlight the profit or loss at different output levels and must be ascertained by comparing the differences between the total cost and total revenue lines. The profit–volume graph shows the impact of changes in volume on profits. The profits and losses are plotted for each of the various sales levels and these are connected by a profit line. You should refer to Figures 9.4–9.6 for an illustration of the graphs.

- **Apply cost–volume–profit analysis in a multi-product setting**. Multi-product CVP analysis requires that an assumption is made concerning the expected sales mix. The approach that is used is to convert the multi-product CVP analysis into a single product analysis based on the assumption that output consists of standard batches of the multiple products based on the expected sales mix. However, you should note that the answers change as the sales mix changes.

- **Identify and explain the assumptions on which cost–volume–profit analysis is based**. Cost–volume–profit analysis is based on the following assumptions: (a) all variables, other than volume, remain constant; (b) the sales mix remains constant; (c) total costs and revenues are linear functions of output; (d) profits are calculated on a variable costing basis; (e) costs can be accurately divided into their fixed and variable elements; (f) the analysis applies only to the relevant range; and (g) the analysis applies only to a short-term horizon.

KEY TERMS AND CONCEPTS

Break-even chart a chart that plots total costs and total revenues against sales volume and indicates the break-even point.

Break-even point the level of output at which costs are balanced by sales revenue and neither a profit nor loss will occur.

Contribution graph a graph that plots variable costs and total costs against sales volume and fixed costs represent the difference between the total cost line and the variable cost line.

Contribution margin the margin calculated by deducting variable expenses from sales revenue.

Decreasing returns to scale a situation that arises when unit costs rise as volume increases.

Increasing returns to scale a situation that arises when unit costs fall as volume increases.

Margin of safety the amount by which sales may decrease before a loss occurs

Profit–volume graph a graph that plots profit/losses against volume.

Profit–volume ratio, or **contribution margin ratio** the proportion of sales available to cover fixed costs and provide for profit. It is calculated by dividing the contribution margin by the sales revenue.

Relevant range the output range at which an organization expects to be operating with a short-term planning horizon.

Sensitivity analysis anaylsis that shows how a result will be changed if the original estimates or underlying assumption changes.

KEY EXAMINATION POINTS

Students tend to experience little difficulty in preparing break-even charts, but many cannot construct profit–volume charts. Remember that the horizontal axis represents the level of activity, while profit/losses are shown on the vertical axis. The maximum loss is at zero activity, and is equal to fixed costs. For practice on preparing a profit–volume chart you should attempt Review problem 9.21 and compare your answer with the solution. Students also experience difficulty with the following:

1 coping with multi-product situations;

2 calculating the break-even point when total sales and costs are given but no information is given on the unit costs;

3 explaining the assumptions of CVP analysis.

For multi-product situations you should base your answer on the average contribution per unit, using the approach shown in Example 9.2. Review problem 9.24 requires the computation of a break-even point in a multi-product setting. When unit costs are not given the break-even point in sales value can be calculated as follows:

$$\text{Fixed costs} \times \frac{\text{total estimated sales}}{\text{total estimated contribution}}$$

or

$$\frac{\text{Fixed costs}}{\text{profit/volume ratio}}$$

You should refer to the solutions to Review problem 9.22 for an illustration of the application of the above approach.

ASSESSMENT MATERIAL

The review questions are short questions that enable you to assess your understanding of the main topics included in the chapter. The numbers in parentheses provide you with the page numbers to refer to if you cannot answer a specific question.

The review problems are more complex and require you to relate and apply the chapter content to various business problems. The problems are graded by their level of difficulty. The multiple-choice questions are the least demanding and normally take less than 10 minutes to complete. Fully worked solutions to the review problems are provided in a separate section at the end of the book. Further review problems with solutions for this chapter are available on the accompanying website www.drury-online.com. The website includes a *Student's Manual* and an *Instructor's Manual*. Students can access both questions and answers from the *Student's Manual* and the questions from the *Instructor's Manual*. The answers to problems in the *Instructor's Manual* are available only to lecturers on the lecturer's password-protected section of the website.

The website also includes over 20 case study problems. A list of these cases is provided on pages 427–30. Several cases are relevant to the content of this chapter. Examples include Dumbellow Ltd, Hardhat Ltd and Merrion Products Ltd.

REVIEW QUESTIONS

9.1 Provide examples of how cost–volume–profit analysis can be used for decision-making. *(p. 209)*

9.2 Explain what is meant by the term 'relevant range'. *(p. 212)*

9.3 Define the term 'contribution margin'. *(p. 213)*

9.4 Define the term 'profit–volume ratio' and explain how it can be used for cost–volume–profit analysis. *(p. 216)*

9.5 Describe and distinguish between the three different approaches to presenting cost–volume–profit relationships in graphical format. *(pp. 217–20)*

9.6 How can a company with multiple products use cost–volume–profit analysis? *(pp. 220–22)*

9.7 Explain why the break-even point changes when there is a change in sales mix. *(pp. 221–22)*

9.8 Describe the assumptions underlying cost–volume–profit analysis. *(pp. 223–24)*

9.9 How can sensitivity analysis be used in conjunction with cost–volume–profit analysis? *(p. 224)*

REVIEW PROBLEMS

9.10 Four lines representing expected costs and revenue have been drawn on the following break-even chart:

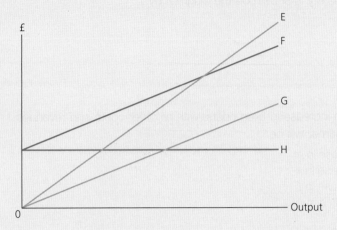

Which statement is correct?

(a) Line F represents total variable cost.

(b) The break-even point occurs at the intersection of lines E and F.

(c) Line G represents total revenue.

(d) The break-even point occurs at the intersection of lines G and H.

ACCA Financial Information for Managers

9.11 The following information is required for sub-questions (a) and (b)

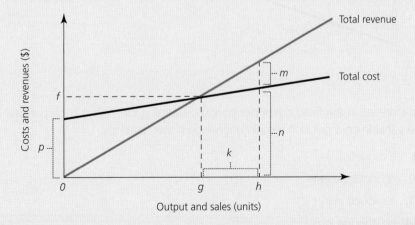

The company expects to sell *h* units in the next accounting period.

(a) The margin of safety is shown on the diagram by:

A k
B m
C n
D p

(b) The effect of an increase in fixed costs, with all other costs and revenues remaining the same, will be:

A   an increase in m
B   an increase in k
C   an increase in f
D   a reduction in p

CIMA – Management Accounting Fundamentals

9.12 The diagram shows the profit–volume chart of Z Ltd for its last accounting period. The company made a profit of $\$w$ during the period.

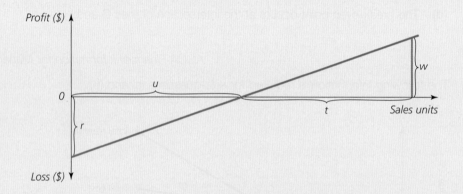

(a) An increase in the fixed costs per period (assuming the selling price per unit and the variable cost per unit remain unchanged), will result in:

(i) a reduction in r

(ii) an increase in w

(iii) a reduction in t

(iv) no change in u

(b) The following results were achieved in the last accounting period:

$r = \$50\,000$ $w = \$16\,000$ $t = 800$ units $u = 2500$ units

The company expects to make and sell an additional 1400 units in the next accounting period. If variable cost per unit, selling price per unit and total fixed costs remain unchanged, the effect on profit will be:

(i)   an increase of $10 500

(ii)   an increase of $21 210

(iii)   an increase of $28 000

(iv)   an increase of $87 500

CIMA Management Accounting Fundamentals

9.13 The profit–volume chart for a single product company is as follows:

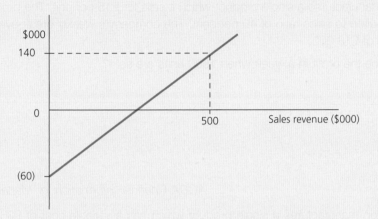

What is the product's contribution to sales ratio (expressed as a %)?

(a)   16%

(b)   28%

(c)   40%

(d)   72%

ACCA – Financial Information for Managers

9.14 A company has established a budgeted sales revenue for the forthcoming period of £500 000 with an associated contribution of £275 000. Fixed production costs are £137 500 and fixed selling costs are £27 500.

What is the break-even sales revenue?

(a)   £75 625

(b)   £90 750

(c)   £250 000

(d)   £300 000

ACCA – Financial Information for Management

9.15 A company wishes to make a profit of £150 000. It has fixed costs of £75 000 with a C/S ratio of 0.75 and a selling price of £10 per unit.

How many units would the company need to sell in order to achieve the required level of profit?

(a) 10 000 units

(b) 15 000 units

(c) 22 500 units

(d) 30 000 units

ACCA – Financial Information for Management

9.16 A company manufactures a single product which it sells for £15 per unit. The product has a contribution to sales ratio of 40 per cent. The company's weekly break-even point is sales of £18 000.

What would be the profit in a week when 1500 units are sold?

(a) £900

(b) £1800

(c) £2700

(d) £4500

ACCA Financial Information for Managers

9.17 An organization manufactures a single product which has a variable cost of £36 per unit. The organization's total weekly fixed costs are £81 000 and it has a contribution to sales ratio of 40 per cent.

This week it plans to manufacture and sell 5000 units. What is the organization's margin of safety this week (in units)?

(a) 1625

(b) 2750

(c) 3375

(d) 3500

ACCA Financial Information for Managers

9.18 An organization manufactures and sells a single product which has a variable cost of £24 per unit and a contribution to sales ratio of 40 per cent. Total monthly fixed costs are £720 000.

What is the monthly breakeven point (in units)?

(a) 18 000

(b) 20 000

(c) 30 000

(d) 45 000

ACCA Financial Information for Managers

9.19   Z plc currently sells products Aye, Bee and Cee in equal quantities and at the same selling price per unit. The contribution to sales ratio for product Aye is 40 per cent; for product Bee it is 50 per cent and the total is 48 per cent. If fixed costs are unaffected by mix and are currently 20 per cent of sales, the effect of changing the product mix to:

Aye   40%
Bee   25%
Cee   35%

is that the total contribution/total sales ratio changes to:

(a)   27.4%

(b)   45.3%

(c)   47.4%

(d)   48.4%

(e)   68.4%

CIMA Stage 2

9.20   The following information is required for sub-questions (a) and (b).
W Ltd makes leather purses. It has drawn up the following budget for its next financial period:

Selling price per unit	$11.60
Variable production cost per unit	$3.40
Sales commission	5% of selling price
Fixed production costs	$430 500
Fixed selling and administration costs	$198 150
Sales	90 000 units

(a)   The margin of safety represents:

(i)   5.6% of budgeted sales

(ii)   8.3% of budgeted sales

(iii)   11.6% of budgeted sales

(iv)   14.8% of budgeted sales

(b)   The marketing manager has indicated that an increase in the selling price to $12.25 per unit would not affect the number of units sold, provided that the sales commission is increased to 8 per cent of the selling price.

These changes will cause the break-even point (to the nearest whole number) to be:

(i)   71 033 units

(ii)   76 016 units

(iii)   79 879 units

(iv)   87 070 units

CIMA – Management Accounting Fundamentals

9.21   Preparation of break-even and profit–volume graphs

ZED plc manufactures one standard product, which sells at £10. You are required to:

(a)   prepare from the data given below, a break-even and profit–volume graph showing the results for the six months ending 30 April and to determine:

   (i)   the fixed costs;

   (ii)   the variable cost per unit;

   (iii) the profit–volume ratio;

   (iv)   the break-even point;

   (v)   the margin of safety;

Month	Sales (units)	Profit/(loss) (£)
November	30 000	40 000
December	35 000	60 000
January	15 000	(20 000)
February	24 000	16 000
March	26 000	24 000
April	18 000	(8000)

(b)   discuss the limitations of such a graph;

(c)   explain the use of the relevant range in such a graph.

(20 marks)

CIMA Cost Accounting 2

9.22   Preparation of a contribution graph

Z plc operates a single retail outlet selling direct to the public. Profit statements for August and September are as follows:

	August	September
Sales	80 000	90 000
Cost of sales	50 000	55 000
Gross profit	30 000	35 000
Less:		
Selling and distribution	8000	9000
Administration	15 000	15 000
Net profit	7000	11 000

Required:

(a)   Use the high- and low-points technique (see Chapter 10) to identify the behaviour of:

   (i)   cost of sales;

   (ii)   selling and distribution costs;

   (iii) administration costs.

(4 marks)

(b) Draw a contribution break-even chart and identify the monthly break-even sales value and area of contribution.

(10 marks)

(c) Assuming a margin of safety equal to 30 per cent of the break-even value, calculate Z plc's annual profit.

(2 marks)

(d) Z plc is now considering opening another retail outlet selling the same products. Z plc plans to use the same profit margins in both outlets and has estimated that the specific fixed costs of the second outlet will be £100 000 per annum.

Z plc also expects that 10 per cent of its annual sales from its existing outlet would transfer to this second outlet if it were to be opened.

Calculate the annual value of sales required from the new outlet in order to achieve the same annual profit as previously obtained from the single outlet.

(5 marks)

(e) Briefly describe the cost accounting requirements of organizations of this type.

(4 marks)

CIMA Cost Accounting Stage 2

9.23 Preparation of a break-even chart with step fixed costs

Toowomba manufactures various products and uses CVP analysis to establish the minimum level of production to ensure profitability.

Fixed costs of £50 000 have been allocated to a specific product but are expected to increase to £100 000 once production exceeds 30 000 units, as a new factory will need to be rented in order to produce the extra units. Variable costs per unit are stable at £5 per unit over all levels of activity. Revenue from this product will be £7.50 per unit.

Required:

(a) Formulate the equations for the total cost at:

(i) less than or equal to 30 000 units;

(ii) more than 30 000 units.

(2 marks)

(b) Prepare a break-even chart and clearly identify the break-even point or points.

(6 marks)

(c) Discuss the implications of the results from your graph in (b) with regard to Toowomba's production plans.

(2 marks)

ACCA Paper 1.2 – Financial Information for Management

9.24 Changes in sales mix

XYZ Ltd produces two products and the following budget applies:

	Product X (£)	Product Y (£)
Selling price	6	12
Variable costs	2	4
Contribution margin	4	8
Fixed costs apportioned	£100 000	£200 000
Units sold	70 000	30 000

You are required to calculate the break-even points for each product and the company as a whole and comment on your findings.

9.25 Non-graphical CVP analysis

The summarized profit and loss statement for Exewye plc for the last year is as follows:

	(£000)	(£000)
Sales (50 000 units)		1000
Direct materials	350	
Direct wages	200	
Fixed production overhead	200	
Variable production overhead	50	
Administration overhead	180	
Selling and distribution overhead	120	1100
Profit/(loss)		(100)

At a recent board meeting the directors discussed the year's results, following which the chairman asked for suggestions to improve the situation.

You are required as management accountant, to evaluate the following alternative proposals and to comment briefly on each:

(a) Pay salesmen a commission of 10 per cent of sales and thus increase sales to achieve break-even point.

(5 marks)

(b) Reduce selling price by 10 per cent, which it is estimated would increase sales volume by 30 per cent.

(3 marks)

(c) Increase direct wage rates from £4 to £5 per hour, as part of a productivity/pay deal. It is hoped that this would increase production and sales by 20 per cent, but advertising costs would increase by £50 000.

(4 marks)

(d) Increase sales by additional advertising of £300 000, with an increased selling price of 20 per cent, setting a profit margin of 10 per cent.

(8 marks)
CIMA P1 Cost Accounting

CHAPTER 10
COST ESTIMATION AND COST BEHAVIOUR

LEARNING OBJECTIVES

After studying this chapter, you should be able to:

- identify and describe the different methods of estimating costs;
- calculate regression equations using the high–low, scattergraph and least-squares techniques;
- explain, calculate and interpret tests of reliability;
- explain the meaning of the term 'correlation coefficient';
- identify and explain the six steps required to estimate cost functions from past data.

Determining how cost will change with output or other measurable factors of activity is of vital importance for decision-making, planning and control. The preparation of budgets, the production of performance reports, and the provision of relevant costs for decisions all depend on reliable estimates of costs and also on distinguishing between fixed and variable costs, at different activity levels.

Unfortunately, costs are not always easy to predict, since they behave differently under different circumstances. For example, direct labour can be classified as a variable cost where a company uses casual labour hired on a daily basis so that the employment of labour can be exactly matched to meet the production requirements. In contrast, direct labour may be classified as a step-fixed cost for activities where a fixed number of people are employed and this number is maintained even when there is a temporary reduction in the quantity of the activity used. Depreciation is often quoted as a non-variable cost (also known as a fixed cost), but it may well be variable if asset value declines in direct proportion to usage. We should therefore be careful not to automatically categorize direct labour as a variable cost and depreciation as a non-variable cost.

Many costs are fairly easy to classify as purely variable (e.g. direct materials), fixed (e.g. rental of equipment), or step-fixed (e.g. labour costs) but others fall into a mixed-cost category (also known as semi-variable costs). In Chapter 2 we explained that a semi-variable cost is a cost that has both a fixed and variable component. For example, the cost of maintenance is a semi-variable cost consisting of planned maintenance that is undertaken whatever the activity, and a variable element that is directly related to activity. We need to separate semi-variable costs into their fixed and variable categories.

Frequently the only information that is available for a semi-variable cost is the cost of the activity and a measure of activity usage. For example, records may only be available for the total cost of the maintenance activity for a given period and the number of maintenance hours used during that period. To separate the total cost into its fixed and variable elements it is necessary to use one of the techniques described in this chapter.

A major objective of this chapter is to ascertain the **activity measure** or **cost driver** that exerts the major influence on the cost of a particular activity. A cost driver can be defined as any factor whose change causes a change in the total cost of an activity. Examples of cost drivers include direct labour hours, machine hours, units of output and number of production run set-ups. Throughout this chapter the terms 'cost driver' and 'activity measure' will be used synonymously.

GENERAL PRINCIPLES APPLYING TO ESTIMATING COST FUNCTIONS

Before we consider the various methods of estimating costs, we need to look at some of the terms that will be used. A **regression equation** identifies an estimated relationship between a dependent variable (cost) and one or more independent variables (i.e. an activity measure or cost driver) *based on past observations.* When the equation includes only one independent variable, it is referred to as **simple regression** and it is possible in this situation to plot the regression equation on a graph as a regression line. When the equation includes two or more independent variables, it is referred to as **multiple regression**. If there is only one independent variable and the relationship is linear, the regression line can be described by the equation for a straight line:

$$y = a + bx$$

Assuming that we wish to express the relationship between the dependent variable (cost) and the independent variable (activity), then:

y = total cost for the period at an activity level of x
a = total non-variable (fixed) cost for the period
b = average variable cost per unit of activity
x = volume of activity levels or cost driver for the period

If non-variable (fixed) costs for a particular period are £5000, the average unit variable cost is £1, and direct labour hours represent the cost driver, then:

$$\text{total cost} = £5000 + [£1 \times \text{direct labour hours}(\times)]$$

or

$$y = a + bx$$

so that

$$y = £5000 + £1x$$

A regression equation that describes the relationship between a dependent variable and one or more independent variables is also known as a **cost function**. Cost functions are normally estimated from past cost data and activity levels. Cost estimation begins with measuring *past* relationships between total costs and the potential drivers of those costs. The objective is to use past cost behaviour patterns as an aid to predicting future costs. Of course, any expected changes of circumstances in the future will require past data to be adjusted in line with future expectations.

There is a danger that cost functions derived from past data may be due to a spurious correlation in the data which may not hold good in the future. Cost functions should not be derived solely on the basis of past observed statistical relationships. The nature of the observed statistical relationship should make sense and be economically plausible.

Economic plausibility exists when knowledge of operations or logic implies that a cause-and-effect relationship may exist. For example, the number of component parts is a potential cost driver for material handling costs since the greater the number of parts the higher the material handling costs. Logic suggests that a potential cause-and-effect relationship exists.

COST ESTIMATION METHODS

The following approaches to cost estimation will be examined:

1 engineering methods;
2 inspection of the accounts method;
3 graphical or scattergraph method;
4 high–low method;
5 least-squares method.

These approaches differ in terms of the costs of undertaking the analysis and the accuracy of the estimated cost functions. They are not mutually exclusive and different methods may be used for different cost categories.

Engineering methods

Engineering methods of analysing cost behaviour are based on the use of engineering analyses of technological relationships between inputs and outputs – for example, work sampling and time and motion studies. The approach is appropriate when there is a physical relationship between costs and the cost driver. The procedure involves making an analysis based on *direct* observations of the underlying physical quantities required for an activity and then converting the results into cost estimates. Engineers, who are familiar with the technical requirements, estimate the quantities of materials and the labour and machine hours required for various operations; prices and rates are then applied to the physical measures to obtain the cost estimates.

The engineering method is useful for estimating costs of repetitive processes where input–output relationships are clearly defined. It is usually appropriate when estimating costs that are associated with direct materials, labour and machine time, because these items can be directly observed and measured. However, the engineering method cannot be used for separating semi-variable costs into their fixed and variable elements.

The engineering method is not restricted to manufacturing activities. It can also be applied to well-structured administrative and selling activities such as typing, invoicing and purchasing. It is not generally appropriate, however, for estimating overhead costs that are difficult to associate directly with individual units of output, since these items cannot easily be directly observed and measured.

Inspection of the accounts

The **inspection of accounts method** requires that the departmental manager and the accountant inspect the accounts for a particular period, and then classify each item of expense as a wholly fixed, wholly variable or a semi-variable cost. A single average *unit* cost figure is selected for the items that are categorized as variable, whereas a single *total* cost for the period is used for the items that are categorized as fixed. For semi-variable items the departmental manager and the accountant agree on a cost function that appears to best describe the cost behaviour. The process is illustrated in Example 10.1.

Note that repairs and maintenance have been classified as a semi-variable cost consisting of a variable element of £0.50 per unit of output plus £5000 non-variable cost. A check on the total cost calculation indicates that the estimate of a unit variable cost of £24.50 will give a total variable cost of £245 000 at an output level of 10 000 units. The non-variable costs of £50 000 are added to this to produce an estimated total cost of £295 000. The cost function is therefore $y = 50\ 000 + £24.50x$. This cost function is then used for estimating total cost centre costs at other output levels.

One problem with this method is that the analysis of costs into their variable and non-variable elements can be very subjective. Also, costs are normally based on the latest details that are available from the accounts, and these figures may not be typical of either past or future cost behaviour. Whenever possible, cost estimates should be based on a series of observations.

Graphical or scattergraph method

This method involves plotting the total costs for each activity level on a graph. The total cost is represented on the vertical (Y axis) and the activity levels are recorded on the horizontal (X axis). A straight line is fitted to the scatter of plotted points by visual approximation. Figure 10.1 illustrates the procedure using the data presented in Example 10.2.

EXAMPLE 10.1

The following cost information has been obtained from the latest monthly accounts for an output level of 10 000 units for a cost centre.

	(£)
Direct materials	100 000
Direct labour	140 000
Indirect labour	30 000
Depreciation	15 000
Repairs and maintenance	10 000
	295 000

The departmental manager and the accountant examine each item of expense and analyze the expenses into their variable and non-variable elements. The analysis might be as follows:

	Unit variable cost (£)	Total non-variable cost (£)
Direct materials	10.00	
Direct labour	14.00	
Indirect labour		30 000
Depreciation		15 000
Repairs and maintenance	0.50	5 000
	24.50	50 000

You will see by referring to Figure 10.1 that the maintenance costs are plotted for each activity level, and a straight line is drawn through the middle of the data points as closely as possible so that the distances of observations above the line are equal to the distances of observations below the line.

The point where the straight line in Figure 10.1 cuts the vertical axis (i.e. £240) represents the non-variable costs, item a in the regression formula $y = a + bx$. The unit variable cost b is found by observing the differences between any two points on the straight line (see the dashed line in Figure 10.1 for observations of 160 and 240 hours) and completing the following calculations:

$$\frac{\text{difference in cost}}{\text{difference inactivity}} = \frac{£720 - £560}{240 \text{ hours} - 160 \text{ hours}} = £2 \text{ per hour}$$

This calculation is based on a comparison of the changes in costs that can be observed on the straight line between activity levels of 160 and 240 hours. This gives a regression formula:

$$y = £240 + £2x$$

If x is assigned a value of 100 hours then:

$$y = 240 + (2 \times 100) = £440$$

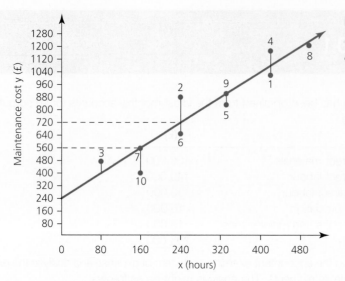

FIGURE 10.1
Graph of maintenance costs at different activity levels

The graphical method is simple to use, and it provides a useful visual indication of any lack of correlation or erratic behaviour of costs. However, the method suffers from the disadvantage that the determination of exactly where the straight line should fall is subjective, and different people will draw different lines with different slopes, giving different cost estimates. To overcome this difficulty, it is preferable to determine the line of best fit mathematically using the least-squares method, which we will describe a little later in this chapter.

EXAMPLE 10.2

The total maintenance costs and the machine hours for the past ten four-weekly accounting periods were as follows:

Period	Machine hours x	Maintenance cost y
1	400	960
2	240	880
3	80	480
4	400	1200
5	320	800
6	240	640
7	160	560
8	480	1200
9	320	880
10	160	440

You are required to estimate the regression equation using the graphical method.

High–low method

The **high–low method** consists of selecting the periods of highest and lowest activity levels and comparing the changes in costs at these two levels. This approach is illustrated in Example 10.3.

The non-variable (fixed) cost can be estimated at any level of activity (assuming a constant unit variable cost) by subtracting the variable cost portion from the total cost. At an activity level of 5000 units the total cost is £22 000 and the total variable cost is £10 000 (5000 units at £2 per unit). The balance of £12 000 is therefore assumed to represent the non-variable cost. The cost function is therefore:

$$y = £12\,000 + £2x$$

The method is illustrated in Figure 10.2, with points A and B representing the lowest and highest output levels, and TC_1 and TC_2 representing the total cost for each of these levels. The other crosses represent past cost observations for other output levels. The higher straight line joining the observations for the lowest and highest activity levels represent the costs that would be estimated for each activity level when the high–low method is used.

EXAMPLE 10.3

The monthly recordings for output and maintenance costs for the past 12 months have been examined and the following information has been extracted for the lowest and highest output levels:

	Volume of production (units)	Maintenance costs (£)
Lowest activity	5 000	22 000
Highest activity	10 000	32 000

The variable cost per unit is calculated as follows:

$$\frac{\text{difference in cost}}{\text{difference in activity}} = \frac{£10\,000}{5000} = £2 \text{ variable cost per unit of output}$$

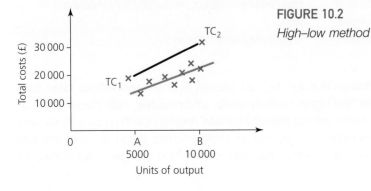

FIGURE 10.2

High–low method

REAL WORLD VIEWS 10.1

Construction cost estimation

Anyone who has ever built their own house knows that cost overruns are a common feature. Building contractors often run into problems and delays, which increase the build time or cost. As the new owner, you will try to avoid overruns, but some are always likely. If we stop to think about it, building a house is a difficult thing to cost with 100 per cent accuracy. If might be that material costs increase if the build is delayed, or costs might increase due to last minute design changes. For the building contractor too, estimated costs will not be perfect but this does not stop a contractor from doing a cost estimate and ultimately giving a price.

To cost the construction of a new house, a building contractor will take into account material, labour and other costs, as well as factors like the location, e.g. build costs are usually higher in urban areas. Materials costs can be estimated from the house plans. For example, the cost of blocks can be estimated based on the height and width of walls from the plans – the holes where windows and doors will be, are assumed as built-up for costing purposes. Typically, building contractors have a cost per square foot/square metre and apply this to the plans to quote a basic finished price. This price will increase depending on additional finishes (e.g. wood-coloured PVC windows, a fitted kitchen) and on location. Some websites are available free to help prospective home owners do their own calculations, which are based on the area of the house.

Building a house is a relatively simple project in terms of the overall construction sector. Infrastructure projects like roads, bridges and tunnels may pose greater cost estimation problems. Such projects are also typically subject to a tendering process where governments or local authorities award work based on cost. Therefore, cost estimation for such projects needs to be as accurate as possible, taking into account the nature of the work involved. Take motorway construction as an example. It may be relatively easy to cost the materials involved to calculate a material cost per kilometre/mile, but no two motorway projects are the same, meaning cost estimation needs to be detailed and fully inclusive. In March 2008, France's largest motorway project to date was announced which involved construction of 100km (approx. 62 miles) of road near Paris at an estimated cost of €675m. One year earlier, an 80km (approx 50 miles) motorway-widening project between Birmingham and Manchester in the UK was costed at £2.1bn. Ignoring exchange rates and other factors, the cost difference seems quite large for a relatively similar length of motorway. However, the UK project had the additional costs of working in a live motorway environment included in the cost estimates. The French project was completely new, on greenfield sites, and did not include costs like temporary lane construction and traffic management.

Discussion points

1   Can a construction company be sure that its cost estimates are reliable enough to allow the business to make a profit?

2   Do you think constructions companies can use data from external sources to help them estimate quantities of materials needed and thus cost materials?

References

http://www.eib.org/projects/press/2008/2008-019-eur-200-m-eib-loan-for-frances-biggest-motorway-project-the-a-19.htm
http://www.guardian.co.uk/uk/2007/jul/31/transport.world
http://www.plan-a-home.ie

You will see from this illustration that the method ignores all cost observations other than the observations for the lowest and highest activity levels. Unfortunately, cost observations at the extreme ranges of activity levels are not always typical of normal operating conditions, and therefore may reflect abnormal rather than normal cost relationships. If you compare the two straight lines in Figure 10.2 you can see how the high–low method can give inaccurate cost estimates. The lower straight line, using the graphical or scattergraph approach described in the previous section, incorporates all of the observations. It is likely to provide a better estimate of the cost function than a method that relies on only two observations. The high–low method cannot therefore be recommended.

The least-squares method

This is a mathematical method of determining the regression line of best fit. It is important for you to understand how this method works, although you are unlikely to be asked to compute these values without help. Spreadsheet packages have regression routines that will perform these calculations for you. You should also note that examination questions generally provide you with formulae 10.1 and 10.2 and the associated values for the variables shown in Exhibit 10.1. It is most unlikely that you will be required to compute the values shown in Exhibit 10.1.

The **least squares method** is based on the principle that the sum of the squares of the vertical deviations from the line that is established using the method is less than the sum of the squares of the vertical deviations from any other line that might be drawn. The regression equation for a straight line that meets this requirement can be found from the following two equations by solving for a and b:

$$a = \frac{\sum y}{n} - \frac{b \sum x}{n} \qquad (10.1)$$

$$b = \frac{n \sum xy - \sum x \sum y}{n \sum x^2 - (\sum x)^2} \qquad (10.2)$$

where n is the number of observations and $\sum$ represents the sum of the variables specified in the above formulae.

Hours x	Maintenance cost y (£)	x^2	xy	y^2
90	1 500	8 100	135 000	2 250 000
150	1 950	22 500	292 500	3 802 500
60	900	3 600	54 000	810 000
30	900	900	27 000	810 000
180	2 700	32 400	486 000	7 290 000
150	2 250	22 500	337 500	5 062 500
120	1 950	14 400	234 000	3 802 500
180	2 100	32 400	378 000	4 410 000
90	1 350	8 100	121 500	1 822 500
30	1 050	900	31 500	1 102 500
120	1 800	14 400	216 000	3 240 000
60	1 350	3 600	81 000	1 822 500
$\sum x = 1260$	$\sum y = 19\,800$	$\sum x^2 = 163\,800$	$\sum xy = 2\,394\,000$	$\sum y^2 = 36\,225\,000$

EXHIBIT 10.1

The least square method

We will use Exhibit 10.1 to illustrate the least-squares method. It is assumed that past information is available for total maintenance cost and machine hours used. We can now insert the data derived from Exhibit 10.1 into the above formulae.

Applying the above formulae 10.1 and 10.2 we must first calculate the value of '*b*' using formula 10.2:

$$b = \frac{12(2\ 394\ 000)-(1260)(19\ 800)}{12(163\ 800)-(1260)^2} = 3\ 780\ 000/378\ 000 = £10$$

$$a = \frac{19\ 800}{12} - \frac{(10)(1260)}{12} = £600$$

We can now use the above cost function (*y* = £600 + £10*x*) to predict the cost incurred at different activity levels, including those for which we have no past observations. For example, at an activity level of 100 hours the cost prediction is £600 non-variable cost, plus £1000 variable cost (100 hours × £10). The regression line and the actual observations (represented by the dots) are recorded in Figure 10.3. The closer the vertical distances of the plotted actual observations are to the straight line the more reliable is the estimated cost function in predicting cost behaviour. In other words, the closer the observations are to the line the stronger the relationship between the independent variable (machine hours in our example) and the dependent variable (i.e. total maintenance cost).

TESTS OF RELIABILITY

In Exhibit 10.1 the cost function was derived using machine hours as the activity measure/cost driver. However a number of other potential cost drivers exist, such as direct labour hours, units

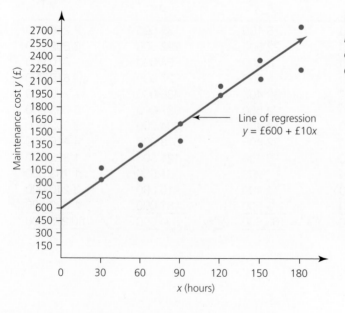

FIGURE 10.3

Regression line y = 600 + 10x compared with actual observations

of output and number of production runs. Various **tests of reliability** can be applied to see how reliable potential cost drivers are in predicting the dependent variable. The most simplistic approach is to plot the data for each potential cost driver and examine the distances from the straight line derived from a visual fit (using the graphical method) or the least squares regression equation. A more sophisticated approach is to compute the **coefficient of variation** (known as r^2). This is also known as the **coefficient of determination** and is the square of the **correlation coefficient** (known as r). It measures how well the predicted values of the dependent variable (i.e. the estimated cost observations represented by y), based on the chosen independent variable (i.e. machine hours (x) in our example shown in Exhibit 10.1), matches the actual cost observations (y). In particular, the coefficient of variation measures the percentage variation in the dependent variable that is explained by the independent variable.

When you are required to calculate the coefficient of determination , most examination questions provide you with the following formula for the correlation coefficient (r):

$$r = \frac{n \sum xy - \sum x \sum y}{\sqrt{(n \sum x^2 - (\sum x)^2)(n \sum y^2 - (\sum y)^2)}} \tag{10.3}$$

Applying the above formula:

$$r = \frac{12(2\ 394\ 000) - (1260)(19\ 800)}{\sqrt{[12(163\ 800) - (1260)^2][12 \times 36\ 225\ 000)(19\ 800)^2]}}$$

$$= \frac{3\ 780\ 000}{4\ 015\ 654} = 0.941$$

so that $r^2 = (0.941)^2 = 0.8861$

You should note that the values computed in Exhibit 10.1 are normally provided in examination questions. What does a coefficient of determination of 0.8861 mean? In percentage terms it means that 88.61 per cent of the variation in total cost is explained by variations in the activity base (cost driver) and the remaining 11.39 per cent is explained by random variation, plus the combined effect that other omitted explanatory variables have on the dependent variable (total cost). The higher the coefficient of variation the stronger is the relationship between the independent and the dependent variable.

The correlation coefficient (r) represents the degree of association between two variables, such as cost and activity. If the degree of association between two variables is very close it will be almost possible to plot the observations on a straight line, and r and r^2 will be very near to 1. In this situation a very strong positive association exists between activity and costs, as illustrated in Figure 10.4. A positive correlation exists when an increase in one variable is associated with an increase in the other variable and a negative correlation exists when an increase in one variable is associated with a decrease in the other variable. Alternatively, the costs may be so randomly distributed that there is little or no correlation between costs and the activity base selected. Thus r and r^2 will be near to zero. An illustration of the situation where no correlation exists is shown in Figure 10.5.

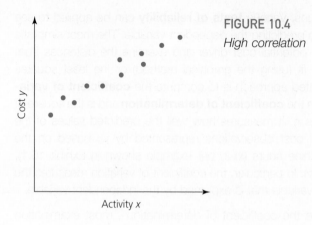

FIGURE 10.4
High correlation

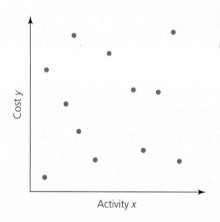

FIGURE 10.5
No correlation

A SUMMARY OF THE STEPS INVOLVED IN ESTIMATING COST FUNCTIONS

We can now summarize the stages involved in the estimation of a cost function based on the analysis of past data. They are:

1 Select the dependent variable *y* (the cost variable) to be predicted.
2 Select the potential cost drivers.
3 Collect data on the dependent variable and cost drivers.
4 Plot the observations on a graph.
5 Estimate the cost function.
6 Test the reliability of the cost function.

It may be necessary to undertake each of these stages several times for different potential cost drivers before an acceptable cost function can be identified.

1 *Select the dependent variable y:* The choice of the cost (or costs) to be predicted will depend upon the purpose of the cost function. If the purpose is to estimate the indirect costs of a production or activity cost centre then all indirect costs associated with the production (activity) centre that are considered to have the same cause-and-effect relationship with the potential costs drivers should be grouped together. In some situations it may be necessary to establish more than one cost function. For example, if certain overheads are considered to be related to performing production set-ups and others are related to machine running hours then it may be necessary to establish two cost pools (centres): one for set-up-related costs and another for machine-related costs. A separate cost function would be established for each cost pool.

2 *Select potential cost drivers:* Examples of potential cost drivers include direct labour hours, machine hours, direct labour cost, number of units of output, number of production run set-ups, number of orders processed and weight of materials.

3 *Collect data on the dependent variable and cost drivers:* A sufficient number of past observations must be obtained to derive acceptable cost functions. The data should be adjusted to reflect any changes of circumstance, such as price changes or changes in the type of equipment used.

4 *Plot the observations on a graph:* A general indication of the relationship between the dependent variable and the cost driver can be observed from the graph. The graph will provide a visual indication as to whether a linear cost function can approximate the cost behaviour and also highlight extreme or abnormal observations. These observations should be investigated to ascertain whether they should be excluded from the analysis.

5 *Estimate the cost function:* The cost function should be estimated using the approaches described in this chapter.

6 *Test the reliability of the cost function:* The reliability of the cost function should be tested using the method described in the previous section. The cost function should be plausible. Cost functions should not be derived solely on the basis of observed past statistical relationships. Instead, they should be used to confirm or reject beliefs that have been developed from a study of the underlying process. The nature of the statistical relationship should be understood and make economic sense.

SUMMARY

The following items relate to the learning objectives listed at the beginning of the chapter.

- **Identify and describe the different methods of estimating costs.** The following approaches can be used to estimate costs: (a) engineering methods; (b) inspection of accounts method; (c) graphical or scattergraph method; (d) high–low method; (e) least squares method; and (f) multiple regression analysis. With engineering studies a detailed study of each operation is undertaken under controlled conditions, based on high levels of efficiency, to ascertain the quantities of labour and materials required. Target prices are then applied based on efficient purchasing to ascertain the standard costs. The engineering method is most appropriate for estimating direct costs for repetitive processes where input–output relationships are clearly defined. The inspection of accounts method requires that a subjective estimate is made of the fixed and variable elements for each item of expenditure within the accounts for a particular period. The remaining four methods are described below.

- **Calculate regression equations using high–low, scattergraph and least squares techniques.** The high–low method consists of selecting the periods of highest and lowest activity levels and comparing the changes in costs that result from these two levels. The variable cost per unit is derived by dividing the difference in cost between the two levels by the differences in activity. Fixed costs are computed by deducting the derived variable cost from total cost at either the lowest or highest output level (see Example 10.3 for an illustration of the calculations). The scattergraph method involves plotting on a graph the total cost for each observed activity level. A straight line is drawn through the middle of the scatter of points so that the distances of observations below the line are equal to the distances above the line. The variable cost per unit is derived from the straight line by dividing the difference in cost by the difference in activity. The intercept gives the estimated fixed cost (see Example 10.2 and Figure 10.1 for an illustration of the computations). The least squares method determines mathematically the line of best fit. It is based on the principle that the sum of the squares of the vertical deviations from the line that is established using this method is less than the sum of the squares of the vertical deviations from any other line that might be drawn (see Exhibit 10.1 for an illustration of the computations). Because this method uses all of the observations and determines the line of best fit mathematically it is considered superior to the high–low or scattergraph methods.

- **Explain, calculate and interpret tests of reliability.** Various tests of reliability can be applied to ascertain how reliable potential independent variables (i.e. cost drivers) are in predicting the dependent variable (i.e. the actual cost observations). One such test is the coefficient of determination (r^2). It is a goodness of fit measure that indicates how well the predicted values of the dependent variable, based on the chosen independent variable, matches the actual cost observations (Y). In particular, the coefficient of determination measures the percentage variation in the dependent variable that is explained by the independent variable. You should refer to Exhibit 10.1 and formula 10.3 for an illustration of the calculation of the coefficient of determination.

- **Explain the meaning of the term correlation coefficient.** The correlation coefficient measures the degree of association between two variables. If the degree of association between the two variables is very close it will almost be possible to plot the relationship on a straight line and the correlation coefficient will be very close to 1. A positive correlation exists when an increase in one variable is associated with an increase in the other variable, whereas a negative correlation exists when an increase/decrease in one variable is associated with a decrease/increase in the other variable. Alternatively, zero correlation exists where there is little or no association between two variables.

- **Identify and explain the six steps required to estimate cost functions from past data.** The following six steps are required: (a) select the cost (dependent) variable to be predicted; (b) select potential cost drivers (i.e. the causes of costs); (c) collect data on the dependent variable and the selected cost driver; (d) plot the observations on a graph; (e) estimate the cost function; and (f) test the reliability of the cost function.

KEY TERMS AND CONCEPTS

Activity measure or **cost driver** any factor (measure) that, when it changes, causes a change in the total cost of an activity.

Coefficient of variation, coefficient of determination or **the correlation coefficient** specific measures of how well the independent variable predicts the values of the dependent variable.

Cost function a term used to describe a relationship between a dependent variable and one or more independent variables.

Engineering methods forms of cost estimation that involve analyzing cost behaviour derived from examining the technological relationships between inputs and outputs.

High–low method a form of cost estimation based on a comparison of the changes in costs for the highest and lowest levels of activity.

Inspection of accounts method a method of cost estimation that involves the examination and subjective classification of all items of expenditure within the accounts into their fixed and variable elements.

Least squares method a mathematical method to determine the regression line of best fit on a graph.

Multiple regression a regression equation with two or more independent variables.

Regression equation an equation that identifies an estimated relationship between a dependent variable and one or more independent variables.

Simple regression a regression equation with one independent variable.

Tests of reliability the measures that can be applied to ascertain how reliable potential cost drivers are in predicting the dependent variable.

KEY EXAMINATION POINTS

In recent years emphasis has switched from calculation to interpretation. Do make sure you can interpret regression equations and explain the meaning of the various statistical tests of reliability. Different formulae can be used to calculate regression equations and r^2 but the formulae specified in the chapter should normally be given in a formulae sheet accompanying the examination paper (see answers to problems 10.14–10.17). The examiner will have set the question assuming you will use the formula. Do not worry if you are unfamiliar with the formula. All that is necessary is for you to enter the figures given in the question into it.

ASSESSMENT MATERIAL

The review questions are short questions that enable you to assess your understanding of the main topics included in the chapter. The numbers in parentheses provide you with the page numbers to refer to if you cannot answer a specific question.

The review problems are more complex and require you to relate and apply the chapter content to various business problems. The problems are graded by their level of difficulty. The multiple-choice questions are the least demanding and normally take less than 10 minutes to complete. Fully worked solutions to the review problems are provided in a separate section at the end of the book. Further review problems with solutions for this chapter are available on the accompanying website www.drury-online.com. The website includes a *Student's Manual* and an *Instructor's Manual*. Students can access both questions and answers from the *Student's Manual* and the questions from the *Instructor's Manual*. The answers to problems in the *Instructor's Manual* are available only to lecturers on the lecturer's password-protected section of the website.

The website also includes over 20 case study problems. A list of these cases is provided on pages 427–30. The Beta Company is a case that is relevant to the content of this chapter.

REVIEW QUESTIONS

10.1 Explain what is meant by the term 'cost function'. *(pp. 238–39)*

10.2 Under what circumstances can the engineering method be used to estimate costs? *(pp. 239–40)*

10.3 Describe the high–low method. *(pp. 243–45)*

10.4 What is the major limitation of the high–low method? *(p. 245)*

10.5 Describe how the scattergraph method is used to analyze costs into their fixed and variable elements. *(pp. 240–42)*

10.6 Describe the least squares method. Why is this method better than the high–low and scattergraph methods? *(pp. 245–46)*

10.7 Describe the steps that should be followed in estimating cost functions. *(pp. 248–49)*

10.8 Why is a scattergraph a useful first step in estimating cost functions? *(p. 248)*

10.9 Explain the meaning of 'coefficient of determination'. *(p. 247)*

REVIEW PROBLEMS

10.10 A hospital's records show that the cost of carrying out health checks in the last five accounting periods have been as follows:

Period	Number of patients seen	Total cost ($)
1	650	17 125
2	940	17 800
3	1260	18 650
4	990	17 980
5	1150	18 360

Using the high–low method and ignoring inflation, the estimated cost of carrying out health checks on 850 patients in period 6 is:

(a) $17 515

(b) $17 570

(c) $17 625

(d) $17 680

CIMA – Management Accounting Fundamentals

10.11 An organization has the following total costs at two activity levels:

Activity level (units)	15 000	24 000
Total costs	£380 000	£470 000

Variable cost per unit is constant in this activity range but there is a step up of £18 000 in the total fixed costs when the activity exceeds 20 000 units.

What are the total costs at an activity level of 18 000 units?

(a) £404 000

(b) £410 000

(c) £422 000

(d) £428 000

ACCA – Financial Information for Management

10.12 The following production and total cost information relates to a single product organization for the last three months:

Month	Production units	Total cost £
1	1200	66 600
2	900	58 200
3	1400	68 200

The variable cost per unit is constant up to a production level of 2000 units per month but a step up of £6000 in the monthly total fixed cost occurs when production reaches 1100 units per month.

What is the total cost for a month when 1000 units are produced?

(a) £54 200

(b) £55 000

(c) £59 000

(d) £60 200

ACCA – Financial Information for Management

10.13 Regression analysis is being used to find the line of best fit ($y = a + bx$) from five pairs of data. The calculations have produced the following information:

$$\sum x = 129 \qquad \sum y = 890 \qquad \sum xy = 23\,091 \qquad \sum x^2 = 3433 \qquad \sum y^2 = 29\,929$$

What is the value of 'a' in the equation for the line of best fit (to the nearest whole number)?

(a) 146

(b) 152

(c) 210

(d) 245

ACCA – Financial Information for Management

10.14 Brisbane Limited has recorded the following sales information for the past six months:

Month	Advertising expenditure £000	Sales revenue £000
1	1.5	30
2	2	27
3	1.75	25
4	3	40
5	2.5	32
6	2.75	38

The following has also been calculated:

$\sum$ (Advertising expenditure) = £13 500
$\sum$ (Sales revenue) = £192 000
$\sum$ (Advertising expenditure x Sales revenue) = £447 250 000
$\sum$ (Sales revenue^2) = £6 322 000 000
$\sum$ (Advertising expenditure^2) = £32 125 000

What is the value of b, i.e. the gradient of the regression line (see formulae 10.1 and 10.2)?

(a) 0.070

(b) 0.086

(c) 8.714

(d) 14.286

ACCA – Financial Information for Management

10.15 A company is seeking to establish whether there is a linear relationship between the level of advertising expenditure and the subsequent sales revenue generated. Figures for the last eight months are as follows:

Month	Advertising expenditure £000	Sales revenue £000
1	2.65	30.0
2	4.25	45.0
3	1.00	17.5
4	5.25	46.0
5	4.75	44.5
6	1.95	25.0
7	3.50	43.0
8	3.00	38.5
Total	26.35	289.5

Further information is available as follows:

$\sum$(Advertising expenditure $\times$ Sales revenue) = £1055.875
$\sum$ (Advertising expenditure)^2 = £101.2625
$\sum$ (Sales revenue)^2 = £11 283.75

All of the above are given in £ million.

Required:

(a) On a suitable graph plot advertising expenditure against sales revenue or *vice versa* as appropriate. Explain your choice of axes.

(5 marks)

(b) Using regression analysis calculate using the formulae given in this chapter a line of best fit. Plot this on your graph from (a).

(5 marks)

ACCA – Financial Information for Management

10.16 **Cost estimation using the linear regression formula**

The management accountant at Josephine Ltd is trying to predict the quarterly total maintenance cost for a group of similar machines. She has extracted the following information for the last eight quarters:

Quarter number	1	2	3	4	5	6	7	8
Total maintenance cost (£000)	265	302	222	240	362	295	404	400
Production units (000)	20	24	16	18	26	22	32	30

The effects of inflation have been eliminated from the above costs.

The management accountant is using linear regression to establish an equation of the form $y = a + bx$ and has produced the following preliminary calculations:

$$\sum(\text{total maintenance cost} \times \text{production units}) = £61\ 250 \text{ million}$$

$$\sum(\text{total maintenance cost})^2 = £809\ 598 \text{ million}$$

$$\sum(\text{production units}) = 4640 \text{ million}$$

Required:

(a) Using the formulae given in this chapter establish the equation which will allow the management accountant to predict quarterly total maintenance costs for given level of production. Interpret your answer in terms of fixed and variable maintenance costs.

(7 marks)

(b) Using the equation established in (a), predict the total maintenance cost for the next quarter when planned production is 44 000 units. Suggest a major reservation, other than the effect of inflation, you would have about this prediction.

(3 marks)

(10 marks)

ACCA – Financial Information for Management

CHAPTER 11
MEASURING RELEVANT COSTS AND REVENUES FOR DECISION-MAKING

LEARNING OBJECTIVES

After studying this chapter you should be able to:

- distinguish between relevant and irrelevant costs and revenues;
- explain the importance of qualitative factors;
- distinguish between the relevant and irrelevant costs and revenues for the five decision-making problems described;
- describe the key concept that should be applied for presenting information for product mix decisions when capacity constraints apply;
- explain why the book value of equipment is irrelevant when making equipment replacement decisions;
- describe the opportunity cost concept.

The provision of relevant information for decision-making is one of the most important functions of management accounting. Decision-making involves choosing between alternatives. For example, managers may be faced with decisions as to whether to discontinue a product or a channel of distribution, make a component within the company or buy from an outside supplier, introduce a new product or service, and/or replace existing equipment. Something that these decisions have in common is that they are not routine. When decisions of this kind are being considered, **special studies** are undertaken.

Making decisions requires that only those costs and revenues that are relevant to the alternatives are considered. If irrelevant cost and revenue data are included, the wrong decisions may be made. It is therefore essential to identify the relevant costs and revenues that are applicable to the alternatives being considered. The purpose of this chapter is to enable you to distinguish between relevant costs and revenues for various decision-making situations.

Special studies focus on whatever planning time horizon the decision-maker considers appropriate for a given situation. However, it is important not to focus excessively on the short term, because the objective is to maximize long-term benefits. We begin by explaining the concept of relevant cost and applying this principle to special studies relating to the following:

1 special selling price decisions;

2 product mix decisions when capacity constraints exist;

3 decisions on replacement of equipment;

4 outsourcing (make or buy) decisions;

5 discontinuation decisions.

IDENTIFYING RELEVANT COSTS AND REVENUES

The **relevant costs and revenues** required for decision-making are only those that will be affected by the decision. Costs and revenues that are independent of a decision are not relevant and need not be considered when making that decision. The relevant financial inputs for decision-making purposes are therefore future cash flows, which will differ between the various alternatives being considered. In other words, only **differential (or incremental) cash flows** should be taken into account, and cash flows that will be the same for all alternatives are irrelevant. To keep things simple we shall focus on relevant costs. You should remember, however, that the same principles also apply to relevant revenues.

Because decision-making is concerned with choosing between future alternative courses of action, and nothing can be done to alter the past, then past costs (also known as sunk costs) are not relevant for decision-making. In Chapter 2 it was pointed out that sunk costs have already been incurred and cannot be avoided regardless of the alternatives being considered.

Allocated common fixed costs are also irrelevant for decision-making. **Facility sustaining costs**, such as general administrative and property costs, are examples of common costs. They are incurred to support the organization as a whole and generally will not change whichever alternative is chosen. They will only change if there is a dramatic change in organizational activity resulting in an expansion or contraction in the business facilities. Common fixed costs may be allocated (i.e. apportioned) to cost objects but they should be disregarded for decision-making. This is because decisions merely lead to a redistribution of the same sunk cost between cost objects – they do not affect the level of cost to the company as a whole.

We can illustrate the identification of relevant costs in a non-business setting. Consider a situation where an individual is uncertain as to whether he or she should purchase a monthly rail ticket to travel to work or use their car. Assuming that the individual already owns and will keep the car, whether or not he or she travels to work by train, the cost of the road fund licence and insurance will be irrelevant. They are sunk costs and will remain the same irrespective of the mode of travel. The cost of fuel will, however, be relevant, because this is a future cost that will differ depending on which alternative method of transport is chosen.

The following general principles can therefore be applied in identifying relevant and irrelevant costs:

1 relevant costs are future costs that differ between alternatives;
2 irrelevant costs consist of sunk costs, allocated costs and future costs that do not differ between alternatives.

IMPORTANCE OF QUALITATIVE FACTORS

In many situations it is difficult to quantify all the important elements of a decision in monetary terms. Those factors that cannot be expressed in monetary terms are classified as **qualitative factors**. An example might be the decline in employee morale that results from redundancies arising from a closure decision. It is essential that qualitative factors be brought to the attention of management during the decision-making process, because otherwise there may be a danger that a wrong decision will be made. For example, the cost of manufacturing a component internally may be more expensive than purchasing from an outside supplier. However, the decision to purchase from an outside supplier could result in the closing down of the company's facilities for manufacturing the component. The effect of such a decision might lead to redundancies and a decline in employee morale, which could affect future output. In addition, the company will now be at the mercy of the supplier who might seek to increase prices on subsequent contracts and/or may not always deliver on time. The company may not then be in a position to meet customers' requirements. In turn, this could result in a loss of customer goodwill and a decline in future sales.

Qualitative factors such as these must be taken into account in the decision-making process. Management must consider the availability of future supplies and the likely effect on customer goodwill if there is a delay in meeting orders. If the component can be obtained from many suppliers and repeat orders for the company's products from customers are unlikely, then the company may give little weighting to these qualitative factors. However, if the component can be obtained from only one supplier and the company relies heavily on repeat sales to existing customers, then the qualitative factors will be of considerable importance. In the latter situation the company may consider that the quantifiable cost savings from purchasing the component from an outside supplier are insufficient to cover the risk of the qualitative factors occurring.

We shall now move on to apply the relevant cost approach to a variety of decision-making problems. We shall concentrate on measuring the financial outcomes but you should remember that they do not always provide the full story. Qualitative factors should also be taken into account in the decision-making process.

SPECIAL PRICING DECISIONS

Special pricing decisions relate to pricing decisions outside the main market. Typically they involve one-time only orders or orders at a price below the prevailing market price. Consider the information presented in Example 11.1.

EXAMPLE 11.1

The Caledonian Company is a manufacturer of clothing that sells its output directly to clothing retailers in the UK. One of its departments manufactures sweaters. The department has a production capacity of 50 000 sweaters per month. Because of the liquidation of one of its major customers the company has excess capacity. For the next quarter, current monthly production and sales volume is expected to be 35 000 sweaters at a selling price of £40 per sweater. Expected *monthly* costs and revenues for an activity level of 35 000 sweaters are as follows:

	(£)	(£ per unit)
Direct labour	420 000	12
Direct materials	280 000	8
Variable manufacturing overheads	70 000	2
Manufacturing fixed (non-variable) overheads	280 000	8
Marketing and distribution fixed (non-variable) costs	105 000	3
Total costs	1 155 000	33
Sales	1 400 000	40
Profit	245 000	7

Caledonian is expecting an upsurge in demand and considers that the excess capacity is temporary. Therefore, even though there is sufficient direct labour capacity to produce 50 000 sweaters, Caledonian intends to retain the temporary excess supply of direct labour for the expected upsurge in demand. A leisure company located overseas has offered to buy 15 000 sweaters each month for the next three months at a price of £20 per sweater. The company would pay for the transportation costs and thus no additional marketing and distribution costs will be incurred. No subsequent sales to this customer are anticipated. The company would require its company logo inserting on the sweater and Caledonian has predicted that this will cost £1 per sweater. Should Caledonian accept the offer from the company?

At first glance it looks as if the order should be rejected since the proposed selling price of £20 is less than the total unit cost of £33. A study of the cost estimates, however, indicates that for the next quarter direct labour will remain unchanged. It is therefore a fixed cost for the period under consideration. Manufacturing fixed overheads and the marketing and distribution costs are also fixed costs for the period under consideration. These costs will thus remain the same irrespective of whether or not the order is accepted. Hence they are irrelevant for this decision. All of the variable costs (i.e. the direct material costs, variable manufacturing overheads and the cost of adding the leisure company's logo) will be different if the order is accepted. Therefore, they are relevant costs for making the decision. The relevant revenue and costs per unit for the decision are:

Selling price		20
Less: Direct materials	8	
Variable overheads	2	
Inserting company logo	1	11
Contribution to fixed costs and profit		9

For sales of 15 000 sweaters Caledonian will obtain an additional contribution of £135 000 per month (15 000 × £9). In Example 11.1none of the fixed costs are relevant for the decision. It is appropriate to unitize variable costs because they are constant per unit but fixed costs should not be unitized since (you will recall from Chapter 2) they are not constant per unit of output. You should present unit relevant costs and revenues (as shown above) only when all fixed costs are irrelevant for decision-making. In most circumstances you are likely to be faced with situations where some of the fixed costs are relevant. Therefore it is recommended that you avoid using unit costs for decision-making and instead adopt the approach presented in Exhibit 11.1, where total costs are used.

Note from Exhibit 11.1 that in columns (1) and (2) both relevant and irrelevant *total* costs are shown for all alternatives under consideration. If this approach is adopted the *same* amounts for the irrelevant items (i.e. those items that remain unchanged as a result of the decision, which are direct labour, and manufacturing and marketing non-variable overheads) are included for all alternatives, thus making them irrelevant for decision-making. Alternatively, you can omit the irrelevant costs in columns (1) and (2) because they are the same for both alternatives. A third approach, which is shown in column (3), involves only presenting the relevant (i.e. differential) costs and revenues.

Note that column (3) represents the difference between columns (1) and (2). You will see that a comparison of columns (1) and (2), or presenting only the relevant items in column (3), shows that the company is better off by £135 000 per month if the order is accepted.

Four important factors must be considered before recommending acceptance of the order. Most of them relate to the assumption that there are no long-run consequences of accepting the offer at a selling price of £20 per sweater. First, it is assumed that the future selling price will not be affected by selling some of the output at a price below the going market price. If this assumption is incorrect then competitors may engage in similar practices of reducing their

Monthly sales and production in units	(1) Do not accept order 35 000 (£)	(2) Accept the order 50 000 (£)	(3) Difference in relevant costs/(revenues) 15 000 (£)
Direct labour	420 000	420 000	—
Direct materials	280 000	400 000	120 000
Variable manufacturing overheads	70 000	100 000	30 000
Manufacturing non-variable overheads	280 000	280 000	—
Inserting company logo		15 000	15 000
Marketing and distribution costs	105 000	105 000	—
Total costs	1 155 000	1 320 000	165 000
Sales revenues	1 400 000	1 700 000	(300 000)
Profit per month	245 000	380 000	135 000
Difference in favour of accepting the order		135 000	

EXHIBIT 11.1
Evaluation of three month order from the company in the leisure industry

selling prices in an attempt to unload spare capacity. This may lead to a fall in the market price, which in turn would lead to a fall in profits from future sales. The loss of future profits may be greater than the short-term gain obtained from accepting special orders at prices below the existing market price. However, given that Caledonian has found a customer outside its normal market, it is unlikely that the market price would be affected. However, if the customer had been within Caledonian's normal retail market there would be a real danger that the market price would be affected. Second, the decision to accept the order prevents the company from accepting other orders that may be obtained during the period at the going price. In other words, it is assumed that no better opportunities will present themselves during the period. Third, it is assumed that the company has unused resources that have no alternative uses that will yield a contribution to profits in excess of £135 000 *per month*. Finally, it is assumed that the fixed costs are unavoidable for the period under consideration. In other words, we assume that the direct labour force and the fixed overheads cannot be reduced in the short term, or that they are to be retained for an upsurge in demand, which is expected to occur in the longer term.

Evaluation of a longer-term order

In Example 11.1 we focused on a short-term time horizon of three months. Capacity could not easily be altered in the short term and therefore direct labour and fixed costs were irrelevant costs with respect to the short-term decision. In the longer term, however, it may be possible to reduce capacity and spending on fixed costs and direct labour. Example 11.2 uses the

EXAMPLE 11.2

Assume that the department within Caledonian Company has a *monthly* production capacity of 50 000 sweaters. Liquidation of a major customer has resulted in expected future demand being 35 000 sweaters per *month*. Caledonian has not been able to find any customers for the excess capacity of 15 000 sweaters apart from a company located overseas that would be prepared to enter into a contractual agreement for a three-year period for a supply of 15 000 sweaters per month at an agreed price of £25 per sweater. The company would require that a motif be added to each sweater and Caledonian has predicted that will cost £1 per sweater. The company would pay for the transportation costs and thus no additional marketing and distribution costs will be incurred.

Direct materials and variable overheads are predicted to be £8 and £2, respectively, per sweater (the same as Example 11.1) and fixed manufacturing (£280 000), marketing and distribution costs (£105 000) and direct labour (£420 000) are also currently the same as the costs used in Example 11.1. However, if Caledonian does not enter into a contractual agreement it will reduce the direct labour force by 30 per cent (to reflect a capacity reduction from 50 000 to 35 000 sweaters). Therefore, monthly direct labour costs will decline by 30 per cent, from £420 000 to £294 000. Further investigations indicate that manufacturing non-variable costs of £70 000 per month could be saved if a decision was made to reduce capacity by 15 000 sweaters per month. For example, the rental contracts for some of the machinery will not be renewed. Also some savings will be made in supervisory labour and support costs. Savings in marketing and distribution costs would be £20 000 per month. Assume also that if the capacity was reduced, factory rearrangements would result in part of the facilities being rented out at £25 000 per month. Should Caledonian accept the offer from the overseas company?

same cost data as Example 11.1 but presents a revised scenario of a longer time horizon so that some of the costs that were fixed in the short term in Example 11.1 can now be changed in the longer term. You will see from Example 11.2 that Caledonian is faced with the following two alternatives:

1 do not accept the overseas order and reduce monthly capacity from 50 000 to 35 000 sweaters;

2 accept the overseas order of 15 000 sweaters per month and retain capacity at 50 000 sweaters per month.

The appropriate financial data for the analysis is shown in Exhibit 11.2. Note that column (1) incorporates the reduction in direct labour and fixed costs if capacity is reduced from 50 000 to 35 000 sweaters. A comparison of the monthly outcomes reported in columns (1) and (2) of Exhibit 11.2 shows that the company is better off by £31 000 per month if it reduces capacity to 35 000 sweaters, assuming that there are no qualitative factors to be taken into consideration. Column (3) presents only the differential (relevant) costs and revenues. This approach also indicates that the company is better off by £31 000 per month.

Note that the entry in column (3) of £25 000 is the lost revenues from the rent of the unutilized capacity if the company accepts the orders. This represents the opportunity cost of accepting the orders. In Chapter 2 it was pointed out that where the choice of one course of action requires that an alternative course of action is given up, the financial benefits that are foregone or sacrificed are known as **opportunity costs**. They only arise when resources are scarce *and* have alternative uses. Thus, in our illustration the capacity allocated to producing 15 000 sweaters results in an opportunity cost (i.e. the lost revenues from the rent of the capacity) of £25 000 per month.

In Exhibit 11.2 all of the costs and revenues are relevant to the decision because some of the costs that were fixed in the short term could be changed in the longer term. The relevance

Monthly sales and production in units	(1) Do not accept order 35 000 (£)	(2) Accept the order 50 000 (£)	(3) Difference in relevant costs/ (revenues) 15 000 (£)
Direct labour	294 000	420 000	126 000
Direct materials	280 000	400 000	120 000
Variable manufacturing overheads	70 000	100 000	30 000
Manufacturing non-variable overheads	210 000	280 000	70 000
Inserting motif		15 000	15 000
Marketing and distribution costs	85 000	105 000	20 000
Total costs	939 000	1 320 000	381 000
Revenues from rental of facilities	25 000		25 000
Sales revenues	1 400 000	1 775 000	(375 000)
Profit per month	486 000	455 000	31 000
Difference in favour of rejecting the order		31 000	

EXHIBIT 11.2

Evaluation of orders for the unutilized capacity over a three-year time horizon

REAL WORLD VIEWS 11.1

Measures of product attractiveness in retail operations

Shelf space limits the quantity and variety of products offered by a retail operation. The visibility of a particular stock-keeping unit (SKU) and probability of a stock-out are related to the space allocated to the SKU. Total contribution for the retail operation is influenced by how shelf space is allocated to the SKUs. For retailers, shelf space 'is their life blood – and it's very limited and expensive'. Shelf space, accordingly, can be treated as a constraint in retailing operations. The most attractive SKU is the SKU that generates the greatest contribution per unit of space (square foot or cubic foot). To calculate contribution, all incremental expenses are deducted from incremental revenue. Incremental revenues include retail price and other direct revenue such as deals, allowances, forward-buy and prompt-payment discounts. Incremental expenses include any money paid out as a result of selling one unit of a particular item. Included in the incremental expenses would be the invoice unit cost and other invoiced amounts (ship-ping charges, for example) that can be traced directly to the sale of the particular item. Incremental revenues and expenses are found by dividing case values by the number of units per case.

If capacity is not changed, then the relevant costs are the incremental costs rather than full costs. The choice of low direct product cost items (i.e. a full product cost including a share of the fixed warehouse, transport and storage costs) over high direct product cost items is essentially a choice to use less of the capacity that has already been paid for. If the costs of capacity are fixed, then using less capacity will not save money. Like the product mix problem, the answer to the space management problem is how to allocate existing capacity so that profit is maximized. To maximize profits where profits are constrained by space limitations, capacity should be allocated on the basis of the SKU that generates the greatest contribution per unit of space.

Discussion point

1 What are the relevant costs and revenues applicable to retail operations?

SOURCE: ADAPTED FROM GARDNER, S. C. MEASURES OF PRODUCT ATTRACTIVENESS AND THE THEORY OF CONSTRAINTS, INTERNATIONAL JOURNAL OF RETAIL AND DISTRIBUTION, 1983. VOL 21. NO. 7, PP 37-40. EMERALD PUBLISHERS WWW.EMERALDINSIGHT.COM/IJRD/HTML

of a cost often depends on the time horizon under consideration. It is therefore important to make sure that the information presented for decision-making relates to the appropriate time horizon. If inappropriate time horizons are selected there is a danger that misleading information will be presented. Remember that our aim should always be to maximize *long-term* net cash inflows.

PRODUCT MIX DECISIONS WHEN CAPACITY CONSTRAINTS EXIST

In the short term sales demand may be in excess of current productive capacity. For example, output may be restricted by a shortage of skilled labour, materials, equipment or space. When sales demand is in excess of a company's productive capacity, the resources responsible for limiting the output should be identified. These scarce resources are known as **limiting factors**. Within a short-term time period it is unlikely that constraints can be removed and additional resources acquired. Where limiting factors apply, profit is maximized when the greatest possible contribution to profit is obtained each time the scarce or limiting factor is used. Consider Example 11.3.

In this situation the farmer's ability to increase output and profits/net cash inflows is limited in the short term by the availability of land for growing crops. At first glance, you may think that the farmer should give top priority to producing maize, since this yields the highest contribution per tonne sold, but this assumption would be incorrect. To produce a tonne of maize, 80 scarce m^2 are required, whereas potatoes, barley and wheat require only $32m^2$, $24m^2$ and $16m^2$ respectively of scarce land. By concentrating on growing potatoes, barley and wheat, the farmer can sell 3000 tonnes of each crop and still have some land left to grow maize. On the other hand, if the farmer concentrates on growing maize it will only be possible to meet the maximum sales demand of maize, and there will be no land available to grow the remaining crops. The way in which you should determine the optimum output to maximize profits is to calculate the contribution per limiting factor for each crop and then to rank the crops in order of profitability based on this calculation.

Using the figures in the present example the result would be as follows:

	Maize	Potatoes	Barley	Wheat
Contribution per tonne of output	$160	$112	$96	$80
m^2 required per tonne of output	80	32	24	16
Contribution per m^2	$2	$3.50	$4	$5
Ranking	4	3	2	1

The farmer can now allocate the 240 000m^2 of land in accordance with the above rankings. The first choice should be to produce as much wheat as possible. The maximum sales are 3000 tonnes, and production of this quantity will result in 48 000m^2 of land being used. The second choice should be to grow barley and the maximum sales demand of 3000 tonnes will result in a further 72 000m^2 of land being used. The third choice is to grow potatoes. To meet the maximum sales demand for potatoes a further 96 000m^2 of land will be required. Growing 3000 tonnes of wheat, barley and potatoes requires 216 000m^2 of land, leaving a balance of 24 000m^2 for growing maize, which will enable 300 tonnes of maize to be grown.

We can now summarize the allocation of the 240 000m^2 of land:

Production	m^2 of land used	Balance of unused land (m^2)
3000 tonnes of wheat	48 000	192 000
3000 tonnes of barley	72 000	120 000
3000 tonnes of potatoes	96 000	24 000
300 tonnes of maize	24 000	—

The above allocation results in the following total contribution:

	$
3000 tonnes of wheat at $80 per tonne contribution	240 000
3000 tonnes of barley at $96 per tonne contribution	288 000
3000 tonnes of potatoes at $112 per tonne contribution	336 000
300 tonnes of maize at $160 per tonne contribution	48 000
Total contribution	912 000

Contrast the above contribution with the contribution that would have been obtained if the farmer had ranked crop profitability by their contributions per tonne of output. This would have

EXAMPLE 11.3

A farmer in Ruritania has 240 000 square metres (m^2) of land on which he grows maize, barley, potatoes and wheat. He is planning his production for the next growing season. The following information is provided relating to the anticipated demand and productive capacity for the next season:

	Maize	Potatoes	Barley	Wheat
Contribution per tonne of output in Ruritanian dollars	$160	$112	$96	$80
m^2 required per tonne of output	80	32	24	16
Estimated sales demand (tonnes)	3000	3000	3000	3000
Required area to meet sales demand (m^2)	240 000	96 000	72 000	48 000

It is not possible in the short run to increase the area of land beyond 240 000m^2 for growing the above crops. You have been asked to advise on the mix of crops that should be produced during the period.

resulted in maize being ranked as the most profitable crop and all of the available land would have been used to grow 3000 tonnes of maize, giving a total contribution of $480 000 (3000 tonnes × $160).

Always remember to consider other qualitative factors before the final production programme is determined. For example, customer goodwill may be lost causing a fall in future sales if the farm is unable to supply all four crops to, say, 50 of its regular customers. Difficulties may arise in applying this procedure when there is more than one scarce resource. It could not be applied if, for example, labour hours were also scarce and maize had the highest contribution per scarce labour hour. In situations where more than one resource is scarce, it is necessary to resort to linear programming methods in order to determine the optimal production programme. For an explanation of how linear programming can be applied when there is more than one scarce resource, you should refer to Learning Note 11.1 on the dedicated open access website (see Preface for details).

Finally, it is important that you remember that the approach outlined in this section applies only to those situations where capacity constraints cannot be removed in the short term. In the longer term additional resources should be acquired if the contribution from the extra capacity exceeds the cost of acquisition.

REPLACEMENT OF EQUIPMENT – THE IRRELEVANCE OF PAST COSTS

Replacement of equipment is a capital investment or long-term decision but one aspect of asset replacement decisions that we will consider at this stage is how to deal with the book value (i.e. the **written down value**) of old equipment. This is a problem that has been known to cause difficulty, but the correct approach is to apply relevant cost principles (i.e. past or sunk costs are irrelevant for decision-making). We shall now use Example 11.4 to illustrate the irrelevance of the book value of old equipment in a replacement decision.

EXAMPLE 11.4

Three years ago the Anytime Bank purchased a cheque sorting machine for £120 000. Depreciation using the straight line basis, assuming a life of six years and no salvage value, has been recorded each year in the financial accounts. The present written down value of the machine is £60 000 and it has a remaining life of three years. Recently a new sorting and imaging machine has been marketed that will cost £50 000 and have an expected life of three years with no scrap value. It is estimated that the new machine will reduce variable operating costs from £50 000 to £30 000 per annum. The current sales value of the old machine is £5000 and will be zero in three years' time.

You will see from an examination of Example 11.4 that the total costs over a period of three years for each of the alternatives are as follows:

	(1) Retain present machine (£)	(2) Buy replacement machine (£)	(3) Difference relevant costs/ (benefits) (£)
Variable/incremental operating costs:			
£50 000 for 3 years	150 000		
£30 000 for 3 years		90 000	(60 000)
Old machine book value:			
3-year annual depreciation charge	60 000		
Lump sum write-off		60 000	
Old machine disposal value		(5000)	(5000)
Initial purchase price of new machine		50 000	50 000
Total cost	210 000	195 000	(15 000)

You can see from the above analysis that the £60 000 book value of the old machine is irrelevant to the decision. Book values are not relevant costs because they are past or sunk costs and are therefore the same for all potential courses of action. If the present machine is retained, three years' depreciation at £20 000 per annum will be written off annually, whereas if the new machine is purchased the £60 000 will be written off as a lump sum if it is replaced. Note that depreciation charges for the new machine are not included in the analysis since the cost of purchasing the machine is already included. The sum of the annual depreciation charges is equivalent to the purchase cost. Thus, including both items would amount to double counting.

The above analysis shows that the costs of operating the replacement machine are £15 000 less than the costs of operating the existing machine over the three-year period. Again there are several different methods of presenting the information. They all show a £15 000 advantage in favour of replacing the machine. You can present the information shown in columns (1) and (2) above, as long as you ensure that the same amount for the irrelevant items is included for all alternatives. Alternatively, you can present columns (1) and (2) with the irrelevant item (i.e. the £60 000) omitted or you can present the differential items listed in column (3). However, if you adopt the latter approach you will probably find it more meaningful to restate column (3) as follows:

	£
Savings on variable operating costs (3 years)	60 000
Sale proceeds of existing machine	5000
	65 000
Less purchase cost of replacement machine	50 000
Savings on purchasing replacement machine	15 000

OUTSOURCING AND MAKE OR BUY DECISIONS

Outsourcing is the process of obtaining goods or services from outside suppliers instead of producing the same goods or providing the same services within the organization. Decisions on whether to produce components or provide services within the organization or to acquire them from outside suppliers are called outsourcing or 'make or buy' decisions. Many organizations outsource some of their activities such as their payroll and purchasing functions

REAL WORLD VIEWS 11.2

Outsourcing at IBM

Krakow, Poland is a location used by many global firms to locate outsourced activities like software development, technical support or billing and accounts receivable. The city has over 150 000 students, who provide a suitable skill base for employers. Another location often used is Bangalore, India where labour costs are cheaper still. Since Poland joined the European Union in 2004, labour costs have steadily increased (7 per cent per annum on average) towards Western European levels, perhaps making Krakow a less attractive location for outsourced activities.

Not so according to IBM. IBM has outsourced activities in both Krakow and Bangalore. It realized that no one location can provide everything and it is not just about cost. In Krakow, for example, the local universities generate a ready supply of graduates – just what IBM needs to staff its software lab. Graduates are also readily available with expertise in US accounting and legal disciplines. The idea is to develop 'centres of competence' less vulnerable to competition based on labour costs alone. 'Even if you're a very well-organized company, it takes time to build a team with experienced people,' says Aleksandra Lichon, human resources director for IBM business consulting services in Krakow.

Moreover, IBM needs to challenge its employees to retain them in an increasingly competitive job market. Polish workers do not want to be seen as cheap labour, but as full members of the team.

In addition to IBM, Krakow also hosts outsourced operations of organizations like KPMG and Motorola, and outsourcing specialists like Cap Gemini, one of the world's leading outsourcing vendors. It seems the availability of well-educated staff outweighs the higher labour cost.

Discussion points

1 Other than those mentioned, what kind of business activities would be best suited to outsourcing?

2 Strategically, do you think outsourcing is a good idea? Does it deliver value financially, operationally and strategically?

References

Spiegel Online International, 26 September 2007 (http://www.spiegel.de/international/business/0,1518, 508014,00.html).

EXAMPLE 11.5

Case A

One of the divisions within Rhine Autos is currently negotiating with another supplier regarding out-sourcing component A that it manufactures. The division currently manufactures 10 000 units per annum of the component. The costs currently assigned to the components are as follows:

	Total costs of producing 10 000 components (£)	Unit cost (£)
Direct materials AB	120 000	12
Direct labour	100 000	10
Variable manufacturing overhead costs (power and utilities)	10 000	1
Fixed manufacturing overhead costs	80 000	8
Share of non-manufacturing overheads	50 000	5
Total costs	360 000	36

The above costs are expected to remain unchanged in the foreseeable future if the Rhine Autos division continues to manufacture the components. The supplier has offered to supply 10 000 components per annum at a price of £30 per unit, guaranteed for a minimum of three years. If Rhine Autos outsources component A the direct labour force currently employed in producing the components will be made redundant. No redundancy costs will be incurred. Direct materials and variable overheads are avoidable if component A is outsourced. Fixed manufacturing overhead costs would be reduced by £10 000 per annum but non-manufacturing costs would remain unchanged. Assume initially that the capacity that is required for component A has no alternative use. Should the division of Rhine Autos make or buy the component?

Case B

Assume now that the extra capacity that will be made available from outsourcing component A can be used to manufacture and sell 10 000 units of component Z at a price of £34 per unit. All of the labour force required to manufacture component A would be used to make component Z. The variable manufacturing overheads, the fixed manufacturing overheads and non-manufacturing overheads would be the same as the costs incurred for manufacturing component A. Materials AB required to manufacture component A would not be required but additional materials XY required for making component Z would cost £13 per unit. Should Rhine Autos outsource component A?

or the purchase of speciality components. Increasingly, municipal local services such as waste disposal, highways and property maintenance are being outsourced. Consider the information presented in Example 11.5 (Case A).

At first glance it appears that the component should be outsourced since the purchase price of £30 is less than the current total unit cost of manufacturing. However, the unit costs include some costs that will be unchanged whether or not the components are outsourced. These costs are therefore not relevant to the decision. We are also assuming that there are no alternative uses of the released capacity if the components are outsourced. The appropriate cost information is presented in Exhibit 11.3 (Section A). Alternative approaches to presenting relevant cost and revenue information are presented. In columns (1) and (2) of Exhibit 11.3 cost information is presented that includes both relevant and irrelevant costs for both alternatives under consideration. The same amount for non-manufacturing overheads, which are irrelevant, is included for both alternatives. By including the same amount in both columns the cost is made irrelevant. Alternatively, you can present cost information in columns (1) and (2) that excludes any irrelevant costs and revenues. Adopting either approach will result in a difference of £60 000 in favour of making component A.

Section A – Assuming there is no alternative use of the released capacity

	Total cost of continuing to make 10 000 components (1) (£ per annum)	Total cost of buying 10 000 components (2) (£ per annum)	Difference = Extra costs/ (savings) of buying (3) (£ per annum)
Direct materials AB	120 000		(120 000)
Direct labour	100 000		(100 000)
Variable manufacturing overhead costs (power and utilities)	10 000		(10 000)
Fixed manufacturing overhead costs	80 000	70 000	(10 000)
Non-manufacturing overheads	50 000	50 000	
Outside purchase cost incurred/(saved)		300 000	300 000
Total costs incurred/(saved) per annum	360 000	420 000	60 000
Extra costs of buying = £60 000			

Section B – Assuming the released capacity can be used to make component Z

	(1) Make component A and do not make component Z (£ per annum)	(2) Buy component A and make component Z (£ per annum)	(3) Difference = Extra costs/ (benefits) of buying component A (£ per annum)
Direct materials XY		130 000	130 000
Direct materials AB	120 000		(120 000)
Direct labour	100 000	100 000	
Variable manufacturing overhead costs	10 000	10 000	
Fixed manufacturing overhead costs	80 000	80 000	
Non-manufacturing overheads	50 000	50 000	
Outside purchase cost incurred		300 000	300 000
Revenue from sales of component Z		(340 000)	(340 000)
Total net costs	360 000	330 000	(30 000)

Extra benefits from buying component A and using the released capacity to make component Z = £30 000

EXHIBIT 11.3

Evaluating a make or buy decision

As in earlier exhibits, the third approach is to list only the relevant costs, cost savings and any relevant revenues. This approach is shown in column (3) of Exhibit 11.3 (Section A). This column represents the differential costs or revenues and it is derived from the differences between columns (1) and (2). In column (3) only the information that is relevant to the decision is presented. This approach shows that the additional costs of buying component A are £300 000 but this enables costs of £240 000 associated with making component A to be saved. Therefore the company incurs an extra cost of £60 000 if it buys component A from the outside supplier.

We shall now explore what happens when the extra capacity created from not producing component A has an alternative use. Consider the information presented in Example 11.5 (Case B). The management of Rhine Autos now should consider the following alternatives:

1 make component A and do not make component Z;

2 outsource component A and make and sell component Z.

It is assumed that there is insufficient capacity to make both components A and Z. The appropriate financial information is shown in Exhibit 11.3 (Section B). You will see that the same costs will be incurred for both alternatives for direct labour and all of the overhead costs. Therefore these items are irrelevant and the same amount can be entered in columns (1) and (2) or they can be omitted from both columns. Note that direct materials AB (£120 000) will be incurred only if the company makes component A so an entry of £120 000 is shown in column (1) and no entry is made in column (2). However, if component A is bought from the supplier the capacity will be used to produce component Z and this will result in a purchase cost of £130 000 being incurred for materials XY. Thus £130 000 is entered in column (2) and no entry is made in column (1) in respect of materials XY. Also note that the sales revenue arising from the sale of component Z is shown in parentheses in column (2). A comparison of the totals of columns (1) and (2) indicates that that there is a net benefit of £30 000 from buying component A if the released capacity is used to make component Z.

Instead of presenting the information in columns (1) and (2) you can present the relevant costs and benefits as shown by the differential items in column (3). This column indicates that the extra costs of buying component A and using the released capacity to make component Z are:

	£
Outside purchase cost incurred	300 000
Purchase of materials XY for component Z	130 000
	430 000

The extra benefits are:

	£
Revenues from the sale of component Z	340 000
Savings from not purchasing materials AB	120 000
	460 000

The above alternative analysis also shows that there is a net benefit of £30 000 from buying component A if the released capacity is used to make component Z.

DISCONTINUATION DECISIONS

Most organizations periodically analyze profits by one or more cost objects, such as products or services, customers and locations. Periodic profitability analysis can highlight unprofitable activities that require a more detailed appraisal (sometimes referred to as a special study) to ascertain whether or not they should be discontinued. In this section we shall illustrate how the principle of relevant costs can be applied to discontinuation decisions. Consider Example 11.6. You will see that it focuses on a decision whether to discontinue operating a sales territory, but the same principles can also be applied to discontinuing products, services or customers.

In Example 11.6 Aero Company analyzes profits by locations. Profits are analyzed by regions which are then further analyzed by sales territories within each region. It is apparent from Example 11.6 that the South East Asian region is profitable (showing a budgeted quarterly profit of £202 000) but the profitability analysis suggests that the Bangkok sales territory is unprofitable. A more detailed study is required to ascertain whether it should be discontinued. Let us assume that this study indicates that:

1 Discontinuing the Bangkok sales territory will eliminate cost of goods sold, salespersons' salaries and sales office rent.

2 Discontinuing the Bangkok sales territory will have no effect on depreciation of sales office equipment, warehouse rent, depreciation of warehouse equipment and regional and headquarters expenses. The same costs will be incurred by the company for all of these items even if the sales territory is discontinued.

Note that in the event of discontinuation the sales office will not be required and the rental will be eliminated, whereas the warehouse rent relates to the warehouse for the region as a whole and, unless the company moves to a smaller warehouse, the rental will remain unchanged. It is therefore not a relevant cost. Discontinuation will result in the creation of additional space and if the extra space remains unused there are no financial consequences to take into account. However, if the additional space can be sublet to generate rental income, this income would be incorporated as an opportunity cost for the alternative of keeping the Bangkok territory.

Exhibit 11.4 shows the relevant cost and revenue computations. Column (1) shows the costs incurred and revenues derived by the company if the sales territory is kept open (i.e. the items listed in the final column of Example 11.6) and column (2) shows the costs and revenues that will occur if a decision is taken to drop the sales territory. Therefore, in column (2) only those costs that would be eliminated (i.e. those in item (1) above) are deducted from column (1). For example, Example 11.6 specifies that £240 000 salespersons' salaries will be eliminated if the Bangkok territory is closed so the entry in column (2) is £360 000 (£600 000 – £240 000).

You can see that the company will continue to incur some of the costs (i.e. those in item (2) above) even if the Bangkok territory is closed, and these costs are therefore irrelevant to the decision. Again you can either include, or exclude, the irrelevant costs in columns (1) and (2) as long as you ensure that the same amount of irrelevant costs is included for both alternatives if you adopt the first approach. Both approaches will show that future profits will decline by £154 000 if the Bangkok territory is closed. Alternatively, you can present just the relevant costs and revenues shown in column (3). This approach indicates that keeping the sales territory open results in additional sales revenues of £1 700 000 but additional costs of £1 546 000 are incurred giving a contribution of £154 000 towards fixed costs and profits. We can conclude that the Bangkok sales territory should not be closed.

EXAMPLE 11.6

The Aero Company is a wholesaler that sells its products to retailers throughout the Far East. Aero's headquarters is in Hong Kong. The company has adopted a regional structure with each region consisting of 3–5 sales territories. Each region has its own regional office and a warehouse that distributes the goods directly to the customers. Each sales territory also has an office where the marketing staff are located. The South East Asian region consists of three sales territories with offices located in Singapore, Kuala Lumpur and Bangkok. The budgeted results for the next quarter are as follows:

	Singapore (£000)	Kuala Lumpur (£000)	Bangkok (£000)	Total (£000)
Cost of goods sold	920	1002	1186	3108
Salespersons' salaries	160	200	240	600
Sales office rent	60	90	120	270
Depreciation of sales office equipment	20	30	40	90
Apportionment of warehouse rent	24	24	24	72
Depreciation of warehouse equipment	20	16	22	58
Regional and headquarters costs	360	400	340	1100
Total costs assigned to each location	1564	1762	1972	5298
Reported profit/(loss)	236	238	(272)	202
Sales	1800	2000	1700	5500

Assuming that the above results are likely to be typical of future quarterly performance, should the Bangkok territory be discontinued?

	Total costs and revenues to be assigned		
	(1) Keep Bangkok territory open (£000)	(2) Discontinue Bangkok territory (£000)	(3) Difference in incremental costs and revenues (£000)
Cost of goods sold	3108	1922	1186
Salespersons' salaries	600	360	240
Sales office rent	270	150	120
Depreciation of sales office equipment	90	90	
Apportionment of warehouse rent	72	72	
Depreciation of warehouse equipment	58	58	
Regional and headquarters costs	1100	1100	
Total costs to be assigned	5298	3752	1546
Reported profit	202	48	154
Sales	5500	3800	1700

EXHIBIT 11.4

Relevant cost analysis relating to the discontinuation of the Bangkok territory

DETERMINING THE RELEVANT COSTS OF DIRECT MATERIALS

So far in this chapter we have assumed, when considering various decisions, that any materials required would not be taken from existing stocks but would be purchased at a later date, and so the estimated purchase price would be the relevant material cost. Where materials are taken from existing stock you should remember that the original purchase price represents a past or sunk cost and is therefore irrelevant for decision-making. However, if the materials are to be replaced then the decision to use them on an activity will result in additional acquisition costs compared with the situation if the materials were not used on that particular activity. Therefore the future replacement cost represents the relevant cost of the materials.

Consider now the situation where the materials have no further use apart from being used on a particular activity. If the materials have some realizable value, the use of the materials will result in lost sales revenues, and this lost sales revenue will represent an opportunity cost that must be assigned to the activity. Alternatively, if the materials have no realizable value the relevant cost of the materials will be zero.

DETERMINING THE RELEVANT COSTS OF DIRECT LABOUR

Determining the direct labour costs that are relevant to short-term decisions depends on the circumstances. Where a company has temporary spare capacity and the labour force is to be maintained in the short term, the direct labour cost incurred will remain the same for all alternative decisions. The direct labour cost will therefore be irrelevant for short-term decision-making purposes. However, in a situation where casual labour is used and where workers can be hired on a daily basis, a company may then adjust the employment of labour to exactly the amount required to meet the production requirements. The labour cost will increase if the company accepts additional work, and will decrease if production is reduced. In this situation the labour cost will be a relevant cost for decision-making purposes.

In a situation where full capacity exists and additional labour supplies are unavailable in the short term, and where no further overtime working is possible, the only way that labour resources could then be obtained for a specific order would be to reduce existing production. This would release labour for the order, but the reduced production would result in a lost contribution, and this lost contribution must be taken into account when ascertaining the relevant cost for the specific order. The relevant labour cost per hour where full capacity exists is therefore the hourly labour rate plus an opportunity cost consisting of the contribution per hour that is lost by accepting the order. For a more detailed illustration explaining why this is the appropriate cost you should refer to Learning note 11.2 on the open access website (see Preface for details).

INCORPORATING UNCERTAINTY INTO THE DECISION-MAKING PROCESS

In this chapter and Chapter 9 we have used a single representative set of estimates for predicting future costs and revenues for alternative courses of action. However, the outcome of a particular decision may be affected by an uncertain environment that cannot be predicted, and a single representative estimate does not therefore convey all the information that might reasonably influence a decision.

Consider a situation where a company has two mutually exclusive potential alternatives, A and B, which each yield receipts of £50 000. The estimated costs of alternative A can be predicted with considerable confidence, and are expected to fall in the range of £40 000–£42 000; £41 000 might be considered a reasonable estimate of cost. The estimate for alternative B is subject to much greater uncertainty, since this alternative requires high-precision work involving operations that are unfamiliar to the company's labour force. The estimated costs are between £35 000 and £45 000, but £40 000 is selected as a representative estimate. If we consider single representative estimates alternative B appears preferable, since the estimated profit is £10 000 compared with an estimated profit of £9000 for alternative A; but a different picture may emerge if we take into account the range of possible outcomes.

Alternative A is expected to yield a profit of between £8000 and £10 000 whereas the range of profits for alternative B is between £5000 and £15 000. Management may consider it preferable to opt for a fairly certain profit of between £8000 and £10 000 for alternative A rather than take the chance of earning a profit of £5000 from alternative B (even though there is the possibility of earning a profit of £15 000 at the other extreme).

This example demonstrates that there is a need to incorporate the uncertainty relating to each alternative into the decision-making process. Decision-making under conditions of uncertainty is a topic that is normally included in second-level management accounting courses but recently some professional accounting examining bodies have incorporated this topic in first-level courses. Because this topic is likely to be relevant to a small percentage of the users of this book it is dealt with in Learning Note 11.4 on the dedicated open access website. You should therefore check your course content to ascertain if you need to read Learning Note 11.4.

SUMMARY

The following items relate to the learning objectives listed at the beginning of the chapter.

- **Distinguish between relevant and irrelevant costs and revenues**. Relevant costs/revenues represent those future costs/revenues that will be changed by a particular decision, whereas irrelevant costs/revenues will not be affected by that decision. In the short term total profits will be increased (or total losses decreased) if a course of action is chosen where relevant revenues are in excess of relevant costs.

- **Explain the importance of qualitative factors**. Quantitative factors refer to outcomes that can be measured in numerical terms. In many situations it is difficult to quantify all the important elements of a decision. Those factors that cannot be expressed in numerical terms are called qualitative factors. Examples of qualitative factors include changes in employee morale and the impact of being at the mercy of a supplier when a decision is made to close a company's facilities and sub-contract components. Although qualitative factors cannot be quantified it is essential that they are taken into account in the decision-making process.

- **Distinguish between the relevant and irrelevant costs and revenues for the five decision-making problems described.** The five decision-making problems described were: (a) special selling price decisions; (b) product mix decisions when capacity constraints apply; (c) decisions on the replacement of equipment; (d) outsourcing (make or buy) decisions; and (e) discontinuation decisions. Different approaches can be used for presenting relevant cost and revenue information. Information can be presented that includes both relevant and irrelevant items for all alternatives under consideration. If this approach is adopted the same amount for the irrelevant items (i.e. those items that remain unchanged as a result of the decision) are included for all alternatives, thus making them irrelevant for the decision. Alternatively, information can be presented that lists only the relevant costs for the alternatives under consideration. Where only two alternatives are being considered a third approach is to present only the relevant (differential) items. You can adopt either approach. It is a matter of personal preference. All three approaches were illustrated for the five decision-making problems.

- **Describe the key concept that should be applied for presenting information for product mix decisions when capacity constraints apply.** The information presented should rank the products by the contribution per unit of the constraining or limiting factor (i.e. the scarce resource). The capacity of the scarce resource should be allocated according to this ranking.

- **Explain why the book value of equipment is irrelevant when making equipment replacement decisions.** The book value of equipment is a past (sunk) cost that cannot be changed for any alternative under consideration. Only future costs or revenues that will differ between alternatives are relevant for replacement decisions.

- **Describe the opportunity cost concept.** Where the choice of one course of action requires that an alternative course of action be given up. The financial benefits that are foregone or sacrificed are known as opportunity costs. Opportunity costs thus represent the lost contribution to profits arising from the best alternative foregone. They arise only when the resources are scarce and have alternative uses. Opportunity costs must therefore be included in the analysis when presenting relevant information for decision-making.

- **Additional learning objective presented in Appendix 11.1.** The appendix to this chapter includes the following additional learning objective: calculate the optimal selling price using differential calculus. This topic is normally dealt with in second stage cost and management accounting courses, but recently some professional accountancy examining bodies have included this topic in first stage courses. You should therefore check your course content to ascertain if you will need to read the appendix.

APPENDIX 11.1: CALCULATING OPTIMUM SELLING PRICES USING DIFFERENTIAL CALCULUS

The optimal output is determined at the point where marginal revenue equals marginal cost (see Chapter 2 for an explanation of the terms marginal revenue and marginal cost). The highest selling price at which the optimum output can be sold determines the optimal selling price. If demand and cost schedules are known, it is possible to derive simultaneously the optimum output level and selling price using differential calculus. Consider Example 11A.1.

EXAMPLE 11A.1

A division within the Caspian Company sells a single product. Divisional fixed costs are £700 000 per annum and a variable cost of £70 is incurred for each additional unit produced and sold over a very large range of outputs. The current selling price for the product is £160, and at this price 10 000 units are demanded per annum. It is estimated that for each successive increase in price of £2 annual demand will be reduced by 500 units. Alternatively, for each £2 reduction in price demand will increase by 500 units.

Calculate the optimum output and price for the product assuming that if prices are set within each £2 range there will be a proportionate change in demand.

The first step when calculating the optimum selling price is to calculate total cost and revenue functions. The total cost (TC) function is:

$$TC = £700\ 000 + £70x$$

where x is the annual level of demand and output.

At present the selling price is £160 and demand is 10 000 units. Each increase or decrease in price of £2 results in a corresponding decrease or increase in demand of 500 units. Therefore, if the selling price were increased to £200, demand would be zero. To increase demand by one unit, selling price must be reduced by £0.004 (£2/500 units). Thus the maximum selling price (SP) for an output of x units is:

$$SP = £200 - £0.004x$$

Assuming that the output demanded is 10 000 units SP = £200 − £0.004 (10 000) = £160. Therefore if demand is 10 000 units, the maximum selling price is £160, the same selling price given in Example 11A.1. We shall now use differential calculus to derive the optimal selling price:

$$TC = £700\ 000 + £70x$$
$$SP = £200 - £0.004x$$

Therefore total revenue (TR) for an output of x units = $£200x - £0.004x^2$

$$\text{marginal cost(MC)} = \frac{dTC}{dx} = £70$$

$$\text{marginal revenue (MR)} = \frac{dTR}{dx} = £200 - £0.008x$$

At the optimum output level

$$\frac{dTC}{dx} = \frac{dTR}{dx}$$

And so

$$£70 = £200 - £0.008x$$
$$x = 162\ 500 \text{ units}$$

The highest selling price at which this output can be sold is

$$SP = £200 - £0.004(16\ 250)$$

so

$$SP = £135$$

Thus optimum selling price and output are £135 and 16.250 units respectively.

KEY TERMS AND CONCEPTS

Differential or incremental cash flows the cash-flows that will be affected by a decision that is to be taken.

Facility sustaining costs common costs that are incurred to support the organization as a whole and are irrelevant for decision-making.

Limiting factors scarce resources that constrain the level of output.

Opportunity costs financial benefits that are sacrificed when an alternative course of action is rejected.

Outsourcing the process of obtaining goods or services from outside suppliers instead of producing the same goods or

providing the same services within the organization.

Qualitative factors non-monetary factors that may affect a decision.

Relevant costs and revenues future costs and revenues that will be changed by a particular decision, whereas irrelevant costs and revenues will not be affected by that decision.

Special studies a detailed non-routine study that is undertaken relating to choosing between alternative courses of action.

Written down value of equipment the original cost minus depreciation.

KEY EXAMINATION POINTS

A common mistake that students make when presenting information for decision-making is to compare *unit* costs. With this approach, there is a danger that fixed costs will be unitized and treated as variable costs. In most cases you should compare total amounts of costs and revenues rather than unit amounts. Many students do not present the information clearly and concisely. There are many alternative ways of presenting the information, but the simplest approach is to list future costs and revenues for each alternative in a format similar to Exhibit 11.1. You should exclude irrelevant items or ensure that the same amount for irrelevant items is included for each alternative. To determine the amount to be entered for each alternative, you should ask yourself what difference it will make if the alternative is selected.

Never allocate common fixed costs to the alternatives. You should focus on how each alternative will affect future cash flows of the organization. Changes in the apportionment of fixed costs will not alter future cash flows of the company. Remember that if a resource is scarce, your analysis should recommend the alternative that yields the largest contribution per limiting factor.

You should now attempt the Review Problems and compare your answers with the solutions that are provided. These problems will test your understanding of a variety of decision problems that have been covered in Chapter 11.

ASSESSMENT MATERIAL

The review questions are short questions that enable you to assess your understanding of the main topics included in the chapter. The numbers in parentheses provide you with the page numbers to refer to if you cannot answer a specific question.

The review problems are more complex and require you to relate and apply the chapter content to various business problems. The problems are graded by their level of difficulty. The multiple-choice questions are the least demanding and normally take less than 10 minutes to complete. Fully worked solutions to the review problems are provided in a separate section at the end of the book. Further review problems with solutions for this chapter are available on the accompanying website www.drury-online.com. The website includes a *Student's Manual* and an *Instructor's Manual.* Students can access both questions and answers from the *Student's Manual* and the questions from the *Instructor's Manual.* The answers to problems in the *Instructor's Manual* are available only to lecturers on the lecturer's password-protected section of the website.

The website also includes over 20 case study problems. A list of these cases is provided on pages 427–430. Cases that are relevant to the content of this chapter include Fleet Ltd and High Street Reproduction Furniture Ltd.

REVIEW QUESTIONS

11.1   What is a relevant cost? *(pp. 258–59)*

11.2   Why is it important to recognize qualitative factors when presenting information for decision-making? Provide examples of qualitative factors. *(p. 259)*

11.3   What underlying principle should be followed in determining relevant costs for decision-making? *(p. 259)*

11.4   Explain what is meant by special pricing decisions. *(pp. 259–60)*

11.5   Describe the important factors that must be taken into account when making special pricing decisions. *(pp. 261–62)*

11.6   Describe the dangers involved in focusing excessively on a short-run decision-making time horizon. *(pp. 261–62)*

11.7   Define limiting factors. *(p. 264)*

11.8   How should a company determine its optimal product mix when a limiting factor exists? *(pp. 265–66)*

11.9   Why is the written down value and depreciation of an asset being considered for replacement irrelevant when making replacement decisions? *(pp. 266–67)*

11.10 Explain the importance of opportunity costs for decision-making. *(p. 263)*

11.11 Explain the circumstances when the original purchase price of materials are irrelevant for decision-making. *(p. 274)*

11.12 Why does the relevant cost of labour differ depending upon the circumstances? *(p. 274)*

REVIEW PROBLEMS

11.13 All of a company's skilled labour, which is paid £8 per hour, is fully employed manufacturing a product to which the following data refer:

		£ per unit	£ per unit
Selling price			60
Less	Variable costs:		
	Skilled labour	20	
	Others	15	
			(35)
Contribution			25

The company is evaluating a contract which requires 90 skilled labour hours to complete. No other supplies of skilled labour are available.

What is the total relevant skilled labour cost of the contract?

(a)   £720

(b)   £900

(c)   £1620

(d)   £2160

ACCA – Financial Information for Management

11.14 A company requires 600 kg of raw material Z for a contract it is evaluating. It has 400 kg of material Z in stock which were purchased last month. Since then the purchase price of material Z has risen by 8 per cent to £27 per kg. Raw material Z is used regularly by the company in normal production.

What is the total relevant cost of raw material Z to the contract?

(a)   £15 336

(b)   £15 400

(c)   £16 200

(d)   £17 496

ACCA – Financial Information for Management

11.15 Equipment owned by a company has a net book value of £1800 and has been idle for some months. It could not be used on a six months contract which is being considered. If not used on this contract, the equipment would be sold now for a net amount of £2000. After use on the contract, the equipment would have no saleable value and would be dismantled. The cost of dismantling and disposing of it would be £800.

What is the total relevant cost of the equipment to the contract?

(a)   £1200

(b)   £1800

(c)   £2000

(d)   £2800

ACCA – Financial Information for Management

11.16   A company is considering the costs for a special order. The order would require 1250 kg of material D. This material is readily available and regularly used by the company. There are 265 kg of material D in stock which cost £795 last week. The current market price is £3.24 per kg. Material D is normally used to make product X. Each unit of X requires 3 kg of material D and, if material D is costed at £3 per kg, each unit of X yields a contribution of £15.

The cost of material D to be included in the costing of the special order is nearest to:

(a)   £3990

(b)   £4050

(c)   £10 000

(d)   £10 300

CIMA Management Accounting – Performance Management

11.17   X plc intends to use relevant costs as the basis of the selling price for a special order: the printing of a brochure. The brochure requires a particular type of paper that is not regularly used by X plc although a limited amount is in X plc's inventory which was left over from a previous job. The cost when X plc bought this paper last year was $15 per ream and there are 100 reams in inventory. The brochure requires 250 reams. The current market price of the paper is $26 per ream, and the resale value of the paper in inventory is $10 per ream.

The relevant cost of the paper to be used in printing the brochure is:

(a) $2500

(b) $4900

(c) $500

(d) $6500

CIMA P2 Management Accounting: Decision Management

11.18   A company which manufactures four components (A, B, C and D), using the same skilled labour, aims to maximize its profits. The following information is available:

	A	**B**	**C**	**D**
Variable production cost per unit (£)	60	70	75	85
Purchase price per unit from another supplier (£)	108	130	120	124
Skilled labour hours per unit to manufacture	4	6	5	3

As it has insufficient skilled labour hours available to manufacture all the components required, the company will need to buy some units of one component from the other supplier.

Which component should be purchased from the other supplier?

(a)   Component A

(b)   Component B

(c)   Component C

(d)   Component D

ACCA – Financial Information for Management

11.19 A company manufactures three products, X, Y and Z. The sales demand and the standard unit selling prices and costs for the next accounting period, period 1, are estimated as follows:

	X	Y	Z
Maximum demand (000 units)	**4.0**	**5.5**	**7.0**
	$ per unit	$ per unit	$ per unit
Selling price	28	22	30
Variable costs:			
Raw materials ($1 per kg)	5	4	6
Direct labour ($12 per hour)	12	9	18

(a) If supplies in period 1 are restricted to 90 000 kgs of raw material and 18 000 hours of direct labour, the limiting factor would be:

(i) direct labour

(ii) raw material

(iii) both direct labour and raw material

(iv) neither direct labour nor raw material.

(b) In period 2 the company will have a shortage of raw materials, but no other resources will be restricted. The standard selling prices and costs and the level of demand will remain unchanged. In what order should the materials be allocated to the products if the company wants to maximize profit?

	1st	2nd	3rd
(i)	Z	X	Y
(ii)	Y	Z	X
(iii)	Z	Y	X
(iv)	Y	X	Z

CIMA – Management Accounting Fundamentals

11.20 A company has three shops (R, S and T) to which the following budgeted information relates:

	Shop R £000	Shop S £000	Shop T £000	Total £000
Sales	400	500	600	1500
Contribution	100	60	120	280
Less: Fixed costs	(60)	(70)	(70)	(200)
Profit/loss	40	(10)	50	80

Sixty per cent of the total fixed costs are general company overheads. These are apportioned to the shops on the basis of sales value. The other fixed costs are specific to each shop and are avoidable if the shop closes down.

If shop S closed down and the sales of the other two shops remained unchanged, what would be the revised budgeted profit for the company?

(a) £50 000

(b) £60 000

(c) £70 000

(d) £90 000

ACCA – Financial Information for Management

11.21 The following information relates to questions (i) and (ii):

In the following price, revenue and cost functions, which have been established by an organization for one of its products, Q represents the number of units produced and sold per week:

Price (£ per unit) = 50 – 0·025Q
Marginal revenue (£ per unit) = 50 – 0·05Q
Total weekly cost = 1000 + 15Q

(i) What price per unit should be set in order to maximize weekly profit?

  (a) £15·00

  (b) £17·50

  (c) £25·00

  (d) £32·50

(ii) What would the weekly total contribution be if the price of the product was set at £20 per unit?

  (a) £2000

  (b) £3000

  (c) £5000

  (d) £6000

ACCA – Financial Information for Management

11.22 Relevant costs for labour and materials

Inez Ltd is evaluating the relevant costs of a one-off contract. The following information relates to the materials and labour requirements of the contract:

Materials

The contract required 2500 kg of material R, which is a material regularly used by the company in other production. The company has 4000 kg of R currently in stock. Half of that stock was purchased two months ago for £24 per kg and the other half was purchased last month for £25 per kg. The supplier has recently notified the company that the price of R has risen by 8 per cent compared with last month.

Labour

The contract requires 600 hours of skilled labour which is paid £10 per hour. The company's existing skilled labour is all fully employed in the manufacture of product T and no further supply is available. The following information relates to product T:

		£ per unit	£ per unit
	Selling price		100
Less	Variable costs:		
	Direct materials	40	
	Skilled labour	25	
	Selling	5	
			(70)
			30

Required:

(a) Calculate the total relevant costs for the contract in respect of:

(i) Material R; and

(ii) Skilled labour.

(5 marks)

(b) Explain the basis you would use to determine if any production overhead costs would be relevant to the evaluation of the contract. Illustrate your answer with examples of such costs but no calculations are required.

(3 marks)

(8 marks)

ACCA – Financial Information for Management

11.23 Limiting factor and make or buy decision

Merryl Ltd manufactures four components (E, F, G and H) which are incorporated into different products made by the company. All the components are manufactured using the same general purpose machinery. The following production cost and machine hour data are available:

	E	F	G	H
Variable production cost (£ per unit)	32	27	34	35
Fixed production cost (£ per unit)	6	14	8	16
General purpose machine hours per unit	5	6	7	8

The fixed production costs represent a share of factory-wide costs that have been related to the individual components by using a direct labour hour rate. There are no fixed costs which can be specifically related to individual components.

From next month the company's monthly manufacturing requirements are for 2000 units of each component. The maximum number of machine hours available for component manufacture is 35 000 per month.

The company can purchase any quantity of each component from Sergeant Ltd at the following unit prices next month:

E	F	G	H
£48	£51	£55	£63

Merryl Ltd aims to minimize its monthly costs.

Required:

(a) Calculate the shortfall in general purpose machine hours next month.

(2 marks)

(b) Determine how many units of which components should be purchased from Sergeant Ltd next month.

(4 marks)

(c) Briefly explain THREE other factors that the management of Merryl Ltd should consider before making a final decision to buy in components from Sergeant Ltd for next month.

(3 marks)

(9 marks)

ACCA – Financial Information for Management

11.24 Acceptance of a special order

The production manager of your organization has approached you for some costing advice on project X, a one-off order from overseas that he intends to tender for. The costs associated with the project are as follows:

	(£)
Material A	4000
Material B	8000
Direct labour	6000
Supervision	2000
Overheads	12 000
	32 000

You ascertain the following:

(i) Material A is in stock and the above was the cost. There is now no other use for material A, other than the above project within the factory, and it would cost £1750 to dispose of. Material B would have to be ordered at the cost shown above.

(ii) Direct labour costs of £6000 relate to workers that will be transferred to this project from another project. Extra labour will need to be recruited to the other project at a cost of £7000.

(iii)   Supervision costs have been charged to the project on the basis of $33\frac{1}{3}$ per cent of labour costs and will be carried out by existing staff within their normal duties.

(iv)   Overheads have been charged to the project at the rate of 200 per cent on direct labour.

(v)   The company is currently operating at a point above break-even.

(vi)   The project will need the utilization of machinery that will have no other use to the company after the project has finished. The machinery will have to be purchased at a cost of £10 000 and then disposed of for £5250 at the end of the project.

The production manager tells you that the overseas customer is prepared to pay up to a maximum of £30 000 for the project and a competitor is prepared to accept the order at that price. He also informs you the minimum that he can charge is £40 000 as the above costs show £32 000, and this does not take into consideration the cost of the machine and profit to be taken on the project. Required:

(a)   Cost the project for the production manager, clearly stating how you have arrived at your figures and giving reasons for the exclusion of other figures.

(12 marks)

(b)   Write a report to the production manager stating whether the organization should go ahead with the tender for the project, the reasons why and the price, bearing in mind that the competitor is prepared to undertake the project for £30 000.

(8 marks)

Note: The project should only be undertaken if it shows a profit.

(c)   State four non-monetary factors that should be taken into account before tendering for this project.

(2 marks)

(d)   What would be your advice if you were told that the organization was operating below break-even point? Give reasons for your advice.

(3 marks)

AAT Cost Accounting and Budgeting

11.25   Decision on which of two mutually exclusive contracts to accept
A company in the civil engineering industry with headquarters located 22 miles from London undertakes contracts anywhere in the United Kingdom.

The company has had its tender for a job in north-east England accepted at £288 000 and work is due to begin in March. However, the company has also been asked to undertake a contract on the south coast of England. The price offered for this contract is £352 000. Both of the contracts cannot be taken simultaneously because of constraints on staff site management personnel and on plant available. An escape clause enables the company to withdraw from the contract in the north-east, provided notice is given before the end of November and an agreed penalty of £28 000 is paid.

The following estimates have been submitted by the company's quantity surveyor:

Cost estimates	North-east (£)	South coast (£)
Materials:		
In stock at original cost, Material X	21 600	
In stock at original cost, Material Y		24 800
Firm orders placed at original cost, Material X	30 400	
Not yet ordered – current cost, Material X	60 000	
Not yet ordered – current cost, Material Z		71 200
Labour – hired locally	86 000	110 000
Site management	34 000	34 000
Staff accommodation and travel for site management	6800	5600
Plant on site – depreciation	9600	12 800
Interest on capital, 8%	5120	6400
Total local contract costs	253 520	264 800
Headquarters costs allocated at rate of 5% on total contract costs	12 676	13 240
	266 196	278 040
Contract price	288 000	352 000
Estimated profit	21 804	73 960

Notes:

1 X, Y and Z are three building materials. Material X is not in common use and would not realize much money if re-sold; however, it could be used on other contracts but only as a substitute for another material currently quoted at 10 per cent less than the original cost of X. The price of Y, a material in common use, has doubled since it was purchased; its net realizable value if re-sold would be its new price less 15 per cent to cover disposal costs. Alternatively it could be kept for use on other contracts in the following financial year.

2 With the construction industry not yet recovered from the recent recession, the company is confident that manual labour, both skilled and unskilled, could be hired locally on a sub-contracting basis to meet the needs of each of the contracts.

3 The plant which would be needed for the south coast contract has been owned for some years and £12 800 is the year's depreciation on a straight-line basis. If the north-east contract is undertaken, less plant will be required but the surplus plant will be hired out for the period of the contract at a rental of £6000.

4 It is the company's policy to charge all contracts with notional interest at 8 per cent on estimated working capital involved in contracts. Progress payments would be receivable from the contractee.

5 Salaries and general costs of operating the small headquarters amount to about £108 000 each year. There are usually ten contracts being supervised at the same time.

6 Each of the two contracts is expected to last from March to February which, coincidentally, is the company's financial year.

7 Site management is treated as a fixed cost.

You are required, as the management accountant to the company:

(a) to present comparative statements to show the net benefit to the company of undertaking the more advantageous of the two contracts;

(12 marks)

(b) to explain the reasoning behind the inclusion in (or omission from) your comparative financial statements, of each item given in the cost estimates and the notes relating thereto.

(13 marks)

CIMA Stage 2 Cost Accounting

11.26 Deletion of a product

Blackarm Ltd makes three products and is reviewing the profitability of its product line. You are given the following budgeted data about the firm for the coming year.

	A	B	C
Product sales (in units)	**100 000**	**120 000**	**80 000**
	(£)	(£)	(£)
Revenue	1 500 000	1 440 000	880 000
Costs:			
Material	500 000	480 000	240 000
Labour	400 000	320 000	160 000
Overhead	650 000	600 000	360 000
	1 550 000	1 400 000	760 000
Profit/(Loss)	(50 000)	40 000	120 000

The company is concerned about the loss on product A. It is considering ceasing production of it and switching the spare capacity of 100 000 units to Product C. You are told:

(i) All production is sold.

(ii) 25 per cent of the labour cost for each product is fixed in nature.

(iii) Fixed administration overheads of £900 000 in total have been apportioned to each product on the basis of units sold and are included in the overhead costs above. All other overhead costs are variable in nature.

(iv) Ceasing production of product A would eliminate the fixed labour charge associated with it and one-sixth of the fixed administration overhead apportioned to product A.

(v) Increasing the production of product C by 100 000 units would mean that the fixed labour cost associated with product C would double, the variable labour cost would rise by 20 per cent and its selling price would have to be decreased by £1.50 in order to achieve the increased sales.

Required:

(a) Prepare a marginal cost statement for a unit of each product on the basis of:

(i) the original budget;

(ii) if product A is deleted.

(12 marks)

(b) Prepare a statement showing the total contribution and profit for each product group on the basis of:

(i) the original budget;

(ii) if product A is deleted.

(8 marks)

(c) Using your results from (a) and (b) advise whether product A should be deleted from the product range, giving reasons for your decision.

(5 marks)

(Total 25 marks)

AAT Cost Accounting and Budgeting

11.27 Calculation of the optimum selling price using calculus
Ella Ltd recently started to manufacture and sell product DG. The variable cost of product DG is £4 per unit and the total weekly fixed costs are £18 000.

The company has set the initial selling price of product DG by adding a mark up of 40 per cent to its total unit cost. It has assumed that production and sales will be 3000 units per week.

The company holds no stocks of product DG.

Required:

(a) Calculate for product DG:

(i) the initial selling price per unit; and

(ii) the resultant weekly profit.

(3 marks)

The management accountant has established that a linear relationship between the unit selling price (P in £) and the weekly demand (Q in units) for product DG is given by:

$$P = 20 - 0.002Q$$

The marginal revenue (MR in £ per unit) is related to weekly demand (Q in units) by the equation:

$$MR = 20 - 0.004Q$$

(b) Calculate the selling price per unit for product DG that should be set in order to maximize weekly profit.

(7 marks)

(c) Distinguish briefly between penetration and skimming pricing policies when launching a new product.

(2 marks)

AAT Cost Accounting and Budgeting

CHAPTER 12
ACTIVITY-BASED COSTING

LEARNING OBJECTIVES

After studying this chapter you should be able to:

- explain why a cost accumulation system is required for generating relevant cost information for decision-making;
- describe the differences between activity-based and traditional costing systems;
- explain why traditional costing systems can provide misleading information for decision-making;
- compute product costs using an ABC system;
- identify and explain each of the four stages involved in designing ABC systems;
- describe the ABC cost hierarchy.

The aim of the previous chapter was to provide you with an understanding of the principles that should be used to identify relevant costs and revenues for various types of decisions. Indirect relevant costs can be difficult to identify and measure. This chapter examines the measurement of indirect relevant costs for decision-making using activity-based costing (ABC) and aims to provide you with a conceptual understanding of ABC and to explain how an ABC system operates.

Unless otherwise stated we shall assume that products are the cost objects but the techniques used, and the principles established, can also be applied to other cost objects such as customers, services and locations. We begin with an examination of the role that a cost accumulation system plays in generating relevant cost information for decision-making.

You should note that this chapter extends the material covered in Chapter 4. To understand the content of this chapter it is essential that you thoroughly understand the content of Chapter 4. You are therefore recommended to refresh your memory of the material there and read pages 82–90 prior to reading this chapter.

Finally, ABC is an advanced topic and may not be included as part of your course curriculum. You should check your course content to ascertain if you will need to read this chapter.

THE NEED FOR A COST ACCUMULATION SYSTEM IN GENERATING RELEVANT COST INFORMATION FOR DECISION-MAKING

There is a need to assign indirect costs to cost objects because many indirect costs are relevant for decision-making. If a cost accumulation system that assigns indirect costs to cost objects is not established, there is a danger that only those incremental costs that are uniquely attributable to individual products will be classified as relevant and indirect costs will be classified as irrelevant for decision-making. Direct costs are transparent and how they will be affected by decisions is clearly observable. In contrast, the effect of decisions on indirect costs is not clearly observable. There has been a tendency in the past to assume that these costs are fixed and irrelevant for decision-making. In many organizations, however, these are costs that have escalated over the years. The message is clear – they cannot be assumed to be fixed and irrelevant for decision-making.

Many indirect costs fluctuate in the long term according to the demand for them. The cost of support functions falls within this category. They include activities such as materials procurement, materials handling, production scheduling, warehousing, expediting and customer order processing. The costs of these activities are either not directly traceable to products, or would involve such detailed tracing that the costs of doing so would far exceed their benefits. Product introduction, discontinuation, redesign and mix decisions all determine the demand for support function resources. For example, if a decision results in a 10 per cent reduction in the demand for the resources of a support activity then we would expect, in the long term, some of the costs of that support activity to decline by 10 per cent. Therefore, to estimate the impact that decisions will have on the support activities (and their future costs) a cost accumulation system is required that assigns those indirect costs, using cause-and-effect allocations, to products.

Organizations can use either traditional costing or ABC systems to assign indirect costs to products. In Chapter 4 it was pointed out that traditional product costing systems are generally appropriate for extracting product costs for profit measurement and inventory valuation purposes but are unlikely to generate sufficiently accurate product costs for decision-making. The developments in information technology in the early 1990s and the accompanying reduction in information processing costs resulted in the emergence of ABC; a costing system that more accurately assigns indirect costs to products for decision-making.

A COMPARISON OF TRADITIONAL AND ABC SYSTEMS

Figure 12.1 illustrates the major differences between traditional costing and ABC systems. The upper panel of this diagram is identical to Figure 4.3, used in Chapter 4 to describe a traditional costing system. It is apparent from Figure 12.1 that both systems involve the two-stage allocation process. In the first stage a traditional system allocates overheads to production and service cost centres (typically departments) and then reallocates service cost centre/department costs to the production departments. You should be able to remember from Chapter 4 that the terms cost centres or cost pools are used to describe a location to which overhead costs are initially assigned. Normally cost centres consist of departments, but in some cases they consist of smaller segments such as groups of machines. An ABC system assigns overheads to each major activity (rather than departments). With ABC systems, many activity-based cost centres (alternatively known as activity cost pools) are established, whereas with traditional systems overheads tend to be pooled by departments, although they are normally described as cost centres.

Activities consist of the aggregation of many different tasks and are described by verbs associated with objects. Typical support activities include: schedule production, set-up machines, move materials, purchase materials, inspect items, process supplier records, expedite and process customer orders. Production process activities include machine products and assemble products. Within the production process, activity cost centres are often identical to the cost centres used by traditional cost systems. Support activities are also sometimes identical to cost centres used by traditional systems, such as when the purchasing department and activity are both treated as cost centres. Overall, however, ABC systems will normally have a greater number of cost centres.

The second stage of the two-stage allocation process allocates costs from cost centres (pools) to products or other chosen cost objects. Traditional costing systems trace overheads to products using a small number of second stage allocation bases (normally described as overhead allocation rates), which vary directly with the volume produced. Instead of using the terms 'allocation bases' or 'overhead allocation rates' the term '**cost driver**' is used by ABC systems. You should be able to remember from Chapters 4 and 10 that a cost driver represents a measure that exerts the major influence on the cost of a particular activity. Direct labour and machine hours are the allocation bases that are normally used by traditional costing systems. In contrast, ABC systems use many different types of second-stage cost drivers, including non-volume-based drivers, such as the number of production runs for production scheduling and the number of purchase orders for the purchasing activity.

Therefore the major distinguishing features of ABC systems are that within the two-stage allocation process they rely on:

1 a greater number of cost centres;
2 a greater number and variety of second stage cost drivers.

By using a greater number of cost centres and different types of cost drivers that cause activity resource consumption, and assigning activity costs to cost objects on the basis of cost driver usage, ABC systems can more accurately measure the resources consumed by cost objects. Traditional cost systems report less accurate costs because they use cost drivers where no cause-and-effect relationships exist to assign support costs to cost objects.

(a) Traditional costing systems

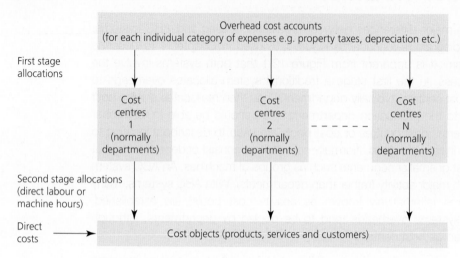

(b) Activity-based costing systems

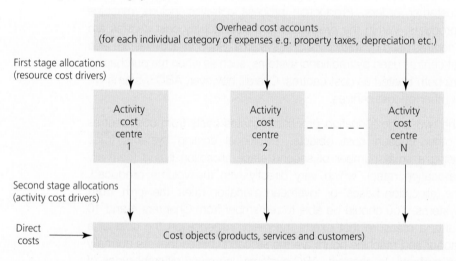

FIGURE 12.1

An illustration of the two-stage allocation process for a traditional and activity-based costing system

VOLUME-BASED AND NON-VOLUME-BASED COST DRIVERS

Our comparison of ABC systems with traditional costing systems indicated that ABC systems rely on a greater number and variety of second stage cost drivers. The term 'variety of cost drivers' refers to the fact that ABC systems use both volume-based and non-volume-based cost drivers. In contrast, traditional systems use only volume-based cost drivers. **Volume-based cost drivers** assume that a product's consumption of overhead resources is directly related to the number of units produced. Typical volume-based cost drivers used by traditional systems are units of output, direct labour hours and machine hours. These cost drivers are appropriate for measuring the consumption of expenses such as machine energy costs, indirect labour employed in production centres and inspection costs where each item produced is subject to final inspection. For example, machine hours are an appropriate cost driver for energy costs since if volume is increased by 10 per cent, machine hours are likely to increase by 10 per cent, thus causing 10 per cent more energy costs to be consumed.

Volume-based drivers are appropriate in the above circumstances because activities are performed each time a unit of the product or service is produced. In contrast, non-volume related activities are not performed each time a unit of the product or service is produced. Consider, for example, the activity of setting up a machine. Set-up resources are consumed each time a machine is changed from one product to another and it costs the same to set-up a machine for 10 or 5000 items. As more set-ups are done more set-up resources are consumed. It is the number of set-ups, rather than the number of units produced, that is a more appropriate measure of the consumption of the set-up activity. For this activity, a **non-volume-based cost driver** such as number of set-ups is needed for the accurate assignment of the costs.

Using only volume-based cost drivers to assign non-volume related overhead costs can result in the reporting of distorted product costs. The extent of distortion depends on what proportion of total overhead costs the non-volume-based overheads represent and the level of product diversity. If a large proportion of an organization's costs are unrelated to volume there is danger that inaccurate product costs will be reported. On the other hand, if non-volume-related overhead costs are only a small proportion of total overhead costs, the distortion of product costs will not be significant. In these circumstances traditional product costing systems are likely to be acceptable.

Product diversity applies when products consume different overhead activities in dissimilar proportions. Differences in product size, product complexity, sizes of batches and set-up times cause product diversity. If all products consume overhead resources in similar proportions product diversity will be low and products will consume non-volume-related activities in the same proportion as volume-related activities. Hence, product cost distortion will not occur with traditional product costing systems. Two conditions are therefore necessary for product cost distortion:

- non-volume-related overhead costs are a large proportion of total overhead costs; and
- product diversity applies.

Where these two conditions exist, traditional product costing systems can result in the overcosting of high volume products and undercosting of low volume products. Consider the information presented in Example 12.1. The reported product costs and profits for the two products are as follows:

	Traditional system		ABC system	
	Product HV **(£)**	**Product LV** **(£)**	**Product HV** **(£)**	**Product LV** **(£)**
Direct costs	310 000	40 000	310 000	40 000
Overheads allocated[a]	300 000 (30%)	50 000 (5%)	150 000 (15%)	150 000 (15%)
Reported profits/(losses)	(10 000)	60 000	140 000	(40 000)
Sales revenues	600 000	150 000	600 000	150 000

Note

[a]Allocation of £1 million overheads using direct labour hours as the allocation base for the traditional system and number of batches processed as the cost driver for the ABC system.

Because product HV is a high volume product that consumes 30 per cent of the direct labour hours whereas product LV, the low volume product consumes only 5 per cent, the traditional system that uses direct labour hours as the allocation base allocates six times more overheads to product HV. However, ABC systems recognize that overheads are caused by other factors, besides volume. In our example, all of the overheads are assumed to be volume-unrelated. They are caused by the number of batches processed and the ABC system establishes a cause-and-effect allocation relationship by using the number of batches processed as the cost driver. Both products require 15 per cent of the total number of batches so they are allocated with an equal amount of overheads.

EXAMPLE 12.1

Assume that the Balearic company has only one overhead cost centre or cost pool. It currently operates a traditional costing system using direct labour hours to allocate overheads to products. The company produces several products, two of which are products HV and LV. Product HV is made in high volumes whereas product LV is made in low volumes. Product HV consumes 30 per cent of the direct labour hours and product LV consumes only 5 per cent. Because of the high-volume production, product HV can be made in large production batches, but the irregular and low level of demand for product LV requires it to be made in small batches. A detailed investigation indicates that the number of batches processed causes the demand for overhead resources. The traditional system is therefore replaced with an ABC system using the number of batches processed as the cost driver. You ascertain that each product accounts for 15 per cent of the batches processed during the period and the overheads assigned to the cost centre that fluctuate in the long term according to the demand for them amount to £1 million. The direct costs and sales revenues assigned to the products are as follows:

	Product HV (£)	Product LV (£)
Direct costs	310 000	40 000
Sales revenues	600 000	150 000

Show the product profitability analysis for products HV and LV using the traditional and ABC systems.

It is apparent from the consumption ratios of the two products that the traditional system based on direct labour hours will overcost high volume products and undercost low volume products. **Consumption ratios** represent the proportion of each activity consumed by a product. If direct labour hours are used as the cost driver the consumption ratios are 0.30 for product HV and 0.05 for product LV, so six times more overheads will be assigned to product HV. When the number of batches processed are used as the cost driver the consumption ratios are 0.15 for each product and an equal amount of overhead will be assigned to each product. Distorted product costs are reported with the traditional costing system that uses the volume-based cost driver because the two conditions specified above apply:

1 non-volume-related overheads are a large proportion of total overheads, being 100 per cent in our example.

2 product diversity exists because the product consumption ratios for the two identified cost drivers are significantly different.

This illustration shows that if the consumption ratios for batches processed had been the same as the ratios for direct labour, the traditional and ABC systems would report identical product costs.

With the traditional costing system misleading information is reported. A small loss is reported for product HV and if it were discontinued the costing system mistakenly gives the impression that overheads will decline in the longer term by £300 000. In contrast, the ABC system allocates overheads on a cause-and-effect basis and more accurately measures the relatively high level of overhead resources consumed by product LV. The message from the profitability analysis is the opposite from the traditional system; that is, product HV is profitable and product LV is unprofitable. If product LV is discontinued, and assuming that the cost driver is the cause of all the overheads then a decision to discontinue product LV should result in the reduction in resource spending on overheads by £150 000.

REAL WORLD VIEWS 12.1

SOURCE: MERZ, M. AND HARDY, A. (1993) ABC PUTS ACCOUNTANTS ON THE DESIGN TEAM AT HP, MANAGEMENT ACCOUNTING (USA) SEPTEMBER, PP. 24–6.

The shift in the assignment of overhead costs at Hewlett-Packard

A division of Hewlett-Packard that manufactures electronic circuit boards faced an environment that conformed closely to the conditions for which ABC is recommended:

- diverse products;
- relatively high overhead costs and for some products, higher than the direct costs;
- production volumes that vary significantly among products;
- the belief by the operating managers that the old traditional system did not give meaningful product costs.

An ABC system was introduced consisting of ten different cost pools and drivers. The composition of the cost pools and selection of the most appropriate drivers resulted from an intense analysis of the production process and cost behaviour patterns. When the company implemented ABC the costs of the old and new system were compared. One circuit board that would have been assigned with overheads of $5 with the old system had a reported total cost of $25 with ABC – an increase of 400 per cent. Another circuit board that would have been assigned an overhead of $123 with the old system was assigned $45 with ABC.

During a six-month forecast and budget cycle, the ABC system resulted in shifting millions of dollars of costs between customers and products and thus had a dramatic impact on product design and pricing decisions.

Discussion points

1 Why do you think that the cost of the circuit boards differed between the old and the new system?

2 What benefits are likely to be obtained from introducing the ABC system?

Example 12.1 is very simplistic. It is assumed that the organization has established only a single cost centre or cost pool, when in reality many will be established with a traditional system, and even more with an ABC system. Furthermore, the data have been deliberately biased to show the superiority of ABC. The aim of the illustration was to highlight the potential cost of errors that can occur when information extracted from simplistic and inaccurate cost systems is used for decision-making.

AN ILLUSTRATION OF THE TWO-STAGE PROCESS FOR AN ABC SYSTEM

Earlier in this chapter Figure 12.1 was used to contrast the general features of ABC systems with traditional costing systems. It was pointed out that ABC systems differ from traditional systems by having a greater number of cost centres in the first stage, and a greater number, and variety, of cost drivers/allocation bases in the second stage of the two-stage allocation process. We shall now look at ABC systems in more detail.

You will see from Figure 12.1 that another major distinguishing feature of ABC is that overheads are assigned to each major activity, rather than departments, which normally represent cost centres with traditional systems. When costs are accumulated by activities they are known as activity cost centres. Production process activities include machine products and assemble products. Thus within the *production process*, activity cost centres may be identical to the cost centres used by traditional cost systems. In contrast, support department cost centres are established for traditional systems whereas, with an ABC system, these centres are often decomposed into many different activity centres.

We shall now use the data presented in Example 4.1 (the Enterprise Company) from Chapter 4 to illustrate ABC in more detail. This example was used to provide the relevant information to compute the overhead rates shown in Exhibit 4.2 for a traditional costing system. To refresh your memory, and to enable you to compare traditional and ABC systems, you should now refer back to Chapter 4 and read pages 84-90 relating to steps 1–4 of the two-stage allocation process for a traditional costing system. Example 4.1 and Exhibit 4.2 are now repeated so that you do not have to be constantly referring back to Chapter 4.

You will see from Exhibit 4.2 that in step 1 total overheads of £11 700 000 are assigned to production and cost centres. Row 1 shows that costs are assigned as follows:

	£
Machine centre X	2 970 000
Machine centre Y	2 690 000
Assembly	2 480 000
Materials procurement	1 760 000
General factory support	1 800 000
	11 700 000

ABC systems have a greater number of cost centres but to keep things simple we shall assume that the three production centre (i.e. the two machining centres and the assembly cost centre) established for the traditional costing system have also been identified as activity cost centres with the ABC system. Therefore the production activity cost centres are identical to the cost centres used by traditional cost systems. However, we shall assume that three activity centres have been established for each of the two support functions. For materials procurement the following activity centres have been established:

Activity	£	Activity cost driver
Purchasing materials	960 000	Number of purchase orders
Receiving materials	600 000	Number of material receipts
Disburse materials	200 000	Number of production runs
	1 760 000	

You can see that the total costs assigned to the purchase, receiving and disburse materials activities total £1 760 000, the same as the total allocated to the materials procurement cost centre by the traditional costing system. The process of allocating the costs to the three activity cost centres is the same as that used to allocate the costs of £1 760 000 to the materials procurement cost centre with the traditional costing system. To simplify the presentation these cost assignments are not shown. To emphasize the point that ABC systems use cause-and-effect second stage allocations, the term cost driver tends to be used instead of allocation base. Cost drivers should be significant determinants of the cost of activities. For example, it is assumed for the Enterprise Company that the cost of processing purchase orders is determined by the number of purchase orders that each product generates, so the number of purchase orders is used to represent the cost driver for the purchasing materials activity. The number of receipts for receiving materials and the number of production runs for the disbursement of materials have been identified as cost drivers for the receipt of materials and disbursement of materials activities.

For the second support department (i.e. general factory support) used as a cost centre with the traditional costing system we shall assume that the following three activity cost centres have been identified:

Activity	£	Activity cost driver
Production scheduling	1 000 000	Number of production runs
Set-up machines	600 000	Number of set-up hours
Quality inspection	200 000	Number of first item inspections
	1 800 000	

You can see that the total costs assigned to the production scheduling, set-up machines and quality inspection activities total £1 800 000, the same as the total allocated to the general factory support cost centre with the traditional costing system.

Exhibit 12.1 shows the product cost calculations for the ABC system. You will see from columns 1 and 3 in the upper section of Exhibit 12.1 that the Enterprise Company has established nine activity cost centres and seven different second stage drivers. Note that the *production* activity cost centres and the cost drivers that have been identified for the ABC system are the same as those used for the traditional costing system. In column 5 in the first section of Exhibit 12.1 cost driver rates are computed by dividing the activity centre cost (column 2) by the quantity of the cost driver used (shown in column 4).

EXAMPLE 4.1

(From Chapter 4). The annual overhead costs for the Enterprise Company which has three production centres (two machine centres and one assembly centre) and two service centres (materials procurement and general factory support) are as follows:

	(£)	(£)
Indirect wages and supervision		
Machine centres: X	1 000 000	
Y	1 000 000	
Assembly	1 500 000	
Materials procurement	1 100 000	
General factory support	1 480 000	6 080 000
Indirect materials		
Machine centres: X	500 000	
Y	805 000	
Assembly	105 000	
Materials procurement	0	
General factory support	10 000	1 420 000
Lighting and heating	500 000	
Property taxes	1 000 000	
Insurance of machinery	150 000	
Depreciation of machinery	1 500 000	
Insurance of buildings	250 000	
Salaries of works management	800 000	4 200 000
		11 700 000

The following information is also available:

	Book value of machinery (£)	Area occupied (sq. metres)	Number of employees	Direct labour hours	Machine hours
Machine shop: X	8 000 000	10 000	300	1 000 000	2 000 000
Y	5 000 000	5 000	200	1 000 000	1 000 000
Assembly	1 000 000	15 000	300	2 000 000	
Stores	500 000	15 000	100		
Maintenance	500 000	5 000	100		
	15 000 000	50 000	1000		

Details of total materials issues (i.e. direct and indirect materials) to the production centres are as follows:

	£
Machine shop X	4 000 000
Machine shop Y	3 000 000
Assembly	1 000 000
	8 000 000

Item of expenditure	Basis of allocation	Total (£)	Production centres			Service centres	
			Machine centre X (£)	Machine centre Y (£)	Assembly (£)	Materials procurement (£)	General factory support (£)
Indirect wage and supervision	Direct	6 080 000	1 000 000	1 000 000	1 500 000	1 100 000	1 480 000
Indirect materials	Direct	1 420 000	500 000	805 000	105 000		10 000
Lighting and heating	Area	500 000	100 000	50 000	150 000	150 000	50 000
Property taxes	Area	1 000 000	200 000	100 000	300 000	300 000	100 000
Insurance of machinery	Book value of machinery	150 000	80 000	50 000	10 000	5 000	5 000
Depreciation of machinery	Book value of machinery	1 500 000	800 000	500 000	100 000	50 000	50 000
Insurance of buildings	Area	250 000	50 000	25 000	75 000	75 000	25 000
Salaries of works management	Number of employees	800 000	240 000	160 000	240 000	80 000	80 000
	(1)	11 700 000	2 970 000	2 690 000	2 480 000	1 760 000	1 800 000
Reallocation of service centre costs							
Materials procurement	Value of materials issued	–	880 000	660 000	220 000	1 760 000	
General factory support	Direct labour hours	–	450 000	450 000	900 000		1 800 000
	(2)	11 700 000	4 300 000	3 800 000	3 600 000	–	–
Machine hours and direct labour hours			2 000 000	1 000 000	2 000 000		
Machine hour overhead rate			£2.15	£3.80			
Direct labour hour overhead rate					£1.80		

EXHIBIT 4.2

Overhead analysis sheet (from Chapter 4)

Activity centre costs are assigned to products by multiplying the cost driver rate by the quantity of the cost driver used by products. These calculations are shown in the second section of Exhibit 12.1. You will see from the first section in Exhibit 12.1 that the costs assigned to the purchasing activity are £960 000 for processing 10 000 purchasing orders, resulting in a cost driver rate of £96 per purchasing order. The second section shows that a batch of 100 units of product A, and 200 units of product B, each require one purchased

(1) Activity	(2) Activity cost £	(3) Activity cost driver	(4) Quantity of activity cost driver	(5) Activity cost driver rate (Col. 2/Col.4)
Production activities:				
Machining: activity centre A	2 970 000	Number of machine hours	2 000 000 machine hours	£1.485 per hour
Machining: activity centre B	2 690 000	Number of machine hours	1 000 000 machine hours	£2.69 per hour
Assembly	2 480 000	Number of direct labour hours	2 000 000 direct lab. hours	£1.24 per hour
	8 140 000			
Materials procurement activities:				
Purchasing components	960 000	Number of purchase orders	10 000 purchase orders	£96 per order
Receiving components	600 000	Number of material receipts	5 000 receipts	£120 per receipt
Disburse materials	200 000	Number of production runs	2 000 production runs	£100 per production run
	1 760 000			
General factory support activities:				
Production scheduling	1 000 000	Number of production runs	2 000 production runs	£500 per production run
Set-up machines	600 000	Number of set-up hours	12 000 set-up hours	£50 per set-up hour
Quality inspection	200 000	Number of first item inspections	1 000 inspections	£200 per inspection
	1 800 000			
Total cost of all manufacturing activities	11 700 000			

Computation of product costs

(1) Activity	(2) Activity cost driver rate (derived from Col. 5 above)	(3) Quantity of cost driver used by 100 units of product A	(4) Quantity of cost driver used by 200 units of product B	(5) Activity cost assigned to product A (Col. 2×Col. 3)	(6) Activity cost assigned to product B (Col. 2×Col. 4)
Machining: activity centre A	£1.485 per hour	500 hours	2 000 hours	742.50	2 970.00
Machining: activity centre B	£2.69 per hour	1 000 hours	4 000 hours	2 690.00	10 760.00
Assembly	£1.24 per hour	1 000 hours	4 000 hours	1 240.00	4 960.00
Purchasing components	£96 per order	1 component	1 component	96.00	96.00
Receiving components	£120 per receipt	1 component	1 component	120.00	120.00
Disburse materials	£100 per production run	5 production runs[a]	1 production run	500.00	100.00
Production scheduling	£500 per production run	5 production runs[a]	1 production run	2 500.00	500.00
Set-up machines	£50 per set-up hour	50 set-up hours	10 set-up hours	2 500.00	500.00
Quality inspection	£200 per inspection	1 inspection	1 inspection	200.00	200.00
Total overhead cost				10 588.50	20 206.00
Units produced				100 units	200 units
Overhead cost *per unit*				£105.88	£101.03
Direct costs *per unit*				100.00	200.00
Total cost *per unit* of output				205.88	301.03

Note
[a] Five production runs are required to machine several unique components before they can be assembled into a final product.

EXHIBIT 12.1

An illustration of cost assignment with an ABC system

component and thus one purchase order. Therefore purchase order costs of £96 are allocated to each batch. Now look at the production scheduling row in the upper section of Exhibit 12.1. You will see that £1 000 000 has been assigned to this activity for 2 000 production runs, resulting in a cost driver rate of £500 per production run. The second section shows that for a batch of 100 units of product A five production runs are required whereas a batch of 200 units of product B requires one production run. Therefore production scheduling activity costs of £2 500 (5 × £500) are allocated to a batch of Product A and £500 to a batch of product B in columns 5 and 6. The same approach is used to allocate the costs of the remaining activities shown in Exhibit 12.1. You should now work through Exhibit 12.1 and study the product cost calculations.

The costs assigned to products using each costing system are as follows:

	Traditional costing system £	ABC system £
Product A	166.75[a]	205.88
Product B	333.50[a]	301.03

Note
[a]Please refer to pages 86–90 in Chapter 4 for the calculations of the product costs for the traditional costing system.

Note that for the traditional system the calculation of the above product costs is shown on page 89 of Chapter 4 and the product costs for the ABC system have been derived from Exhibit 12.1. Compared with the ABC system the traditional system undercosts product A and overcosts product B. By reallocating the service centre costs to the production centres and allocating the costs to products on the basis of either machine hours or direct labour hours the traditional system incorrectly assumes that these allocation bases are the cause of the costs of the support activities. Compared with product A, product B consumes twice as many machine and direct labour hours per unit of output. Therefore, relative to Product A, the traditional costing system allocates twice the amount of support costs to product B.

In contrast, ABC systems create separate cost centres for each major support activity and allocate costs to products using cost drivers that are the significant determinants of the cost of the activities. The ABC system recognizes that a batch of both products consume the same quantity of purchasing, receiving and inspection activities and, for these activities, allocates the same costs to both products. Because product B is manufactured in batches of 200 units, and product A in batches of 100 units, the cost per unit of output for product B is half the amount of Product A for these activities. Product A also has five unique machined components, whereas product B has only one, resulting in a batch of Product A requiring five production runs whereas a batch of Product B only requires one. Therefore, relative to product B, the ABC system assigns five times more costs to product A for the production scheduling and disbursement of materials activities (see columns 5 and 6 in the lower part of Exhibit 12.1). Because product A is a more complex product it requires relatively more support activity resources and the cost of this complexity is captured by the ABC system.

DESIGNING ABC SYSTEMS

The discussion so far has provided a broad overview of ABC. We shall now examine ABC in more detail by looking at the design of ABC systems. Four steps are involved. They are:

1 identifying the major activities that take place in an organization;

2 assigning costs to cost pools/cost centres for each activity;

3 determining the cost driver for each major activity;

4 assigning the cost of activities to products according to the product's demand for activities.

The first two steps relate to the first stage and the final two steps to the second stage of the two-stage allocation process shown in Figure 12.1. Let us now consider each of these steps in more detail.

Step 1: Identifying activities

Activities are composed of the aggregation of units of work or tasks and are described by verbs associated with tasks. For example, purchasing of materials might be identified as a separate activity. This activity consists of the aggregation of many different tasks, such as receiving a purchase request, identifying suppliers, preparing purchase orders, mailing purchase orders and performing follow-ups.

The activities chosen should be at a reasonable level of aggregation based on costs versus benefits criteria. For example, instead of classifying purchasing of materials as an activity, each of its constituent tasks outlined above could be classified as separate activities. However, this level of decomposition would involve the collection of a vast amount of data and is likely to be too costly for product costing purposes. Alternatively, the purchasing activity might be merged with the materials receiving, storage and issuing activities to form a single materials procurement and handling activity. This is likely to represent too high a level of aggregation because a single cost driver is unlikely to provide a satisfactory determinant of the cost of the activity. For example, selecting the number of purchase orders as a cost driver may provide a good explanation of purchasing costs but may be entirely inappropriate for explaining costs relating to receiving and issuing. Therefore, instead of establishing materials procurement and handling as a single activity it may be preferable to decompose it into three separate activities; namely purchasing, receiving and issuing activities, and establish separate cost drivers for each activity.

Recent studies suggest that between 20 and 30 activity centres tend to be the norm. The final choice of activities must be a matter of judgement but it is likely to be influenced by factors such as the total cost of the activity centre (it must be of significance to justify separate treatment) and the ability of a single driver to provide a satisfactory determinant of the cost of the activity.

Step 2: Assigning costs to activity cost centres

After the activities have been identified the cost of resources consumed over a specified period must be assigned to each activity. The aim is to determine how much the organization is spending on each of its activities. Many of the resources will be directly attributable to specific activity centres, but others (such as labour and lighting and heating costs) may be indirect and jointly shared by several activities. These costs should be assigned to activities on the basis of cause-and-effect cost drivers, or interviews with staff who can provide reasonable estimates of the resources consumed by different activities. Arbitrary allocations should not be used. The greater the amount of costs traced to activity centres by cost apportionments at this stage, the more arbitrary and less reliable will be the product cost information generated by ABC systems. Cause-and-effect cost drivers used at this stage to allocate shared resources to individual activities are called **resource cost drivers**.

Step 3: Selecting appropriate cost drivers for assigning the cost of activities to cost objects

In order to assign the costs attached to each activity cost centre to products a cost driver must be selected for each activity centre. Cost drivers used at this stage are called **activity cost drivers**. Several factors must be borne in mind when selecting a suitable cost driver. First, it should provide a good explanation of costs in each activity cost centre. Second, a cost driver should be easily measurable, the data should be relatively easy to obtain and be identifiable with products.

Activity cost drivers consist of transaction and duration drivers.**Transaction drivers**, such as the number of purchase orders processed, number of customer orders processed, number of inspections performed and the number of set-ups undertaken, all count the number of times an activity is performed. Transaction drivers are the least expensive type of cost driver to measure but they are also likely to be the least accurate because they assume that the same quantity of resources is required every time an activity is performed. However, if the variation in the amount of resources required by individual cost objects is not great, transaction drivers will provide a reasonably accurate measurement of activity resources consumed. If this condition does not apply then duration cost drivers should be used.

Duration drivers represent the amount of time required to perform an activity. Examples of duration drivers include set-up hours and inspection hours. For example, if one product requires a short set-up time and another requires a long time then using set-up hours as the cost driver will more accurately measure activity resource consumption than the transaction driver (number of set-ups) which assumes that an equal amount of activity resources are consumed by both products. Using the number of set-ups will result in the product that requires a long set-up time being undercosted whereas the product that requires a short set-up will be overcosted. This problem can be overcome by using set-up hours as the cost driver, but this will increase the measurement costs.

Step 4: Assigning the cost of the activities to products

The final step involves applying the cost driver rates to products. This means that the cost driver must be measurable in a way that enables it to be identified with individual products. Thus, if set-up hours are selected as a cost driver, there must be a mechanism for measuring the set-up hours consumed by each product. Alternatively, if the number of set-ups is selected as the cost driver, measurements by products are not required. The ease and cost of obtaining data on cost driver consumption by products is therefore a factor that must be considered during the third step when an appropriate cost driver is being selected.

ACTIVITY HIERARCHIES

Manufacturing activities can be classified as a cost hierarchy dimension consisting of:

1 unit-level activities;
2 batch-level activities;
3 product-sustaining activities;
4 facility-sustaining activities.

Unit-level activities (also known as volume-related activities) are performed each time a unit of the product or service is produced. Expenses in this category include direct labour, direct materials, energy costs and expenses that are consumed in proportion to machine processing time (such as maintenance). Unit-level activities consume resources in proportion to the number of units of production and sales volume. For example, if a firm produces 10 per cent more units it will consume 10 per cent more labour cost, 10 per cent more machine hours and 10 per cent more energy costs. Typical cost drivers for unit level activities include labour hours, machine hours and the quantity of materials processed. These cost drivers are also used by traditional costing systems. Traditional systems are therefore also appropriate for assigning the costs of unit-level activities to cost objects.

Batch-related activities, such as setting up a machine or processing a purchase order, are performed each time a batch of goods is produced. The cost of batch-related activities varies with the number of batches made, but is common (or fixed) for all units within the batch. For example, set-up resources are consumed when a machine is changed from one product to another. As more batches are produced, more set-up resources are consumed. It costs the same to set-up a machine for 10 or 5000 items. Thus the demands for the set-up resources are independent of the number of units produced after completing the set-up. Similarly, purchasing resources are consumed each time a purchasing order is processed, but the resources consumed are not determined by the number of units included in the purchase order. Other examples of batch-related costs include resources devoted to production scheduling, first-item inspection and materials movement. Traditional costing systems treat batch-related expenses as fixed costs, whereas ABC systems assume that they vary with the number of batches processed.

Product-sustaining activities or **service-sustaining activities** are performed to enable the production and sale of individual products (or services). Examples of product-sustaining activities provided by Kaplan and Cooper (1998) include maintaining and updating product specifications and the technical support provided for individual products and services. The costs of product-sustaining activities are incurred irrespective of the number of units of output or the number of batches processed, and their expenses will tend to increase as the number of products manufactured is increased. ABC uses product-level bases such as number of active part numbers to assign these costs to products.

The final activity category is **facility-sustaining** (or **business-sustaining) activities**. They are performed to support the facility's general manufacturing process and include general administrative staff, plant management and property costs. They are incurred to support the organization as a whole and are common and joint to all products manufactured in the plant. There would have to be a dramatic change in activity, resulting in an expansion or contraction in the size of the plant, for facility-sustaining costs to change. Such events are most unlikely in most organizations. Therefore, these costs should not be assigned to products since they are unavoidable and irrelevant for most decisions. Instead, they are regarded as common costs to *all* products made in the plant and deducted as a lump sum from the total of the operating margins from *all* products.

COST VERSUS BENEFITS CONSIDERATIONS

In Chapter 4 we pointed out that the design of a cost system should be based on cost versus benefit considerations. A sophisticated ABC system should generate the most accurate product costs. The cost of implementing and operating an ABC system is significantly more expensive than operating a traditional costing system. However, the distorted costs reported by traditional systems may result in significant mistakes in decisions (such as selling unprofitable products or dropping profitable products). If the cost of errors arising from using distorted information generated from a traditional costing system exceeds the additional costs of implementing and operating an ABC system then an ABC system ought to be implemented.

The optimal costing system is different for different organizations. A simplistic traditional costing system may report reasonably accurate product costs in organizations that have the following characteristics:

1 low levels of competition;
2 non-volume-related indirect costs that are a low proportion of total indirect costs;
3 a fairly standardized product range all consuming organizational resources in similar proportions (i.e. low product diversity).

In contrast, a sophisticated ABC system may be optimal for organizations having the following characteristics:

1 intensive competition;
2 non-volume-related indirect costs that are a high proportion of total indirect costs;
3 a diverse range of products, all consuming organizational resources in significantly different proportions (i.e. high product diversity).

ABC IN SERVICE ORGANIZATIONS

Kaplan and Cooper (1998) suggest that service companies are ideal candidates for ABC, even more than manufacturing companies. Their justification for this statement is that most of the costs in service organizations are indirect. In contrast, manufacturing companies can trace important components (such as direct materials and direct labour) of costs to

REAL WORLD VIEWS 12.2

ABC at DHL

DHL, part of the Deutsche Post World Net (DPWN) group, is a global leader in the air express industry. The DWPN group posted turnover of €63 billion in 2007, employed more than 500 000 people and operated in 220 countries and territories.

Despite having what might seem a small number of standardized services (e.g., Same Day, Time Definite and Day Definite), DHL realized in 1988 that increasing competition and removal of border controls in the European Union could affect its business. In 1988, DHL implemented activity-based costing (ABC) throughout the organization. It used a spreadsheet-based system to calculate product costs. Initial benefits were gained from the system in the form of supporting pricing policy. Over time, the organization increased its package and mail business. However, the ABC system proved inadequate when the business changed. Between 1994 and 1997 an improved ABC model was deployed in Europe, but this still failed to meet the requirements of a business dealing with 5 million shipments of varying sizes to 200 countries on a daily basis. The deployment of the model in Europe did reveal that differing customer profiles and behaviours had an impact on cost, but not all these drivers could be consistently identified. Thus, the drivers that could be measured contributed to a further revision of the ABC model. From this DHL

was able to launch a strategic customer review initiative that identified problematic customer interfaces contributing to increasing costs. The company also defined a customer negotiation strategy and customer profitability indicators, both of which became cornerstones of the business. Thus from its ABC system, DHL not only developed a reliable costing system, but also a set of tools that can support the pricing of large global tenders.

Discussion points

1 Do you think it is easy to identify the cost drivers of a business?

2 Would it be beneficial for a management accountant to have an extensive knowledge of business operations if he or she were to be involved in implementing an ABC system? Why or why not?

References

1 Bellis-Jones Hill Group, customer case: 'DHL – customer profitability in action' (www.bellisjoneshill.com).

2 DHL *Annual Report* 2007 (available at www.dhl.com).

individual products. Therefore, indirect costs are likely to be a much smaller proportion of total costs.

A UK survey by Drury and Tayles (2005) suggests that service organizations are more likely to implement ABC systems. They reported that 51 per cent of the financial and service organizations surveyed, compared with 15 per cent of manufacturing organizations, had implemented ABC. Kaplan and Cooper (1998) illustrate how ABC was applied in The Co-operative Bank, a medium-sized UK bank. ABC was used for product and customer profitability analysis. The following are some of the activities and cost drivers that were identified:

Activity	Cost driver
Provide ATM services	Number of ATM transactions
Clear debit items	Number of debits processed
Clear credit items	Number of credits processed
Issue cheque books	Number of cheque books issued
Computer processing	Number of computer transactions
Prepare statements of account transactions	Number of statements issued
Administer mortgages	Number of mortgages maintained

Activity costs were allocated to the different savings and loans products based on their demand for the activities using the cost drivers as a measure of resource consumption. Some expenses, such as finance and human resource management, were not assigned to products because they were considered to be for the benefit of the organization as a whole and not attributable to individual products. These business sustaining costs represented approximately 15 per cent of total operating expenses. Profitability analysis was extended to customer segments within product groups. The study revealed that approximately half of the current accounts, particularly those with low balances and high transactions, were unprofitable. By identifying the profitable customer segments the marketing function was able to direct its effort to attracting more new customers, and enhancing relationships with those existing customers whose behaviour would be profitable to the bank.

Significant variations in the usage of ABC both within the same country and across different countries have been reported. These differences may arise from the difficulty in precisely defining the difference between traditional costing systems and ABC systems and the specific time period when the surveys were actually undertaken.

Survey evidence suggests that over the last decade there has been an increasing interest in ABC. In the UK, surveys in the early 1990s reported adoption rates around 10% (Innes and Mitchell, 1991; Nicholls, 1992; Drury et al., 1993). Similar adoption rates of 10% were found in Ireland (Clarke, 1992) and 14% in Canada (Armitage and Nicholson, 1993). In the USA Green and Amenkhienan (1992) claimed that 45% of firms used ABC to some extent. More recent surveys suggest higher ABC adoption rates. In the UK reported usage was 18% (Innes et al., 2000), 22% (Banerjee and Kane, 1996), 21% (Evans and Ashworth, 1996) and 23% (Drury and Tayles, 2000). In the USA Shim and Stagliano (1997) reported a usage rate of 27%.

Reported usage rates for mainland Europe are 19% in Belgium (Bruggeman et al., 1996) and 6% in Finland in 1992, 11% in 1993 and 24% in 1995 (Virtanen et al., 1996). Low usage rates have been reported in Denmark (Israelsen et al., 1996), Sweden (Ask et al., 1996) and Germany (Scherrer, 1996). Activity-based techniques do not appear to have been adopted in Greece (Ballas and Venieris, 1996), Italy (Barbato et al., 1996) or Spain (Saez-Torrecilla et al., 1996).

Other studies have examined the applications of ABC. Innes and Mitchell (1995a) and Innes et al. (2000) found that cost reduction was the most widely-used application. Other widely-used applications included product/service pricing, cost modelling and performance measurement/improvement. ABC was used for stock valuation by 29% of ABC adopters thus suggesting that the majority of ABC users have separate systems for stock valuation and management accounting applications.

EXHIBIT 12.2

Surveys of company practice

ABC COST MANAGEMENT APPLICATIONS

Our aim in this chapter has been to look at how ABC can be used to provide information for decision-making by more accurately assigning costs to cost objects, such as products, customers and locations. In addition, ABC can be used for a range of cost management/cost reduction applications. The decision to implement ABC should not, therefore, be based only on its ability to produce more accurate and relevant decision-making information. Indeed, surveys by Innes and Mitchell (1995a) and Innes *et al.* (2000) on ABC applications suggest that the cost management applications tend to outweigh the product costing applications which were central to ABC's initial development. The ABC applications to cost management are discussed in Learning Note 14.1 on the dedicated website (see Preface for details).

SUMMARY

The following items relate to the learning objectives listed at the beginning of the chapter.

- **Explain why a cost accumulation system is required for generating relevant cost information for decision-making.** Many indirect costs are relevant for decision-making and a costing system is therefore required that provides an estimate of resources consumed by cost objects using cause-and-effect allocations to allocate indirect costs.

- **Describe the differences between activity-based and traditional costing systems.** The major differences relate to the two-stage allocation process. In the first stage, traditional systems allocate indirect costs to cost centres (normally departments) whereas activity-based systems allocate indirect costs to cost centres based on activities rather than departments. Since there are many more activities than departments a distinguishing feature is that activity-based systems will have a greater number of cost centres in the first stage of the allocation process. In the second stage, traditional systems use a limited number of different types of second stage volume-based allocation bases (cost drivers) whereas activity-based systems use many different types of volume-based and non-volume-based cause-and-effect second stage drivers.

- **Explain why traditional costing systems can provide misleading information for decision-making.** Traditional systems often tend to rely on arbitrary allocations of indirect costs. In particular, they rely extensively on volume-based allocations. Many indirect costs are not volume-based but, if volume-based allocation bases are used, high-volume products are likely to be assigned with a greater proportion of indirect costs than they have consumed whereas low-volume products will be assigned a lower proportion. In these circumstances traditional systems will overcost high-volume products and undercost low-volume products. In contrast, ABC systems recognize that many indirect costs vary in proportion to changes other than production volume. By identifying the cost drivers that cause the costs to change and assigning costs to cost objects on the basis of cost driver usage, costs can be more accurately traced. It is claimed that this cause-and-effect relationship provides a superior way of determining relevant costs.

- **Compute product costs using an ABC system.** Cost drivers (overhead allocation rates) are established for each activity cost pool and assigned to cost objects using the two-stage allocation overhead procedure. In the first stage an overhead analysis sheet is used to allocate overheads to activity cost pools using resource cost drivers. The second stage involves (a) the calculation of appropriate activity cost driver rates and (b) the assignment of overheads to products passing through each activity cost centre based on cost driver usage. These steps were illustrated using data presented in Example 4.NaN.

- **Identify and explain each of the four stages involved in designing ABC systems.** The design of ABC systems involves the following four stages: (a) identify the major activities that take place in the organization; (b) create a cost centre/cost pool for each activity; (c) determine the cost driver for each major activity; and (d) trace the cost of activities to the product according to a product's demand (using cost drivers as a measure of demand) for activities.

- **Describe the ABC cost hierarchy.** ABC systems classify activities along a cost hierarchy consisting of unit-level, batch-level, product-sustaining and facility-sustaining activities. Unit-level activities are performed each time a unit of the product or service is produced. Examples include direct labour and energy costs. Batch-level activities are performed each time a batch is produced. Examples include setting up a machine or processing a purchase order. Product-sustaining activities are performed to enable the production and sale of individual products. Examples include the technical support provided for individual products and the resources required performing product enhancements. Facility-sustaining activities are performed to support the facility's general manufacturing process. They include general administrative staff and property support costs.

KEY TERMS AND CONCEPTS

Activities activities in an ABC system are aggregations of events, tasks or units of work that cause the consumption of resources.

Activity cost-driver a cost-driver used to assign costs within an activity centre to products.

Batch-related activity an activity that is performed each time a batch of products or services is produced.

Consumption ratios ratios that show the proportion of each activity within an ABC system that is consumed by a product using a specified cost driver.

Cost-driver a second-stage allocation base within an ABC system that represents a measure that has the major influence on the cost of a particular activity.

Duration driver an activity cost-driver that is based on the amount of time required to perform an activity.

Facility-sustaining, or business-sustaining activities activities that are incurred to support the organization as a whole and are common and joint to all products or services produced by the organization.

Non-volume-based cost-drivers a method of assigning indirect costs that are not performed each time a unit of the product is produced.

Product-sustaining activity or **service-sustaining activity** an activity that is performed to enable the production and sale of an individual product or service.

Resource cost drivers cause-and-effect cost drivers used to allocate shared resources to individual activities.

Transaction driver an activity cost-driver that is based on the number of times that an activity is performed.

Unit-level activity an activity that is performed each time a unit of product or service is produced.

Volume-based cost-drivers a method of assigning indirect costs that assume that a product's consumption of overheads is directly determined to the volume of units produced.

KEY EXAMINATION POINTS

Questions often require you to compute product costs for a traditional system and an activity-based system and explain the difference between the product costs. It is also likely that examiners will require you to outline the circumstances where ABC systems are likely to prove most beneficial.

ASSESSMENT MATERIAL

The review questions are short questions that enable you to assess your understanding of the main topics included in the chapter. The numbers in parentheses provide you with the page numbers to refer to if you cannot answer a specific question.

The review problems are more complex and require you to relate and apply the chapter content to various business problems. The problems are graded by their level of difficulty. The multiple-choice questions are the least demanding and normally take less than 10 minutes to complete. Fully worked solutions to the review problems are provided in a separate section at the end of the book. Further review problems with solutions for this chapter are available on the accompanying website www.drury-online.com. The website includes a *Student's Manual* and an *Instructor's Manual*. Students can access both questions and answers from the *Student's Manual* and the questions from the Instructor's Manual. The answers to problems in the *Instructor's Manual* are available only to lecturers on the lecturer's password-protected section of the website.

REVIEW QUESTIONS

12.1 Explain why a cost accumulation system is required for generating relevant cost information for decision-making. *(p.294)*

12.2 What are the fundamental differences between a traditional and an ABC system? *(p. 295)*

12.3 Define activities and cost drivers. *(p. 295)*

12.4 Distinguish between volume-based and non-volume-based cost drivers. *(pp. 296–7)*

12.5 Describe the circumstances when traditional costing systems are likely to report distorted costs. *(p. 309)*

12.6 Explain how low volume products can be undercosted and high volume products overcosted when traditional costing systems are used. *(pp. 297–9)*

12.7 What is meant by 'product diversity' and why is it important for product costing? *(p. 297)*

12.8 Describe each of the four stages involved in designing ABC systems. *(pp. 306–8)*

12.9 Distinguish between resource cost drivers and activity cost drivers. *(p. 307)*

12.10 Distinguish between transaction and duration cost drivers. *(p. 307)*

12.11 Describe the ABC manufacturing cost hierarchy. *(pp. 308–9)*

12.12 Explain the circumstances when ABC is likely to be preferred to traditional costing systems. *(p. 309)*

12.13 Provide examples of how ABC can be used in service organizations. *(pp. 309–11)*

REVIEW PROBLEMS

12.14 S Ltd manufactures components for the aircraft industry. The following annual information regarding three of its key customers is available:

	W	X	Y
Gross margin	£1 100 000	£1 750 000	£1 200 000
General administration costs	£40 000	£80 000	£30 000
Units sold	1750	2000	1500
Orders placed	1000	1000	1500
Sales visits	110	100	170
Invoices raised	900	1200	1500

The company uses an activity-based costing system and the analysis of customer-related costs is as follows:

Sales visits	£500 per visit
Order processing	£100 per order placed
Despatch costs	£100 per order placed
Billing and collections	£175 per invoice raised

Using customer profitability analysis, the ranking of the customers would be:

	W	X	Y
A	1st	2nd	3rd
B	1st	3rd	2nd
C	2nd	1st	3rd
D	2nd	3rd	1st
E	3rd	2nd	1st

(4 marks)
CIMA Management Accounting

12.15 DRP Limited has recently introduced an activity-based costing system. It manufactures three products, details of which are set out below:

	Product D	Product R	Product P
Budgeted annual production (units)	100 000	100 000	50 000
Batch size (units)	100	50	25
Machine set-ups per batch	3	4	6
Purchase orders per batch	2	1	1
Processing time per unit (minutes)	2	3	3

Three cost pools have been identified. Their budgeted costs for the year ending 30 June are as follows:

Machine set-up costs	£150 000
Purchasing of materials	£70 000
Processing	£80 000

The budgeted machine set-up cost per unit of product R is nearest to:

(a)   £ 0.52

(b)   £ 0.60

(c)   £ 6.52

(d)   £ 26.09

(3 marks)

CIMA Management Accounting – Performance Management

12.16   CJD Ltd manufactures plastic components for the car industry. The following budgeted information is available for three of their key plastic components:

	W £ per unit	X £ per unit	Y £ per unit
Selling price	200	183	175
Direct material	50	40	35
Direct labour	30	35	30
Units produced and sold	10 000	15 000	18 000

The total number of activities for each of the three products for the period is as follows:

Number of purchase requisitions	1200	1800	2000
Number of set ups	240	260	300

Overhead costs have been analyzed as follows:

Receiving/inspecting quality assurance	£1 400 000
Production scheduling/machine set up	£1 200 000

Calculate the budgeted profit per unit for each of the three products using activity based budgeting.

(4 marks)

CIMA P1 Management Accounting: Performance Evaluation

12.17

(a)   Explain the following terms giving an example of each:

(i)   service centre; and

(ii)   production centre.

Explain how the treatment of overheads differs between the two different types of centre.

(6 marks)

(b)   Explain how activity-based costing differs from traditional absorption costing, giving an example.

(4 marks)

ACCA – Financial Information for Management

12.18 It is now fairly widely accepted that conventional cost accounting distorts management's view of business through unrepresentative overhead allocation and inappropriate product costing.

This is because the traditional approach usually absorbs overhead costs across products and orders solely on the basis of the direct labour involved in their manufacture. And as direct labour as a proportion of total manufacturing cost continues to fall, this leads to more and more distortion and misrepresentation of the impact of particular products on total overhead costs.

(From an article in *The Financial Times*)

You are required to discuss the above and to suggest what approaches are being adopted by management accountants to overcome such criticism.

(15 marks)
CIMA Stage 2 Cost Accounting

12.19 Comparison of traditional product costing with ABC

Having attended a CIMA course on activity-based costing (ABC) you decide to experiment by applying the principles of ABC to the four products currently made and sold by your company. Details of the four products and relevant information are given below for one period:

Product	A	B	C	D
Output in units	120	100	80	120
Costs per unit:	(£)	(£)	(£)	(£)
Direct material	40	50	30	60
Direct labour	28	21	14	21
Machine hours (per unit)	4	3	2	3

The four products are similar and are usually produced in production runs of 20 units and sold in batches of 10 units.

The production overhead is currently absorbed by using a machine hour rate, and the total of the production overhead for the period has been analyzed as follows:

	(£)
Machine department costs (rent, business rates, depreciation and supervision)	10 430
Set-up costs	5250
Stores receiving	3600
Inspection/Quality control	2100
Materials handling and despatch	4620

You have ascertained that the 'cost drivers' to be used are as listed below for the overhead costs shown:

Cost	Cost driver
Set-up costs	Number of production runs
Stores receiving	Requisitions raised
Inspection/Quality control	Number of production runs
Materials handling and despatch	Orders executed

The number of requisitions raised on the stores was 20 for each product and the number of orders executed was 42, each order being for a batch of 10 of a product. You are required:

(a) to calculate the total costs for each product if all overhead costs are absorbed on a machine hour basis;

(4 marks)

(b) to calculate the total costs for each product, using activity-based costing;

(7 marks)

(c) to calculate and list the unit product costs from your figures in (a) and (b) above, to show the differences and to comment briefly on any conclusions which may be drawn which could have pricing and profit implications.

(4 marks)
(Total 15 marks)

PART 4
INFORMATION FOR PLANNING, CONTROL AND PERFORMANCE MEASUREMENT

13   The budgeting process

14   Management control systems

15   Standard costing and variance analysis

This section examines the implementation of decisions through the planning and control process. Planning involves systematically looking at the future, so that decisions can be made today which will bring the company its desired results. Control can be defined as the process of measuring and correcting actual performance to ensure that plans for implementing the chosen course of action are carried out.

Part Four contains three chapters. Chapter 13 considers the role of budgeting within the planning process and the relationship between the long-range plan and the budgeting process. Chapters 14 and 15 are concerned with the control process. To fully understand the role that management accounting control systems play in the control process, it is necessary to be aware of how they relate to the entire array of control mechanisms used by organizations. Chapter 14 describes the different types of controls that are used by companies. The elements of management accounting control systems are described within the context of the overall control process. Chapter 15 focuses on the technical aspects of accounting control systems. It describes the major features of a standard costing system: a system that enables the differences between the planned and actual outcomes to be analyzed in detail. The operation of a standard costing system is described and the procedure for calculating the variances explained.

CHAPTER 13
THE BUDGETING PROCESS

LEARNING OBJECTIVES

After studying this chapter, you should be able to:

- explain how budgeting fits into the overall planning and control framework;
- identify and describe the six different purposes of budgeting;
- identify and describe the various stages in the budget process;
- prepare functional and master budgets;
- describe the use of computer-based financial models for budgeting.

In the previous four chapters we have considered how management accounting can assist managers in making decisions. The actions that follow managerial decisions normally involve several aspects of the business, such as the marketing, production, purchasing and finance functions, and it is important that management should coordinate these various interrelated aspects of decision-making. If they fail to do this, there is a danger that managers may each make decisions that they believe are in the best interests of the organization when, in fact, taken together they are not. For example, the marketing department may introduce a promotional campaign that is designed to increase sales demand to a level beyond that which the production department can handle. The various activities within a company should be coordinated by the preparation of plans of actions for future periods. These detailed plans are usually referred to as **budgets**.

Our objective in this chapter is to focus on the planning process within a business organization and to examine the role of budgeting within this process. What do we mean by planning? Planning is the design of a desired future and of effective ways of bringing it about. A distinction is normally made between short-term planning (budgeting) and **long-range planning**, alternatively known as **strategic or corporate planning**. Long-range planning is the systematic and formalized process for purposely directing and controlling future operations towards desired objectives for periods extending beyond one year. Short-term planning or budgeting, on the other hand, must accept the environment of today, and the physical, human and financial resources that are currently available to the firm. These resources are to a considerable extent determined by the quality of the firm's long-range planning efforts.

RELATIONSHIP BETWEEN BUDGETING AND LONG-TERM PLANNING

The annual budget should be set within the context of longer-term plans, which are likely to exist even if they have not been made explicit. Long-term planning involves strategic planning over several years and the identification of the basic strategy of the firm (i.e. the future direction the organization will take) and the gaps which exist between the future needs and present capabilities. A long-term plan is a statement of the preliminary targets and activities required by an organization to achieve its strategic aims together with a broad estimate for each year of the resources required. Because long-term planning involves looking several years into the future the plans tend to be uncertain, general in nature, imprecise and subject to change.

Budgeting is concerned with the implementation of the long-term plan for the year ahead. Because of the shorter planning horizon, budgets are more precise and detailed. Budgets provide a clear indication of what is expected to be achieved during the budget period whereas long-term plans represent the broad directions that top management intend to follow.

The budget is not something that originates 'from nothing' each year – it is developed within the context of ongoing business and is ruled by previous decisions that have been taken within the long-term planning process. When activities are initially approved for inclusion in the long-term plan, they are based on uncertain estimates that are projected for several years. These proposals must be reviewed and revised in the light of more recent information. This review and revision process frequently takes place as part of the annual budgeting process, and it may result in important decisions being taken on possible activity adjustments within the current budget period. The budgeting process cannot therefore be viewed as being purely concerned with the current year – it must be considered as an integrated part of the long-term planning process.

THE MULTIPLE FUNCTIONS OF BUDGETS

Budgets serve a number of useful purposes. They include:

1 *planning* annual operations;
2 *coordinating* the activities of the various parts of the organization and ensuring that the parts are in harmony with each other;
3 *communicating* plans to the various responsibility centre managers;
4 *motivating* managers to strive to achieve the organizational goals;
5 *controlling* activities;
6 *evaluating* the performance of managers.

Let us now examine each of these six factors.

Planning

The major planning decisions will already have been made as part of the long-term planning process. However, the annual budgeting process leads to the refinement of those plans, since managers must produce detailed plans for the implementation of the long-range plan. Without the annual budgeting process, the pressures of day-to-day operating problems may tempt managers not to plan for future operations. The budgeting process ensures that managers do plan for future operations, and that they consider how conditions in the next year might change and what steps they should take now to respond to these changed conditions. This process encourages managers to anticipate problems before they arise, and to respond to changing conditions with reasoned judgement, instead of making hasty decisions that are based on expediency.

Coordination

The budget serves as a vehicle through which the actions of the different parts of an organization can be brought together and reconciled into a common plan. Without any guidance, managers may each make their own decisions, believing that they are working in the best interests of the organization. For example, the purchasing manager may prefer to place large orders so as to obtain large discounts; the production manager will be concerned with avoiding high stock levels; and the accountant will be concerned with the impact of the decision on the cash resources of the business. It is the aim of budgeting to reconcile these differences for the good of the organization as a whole, rather than for the benefit of any individual area. Budgeting therefore compels managers to examine the relationship between their own operations and those of other departments, and, in the process, to identify and resolve conflicts.

Communication

If an organization is to function effectively, there must be definite lines of communication so that all the parts will be kept fully informed of the plans and the policies, and constraints, to which the organization is expected to conform. Everyone in the organization should have a clear understanding of the part they are expected to play in achieving the annual budget. This process will ensure that the appropriate individuals are made accountable for implementing the budget. Through the budget, top management communicates its expectations to lower level management, so that all members of the organization may understand these expectations and can coordinate their activities to attain them. It is not just the budget itself that facilitates communication – much vital information is communicated in the actual act of preparing it.

Motivation

The budget can be a useful device for influencing managerial behaviour and motivating managers to perform in line with the organizational objectives. A budget provides a standard that under the right circumstances, a manager will be motivated to strive to achieve. However, budgets can also encourage inefficiency and conflict between managers. If individuals have actively participated in preparing the budget, and it is used as a tool to assist managers in managing their departments, it can act as a strong motivational device by providing a challenge. However, if the budget is dictated from above, and imposes a threat rather than a challenge, it may be resisted and do more harm than good.

Control

A budget assists managers in managing and controlling the activities for which they are responsible. By comparing the actual results with the budgeted amounts for different categories of expenses, managers can identify costs which do not conform to the original plan and thus require their attention. This process enables management to operate a system of management by exception which means that a manager's attention and effort can be concentrated on significant deviations from the expected results. By investigating the reasons for the deviations, managers may be able to identify inefficiencies such as the purchase of inferior quality materials. When the reasons for the inefficiencies have been found, appropriate control action should be taken to remedy the situation.

Performance evaluation

A manager's performance is often evaluated by measuring his or her success in meeting the budgets. In some companies bonuses are awarded on the basis of an employee's ability to achieve the targets specified in the periodic budgets, or promotion may be partly dependent upon a manager's budget record. In addition, the manager may wish to evaluate his or her own performance. The budget thus provides a useful means of informing managers of how well they are performing in meeting targets that they have previously helped to set.

CONFLICTING ROLES OF BUDGETS

Because a single budget system is normally used to serve several purposes there is a danger that these aims may conflict with each other. For instance, the planning and motivation roles may be in conflict with each other. Demanding budgets that may not be achieved may be appropriate to motivate maximum performance, but they are unsuitable for planning purposes. For these a budget should be set based on easier and more realistic targets that are expected to be met.

There can also be a conflict between the planning and performance evaluation roles. For planning purposes budgets are set in advance of the budget period and are based on an anticipated set of circumstances or environment. Performance evaluation should be based on a comparison of actual performance with an adjusted budget to reflect the circumstances under which managers actually operated. In practice, many firms compare actual performance with the original budget (adjusted to the actual level of activity, i.e. a flexible budget), even though managers may have had no control over any changes to the circumstances or environment that were anticipated when the budget was set.

THE BUDGET PERIOD

The conventional approach is that once a year the manager of each budget centre prepares a detailed budget for one year. For control purposes, the budget is divided into either 12 monthly or 13 four-weekly periods. The preparation of budgets on an annual basis has been strongly criticized on the grounds that it is too rigid and ties a company to a 12 month commitment, which can be risky because the budget is based on uncertain forecasts.

An alternative approach is for the annual budget to be broken down by months for the first three months, and by quarters for the remaining nine months. The quarterly budgets are then developed on a monthly basis as the year proceeds. For example, during the first quarter, the monthly budgets for the second quarter will be prepared; and during the second quarter, the monthly budgets for the third quarter will be prepared. The quarterly budgets may also be reviewed as the year unfolds. For example, during the first quarter, the budget for the next three quarters may be changed as new information becomes available. A new budget for a fifth quarter will also be prepared. This process is known as **continuous or rolling budgeting**, and ensures that a 12 month budget is always available by adding a quarter in the future as the quarter just ended is dropped. Contrast this with a budget prepared once per year. As the year goes by, the period for which a budget is available will shorten until the budget for next year is prepared. Rolling budgets also ensure that planning is not something that takes place once a year when the budget is being formulated. Instead, budgeting is a continuous process, and managers are encouraged to constantly look ahead and review future plans. Another advantage is that actual performance will be compared with a more realistic target, because budgets are being constantly reviewed and updated. The main disadvantage of a rolling budget is that it can create uncertainty for managers because the budget is constantly being changed.

Irrespective of whether the budget is prepared on an annual or a continuous basis, monthly or four-weekly budgets are normally used for *control* purposes.

ADMINISTRATION OF THE BUDGETING PROCESS

It is important that suitable administration procedures exist to ensure that the budget process works effectively. In practice, the procedures should be tailor-made to the requirements of the organization, but as a general rule a firm should ensure that procedures are established for approving the budgets and that the appropriate staff support is available for assisting managers in preparing their budgets.

The budget committee

The budget committee should consist of high-level executives who represent the major segments of the business. Its major task is to ensure that budgets are realistic and that they are coordinated satisfactorily. The normal procedure is for the functional heads to present their budget to the committee for approval. If the budget does not reflect a reasonable level of performance, it will not be approved and the functional head will be required to adjust the budget and re-submit it for approval. It is important that the person whose performance is being measured should agree that the revised budget can be achieved, or it will not act as a motivational device. If budget revisions are made, the budgetees should at least feel that they were given a fair hearing by the committee. We shall discuss budget negotiation in more detail later in this chapter.

The budget committee should appoint a budget officer, who will normally be the accountant. The role of the budget officer is to coordinate the individual budgets into a budget for the whole organization, so that the budget committee and the budgetee can see the impact of an individual budget on the organization as a whole.

Accounting staff

The accounting staff will normally assist managers in the preparation of their budgets. They will, for example, circulate instructions about budget preparation and offer advice on the process, provide past information that may be useful for preparing the present budget, and ensure that managers submit their budgets on time. The accounting staff do not determine the content of the various budgets, but they do provide a valuable advisory and clerical service for the line managers.

Budget manual

A budget manual should be prepared by the accountant and circulated to all managers who are responsible for preparing budgets. This manual will describe the objectives and procedures involved in the budgeting process and will provide a useful reference source for managers responsible for budget preparation. In addition, the manual may include a timetable specifying the order in which the budgets should be prepared and the dates when they should be presented to the budget committee.

STAGES IN THE BUDGETING PROCESS

The important stages are as follows:

1 communicating details of budget policy and guidelines to those people responsible for the preparation of budgets;
2 determining the factor that restricts output;
3 preparation of the sales budget;
4 initial preparation of various budgets;
5 negotiation of budgets with superiors;
6 coordination and review of budgets;
7 final acceptance of budgets;
8 ongoing review of budgets.

Let us now consider each of these stages in more detail.

Communicating details of the budget policy

Many decisions affecting the budget year will already have been taken as part of the long-term planning process. The long-range plan is therefore the starting point for the preparation of the annual budget. Thus, top management must communicate the policy effects of the long-term plan to those responsible for preparing the current year's budgets. Policy effects might include planned changes in sales mix, or the expansion or contraction of certain activities. Any other important guidelines that are to govern the preparation of the budget should also be specified – for example the allowances that are to be made for price and wage increases, and the expected changes in productivity. Also, any expected changes in industry demand and output should be communicated by top management to the managers responsible for budget preparation. It is essential that all managers be made aware of the policy of top management for implementing the long-term plan in the current year's budget so that common guidelines can be established. The process also indicates to the managers responsible for preparing the budgets how they should respond to any expected environmental changes.

REAL WORLD VIEWS 13.1

Budgeting in the movie industry

Preparing a budget, and sticking to it, is quite important in the movie industry. While the large sums of money received by movie stars often make for interesting reading, there are many more costs to be considered when making a movie. Production staff, sets and location costs, to name but a few, are often complicated by multiple locations, currencies and languages. With movies like *Spiderman 3* (released 2007) having a budget of $258 million, cost control and tracking are important.

For the past decade, MovieMagic budgeting software by Entertainment Partners has been the accepted standard budgeting software in the movie industry. The software is used by producers, production managers and production accountants who want easily and accurately to create documentary, film, music video and television budgets. MovieMagic allows the user to create multiple budget scenarios for a single project and can incorporate subgroups such as locations and personnel. It also comes preloaded with the most common expense categories in the industry and 25 standard forms covering movies, television and videos. These can ease the budget preparation process. It also integrates closely with other software used in the movie industry, such as production scheduling software.

Movie budgets tend to increase from the initial concept once production begins. For example, the 1997 movie *Titanic* was 100 per cent over budget. Even with large earnings, the return on such an investment diminishes with such poor budgeting and cost control. Perhaps the use of software like MovieMagic could help avoid such overruns.

Discussion points

1 Do you think costs to make a movie are more uncontrollable than in other businesses?

2 Can you think of an example of differing cost scenarios that might form part of a movie budget in software like MovieMagic?

References

1 http://www.the-numbers.com/movies/records/allbudgets.php

2 http://www.entertainmentpartners.com

3 Studios still fighting battle of the bulging budget, *Los Angeles Times*, 13 January 1998 (http://articles.latimes.com/1998/jan/13/business/fi-7705).

Determining the factor that restricts performance

In every organization there is some factor that restricts performance for a given period. In the majority of organizations this factor is sales demand. However, it is possible for production capacity to restrict performance when sales demand is in excess of available capacity. Prior to the preparation of the budgets, top management needs to determine the factor that restricts performance, since this factor will in turn determine the point at which the annual budgeting process should begin.

Preparation of the sales budget

When sales demand is the factor that restricts output, it is the volume of sales and the sales mix that determine the level of a company's operations. For this reason, the sales budget is the most important plan in the annual budgeting process. This budget is also the most difficult plan to produce, because total sales revenue depends on the actions of customers. In addition, sales demand may be influenced by the state of the economy or the actions of competitors.

Initial preparation of budgets

The managers who are responsible for meeting the budgeted performance should prepare the budget for those areas for which they are responsible. The preparation of the budget should be a 'bottom-up' process. This means that the budget should originate at the lowest levels of management and be refined and coordinated at higher levels. The justification for this approach is that it enables managers to participate in the preparation of their budgets and increases the probability that they will accept the budget and strive to achieve the budget targets.

There is no single way in which the appropriate quantity for a particular budget item is determined. Past data may be used as the starting point, but this does not mean that budgeting is based on the assumption that what has happened in the past will occur in the future. Past information may provide useful guidance, but changes in future conditions must be taken into account. In addition, managers may look to the guidelines provided by top management for determining the content of their budgets. For example, the guidelines may provide specific instructions as to the content of their budgets and the permitted changes that can be made in the prices of purchases of materials and services. For production activities standard costs (see Chapter 15) may be used as the basis for costing activity volumes which are planned in the budget.

Negotiation of budgets

Budgeting should be a participative process. The budget should be originated at the lowest level of management and the managers at this level should submit their budget to their superiors for approval. The superior should then incorporate this budget with other budgets for which he or she is responsible and then submit this budget for approval to his or her superior. The manager who is the superior then becomes the budgetee at the next higher level. The process is illustrated in Figure 13.1. Sizer (1989) describes this approach as a two-way process of a top-down statement of objectives and strategies, bottom-up budget preparation and top-down approval by senior management.

The lower-level managers are represented by boxes 1–8. Managers 1 and 2 will prepare their budgets in accordance with the budget policy and the guidelines laid down by top management. The managers will submit their budget to their supervisor, who is in charge of the whole department (department A). Once these budgets have been agreed by the manager of department A, they will be combined by the departmental manager, who will then present this budget to his or her superior (manager of plant 1) for approval. The manager of plant 1 is also responsible for department B, and will combine the agreed budgets for departments A and B before presenting the combined budget to his or her supervisor (the production manager). The production manager will merge the budget for plants 1 and 2, and this final budget will represent the production budget that will be presented to the budget committee for approval.

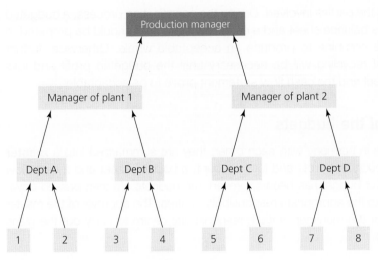

FIGURE 13.1

An illustration of budgets moving up the organization hierarchy

At each of these stages the budgets will be negotiated between the budgetees and their superiors, and eventually be agreed by both parties. Hence the figures that are included in the budget are the result of a bargaining process between a manager and his or her superior. It is important that the budgetees should participate in arriving at the final budget and that the superior does not revise the budget without giving full consideration to the subordinates' arguments for including any of the budgeted items. Otherwise, real participation will not be taking place, and it is unlikely that the subordinate will be motivated to achieve a budget that he or she did not accept.

It is also necessary to be watchful that budgetees do not deliberately attempt to obtain approval for easily attainable budgets. It is equally unsatisfactory for a superior to impose difficult targets in the hope that an authoritarian approach will produce the desired results. The desired results may be achieved in the short term, but only at the cost of a loss of morale and increased labour turnover in the future.

Negotiation is of vital importance in the budgeting process, and can determine whether the budget becomes a really effective management tool or just a routine to follow. If managers are successful in establishing a position of trust and confidence with their sub-ordinates, the negotiation process will produce a meaningful improvement in the budgetary process and outcomes for the period.

Coordination and review of budgets

As the individual budgets move up the organizational hierarchy in the negotiation process, they must be examined in relation to each other. This examination may reveal that some budgets are out of balance with others and need modifying so that they will be compatible with conditions, constraints and plans that are beyond a manager's knowledge or control. For example, a plant manager may include equipment replacement in his or her budget when funds are simply not available. The accountant must identify such inconsistencies and bring them to the attention of the appropriate manager. Any changes in the budgets should be made by the responsible managers, and this may require that the budgets be recycled from the bottom to the top for a second or even a third time until all the budgets are coordinated and are acceptable to all the parties involved. During the coordination process, a budgeted profit and loss account, a balance sheet and a cash flow statement should be prepared to ensure that all the parts combine to produce an acceptable whole. Otherwise, further adjustments and budget recycling will be necessary until the budgeted profit and loss account, the balance sheet and the cash flow statement prove to be acceptable.

Final acceptance of the budgets

When all the budgets are in harmony with each other, they are summarized into a **master budget** consisting of a budgeted profit and loss account, a balance sheet and a cash flow statement. After the master budget has been approved, the budgets are then passed down through the organization to the appropriate responsibility centres. The approval of the master budget is the authority for the manager of each responsibility centre to carry out the plans contained in each budget.

Budget review

The budget process should not stop when the budgets have been agreed. Periodically, the actual results should be compared with the budgeted results. These comparisons should normally be made on a monthly basis and a report should be available on line in the first week of the following month, so that it has the maximum motivational impact. This will enable management to identify the items that are not proceeding according to plan and to investigate the reasons for the differences. If these differences are within the control of management, corrective action can be taken to avoid similar inefficiencies occurring again in the future.

During the budget year, the budget committee should periodically evaluate the actual performance and reappraise the company's future plans. If there are any changes in the actual conditions from those originally expected, this will normally mean that the budget plans should be adjusted. This revised budget then represents a revised statement of formal operating plans for the remaining portion of the budget period. The important point to note is that the budgetary process does not end for the current year once the budget has begun; budgeting should be seen as a continuous and dynamic process.

A DETAILED ILLUSTRATION

Let us now look at an illustration of the procedure for constructing budgets in a manufacturing company, using the information contained in Example 13.1. Note that the level of detail included here is much less than that which would be presented in practice. A truly realistic illustration would fill many pages, with detailed budgets being analyzed in various ways. We shall consider an annual budget, whereas a realistic illustration would analyze the annual budget into 12 monthly periods. Monthly analysis would considerably increase the size of the illustration, but would not give any further insight into the basic concepts or procedures. In addition, we shall assume in this example that the budgets are prepared for only two responsibility centres (namely departments 1 and 2). In practice, many responsibility centres are likely to exist.

SALES BUDGET

The sales budget shows the quantities of each product that the company plans to sell and the intended selling price. It provides the predictions of total revenue from which cash receipts from customers will be estimated, and it also supplies the basic data for constructing budgets for production costs, and for selling, distribution and administrative expenses. The sales budget is, therefore, the foundation of all other budgets, since all expenditure is ultimately dependent on the volume of sales. If the sales budget is not accurate, the other budget estimates will also be unreliable. We will assume that the Enterprise Company has completed a marketing analysis and that the following annual sales budget is based on the result:

Schedule 1 – Sales budget for year ending 200X

Product	Units sold	Selling price (£)	Total revenue (£)
Alpha	8500	400	3 400 000
Sigma	1600	560	896 000
			4 296 000

Schedule 1 represents the *total* sales budget for the year. In practice, the total sales budget will be supported by detailed *subsidiary* sales budgets where sales are analyzed by areas of responsibility, such as sales territories, and into monthly periods analyzed by products.

EXAMPLE 13.1

The Enterprise Company manufactures two products, known as alpha and sigma. Alpha is produced in department 1 and sigma in department 2. The following information is available for 200X.
Standard material and labour costs:

	(£)
Material X	7.20 per unit
Material Y	16.00 per unit
Direct labour	12.00 per hour

Overhead is recovered on a direct labour hour basis.
The standard material and labour usage for each product is as follows:

	Model alpha	Model sigma
Material X	10 units	8 units
Material Y	5 units	9 units
Direct labour	10 hours	15 hours

The balance sheet for the previous year end was as follows:

	(£)	(£)	(£)
Fixed assets:			
Land		170 000	
Buildings and equipment	1 292 000		
Less depreciation	255 000	1 037 000	1 207 000
Current assets:			
Stocks, finished goods	99 076		
raw materials	189 200		
Debtors	289 000		
Cash	34 000		
	611 276		
Less current liabilities			
Creditors	248 800		362 476
Net assets			1 569 476
Represented by shareholder's interest:			
1 200 000 ordinary shares of £1 each		1 200 000	
Reserves		369 476	
			1 569 476

Other relevant data is as follows for the year 200X:

	Finished product	
	Model alpha	Model sigma
Forecast sales (units)	8500	1600
Selling price per unit	£400	£560
Ending inventory required (units)	1870	90
Beginning inventory (units)	170	85

	Direct material	
	Material X	Material Y
Beginning inventory (units)	8500	8000
Ending inventory required (units)	10 200	1700

	Department 1 (£)	Department 2 (£)
Budgeted variable overhead rates (per direct labour hour):		
Indirect materials	1.20	0.80
Indirect labour	1.20	1.20
Power (variable portion)	0.60	0.40
Maintenance (variable portion)	0.20	0.40
Budgeted fixed overheads		
Depreciation	100 000	80 000
Supervision	100 000	40 000
Power (fixed portion)	40 000	2000
Maintenance (fixed portion)	45 600	3196

	(£)
Estimated non-manufacturing overheads:	
Stationery etc. (Administration)	4000
Salaries	
Sales	74 000
Office	28 000
Commissions	60 000
Car expenses (Sales)	22 000
Advertising	80 000
Miscellaneous (Office)	8000
	276 000

Budgeted cash flows are as follows:

	Quarter 1 (£)	Quarter 2 (£)	Quarter 3 (£)	Quarter 4 (£)
Receipts from customers	1 000 000	1 200 000	1 120 000	985 000
Payments:				
Materials	400 000	480 000	440 000	547 984
Payments for wages	400 000	440 000	480 000	646 188
Other costs and expenses	120 000	100 000	72 016	13 642

You are required to prepare a master budget for the year 200X and the following budgets:

1 sales budget;

2 production budget;

3 direct materials usage budget;

4 direct materials purchase budget;

5 direct labour budget;

6 factory overhead budget;

7 selling and administration budget;

8 cash budget.

PRODUCTION BUDGET AND BUDGETED STOCK LEVELS

When the sales budget has been completed, the next stage is to prepare the production budget. This budget is expressed in *quantities only* and is the responsibility of the production manager. The objective is to ensure that production is sufficient to meet sales demand and that economic stock levels are maintained. The production budget (Schedule 2) for the year will be as follows:

Schedule 2 – Annual production budget

	Department 1 (alpha)	Department 2 (sigma)
Units to be sold	8500	1600
Planned closing stock	1870	90
Total units required for sales and stocks	10 370	1690
Less planned opening stocks	170	85
Units to be produced	10 200	1605

The total production for each department should also be analyzed on a monthly basis.

DIRECT MATERIALS USAGE BUDGET

The supervisors of departments 1 and 2 will prepare estimates of the materials which are required to meet the production budget. The materials usage budget for the year will be as follows:

Schedule 3 – Annual direct material usage budget

	Department 1			Department 2					
	Units	Unit price (£)	Total (£)	Units	Unit price (£)	Total (£)	Total units	Total unit price (£)	Total (£)
Material X	102 000[a]	7.20	734 400	12 840[c]	7.20	92 448	114 840	7.20	826 848
Material Y	51 000[b]	16.00	816 000	14 445[d]	16.00	231 120	65 445	16.00	1 047 120
			1 550 400			323 568			1 873 968

[a] 10 200 units production at 10 units per unit of production.
[b] 10 200 units production at 5 units per unit of production.
[c] 1605 units production at 8 units per unit of production.
[d] 1605 units production at 9 units per unit of production.

DIRECT MATERIALS PURCHASE BUDGET

The direct materials purchase budget is the responsibility of the purchasing manager, since it will be he or she who is responsible for obtaining the planned quantities of raw materials to meet the production requirements. The objective is to purchase these materials at the right time at the planned purchase price. In addition, it is necessary to take into account the planned raw material stock levels. The annual materials purchase budget for the year will be as follows:

Schedule 4 – Direct materials purchase budget

	Material X (units)	Material Y (units)
Quantity necessary to meet production requirements as per material usage budget	114 840	65 445
Planned closing stock	10 200	1700
	125 040	67 145
Less planned opening stock	8500	8000
Total units to be purchased	116 540	59 145
Planned unit purchase price	£7.20	£16
Total purchases	£839 088	£946 320

Note that this budget is a summary budget for the year, but for detailed planning and control it will be necessary to analyze the annual budget on a monthly basis.

DIRECT LABOUR BUDGET

The direct labour budget is the responsibility of the respective managers of departments 1 and 2. They will prepare estimates of their departments' labour hours required to meet the planned production. Where different grades of labour exist, these should be specified separately in the budget. The budget rate per hour should be determined by the industrial relations department. The direct labour budget will be as follows:

Schedule 5 – Annual direct labour budget

	Department 1	Department 2	Total
Budgeted production (units)	10 200	1605	
Hours per unit	10	15	
Total budgeted hours	102 000	24 075	126 075
Budgeted wage rate per hour	£12	£12	
Total wages	£1 224 000	£288 900	£1 512 900

FACTORY OVERHEAD BUDGET

The factory overhead budget is also the responsibility of the respective production department managers. The total of the overhead budget will depend on the behaviour of the costs of the individual overhead items in relation to the anticipated level of production. The overheads must also be analyzed according to whether they are controllable or non-controllable for the purpose of cost control. The factory overhead budget will be as follows:

Schedule 6 – Annual factory overhead budget
Anticipated activity – 102 000 direct labour hours (department 1)
24 075 direct labour hours (department 2)

	Variable overhead rate per direct labour hour		Overheads		
	Department 1 (£)	Department 2 (£)	Department 1 (£)	Department 2 (£)	Total (£)
Controllable overheads:					
Indirect material	1.20	0.80	122 400	19 260	
Indirect labour	1.20	1.20	122 400	28 890	
Power (variable portion)	0.60	0.40	61 200	9630	
Maintenance (variable portion)	0.20	0.40	20 400	9630	
			326 400	67 410	393 810
Non-controllable overheads:					
Depreciation			100 000	80 000	
Supervision			100 000	40 000	
Power (fixed portion)			40 000	2000	
Maintenance (fixed portion)			45 600	3196	
			285 600	125 196	410 796
Total overhead			612 000	192 606	804 606
Budgeted departmental overhead rate			£6.00[a]	8.00[b]	

[a] £612 000 total overheads divided by 102 000 direct labour hours.
[b] £192 606 total overheads divided by 24 075 direct labour hours.

The budgeted expenditure for the variable overhead items is determined by multiplying the budgeted direct labour hours for each department by the budgeted variable overhead rate per hour. It is assumed that all variable overheads vary in relation to direct labour hours.

SELLING AND ADMINISTRATION BUDGET

The selling and administration budgets have been combined here to simplify the presentation. In practice, separate budgets should be prepared: the sales manager will be responsible for the selling budget, the distribution manager will be responsible for the distribution expenses and the chief administrative officer will be responsible for the administration budget.

Schedule 7 – Annual selling and administration budget

	(£)	(£)
Selling:		
Salaries	74 000	
Commission	60 000	
Car expenses	22 000	
Advertising	80 000	236 000
Administration:		
Stationery	4000	
Salaries	28 000	
Miscellaneous	8000	40 000
		276 000

DEPARTMENTAL BUDGETS

For cost control the direct labour budget, materials usage budget and factory overhead budget are combined into separate departmental budgets. These budgets are normally broken down into 12 separate monthly budgets, and the actual monthly expenditure is compared with the budgeted amounts for each of the items concerned. This comparison is used for judging how effective managers are in controlling the expenditure for which they are responsible. The departmental budget for department 1 will be as follows:

Department 1 – Annual departmental operating budget

	(£)	Budget (£)	Actual (£)
Direct labour (from schedule 5):			
102 000 hours at £12		1 224 000	
Direct materials (from schedule 3):			
102 000 units of material X at £7.20 per unit	734 400		
51 000 units of material Y at £16 per unit	816 000	1 550 400	
Controllable overheads (from schedule 6):			
Indirect materials	122 400		
Indirect labour	122 400		
Power (variable portion)	61 200		
Maintenance (variable portion)	20 400	326 400	
Uncontrollable overheads (from schedule 6):			
Depreciation	100 000		
Supervision	100 000		
Power (fixed portion)	40 000		
Maintenance (fixed portion)	45 600	285 600	
		3 386 400	

MASTER BUDGET

When all the budgets have been prepared, the budgeted profit and loss account and balance sheet provide the overall picture of the planned performance for the budget period.

Budgeted profit and loss account for the year ending 200X

	(£)	(£)
Sales (schedule 1)		4 296 000
Opening stock of raw materials (from opening balance sheet)	189 200	
Purchases (schedule 4)	1 785 408[a]	
	1 974 608	
Less closing stock of raw materials (schedule 4)	100 640[b]	
Cost of raw materials consumed	1 873 968	
Direct labour (schedule 5)	1 512 900	
Factory overheads (schedule 6)	804 606	
Total manufacturing cost	4 191 474	
Add opening stock of finished goods (from opening balance sheet)	99 076	
Less closing stock of finished goods	665 984[c]	(566 908)
Cost of sales		3 624 566
Gross profit		671 434
Selling and administration expenses (schedule 7)		276 000
Budgeted operating profit for the year		395 434

[a] £839 088 (X) + £946 320 (Y) from schedule 4.

[b] 10 200 units at £7.20 plus 1700 units at £16 from schedule 4.

[c] 1870 units of alpha valued at £332 per unit, 90 units of sigma valued at £501.60 per unit.

The product unit costs are calculated as follows:

	Alpha		Sigma	
	Units	(£)	Units	(£)
Direct materials				
X	10	72.00	8	57.60
Y	5	80.00	9	144.00
Direct labour	10	120.00	15	180.00
Factory overheads:				
Department 1	10	60.00	—	—
Department 2	—	—	15	120.00
		332.00		501.60

Budgeted balance sheet as at 31 December

	(£)	(£)
Fixed assets:		
Land		170 000
Building and equipment	1 292 000	
Less depreciation[a]	435 000	857 000
		1 027 000
Current assets:		
Raw material stock	100 640	
Finished good stock	665 984	
Debtors[b]	280 000	
Cash[c]	199 170	
	1 245 794	937 910
		1 964 910
Current liabilities:		
Creditors[d]	307 884	
Represented by shareholders' interest:		
1 200 000 ordinary shares of £1 each	1 200 000	
Reserves	369 476	
Profit and loss account	395 434	1 964 910

[a] £255 000 + £180 000 (schedule 6) = £435 000.

[b] £289 000 opening balance + £4 296 000 sales − £4 305 000 cash.

[c] Closing balance as per cash budget.

[d] £248 800 opening balance + £1 785 408 purchases + £141 660 indirect materials −
£1 876 984 cash.

CASH BUDGETS

The objective of the **cash budget** is to ensure that sufficient cash is available at all times to meet the level of operations that are outlined in the various budgets. The cash budget for Example 13.1 is presented below and is analyzed by quarters, but in practice monthly or weekly budgets will be necessary. Because cash budgeting is subject to uncertainty, it is necessary to provide for more than the minimum amount required, to allow for some margin of error in planning. Cash budgets can help a firm to avoid cash balances that are surplus to its requirements by enabling management to take steps in advance to invest the surplus cash in short-term investments. Cash deficiencies can also be identified in advance, and steps can be taken to ensure that bank loans will be available to meet any temporary shortfalls. For example, when management examines the cash budget for the Enterprise Company, they may consider that the cash balances are higher than necessary in the second and third quarters of the year, and they may decide to invest part of the cash balance in short-term investments.

The overall aim should be to manage the cash of the firm to attain maximum cash availability and maximum interest income on any idle funds.

Cash budget for year ending 200X

	Quarter 1 (£)	Quarter 2 (£)	Quarter 3 (£)	Quarter 4 (£)	Total (£)
Opening balance	34 000	114 000	294 000	421 984	34 000
Receipts from debtors	1 000 000	1 200 000	1 120 000	985 000	4 305 000
	1 034 000	1 314 000	1 414 000	1 406 984	4 339 000
Payments:					
Purchase of materials	400 000	480 000	440 000	547 984	1 867 984
Payment of wages	400 000	440 000	480 000	646 188	1 966 188
Other costs and expenses	120 000	100 000	72 016	13 642	305 658
	920 000	1 020 000	992 016	1 207 814	4 139 830
Closing balance	114 000	294 000	421 984	199 170	199 170

FINAL REVIEW

The budgeted profit and loss account, the balance sheet and the cash budget will be submitted by the accountant to the budget committee, together with a number of budgeted financial ratios such as the return on capital employed, working capital, liquidity and gearing ratios. If these ratios prove to be acceptable, the budgets will be approved. In Example 13.1 the return on capital employed is approximately 20 per cent, but the working capital ratio (current assets:current liabilities) is over 4:1, so management should consider alternative ways of reducing investment in working capital before finally approving the budgets.

COMPUTERIZED BUDGETING

In the past, budgeting was a task dreaded by many management accountants. You will have noted from Example 13.1 that many numerical manipulations are necessary to prepare the budget. In the real world the process is far more complex, and, as the budget is being formulated, it is usually revised many times.

In today's world, the budgeting process is computerized and instead of being primarily concerned with numerical manipulations, the accounting staff can now become more involved in the real planning process. Computer-based financial models normally consist of mathematical statements of inputs and outputs. By simply altering the mathematical statements budgets can be revised quickly and with little effort. However, the major advantage of computerized budgeting is that management can evaluate many different options before the budget is finally agreed. Establishing a model enables 'What-if?' analysis to be employed. For example, answers to the following questions can be displayed in the form of a master budget: What if sales increase or decrease by 10 per cent? What if unit costs increase or decrease by 5 per cent? What if the credit terms for sales were reduced from 30 to 20 days?

In addition, computerized models can incorporate actual results, period by period, and carry out the necessary calculations to produce budgetary *control* reports. It is also possible

REAL WORLD VIEWS 13.2

SOURCE: ADAPTED FROM HORNYAK, S. (2000), BUDGETING MADE EASY, MANAGEMENT ACCOUNT, OCTOBER 2000.

Using Web technology for the budget process

An e-budgeting solution completely automates the development of an organization's budget and forecast. From anywhere in the world, at all times, participants in the process can log through the internet to access their budget and any pertinent related information so they can work on their plans. Web-based enterprise budgeting systems offer a centrally administered system that provides easy-to-use flexible tools for the end users who are responsible for budgeting. The Web functionality of these applications allows constant monitoring, updates and modelling.

E-budgeting provides the flexibility demanded by modern organizations. For example, the finance department can request across-the-board reallocations of expenditures and model the result immediately. No longer do management accountants have to go back and forth with other managers re-inputting data and retallying results. E-budgeting can eliminate the cumbersome accounting tasks of pulling numbers from disparate files, cutting and pasting, entering and uploading, and constantly performing reconciliation.

Also, a Web-based budgeting application lets managers access data from office or home – wherever they happen to be working. It broadens the system's availability to the user community.

When executives at Toronto-Dominion Bank were searching for a new solution capable of handling the bank's enterprise budgeting and planning function, they turned to the Internet. The company selected Clarus Corporation's Web-deployed, enterprise Clarus™ Budget solution. Its accountant stated 'in the past, we have compiled our business plan using hundreds of spreadsheets, and our analysts have spent a disproportionate amount of their time compiling and verifying data from multiple sources. Implementing a Web-based, enterprise-wide budgeting solution will help us to develop our business plans and allow our analysts to be proactive in monitoring quarterly results.'

Discussion point

What impact does e-budgeting have on the management accounting function?

to adjust the budgets for the remainder of the year when it is clear that the circumstances on which the budget was originally set have changed.

CRITICISMS OF BUDGETING

In recent years criticisms of traditional budgeting have attracted much publicity. Ekholm and Wallin (2000) and Dugdale and Lyne (2006) have reviewed the literature relating to annual budgets. They have identified the following criticisms relating to the annual budgeting process:

- encouraging rigid planning and incremental thinking;
- being time-consuming;
- ignoring key drivers of shareholder value by focusing too much attention on short-term financial numbers;
- being a yearly rigid ritual;

- tying the company to a 12 month commitment, which is risky since it is based on uncertain forecasts;
- meeting only the lowest targets and not attempting to beat the targets;
- spending what is in the budget even if this is not necessary in order to guard against next year's budget being reduced;
- achieving the budget even if this results in undesirable actions.

The term beyond budgeting is used by Hope and Fraser (2003) in relation to alternative approaches that should be used instead of annual budgeting. Rolling forecasts, produced on a monthly or quarterly basis, are suggested as the main alternative to the annual budget. These rolling forecasts should embrace key performance indicators that are necessary to achieve the objectives of the organization and should also incorporate exception-based monitoring. Rolling forecasts are advocated because they do not have the same compulsory and stifling image when compared with the annual budget.

Because of the criticisms of budgeting, and the beyond budgeting movement, Dugdale and Lyne (2006) surveyed financial and non-financial managers in 40 UK companies. Their main conclusion was that budgeting is alive and well. All of the companies surveyed used budgets and, generally, both financial and non-financial managers thought they were important for planning, control, performance measurement, co-ordination and communication. To find out how problematic the respondents viewed their budgets, they were asked whether they agreed with 20 critical propositions. The respondents tended to disagree with all of the propositions.

SUMMARY

The following items relate to the learning objectives listed at the beginning of the chapter.

- **Explain how budgeting fits into the overall planning and control framework.** The annual budget should be set within the context of longer-term plans, which are likely to exist even if they have not been made explicit. A long-term plan is a statement of the preliminary targets and activities required by an organization to achieve its strategic plans, together with a broad estimate for each year of the resources required. Because long-term planning involves 'looking into the future' for several years, the plans tend to be uncertain, general in nature, imprecise and subject to change. Annual budgeting is concerned with the detailed implementation of the long-term plan for the year ahead.

- **Identify and describe the six different purposes of budgeting.** Budgets are used for the following purposes: (a) planning annual operations; (b) coordinating the activities of the various parts of the organization and ensuring that the parts are in harmony with each other; (c) communicating the plans to the managers of the various responsibility centres; (d) motivating managers to strive to achieve organizational goals; (e) controlling activities; and (f) evaluating the performance of managers.

- **Identify and describe the various stages in the budget process.** The important stages are as follows: (a) communicating details of the budget policy and guidelines to those people responsible for the preparation of the budgets; (b) determining the factor that restricts output (normally sales volume); (c) preparation of the sales budget (assuming that sales demand is the factor that restricts output); (d) initial preparation of the various budgets; (e) negotiation of budgets with superiors; (f) coordination and review of budgets; (g) final acceptance of budgets; and (h) ongoing review of budgets. Each of the above stages is described in the chapter.

- **Prepare functional and master budgets.** When all of the budgets have been prepared they are summarized into a master budget consisting in a budgeted profit and loss account, a balance sheet and a cash budget statement. The preparation of functional and master budgets was illustrated using Example 13.1.

- **Describe the use of computer-based financial models for budgeting.** Computer-based financial models are mathematical statements of the inputs and output relationships that affect the budget. These models allow management to conduct sensitivity analysis to ascertain the effects on the master budget of changes in the original predicted data or changes in the assumptions that were used to prepare the budgets.

KEY TERMS AND CONCEPTS

Budget a detailed financial plan for future activities, normally drawn up for a period of up to a year.

Budgeting the process of drawing up detailed financial plans for the year ahead in order to implement long-term objectives.

Cash budget a budget that estimates the inflows and outflows of cash over the budget period.

Continuous budgeting, or rolling budgeting budgeting that ensures that a 12 month budget is always available by add-ing a budget for each quarter in the future as the quarter just ended is dropped.

Long-range planning, or strategic planning or corporate planning the systematic and formalized process for directing and controlling future operations for periods extending beyond a year.

Master budget a document that summarizes the individual budgets and consists of a budgeted profit and loss, balance sheet and cash flow statement.

KEY EXAMINATION POINTS

Examination questions on budgeting frequently require the preparation of functional or cash budgets. A common mistake is to incorrectly deduct closing stocks and add opening stocks when preparing production and material purchase budgets (see Review problems 13.10 and 13.13).

ASSESSMENT MATERIAL

The review questions are short questions that enable you to assess your understanding of the main topics included in the chapter. The numbers in parentheses provide you with the page numbers to refer to if you cannot answer a specific question.

The review problems are more complex and require you to relate and apply the chapter content to various business problems. The problems are graded by their level of difficulty. The multiple-choice questions are the least demanding and normally take less than 10 minutes to complete. Fully worked solutions to the review problems are provided in a separate section at the end of the book. Further review problems with solutions for this chapter are available on the accompanying website www.drury-online.com. The website includes a *Student's Manual* and an *Instructor's Manual.* Students can access both questions and answers from the *Student's Manual* and the questions from the *Instructor's Manual.* The answers to problems in the *Instructor's Manual* are available only to lecturers on the lecturer's password-protected section of the website.

The website also includes over 20 case study problems. A list of these cases is provided on pages 427–30 Cases that are relevant to the content of this chapter include Endeavour Twoplise Ltd and Global Ltd.

REVIEW QUESTIONS

13.1 Define the term 'budget'. How are budgets used in planning? *(pp. 323–4)*

13.2 Distinguish between budgeting and long-range planning. How are they related? *(p. 324)*

13.3 Describe the different purposes of budgeting. *(pp. 324–6)*

13.4 Explain what is meant by the term 'management by exception'. *(p. 326)*

13.5 Describe how the different roles of budgets can conflict with each other. *(p. 326)*

13.6 Distinguish between continuous and rolling budgets. *(pp. 326–7)*

13.7 Describe the different stages in the budgeting process. *(pp. 328–32)*

13.8 All budgets depend on the sales budget. Do you agree? Explain. *(p. 323)*

13.9 What is a master budget? *(p. 332)*

REVIEW PROBLEMS

13.10 When preparing a production budget, the quantity to be produced equals:

    (a) sales quantity + opening stock + closing stock

    (b) sales quantity – opening stock + closing stock

    (c) sales quantity – opening stock – closing stock

    (d) sales quantity + opening stock – closing stock

    (e) sales quantity

CIMA Stage 2

13.11 Which of the following is the responsibility of the budget committee?

(a) Taking corrective action to ensure that sales targets are achieved.

(b) Ensuring the sales budget is consistent with other budgets.

(c) Providing information on sales levels and prices in previous budget periods.

(d) Drawing up the sales budget.

CIMA – Management Accounting Fundamentals

13.12 The benefits of using a computerized budget system as opposed to a manual one are:

(i) data used in drawing up the budget can be processed more quickly;

(ii) budget targets will be more acceptable to the managers responsible for their achievement;

(iii) changes in variables can be incorporated into the budget more quickly;

(iv) the principal budget factor can be identified before budget preparation begins;

(v) continuous budgeting is only possible using a computerized system.

(a) (i) and (iii) only

(b) (i), (ii) and (iii) only

(c) (i), (iii) and (iv) only

(d) (i), (iii) and (v) only

CIMA – Management Accounting Fundamentals

13.13 A company has the following budget for the next month:

Finished product

Sales	7000 units
Production units	7200 units

Materials

Usage per unit	3 kg
Opening stock	400 kg
Closing stock	500 kg

What is the material purchases budget for the month?

(a) 20 900 kg

(b) 21 100 kg

(c) 21 500 kg

(d) 21 700 kg

ACCA – Financial Information for Management

13.14 The following estimates have been prepared for a retailer's next budget period:

	$
Sales	160 000
Opening debtors	27 500
Closing debtors	19 400
Opening stock	16 600
Closing stock	18 700

The gross profit margin on sales is budgeted at 55 per cent.

(a) The cash which the retailer expects to receive from customers during the budget period amounts to:

(i) $88 000

(ii) $151 900

(iii) $157 900

(iv) $168 100

(b) The value of purchases made by the retailer during the budget period is expected to be:

(i) $69 900

(ii) $74 100

(iii) $85 900

(iv) $90 100

CIMA – Management Accounting Fundamentals

13.15 A company manufactured two products P1 and P2 in a factory divided into two cost centres, X and Y. The following budgeted data are available:

	Cost centre	
	X	Y
Allocated and apportioned fixed overhead costs	£88 000	£96 000
Direct labour hours per unit:		
Product P1	3.0	1.0
Product P2	2.5	2.0

Budgeting output is 8000 units of each product. Fixed overhead costs are absorbed on a direct labour hour basis.

What is the budgeted fixed overhead cost per unit for Product P2?

(a) £10

(b) £11

(c) £12

(d) £13

13.16   D plc operates a retail business. Purchases are sold at cost plus 25 per cent. The management team are preparing the cash budget and have gathered the following data:

1   The budgeted sales are as follows:

Month	£000
July	100
August	90
September	125
October	140

2   It is management policy to hold inventory at the end of each month which is sufficient to meet sales demand for the next half month. Sales are budgeted to occur evenly during each month.

3   Creditors are paid one month after the purchase has been made.

Calculate the entries for purchases that will be shown for August, September and October.

(3 marks)
CIMA P1 Management Accounting: Performance Evaluation

13.17   **Preparation of functional budgets, cash budget and master budget**
The budgeted balance sheet data of Kwan Tong Umbago Ltd is as follows:

	1 March Cost (£)	Depreciation to date (£)	Net (£)
Fixed assets			
Land and buildings	500 000	—	500 000
Machinery and equipment	124 000	84 500	39 500
Motor vehicles	42 000	16 400	25 600
	666 000	100 900	565 100
Working capital: current assets			
Stock of raw materials			
(100 units)		4320	
Stock of finished goods			
(110 units)[a]		10 450	
Debtors (January £7680		18 080	
February £10 400)			
Cash and bank		6790	
		39 640	
Less current liabilities			
Creditors		3900	35 740
(raw materials)			600 840
Represented by:			
Ordinary share capital (fully paid) £1 shares			500 000
Share premium			60 000
Profit and loss account			40 840
			600 840

[a] The stock of finished goods was valued at marginal cost.

The estimates for the next four-month period are as follows:

	March	April	May	June
Sales (units)	80	84	96	94
Production (units)	70	75	90	90
Purchases of raw materials (units)	80	80	85	85
Wages and variable overheads at £65 per unit	£4550	£4875	£5850	£5850
Fixed overheads	£1200	£1200	£1200	£1200

The company intends to sell each unit for £219 and has estimated that it will have to pay £45 per unit for raw materials. One unit of raw material is needed for each unit of finished product.

All sales and purchases of raw materials are on credit. Debtors are allowed two months' credit and suppliers of raw materials are paid after one month's credit. The wages, variable overheads and fixed overheads are paid in the month in which they are incurred.

Cash from a loan secured on the land and buildings of £120 000 at an interest rate of 7.5 per cent is due to be received on 1 May. Machinery costing £112 000 will be received in May and paid for in June.

The loan interest is payable half yearly from September onwards. An interim dividend to 31 March of £12 500 will be paid in June.

Depreciation for the four months, including that on the new machinery, is:

Machinery and equipment	£15 733
Motor vehicles	£3500

The company uses the FIFO method of stock valuation. Ignore taxation.
Required:

(a) Calculate and present the raw materials budget and finished goods budget in terms of units, for each month from March to June inclusive.

(5 marks)

(b) Calculate the corresponding sales budgets, the production cost budgets and the budgeted closing debtors, creditors and stocks in terms of value.

(5 marks)

(c) Prepare and present a cash budget for each of the four months.

(6 marks)

(d) Prepare a master budget, i.e. a budgeted trading and profit and loss account, for the four months to 30 June, and budgeted balance sheet as at 30 June.

(10 marks)

(e) Advise the company about possible ways in which it can improve its cash management.

(9 marks)

ACCA Paper 8 Managerial Finance

13.18 Budget preparation and comments on sales forecasting methods

You have recently been appointed as the management accountant to Alderley Ltd, a small company manufacturing two products, the Elgar and the Holst. Both products use the same type of material and labour but in different proportions. In the past, the company has had poor control over its working capital. To remedy this, you have recommended to the directors that a budgetary control system be introduced. This proposal has now been agreed.

Because Alderley Ltd's production and sales are spread evenly over the year, it was agreed that the annual budget should be broken down into four periods, each of 13 weeks, and commencing with the 13 weeks ending 4 April. To help you in this task, the sales and production directors have provided you with the following information:

1 Marketing and production data

	Elgar	Holst
Budgeted sales for 13 weeks (units)	845	1235
Material content per unit (kilograms)	7	8
Labour per unit (standard hours)	8	5

2 Production labour

The 24 production employees work a 37-hour, five-day week and are paid £8 per hour. Any hours in excess of this involve Alderley in paying an overtime premium of 25 per cent. Because of technical problems, which will continue over the next 13 weeks, employees are only able to work at 95 per cent efficiency compared to standard.

3 Purchasing and opening stocks

The production director believes that raw material will cost £12 per kilogram over the budget period. He also plans to revise the amount of stock being kept. He estimates that the stock levels at the commencement of the budget period will be as follows:

Raw materials	Elgar	Holst
2328 kilograms	163 units	361 units

4 Closing stocks

At the end of the 13-week period closing stocks are planned to change. On the assumption that production and sales volumes for the second budget period will be similar to those in the first period:

- raw material stocks should be sufficient for 13 days' production;

- finished stocks of the Elgar should be equivalent to 6 days' sales volume;

- finished stocks of the Holst should be equivalent to 14 days' sales volume.

Task 1

Prepare in the form of a statement the following information for the 13-week period to 4 April:

(a) the production budget in units for the Elgar and Holst;

(b) the purchasing budget for Alderley Ltd in units;

(c) the cost of purchases for the period;

(d) the production labour budget for Alderley Ltd in hours;

(e) the cost of production labour for the period.

Note: Assume a five-day week for both sales and production.

The managing director of Alderley Ltd, Alan Dunn, has also only recently been appointed. He is keen to develop the company and has already agreed to two new products being developed. These will be launched in 18 months' time. While talking to you about the budget, he mentions that the quality of sales forecasting will need to improve if the company is to grow rapidly. Currently, the budgeted sales figure is found by initially adding 5 per cent to the previous year's sales volume and then revising the figure following discussions with the marketing director. He believes this approach is increasingly inadequate and now requires a more systematic approach.

A few days later, Alan Dunn sends you a memo. In that memo, he identifies three possible strategies for increasing sales volume. They are:

● more sales to existing customers;

● the development of new markets;

● the development of new products.

He asks for your help in forecasting likely sales volumes from these sources.

Task 2

Write a brief memo to Alan Dunn. Your memo should:

(a) identify *four* ways of forecasting future sales volume;

(b) show how each of your four ways of forecasting can be applied to *one* of the sales strategies identified by Alan Dunn and justify your choice;

(c) give *two* reasons why forecasting methods might not prove to be accurate.

AAT

13.19 X Plc manufactures specialist insulating products that are used in both residential and commercial buildings. One of the products, Product W, is made using two different raw materials and two types of labour. The company operates a standard absorption costing system and is now preparing its budgets for the next four quarters. The following information has been identified for Product W:

Sales

Selling price	£220 per unit

Sales demand

Quarter 1	2250 units
Quarter 2	2050 units
Quarter 3	1650 units
Quarter 4	2050 units
Quarter 5	1250 units
Quarter 6	2050 units

Costs

Materials

A	5 kgs per unit @ £4 per kg
B	3 kgs per unit @ £7 per kg

Labour

Skilled	4 hours per unit @ £15 per hour
Semi-skilled	6 hours per unit @ £9 per hour
Annual overheads	£280,000
	40% of these overheads are fixed and the remainder varies with total labour hours. Fixed overheads are absorbed on a unit basis.

Inventory holding policy

Closing inventory of finished goods	30% of the following quarter's sales demand
Closing inventory of materials	45% of the following quarter's materials usage

The management team are concerned that X Plc has recently faced increasing competition in the market place for Product W. As a consequence there have been issues concerning the availability and costs of the specialized materials and employees needed to manufacture Product W, and there is concern that these might cause problems in the current budget setting process.

(a)   Prepare the following budgets for each quarter for X Plc:

   (i)   Production budget in units;

   (ii)   Raw material purchases budget in kgs and value for Material B.

(5 marks)

(b)   X Plc has just been informed that Material A may be in short supply during the year for which it is preparing budgets. Discuss the impact this will have on budget preparation and other areas of X Plc.

(5 marks)

Actual production	7250 units
Actual overheads	
Variable	£185 000
Fixed	£105 000
Actual labour costs	
Skilled – £16.25 per hour	£568 750
Semi-skilled – £8 per hour	£332 400

(c) Assuming that the budgeted production of Product W was 7700 units and that the following actual results were incurred for labour and overheads in the year: Prepare a flexible budget statement for X Plc showing the total variances that have occurred for the above four costs only.

(5 marks)

(d) Explain how rolling budgets are used and why they should be suitable for X Plc.

(5 marks)

CIMA P1 Management Accounting: Performance Evaluation

CHAPTER 14
MANAGEMENT CONTROL SYSTEMS

LEARNING OBJECTIVES

After studying this chapter you should be able to:

- describe the three different types of controls used in organizations;
- distinguish between feedback and feed-forward controls;
- define the four different types of responsibility centres;
- explain the different elements of management accounting control systems;
- describe the controllability principle and the methods of implementing it;
- describe the different approaches that can be used to determine financial performance targets and discuss the impact of their level of difficulty on motivation and performance;
- describe the influence of participation in the budgeting process;
- explain why a performance measurement system should also incorporate non-financial measures.

Control is the process of ensuring that a firm's activities conform to its plan and that its objectives are achieved. In an article published many years ago Drucker (1964) distinguished between 'controls' and 'control'. 'Controls' refer to measurement and information, whereas control means direction. In other words, 'controls' are purely a means to an end; the end is control. '**Control**' is the function that makes sure that actual work is done to fulfil the original intention, and 'controls' are used to provide information to assist in determining the control action to be taken. For example, material costs may be greater than budget. 'Controls' will indicate that costs exceed budget and that this may be because the purchase of inferior quality materials causes excessive wastage. 'Control' is the action that is taken to purchase the correct quality materials in the future to reduce excessive wastage.

'Controls' encompass all the methods and procedures that direct employees towards achieving the organization objectives. The management accounting control system is only one of the many different control mechanisms that companies use to control their managers and employees. To fully understand the role that management accounting control systems play, it is necessary to be aware of how they relate to the entire array of control mechanisms used by organizations. Note that the term **management control system** is used to refer to the entire array of controls used by an organization.

DIFFERENT TYPES OF CONTROLS

To make sense of the vast number of control mechanisms that are used by companies we shall classify them into three categories using approaches that have been adopted by Ouchi (1979) and Merchant (1998). They are:

1 action (or behavioural) controls;

2 personnel, cultural and social controls;

3 results (or output) controls.

You should note that management accounting systems are normally synonymous with output controls whereas management control systems encompass all of the above categories.

Action or behavioural controls

Behavioural controls also known as **action controls** involve observing the actions of individuals as they go about their work. They are appropriate where cause and effect relationships are well understood, so that if the correct means are followed, the desired outcomes will occur. Under these circumstances effective control can be achieved by having superiors watch and guide the actions of subordinates. For example, if the supervisor watches the workers on the assembly line and ensures that the work is done exactly as prescribed, then the expected quality and quantity of work should ensue. Forms of action controls described by Merchant include behavioural constraints, preaction reviews and action accountability.

The aim of *behavioural constraints* is to prevent people from doing things that should not be done. They include physical constraints, such as computer passwords that restrict access to authorized personnel, and administrative constraints such as imposing ceilings on the amount of capital expenditure that managers may authorize.

Preaction reviews involve the scrutiny and approval of action plans of the individuals being controlled before they can undertake a course of action. Examples include the approval by municipal authorities of plans for the construction of properties prior to building commencing, or the approval by a tutor of a dissertation plan prior to the student being authorized to embark on the dissertation.

Action accountability involves defining actions that are acceptable or unacceptable, observing the actions and rewarding acceptable or punishing unacceptable actions. Examples of action accountability include establishing work rules and procedures and company codes of conduct that employees must follow. Budgets are another form of action accountability whereby an upper limit of expense category is given for the budget period. If managers exceed these limits they are held accountable and required to justify their actions.

Personnel, cultural and social controls

Social controls involve the selection of people who have already been socialized into adopting particular norms and patterns of behaviour to perform particular tasks. For example, if the only staff promoted to managerial level are those who display a high commitment to the firm's objectives then the need for other forms of controls can be reduced.

Personnel controls involve helping employees do a good job by building on employees' natural tendencies to control themselves. In particular, they ensure that the employees have the capabilities (in terms of intelligence, qualifications and experience) and the resources needed to do a good job. Merchant identifies three major methods of implementing personnel controls. They are selection and placement, training and job design and the provision of the necessary resources. Selection and placement involves finding the right people to do a specified job. Training can be used to ensure that employees know how to perform the assigned tasks and to make them fully aware of the results and actions that are expected from them. Job design entails designing jobs in such a way that employees are able to undertake their tasks with a high degree of success. This requires that jobs are not made too complex, onerous or badly defined so that employees do not know what is expected of them.

Cultural controls represent a set of values, social norms and beliefs that are shared by members of the organization and that influence their actions. Cultural controls are exercised by individuals over one another – for example, procedures used by groups within an organization to regulate performance of their own members and to bring them into line when they deviate from group norms. Cultural controls are virtually the same as social controls.

Results or output controls

Results or output controls involve collecting and reporting information about the outcomes of work effort. The major advantage of results controls is that senior managers do not have to be knowledgeable about the means required to achieve the desired results or be involved in directly observing the actions of subordinates. They merely rely on output reports to ascertain whether or not the desired outcomes have been achieved. Management accounting control systems can be described as a form of output controls. They are mostly defined in monetary terms such as revenues, costs, profits and ratios such as return on investment. Results measures can also include non-accounting measures such as the number of units of defective production, the number of loan applications processed or ratio measures such as the number of customer deliveries on time as a percentage of total deliveries. Results controls involve the following stages:

1 establishing results (i.e. performance) measures that minimize undesirable behaviour;
2 establishing performance targets;
3 measuring performance;
4 providing rewards or punishment.

REAL WORLD VIEWS 14.1

Crime-fighting targets lead to 'dysfunctional' policing says police chief

Government crime-fighting targets are a shambles and should be scrapped, claims Chief Superintendent Ian Johnston. Mr Johnston was speaking ahead of the Police Superintendents' Association's 2007 annual conference, when he will ask the police minister to scrap the current targets regime.

'I believe we should abolish the performance framework in its entirety,' Mr Johnston said. 'It sounds radical, but it would be very warmly welcomed by the police service and would allow us, the professionals, to make judgements. We want to reclaim policing for the police.' He added: 'Centrally imposed targets are preventing senior police officers from delivering the policing that the public wants and deserves. We need to restore discretion to senior police officers enabling them to make decisions that relate to local policing issues, ensuring that we deliver a high standard of quality policing.'

In May 2007, the leaders of rank-and-file police officers made a similar demand to reverse the target driven culture that has forced them to make 'ludicrous' decisions such as a case in Kent where a child was arrested for throwing cream buns at a bus. The Police Federation said judging officers purely on how many arrests, cautions or on-the-spot fines they can deliver was making a mockery of the criminal justice system. The drive to meet Whitehall performance targets was compelling officers to criminalize middle England, they added.

The organization published a dossier of ridiculous cases they claimed resulted from Home Office targets placed on beat bobbies. The cases included a Cheshire man who was cautioned by police for being found in possession of an egg with intent to throw, and a West Midlands woman arrested on her wedding day for criminal damage to a car park barrier when her foot slipped on her accelerator.

Today, Mr Johnston said, 'current Home Office targets have made some senior officers seriously ill from the stress of managing a wide range of competing demands. More than 70 per cent of basic command unit commanders believe national targets have had a negative impact on service delivery. We are obliged to count everything and in order to account for our performance we are not addressing a lot of the issues that the public see as far more important.' He added: 'The time has come for someone to say that the performance framework and the red tape and the bureaucracy have got to go. The government's focus on volume crime targets is skewing all police activity in a way that our members see as increasingly dysfunctional.'

Discussion point

How might the dysfunctional effects of the performance system in the police force be minimized?

SOURCE: DAILY MAIL, 7 SEPTEMBER 2007 (WWW.DAILYMAIL.CO.UK/NEWS/ARTICLE-480296).

The *first stage* involves selecting performance measures for those aspects of activities that the organization wishes to monitor. Ideally desirable behaviour should result in improvements in the performance measure and undesirable behaviour should have a detrimental effect on the measure. The *second stage* requirement of a pre-set performance target tells individuals what to aim for and allows employees and their superiors to interpret performance. The *third stage* relates to measuring performance. Ability to measure the outputs of activities constrains the use of output measures for these activities. For example, the accomplishments of a personnel department can be difficult to measure and other forms of control are likely to be preferable. The *final stage* of results controls involves encouraging employees to achieve organizational goals by having rewards (or punishments) linked to their success (or failure) in achieving the results measures. Organizational rewards include salary increases, bonuses, promotions and recognition. Employees can also derive intrinsic rewards through a sense of accomplishment and achievement. Punishments include demotions, failure to obtain the rewards and possibly the loss of one's job.

FEEDBACK AND FEED-FORWARD CONTROLS

Feedback control involves monitoring outputs achieved against desired outputs and taking corrective action if a deviation exists. In **feed-forward control**, predictions are made of what outputs are expected to be at some future time. If these expectations differ from what is desired, control actions are taken that will minimize these differences. The objective is for control to be achieved before any deviations from desired outputs actually occur. In other words, with feed-forward controls likely errors can be anticipated and steps taken to avoid them, whereas with feedback controls actual errors are identified after the event and corrective action is taken to implement future actions to achieve the desired outputs.

A major limitation of feedback control is that errors are identified after they have occurred. However, this is not usually a significant problem when there is a short time lag between the occurrence of an error and the identification and implementation of corrective action. Feed-forward control is therefore preferable when a significant time lag occurs. The budgeting process is a feed-forward control system. To the extent that outcomes fall short of what is desired, alternatives are considered until a budget is produced that is expected to achieve what is desired. The comparison of actual results with budget, in identifying variances and taking remedial action to ensure that future outcomes will conform with budgeted outcomes, is an illustration of a feedback control system. Thus accounting control systems consist of both feedback and feed-forward controls.

MANAGEMENT ACCOUNTING CONTROL SYSTEMS

Up to this point in the chapter, we have been looking at the broad context of management control systems. We shall now concentrate on management accounting control systems which represent the predominant controls in most organizations.

Why are accounting controls the predominant controls? There are several reasons. First, all organizations need to express and aggregate the results of a wide range of dissimilar activities using a common measure. The monetary measure meets this requirement. Second, profitability and liquidity are essential to the success of all organizations and financial measures relating to these and other areas are closely monitored by stakeholders. It is therefore natural that managers will wish to monitor performance in monetary terms. Third, financial measures also enable a common decision rule to be applied by all managers when considering alternative courses of action. That is, a course of action will normally benefit a firm only if it results in an improvement in its financial performance. Finally, measuring results in financial terms enables managers to be given more autonomy. Focusing on the outcomes of managerial actions, summarized in financial terms, gives managers the freedom to take whatever actions they consider to be appropriate to achieve the desired results.

RESPONSIBILITY CENTRES

The complex business environment of today makes it virtually impossible for most firms to be controlled centrally. It is simply not possible for central management to have all the relevant information and time to determine the detailed plans for the entire organization. Some degree of decentralization is essential for all but the smallest firms. Organizations decentralize by creating responsibility centres. A **responsibility centre** may be defined as a unit of a firm where an individual manager is held responsible for the unit's performance. There are four types of responsibility centres. They are:

1 cost or expense centres;
2 revenue centres;
3 profit centres;
4 investment centres.

The creation of responsibility centres is a fundamental part of management accounting control systems. It is therefore important that you can distinguish between the various forms of responsibility centres.

Cost or expense centres

Cost or **expense centres** are responsibility centres whose managers are normally accountable for only those costs that are under their control. We can distinguish between two types of cost centres – standard cost centres and discretionary cost centres. The main features of **standard cost centres** are that output can be measured and the input required to produce each unit of output can be specified. Control is exercised by comparing the standard cost (that is, the cost of the inputs that *should* have been consumed in producing the output) with the cost that was *actually* incurred. The difference between the actual cost and the standard cost is described as the 'variance'. Standard cost centres and variance analysis will be discussed extensively in the next chapter.

Standard cost centres are best suited to units within manufacturing firms but they can also be established in service industries such as units within banks, where output can be measured in terms of the number of cheques or the number of loan applications processed, and there are also well defined input–output relationships. Although cost centre managers are not accountable for sales revenues they can affect the amount of sales revenue generated if quality standards are not met and outputs are not produced according to schedule. Therefore, non-financial performance measures that relate to quality and timeliness are also required alongside financial measures.

Discretionary expense centres are those responsibility cost centres where output cannot be measured in financial terms and there are no clearly observable relationships between inputs (the resources consumed) and the outputs (the results achieved). Control normally takes the form of ensuring that actual expenditure adheres to budgeted expenditure for each expense category and also ensuring that the tasks assigned to each centre have been successfully accomplished. Examples of discretionary centres include advertising and publicity and research and development departments.

One of the major problems arising in discretionary expense centres is measuring the effectiveness of expenditures. For example, the marketing support department may not have exceeded an advertising budget but this does not mean that the advertising expenditure has been effective. The advertising may have been incorrectly timed, it may have been directed to the wrong audience, or it may have contained the wrong message. Determining the effectiveness and efficiency of discretionary expense centres is one of the most difficult areas of management control.

Revenue centres

Revenue centres are responsibility centres where managers are mainly accountable only for financial outputs in the form of sales revenues. Typical examples of revenue centres are where regional sales managers are accountable for sales within their regions. Revenue centre managers may also be held accountable for selling expenses, such as salesperson salaries, commissions and order-getting costs. They are not, however, made accountable for the cost of the goods and services that they sell.

Profit centres

Both cost and revenue centre managers have limited decision-making authority. Cost centre managers are accountable only for managing inputs of their centres and decisions relating to outputs are made by other units within the firm. Revenue centres are accountable for selling the products or services but they have no control over their manufacture. A significant increase in managerial autonomy occurs when unit managers are given responsibility for both production and sales. In this situation managers are normally free to set selling prices, choose which markets to sell in, make product-mix and output decisions and select suppliers. Units within an organization whose managers are accountable for both revenues and costs are called **profit centres**.

Investment centres

Investment centres are responsibility centres whose managers are responsible for both sales revenues and costs and, in addition, have responsibility and authority to make working capital and capital investment decisions. Typical investment centre performance measures include return on investment (ROI) and economic value added (EVA) (see Learning Note 14.1 on the open access website for an explanation of ROI and EVA). These measures are influenced by revenues, costs and assets employed and thus reflect the responsibility that managers have for both generating profits and managing the investment base. Investment centres represent the highest level of managerial autonomy. They include the company as a whole, operating subsidiaries, operating groups and divisions. The additional issues relating to aspects of control in profit and investment centres are generally covered on second level cost and management accounting courses. However, some of the professional examining bodies have begun to examine this topic on first level courses. To accommodate the different requirements of readers, responsibility accounting in profit and investment centres is covered in Learning Note 14.1 on the open access website (see Preface for details).

THE NATURE OF MANAGEMENT ACCOUNTING CONTROL SYSTEMS

Management accounting control systems have two core elements. The first is the formal planning processes such as budgeting and long-term planning that were described in the previous chapter. These processes are used for establishing performance expectations for evaluating performance. The second is **responsibility accounting** which involves the creation of responsibility centres. Responsibility centres enable accountability for financial results and outcomes to be allocated to individuals throughout the organization. The objective of responsibility accounting is to accumulate costs and revenues for each individual responsibility centre so that the deviations from a performance target (typically the budget) can be attributed to the individual who is accountable for the responsibility centre. For each responsibility centre the process involves setting a performance target, measuring performance, comparing performance against the target, analyzing the variances and taking action where significant variances exist between actual and target performance.

Responsibility accounting is implemented by issuing performance reports at frequent intervals (normally monthly) that inform responsibility centre managers of the deviations from budgets for which they are accountable and are required to take action. An example of a performance report issued to a cost centre manager is presented in the lower section of Exhibit 14.1. You should note that at successively higher levels of management less detailed information is reported. You can see from the upper sections of Exhibit 14.1 that the information is condensed and summarized as the results relating to the responsibility centre are reported at higher levels. Exhibit 14.1 only includes financial information. In addition non-financial measures such as those relating to quality and timeliness may be reported. We shall look at non-financial measures in more detail at the end of this chapter.

Responsibility accounting involves:

1 distinguishing between those items which managers can control and for which they should be held accountable and those items over which they have no control and for which they are not held accountable (i.e. applying the controllability principle);

2 setting financial performance targets and determining how much influence managers should have in the setting of financial targets;

3 determining how much influence managers should have in setting financial targets.

We shall now examine each of these items in detail.

THE CONTROLLABILITY PRINCIPLE

Responsibility accounting is based on the application of the **controllability principle** which means that it is appropriate to charge to an area of responsibility only those costs that are significantly influenced by the manager of that responsibility centre. The controllability principle can be implemented by either eliminating the uncontrollable items from the areas for which managers are held accountable, or calculating their effects so that the reports distinguish between controllable and uncontrollable items.

Applying the controllability principle is difficult in practice because many areas do not fit neatly into either controllable or uncontrollable categories. Instead, they are partially controllable. Even when outcomes are affected by occurrences outside a manager's control, such as competitors' actions, price changes and supply shortages, a skilful manager can take action to reduce their adverse effects. He or she can substitute alternative materials where the prices of raw materials change or monitor and respond to competitors' actions. If these factors are categorized as uncontrollables managers will not be motivated to try and influence them.

Performance report to managing director

		Budget		Variance[a] F (A)	
		Current month (£)	Year to date (£)	This month (£)	Year to date (£)
Managing director	Factory A	453 900	6 386 640	80 000(A)	98 000(A)
	Factory B	X	X	X	X
	Factory C	X	X	X	X
	Administration costs	X	X	X	X
	Selling costs	X	X	X	X
	Distribution costs	X	X	X	X
		2 500 000	30 000 000	400 000(A)	600 000(A)

Performance report to production manager of factory A

Production manager	Works manager's office	X	X	X	X
	Machining department 1	165 600	717 600	32 760(A)	89 180(A)
	Machining department 2	X	X	X	X
	Assembly department	X	X	X	X
	Finishing department	X	X	X	X
		453 900	6 386 640	80 000(A)	98 000(A)

Performance report to head of responsibility centre

Head of responsibility centre	Direct materials	X	X	X	X
	Direct labour	X	X	X	X
	Indirect labour	X	X	X	X
	Indirect materials	X	X	X	X
	Power	X	X	X	X
	Maintenance	X	X	X	X
	Idle time	X	X	X	X
	Other	X	X	X	X
		165 600	717 600	32 760(A)	89 180(A)

EXHIBIT 14.1
Responsibility accounting monthly performance reports

[a]F indicates a favourable variance (actual cost less than budgeted cost) and (A) indicates an adverse budget (actual cost greater than budget cost). Note that, at the lowest level of reporting, the responsibility centre head's performance report contains detailed information on operating costs. At successively higher levels of management less detail is reported. For example, the managing director's information on the control of activities consists of examining those variances that represent significant departures from the budget for each factory and functional area of the business and requesting explanations from the appropriate managers.

Dealing with the distorting effects of uncontrollable factors before the measurement period

Management can attempt to deal with the distorting effects of uncontrollables by making adjustments either before or after the measurement period. Uncontrollable and controllable factors can be determined prior to the measurement period by specifying which budget line items are to be regarded as controllable and uncontrollable. Uncontrollable items can either be excluded from performance reports or shown in a separate section within the performance report so that they are clearly identifiable. The latter approach has the advantage of drawing managerial attention to those costs that a company incurs to support their activities. Managers may be able to indirectly influence these costs if they are made aware of the sums involved.

How do we distinguish between controllable and uncontrollable items? Merchant suggests that the following general rule should be applied to all employees – 'Hold employees accountable for the performance areas you want them to pay attention to'. Applying this rule explains why some organizations assign the costs of shared resource pools, such as administrative costs relating to personnel and data processing departments, to responsibility centres. Assigning these costs authorizes managers of the user responsibility centres to question the amount of the costs and the quantity and quality of services supplied. In addition, responsibility centres are discouraged from making unnecessary requests for the use of these services.

Dealing with the distorting effects of uncontrollable factors after the measurement period

Variance analysis and flexible performance standards can be used to remove the effects of uncontrollable factors from the results measures after the measurement period. Variance analysis seeks to analyze the factors that cause the actual results to differ from predetermined

REAL WORLD VIEWS 14.2

Responsibility cost control systems in China

Because of the previous lack of effective control of expenditure by the Han Dan Company a system of responsibility accounting and standard costing was introduced. The basic principles underlying the responsibility cost control system included: (1) setting cost and profit targets (responsibility standards) that take into account market pressures; (2) assigning target costs to various levels of responsibility centre; (3) evaluating performance based on fulfilment of the responsibility targets; and (4) implementing a reward scheme with built-in incentive mechanisms. In order to facilitate performance measurement and evaluation, non-controllable common costs were excluded from the responsibility costs decomposed within primary production factories. Responsibility contracts between factory managers and managers at lower levels must also be signed. Breakdown of the aggregated respon-

sibility targets to all profit centres and their subordinates are conducted by the Department of Finance and Accounting. In addition, the department is responsible for monthly and yearly reporting of the execution results of the responsibility cost control system. It also reports and analyzes the variances between actual outcomes and responsibility targets, and determines the necessary bonus rewards (or penalty) for each responsibility centre in terms of the fulfilment of the cost and profit targets signed by managers. If a responsibility centre or individual worker fails to meet the cost targets specified in the responsibility contracts, all bonus and other benefits relating to the responsibility unit or worker will be forfeited.

Discussion point

What are the limitations of linking bonuses to meeting cost targets?

SOURCE: ADAPTED FROM Z. JUN LIN AND Z. YU (2002), RESPONSIBILITY COST CONTROL SYSTEM IN CHINA: A CASE OF MANAGEMENT ACCOUNTING APPLICATION, *MANAGEMENT ACCOUNTING RESEARCH*, VOL. 13, NO. 4, PP 447–67.

budgeted targets. In particular, it helps to distinguish between controllable and uncontrollable items and identify those individuals who are accountable for the variances. Variance analysis will be discussed extensively in the next chapter.

Flexible performance standards apply when targets are adjusted to reflect uncontrollable factors arising from the circumstances not envisaged when the targets were set. The most widely used flexible performance standard is to use **flexible budgets** in which the uncontrollable volume effects on cost behaviour are removed from the manager's performance reports. Because some costs vary with changes in the level of activity, it is essential when applying the controllability principle to take into account the variability of costs. For example, if the actual level of activity is greater than the budgeted level of activity then those costs that vary with activity will be greater than the budgeted costs purely because of changes in activity. Let us consider the simplified situation presented in Example 14.1.

EXAMPLE 14.1

An item of expense that is included in the budget for a responsibility centre varies directly in relation to activity at an estimated cost of £5 per unit of output. The budgeted monthly level of activity was 20 000 units and the actual level of activity was 24 000 units at a cost of £105 000.

Assuming that the increase in activity was due to an increase in sales volume greater than that anticipated when the budget was set, then the increases in costs arising from the volume change are beyond the control of the responsibility centre manager. It is clearly inappropriate to compare actual *variable* costs of £105 000 from an activity level of 24 000 units with budgeted *variable* costs of £100 000 from an activity level of 20 000 units. This would incorrectly suggest an overspending of £5000. If managers are to be made responsible for their costs, it is essential that they are responsible for performance under the conditions in which they worked, and not for a performance based on conditions when the budget was drawn up. In other words, it is misleading to compare actual costs at one level of activity with budgeted costs at another level of activity. At the end of the period the original budget must be adjusted to the actual level of activity to take into account the impact of the uncontrollable volume change on costs. This procedure is called flexible budgeting. In Example 14.1 the performance report should be as follows:

Budgeted expenditure	Actual expenditure
(flexed to 24 000 units)	(24 000 units)
£120 000	£105 000

The budget is adjusted to reflect what the costs should have been for an actual activity of 24 000 units. This indicates that the manager has incurred £15 000 less expenditure than would have been expected for the actual level of activity, and a favourable variance of £15 000 should be recorded on the performance report, not an adverse variance of £5000, which would have been recorded if the original budget had not been adjusted.

In Example 14.1 it was assumed that there was only one variable item of expense, but in practice the budget will include many different expenses including fixed, semi-variable and variable expenses. You should note that fixed expenses do not vary in the short-term with activity and therefore the budget should remain unchanged for these expenses. The budget should be flexed only for variable and semi-variable expenses.

Guidelines for applying the controllability principle

Dealing with uncontrollables represents one of the most difficult areas for the design and operation of management accounting control systems. The following guidelines published by the American Accounting Association (Report of Cost Concepts and Standards) in 1957 still continues to provide useful guidance:

1   If a manager *can control the quantity and price paid* for a service then the manager is responsible for all the expenditure incurred for the service.

2   If the manager *can control the quantity of the service but not the price paid* for the service then only that amount of difference between actual and budgeted expenditure that is due to usage should be identified with the manager.

3   If the manager *cannot control either the quantity or the price paid* for the service then the expenditure is uncontrollable and should not be identified with the manager.

An example of the latter situation is when the costs of an industrial relations department are apportioned to a department on an arbitrary basis that results in an allocation of expenses that the managers of responsibility centres may not be able to influence. In addition to the above guidelines Merchants's general rule should also be used as a guide – 'Hold employees accountable for the performance areas you want them to pay attention to'.

SETTING FINANCIAL PERFORMANCE TARGETS AND DETERMINING HOW CHALLENGING THE TARGETS SHOULD BE

There are three approaches that can be used to set financial targets. They are targets derived from engineering studies of input–output relationships, targets derived from historical data and targets derived from negotiations between superiors and subordinates.

Engineered targets can be used when there are clearly defined and stable input–output relationships such that the inputs required can be estimated directly from product specifications. For example, in a fast-food restaurant it is possible to estimate the inputs required for a given output of hamburgers because there is a physical relationship between the ingredients such as meats, buns, condiments and packaging and the number of hamburgers made. Input–output relationships can also be established for labour by closely observing the processes to determine the quantity of labour that will be required for a given output.

Where clearly defined input–output relationships do not exist other approaches must be used to set financial targets. One approach is to use **historical targets** derived directly from the results of previous periods. Previous results plus an increase for expected price changes may form the basis for setting the targets or an improvement factor may be incorporated into the estimate, such as previous period costs less a reduction of 10 per cent. The disadvantage of using historical targets is that they may include past inefficiencies. Also, if the outcome of efficient performance in a previous period is used as a basis for setting a more demanding target in the next period, employees may be encouraged to underperform.

Negotiated targets are set based on negotiations between superiors and subordinates. The major advantage of negotiated targets is that they address the information asymmetry gap that can exist between superior and subordinate. This gap arises because subordinates have more information than their superiors on the relationships between outputs and inputs and the constraints that exist at the operating level, whereas superiors have a broader view of the organization as a whole and the resource constraints that apply. You should refer back to the previous chapter for a more detailed discussion of the negotiation process.

The effect of the level of budget difficulty on motivation and performance

The fact that a financial target represents a specific quantitative goal gives it a strong motivational potential, but the targets set must be accepted if managers are to be motivated to achieve higher levels of performance. Unfortunately, it is not possible to specify exactly the optimal degree of difficulty for financial targets, since task uncertainty and cultural, organizational and personality factors all affect an individual manager's reaction to a financial target.

Figure 14.1, derived from Otley (1987), shows the theoretical relationship between budget difficulty, aspiration levels and performance. In Figure 14.1 it is assumed that performance and aspiration levels are identical. Note that the **aspiration level** relates to the personal goal of the budgetee (that is, the person who is responsible for the budget). In other words, it is the level of performance that they hope to attain. You will see from Figure 14.1 that as the level of budget difficulty is increased both the budgetees' aspiration level and performance increases. However, there becomes a point where the budget is perceived as impossible to achieve and the aspiration level and performance decline dramatically.

To motivate the highest level of actual performance, demanding budgets should be set and small adverse variances should be regarded as a healthy sign and not as something to be

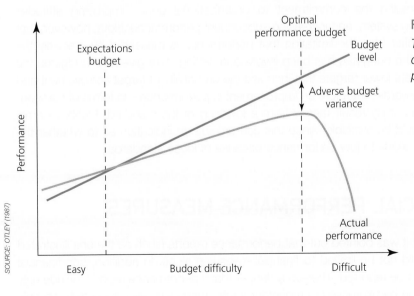

FIGURE 14.1

The effect of budget difficulty on performance.

avoided. If budgets are always achieved with no adverse variances, this indicates that the standards are too loose to motivate the best possible results.

PARTICIPATION IN THE BUDGETING AND TARGET-SETTING PROCESS

Participation relates to the extent that subordinates or budgetees are able to influence the figures that are incorporated in their budgets or targets. Participation is sometimes referred to as **bottom-up budget setting** whereas a non-participatory approach whereby subordinates have little influence on the target-setting process is sometimes called **top-down budget setting**.

Allowing individuals to participate in the setting of performance targets has several advantages. First, individuals are more likely to accept the targets and be committed to achieving them if they have been involved in setting them. Second, participation can reduce the information asymmetry gap that can occur when standards are imposed from above. This information sharing process enables more effective targets to be set that reflect both operational and organizational constraints. Finally, imposed standards can encourage negative attitudes and result in demotivation and alienation. This in turn can lead to a rejection of the targets and poor performance.

Participation has been advocated by many writers as a means of making tasks more challenging and giving individuals a greater sense of responsibility. For many years participation in decision-making was thought to be a panacea for effective organizational effort but this school of thought was later challenged. The debate has never been resolved. The believers have never been able to demonstrate that participation really does have a positive effect on productivity and the sceptics have never been able to prove the opposite (Macintosh, 1985).

Because of the conflicting findings relating to the effectiveness of participation, research has tended to concentrate on studying how various factors influence the effectiveness of participation. If participation is used selectively in the right circumstances it has an enormous potential for encouraging the commitment to organizational goals, improving attitudes towards the budgeting system, and increasing subsequent performance. Note, however, that participation does suffer from the limitation that performance is measured by precisely the same standard that the budgetee has been involved in setting. This gives the budgetee the opportunity to negotiate lower targets that increase the probability of target achievement and the accompanying rewards. Therefore an improvement in performance – in terms of comparison with the budget – may result merely from a lowering of the standard. Ideally external reference points should be available, since this can provide an indication as to whether the participation process leads to low performance because of loose standards.

NON-FINANCIAL PERFORMANCE MEASURES

Earlier in this chapter it was pointed out that performance reports (such as the one illustrated in Exhibit 14.1) should not be limited to financial measures alone. In addition, non-financial measures should also be reported. There is a danger that if performance reports include only those items which can be expressed in monetary terms, managers will concentrate on only these variables and ignore other important variables that cannot easily be quantified in monetary terms. It is always possible to obtain short-term improvements in cost control by hierarchical pressure to cut costs and raise productivity, but this will eventually have negative effects on managerial performance in the form of adverse motivational changes, increased labour turnover and reduced product quality. The problem is that reductions in costs are measured and included in performance reports, but the state of the morale of a department cannot easily be measured. Performance reports should, therefore, be broadened to incorporate other variables besides costs and revenues. Unfortunately, performance reports based only on costs and revenues do not give a sufficient indication of the future results that can be expected from present actions.

Financial summaries of performance provide only a limited view of the efficiency and effectiveness of actual operations. Consider a situation where a purchasing department regularly achieved the budget for all expense items. The message from a responsibility performance reporting system that incorporates only financial measures suggests that the department was well managed. However, the department provided a poor service to the production departments. Low-cost suppliers were selected who provided poor-quality materials and frequently failed to meet delivery dates. This caused much wasted effort in chasing up orders and prejudiced the company's ability to deliver to its customers on time. In this situation there is clearly a need to incorporate non-financial measures that provide information on the quality of the service provided by the department.

In recent years there has been a shift from treating financial figures as the foundation for performance measurement and control to treating them as one among a broader set of measures. In today's worldwide competitive environment companies are competing in terms of product quality, delivery, reliability, after-sales service and customer satisfaction. None of these variables is directly measured by responsibility performance reporting systems that rely solely on financial measures, despite the fact that they represent major goals of world-class manufacturing companies. By focusing mainly on measuring costs, there is a danger that the performance reporting system will motivate managers to focus exclusively on cost reduction and ignore other important strategic manufacturing goals.

The changes described above have resulted in much greater emphasis being placed on non-financial performance measures, such as quality, reliability, flexibility and delivery, that provide feedback on the key variables required to compete successfully in today's environment.

ACTIVITY-BASED COST MANAGEMENT

So far in this chapter the major features of traditional management accounting control systems and the mechanisms that can be used to control costs have been described. Traditional management accounting control systems focus mainly on comparing actual results against a preset standard (typically the budget), identifying and analysing variances and taking remedial action to ensure that future outcomes conform with budgeted outcomes. Traditional systems have been criticized because they tend to be based on the preservation of the status quo and the ways of performing existing activities are not reviewed. The emphasis is on cost containment rather than cost reduction. During the 1990s increasing emphasis has been given to **cost management** (also known as **activity-based management (ABM) or**

activity-based cost management (ABCM)) where the focus is on cost reduction and continuous improvement and change, rather than cost containment. Cost management is generally applicable only to advanced courses. Therefore, this topic is presented in Learning Note 14.2 on the open access website (see Preface for details). You should check your course content to ascertain if this topic is relevant to you.

SUMMARY

The following items relate to the learning objectives listed at the beginning of the chapter.

- **Describe the three different types of controls used in organizations.** Three different categories of controls are used – action/behavioural controls, personnel and cultural controls and results/output controls. With action controls the actions themselves are the focus of controls. Personnel controls help employees do a good job by building on employees' natural tendencies to control themselves. They include selection and placement, training and job design. Cultural controls represent a set of values, social norms and beliefs that are shared by members of the organization and that influence their actions. Output or results controls involve collecting and reporting information about the outcomes of work effort.

- **Distinguish between feedback and feed-forward controls.** Feedback control involves monitoring outputs achieved against desired outputs and taking whatever corrective action is necessary if a deviation exists. In feedforward control, instead of actual outputs being compared against desired outputs, predictions are made of what outputs are expected to be at some future time. If these expectations differ from what is desired, control actions are taken that will minimize these differences. The objective is for control to be achieved before any deviations from desired outputs actually occur. The budgeting planning process is a feed-forward control system. The budgetary control process involving the comparison of actual results with budget, in identifying variances and taking remedial action to ensure future outcomes will conform with budgeted outcomes, is an illustration of a feedback control system.

- **Define the four different types of responsibility centres.** A responsibility centre may be defined as a unit of a firm where an individual manager is held accountable for the unit's performance. There are four types of responsibility centres – cost or expense centres, revenue centres, profit centres and investment centres. Cost or expense centres are responsibility centres whose managers are normally accountable for only those costs that are under their control. Revenue centres are responsibility centres where managers are accountable only for financial outputs in the form of generating sales revenues. A significant increase in managerial autonomy occurs when unit managers are given responsibility for both production and sales. Units within an organization whose managers are accountable for both revenues and costs are called profit centres. Investment centres are responsibility centres whose managers are responsible for both sales revenues and costs and, in addition, have responsibility and authority to make working capital and capital investment decisions.

- **Explain the different elements of management accounting control systems.** Management accounting control systems have two core elements. The first is the formal planning processes such as budgeting and long-term planning. These processes are used for establishing performance expectations for evaluating performance. The second is responsibility accounting, which involves the creation of responsibility centres.

Responsibility centres enable accountability for financial results/outcomes to be allocated to individuals throughout the organization. Responsibility accounting involves: (a) distinguishing between those items which managers can control and for which they should be held accountable, and those items over which they have no control and for which they are not held accountable; (b) determining how challenging the financial targets should be; and (c) determining how much influence managers should have in the setting of financial targets.

- **Describe the controllability principle and the methods of implementing it.** The controllability principle states that it is appropriate to charge to an area of responsibility only those costs that are significantly influenced by the manager of that responsibility centre. The controllability principle can be implemented by either eliminating the uncontrollable items from the areas that managers are held accountable for or calculating their effects so that the reports distinguish between controllable and uncontrollable items.

- **Describe the different approaches that can be used to determine financial performance targets and discuss the impact of their level of difficulty on motivation and performance.** There are three approaches that can be used to set financial targets. They involve targets derived from engineering studies of input–output relationships, targets derived from historical data and targets derived from negotiations between superiors and subordinates. Different types of financial performance targets can be set ranging from easily achievable to difficult to achieve.

- **Describe the influence of participation in the budgeting process.** Participation relates to the extent that budgetees are able to influence the figures that are incorporated in their budgets or targets. Allowing individuals to participate in the setting of performance targets has the following advantages: (a) individuals are more likely to accept the targets and be committed to achieving them if they have been involved in the target setting process; (b) participation can reduce the information asymmetry gap that applies when standards are imposed from above; and (c) imposed standards can encourage negative attitudes and result in demotivation and alienation. Participation, however, is subject to the limitation that performance is measured by precisely the same standard that the budgetee has been involved in setting. Participation must be used selectively; but if it is used in the right circumstances, it has an enormous potential for encouraging the commitment to organizational goals.

- **Explain why a performance measurement system should also incorporate non-financial measures.** There is a danger that if performance reports include only those items which can be expressed in monetary terms, managers will concentrate only on these variables and ignore other measures that are critical to the long-term success of the business. Key non-financial measures should be incorporated into the performance measurement systems that focus on areas such as competitiveness, product leadership, productivity, quality, delivery performance and innovation. If managers focus excessively on financial measures there is a danger that short-term performance will be emphasized at the expense of long-term performance.

KEY TERMS AND CONCEPTS

Aspiration level the level of performance that the person who is responsible for achieving the budget hopes to attain.

Behavioural controls, or **action controls** the observation of the actions of employees as they go about their work.

Bottom-up budget setting budgeting that allowing budgetees to influence the figures that are incorporated in their budgets or targets.

Control the process of ensuring that an organization's activities conform to its plan and that its objectives are achieved.

Controllability principle the process of only charging those costs to a responsibility centre that can be significantly influenced by the manager of that centre.

Cost centre, or **expense centres** responsibility centres whose managers are accountable for those costs (or expenses) that are under their control.

Cost management (also known as activity-based management (ABM) or activity-based cost management (ABCM) focuses on cost reduction, continuous improvement and change in business processes/activities rather than just cost containment.

Cultural controls the values, social norms and beliefs that are shared by members of an organization and which influence their behaviour.

Discretionary expense centres responsibility centres where output cannot be measured in financial terms and there are no clearly observable relationships between inputs and outputs.

Engineered targets targets that are derived from engineering studies of input–output relationships.

Feedback control the monitoring of outputs against desired outputs and correcting deviations when they are discovered.

Feed-forward control predicting outcomes, comparing them with desired outcomes and taking control action where necessary.

Flexible budget a budget in which targets have been adjusted to reflect changes in the level of activity that were not envisaged when the targets were set.

Historical targets targets that are derived directly from the results of previous periods.

Investment centres responsibility centres where managers are responsible for sales revenues and costs and also for investment of capital.

Management control system the entire range of controls that an organization uses.

Negotiated targets targets that are based on the results of negotiations between managers and subordinates.

Participation the extent to which budgetees are able to influence the figures that are incorporated in their budgets or targets.

Personnel controls supporting people's natural tendency to perform well at work.

Profit centres responsibility centres where managers have responsibility for both revenues and costs.

Responsibility accounting the element of management accounting control systems that involves setting up and monitoring the activities of responsibility centres.

Responsibility centre a unit of a firm where an individual manager is held responsible for the unit's performance.

Results controls, or **output controls** the collecting and reporting information about the outcomes of activities to ascertain whether or not desired outcomes have been achieved.

Revenue centres responsibility centres where the main responsibility of managers is for financial outputs in the form of sales revenues.

Social controls the selection of staff who are already socialized into adopting the behaviour considered appropriate for particular roles.

Standard cost centres responsibility centres where output can be measured and the input required to produce each unit of output can be specified.

Top-down budgeting budgeting that involves imposing budgets and targets from above.

Variance analysis seeks to determine and analyze the factors that cause actual results to differ from predetermined targets.

KEY EXAMINATION POINTS

Essay questions are extensively used in second year management accounting courses. They tend not to be widely used for first year courses. The most frequently examined topic on first year courses is to prepare flexible budgets (see solution to Review problem 14.17). If you are required to prepare flexible budgets remember to flex the budget on the basis of target cost for actual output rather than input measures, such as direct labour or input hours. Also questions requiring you to comment on, or redraft performance reports, are sometimes set (e.g. Review problem 14.19). It is important that you distinguish between controllable and non-controllable expenses and stress the need to incorporate non-financial measures. A common error is to compare actual performance with an unflexed budget.

The review questions are short questions that enable you to assess your understanding of the main topics included in the chapter. The numbers in parentheses provide you with the page numbers to refer to if you cannot answer a specific question.

The review problems are more complex and require you to relate and apply the chapter content to various business problems. The problems are graded by their level of difficulty. The multiple-choice questions are the least demanding and normally take less than 10 minutes to complete. Fully worked solutions to the review problems are provided in a separate section at the end of the book. Further review problems with solutions for this chapter are available on the accompanying website www.drury-online.com. The website includes a *Student's Manual* and an *Instructor's Manual.* Students can access both questions and answers from the *Student's Manual* and the questions from the *Instructor's Manual.* The answers to problems in the *Instructor's Manual* are available only to lecturers on the lecturer's password-protected section of the website.

REVIEW QUESTIONS

14.1 Distinguish between 'controls' and 'control'. *(pp. 355–6)*

14.2 Identify and describe three different types of control mechanisms used by companies. *(pp. 356–9)*

14.3 Provide examples of behavioural, action, social, personnel and cultural controls. *(pp. 356–7)*

14.4 Describe the different stages that are involved with output/results controls. *(pp. 357–9)*

14.5 Distinguish between feedback and feed-forward controls. Provide an example of each type of control. *(p. 359)*

14.6 Describe the four different types of responsibility centres. *(pp. 360–1)*

14.7 Explain what is meant by the term 'responsibility accounting'. *(p. 362)*

14.8 What factors must be taken into account when operating a responsibility accounting system? *(p. 362)*

14.9 What is the 'controllability principle'? Describe the different ways in which the principle can be applied. *(pp. 362–6)*

14.10 What are flexible budgets? Why are they preferred to fixed (static budgets)? *(pp. 365–6)*

14.11 What is meant by the term 'aspiration level'? *(p. 367)*

14.12 Describe the effect of the level of budget difficulty on motivation and performance. *(p. 367)*

14.13 Distinguish between participation and top-down budget setting. *(p. 368)*

14.14 Describe the factors influencing the effectiveness of participation in the budget process. *(p. 368)*

14.15 What are the limitations of participation in the budget process? *(p. 368)*

REVIEW PROBLEMS

14.16 Reginald is the manager of production department M in a factory which has ten other production departments. He receives monthly information that compares planned and actual expenditure for department M. After department M, all production goes into the factory departments to be completed prior to being dispatched to customers. Decisions involving capital expenditure in department M are not taken by Reginald. Which of the following describes Reginald's role in department M?

(a) A cost centre manager

(b) An investment centre manager

(c) A profit centre manager

(d) A revenue centre manager

ACCA Financial Information for Management

14.17 Flexible budgets and variance analysis
A company has obtained the following information regarding costs and revenue for the past financial year:

Original budget:

Sales	10 000 units
Production	12 000 units

Standard cost per unit:

	£
Direct materials	5
Direct labour	9
Fixed production overheads	8
	22
Selling price	30

Actual results:

Sales	9750 units
Revenue	£325 000
Production	11 000 units
Material cost	£65 000
Labour cost	£100 000
Fixed production overheads	£95 000

There were no opening stocks.

Required:

(a) Produce a flexed budget statement showing the flexed budget and actual results. Calculate the variances between the actual and flexed figures for the following:

- sales;

- materials;

- labour; and

- fixed production overhead.

(7 marks)

(b) Explain briefly how the sales and materials variances calculated in (a) may have arisen.

(3 marks)
ACCA Paper 1.2 – Financial Information for Management

14.18 Performance reporting

M plc designs, manufactures and assembles furniture. The furniture is for home use and therefore varies considerably in size, complexity and value. One of the departments in the company is the Assembly Department. This department is labour intensive; the workers travel to various locations to assemble and fit the furniture using the packs of finished timbers that have been sent to them. Budgets are set centrally and they are then given to the managers of the various departments who then have the responsibility of achieving their respective targets. Actual costs are compared against the budgets and the managers are then asked to comment on the budgetary control statement.

The statement for April for the Assembly Department is shown below.

	Budget	Actual	Variance	
Assembly labour hours	6400	7140		
	$	$	$	
Assembly labour	51 970	58 227	6257	Adverse
Furniture packs	224 000	205 000	19 000	Favourable
Other materials	23 040	24 100	1060	Adverse
Overheads	62 060	112 340	50 280	Adverse
Total	361 070	399 667	38 597	Adverse

Note: the costs shown are for assembling and fitting the furniture (they do not include time spent travelling to jobs and the related costs). The hours worked by the Manager are not included in the figure given for the assembly labour hours.

The Manager of the Assembly Department is new to the job and has very little previous experience of working with budgets but he does have many years' experience as a supervisor in assembly departments. Based on that experience he was sure that the department had performed well. He has asked for your help in replying to a memo he has just received asking him to 'explain the serious overspending of his department'. He has sent your some additional information about the budget.

1 The budgeted and actual assembly labour costs include the fixed salary of $2050 for the Manager of the Assembly Department. All of the other labour is paid for the hours they work.

2 The cost of the furniture packs and the other materials is assumed by the central finance office of M plc to vary in proportion to the number of assembly hours worked.

3 The budgeted overhead costs are made up of three elements: a fixed cost of $9000 for services from central headquarters, a stepped fixed cost which changes when the assembly hours exceed 7000 hours, and some variable overheads. The variable overheads are assumed to vary in proportion to the number of assembly labour hours. Working papers for the budget showed the impact of the overhead costs differing amounts of assembly labour hours:

Assembly labour hours	5000	7500	10 000
Overhead costs	$54 500	$76 500	$90 000

The actual fixed costs for April were as budgeted.
Required:

(a) Prepare, using the additional information that the Manager of the Assembly Department have given you, a budgetary control statement that would be more helpful to him.

(7 marks)

(b) (i) Discuss the differences between the format of the statement that you have produced and that supplied by M plc.

(4 marks)

(ii) Discuss the assumption made by the central office of M plc that costs vary in proportion to assembly labour hours

(3 marks)

(c) Discuss whether M plc should change to a system of participative budgeting.

(6 marks)
CIMA P1 Management Accounting: Performance Evaluation

14.19 Comments on a performance report

The Victoria Hospital is located in a holiday resort that attracts visitors to such an extent that the population of the area is trebled for the summer months of June, July and August. From past experience, this influx of visitors doubles the activity of the hospital during these months. The annual budget for the hospital's laundry department is broken down into four quarters, namely April–June, July–September, October–December and January–March, by dividing the annual budgeted figures by four. The budgeting work has been done for the current year by the secretary of the hospital using the previous year's figures and adding 3 per cent for inflation. It is realized by the Hospital Authority that management information for control purposes needs to be improved, and you have been recruited to help to introduce a system of responsibility accounting.

You are required, from the information given, to:

(a) comment on the way in which the quarterly budgets have been prepared and to suggest improvements that could be introduced when preparing the budgets for the next financial year;

(b) state what information you would like to flow from the actual against budget comparison (note that calculated figures are *not* required);

(c) state the amendments that would be needed to the current practice of budgeting and reporting to enable the report shown below to be used as a measure of the efficiency of the laundry manager.

Victoria Hospital – Laundry department
Report for quarter ended 30 September

	Budget	Actual
Patients days	9000	12 000
Weight processed (kg)	180 000	240 000
	(£)	**(£)**
Costs:		
Wages	8800	12 320
Overtime premium	1400	2100
Detergents and other supplies	1800	2700
Water, water softening and heating	2000	2500
Maintenance	1000	1500
Depreciation of plant	2000	2000
Manager's salary	1250	1500
Overhead, apportioned:		
for occupancy	4000	4250
for administration	5000	5750

(15 marks)
CIMA Cost Accounting 1

14.20 Flexible budgets and the motivational role of budgets

Club Atlantic is an all-weather holiday complex providing holidays throughout the year. The fee charged to guests is fully inclusive of accommodation and all meals. However, because the holiday industry is so competitive, Club Atlantic is only able to generate profits by maintaining strict financial control of all activities.

The club's restaurant is one area where there is a constant need to monitor costs. Susan Green is the manager of the restaurant. At the beginning of each year she is given an annual budget which is then broken down into months. Each month she receives a statement monitoring actual costs against the annual budget and highlighting any variances. The statement for the month ended 31 October is reproduced below along with a list of assumptions:

Club Atlantic Restaurant Performance Statement
Month to 31 October

	Actual	Budget	Variance (over)/under
Number of guest days	11 160	9600	(1560)
	(£)	(£)	(£)
Food	20 500	20 160	(340)
Cleaning materials	2232	1920	(312)
Heat, light and power	2050	2400	350
Catering wages	8400	7200	(1200)
Rent rates, insurance and depreciation	1860	1800	(60)
	35 042	33 480	(1562)

Assumptions:

(a) The budget has been calculated on the basis of a 30-day calendar month with the cost of rents, insurance and depreciation being an apportionment of the fixed annual charge.

(b) The budgeted catering wages assume that:

(i) there is one member of the catering staff for every 40 guests staying at the complex;

(ii) the daily cost of a member of the catering staff is £30.

(c) All other budgeted costs are variable costs based on the number of guest days.

Task 1
Using the data above, prepare a revised performance statement using flexible budgeting. Your statement should show both the revised budget and the revised variances. Club Atlantic uses the existing budgets and performance statements to motivate its managers as well as for financial control. If managers keep expenses below budget they receive a bonus in addition to their salaries. A colleague of Susan is Brian Hilton. Brian is in charge of the swimming pool and golf course, both of which have high levels of fixed costs. Each month he manages to keep expenses below budget and in return enjoys regular bonuses. Under the current reporting system, Susan Green only rarely receives a bonus.

At a recent meeting with Club Atlantic's directors Susan Green expressed concern that the performance statement was not a valid reflection of her management of the restaurant. You are currently employed by Hall and Co., the club's auditors, and the directors of Club Atlantic have asked you to advice them whether there is any justification for Susan Green's concern.

At the meeting with the Club's directors, you were asked the following questions:

(a) Do budgets motivate managers to achieve objectives?

(b) Does motivating managers lead to improved performance?

(c) Does the current method of reporting performance motivate Susan Green and Brian Hilton to be more efficient?

Task 2

Write a *brief* letter to the directors of Club Atlantic addressing their question and justifying your answers.

Note: You should make use of the data given in this task plus your findings in Task 1.

AAT Technicians Stage

CHAPTER 15
STANDARD COSTING AND VARIANCE ANALYSIS

LEARNING OBJECTIVES

After studying this chapter you should be able to:

- explain how a standard costing system operates;
- explain how standard costs are set;
- explain the meaning of standard hours produced;
- identify and describe the purposes of a standard costing system;
- calculate labour, material, overhead and sales margin variances and reconcile actual profit with budgeted profit;
- identify the causes of labour, material, overhead and sales margin variances;
- distinguish between standard variable costing and standard absorption costing;
- prepare a set of accounts for a standard costing system.

In the previous chapter we examined the major features of management accounting control systems. We adopted a broad approach in order to describe management accounting control in the context of the overall control process. In this chapter we shall focus in more detail on the financial controls that are used by organizations.

We shall describe standard costing, a financial control system that enables the deviations from budget to be analyzed in detail, thus enabling costs to be controlled more effectively. In particular, we shall examine how a standard costing system operates and how the variances are calculated. Standard costing systems are applied in cost centres where the output can be measured and the input required to produce each unit of output can be specified. Standard costing is generally applied to manufacturing activities. However, the sales variances that are described in this chapter can also be applied in revenue centres.

Standard costs are predetermined costs; they are target costs that should be incurred under efficient operating conditions. They are not the same as **budget costs**. A budget relates to an entire activity or operation; a standard presents the same information on a per unit basis. A standard therefore provides cost expectations per *unit* of activity and a budget provides the cost expectation for the *total* activity. If the budget output for a product is for 10 000 units and the standard cost is £3 per unit, budgeted cost will be £30 000. We shall see that establishing standard costs for each unit produced enables a detailed analysis to be made of the difference between the budgeted cost and the actual cost so that costs can be controlled more effectively.

In the first part of the chapter (pages 382–403) we shall concentrate on those variances that are likely to be useful for cost control purposes. The second part describes those variances that are required for financial accounting purposes but that are not particularly useful for cost control. If your course does not relate to the disposition of variances for financial accounting purposes, or the recording of standard costs in the accounts, you can omit pages 403–414.

OPERATION OF A STANDARD COSTING SYSTEM

Standard costing is most suited to an organization whose activities consist of a series of *common* or *repetitive* operations and where the input required to produce each unit of output can be specified. It is therefore relevant in manufacturing companies, since the processes involved are often of a repetitive nature. Standard costing procedures can also be applied in service industries such as units within banks, where output can be measured in terms of the number of cheques or the number of loan applications processed, and there are also well-defined input–output relationships. Standard costing cannot, however, be applied to activities of a non-repetitive nature, since there is no basis for observing repetitive operations and consequently standards cannot be set.

A standard costing system can be applied to organizations that produce many different products, as long as production consists of a series of common operations. For example, if the output from a factory is the result of five common operations, it is possible to produce many different product variations from these operations. It is therefore possible that a large product range may result from a small number of common operations. If standard costs are developed for repetitive operations, product standard costs can be derived simply by combining the standard costs from the operations that are necessary to make the product. This process is illustrated in Exhibit 15.1.

It is assumed that the standard costs are £20, £30, £40 and £50 for each of the operations 1 to 4. The standard cost for *product* 100 is therefore £110, which consists of £20 for operation 1, plus £40 and £50 for operations 3 and 4. The standard costs for each of the other products are calculated in a similar manner. In addition, the total standard cost for the total output of each operation for the period has been calculated. For example, six items of operation number 1 have been completed, giving a total standard cost of £120 for this operation (six items at £20 each). Three items of operation 2 have been completed, giving a total standard cost of £90, and so on.

Responsibility centre	Operation no. and standard cost		Products							Total standard cost	Actual cost
	No.	(£)	100	101	102	103	104	105	106	(£)	
A	1	20	✓	✓		✓	✓	✓	✓	120	
B	2	30		✓		✓		✓		90	
C	3	40	✓		✓		✓			120	
D	4	50	✓	✓	✓				✓	200	
Standard product cost			£110	£100	£90	£50	£60	£50	£70	530	

EXHIBIT 15.1

Standard costs analyzed by operations and products

Variances allocated to responsibility centres

You can see from Exhibit 15.1 that different responsibility centres are responsible for each operation. For example, responsibility centre A is responsible for operation 1, responsibility centre B for operation 2, and so on. Consequently, there is no point in comparing the actual cost of *product* 100 with the standard cost of £110 for the purposes of control, since responsibility centres A, C and D are responsible for the variance. None of the responsibility centres is solely answerable for the variance. Cost control requires that responsibility centres be identified with the standard cost for the output achieved. Therefore if the actual costs for responsibility centre A are compared with the standard cost of £120 for the production of the six items (see first row of Exhibit 15.1), the manager of this responsibility centre will be answerable for the full amount of the variance. Only by comparing total actual costs with total standard costs *for each operation or responsibility centre* for a period can control be effectively achieved. A comparison of standard product costs that involves several different responsibility centres is clearly inappropriate.

Figure 15.1 provides an overview of the operation of a standard costing system. You will see that the standard costs for the actual output for a particular period are traced to the managers of responsibility centres who are responsible for the various operations. The actual costs for the same period are also charged to the responsibility centres. Standard and actual costs are compared and the variance is reported. For example, if the actual cost for the output of the six items produced in responsibility centre A during the period is £220 and the standard cost is £120 (Exhibit 15.1), a variance of £100 will be reported.

Detailed analysis of variances

The box below the first arrow in Figure 15.1 indicates that the operation of a standard costing system also enables a detailed analysis of the variances to be reported. Variances for each responsibility centre can be identified by each element of cost and analyzed according to the price and quantity content. The accountant assists managers by pinpointing where the variances have arisen and the responsibility managers can undertake the appropriate

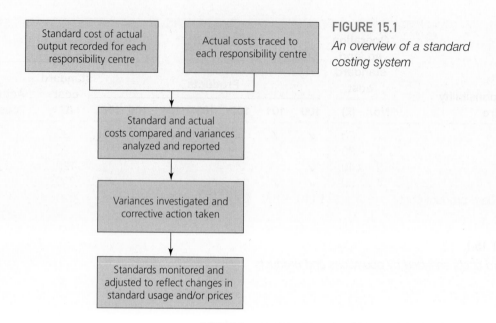

FIGURE 15.1

An overview of a standard costing system

investigations to identify the reasons for the variance. For example, the accountant might identify the reason for a direct materials variance as being excessive usage of a certain material in a particular process, and the responsibility centre manager would then investigate this process and identify the reasons for the excessive usage. Such an investigation should result in appropriate remedial action being taken or, if it is found that the variance is due to a permanent change in the standard, the standard should be changed.

Actual product costs are not required

It is questionable whether the allocation of actual costs to products serves any useful purpose. Because standard costs represent *future* target costs, they are preferable to actual *past* costs for decision-making. Also, the external financial accounting regulations in most countries specify that if standard product costs provide a reasonable approximation of actual product costs, they are acceptable for inventory valuation calculations for external reporting.

There are therefore strong arguments for not producing actual *product* costs when a standard costing system exists, including the fact that this will lead to a large reduction in information processing costs. However, it must be stressed that actual costs must be accumulated periodically for each operation or responsibility centre, so that comparisons can be made with standard costs. Nevertheless, there will be considerably fewer responsibility centres than products, and the accumulation of actual costs is therefore much less time-consuming.

ESTABLISHING COST STANDARDS

Control over costs is best effected through action at the point where the costs are incurred. Hence the standards should be set for the quantities of material, labour and services to be consumed in performing an *operation*, rather than the complete *product* cost standards. Variances from these standards should be reported to show causes and responsibilities for deviations from standard. Product cost standards are derived by listing and adding the standard costs of operations required to produce a particular product. For example, you will see by referring to Exhibit 15.1 that the standard cost of product 100 is £110 and is derived from the sum of the standard costs of operations 1, 3 and 4.

There are two approaches that can be used to set standard costs. First, past historical records can be used to estimate labour and material usage. Second, standards can be set based on **engineering studies**. This involves a detailed study of each operation, based on careful specifications of materials, labour and equipment and on controlled observations of operations. If historical records are used to set standards, there is a danger that past inefficiencies will affect the standards. If historical records are used, standards are set based on average past performance for the same or similar operations.

The disadvantage of this method is that, unlike the engineering method, it does not focus attention on finding the best combination of resources, production methods and product quality. Nevertheless, standards derived from average historical usage do appear to be widely used in practice. (See Exhibit 15.3 on page 389.)

Let us now consider how standards are established for each operation for direct labour, direct materials and overheads using the engineering studies approach. Note that the standard cost for each operation is derived from multiplying the quantity of input that should be used per unit of output (i.e. the quantity standard) by the amount that should be paid for each unit of input (i.e. the price standard).

Direct material standards

These are based on product specifications derived from an intensive study of the input *quantity* necessary for each operation. This study should establish the most suitable materials for each operation, based on product design and quality policy, and also the optimal quantity that should be used after taking into account any unavoidable wastage or loss. Material quantity standards are usually recorded on a **bill of materials**. This states the required quantity of materials for each operation to complete the product. A separate bill of materials is maintained for each product. The standard material product cost is then found by multiplying the standard quantities by the appropriate standard prices.

The standard *prices* are obtained from the purchasing department. The standard material prices are based on the assumption that the purchasing department has carried out a suitable search of alternative suppliers and has selected suppliers who can provide the required quantity of sound quality materials at the most competitive price. Standard prices then provide a suitable base against which actual prices paid for materials can be evaluated.

Direct labour standards

To set labour standards, activities should be analyzed by the different operations. Each operation is studied and an allowed time computed. The normal procedure for such a study is to analyze each operation to eliminate any unnecessary elements and to determine the most efficient production method. The most efficient methods of production, equipment and operating conditions are then standardized. This is followed by time measurements that are made to determine the number of standard hours required by an average worker to complete the job. Unavoidable delays such as machine breakdowns and routine maintenance are included in the standard time. The wage rates are applied to the standard time to determine the standard labour cost for each operation.

Overhead standards

The procedure for establishing standard manufacturing overhead rates for a standard costing system is the same as that which is used for establishing *predetermined* overhead rates as described in Chapter 4. Separate rates for fixed and variable overheads are essential for planning and control. With traditional costing systems the standard overhead rate will be based on a rate per direct labour hour or machine hour of input.

Fixed overheads are largely independent of changes in activity, and remain constant over wide ranges of activity in the short term. It is therefore inappropriate to unitize fixed overheads for short-term cost control purposes to derive a fixed overhead rate per unit of activity. However, in order to meet the external financial reporting stock valuation requirements, fixed manufacturing overheads must be traced to products. It is therefore necessary to unitize fixed overheads for stock valuation purposes.

The main difference with the treatment of overheads under a standard costing system as opposed to a non-standard costing system is that the product overhead cost is based on the hourly overhead rates multiplied by the *standard hours* (that is, hours that should have been used) rather than the *actual hours* used.

A standard cost card should be maintained for each product and operation. It reveals the quantity of each unit of input that should be used to produce one unit of output. A typical product standard cost card is illustrated in Exhibit 15.2. In most organizations standard cost cards are now in computerized format. Standards should be continuously reviewed, and, where significant changes in production methods or input prices occur, they should be changed in order to ensure that standards reflect current targets.

Standard hours produced

It is not possible to measure *output* in terms of units produced for a department making several different products or operations. For example, if a department produces 100 units of product X, 200 units of product Y and 300 units of product Z, it is not possible to add the production of these items together, since they are not homogeneous. This problem can be overcome by ascertaining the amount of time, working under efficient conditions, it should take to make each product. This time calculation is called standard hours produced. In other words, **standard hours** are an *output* measure that can act as a common denominator for adding together the production of unlike items.

Let us assume that the following standard times are established for the production of one unit of each product:

Product X	5 standard hours
Product Y	2 standard hours
Product Z	3 standard hours

Date standard set								Product: sigma	
Direct materials			**Standard**	**Department**				**Totals**	
Operation	**Item**	**Quantity**	**price**						
no.	**code**	**(kg)**	**(£)**	**A**	**B**	**C**	**D**	**(£)**	
1	5.001	5	3	£15					
2	7.003	4	4		£16				
								31	
Direct labour									
Operation	**Standard**	**Standard**							
no.	**hours**	**rate (£)**							
1	7	9		£63					
2	8	9			£72				
								135	
Factory overhead									
Operation	**Standard**	**Standard**							
no.	**hours**	**rate (£)**							
1	7	3		£21					
2	8	4			£32				
								53	
Total manufacturing cost per unit (£)								219	

EXHIBIT 15.2

An illustration of a standard cost card

This means that it should take five hours to produce one unit of product X under efficient production conditions. Similar comments apply to products Y and Z. The production for the department will be calculated in standard hours as follows:

Product	Standard time per unit produced (hours)	Actual output (units)	Standard hours produced
X	5	100	500
Y	2	200	400
Z	3	300	900
			1800

Remember that standard hours produced is an output measure, and flexible budget allowances should be based on this. In the illustration we should expect the *output* of 1800 standard hours to take 1800 direct labour hours of *input* if the department works at the prescribed level of efficiency. The department will be inefficient if 1800 standard hours of output are produced using, say, 2000 direct labour hours of input. The flexible budget allowance should therefore be based on 1800 standard hours produced to ensure that no extra allowance is given for the 200 excess hours of input. Otherwise, a manager will obtain a higher budget allowance through being inefficient.

REAL WORLD VIEWS 15.1

The effect of standards on product and service quality

Setting standards in an organization may be primarily to assist in the calculation of a standard cost for the product or service for management accounting purposes. Standards are also relevant for operational and customer service managers as they may affect the manufacture of the product or the quality of the service.

Take McDonald's, Burger King or Coca-Cola for example. All three companies produce products that adhere to standard ingredients, albeit with some minimal regional variation. A BigMac or Whopper for example, will contain a beef patty that is manufactured to an exact uncooked weight. Similarly, every bottle of Coca-Cola will contain a similar amount of cola concentrate. As the ingredients are standardized according to 'recipes', a standard cost can be readily calculated and used for cost control and performance reporting. Perhaps more importantly, the customer is confident of getting a similar product on each purchase.

In comparison, consider a car-hire company like Hertz or a bank like HSBC. Most service organizations will have a customer care (HSBC) or reservations (Hertz) call centre. Staff at these centres will have a standard customer handling time to adhere to – perhaps three minutes. It is not always possible to deal with customer issues or make a sale in the allotted time. Exceeding the standard handling time ultimately increases cost as more staff may be needed to handle customer call volume. On the other hand, by strictly adhering to a standard handling time, customer satisfaction and quality of service may be reduced. Thus, in a service company scenario, a fine balance between standards and quality must be achieved to ensure customer satisfaction in the longer term.

Discussion points

1 Do you think it is plausible to set standards for delivery of a service, which are primarily dictated by cost?

2 Is it possible to measure the delivery of a service (e.g. a mortgage application) against a set standard?

PURPOSES OF STANDARD COSTING

Standard costing systems are widely used because they provide cost information for many different purposes, such as the following:

● Providing a prediction of future costs that can be used for *decision-making purposes*. Standard costs can be derived from either traditional or activity-based costing systems. Because standard costs represent *future* target costs based on the elimination of avoidable inefficiencies, they are preferable to estimates based on adjusted past costs which may incorporate inefficiencies For example, in markets where competitive prices do not exist products may be priced on a bid basis. In these situations standard costs provide more appropriate information because efficient competitors will seek to eliminate avoidable costs. It is therefore unwise to assume that inefficiencies are recoverable within the bid price.

EXHIBIT 15.3
*Surveys of
company practice*

Since its introduction in the early 1900s standard costing has flourished and is now one of the most widely used management accounting techniques. Three independently conducted surveys of USA practice indicate highly consistent figures in terms of adopting standard costing systems. Cress and Pettijohn (1985) and Schwarzbach (1985) report an 85 per cent adoption rate, while Cornick *et al.* (1988) found that 86 per cent of the surveyed firms used a standard costing system. A Japanese survey by Scarborough *et al.* (1991) reported a 65 per cent adoption rate. Surveys of UK companies by Drury *et al.* (1993) and New Zealand companies by Guilding *et al.* (1998), reported adoption rates of 76 per cent and 73 per cent respectively.

A CIMA sponsored study of 41 UK manufacturing organizations by Dugdale *et al.* (2006) reported that 30 of the firms employed standard costing. The majority of these firms (26) set standard costs for materials and labour and a smaller majority (20) also set standard overhead costs. They conclude that despite the huge changes in the manufacturing environment, standard costing is alive and well.

In relation to the methods to set labour and material standards Drury *et al.* reported the following usage rates:

	Extent of use (%)				
	Never	**Rarely**	**Sometimes**	**Often**	**Always**
Standards based on design/ engineering studies	18	11	19	31	21
Observations based on trial runs	18	16	36	25	5
Work study techniques	21	18	19	21	21
Average of historic usage	22	11	23	35	9

In the USA Lauderman and Schaeberle (1983) reported that 43 per cent of the respondents used average historic usage, 67 per cent used engineering studies, 11 per cent used trial runs under controlled conditions and 15 per cent used other methods. The results add up to more than 100 per cent because some companies used more than one method.

- Providing a *challenging target* that individuals are motivated to achieve. For example, research evidence suggests that the existence of a defined quantitative goal or target is likely to motivate higher levels of performance than would be achieved if no such target was set.

- Assisting in *setting budgets* and evaluating managerial performance. Standard costs are particularly valuable for budgeting because they provide a reliable and convenient source of data for converting budgeted production into physical and monetary resource requirements. Budgetary preparation time is considerably reduced if standard costs are available because the standard costs of operations and products can be readily built up into total costs of any budgeted volume and product mix.

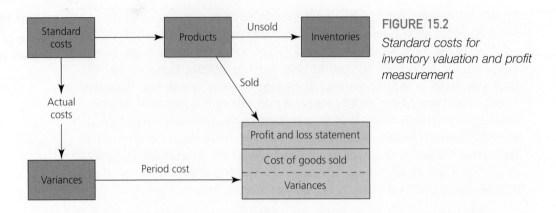

FIGURE 15.2

Standard costs for inventory valuation and profit measurement

- Acting as a *control device* by highlighting those activities that do not conform to plan and thus alerting managers to those situations that may be 'out of control' and in need of corrective action. With a standard costing system variances are analyzed in great detail and useful feedback is provided to help pinpoint areas where variances have arisen.

- Simplifying the task of tracing costs to products for *profit measurement and inventory valuation* purposes. Besides preparing annual financial accounting profit statements most organizations also prepare monthly internal profit statements. If actual costs are used a considerable amount of time is required in tracking costs so that monthly costs can be allocated between cost of sales and inventories. A data processing system is required that can track monthly costs in a resource-efficient manner. Standard costing systems meet this requirement. You will see from Figure 15.2 that product costs are maintained at standard cost. Inventories and cost of goods sold are recorded at standard cost and a conversion to actual cost is made by writing off all variances arising during the period as a period cost. Note that the variances from standard cost are extracted by comparing actual with standard costs at the responsibility centre level, and not at the product level, so that actual costs are not assigned to individual products.

VARIANCE ANALYSIS

It is possible to compute variances simply by committing to memory a series of variance formulae. If you adopt this approach, however, it will not help you to understand what a variance is intended to depict and what the relevant variables represent. In our discussion we shall therefore concentrate on the fundamental meaning of the variance, so that you can logically deduce the variance formulae as we go along.

All of the variances presented in this chapter are illustrated from the information contained in Example 15.1. Note that the level of detail presented is highly simplified. A truly realistic situation would involve many products, operations and responsibility centres but would not give any further insights into the basic concepts or procedures.

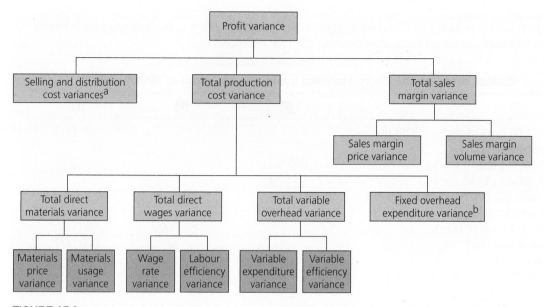

FIGURE 15.3

Variance analysis for a variable costing system

[a] Selling and distribution cost variances are not presented in this chapter. If activities are of a repetitive nature, standards can be established and variances can be calculated in a similar manner to production cost variances. If standards cannot be established, costs should be controlled by comparing budgeted and actual costs.

[b] With an absorption costing system, the summary of fixed overhead variances presented in Exhibit 15.6 would replace this box.

Figure 15.3 shows the breakdown of the profit variance (the difference between budgeted and actual profit) into the component cost and revenue variances that can be calculated for a standard variable costing system. We shall now calculate the variances set out in Figure 15.3 using the data presented in Example 15.1.

EXAMPLE 15.1

Alpha manufacturing company produces a single product, which is known as sigma. The product requires a single operation, and the standard cost for this operation is presented in the following standard cost card:

Standard cost card for product sigma	(£)
Direct materials:	
2 kg of A at £10 per kg	20.00
1 kg of B at £15 per kg	15.00
Direct labour (3 hours at £9 per hour)	27.00
Variable overhead (3 hours at £2 per direct labour hour)	6.00
Total standard variable cost	68.00
Standard contribution margin	20.00
Standard selling price	88.00

(Continued)

Alpha Ltd plans to produce 10 000 units of sigma in the month of April, and the budgeted costs based on the information contained in the standard cost card are as follows:

Budget based on the above standard costs and an output of 10 000 units

	(£)	(£)	(£)
Sales (10 000 units of sigma at £88 per unit)			880 000
Direct materials:			
A: 20 000 kg at £10 per kg	200 000		
B: 10 000 kg at £15 per kg	150 000	350 000	
Direct labour (30 000 hours at £9 per hour)		270 000	
Variable overheads (30 000 hours at £2 per direct labour hour)		60 000	680 000
Budgeted contribution			200 000
Fixed overheads			120 000
Budgeted profit			80 000

Annual budgeted fixed overheads are £1 440 000 and are assumed to be incurred evenly throughout the year. The company uses a variable costing system for internal profit measurement purposes.

The actual results for April are:

	(£)	(£)
Sales (9000 units at £90)		810 000
Direct materials:		
A: 19 000 kg at £11 per kg	209 000	
B: 10 100 kg at £14 per kg	141 400	
Direct labour (28 500 hours at £9.60 per hour)	273 600	
Variable overheads	52 000	676 000
Contribution		134 000
Fixed overheads		116 000
Profit		18 000

Manufacturing overheads are charged to production on the basis of direct labour hours. Actual production and sales for the period were 9000 units.

MATERIAL VARIANCES

The costs of the materials used in a manufactured product are determined by two basic factors: the price paid for the materials, and the quantity of materials used in production. This gives rise to the possibility that the actual cost will differ from the standard cost because the *actual quantity* of materials used will be different from the *standard quantity* and/or that the actual price paid will be different from the *standard price*. We can therefore calculate a material usage and a material price variance.

MATERIAL PRICE VARIANCES

The starting point for calculating this variance is simply to compare the standard price per unit of materials with the actual price per unit. Refer again to Example 15.1. You will see that the standard price for material A is £10 per kg, but the actual price paid was £11 per kg. The price variance is £1 per kg. This is of little consequence if the excess purchase price has been paid only for a small number of units or purchases. But the consequences are important if the excess purchase price has been paid for a large number of units, since the effect of the variance will be greater.

The difference between the standard material price and the actual price per unit should therefore be multiplied by the quantity of materials purchased. For material A the price variance is £1 per unit; but since 19 000 kg were purchased, the excess price was paid out 19 000 times. Hence the total material price variance is £19 000 adverse. The formula for the material price variance now follows logically:

> The **material price variance** is equal to the difference between the standard price (SP) and the actual price (AP) per unit of materials multiplied by the quantity of materials purchased (QP):
>
> $$(SP - AP) \times QP$$

Now refer to material B in Example 15.1. The standard price is £15, compared with an actual price of £14, giving a £1 saving per kg. As 10 100 kg were purchased, the total price variance will be £10 100 (10 100 kg at £1). The variance for material B is favourable and that for material A is adverse. The normal procedure is to present the amount of the variances followed by symbols A or F to indicate either adverse or favourable variances.

An adverse price variance may reflect a failure by the purchasing department to seek the most advantageous sources of supply. However, it is incorrect to assume that the level of the material price variance will always indicate the efficiency of the purchasing department. Actual prices may exceed standard prices because of a change in market conditions that causes a general price increase for the type of materials used. The price variance might therefore be beyond the control of the purchasing department. A favourable price variance might be due to the purchase of inferior quality materials, which may lead to inferior product quality or more wastage. For example, the price variance for material B is favourable, but we shall see in the next section that this is offset by excess usage. If the reason for this excess usage is the purchase of inferior quality materials then the material usage variance should be charged to the purchasing department.

Calculation on quantity purchased or quantity used

It is important that variances are reported as quickly as possible so that any inefficiencies can be identified and remedial action taken. A problem occurs, however, with material purchases in that there may be a considerable delay before materials are actually used: materials may be purchased in one period and used in a subsequent period. For example, if 10 000 units of a material are purchased in period 1 at a price of £1 per unit over standard and 2000 units are used in each of periods 1 to 5, the following alternatives are available for calculating the price variance:

1 The full amount of the price variance of £10 000 is reported in *period 1* with quantity being defined as the *quantity purchased*.

2 The price variance is calculated with quantity being defined as the *quantity used*. The unit price variance of £1 is multiplied by the quantity used (i.e. 2000 units), which means that a price variance of £2000 will be reported for each of *periods 1 to 5*.

Method 1 is recommended, because the price variance can be reported in the period in which it is incurred, and reporting of the total variance is not delayed until months later when the materials are used. Also, adopting this approach enables corrective action to be taken earlier. For the sake of simplicity we shall assume in Example 15.1 that the actual purchases are identical with the actual usage.

MATERIAL USAGE VARIANCES

The starting point for calculating this quantity variance is simply to compare the standard quantity that should have been used with the actual quantity that has been used. Refer again to Example 15.1. You will see that the standard usage for the production of one unit of sigma is 2 kg for material A. As 9000 units of sigma are produced, 18 000 kg of material A should have been used; however, 19 000 kg are actually used, which means there has been an excess usage of 1000 kg.

The importance of this excess usage depends on the price of the materials. For example, if the price is £0.01 per kg then an excess usage of 1000 kg will not be very significant, but if the price is £10 per unit then an excess usage of 1000 kg will be very significant. It follows that to assess the importance of the excess usage, the variance should be expressed in monetary terms.

Should the standard material price per kg or the actual material price per kg be used to calculate the variance? The answer is the standard price. If the *actual* material price is used, the usage variance will be affected by the efficiency of the purchasing department, since any excess purchase price will be assigned to the excess usage. It is therefore necessary to remove the price effects from the usage variance calculation, and this is achieved by valuing the variance at the standard price. Hence the 1000 kg excess usage of material A is multiplied by the standard price of £10 per unit, which gives an adverse usage variance of £10 000. The formula for the variance is:

the **material usage variance** is equal to the difference between the standard quantity (SQ) required for actual production and the actual quantity (AQ) used multiplied by the standard material price (SP):

$$(SQ - AQ) \times SP$$

For material B you will see from Example 15.1 that the standard quantity is 9000 kg (9000 units × 1 kg), but 10 100 kg have been used. The excess usage of 1100 kg is multiplied by the standard price of £15 per kg, which gives an adverse variance of £16 500. Note that the principles of flexible budgeting described in the previous chapter also apply here, with *standard quantity being based on actual production and not budgeted production*. This ensures that a manager is evaluated under the conditions in which he or she actually worked and not those envisaged at the time the budget was prepared.

The material usage variance is normally controllable by the manager of the appropriate production responsibility centre. Common causes of material usage variances include the careless handling of materials by production personnel, the purchase of inferior quality materials, pilferage, changes in quality control requirements, or changes in methods of production. Separate material usage variances should be calculated for each type of material used and allocated to each responsibility centre.

TOTAL MATERIAL VARIANCES

From Figure 15.3 above you will see that this variance is the total variance before it is analyzed into the price and usage elements. The formula for the variance is:

the **total material variance** is the difference between the standard material cost (SC) for the actual production and the actual cost (AC):

$$SC - AC$$

To compute the total material variance we need to determine what the standard cost of materials should be for the actual production. For material A the standard material cost is £20 per unit (see Example 15.1), giving a total standard material cost of £180 000 (9000 units × £20). The actual cost is £209 000, and therefore the variance is £29 000 adverse. The price variance of £19 000 plus the usage variance of £10 000 agrees with the total material variance. Similarly, the total material variance for material B is £6400, consisting of a favourable price variance of £10 100 and an adverse usage variance of £16 500.

Note that if the price variance is calculated on the actual quantity *purchased* instead of the actual quantity *used*, the price variance plus the usage variance will agree with the total variance only when the quantity purchased is equal to the quantity that is used in the particular accounting period. Reconciling the price and usage variance with the total variance is merely a formal exercise, and you should not be concerned if reconciliation of the sub-variances with the total variance is not possible.

WAGE RATE VARIANCES

The cost of labour is determined by the price paid for labour and the quantity of labour used. Thus a price and quantity variance will also arise for labour. The price (wage rate) variance is calculated by comparing the standard price per hour with the actual price paid per hour. In Example 15.1 the standard wage rate per hour is £9 and the actual wage rate is £9.60 per hour, giving a wage rate variance of £0.60 per hour. To determine the importance of the variance, it is necessary to ascertain how many times the excess payment of £0.60 per hour is paid. As 28 500 labour hours are used (see Example 15.1), we multiply 28 500 hours by £0.60. This gives an adverse wage rate variance of £17 100. The formula for the wage rate variance is:

the **wage rate variance** is equal to the difference between the standard wage rate per hour (SR) and the actual wage rate (AR) multiplied by the actual number of hours worked (AH):

$$(SR - AR) \times AH$$

Note the similarity between this variance and the material price variance. Both variances multiply the difference between the standard price and the actual price paid for a unit of a resource by the actual quantity of resources used.

The wage rate variance is probably the one that is least subject to control by management. In most cases the variance is due to wage rate standards not being kept in line with changes in actual wage rates, and for this reason it is not normally controllable by departmental managers.

LABOUR EFFICIENCY VARIANCE

The labour efficiency variance represents the quantity variance for direct labour. The quantity of labour that should be used for the actual output is expressed in terms of *standard hours produced*. In Example 15.1 the standard time for the production of one unit of sigma is three hours. Thus a production level of 9000 units results in an output of 27 000 standard hours. In other words, working at the prescribed level of efficiency, it should take 27 000 hours to produce 9000 units. However, 28 500 direct labour hours are actually required to produce this output, which means that 1500 excess direct labour hours are used. We multiply the excess direct labour hours by the standard wage rate of £9 per hour to calculate the variance. This gives an adverse variance of £13 500. The formula for calculating the labour efficiency variance is:

the **labour efficiency variance** is equal to the difference between the standard labour hours for actual production (SH) and the actual labour hours worked (AH) during the period multiplied by the standard wage rate per hour (SR):

$$(SH - AH) \times SR$$

This variance is similar to the material usage variance. Both variances multiply the difference between the standard quantity and actual quantity of resources consumed by the standard price.

The labour efficiency variance is normally controllable by the manager of the appropriate production responsibility centre and may be due to a variety of reasons. For example, the use of inferior quality materials, different grades of labour, failure to maintain machinery in proper condition, the introduction of new equipment or tools and changes in the production processes will all affect the efficiency of labour. An efficiency variance may not always be controllable by the production supervisors; it may be due, for example, to poor production scheduling by the planning department, or to a change in quality control standards.

TOTAL LABOUR VARIANCE

From Figure 15.3 you will see that this variance represents the total variance before analysis into the price and quantity elements. The formula for the variance is:

the **total labour variance** is the difference between the standard labour cost (SC) for the actual production and the actual labour cost (AC):

$$SC - AC$$

SOURCE: SHANK, J. K. AND FISHER, J. (1999), TARGET COSTING AS A STRATEGIC TOOL, *SLOAN MANAGEMENT REVIEW*, FALL, VOL. 4 ISSUE 1, PP. 73–82

REAL WORLD VIEWS 15.2

Standard costing at Montclair Papers Division of Mohawk Forest Products

Montclair produces 1500 different products, including Forest Green Carnival. Its standard cost of $2900 per ton is derived from:

- Union wage rates for labour costs ('Pattern bargaining' virtually assured comparable labour costs among the major union firms, all of which were unionized);

- Standard yield rates for all manufacturing steps, based on latest performance measured against long-standing norms at the Montclair mill;

- Current market prices for all purchased components;

- Generally accepted industry procedures for building the 'normal' cost of scrap into the standard cost, after deducting the offset for the market value of the scrap generated.

The standards were updated annually for changes in purchase prices, process flows and yield targets. With more than 1500 products manufactured in the mill, more frequent updating was deemed unfeasible.

Manufacturing management accepted that the standard cost represented best practices of the mill and thus was an appropriate basis for monitoring monthly performance. Standard costs were also helpful to simplify calculating the month-end cost of goods sold and the ending inventory for financial statements. Updated only once a year, the standard cost was stable from month to month. Management viewed this stability as a positive feature in monitoring monthly performance against the annual plan.

Discussion points

1 Why do some companies find it inappropriate to implement a standard costing system?

2 Can you think of any other uses of standard costing at Montclair?

In Example 15.1 the actual production was 9000 units, and, with a standard labour cost of £27 per unit, the standard cost is £243 000 (9000 × £27). The actual cost is £273 600, which gives an adverse variance of £30 600. This consists of a wage rate variance of £17 100 and a labour efficiency variance of £13 500.

VARIABLE OVERHEAD VARIANCES

A total variable overhead variance is calculated in the same way as the total direct labour and material variances. In Example 15.1 the output is 9000 units and the standard variable overhead cost is £6 *per unit* produced. The standard cost for the production of 9000 units for variable overheads is thus £54 000. The actual variable overheads incurred are £52 000, giving a favourable variance of £2000. The formula for the variance is:

the **total variable overhead variance** is the difference between the standard variable overheads charged to production (SC) and the actual variable overheads incurred (AC):

$$SC - AC$$

Where variable overheads vary with direct labour or machine hours of *input* the total variable overhead variance will be due to one or both of the following:

1 A *price* variance arising from actual expenditure being different from budgeted expenditure.

2 A *quantity* variance arising from actual direct labour or machine hours of input being different from the hours of input, which *should* have been used.

These reasons give rise to the two sub-variances, which are shown in Figure 15.3: the variable overhead expenditure variance and the variable overhead efficiency variance.

Variable overhead expenditure variance

To compare the actual overhead expenditure with the budgeted expenditure, it is necessary to flex the budget. Because it is assumed in Example 15.1 that variable overheads will vary with direct labour hours of *input* the budget is flexed on this basis. Actual variable overhead expenditure is £52 000, resulting from 28 500 direct labour hours of input. For this level of activity variable overheads of £57 000, which consist of 28 500 input hours at £2 per hour, should have been spent. Spending was £5000 less than it should have been, and the result is a favourable variance.

If we compare the budgeted and the actual overhead costs for 28 500 direct labour hours of input, we shall ensure that any efficiency content is removed from the variance. This means that any difference must be due to actual variable overhead spending being different from the budgeted variable overhead spending. The formula for the variance is:

the **variable overhead expenditure variance** is equal to the difference between the budgeted flexed variable overheads (BFVO) for the actual direct labour hours of input and the actual variable overhead costs incurred (AVO):

$$BFVO - AVO$$

Variable overhead represents the aggregation of a large number of individual items, such as indirect labour, indirect materials, electricity, maintenance and so on. The variable overhead variance can arise because the prices of individual items have changed. It can also be affected by how efficiently the individual variable overhead items are used. Waste or inefficiency, such as using more kilowatt-hours of power than should have been used, will increase the cost of power and, thus, the total cost of variable overhead. The variable overhead expenditure on its own is therefore not very informative. Any meaningful analysis of this variance requires a comparison of the actual expenditure for each individual item of variable overhead expenditure against the budget.

Variable overhead efficiency variance

In Example 15.1 it is assumed that variable overheads vary with direct labour hours of input. The variable overhead efficiency variance arises because 28 500 direct labour hours of input were required to produce 9000 units. Working at the prescribed level of efficiency (3 hours per unit of output), it should take 27 000 hours to produce 9000 units of output. Therefore an extra 1500 direct labour hours of input were required. Because variable overheads are assumed to vary with direct labour hours of input, an additional £3000 (1500 hours at £2) variable overheads will be incurred. The formula for the variance is:

the **variable overhead efficiency variance** is the difference between the standard hours of output (SH) and the actual hours of input (AH) for the period multiplied by the standard variable overhead rate (SR):

$$(SH - AH) \times SR$$

You should note that if it is assumed that variable overheads vary with direct labour hours of input, this variance is identical to the labour efficiency variance. Consequently, the reasons for the variance are the same as those described previously for the labour efficiency variance. If you refer again to Figure 15.3, you will see that the variable overhead expenditure variance (£5000 favourable) plus the variable efficiency variance (£3000 adverse) add up to the total variable overhead variance of £2000 favourable.

SIMILARITIES BETWEEN MATERIALS, LABOUR AND OVERHEAD VARIANCES

So far, we have calculated price and quantity variances for direct material, direct labour and variable overheads. You will have noted the similarities between the computations of the three quantity and price variances. We calculated the quantity variances (i.e. material usage, labour efficiency and variable overhead efficiency variances) by multiplying the difference between the standard quantity (SQ) of resources consumed for the actual production and the actual quantity (AQ) of resources consumed by the standard price (SP) per unit of the resource. Thus, the three quantity variances can be formulated as:

$$(SQ - AQ) \times SP$$

Note that the standard quantity is derived from determining the quantity that should be used *for the actual production* for the period so that the principles of flexible budgeting are applied.

The price variances (i.e. material price, wage rate and variable overhead expenditure variances) were calculated by multiplying the difference between the standard price (SP) and the actual price (AP) per unit of a resource by the actual quantity (AQ) of resources acquired/used. The price variances can be formulated as:

$$(SP - AP) \times AQ$$

This can be re-expressed as:

$$(AQ \times SP) - (AQ \times AP)$$

Note that the first term in this formula (with AQ representing actual hours) is equivalent to the budgeted flexed variable overheads that we used to calculate the variable overhead expenditure variance. The last term represents the actual cost of the resources consumed.

We can therefore calculate all the price and quantity variances illustrated so far in this chapter by applying the two formulae outlined above.

FIXED OVERHEAD EXPENDITURE OR SPENDING VARIANCE

The final production variance shown in Figure 15.3 is the fixed overhead expenditure variance. With a direct costing system, fixed manufacturing overheads are not unitized and allocated to products. Instead, the total fixed overheads for the period are charged as an expense to the period in which they are incurred. Fixed overheads are assumed to remain unchanged in the short term in response to changes in the level of activity, but they may change in response to other factors. For example, price increases may cause expenditure on fixed overheads to rise. The fixed overhead expenditure variance therefore explains the difference between budgeted fixed overheads and the actual fixed overheads incurred. The formula for the **fixed overhead expenditure variance** is the difference between the budgeted fixed overheads (BFO) and the actual fixed overhead (AFO) spending:

$$BFO - AFO$$

In Example 15.1 budgeted fixed overhead expenditure is £120 000 and actual fixed overhead spending £116 000. Therefore, the fixed overhead expenditure variance is £4000. Whenever the actual fixed overheads are less than the budgeted fixed overheads, the variance will be favourable. The total of the fixed overhead expenditure variance on its own is not particularly informative. Any meaningful analysis of this variance requires a comparison of the actual expenditure for each individual item of fixed overhead expenditure against the budget. The difference may be due to a variety of courses, such as changes in salaries paid to employees, or the appointment of additional supervisors. Only by comparing individual items of expenditure and ascertaining the reasons for the variances, can one determine whether the variance is controllable or uncontrollable. Generally, this variance is likely to be uncontrollable in the short term.

SALES VARIANCES

Sales variances can be used to analyze the performance of the sales function or revenue centres on broadly similar terms to those for manufacturing costs. The most significant feature of sales variance calculations is that they are calculated in terms of profit contribution margins rather than sales values. Consider Example 15.2.

EXAMPLE 15.2

The budgeted sales for a company are £110 000 consisting of 10 000 units at £11 per unit. The standard cost per unit is £7. Actual sales are £120 000 (12 000 units at £10 per unit) and the actual cost per unit is £7.

You will see that when the variances are calculated on the basis of sales *value*, it is necessary to compare the budgeted sales *value* of £110 000 with the actual sales of £120 000. This gives a favourable variance of £10 000. This calculation, however, ignores the impact of the sales effort on profit. The budgeted profit contribution is £40 000, which consists of 10 000 units at £4 per unit, but the actual impact of the sales effort in terms of profit margins indicates a profit contribution of £36 000, which consists of 12 000 units at £3 per unit, indicating an adverse variance of £4000. If we examine Example 15.2, we can see that compared with the budget the selling price has been reduced, and that this has led not only to an increase in the total sales revenue but also to a reduction in total profits. The objective of the selling function is to influence favourably total profits. Thus a more meaningful performance measure will be obtained by comparing the results of the sales function in terms of profit contribution margins rather than sales revenues. Let us now calculate the sales variances from the information contained in Example 15.1.

Total sales margin variance

The total sales margin variance seeks to identify the influence of the sales function on the difference between budget and actual profit contribution. In Example 15.1 the budgeted profit contribution is £200 000, which consists of budgeted sales of 10 000 units at a contribution of £20 per unit. This is compared with a contribution derived from the actual sales volume of 9000 units. Because the sales function is responsible for the sales volume and the unit selling price, but not the unit manufacturing costs, the standard cost of sales and not the actual cost of sales is deducted from the actual sales revenue. The calculation of the contribution for ascertaining the total sales margin variance will therefore be as follows:

	(£)
Actual sales revenue (9000 units at £90)	810 000
Standard variable cost of sales for actual sales volume (9000 units at £68)	612 000
Profit contribution margin	198 000

To calculate the total sales margin variance we deduct the budgeted contribution for the period of £200 000 from the actual profit contribution of £198 000. This gives an adverse variance of £2000.

The formula for calculating the variance is as follows:

the **total sales margin variance** is the difference between actual sales revenue (ASR) less the standard variable cost of sales (SCOS) and the budgeted contribution (BC):

$$(ASR - SCOS) - BC$$

Using the standard cost of sales in the above formula and calculation ensures that production variances do not distort the calculation of the sales variances. This means that sales variances arise only because of changes in those variables controlled by the sales function (i.e. selling prices and sales quantity). Figure 15.3 indicates that it is possible to analyze the total sales margin variance into two sub-variances – a sales margin price variance and a sales margin volume variance.

Sales margin price variance

In Example 15.1 the actual selling price is £90 and the standard selling price is £88. In order to ensure that production variances do not distort the calculation of the sales margin price variance, the standard unit variable cost of £68 should be deducted from both the actual and the standard selling prices. This gives a contribution of £22 that is derived from the actual selling price and a contribution of £20 derived from the standard selling price. Because the actual sales volume is 9000 units, the increase in selling price means that the increase in contribution of £2 per unit is obtained 9000 times, giving a favourable sales margin variance of £18 000. In formula terms the variance is calculated as follows:

$$[(\text{Actual selling price} - \text{Standard variable cost}) - (\text{Standard selling price} - \text{Standard variable cost})] \times \text{Actual sales volume}$$

Since the standard variable cost is deducted from both the actual and standard selling price, the formula above can be simplified by omitting standard variable cost so that:

the **sales margin price variance** is the difference between the actual selling price (ASP) and the standard selling price (SSP) multiplied by the actual sales volume (AV):

$$(\text{ASP} - \text{SSP}) \times \text{AV}$$

Sales margin volume variance

To ascertain the effect of changes in the sales volume on the difference between the budgeted and the actual contribution, we must compare the budgeted sales volume with the actual sales volume. You will see from Example 15.1 that the budgeted sales are 10 000 units but the actual sales are 9000 units, and to enable us to determine the impact of this reduction in sales volume on profit, we must multiply the 1000 units by the standard contribution margin of £20. This gives an adverse variance of £20 000.

The use of the standard margin (standard selling price less standard cost) ensures that the volume variance will not be affected by any *changes* in the actual selling prices. The formula for calculating the variance is:

the **sales margin volume variance** is the difference between the actual sales volume (AV) and the budgeted volume (BV) multiplied by the standard contribution margin (SM):

$$(\text{AV} - \text{BV}) \times \text{SM}$$

Difficulties in interpreting sales margin variances

The favourable sales margin price variance of £18 000 plus the adverse volume variance of £20 000 add up to the total adverse sales margin variance of £2000. It may be argued that it is not very meaningful to analyze the total sales margin variance into price and volume components, since changes in selling prices are likely to affect sales volume. A favourable price variance will tend to be associated with an adverse volume variance, and vice versa. It may be unrealistic to expect to sell more than the budgeted volume when selling prices have increased.

	(£)	(£)	(£)
Budgeted net profit			80 000
Sales variances:			
Sales margin price	18 000F		
Sales margin volume	20 000A	2000A	
Direct cost variances:			
Material: Price	8900A		
Usage	26 500A	35 400A	
Labour: Rate	17 100A		
Efficiency	13 500A	30 600A	
Manufacturing overhead variances:			
Fixed overhead expenditure	4000F		
Variable overhead expenditure	5000F		
Variable overhead efficiency	3000A	6000F	62 000A
Actual profit			18 000

A further problem with sales variances is that the variances may arise from external factors and may not be controllable by management. For example, changes in selling prices may be a reaction to changes in selling prices of competitors. Alternatively, a reduction in both selling prices and sales volume may be the result of an economic recession that was not foreseen when the budget was prepared. For control and performance appraisal it may be preferable to compare actual market share with target market share for each product. In addition, the trend in market shares should be monitored and selling prices should be compared with competitors' prices.

RECONCILING BUDGETED PROFIT AND ACTUAL PROFIT

Top management will be interested in the reason for the actual profit being different from the budgeted profit. By adding the favourable production and sales variances to the budgeted profit and deducting the adverse variances, the reconciliation of budgeted and actual profit shown in Exhibit 15.4 can be presented in respect of Example 15.1.

Example 15.1 assumes that Alpha Ltd produces a single product consisting of a single operation and that the activities are performed by one responsibility centre. In practice, most companies make many products, which require operations to be carried out in different responsibility centres. A reconciliation statement such as that presented in Exhibit 15.4 will, therefore, normally represent a summary of the variances for many responsibility centres. The reconciliation statement thus represents a broad picture to top management that explains the major reasons for any difference between the budgeted and actual profits.

STANDARD ABSORPTION COSTING

The external financial accounting regulations in most countries require that companies should value inventories at full absorption manufacturing cost. The effect of this is that fixed overheads should be allocated to products and included in the closing inventory valuations. With the variable costing system, fixed overheads are not allocated to products. Instead, the total fixed costs are charged as an expense to the period in which they are incurred. (For a discussion of the differences between variable and absorption costing systems you should refer back to Chapter 8.) With an absorption costing system, an additional fixed overhead variance is calculated. This variance is called a volume variance. In addition, the sales margin variances must be expressed in unit *profit* margins instead of *contribution* margins. These variances are not particularly useful for control purposes. If your course does not relate to the disposition of variances to meet financial accounting requirements (i.e. standard absorption costing), you can omit pages 404–14.

With a standard absorption costing system, predetermined fixed overhead rates are established by dividing annual budgeted fixed overheads by the budgeted annual level of activity. We shall assume that in respect of Example 15.1, budgeted annual fixed overheads are £1 440 000 (£120 000 per month) and budgeted annual activity is 120 000 units (10 000 units per month). The fixed overhead rate per unit of output is calculated as follows:

$$\frac{\text{budgeted fixed overheads (£1 440 000)}}{\text{budgeted activity (120 000 units)}} = \text{£12 per unit of sigma produced}$$

Where different products are produced, units of output should be converted to standard hours. In Example 15.1 the output of one unit of sigma requires 3 direct labour hours. Therefore, the budgeted output in standard hours is 360 000 hours (120 000 × 3 hours). The fixed overhead rate per standard hour of output is:

$$\frac{\text{budgeted fixed overheads (£1 440 000)}}{\text{budgeted standard hours (360 000)}} = \text{£4 per standard hour}$$

By multiplying the number of hours required to produce one unit of sigma by £4 per hour, we also get a fixed overhead allocation of £12 for one unit of sigma (3 hours × £4). For the remainder of this chapter output will be measured in terms of standard hours produced.

We shall assume that production is expected to occur evenly throughout the year. Monthly budgeted production output is therefore 10 000 units, or 30 000 standard direct labour hours. At the planning stage an input of 30 000 direct labour hours (10 000 × 3 hours) will be included as the company will budget at the level of efficiency specified in the calculation of the product standard cost. Thus the *budgeted hours of input* and the *budgeted hours of output* (i.e. the standard hours produced) will be the same at the planning stage. In contrast, the *actual* hours of input may differ from the *actual* standard hours of output. In Example 15.1 the actual direct labour hours of input are 28 500, and 27 000 standard hours (9 000 units of output requiring 3 hours per unit) were actually produced.

With an absorption costing system, fixed overheads of £108 000 (27 000 standard hours of output at a standard rate of £4 per hour) will have been charged to products for the month of April. Actual fixed overhead expenditure was £116 000. Therefore, £8000 has not been allocated to products. In other words, there has been an under-recovery of fixed overheads. Where the fixed overheads allocated to products exceeds the overhead incurred, there will be an over-recovery of fixed overheads. The under- or over-recovery of fixed overheads represents the total fixed overhead variance for the period. The total fixed overhead variance is calculated using a formula similar to those for the total direct labour and total direct materials variances:

the **total fixed overhead variance** is the difference between the standard fixed overhead charged to production (SC) and the actual fixed overhead incurred (AC):

$$SC\ (£108\ 000)\ -\ AC\ (£116\ 000) = £8000A$$

Note that the standard cost for the actual production can be calculated by measuring production in standard hours of output (27 000 hours × £4 per hour) or units of output (9000 units × £12 per unit).

The under- or over-recovery of fixed overheads (i.e. the fixed overhead variance) arises because the fixed overhead rate is calculated by dividing *budgeted* fixed overheads by *budgeted* output. If actual output or fixed overhead expenditure differs from budget, an under- or over-recovery of fixed overheads will arise. In other words, the under- or over-recovery may be due to the following:

1 A fixed overhead expenditure variance of £4000 arising from actual *expenditure* (£116 000) being different from budgeted *expenditure* (£120 000).

2 A fixed overhead volume variance arising from actual *production* differing from budgeted production.

The fixed overhead expenditure variance also occurs with a variable costing system. The favourable variance of £4000 was explained earlier in this chapter. The volume variance arises only when inventories are valued on an absorption costing basis.

VOLUME VARIANCE

This variance seeks to identify the portion of the total fixed overhead variance that is due to actual production being different from budgeted production. In Example 15.2 the standard fixed overhead rate of £4 per hour is calculated on the basis of a normal activity of 30 000 standard hours per month. Only when actual standard hours produced are 30 000 will the budgeted monthly fixed overheads of £120 000 be exactly recovered. Actual output, however, is only 27 000 standard hours. The fact that the actual production is 3000 standard hours less than the budgeted output hours will lead to a failure to recover £12 000 fixed overhead (3000 hours at £4 fixed overhead rate per hour). The formula for the variance is:

the **volume variance** is the difference between actual production (AP) and budgeted production (BP) for a period multiplied by the standard fixed overhead rate (SR):

$$(AP - BP) \times SR$$

The volume variance reflects the fact that fixed overheads do not fluctuate in relation to output in the short term. Whenever actual production is less than budgeted production, the fixed overhead charged to production will be less than the budgeted cost, and the volume variance will be adverse. Conversely, if the actual production is greater than the budgeted production, the volume variance will be favourable.

When the adverse volume variance of £12 000 is netted with the favourable expenditure variance of £4000, the result is equal to the total fixed overhead adverse variance of £8000. It is also possible to analyze the volume variance into two further sub-variances – the volume efficiency variance and the capacity variance.

VOLUME EFFICIENCY VARIANCE

If we wish to identify the reasons for the volume variance, we may ask why the actual production was different from the budgeted production. One possible reason may be that the labour force worked at a different level of efficiency from that anticipated in the budget.

The actual number of direct labour hours of input was 28 500. Hence, one would have expected 28 500 hours of output (i.e. standard hours produced) from this input, but only 27 000 standard hours were actually produced. Thus, one reason for the failure to meet the budgeted output was that output in standard hours was 1500 hours less than it should have been. If the labour force had worked at the prescribed level of efficiency, an additional 1500 standard hours would have been produced, and this would have led to a total of £6000 (£1500 hours at £4 per standard hour) fixed overheads being absorbed. The inefficiency of labour is therefore one of the reasons why the actual production was less than the budgeted production, and this gives an adverse variance of £6000. The formula for the variance is:

the **volume efficiency variance** is the difference between the standard hours of output (SH) and the actual hours of input (AH) for the period multiplied by the standard fixed overhead rate (SR):

$$(SH - AH) \times SR$$

You may have noted that the physical content of this variance is a measure of labour efficiency and is identical with the labour efficiency variance. Consequently, the reasons for this variance will be identical with those previously described for the labour efficiency variance.

VOLUME CAPACITY VARIANCE

This variance indicates the second reason why the actual production might be different from the budgeted production. The budget is based on the assumption that the direct labour hours of input will be 30 000 hours, but the actual hours of input are 28 500 hours. The difference of 1500 hours reflects the fact that the company has failed to utilize the planned capacity. If we assume that the 1500 hours would have been worked at the prescribed level of efficiency, an additional 1500 standard hours could have been produced and an additional £6000 fixed overhead could have been absorbed. Hence the capacity variance is £6000 adverse. Whereas the volume efficiency variance indicated a failure to utilize capacity *efficiently,* the volume capacity variance indicates a failure to utilize capacity *at all.* The formula is:

the **volume capacity variance** is the difference between the actual hours of input (AH) and the budgeted hours of input (BH) for the period multiplied by the standard fixed overhead rate (SR):

$$(AH - BH) \times SR$$

A failure to achieve the budgeted capacity may be for a variety of reasons. Possible causes include machine breakdowns, material shortages, poor production scheduling, labour disputes and a reduction in sales demand.

The volume efficiency variance is £6000 adverse, and the volume capacity variance is also £6000 adverse. When these two variances are added together, they agree with the fixed

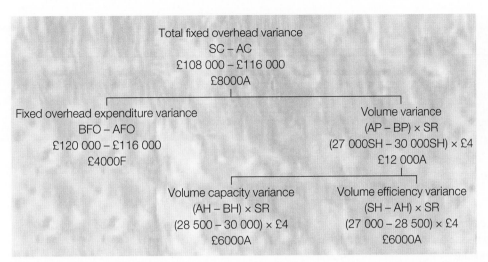

EXHIBIT 15.5
Diagram of fixed overhead variances

overhead volume variance of £12 000. Exhibit 15.5 summarizes the variances that we have calculated in this section.

You should note that the volume variance and its two sub-variances (capacity and efficiency) are sometimes restated in non-monetary terms as follows;

$$\text{production volume ratio} = \frac{\text{standard hours of actual output (27 000)}}{\text{budgeted hours of output (30 000)}} \times 100$$

$$= 90\%$$

$$\text{production efficency ratio} = \frac{\text{standard hours of actual output (27 000)}}{\text{actual hours worked (28 500)}} \times 100$$

$$= 94.7\%$$

$$\text{capacity usage ratio} = \frac{\text{actual hours worked (28 500)}}{\text{budgeted hours of input (30 000)}} \times 100$$

$$= 95\%$$

RECONCILIATION OF BUDGETED AND ACTUAL PROFIT FOR A STANDARD ABSORPTION COSTING SYSTEM

The reconciliation of the budgeted and actual profits is shown in Exhibit 15.6. You will see that the reconciliation statement is identical with the variable costing reconciliation statement, apart from the fact that the absorption costing statement includes the fixed overhead volume variance and values the sales margin volume variance at the standard profit margin per unit instead of the contribution per unit. If you refer back to Example 15.1 on page 391, you will see that the contribution margin for sigma is £20 per unit sold whereas the profit margin per unit after deducting fixed overhead cost (£12 per unit) is £8. Multiplying the difference in budgeted and actual sales volumes of 1000 units by the standard profit margin gives a sales volume margin variance of £8000. Note that the sales margin price variance is identical for both systems.

	(£)	(£)	(£)	(£)
Budgeted net profit				80 000
Sales variances:				
Sales margin price		18 000F		
Sales margin volume		8000A	10 000F	
Direct cost variances:				
Material – Price: Material A	19 000A			
Material B	10 100F	8900A		
– Usage: Material A	10 000A			
Material B	16 500A	26 500A	35 400A	
Labour – Rate		17 100A		
Efficiency		13 500A	30 600A	
Manufacturing overhead variances:				
Fixed – Expenditure	4000F			
Volume	12 000A	8000A		
Variable – Expenditure	5000F			
Efficiency	3000A	2000F	6000A	62 000A
Actual profit				18 000

EXHIBIT 15.6

Reconciliation of budgeted and actual profits for a standard absorption costing system

RECORDING STANDARD COSTS IN THE ACCOUNTS

If you are not studying for a specialist accounting qualification it is possible that your curriculum may not include the recording of standard costs. You should therefore check whether or not this topic is included in your curriculum to ascertain if you need to read this section. Standard costs can be used for planning, control, motivation and decision-making purposes without being entered into the books. However, the incorporation of standard costs into the cost accounting system greatly simplifies the task of tracing costs for inventory valuation and saves a considerable amount of data processing time. For example, if raw material stocks are valued at standard cost, the stock records may be maintained in terms of physical quantities only. The value of raw materials stock may be obtained simply by multiplying the physical quantity of raw materials in stock by the standard cost per unit. This avoids the need to record stocks on a first in, first out or average cost basis. The financial accounting regulations in most countries specify that inventory valuations based on standard costs may be included in externally published financial statements, provided the standard costs used are current and attainable. Most companies that have established standard costs therefore incorporate them into their cost accounting recording system.

Variations exist in the data accumulation methods adopted for recording standard costs, but these variations are merely procedural and the actual inventory valuations and profit calculations will be the same whichever method is adopted. In this chapter we shall illustrate a standard absorption costing system that values all inventories at standard cost, and all entries that are recorded in the inventory accounts will therefore be at *standard prices*. Any differences between standard costs and actual costs are debited or credited to variance accounts. Adverse variances will appear as debit balances, since they are additional costs in excess of standard. Conversely, favourable variances will appear as credit balances. Only production variances are recorded, and sales variances are not entered in the accounts.

Let us now consider the cost accounting records for Example 15.1, which was presented earlier in this chapter. We shall assume that the company operates an integrated cost accounting system. The variances recorded in the accounts are those for an absorption costing system summarized in the reconciliation statement presented in Exhibit 15.6. The appropriate ledger entries are presented in Exhibit 15.7 (pages 412–13). Each ledger and journal entry has been labelled with numbers from 1 to 13 to try to give you a clear understanding of each accounting entry.

Purchase of materials

19 000 kg of raw material A at £11 per kg and 10 100 kg of raw material B at £14 per kg were purchased. This gives a total purchase cost of £209 000 for A and £141 400 for B. The standard prices were £10 per kg for A and £5 per kg for B. The accounting entries for material A are:

1. Dr Stores ledger control account (AQ × SP)	190 000	
1. Dr Material price variance account	19 000	
1. Cr Creditors control account (AQ × AP)		209 000

You will see that the stores ledger control account is debited with the standard price (SP) for the actual quantity purchased (AQ), and the actual price (AP) to be paid is credited to the creditors control account. The difference is the material price variance. The accounting entries for material B are:

2. Dr Stores ledger control account (AQ × SP)	151 500	
2. Cr Material price variance account		10 100
2. Cr Creditors (AQ × AP)		141 400

Usage of materials

19 000 kg of A and 10 100 kg of B were actually issued, and the standard usage (SQ) was 18 000 and 9000 kg at standard prices of £10 and £15. The accounting entries for material A are:

3. Dr Work in progress (SQ × SP)	180 000	
3. Dr Material usage variance	10 000	
3. Cr Stores ledger control account (AQ × SP)		190 000

Work in progress is debited with the standard quantity of materials at the standard price and the stores ledger account is credited with the actual quantity issued at the standard price. The difference is the material usage variance. The accounting entries for material B are:

4. Dr Work in progress (SQ × SP)	135 000	
4. Dr Material usage variance	16 500	
4. Cr Stores ledger control account (AQ × SP)		151 500

Direct wages

The actual hours worked were 28 500 hours for the month. The standard hours produced were 27 000. The actual wage rate paid was £9.60 per hour, compared with a standard rate of £9 per hour. The actual wages cost is recorded in the same way in a standard costing system as an actual costing system. The accounting entry for the actual wages paid is:

5. Dr Wages control account	273 600	
5. Cr Wages accrued account		273 600

The wages control account is then cleared as follows:

6. Dr Work in progress (SQ × SP)	243 000	
6. Cr Wages control account		243 000
6. Dr Wage rate variance	17 100	
6. Dr Labour efficiency variance	13 500	
6. Cr Wages control account		30 600

The wages control account is credited and the work in progress account is debited with the standard cost (i.e. standard hours produced times the standard wage rate). The wage rate and labour efficiency variance accounts are debited, since they are both adverse variances and account for the difference between the actual wages cost (recorded as a debit in the wages control account) and the standard wages cost (recorded as a credit in the wages control account).

Manufacturing overhead costs incurred

The actual manufacturing overhead incurred is £52 000 for variable overheads and £116 000 for fixed overheads. The accounting entries for actual overhead *incurred* are recorded in the same way in a standard costing system as in an actual costing system. That is:

7. Dr Factory variable overhead control account	52 000	
7. Dr Factory fixed overhead control account	116 000	
7. Cr Expense creditors		168 000

Absorption of manufacturing overheads and recording the variances

Work in progress is debited with the standard manufacturing overhead cost for the output produced. The standard overhead rates were £4 per standard hour for fixed overheads and £2 per standard hour for variable overheads. The actual output was 27 000 standard hours. The standard fixed overhead cost is therefore £108 000 (27 000 standard hours at £4 per hour) and the variable overhead cost is £54 000. The accounting entries for fixed overheads are:

8. Dr Work in progress (SQ × SP)	108 000	
8. Dr Volume variance	12 000	
8. Cr Factory fixed overhead control account		120 000
8. Dr Factory fixed overhead control account	4000	
8. Cr Fixed overhead expenditure variance		4000

You will see that the debit of £108 000 to the work in progress account and the corresponding credit to the factory fixed overhead control account represents the standard fixed overhead cost of production. The difference between the debit entry of £116 000 in the factory fixed overhead control account in Exhibit 15.7 for the *actual* fixed overheads incurred, and the credit entry of £108 000 for the *standard* fixed overhead cost of production is the total fixed overhead variance, which consists of an adverse volume variance of £12 000 and a favourable expenditure variance of £4000. This is recorded as a debit to the volume variance account and a credit to the expenditure variance account. The accounting entries for variable overheads are:

9. Dr Work in progress account (SQ × SP)	54 000	
9. Dr Variable overhead efficiency variance	3000	
9. Cr Factory variable overhead control account		57 000
9. Dr Factory variable overhead control account	5000	
9. Cr Variable overhead expenditure variance account		5000

The same principles apply with variable overheads. The debit to work in progress account and the corresponding credit to the factory variable overhead control account of £54 000 is the standard variable overhead cost of production. The difference between the debit entry of £52 000 in the factory variable overhead account in Exhibit 15.7 for the *actual* variable overheads incurred and the credit entry of £54 000 for the *standard* variable overhead cost of production is the total variable overhead variance, which consists of an adverse efficiency variance of £3000 and a favourable expenditure variance of £5000.

Completion of production

In Exhibit 15.7 the total amount recorded on the debit side of the work in progress account is £720 000. As there are no opening or closing stocks, this represents the total standard cost of production for the period, which consists of 9000 units at £80 per unit. When the completed production is transferred from work in progress to finished goods stock, the accounting entries will be as follows:

10. Dr Finished stock account	720 000	
10. Cr Work in progress account		720 000

Because there are no opening or closing stocks, both the work in progress account and the stores ledger account will show a nil balance.

Sales

Sales variances are not recorded in the accounts, so actual sales of £810 000 for 9000 units will be recorded as:

11. Dr Debtors	810 000	
11. Cr Sales		810 000

Stores ledger control account

1. Creditors (material A)	190 000	3. Work in progress (material A)	180 000
2. Creditors (material B)	151 500		
		3. Material usage variance (material A)	10 000
		4. Work in progress (material B)	135 000
		4. Material usage variance (material B)	16 500
	341 500		341 500

Creditors control account

2. Material price variance (material B)	10 100	1. Stores ledger control (material A)	190 000
		1. Material price variance (material A)	19 000
		2. Stores ledger control (material B)	151 500

Variance accounts

1. Creditors (material A)	19 000	2. Creditors (material price B)	10 100
3. Stores ledger control (material A usage)	10 000	8. Fixed factory overhead (expenditure)	4000
4. Stores ledger control (material B usage)	16 500	9.Variable factory overhead (expenditure)	5000
6. Wages control (wage rate)	17 100		19 100
6. Wages control (lab. effic'y)	13 500	13. Costing P + L a/c (balance)	72 000
8. Fixed factory overhead (volume)	12 000		
9. Variable factory overhead (effic'y)	3000		
	91 100		91 100

Work in progress control account

3. Stores ledger (material A)	180 000	10. Finished goods stock account	720 000
4. Stores ledger (material B)	135 000		
6. Wages control	243 000		
8. Fixed factory overhead	108 000		
9. Variable factory overhead	54 000		
	720 000		720 000

Wages control account

5. Wages accrued account	273 600	6. WIP	243 000
		6. Wage rate variance	17 100
		6. Labour efficiency variance	13 500
	273 600		273 600

Fixed factory overhead control account

7. Expense creditors	116 000	8. WIP	108 000
8. Expenditure variance	4000	8. Volume variance	12 000
	120 000		120 000

EXHIBIT 15.7

Accounting entries for a standard costing system

Variable factory overhead control account

7. Expense creditors	52 000	9. WIP	54 000
9. Expenditure	5000	9. Efficiency variance	3000
	57 000		57 000

Finished goods stock control account

10. WIP	720 000	12. Cost of sales	720 000

Cost of sales account

12. Finish goods stock	720 000	13. Costing P + L a/c	720 000

Costing P + L Account

12. Cost of sales at standard cost	720 000	11. Sales	810 000
13. Variance account (net variances)	72 000		
Profit for period	18 000		
	810 000		810 000

EXHIBIT 15.7

(Continued)

As all the production for the period has been sold, there will be no closing stock of finished goods, and the standard cost of production for the 9000 units will be transferred from the finished goods account to the cost of sales account:

12. Dr Cost of sales account   288 000
    12. Cr Finished goods account   288 000

Finally, the cost of sales account and the variance accounts will be closed by a transfer to the costing profit and loss account (the item labelled 13 in Exhibit 15.7). The balance of the costing profit and loss account will be the *actual* profit for the period.

Calculation of profit

To calculate the profit, we must add the adverse variances and deduct the favourable variances from the standard cost of sales, which is obtained from the cost of sales account. This calculation gives the actual cost of sales for the period, which is then deducted from the actual sales to produce the actual profit for the period. The calculations are as follows:

	(£)	(£)	(£)
Sales			810 000
Less standard cost of sales		720 000	
Plus adverse variances:			
Material A price variance	19 000		
Material usage variance	26 500		
Wage rate variance	17 100		
Labour efficiency variance	13 500		
Volume variance	12 000		
Variable overhead efficiency variance	3000	91 100	
		811 100	
Less favourable variances:			
Material B price variance	10 100		
Fixed overhead expenditure variance	4000		
Variable overhead expenditure variance	5000	19 100	
Actual cost of sales			792 000
Actual profit			18 000

SUMMARY

The following items relate to the learning objectives listed at the beginning of the chapter.

- **Explain how a standard costing system operates.** Standard costing is most suited to an organization whose activities consist of a series of repetitive operations and the input required to produce each unit of output can be specified. A standard costing system involves the following: (a) the standard costs for the actual output are recorded for each operation for each responsibility centre; (b) actual costs for each operation are traced to each responsibility centre; (c) the standard and actual costs are compared; (d) variances are investigated and corrective action is taken where appropriate; and (e) standards are monitored and adjusted to reflect changes in standard usage and/or prices.

- **Explain how standard costs are set.** Standards should be set for the quantities and prices of materials, labour and services to be consumed in performing each operation associated with a product. Product standard costs are derived by listing and adding the standard costs of operations required to produce a particular product. Two approaches are used for setting standard costs. First, past historical records can be used to estimate labour and material usage. Second, standards can be set based on engineering studies. With engineering studies a detailed study of each operation is undertaken under controlled conditions, based on high levels of efficiency, to ascertain the quantities of labour and materials required. Target prices are then applied to ascertain the standard costs.

- **Explain the meaning of standard hours produced.** It is not possible to measure output in terms of units produced for a department making several different products or operations. This problem is overcome by ascertaining the amount of time, working under efficient operating conditions, it should take to make each product. This time calculation is called standard hours produced. Standard hours thus represents an output measure that acts as a common denominator for adding together the production of unlike items.

- **Identify and describe the purposes of a standard costing system.** Standard costing systems can be used for the following purposes: (a) providing a prediction of future costs that can be used for decision-making; (b) providing a challenging target that individuals are motivated to achieve; (c) providing a reliable and convenient source of data for budget preparation; (d) acting as a control device by highlighting those activities that do not conform to plan and thus alerting managers to those situations that may be 'out of control' and in need of corrective action; and (e) simplifying the task of tracing costs to products for profit measurement and inventory valuation purpose.

- **Calculate labour, material, overhead and sales margin variances and reconcile actual profit with budgeted profit.** To reconcile actual profit with budget profit the favourable variances are added to the budgeted profit and adverse variances are deducted. The end result should be the actual profit. A summary of the formulae for the computation of the variances is presented in Exhibit 15.8. In each case the formula is presented so that a positive variance is favourable and a negative variance unfavourable.

- **Identify the causes of labour, material, overhead and sales margin variances.** Quantities cost variances arise because the actual quantity of resources consumed exceeds actual usage. Examples include excess usage of materials and labour arising from the usage of inferior materials, careless handling of materials and failure to maintain machinery in proper condition. Price variances arise when the actual prices paid for resources exceed the standard prices. Examples include the failure of the purchasing function to seek the most efficient sources of supply or the use of a different grade of labour to that incorporated in the standard costs.

- **Distinguish between standard variable costing and standard absorption costing.** With a standard variable costing system, fixed overheads are not allocated to products. Sales margin variances are therefore reported in terms of contribution margins and a single fixed overhead variance, that is, the fixed overhead expenditure variance is reported. With a standard absorption costing system, fixed overheads are allocated to products and this process leads to the creation of a fixed overhead volume variance and the reporting of sales margin variances measured in terms of profit margins. The fixed overhead volume variance is not particularly helpful for cost control purposes, but this variance is required for financial accounting purposes.

- **Prepare a set of accounts for a standard costing system.** The method used in the chapter to illustrate the recording of standard costs valued all inventories at standard cost with all entries being recorded in the inventory accounts at standard prices. Any differences between standard costs and actual costs are debited or credited to variance accounts. Adverse variances appear as debit balances and favourable variances as credit balances. The preparation of a set of accounts for a standard costing system was illustrated in Exhibit 15.7.

The following variances are reported for both variable and absorption costing systems:

Materials and labour

1	Material price variance	=	(standard price per unit of material – actual price) × quantity of materials purchased
2	Material usage variance	=	(standard quantity of materials for actual production – actual quantity used) × standard price per unit
3	Total materials cost variance	=	(actual production × standard material cost per unit of production) – actual materials cost
4	Wage rate variance	=	(standard wage rate per hour – actual wage rate) × actual labour hours worked
5	Labour efficiency variance	=	(standard quantity of labour hours for actual production – actual labour hours) × standard wage rate
6	Total labour cost variance	=	(actual production × standard labour cost per unit of production) – actual labour cost

Fixed production overhead

7	Fixed overhead expenditure variance	=	budgeted fixed overheads – actual fixed overheads

Variable production overhead

8	Variable overhead expenditure variance	=	(budgeted variable overheads for actual input volume – actual variable overhead cost)
9	Variable overhead efficiency variance	=	(standard quantity of input hours for actual production – actual input hours) × variable overhead rate
10	Total variable overhead variance	=	(actual production × standard variable overhead rate per unit) – actual variable overhead cost

Sales margins

11	Sales margin price variance	=	(actual selling price – standard selling price) × actual sales volume
12	Sales margin volume variance	=	(actual sales volume – budgeted sales volume) × standard contribution margin
13	Total sales margin variance	=	(actual sales revenue – standard variable cost of sales) – total budgeted contribution

With a standard absorption costing system profit margins are used instead of contribution margins for the sales variances and the following additional variances are reported:

14	Fixed overhead volume variance	=	(actual production – budgeted production) × standard fixed overhead rate
15	Volume efficiency variance	=	(standard quantity of input hours for actual production – actual input hours) × standard fixed overhead rate
16	Volume capacity variance	=	(actual hours of input – budgeted hours of input) × standard fixed overhead rate
17	Total fixed overhead variance	=	(actual production × standard fixed overhead rate per unit) – actual fixed overhead cost

EXHIBIT 15.8

Summary of the formulae for the computation of the variances

KEY TERMS AND CONCEPTS

Bill of materials a description of the required quantity of materials needed for each operation to complete a product.

Budget costs predicted total costs for products or activities.

Capacity usage ratio the actual hours worked expressed as a percentage of the budgeted hours of input.

Engineering studies detailed studies of operations, based on careful specifications of materials, labour and equipment and on controlled observations of operations.

Fixed overhead expenditure variance the difference between the budgeted fixed overheads and the actual fixed overhead expenditure.

Labour efficiency variance the difference between the standard labour hours for actual production and the actual labour hours, multiplied by the standard hourly wage rate.

Material price variance the difference between the standard price and the actual price per unit of materials multiplied by the quantity of materials purchased.

Material usage variance the difference between the standard quantity required for actual production and the actual quantity used multiplied by the standard material price.

Production efficiency ratio the standard hours for the actual output expressed as a percentage of the actual hours worked.

Production volume ratio the standard hours for the actual output expressed as a percentage of the budgeted hours of output.

Sales margin price variance the difference between the actual selling price and the standard selling price multiplied by the actual sales volume.

Sales margin volume variance the difference between the actual sales volume and the budget volume multiplied by the standard contribution margin.

Standard costs target costs that should be incurred under efficient operating conditions.

Standard hours an output measure that can act as a common denominator for measuring the output of unlike items.

Total fixed overhead variance the difference between the standard fixed overhead charged to production and the actual fixed overhead incurred.

Total labour variance the difference between the standard labour cost for actual production and the actual labour cost.

Total material variance the difference between the standard material cost for the actual production and the actual cost.

Total sales margin variance the difference between actual sales revenue less the standard variable cost of sales and the budgeted contribution.

Total variable overhead variance the difference between the standard variable overheads charged to production and the actual variable overheads incurred.

Variable overhead efficiency variance the difference between the standard hours of output and the actual hours of input for the period, multiplied by the standard variable overhead rate.

Variable overhead expenditure variance the difference between the budgeted flexed variable overheads for the actual direct labour hours of input and the actual variable overhead costs incurred.

Volume capacity variance the difference between the actual hours of input and the budgeted hours of input for the period multiplied by the standard fixed overhead rate.

Volume efficiency variance the difference between the standard hours of output and the actual hours of input for the period multiplied by the standard fixed overhead rate.

Volume variance the difference between actual production and budgeted production for a period multiplied by the standard fixed overhead rate.

Wage rate variance the difference between the standard hourly wage rate and the actual wage rate, multiplied by the actual number of hours worked.

KEY EXAMINATION POINTS

A common error that students make is to calculate variances based on the original fixed budget. Remember to flex the budget. Therefore the starting point when answering a standard costing question should be to calculate actual production. If more than one product is produced, output should be expressed in standard hours. If standard overhead rates are not given, you can calculate the rates by dividing budgeted fixed and variable overheads by the budgeted output. Remember that output can be measured by units produced or standard hours produced. Make sure you are consistent and use overhead rates per standard hours if production is measured in standard hours, or overhead rates per unit produced if output is measured in terms of units produced. You should always express output in standard hours if the question requires the calculation of overhead efficiency variances. If the question does not specify whether you should calculate the variances on an absorption costing or variable costing basis, choose your preferred method and state the approach you have selected in your answer.

Frequently questions are set that give you the variances but require calculations of actual costs and inputs (see Review problem 15.28). Students who calculate variances simply by committing to memory a series of variance formulae experience difficulties in answering these questions. Make sure you understand how the variances are calculated, and check your answers with the solutions to the Review problems.

ASSESSMENT MATERIAL

The review questions are short questions that enable you to assess your understanding of the main topics included in the chapter. The numbers in parentheses provide you with the page numbers to refer to if you cannot answer a specific question.

The review problems are more complex and require you to relate and apply the chapter content to various business problems. The problems are graded by their level of difficulty. The multiple-choice questions are the least demanding and normally take less than 10 minutes to complete. Fully worked solutions to the review problems are provided in a separate section at the end of the book. Further review problems with solutions for this chapter are available on the accompanying website www.drury-online.com. The website includes a *Student's Manual* and an *Instructor's Manual*. Students can access both questions and answers from the *Student's Manual* and the questions from the *Instructor's Manual* The answers to problems in the *Instructor's Manual* are available only to lecturers on the lecturer's password-protected section of the website.

The website also includes over 20 case study problems. A list of these cases is provided on pages 427–30. Anjo Ltd and the Berkshire Toy Company are cases that are relevant to the content of this chapter.

REVIEW QUESTIONS

15.1 Describe the difference between budgeted and standard costs. *(p. 382)*

15.2 Explain how a standard costing system operates. *(pp. 382–4)*

15.3 Describe how standard costs are established using engineering studies. *(pp. 385–6)*

15.4 What are standard hours produced? What purpose do they serve? *(pp. 386–7)*

15.5 Describe the different purposes of a standard costing system. *(pp. 388–90)*

15.6 What are the possible causes of (a) material price and (b) material usage variances? *(pp. 393, 395)*

15.7 Explain why it is preferable for the material price variance to be computed at the point of purchase rather than the point of issue. *(pp. 393–94)*

15.8 What are the possible causes of (a) wage rate and (b) labour efficiency variances? *(p. 396)*

15.9 Explain how variable overhead efficiency and expenditure variances are computed. What are the possible causes of each of these variances? *(pp. 397–9)*

15.10 Why are sales variances based on contribution margins rather than sales revenues? *(pp. 400–01)*

15.11 Distinguish between a standard absorption and a standard variable costing system (pp. 403–4)

15.12 What additional variances arise with a standard absorption costing system? (pp. 404–6)

15.13 How do sales variances differ between a standard absorption and a variable costing system? (p. 407)

15.14 Explain what is meant by a volume variance. Does the volume variance provide any meaningful information for cost control? (p. 405)

REVIEW PROBLEMS

15.15 A company has a budgeted material cost of £125 000 for the production of 25 000 units per month. Each unit is budgeted to use 2 kg of material. The standard cost of material is £2.50 per kg.

Actual materials in the month cost £136 000 for 27 000 units and 53 000 kg were purchased and used.

(a) What was the adverse material price variance?

  (i) £1000

  (ii) £3500

  (iii) £7500

  (iv) £11 000

(b) What was the favourable material usage variance?

  (i) £2500

  (ii) £4000

  (iii) £7500

  (iv) £10 000

ACCA – Financial Information for Management

15.16 The following information relates to labour costs for the past month:

Budget	Labour rate	£10 per hour
	Production time	15 000 hours
	Time per unit	3 hours
	Production units	5000 units
Actual	Wages paid	£176 000
	Production	5500 units
	Total hours worked	14 000 hours

There was no idle time.
What were the labour rate and efficiency variances?

	Rate variance	Efficiency variance
(a)	£26 000 adverse	£25 000 favourable
(b)	£26 000 adverse	£10 000 favourable
(c)	£36 000 adverse	£2500 favourable
(d)	£36 000 adverse	£25 000 favourable

ACCA – Financial Information for Management

15.17 G Ltd repairs electronic calculators. The wages budget for the last period was based on a standard repair time of 24 minutes per calculator and a standard wage rate of $10.60 per hour.

Following the end of the budget period, it was reported that:

Number of repairs	31 000
Labour rate variance	$3100 (A)
Labour efficiency variance	Nil

Based on the above information, the actual wage rate during the period was:

A $10.35 per hour

B $10.60 per hour

C $10.85 per hour

D $11.10 per hour

CIMA – Management Accounting Fundamentals

15.18 Q plc used standard costing. The details for April were as follows:

Budgeted output	15 000	units
Budgeted labour hours	60 000	hours
Budgeted labour cost	£540 000	
Actual output	14 650	units
Actual labour hours paid	61 500	hours
Productive labour hours	56 000	hours
Actual labour cost	£522 750	

Calculate the idle time and labour efficiency variances for April

(4 marks)
CIMA P1 Management Accounting: Performance Evaluation

15.19 A manufacturing company operates a standard absorption costing system. Last month 25 000 production hours were budgeted and the budgeted fixed production overhead cost was $125 000. Last month the actual hours worked were 24 000 and the standard hours for actual production were 27 000.

What was the fixed production overhead capacity variance for last month?

A $5 000 Adverse

B $5 000 Favourable

C $10 000 Adverse

D $10 000 Favourable

ACCA F2 – Management Accounting

15.20 A company operates a standard marginal costing system. Last month actual fixed overhead expenditure was 2 per cent below budget and the fixed overhead expenditure variance was £1250.

What was the actual fixed overhead expenditure for last month?

A £61 250

B £62 475

C £62 500

D £63 750

ACCA Financial Information for Management

15.21 If fixed production overhead is over-absorbed in an accounting period, which ONE of the following combinations could have caused this result?

Fixed overhead expenditure variance	and	Fixed overhead volume variance
A $4200 (A)		$3750 (F)
B $3250 (A)		$4170 (F)
C $2240 (A)		$1870 (A)
D $2980 (F)		$3690 (A)

CIMA – Management Accounting Fundamentals

15.22 A company uses standard absorption costing. The following information was recorded by the company for October:

	Budget	Actual
Output and sales (units)	8 700	8 200
Selling price per unit	£28	£31
Variable cost per unit	£10	£10
Total fixed overheads	£34 800	£37 000

(a) The sales price variance for October was:

(i) £38 500 Favourable

(ii) £41 000 Favourable

(iii) £41 000 Adverse

(iv) £65 600 Adverse

(b) The sales volume profit variance for October was:

(i) £6000 Adverse

(ii) £6000 Favourable

(iii) £8000 Adverse

(iv) £8000 Favourable

(c) The fixed overhead volume variance for October was:

(i) £2000 Adverse

(ii) £2200 Adverse

(iii) £2200 Favourable

(iv) £4200 Adverse

CIMA P1 Management Accounting: Performance Evaluation

15.23 A company operates a standard marginal costing system. Last month the company sold 200 units more than it planned to sell. The following data relate to last month:

	Standard £	Actual £
Selling price per unit	40	38
Variable cost per unit	30	29

What was the favourable sales volume contribution variance last month?

(a) £1600

(b) £1800

(c) £2000

(d) £2200

ACCA Financial Information for Management

15.24 A company uses standard absorption costing. The following data relate to last month:

	Budget	Actual
Sales and production (units)	1000	900

	Standard £	Actual £
Selling price per unit	50	52
Total production cost per unit	39	40

What was the adverse sales volume profit variance last month?

(a) £1000

(b) £1100

(c) £1200

(d) £1300

ACCA Financial Information for Management

15.25 **Labour, material and variable overhead variances**
Casilda Ltd manufactures gonds, which have a standard selling price of £120 per gond. The company operates a standard marginal costing system and values stocks at standard cost.

The standard variable cost of a gond is as follows:

	£ per gond
Direct material	20
Direct labour (6 hours at £8 per hour)	48
Production overhead	24
	92

The budgeted and actual activity levels for last month were as follows:

	Budget units	Actual units
Sales	25 000	25 000
Production	25 000	26 000

The actual sales and variable costs for last month were as follows:

	£
Sales	2 995 000
Direct labour (purchased and used)	532 800
Direct labour (150 000 hours)	1 221 000
Variable production overhead	614 000

Required:

(a) Calculate the following cost variances for last month:

   (i) Total direct materials;

   (ii) Total variable production overhead;

   (iii) Direct labour rate;

   (iv) Direct labour efficiency.

(4 marks)

(b) Prepare a statement that reconciles the budgeted contribution with the actual contribution for last month and which incorporates the variances calculated in (a).

(6 marks)

(c) Suggest ONE possible explanation of how the direct labour variance calculated in (a) could be interrelated.

(2 marks)

(12 marks)

ACCA Financial Information for Management

15.26   **Sales variances**

Fairfax Ltd manufactures a single product which has a standard selling price of £22 per unit. It operates a standard marginal costing system. The standard variable production cost is £9 per unit. Budgeted annual production is 360 000 units and budgeted non-production costs of £1 152 000 per annum are all fixed.
The following data relate to last month:

	Budget units	Actual units
Production	30 000	33 000
Sales	32 000	34 000

Required:

(a) Calculate the sales price and sales volume contribution variances for last month showing clearly whether each variance is favourable or adverse.

(4 marks)

(b) Explain how the two variances calculated in (a) could be interrelated.

(3 marks)

(c) Calculate the BUDGETED profit for last month assuming that the company was using absorption costing.

(4 marks)

ACCA Financial Information for Management

15.27 **Variance analysis and reconciliation of actual and budgeted profit**
BS Limited manufactures one standard product and operates a system of variance accounting using a fixed budget. As assistant management accountant, you are responsible for preparing the monthly operating statements. Data from the budget, the standard product cost and actual data for the month ended 31 October are given below.

Using the data given, you are required to prepare the operating statement for the month ended 31 October to show the budgeted profit; the variances for direct materials, direct wages, overhead and sales, each analyzed into causes; and actual profit.

Budgeted and standard cost data:
Budgeted sales and production for the month: 10 000 units
Standard cost for each unit of product:

Direct material:	X:	10 kg at £1 per kg
	Y:	5 kg at £5 per kg
Direct wages:		5 hours at £8 per hour

Budgeted fixed overheads are £300 000
Budgeted sales price has been calculated to give a contribution of 50 per cent of the selling price.

Actual data for the month ended 31 October:
Production: 9500 units sold at a price of £160
Direct materials consumed:
 X: 96 000 kg at £1.20 per kg
 Y: 48 000 kg at £4.70 per kg

Direct wages incurred 46 000 hours at £8.20 per hour
Fixed production overhead incurred £290 000

(30 marks)

15.28 **Calculation of actual input data working back from variances**
The following data relate to actual output, costs and variances for the four-weekly accounting period number 4 of a company that makes only one product. Opening and closing work in progress figures were the same.

	(£000)
Actual production of product XY	18 000 units
Actual costs incurred:	
Direct materials purchased and used (150 000 kg)	210
Direct wages for 32 000 hours	264
Variable production overhead	38

	(£000)
Variances:	
Direct materials price	15 F
Direct materials usage	9 A
Direct labour rate	8 A
Direct labour efficiency	32 F
Variable production overhead expenditure	6 A
Variable production overhead efficiency	4 F

Variable production overhead varies with labour hours worked.
A standard marginal costing system is operated.

You are required to:

(a) present a standard product cost sheet for one unit of product XY;

(16 marks)

(b) describe briefly *three* types of standard that can be used for a standard costing system, stating which is usually preferred in practice and why.

(9 marks)
(Total 25 marks)

15.29 Accounting entries for a standard costing system
Bronte Ltd manufactures a single product, a laminated kitchen unit with a standard cost of £110 made up as follows:

	(£)
Direct materials (15 sq. metres at £3 per sq. metre)	45
Direct labour (5 hours at £10 per hour)	50
Variable overheads (5 hours at £2 per hour)	10
Fixed overheads (5 hours at £1 per hour)	5
	110

The standard selling price of the kitchen unit is £130. The monthly budget projects production and sales of 1000 units. Actual figures for the month of April are as follows:

Sales 1200 units at £132
Production 1400 units
Direct materials 22 000 sq. metres at £4 per sq. metre
Direct wages 6800 hours at £11
Variable overheads £11 000
Fixed overheads £6000

There were no opening stocks at the beginning of the period.
You are required to prepare:

(a) a trading account reconciling actual and budgeted profit and showing all the appropriate variances

(13 marks)

(b) ledger accounts in respect of the above transactions.

ICAEW Accounting Techniques

The dedicated website for this book includes over 20 case studies. Both students and lecturers can download these case studies from the open access website. The authors of the cases have provided teaching notes for each case and these can be downloaded only by lecturers from the password-protected lecturers' section of the website.

The cases generally cover the content of several chapters and contain questions to which there is no ideal answer. They are intended to encourage independent thought and initiative and to relate and apply the content of this book to more uncertain situations. They are also intended to develop critical thinking and analytical skills. Details relating to the cases that are available from the website are as follows:

Anjo Ltd

Lin Fitzgerald, Loughborough University Business School

Variance analysis that provides the opportunity for the case to be used as a role-playing exercise.

Berkshire Threaded Fasteners Company

John Shank, The Amos Tuck School of Business Administration, Dartmouth College

Cost analysis for dropping a product, for pricing, for product mix and product improvement.

Berkshire Toy Company

D. Crawford and E.G. Henry, State University of New York (SUNY) at Oswego

Variance analysis, performance evaluation, responsibility accounting and the balanced scorecard.

Blessed Farm Partnership

Rona O'Brian, Sheffield Hallam University

Strategic decision-making, evaluation of alternatives, ethics, sources of information.

Bohemia Industries

Colin Drury, Huddersfield University Business School

The application of variable and absorption costing for internal monthly profit reporting.

Chadwick's Department Store

Lewis Gordon, Liverpool John Moores University

The application of budget-building techniques and spreadsheet skills to a retail sector situation.

Company A

Mike Tayles, University of Hull Business School and Paul Walley, Warwick Business School.

Evaluation of a product costing system and suggested performance measures to support key success factors.

Company B

Mike Tayles, University of Hull Business School and Paul Walley, Warwick Business School.

The impact of a change in manufacturing strategy and method upon product costing and performance measurement systems.

Dumbellow Ltd

Stan Brignall, Aston Business School

Marginal costing versus absorption costing, relevant costs and cost–volume–profit analysis.

Edit 4U Ltd

Rona O'Brien, Sheffield Hallam University

The case study explores and evaluates the role of management accounting information in a small business context.

Electronic Boards plc

John Innes, University of Dundee, and Falconer Mitchell, University of Edinburgh

A general case that may be used at an introductory stage to illustrate the basics of management accounting and the role it can play within a firm.

Endeavour Twoplise Ltd

Antony Head, Brenda McDonnell, Jayne Rastrick, Sheffield Hallam University, and Susan Richardson, University of Bradford Management Centre

Functional budget and master budget construction, budgetary control and decision-making.

Fleet Ltd

Lin Fitzgerald, Loughborough University Business School

Outsourcing decision involving relevant costs and qualitative factors.

Global Ltd

Susan Richardson, University of Bradford Management Centre

Cash budgeting, links between cash and profit, pricing/bidding, information system design and behavioural aspects of management control.

Hardhat Ltd

Stan Brignall, Aston Business School

Cost–volume–profit analysis.

High Street Reproduction Furniture Ltd

Antony Head, Rona O'Brian, Jayne Rastrick, Sheffield Hallam University, and Susan Richardson, University of Bradford Management Centre

Relevant costs, strategic decision-making and limiting factors.

Majestic Lodge

John Shank, The Amos Tuck School of Business Administration, Dartmouth College

Relevant costs and cost–volume–profit analysis.

Merrion Products Ltd

Peter Clarke, University College Dublin

Cost–volume–profit analysis, relevant costs and limiting factors.

Moult Hall

Antony Head, Brenda McDonnell, Jayne Rastrick, Sheffield Hallam University, and Susan Richardson, University of Bradford Management Centre

Organizational objectives, strategic decision-making, evaluation of alternatives, relevant costs, debating the profit ethos, break-even analysis.

Oak City

R.W. Ingram and W.C. Parsons, University of Alabama, and W.A. Robbins, Attorney, Pearson and Sutton

Cost allocation in a government setting to determine the amount of costs that should be charged to business for municipal services. The case also includes ethical considerations.

Quality Shopping

Rona O'Brian, Sheffield Hallam University

Departmental budget construction, credit checking, environmental issues, behavioural issues and management control systems.

Rogatec Ltd

Antony Head, Brenda McDonnell, Jayne Rastrick, Sheffield Hallam University, and Susan Richardson, University of Bradford Management Centre

Standard costing and variance analysis, budgets, ethics, sources of information.

The Beta Company

Peter Clarke, University College Dublin

Cost estimation involving regression analysis and relevant costs.

Traditions Ltd

Antony Head, Brenda McDonnell, Jayne Rastrick, Sheffield Hallam University, and Susan Richardson, University of Bradford Management Centre

Relevant cost analysis relating to a discontinuation decision and budgeting.

BIBLIOGRAPHY

Al-Omiri, M. and Drury, C. (2007), A survey of the factors influencing the choice of product costing systems in UK organizations, *Management Accounting Research,* 18(4), 399–424.

American Accounting Association (1957) *Accounting and Reporting Standards for Corporate Financial Statements and Preceding Statements and Supplements,* 4.

American Accounting Association (1966) *A Statement of Basic Accounting Theory,* American Accounting Association.

Armitage, H.M. and Nicholson, R. (1993) Activity based costing: a survey of Canadian practice, Issue Paper No. 3, Society of Management Accountants of Canada.

Ask, U. and Ax, C. (1992) Trends in the Development of Product Costing Practices and Techniques – A Survey of Swedish Manufacturing Industry, Paper presented at the 15th Annual Congress of the European Accounting Association, Madrid.

Ask, U., Ax, C. and Jonsson, S. (1996) Cost management in Sweden: from modern to post-modern, in Bhimani, A. (ed.) *Management Accounting: European Perspectives,* Oxford, Oxford University Press, 199–217.

Ballas, A. and Venieris, G. (1996) A survey of management accounting practices in Greek firms, in Bhimani, A. (ed.) *Management Accounting: European Perspectives,* Oxford, Oxford University Press, 123–39.

Banerjee, J. and Kane, W. (1996) *Report on CIMA/JBA survey, Management Accounting,* October, 30, 37.

Barbato, M.B., Collini, P. and Quagli, C. (1996) Management accounting in Italy, in Bhimani, A. (ed.) *Management Accounting: European Perspectives,* Oxford, Oxford University Press, 140–63.

Barrett, M.E. and Fraser, L.B. (1977) Conflicting roles in budget operations, *Harvard Business Review,* July-August, 137–46.

Berliner, C. and Brimson, J.A. (1988) *Cost Management for Today's Advanced Manufacturing,* Harvard Business School Press.

Bjornenak, T. (1997a) Diffusion and accounting: the case of ABC in Norway, *Management Accounting Research,* 8(1), 3–17.

Bjornenak, T. (1997b) Conventional wisdom and accounting practices, *Management Accounting Research,* 8(4), 367–82.

Blayney, P. and Yokoyama, I. (1991) Comparative analysis of Japanese and Australian cost accounting and management practices, *Working paper,* University of Sydney, Australia.

Boons, A., Roozen, R.A. and Weerd, R.J. de (1994) Kosteninformatie in de Nederlandse Industrie, in *Relevantie methoden en ontwikkelingen* (Rotterdam: Coopers and Lybrand).

Brealey, J.A. (2006) The calculation of product costs and their use in decision-making in the British Manufacturing Industry, PhD dissertation, University of Huddersfield.

Brounen, D., de Jong, A. and Koedijk, K. (2004) Corporate Finance in Europe: confronting theory with practice, *Financial Management,* 33(4), 71–101.

Bruggeman, W., Slagmulder, R. and Waeytens, D. (1996) Management accounting changes; the Belgian experience, in Bhimani, A. (ed.) *Management Accounting: European Perspectives,* Oxford, Oxford University Press, 1–30.

Cats-Baril, W.L. Gatti, J.F. and Grinell, D.J. (1986) Joint product costing in the semiconductor industry, Management Accounting (USA), 28–35.

Chartered Institute of Management Accountants (2005) *Management Accounting: Official Terminology,* CIMA.

Clarke, P.J. (1992) Management Accounting Practices and Techniques in Irish Manufacturing Firms, *The 15th Annual Congress of the European Accounting Association*, Madrid, Spain.

Clarke, P. (1995) Management accounting practices and techniques in Irish manufacturing companies, *Working paper,* Trinity College, Dublin.

Cooper, R. (1990a) Cost classifications in unit-based and activity-based manufacturing cost systems, *Journal of Cost Management,* Fall, 4–14.

Cooper, R. (1990b) Explicating the logic of ABC, *Management Accounting,* November, 58–60.

Cooper, R. and Kaplan, R.S. (1987) How cost accounting systematically distorts product costs, in *Accounting and Management: Field Study Perspectives* (eds W J. Bruns and R.S. Kaplan), Harvard Business School Press, Ch. 8.

Cooper, R. and Kaplan, R.S. (1988) Measure costs right: make the right decisions, *Harvard Business Review,* September/October, 96–103.

Cooper, R. and Kaplan, R.S. (1991) *The Design of Cost Management Systems: Text, Cases and Readings,* Prentice-Hall.

Cooper, R. and Kaplan, R.S. (1992) Activity based systems: measuring the costs of resource usage, *Accounting Horizons,* September, 1–13.

Cornick, M., Cooper, W. and Wilson, S. (1988) How do companies analyse overhead?, *Management Accounting,* June, 41–3.

Cress, W. and Pettijohn, J. (1985) A survey of budget-related planning and control policies and procedures, *Journal of Accounting Education,* 3, Fall, 61–78.

Drucker, P.F. (1964) Controls, control and management, in *Management Controls: New Directions in Basic Research* (eds C.P. Bonini, R. Jaedicke and H. Wagner), McGraw-Hill.

Drury, C. (2008) *Management and Cost Accounting,* Cengage Learning EMEA.

Drury, C. and Tayles, M. (1994) Product costing in UK manufacturing organisations, *The European Accounting Review,* 3(3), 443–69.

Drury, C. and Tayles, M. (2000) *Cost system design and profitability analysis in UK companies,* Chartered Institute of Management Accountants.

Drury, C. and Tayles, M. (2005) Explicating the design of overhead absorption procedures in UK organizations, *British Accounting Review,* 37(1), 47–84.

Drury, C. and Tayles, M. (2006) Profitability analysis in UK organizations: An exploratory study, *British Accounting Review,* 38(4), 405–25.

Drury, C., Braund, S., Osborne, P. and Tayles, M. (1993) A survey of management accounting practices in UK manufacturing companies, ACCA Research Paper, Chartered Association of Certified Accountants.

Dugdale, D., Jones, T.C. and Green, S. (2006) *Contemporary management accounting practices in UK manufacturing companies*, Chartered Institute of Management Accountants.

Dugdale, D. and Lyne, S. (2006) Are budgets still needed?, *Financial Management*, November, 32–35.

Ekholm, B-G. and Wallin, J. (2000) Is the annual budget really dead?, *The European Accounting Review*, 9(4), 519–39.

Evans, H. and Ashworth, G. (1996) Survey conclusions: wakeup to the competition, *Management Accounting* (UK), May, 16–18.

Friedman, A.L. and Lynne, S.R. (1995) *Activity-based Techniques: The Real Life Consequences,* Chartered Institute of Management Accountants.

Friedman, A.L. and Lynne, S.R. (1997) Activity-based techniques and the death of the beancounter, *The European Accounting Review*, 6(1), 19–44.

Friedman, A.L. and Lynne, S.R. (1999) *Success and Failure of Activity-based Techniques: A long-term perspective,* Chartered Institute of Management Accountants.

Granlund, M. and Lukka, K. (1998) It's a small world of management accounting practices, *Journal of Management Accounting Research,* 10, 151–79.

Green, F.B. and Amenkhienan, F.E. (1992) Accounting innovations: A cross sectional survey of manufacturing firms, *Journal of Cost Management for the Manufacturing Industry,* Spring 58–64.

Guilding, C., Lamminmaki, D. and Drury, C. (1998) Budgeting and standard costing practices in New Zealand and the United Kingdom, *The International Journal of Accounting,* 33(5), 41–60.

Gurton, A. (1999) Bye bye budget: the annual budget is dead, *Accountancy*, March, 60.

Hope, J. and Fraser, R. (2003) Who needs budgets?, *Harvard Business Review*, February, 42–8.

Hopper, T., Kirkham, L., Scapens, R.W. and Turley, S. (1992) Does financial accounting dominate management accounting – A research note, *Management Accounting Research*, 3(4), 307–11.

Innes, J. and Mitchell, F. (1991) ABC: A survey of CIMA members, *Management Accounting*, October, 28–30.

Innes, J. and Mitchell, F. (1995a) A survey of activity-based costing in the UK's largest companies, *Management Accounting Research*, June, 137–54.

Innes, J. and Mitchell, F. (1995b) Activity-based costing, in *Issues in Management Accounting* (eds D. Ashton, T. Hopper and R.W. Scapens), Prentice-Hall, 115–36.

Innes, J., Mitchell, F. and Sinclear, D. (2000) Activity-based costing in the UK's largest companies: a comparison of 1994 and 1999 survey results, *Management Accounting Research*, 11(3), 349–62.

Israelsen, P., Anderson, M., Rohde, C. and Sorensen, P.E. (1996) Management accounting in Denmark: theory and practice, in Bhimani, A. (ed.) *Management Accounting: European Perspectives,* Oxford, Oxford University Press, 31–53.

Kaplan, R.S. and Cooper, R. (1998) *Cost and Effect: Using Integrated Systems to Drive Profitability and Performance,* Harvard Business School Press.

Kennedy, A. and Dugdale, D. (1999) Getting the most from budgeting, *Management Accounting (UK),* February, 22–4.

Lauderman, M. and Schaeberle, F.W. (1983) The cost accounting practices of firms using standard costs, *Cost and Management* (Canada), July/August, 21–5.

Lukka, K. and Granlund, M. (1996) Cost accounting in Finland: Current practice and trends of development, *The European Accounting Review,* 5(1), 1–28.

Macintosh, N.B. (1985) *The Social Software of Accounting and Information Systems,* Wiley.

Merchant, K.A. (1998) *Modern Management Control Systems: Text and Cases,* Prentice-Hall, New Jersey.

Merz, M. and Hardy, A. (1993) ABC puts accountants on the design team at HP, *Management Accounting (USA),* September, 24–6.

Nicholls, B. (1992) ABC in the UK – a status report, *Management Accounting,* May, 22–3.

Otley, D.T. (1987) *Accounting Control and Organizational Behaviour,* Heinemann.

Ouchi, W.G. (1979) A conceptual framework for the design of organizational control mechanisms, *Management Science,* 833–48.

Saez-Torrecilla, A., Fernandez-Fernandez, A., Texeira-Quiros, J. and Vaquera-Mosquero, M. (1996) Management accounting in Spain: trends in thought and practice, in Bhimani, A. (ed.) *Management Accounting: European Perspective 3,* Oxford, Oxford University Press, 180–90.

Scapens, R., Jazayeri, M. and Scapens, J. (1998) SAP: Integrated information systems and the implications for management accountants, *Management Accounting (UK),* September, 46–8.

Scarborough, P.A., Nanni, A. and Sakurai, M. (1991) Japanese management accounting practices and the effects of assembly and process automation, *Management Accounting Research,* 2, 27–46.

Scherrer, G. (1996) Management accounting: a German perspective, in Bhimani, A. (ed.), *Management Accounting: European Perspectives,* Oxford, Oxford University Press, 100–22.

Schwarzbach, H.R. (1985) The impact of automation on accounting for direct costs, *Management Accounting* (USA), 67(6), 45–50.

Shim, E. and Stagliano, A. (1997) A survey of US manufacturers on implementation of ABC, *Journal of Cost Management,* March/April, 39–41.

Simon, H.A. (1959) Theories of decision making in economics and behavioural science, *The American Economic Review,* June, 233–83.

Sizer, J. (1989) *An Insight into Management Accounting*, Penguin, Chs 11, 12.

Slater, K. and Wootton, C. (1984) *Joint and By-product Costing in the UK,* Institute of Cost and Management Accounting.

Virtanen, K., Malmi, T., Vaivio, J. and Kasanen, E. (1996) Drivers of management accounting in Finland, in Bhimani, A. (ed.) *Management Accounting: European Perspectives,* Oxford, Oxford University Press, 218–41.

Chapter 2

2.14 **(a)** SV (or variable if direct labour can be matched exactly to output)
   (b) F
   (c) F
   (d) V
   (e) F (Advertising is a discretionary cost. See Chapter 14 for an explanation of this cost.)
   (f) SV
   (g) F
   (h) SF
   (i) V

2.15 Controllable (c), (d), (f)
   Non-controllable (a), (b), (e), (g), (h)

2.16 It is assumed that cost object for (d) is the specific road haulage journey so that the driver's wages can be assigned to each specific journey, whereas the cost objective in the power generation organization is each specific unit of output. The cost of maintenance workers cannot be identified with a specific cost unit. It will therefore be an indirect cost so the Answer = (c)

2.17 Answer = (d)

2.18 Total variable overheads = 17 000 × £3.50 = £59 500
   Total variable overhead (£59 500) + Total fixed overhead = Total overhead (£246 500)
   Total fixed overhead = £246 500 − £59 500 = £187 000
   Answer = (c)

2.19 Answer = (b)

2.20 Answer = (b)

2.21 Answer = (b)

2.22 See the description of cost behaviour in Chapter 2 for the answer to these questions. In particular the answer should provide graphs for fixed costs, variable costs, semi-fixed costs and semi-variable costs.

2.23 You will find the answer to this question in Chapter 2. In particular the answer should describe the classification of costs for stock valuation and profit measurement; classification for decision-making and planning; classification for control. In addition the answer should illustrate methods of classification (see Chapter 2 for examples) within the above categories

and describe the benefits arising from classifying costs in the manner illustrated.

2.24 See Chapter 2 for the answer to this question.

2.25 **(a)** See 'Functions of management accounting' in Chapter 1 for the answer to this question. In particular your answer should stress that the cost accountant provides financial information for stock valuation purposes and also presents relevant information to management for decision-making and planning and cost control purposes. For example, the cost accountant provides information on the costs and revenues of alternative courses of action to assist management in selecting the course of action which will maximize future cash flows. By coordinating plans together in the form of budgets, and comparing actual performance with plans, the accountant can pinpoint those activities which are not proceeding according to plan.

   (b) **(i)** Direct costs are those costs which can be traced to a cost objective. If the cost objective is a sales territory then *fixed* salaries of salesmen will be a direct cost. Therefore the statement is incorrect.

   (ii) Whether a cost is controllable depends on the level of authority and time span being considered. For example, a departmental foreman may have no control over the number of supervisors employed in his department but this decision may be made by his superior. In the long term such costs are controllable.

   (iii) This statement is correct. See 'sunk costs' in Chapter 2 for an explanation of why this statement is correct.

2.26 **(i)** See Chapter 2 for a definition of opportunity cost and sunk cost.
   (ii) *Opportunity cost:* If scarce resources such as machine hours are required for a special contract then the cost of the contract should include the lost profit that would have been earned on the next best alternative. This should be recovered in the contract price.
   Sunk cost: The original cost of equipment used for a contract is a sunk cost and should be ignored. The change in the resale value resulting

from the use of the equipment represents the relevant cost of using the equipment.

(iii) The significance of opportunity cost is that relevant costs do not consist only of future cash outflows associated directly with a particular course of action. Imputed costs must also be included. The significance of sunk costs is that past costs are not relevant for decision-making.

2.27 See Chapter 2 for an explanation of the terms avoidable costs and unavoidable costs and Chapter 4 for an explanation of cost centres. A cost unit is a unit of product or service for which costs are ascertained. In a manufacturing organization a cost unit will be a unit of output produced within a cost centre. In a service organization, such as an educational establishment, a cost unit might be the cost per student.

2.28 Variable costs are constant per unit of output. The costs per unit of output are as follows:

	Cost per unit 125 units (£)	Cost per unit 180 units (£)
T1	8.00	7.00
T2	14.00	14.00
T3	19.80	15.70
T4	25.80	25.80

Answer = (c)

2.29 (a) (i) Schedule of annual mileage costs

	5000 miles (£)	10 000 miles (£)	15 000 miles (£)	30 000 miles (£)
Variable costs				
Spares	100	200	300	600
Petrol	380	760	1140	2280
Total variable cost	480	960	1440	2880
Variable cost per mile	0.096	0.096	0.096	0.096
Fixed costs				
Depreciation[a]	2000	2000	2000	2000
Maintenance	120	120	120	120
Vehicle licence	80	80	80	80
Insurance	150	150	150	150
Tyres[b]	—	—	75	150
	2350	2350	2425	2500
Fixed cost per mile	0.47	0.235	0.162	0.083
Total cost	2830	3310	3865	5380
Total cost per mile	0.566	0.331	0.258	0.179

Notes
[a]Annual depreciation

$$= \frac{£5500 \text{ (cost)} - £1500 \text{ (trade-in price)}}{2 \text{ years}} = £2000$$

[b]At 15 000 miles per annum tyres will be replaced once during the two-year period at a cost of £150. The average cost per year is £75. At 30 000 miles per annum tyres will be replaced once each year.

Comments
Tyres are a semi-fixed cost. In the above calculations they have been regarded as a step fixed cost. An alternative approach would be to regard the semi-fixed cost as a variable cost by dividing £150 tyre replacement by 25 000 miles. This results in a variable cost per mile of £0.006.

Depreciation and maintenance cost have been classified as fixed costs. They are likely to be semi-variable costs, but in the absence of any additional information they have been classified as fixed costs.

(ii) See Figure 2.29.

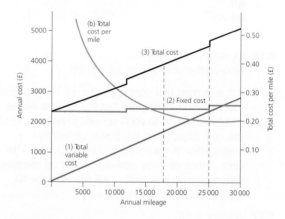

FIGURE 2.29

The step increase in fixed cost is assumed to occur at an annual mileage of 12 500 and 25 000 miles, because tyres are assumed to be replaced at this mileage

(iii) The respective costs can be obtained from the vertical dashed lines in the graph (Figure 2.29).

(b) The *cost per mile* declines as activity increases. This is because the majority of costs are fixed and do not increase when mileage increases. However, *total cost* will increase with increases in mileage.

2.30 (a) (i) For an explanation of sunk and opportunity costs see Chapter 2. The down payment of £5000 represents a sunk cost. The lost profit from subletting the shop of £1600 p.a. ((£550 × £12) − £5000) is an example of an opportunity cost. Note that only the £5000 additional rental is included in the opportunity cost calculation. (The £5000 sunk cost is excluded from the calculation.)

(ii) The relevant information for running the shop is:

	(£)
Net sales	100 000
Costs (£87 000 – £5000 sunk cost)	82 000
	18 000
Less opportunity cost from subletting	1600
Profit	16 400

The above indicates that £16 400 additional profits will be obtained from using the shop for the sale of clothing. It is assumed that Mrs Johnson will not suffer any other loss of income if she devotes half her time to running the shop.

(b) The CIMA terminology defines a notional cost as 'A hypothetical cost taken into account in a particular situation to represent a benefit enjoyed by an entity in respect of which no actual expense is incurred.'

Examples of notional cost include:

(i) Interest on capital to represent the notional cost of using an asset rather than investing the capital elsewhere.

(ii) Including rent as a cost for premises owned by the company so as to represent the lost rent income resulting from using the premises for business purposes.

Chapter 3

3.14 Overtime premium = hours overtime at $5.10 = $35.70
Answer = (b)

3.15

	$	$
Direct materials		5500
Direct expenses		14 500
Staff salaries:		
1020 hours × $24.00	24 480	
Overtime hours 40 hours ×	240	24 720
$6.00		44 720

Answer = (c)

3.16 Production will be charged at the most recent (higher prices) resulting in lower profits, and stocks will consist of the earlier (lower prices). Therefore Answer = (a).

3.17 Closing stock in units = 100 opening balance + 200 receipts – 150 issues = 150 units
LIFO valuation = (100 × £62) + (50 × £6700/100)
= £9550
FIFO valuation = 150 × £62 = £9 300
Therefore the LIFO valuation is greater than FIFO valuation by £250
Answer = (b)

3.18 Average price per unit after the issue on the 5th = [(100 units × £2900/200) = £1 450
Average price after the receipt on the 7th = [(400 × £17.50) + £1450]/500 = £16.90
Value of issues = (100 × £2900/200) + (360 × £16.90)
= £7534
Answer = (b)

3.19 Closing stock (units) = 300 + 400 + 500 – 600 – 300
= 300
The issue of 600 kg on the 13th will consist of the 400 kg on the 4th and 200 kg of the opening stock and the issue of the 300 kg on the 25th will be from the 500kg purchased on the 18th
Therefore the closing stock will consist of 100 kg of the opening stock and 200 kg from the purchase on the 18th
Valuation = (100 × £11) + (200 × £13) = £3 700
Answer = (c)

3.20 **(a)** Purchases are 460 units and issues are 420 units resulting in a closing stock of 40 units. Therefore closing stock valuation = 40 units at the latest purchase price ($1.90) = $76. Therefore Answer = (d)

(b) Answer = (c) (see outcomes for Example 3.2 in the text)

3.21 Re-order level = Maximum usage × Maximum lead time
= 95 × 18 = 1710
Answer = (c)

3.22 **(i)** Answer = (c)
(ii) Maximum stock = Re-order level + Re-Order quantity
– Minimum usage during minimum lead time
= 1710 + 1750 – (50 × 12)
= 2860
Answer = (b)

3.23 The average annual stock in units consists of the buffer inventory (maintained throughout the year) plus half of the EOQ giving 1500 units
Therefore the annual holding cost = 1500 units × £2 = $3000
Answer = (c)

3.24 EOQ = $\sum[(2 \times 20\ 000 \times 4 \times £20)/(0.06 \times 25)]$
= 1461 units
Answer = (c)

3.25 Answer = (d)

3.26 The following formula (see 'Key examination points' at the end of Chapter 3) should be used:
Maximum stock level = Re-order level (1800) + EOQ (2000) – minimum usage for the minimum lead time (50 × 11)
= 3250 units
Answer = (c)

3.27 (a) EOQ = $\sqrt{(2 \times 15\,000 \times 80)/(0.1333 \times 200)}$
= 300 units
Number of orders per year = 15 000/300
= 50 orders

(b) EOQ = $\sqrt{(2 \times 2800 \times 28)/(25 \times .08)}$
= 280 units
Holding cost = 280/2 × £2 = $280

3.28 (a) (i) EOQ = $\sqrt{[(2 \times 48\,000 \times 120)/(0.10 \times £80)]}$
= 1200 units

(ii)

	£
Purchasing cost (48 000 × £80)	3 840 000
Ordering cost (48 000/1200) × £120	4800
Holding cost (1200/2) × £80 × 0.10	4800
Total cost	3 849 600

(b)

	£
Purchasing cost (48 000 × £80 × 0.99)	3 801 600
Ordering cost (48 000/2 000) × £120	2880
Holding cost (2000/2) × £80 × 0.99 × 0.10	7920
Total cost	3 812 400

Annual saving = (£3 849 600–£3 812 400) = £37 200

(c) opportunity cost of investment in stocks (i.e. interest on capital tied up in stocks);
incremental insurance costs;
incremental warehouse and storage costs;
costs of obsolescence and deterioration of stocks.

3.29 (a) (i) EOQ = $\sqrt{[(2 \times 8760 \times 12.50)/(0.05 \times £80)]}$
= 234 units

(b) Daily usage = 24 units (8760/365)
Re-order level = 504 units (21 days × 24 units)

(c) (i) A stockout occurs when a company runs out of stocks. To avoid the costs associated with running out of stocks (e.g. lost sales arising from the loss of customer goodwill) companies carry buffer/safety stocks to cover emergency situations arising from demand or lead times being greater than the anticipated levels.

(ii) The company should establish a buffer stock if periodic demand for component RB fluctuates from period to period or the lead time fluctuates from its present constant level of 21 days.

3.30 (i) Current average maximum production = 30 × 55 hrs × 6 units = 9900 units. Proposed maximum production = 30 × 55 hrs × 8 units = 13 200 units

Existing payment system: Output level (units) 7

Output level (units)	7000	9600	9900
	£	£	£
Sales value (£11 per unit)	77 000	105 600	108 900
Pre-finishing VC	56 000	76 800	79 200
Direct labour:			
Guaranteed	9600	9600	9600
Overtime (W1)	—	4800	5400
Variable overhead (W2)	560	768	792
Fixed overhead	9000	9000	9000
Total cost	75 160	100 968	103 992
Profit	1840	4632	4908

Proposed scheme:

Output level (units)	7000	9600	9900	12 000
	£	£	£	£
Sales value	77 000	105 600	108 900	132 000
Pre-finishing VC	56 000	76 800	79 200	96 000
Direct labour at £1.40 per unit	9800	13 440	13 860	16 800
Variable overhead (W3)	420	576	594	720
Fixed overhead	9000	9000	9000	9000
Total cost	75 220	99 816	102 654	122 520
Profit	1780	5784	6246	9480

Working:
(W1) 9600 units requires 1600 hrs (9600/6)
∴ (Overtime = 400 hrs × £12
9900 units requires 1650 hrs (9900/6)
∴ (Overtime = 450 hrs × £12
Basic hours = 1200 hrs
(W2) 7000 units = 7000/6 × £0.48
9600 units = 9600/6 × £0.48
9900 units = 9900/6 × £0.48
(W3) 7000 units = 7000/8 × £0.48
9600 units = 9600/8 × £0.48
9900 units = 9900/8 × £0.48
12 000 units = 12 000/8 × £0.48

(ii) At low output levels the average wage rate per unit is £1.33 (£8/6 units), compared with £1.40 with the incentive scheme. However, once overtime is worked, the wage rate per unit of output exceeds £1.40 per unit under the incentive scheme. For example, at an output level of 9600 units the wage rate per unit of output is £1.50 (£14 400/9600).
Variable overheads vary with productive hours. Therefore variable overhead per unit will be

£0.08 (£0.48/6) under the old scheme and £0.06 per unit under the new scheme (£0.48/8). The proposed incentive scheme will also enable the maximum output level to be achieved, thus enabling maximum sales to be achieved.

Chapter 4

4.11 Answer = (a)

4.12 (i) Budgeted overhead rates and not actual overhead rates should be used as indicated in Chapter 3

Overhead rate = £148 750/8500 hours
= £17.50 per hour.

Answer = (a)

(ii)

	(£)
Actual overheads incurred	146 200
Overheads absorbed (7928 × £17.50)	138 740
Under-absorbed overheads	7460

Answer = (d)

4.13 Budgeted machine hour rate = $3.60($180 000/ 50 000 hours) Standard machine hours per unit = 1.25(50 000 hours/40 000 units)

	$
Overheads incurred	178 080
Overheads absorbed (38 760 units × 1.25 hours × $3.60) =	174 420
Under absorbed overheads	3660

Answer = (b)

4.14 Items that contribute to the over-absorption of overheads are if actual production exceeds budgeted production or actual overhead expenditure is less than budgeted expenditure. When both of these items occur overheads will be over-absorbed. Therefore the answer is D.

4.15

Direct materials	10 650
Direct labour	3260
Prime cost	13 910
Production overhead (140 × $8.50)	1190
Non-manufacturing overheads and profit (60% × $13 910)	8346
Estimated price	23 446

Answer = (c)

4.16 Cost centre G = 40 000 + (0.50 × £18 000) + 0.3 [£30 000 + (0.10 × £18 000)] = £58 540

Answer = (b)

4.17 (a)

	Total (£)	A (£)	Departments B (£)	C (£)	X (£)	Y (£)
Rent and rates[a]	12 800	6000	3600	1200	1200	800
Machine insurance[b]	6000	3000	1250	1000	500	250
Telephone charges[c]	3200	1500	900	300	300	200
Depreciation[b]	18 000	9000	3750	3000	1500	750
Supervisors' salaries[d]	24 000	12 800	7200	4000		
Heat and light[a]	6400	3000	1800	600	600	400
	70 400					
Allocated		2800	1700	1200	800	600
		38 100	20 200	11 300	4900	3000
Reapportionment of X		2450 (50%)	1225 (25%)	1225 (25%)	(4900)	
Reapportionment of Y		600 (20%)	900 (30%)	1500 (50%)		(3000)
		£41 150	£22 325	£14 025		
Budgeted D.L. hours[e]		3200	1800	1000		
Absorption rates		£12.86	£12.40	£14.02		

Notes
[a] Apportioned on the basis of floor area.
[b] Apportioned on the basis of machine value.
[c] Should be apportioned on the basis of the number of telephone points or estimated usage. This information is not given and an alternative arbitrary method of apportionment should be chosen. In the above analysis telephone charges have been apportioned on the basis of floor area.
[d] Apportioned on the basis of direct labour hours.
[e] Machine hours are not given but direct labour hours are. It is assumed that the examiner requires absorption to be on the basis of direct labour hours.

(b)

	Job 123 (£)	Job 124 (£)
Direct material	154.00	108.00
Direct labour:		
Department A	76.00	60.80
Department B	42.00	35.00
Department C	34.00	47.60
Total direct cost	306.00	251.40
Overhead:		
Department A	257.20	205.76
Department B	148.80	124.00
Department C	140.20	196.28
Total cost	852.20	777.44
Profit	284.07	259.15

(c) Listed selling price   1136.27   1036.59
Note
Let SP represent selling price.

Cost + 0.25SP = SP
Job 123: £852.20 +0.25SP = 1SP
0.75SP = £852.20

Hence SP = £1136.27
For Job 124:   0.75SP = £777.44
Hence SP = £1036.59

(d) For the answer to this question see sections on materials recording procedure and pricing the issues of materials in Chapter 3.

4.18 **(i)** Percentage of direct material cost $= \dfrac{£250\,000}{£100\,000}$
$\times 100 = 250\%$

Direct labour hour rate $= £250\,000/$
$50\,000$ hours $= £5$ per hour

(ii) Percentage material cost $= 250\% \times £7000$
$= £17\,500$

Direct labour cost $= 800 \times £5 = £4000$

(iii) Overhead incurred £350 000
Overhead absorbed £275 000 (55 000 × £5)
Under absorption of overhead £75 000
The under absorption of overhead should be regarded as a period cost and charged to the profit and loss account.

(iv) The answer should stress the limitations of the percentage of direct material cost method and justify why the direct labour hour method is the most frequently used method in non-machine paced environments. See Learning Note 4.1 for a more detailed answer to this question.

4.19 (a)

(i) Calculation of budgeted overhead absorption rates:

Apportionment of overheads to production departments

	Machine shop	Fitting section	Canteen	Machine maintenance section	Total
	(£)	(£)	(£)	(£)	(£)
Allocated overheads	27 660	19 470	16 600	26 650	90 380
Rent, rates, heat and light[a]	9000	3500	2500	2000	17 000
Depreciation and insurance of equipment[a]	12 500	6250	2500	3750	25 000
	49 160	29 220	21 600	32 400	132 380
Service department apportionment					
Canteen[b]	10 800	8400	(21 600)	2400	—
Machine maintenance section	24 360	10 440	—	(34 800)	—
	84 320	48 060	—	—	132 380

Calculation of absorption bases

Product	Budgeted production	Machine shop Machine hours per product	Total machine hours	Fitting section Direct labour cost per product (£)	Total direct wages (£)
X	4200 units	6	25 200	12	50 400
Y	6900 units	3	20 700	3	20 700
Z	1700 units	4	6800	21	35 700
			52 700		106 800

Budgeted overhead absorption rates

Machine shop

$\dfrac{\text{budgeted overheads}}{\text{budgeted machine hours}} = \dfrac{£84\,320}{£52\,700}$
$= £1.60$ per machine hour

Fitting section

$\dfrac{\text{budgeted overheads}}{\text{budgeted direct wages}} = \dfrac{48\,320}{106\,800}$
$= 45\%$ of direct wages

Notes
[a]Rents, rates, heat and light are apportioned on the basis of floor area. Depreciation and insurance of equipment are apportioned on the basis of book value.
[b]Canteen costs are reapportioned according to the number of employees. Machine maintenance section costs are reapportioned according to the percentages given in the question.

(ii) The budgeted manufacturing overhead cost for producing one unit of product X is as follows:

	(£)
Machine shop: 6 hours at £1.60 per hour	9.60
Fittings section: 45% of £12	5.40
	15.00

(b) The answer should discuss the limitations of blanket overhead rates and actual overhead rates. See 'Blanket overhead rates' and 'Budgeted overhead rates' in Chapter 4 for the answer to this question.

4.20 (a) The calculation of the overhead absorption rates are as follows:
Forming department machine hour rate = £6.15 per machine hour (£602 700/98 000 hours)
Finishing department labour hour rate = £2.25 per labour hour (£346 500/154 000 hours)
The forming department is mechanized, and it is likely that a significant proportion of overheads will be incurred as a consequence of employing and running the machines. Therefore a machine hour rate has been used. In the finishing department several grades of labour are used. Consequently the direct wages percentage method is inappropriate, and the direct labour hour method should be used.

(b) The decision should be based on a comparison of the incremental costs with the purchase price of an outside supplier if spare capacity exists. If no spare capacity exists then the lost contribution on displaced work must be considered. The calculation of incremental costs requires that the variable element of the total overhead absorption rate must be calculated. The calculation is:
Forming department variable machine hour rate = £2.05 (£200 900/98 000 hours)
Finishing department variable direct labour hour rate = £0.75 (£115 500/154 000 hours)
The calculation of the variable costs per unit of each component is:

	A (£)	B (£)	C (£)
Prime cost	24.00	31.00	29.00
Variable overheads: Forming	8.20	6.15	4.10
Finishing	2.25	7.50	1.50
Variable unit manufacturing cost	34.45	44.65	34.60
Purchase price	£30	£65	£60

On the basis of the above information, component A should be purchased and components B and C manufactured. This decision is based on the following assumptions:

(i) Variable overheads vary in proportion to machine hours (forming department) and direct labour hours (finishing department).

(ii) Fixed overheads remain unaffected by any changes in activity.

(iii) Spare capacity exists.

For a discussion of make-or-buy decisions see Chapter 11.

(c) Production overhead absorption rates are calculated in order to ascertain costs per unit of output for stock valuation and profit measurement purposes. Such costs are inappropriate for decision-making and cost control. For an explanation of this see the section in Chapter 4 titled 'Different costs for different purposes'.

4.21 (a)

Cost centre	P1 £	P2 £	S1 £	S2 £
Allocated and apportioned overheads	477 550	404 250	132 000	96 000
Reapportionment of S1 (30:65:15)	36 000	78 000	(132 000)	18 000
Reapportionment of S2 (5:3)	71 250	42 750	—	—
	584 800	525 000	—	—
Machine hours (P1)	68 000			
Direct labour hours (P2)		14 000		
Absorption rate:				
Per machine hour	£8.60			
Per direct labour hour		£37.50		

(b) See 'Step 2 – Reallocating the costs assigned to service cost centres to production cost centres' and 'Assignment of direct and indirect costs' in Chapter 4 for the answer to this question.

Chapter 5

5.9 Answer = (b)

5.10 Answer = (d)

5.11 The profits in the financial accounts exceed the profits in the cost accounts by £4 958 (£79 252–£74 294). A stock increase represents a reduction in the cost of sales and thus an increase in profits. Therefore the stock increase in the financial accounts must have been £4 958 greater than the increase in the cost accounts. The stock increase in the cost accounts was £13 937 (£24 053–£10 116) so the increase in the financial accounts was £18 895 (£13 937 + £4 958). Thus, the closing stock in the financial accounts was £28 112 (£9 217 + £18 895).

Answer = (d)

5.12 In the financial accounts there is a total stock decrease of £2 900 (£1000 materials and £1 900 finished goods) and a decrease of £3 200 in the costs accounts (£1 200 materials and £2 000 finished goods). Since a stock decrease represents an increase in cost of goods sold and a decrease in profits the cost accounting profit will be £300 less than the financial accounting profit. In other words, the financial accounting profit will be £300 greater than the cost accounting profit.

Answer = (a)

5.13

	Cost accounts	Financial accounts	Difference
Stock increase	£33 230	£15 601	£17 629

The stock increase shown in the cost accounts is £17 629 more than the increase shown in the financial accounts. Closing stocks represent expenses to be deferred to future accounting periods. Therefore the profit shown in the cost accounts will be £176 129 (£158 500 + £17 629).

Answer = (c)

5.14 Where substantial costs have been incurred on a contract and it is nearing completion the following formula is often used to determine the attributable profit to date:

$$2/3 \times \text{Notional profit} \times \frac{\text{cash received}}{\text{value of work certified}}$$

$$= 2/3 \times (£1.3\text{m} - £1\text{m}) \times £1.2\text{m}/£1.3\text{m} = £276\,923$$

Answer = (b)

5.15 Answer = (a) (Note that if half of the contract is complete the prudence concept advocates that less than half of the profit should be taken).

5.16 Answer = (d)

5.17 The company's cost accounts are not integrated with the financial accounts. For a description of a non-integrated accounting system see 'Interlocking accounts' in Chapter 5. The following accounting entries are necessary:

Cost ledger control account

	(£)			(£)
Sales a/c	410 000	1.5.00	Balance b/f	302 000
Capital under construction a/c	50 150		Stores ledger a/c – Purchases	42 700
Balance c/f	237 500		Wages control a/c	124 000
			Production overhead a/c	152 350
			WIP a/c–Royalty	2150
			Selling overhead a/c	22 000
			Profit	52 450
	697 650			697 650

Stores ledger control account

	(£)		(£)
1.5.00 Balance b/f	85 400	WIP a/c	63 400
Cost ledger control a/c – Purchases	42 700	Production overhead a/c	1450
		Capital a/c	7650
		31.5.X0 Balance c/f	55 600
	£128 100		£128 100

Wages control account

	(£)		(£)
Cost ledger control a/c	124 000	Capital a/c Production	12 500
		Production	35 750
		WIP a/c	7550
	£124 000		£124 000

Production overhead control account

	(£)		(£)
Stores ledger a/c	1450	Capital a/c	30 000
Wages control a/c	35 750	WIP a/c – Absorption (balancing figure)	152 000
Cost ledger control a/c	152 350	Costing P/L a/c (under absorption)	7550
	£189 550		£189 550

Work in progress control account

	(£)		(£)
1.5.00 Balance b/f	167 350	Finished goods control a/c (balancing figure)	281 300
Stores ledger a/c – Issues	63 400		
Wages control a/c	75 750	31.5.%X0 Balance c/f [a]	179 350
Production overhead absorbed	152 000		
Cost ledger control a/c – Royalty	2150		
	£460 650		£460 650

Finished goods control account

	(£)		(£)
1.5.00 Balance b/f	49 250	Cost sales a/cb	328 000
WIP a/c	281300	31.5.X0 Balance c/f	2550
	£330 550		£330 550

Capital under construction account

	(£)		(£)
Stores ledger a/c	7650	Cost ledger control a/c	50 150
Wages control a/c	12 500		
Production overhead absorbed	30 000		
	£50 150		£50 150

Sales account

	(£)		(£)
Costing P/L a/c	£410 000	Cost ledger control a/c	£410 000

Cost of sales account

	(£)		(£)
Finished goods a/c[b]	£328 000	Cost P/L a/c	£328 000

Selling overhead account

	(£)		(£)
Cost ledger control a/c	£22 000	Costing P/L a/c	£22 000

Costing profit and loss account

	(£)		(£)
Selling overhead a/c	22 000	Sales a/c	410 000
Production overhead (under absorbed)	7550		
Cost of sales a/c	328 000		
Profit – Cost ledger control a/c	52 450		
	£410 000		£410 000

Notes
[a] Closing balance of work in progress = £167 350 (opening balance)
£12 000 (increase per question)
£179 350
[b] Transfer from finished goods stock to cost of sales account:
£410000 sales × (100/125) = £328000

5.18 (a) Stores ledger control account

	(£)		(£)
Opening balances b/f	24 175	Materials issued:	
Creditors – materials purchased	76 150	Work in progress control	26 350
		Production overhead control	3280
		Closing stock c/f	70 695
	£100 325		£100 325

Wages control account

	(£)		(£)
Direct wages:		WIP	15 236
Wages accrued a/c	17 646	Capital equipment a/c	2670
Employees' contributions a/c	4364	Factory overhead (idle time)	5230
Indirect wages:	3342	Factory overhead (indirect wages)	4232
Wages accrued a/c			
Employees' contributions a/c	890		
Balances (Wages accrued a/c)	1126		
	27 368		27 368

Work in progress control account

	(£)		(£)
Opening balance b/f	19 210	Finished goods control – cost of goods	
Stores ledger – materials issued	26 350	transferred	62 130
Wages control direct wages	15 236	Closing stock c/f	24 360
Production overhead control:	22 854		
overhead absorbed (15 236 × 150%)			
Profit and loss a/c: stock gain[a]	2840		
	£86 490		£86 490

Finished goods control account

	(£)		(£)
Opening balance b/f	34 164	Profit and loss a/c: cost of sales	59 830
Working in progress: cost of goods sold	62 130	Closing stock c/f (difference)	36 464
	£96 294		£96 294

Production overhead control account

	(£)		(£)
Prepayments b/f	2100	Work in progress:	
Stores ledger: materials issued for repairs	3280	absorbed overheads (15 236 × 150%)	22 854
Wages control: idle time of direct workers	5230	Capital under construction a/c: overheads absorbed (2670 × 150%)	4005
Wages control: indirect workers' wages (3342 + 890)	4232	Profit and loss a/c: underabsorbed overhead balance	183
Cash/creditors: other overheads incurred	12 200		
	£27 042		£27 042

Profit and loss account

	(£)		(£)
Cost of goods sold	59 830	Sales	75 400
Gross profit c/f	15 570		
	£75 400		75 400
Selling and distribution overheads		Gross profit b/f	15 570
	5240	Stock gain[a]: WIP control	2840
Production overhead control: underabsorbed overhead	183		
Net profit c/f	12 987		
	£18 410		£18 410

Notes

[a]The stock gain represents a balancing figure. It is assumed that the stock gain arises from ___ ___ count of closing stocks at the end of the period.

Note that value of materials transferred between batches will be recorded in the subsidiary records, but will not affect the control (total) accounts.

(b) **(i)** Large increase in raw material stocks. Is this due to maintaining uneconomic stock levels or is it due to an anticipated increase in production to meet future demand?

(ii) WIP stock gain.

(iii) Idle time, which is nearly 25% of the total direct wages cost.

(iv) The gross direct wages are £22 010 (£17 646 + £4364), but the allocation amounts to £23136 (£15 236 + £5230 + £2670).

(c) Stocks are valued at the end of the period because they represent unexpired costs, which should not be matched against sales for the purpose of calculating profits. Stocks represent unexpired costs, which must be valued for inclusion in the balance sheet. Manufacturing expense items such as factory rent are included in the stock valuations because they represent resources incurred in transforming the materials into a more valuable finished product. The UK financial accounting regulations (SSAP 9) states that 'costs of stocks (and WIP) should comprise those costs which have been incurred in bringing the product to its present location and condition, including all related production overheads.'

5.19 (a) Raw materials stores account

	(£)		(£)
Balance b/d	49 500	Work in progress	104 800
Purchases	108 800	Loss due to flood to P&L a/c	2400
		Balance c/d	51 100
	£158 300		£158 300
Balance b/d	51 100		

Work in progress control account

	(£)		(£)
Balance b/d	60 100	Finished goods	222 500
Raw materials	104 800	Balance c/d	56 970
Direct wages	40 200		
Production overhead	74 370		
	£279 470		£279 470
Balance b/d	56 970		

Finished goods control account

	(£)		(£)
Balance b/d	115 400	Cost of sales	212 100
Work in progress	222 500	Balance c/d	125 800
	£337 900		£337 900
Balance b/d	125 800		

Production overhead

	(£)		(£)
General ledger control	60 900	Work in progress (185% × £40 200)	74 370
Notional rent (3 × £4000)	12 000		
Overhead over absorbed	1470		
	£74 370		£74 370

General ledger control account

	(£)		(£)
Sales	440 000	Balance b/d (49 500 + 60 100 + 115 400)	225 000
Balance c/d	233 870		
		Purchases	108 800
		Direct wages	40 200
		Production overhead	60 900
		Notional rent	12 000
		P & L a/c (profit for period: see (b))	226 970
	673 870		673 870

(b) *Calculation of profit in cost accounts*

	(£)	(£)
Sales		440 000
Cost of sales	212 000	
Loss of stores	2400	
Less overhead over absorbed	214 500	
Profit	1470	213 030
		226 970

Reconciliation statement[a]

	(£)	(£)	(£)
Profit as per cost accounts			226 970
Differences in stock values:			
Raw materials opening stock	1500		
Raw materials closing stock	900		
WIP closing stock	1030	3430	
WIP opening stock	3900		
Finished goods opening stock	4600		
Finished goods closing stock	3900	(12 400)	(8970)
Add items not included in financial accounts:			
Notional rent		12 000	
Profit as per financial accounts		230 000	

Note

[a]Stock valuations in the financial accounts may differ from the valuation in the cost accounts. For example, raw materials may be valued on a LIFO basis in the cost accounts, whereas FIFO or weighted average may be used in the financial accounts. WIP and finished stock may be valued on a marginal (variable costing) basis in the cost accounts, but the valuation may be based on an absorption costing basis in the financial accounts. To reconcile the profits, you should start with the profit from the cost accounts and consider what the impact would be on the profit calculation if the financial accounting stock valuations were used. If the opening stock valuation in the financial accounts exceeds the valuation in the cost accounts then adopting the financial accounting stock valuation will reduce the profits. If the closing stock valuation in the financial accounts exceeds the valuation in the cost accounts then adopting the financial accounting stock valuation will increase profits. Note that the notional rent is not included in the financial accounts and should therefore be deducted from the costing profit in the reconciliation statement.

(c) The over recovery of overhead could be apportioned between cost of goods sold for the current period and closing stocks. The justification for this is based on the assumption that the under/over recovery is due to incorrect estimates of activity and overhead expenditure, which leads to incorrect allocations being made to the cost of sales and closing stock accounts. The proposed adjustment is an attempt to rectify this incorrect allocation. The alternative treatment is for the full amount of the under/over recovery to be written off to the cost accounting profit and loss account in the current period as a period cost. This is the treatment recommended by SSAP 9.

5.20 (a) *HR Construction plc – Contract Accounts*

	A (£000)	B (£000)		A (£000)	B (000)
Stores	700	150	Stores returns	80	30
Plant	1000	150	Transfers to B	40	—
Transfers from A	—	40	Materials c/fwd	75	15
Plant hire	200	30	Plant c/fwd[a]	880	144
Labour	300	270	Cost of work not certified c/fwd	160	20
Overhead	75	18			
Direct expenses	25	4	Balance – Cost of work certified c/fwd	1065	453
	2300	662		2300	662
Cost of work certified b/fwd	1065	453	Attributable sales revenue[c]	1545	420
			Loss recognized this period[b]		33
Profit recognized this period[b]	480				
	1545	453		1545	453
Cost of work not certified c/fwd	160	20			
Plant b/fwd	880	144			
Materials b/fwd	75	15			

Notes

[a]Value at the start of the year less one year's depreciation for Contract A and 3 months' depreciation for Contract B.

[b]The profits/(losses) recognized for the period are calculated as follows:

	Contract A (£000)	Contract B (£000)
Cost of work certified	1065	453
Cost of work not certified	160	20
Estimated costs to complete	135	110
Estimated cost of the contracts	1360	583
Contract price	2000	550
Estimated profit/(loss)	640	(33)

Profit recognized (Value certified (1500)/Contract price (£2000) × £640 = £480 000 for Contract A).

An alternative more prudent approach would have been to multiply the estimated profit by cash received/contract price.

Applying the prudence concept the full anticipated loss is recognized in the current period.

[c]Profit recognized plus cost of work certified for A Cost of work certified less loss recognized for B.

(b) *Balance sheet extracts*

	Contract A (£000)	Contract B (£000)
Fixed assets		
Plant at cost	1000	150
Depreciation	120	6
Written down value	880	144
Debtors		
Attributable sales	1545	420
Less cash received	1440	460
	105	(40)
Work-in-progress		
Total costs incurred to date	1225	473
Included in cost of sales	1065	453
	160	20

The loss of 33 000 for Contract A will be shown as a deduction from the total company profits. Alternatively, the loss can be deducted from the total costs incurred to date thus reflecting the fact that £33 000 of the total losses have been recognized during the current period.

(c) See 'job costing systems and process costing systems' in Chapter 6 and 'contract costing' in Chapter 5 for the answer to this question.

Chapter 6

6.11

	Units
Opening stock	400
Input	3000
	3400
Closing stock	(200)
Actual losses (normal + abnormal)	(400)
Output	2800

Answer = (a)

6.12 The input cost consists of materials of £9000 plus conversion costs of £13 340 giving a total of £22 340.

Cost per unit =

$$\frac{\text{Input cost (£22 340) less scrap value of normal loss } (100 \times £3)}{\text{Expected output } (200 \times 0.95 = 1900 \text{ units})}$$

= £11.60

Answer = (b)

6.13 Abnormal gain debited to process account and credited to abnormal gain account:

	(£)	(£)
Materials (160 × £9.40)	1504	
Conversion cost (160 × 0.75 × £11.20)	1344	
		2848
Lost sales of scrap (180 × £2)		(360)
Net cost credited to profit and loss account		2528

Answer = (c)

6.14 Input = Opening WIP (2000 units)
+ Material input (24 000) = 26 000
Output = Completed units (19 500) + Closing WIP (3000)
+ Normal Loss (2400) = 24 900
Abnormal Loss = 1100 units
(Balance of 26 000 – 24 900)

Equivalent units (FIFO)

	Completed units less Opening WIP equiv.units	Closing WIP equiv. units	Abnormal loss equiv. units	Total equiv. units
Materials	17 500 (19 500 − 2000)	3000 (100%)	1100 (100%)	21 600
Conversion	18 700 (19 500 − 800)	1350 (45%)	1100 (100%)	21 150

It is assumed that losses are detected at the end of the process and that the answer should adopt the short-cut method and ignore the normal loss in the cost per unit calculations.
Answer = (c)

6.15 Closing stock = Opening stock (Nil) + Input (13 500)
– Completed units (11 750) = 1750 units

It is assumed that materials are fully complete (£5.75) and labour and overheads are partly complete (£2.50)
Value of closing stock = (1750 × £5.75)
+ (1750 × £2.50) = £14 437.50
Answer = (b)

6.16 *Process F*
Expected output = 59 800 (0.92 × 65 000)
Actual output = 58 900
Abnormal loss = 900
Process G
Expected output = 35 625
Actual output = 35 700
Abnormal gain = 75
Answer = (c)

6.17 Input = Opening WIP (2400) + Material input
(58 000) = 60 400 litres
Output = Completed units (52 500) + Normal loss
(5% × 58 000 = 2900) + Closing WIP (3000)
= 58 400
Abnormal loss = 60 400 – 58 400 = 2000 litres

It is assumed that the short-cut method described in Appendix 6.1 is adopted whereby the normal loss is not included in the equivalent units calculation. The computation of equivalent units is as follows:

Cost element	Completed units	Abnormal loss equivalent units	Closing WIP equivalent units	Total equivalent units
Materials	52 500	2000	3000	57 500
Conversion cost	52 500	2000	1500	56 000

Answer = (d)

6.18 **(a)** The debit side (input) indicates that 4000 units were input into the process but the output recorded on the credit side is 3850 units thus indicating that the balance must represent an abnormal loss of 150 units. The accounting entries for abnormal losses are to debit the abnormal loss account and credit the process account. Therefore the answer is A.

(b) and **(c)**
The calculation of the closing WIP value and the cost of finished goods is as follows:

Cost element	Total cost ($)	Completed units	Abnormal loss equivalent units	Closing WIP equivalent units	Total equivalent units	Cost per unit ($)	Closing WIP ($)
Materials[a]	15 300	2750	150	700	3600	4.25	2 975.00
Labour	8125	2750	150	350	3250	2.50	875.00
Production overhead	3498	2750	150	280	3180	1.10	308.00
	27 923					7.85	4 158.00

Finished goods (2750 × $7.85) 21 587.50
Abnormal loss (150 × $7.85) 1177.50
27 923.00

Note

[a]£16 000 materials less £700 scrap value of the normal loss. The above computation is based on the short-cut method described in the Appendix of Chapter 6.

Therefore the answer is B for part both parts (b) and (c).

6.19 **(a)** Input = 15 000 (14 000 + 3000 − 2000)
Answer = (c)

(b) Equivalent production for materials
= 14 000 completed units − opening WIP (2000) + closing WIP (3000) = 15 000 units
Materials cost per unit = £3.40 (£51 000/15 000)
Equivalent production for conversion costs
= 14 000 completed units − opening WIP (2000 × 0.6) + closing WIP (3000 × 0.3)
= 13 700 units
Cost per unit = £14.10 (£193 170/13 700)

Closing stock = (3000 × £3.40) + (900 × £14.10)
= £22 890
Answer = (d)

6.20 **(a)** Closing WIP = 160 units (200 + 1000 − 1040)
WIP value = £1280 (160 × 0.40 × £20)
Answer = (b)

(b) Completed production equivalent units
= 960 [1040 − (0.4 × 200)]
Cost of completed production = (960 × £20) + £1530 opening WIP = £20 730
Answer = (c)

6.21 The normal loss is 180 units (10% of 1800 units) and the actual loss is 180 units. Therefore there are no abnormal losses in process. It is assumed that the sale proceeds from the normal loss relates primarily to the materials input. Hence the sales proceeds are deducted from materials in the unit cost calculation. Assuming that losses occur prior to the WIP stage of completion it is appropriate to use the short cut method to compute the unit costs. The calculations are as follows:

Cost element	Total cost (£)	Completed units	WIP equiv. units	Total equiv. units	Cost per unit (£)
Materials	484 000[a]	1920	500	2420	200
Labour	322 320[b]	1920	450	2370	136
Overhead costs	156 880[b]	1920	200	2120	74
					410

Notes
[a]Opening WIP plus current cost less sales value of normal loss
[b]Opening WIP plus current cost

Cost of completed production = 1920 units × £410
= £787200

6.22 **(a)**

	Litres	£	Process 1	Litres	£
Input	50 000	365 000	Output (W1)	47 000	634 500
Conversion		265 000	Normal loss (0.08 × 50 000)	4000	—
Abnormal gain (W2)	1000	13 500			
	51 000	634 500		51 000	634 500

Workings
W1 Cost per litre =
(£365 000 + £256 000)/(0.92 × 50 000) = £13.50
Completed production = 47 000 × £13.50 = £634 500
W2 (50 000 × 0.92) expected production
compared with an actual production of 46 000 litres

(b)

Cost element	Current period costs (£)	Completed units less opening WIP equiv. units	Closing WIP equiv. units	Current total equiv. units (£)	Cost per unit (£)
Previous process cost	634 500	45 000	2000	47 000	13.50
Conversion cost	392 000	48 000	1000	49 000	8.00

(i) Cost of completed production = opening WIP
(£80 000) + previous process cost (45 000 × £13.50)
+ conversion cost (48 000 × £8) = £1 071 500

(ii) Value of closing WIP
= previous process cost (2000 × £13.50)
+ conversion cost (1000 × £8) = £35 000

(c) The disposal costs should be debited to the process account as an expense of the process

6.23 (a) Opening WIP (100) + input − closing WIP (200)
= Normal loss (0.10 × input) + output (1250)
Input − Normal loss (0.10 × input)
= 1250 − 100 + 200
0.90 input = 1350
Input = 1500 (1350/0.9)

(b) The short cut approach is adopted resulting in the normal loss not being included in the calculation of equivalent units (see Appendix 6.1).

	Completed units less opening WIP equivalent units	Closing WIP equiv. units	Current total equiv. units
Materials	1150 (1250 − 100)	200	1350
Conversion cost	1220 (1250 − 30)	80 (200 × 40%)	1300

(c) Cost per unit =
Input cost/current total equivalent units
Conversion cost = 1300 × £1.50 = £1950
With materials the normal loss will be deducted from the input cost to derive the cost per unit so that:
Materials = 1350 × £2.60 = £3510 + (10% × 1500 × £2)
= £3810

6.24 (a) *Calculation of input for process 1*

	(litres)	(£)
Opening stock	4000	10 800
Receipts	20 000	61 000
Less closing stock	(8000)	(24 200)
Process input	16 000	47 600

Output	(litres)
Completed units	8000
Closing WIP	5600
Normal loss (15% of input)	2400
	16 000

Because input is equal to output, there are no abnormal gains or losses.

Calculation of cost per unit (Process 1)
It is assumed that the loss occurs at the point of inspection. Because WIP has passed the inspection point, the normal loss should be allocated to both completed units and WIP. The calculation using the short-cut method is as follows:

Element of cost	Completed units (£)	Closing WIP	Total equiv. units	Cost per unit (£)	WIP (£)
Materials	47 600	8000	5600	13 600	3.50	19 600
Conversion cost	21 350	8000	4200	12 200	1.75	7350
					£5.25	£26 950

Completed units 8000 × £5.25 = £42 000

Process 1 account – May

	(litres)	(£)		(litres)	(£)
Materials	16 000	47 600	Transfers to process 2	8000	42 000
Labour		4880	Normal loss	2400	—
Direct expenses		4270	Closing stock C/f	5600	26 950
Overheads absorbed		12 200			
	16 000	68 950		16 000	68 950

With process 2, there is no closing WIP. Therefore it is unnecessary to express output in equivalent units. The cost per unit is calculated as follows:

$$\frac{\text{cost of production less scrap value of normal loss}}{\text{expected output}}$$

$$= \frac{£54000^a}{(90\% \times 8000)} = £7.50$$

Note

[a] Cost of production = transferred in cost from process 1 (42 000) + labour (£6000) + overhead (£6000)

Process 2 account

	Litres	(£)		Litres	(£)
Transferred from Process	1 8000	42 000	Finished goods store[b]	7500	56 250
Labour		6000	Normal loss	800	
Overheads absorbed		6000	Closing stock	–	–
Abnormal gain[a]	300	2250			
	8300	56 250		8300	56 250

Finished goods account

	Litres	(£)
Ex Process 2	7500	56 250

Abnormal gain account

	(£)		Litres	(£)
Profit and loss account	2 250	Process 2 account	300	2250

Notes
a Input = 8000 litres.
  Normal output = 90% × 8000 litres = 7200 litres.
  Actual output = 7500 litres.
  Abnormal gain = 300 litres × £7.50 per litre = £2250
b 7500 litres at × £7.50 per litre.

6.25 (a)

Process G Account

	Litres	£		Litres	£
Opening WIP	2000	24 600	Output (W4): Ex opening WIP	2000	
Costs arising:			Started and finished in month		
Direct materials	12 500	99 600		8000	
Conversion		155 250		10 000	221 520
			Normal loss (0.08 × 12 500)	1000	3000
			Abnormal loss (W2)	500	11 100
			Closing WIP (W3)	3000	43 830
	14 500	279 450		14 500	279 450

Workings
W1 Calculation of cost per equivalent unit

Cost element	Current period costs (£)	Completed units less opening WIP equiv. units	Closing WIP equiv. units	Abnormal loss equiv. units[a]	Current total equiv. units (£)	Cost per unit (£)
Materials	96 600[b]	8000	3000	500	11 500	8.40
Conversion cost	155 250	9400	1350	500	11 250	13.80

Notes
[a] £99 600 current period cost – scrap value of normal loss (12 500 × 0.08 × £3)

[b] Input = Opening WIP (2000 litres) + Material input (12 500) = 14 500

Output = Completed unit (10 000) + Closing WIP (3000) + Normal Loss (1000) = 14 000

Abnormal Loss = 500 units (Balance of 14 500 – 14 000)

W2 Value of abnormal loss = 500 × (£8.40 + £13.80)
$$= £11 100$$

W3 Value of closing stock = (3 000 × £8.40) + (1350 × £13.80) = £43 830

W4 Value of completed production = (8000 × £8.40) + (9400 × £13.80) + Opening WIP (£24 600) = £221 520

(b) Organizations where it would be appropriate to use service costing include hospitals and hotels. Typical cost units include inpatient days and occupied rooms per night.

Chapter 7

7.10 Joint costs to be allocated = $140 000
less by product revenues (6000 × $3) = $122 000
Sales value of X = $125 000 (2500 × $50)
Sales value of Y = $210 000 (3500 × $60)
Total sales value = $335 000
Costs allocated to X = ($125 000/$335 000 × $122 000) + $24 000 = $69 522
Costs allocated to Y = ($210 000/335 000 × $122 000) + $46 000 = $122 478

7.11 Production = units sold + closing stock – opening stock
J = 6000 + 300 – 100 = 6200
K = 4000 + 200 – 400 = 3800
Apportioned to J = (6200/10 000) × £110 000 = £68 200
Answer = (d)

7.12 Sales value of production:
W = $120 000 (12 000 × $10)
X = $120 000 (10 000 × £12)

Joint costs will therefore be apportioned to each product in the ratio of 1:1 so the amount apportioned to product X will be $388 080 ($776 160/2)
Closing inventory of X = $77 616 (0.2 × $388 080)
Answer = (d)

7.13 Answer = (d)

7.14 Sales value after further processing = (9000 × 0.9) × £12 = £97 200
Sales value without further processing = (9000 × £10) = £90 000
Increase in sales revenue £7200
Further processing cost = £9000 (9000 × £1)

Decrease in profit by further processing £1800

Answer = (d)

7.15 (a) See Chapters 6 and 7 for an explanation of the meaning of each of these terms.

(b) No specific apportionment method is asked for in this problem. It is recommended that the joint costs should be apportioned (see Chapter 7) according to the sales value at split-off point:

Product	Sales value (£)	Proportion to total (%)	Joint costs apportioned (£)
A	60 000	20	40 000
B	40 000	13.33	26 660
C	200 000	66.67	133 340
	300 000	100.00	200 000

(c) Assuming all of the output given in the problem can be sold, the initial process is profitable – the sales revenue is £300 000 and the joint costs are £200 000. To determine whether further processing is profitable the additional revenues should be compared with the additional relevant costs:

	A (£)	B (£)	C (£)
Additional relevant revenues	10 (20 – 10)	4 (8 – 4)	6 (16 – 10)
Additional relevant costs	14	2	6
Excess of relevant revenue over costs	(4)	2	—

Product B should be processed further, product A should not be processed further, and if product C is processed further, then profits will remain unchanged.

7.16 (a)

Process G

	Litres	£		Litres	£
			Output (W3)		
Raw material	60 000	381 000			
Direct labour		180 000	P1 (W4)	36 250	507 500
Direct expenses		54 000	P2 (W4)	21 750	304 500
Production overheads (W1)		198 000	Normal loss (W2)	3000	15 000
Abnormal gain (W4)	1000	14 000			
	61 000	827 000		61 000	827 000

Workings

W1 Production overheads = 110% × 180 000
    = £198 000

W2 Normal loss = 5% × 60 000 = 3000 litres at £5
    = £15 000

W3 Total output = 61 000 (input + abnormal gain)
    – 3000 normal loss = 58 000 litres
P1 and P2 is produced in the ratio 5 : 3
P1 = (5/8) × 58 000 = 36 250 litres
P2 = (3/8) × 58 000 = 21 750 litres

W4 Cost per litre:
   Net total cost = Input cost (381 000 + 180 000 + 54 000
   + 198 000) – value of normal loss 15 000 = £798 000
   Expected output = 60 000 × 95% = 57 000 litres
   Cost per litre = £798 000/57 000 = £14
   Abnormal gain = 1000 × £14 = £14 000

Joint products:
P1 36 250 × £14 = £507 500
P2 21 750 × £14 = £304 500

(b) Each 100 litres of product P1 sold at point of split-off without further processing generates revenue of £2000 (100 × £20)
The revenue (from PP1) arising from further processing is £2340 (100 × 0.9) × £26 resulting in additional revenue of £340 but the additional cost of further processing is £400 (100 × £4).
Therefore product P1 should not be further processed into product PP1.

(c) (i) Direct expenses are costs, other than material and labour, which are specifically identifiable with process G. An example of such a cost would be the cost of hiring special equipment that is required only for process G.

(c) (ii) Production overheads are general factory wide costs that cannot be specifically identified with individual processes.

7.17 (a)

Process K account

	Litres	£		Litres	£
Materials input	90 000	450 000	Normal loss (4% × 90 000)	3600	18 00
Conversion costs		216 000	Abnormal loss [W1] (4 800 – 3 600)	1200	9000
			Output:		
			Product P1 [W2]	56 800	355 000
			Product P2 [W2]	28 400	284 000
	90 000	666 000		90 000	666 000

W1 The expected output is 86 400 litres (90 000 × 0.96) and the actual output is 85 200 litres resulting in an abnormal loss of 1200 litres.
Cost per unit of output = Input cost (£666 000 – value of normal loss of £18 000) divided by the expected output of 86 400 litres = £7.50
Abnormal loss valuation = £9000 (1200 × 7.50)

W2 The total output (85 200) is in the ratio 2 :1 (P1 : P2)
giving 56 800 litres of P1 and 28 400 litres of P2
The combined total output of P1 and P2 is valued at
£639 000 (85 200 × 7.50) and is allocated to P1 and P2 in
the ratio of the sales value of production.
P1 : P2 = (56 800 × £25) : (28 400 × £40) = 1.25 : 1
Product P1 valuation = (1.25/2.25) × £639 000 = £355 000
Product P2 valuation = (1.00/2.25) × £639 000 = £284 000

(b) Each 100 litres of product P1 sold at point of split-off without further processing generates revenue of £2500 (100 × £25)
The revenue (from XP1) arising from further processing is £2760 [(100 × 0.92) × £30] resulting in additional revenue of £260 but the additional cost of further processing is £300 (100 × £3).
Therefore product P1 should not be further processed into product XP1.

Chapter 8

8.9 Fixed overhead rate = £250 per unit
Inventories decreased by 300 units resulting in an extra £75 000 (300 × £250) being charged as a production cost with an absorption costing system. Therefore profits will be £75 000 lower with an absorption costing system (i.e. Answer = (b))

8.10 When production volume equals sales volume marginal (variable) and absorption costing profit s will be identical. Production exceeds sales by 2000 units resulting in additional manufacturing overheads of £9000 (2000 × £63 000/14 000) being deferred as an expense and included in the closing stock valuation. Therefore profits will be £9000 lower with the variable costing system (i.e. £27 000) so the answer will be B.

8.11 The difference between the marginal (variable) costing loss and the absorption costing profit is $5000. The absorption costing profit is higher indicating that there was an increase in inventories arising from production volume exceeding sales volume. Given that the fixed production cost is $2 per unit production will have exceeded sales by 2500 units ($5000/$2) so that actual production was 12 500 units. Therefore Answer = (d)

8.12 Because closing inventory exceeds opening inventory, production exceeds sales so that absorption costing will be greater than the marginal costing profit by the amount of fixed overheads included in the increase in inventories. Therefore the absorption profit is:
Marginal costing profit (37 500) + fixed overheads *included in the increase in inventories* (£4 × 250 units) = £38 500.
Answer = (c)

8.13 **(a)** Fixed overheads per unit = $15 000/10 000 units = $1.50
Production exceeds sales so that absorption costing will be greater than the marginal costing profit by the amount of fixed overheads included in the increase in inventories. Therefore the absorption profit will exceed the marginal costing profit by $750 (500 units × $1.50).
Answer = (iii)

(b)

	$	$
Sales (10 300 × $6.40)		65 920
Cost of sales:		
Variable costs (10 300 × $3.60)	37 080	
Fixed overheads (10 300 × $1.50)	15 450	
	52 530	
Under-absorbed fixed overheads	700	53 230
($15 700 – $15 000)		
Profit		12 690

Answer = (ii)

8.14 The profit difference is due to the fixed overheads being incorporated in the stock movements with the absorption costing system.
Profit difference = £9750 (£60 150 – £50 400)
Fixed overheads in stock movement = £9750
Physical stock movement = 1500 units
Fixed overhead rate per unit = £9750/1500 units = £6.50

Answer = (d)

8.15 **(a)**

	£000	£000
Sales (24 000)		864
Less: Production cost of sales:		
Opening stock (3000 × 28) [W1]	84	
Production (22 000 × 28)	616	
Closing stock (1000 × 28)	(28)	
	—	(672)
		192
Less: Under absorption of fixed production overhead cost [W2] (3 000 × 5)		(15)
Gross profit		177
Less: Non-production costs:		
Variable selling cost	60	
Fixed selling and admin costs	40	
	—	(100)
Net profit		77

Workings
W1 Variable production cost per unit
= £23 (£506 000/22 000 units)
Fixed production overhead cost per unit
= £5 (£125 000/5000 units)
Total production cost per unit = £28

W2 3000 units (normal production of 25 000 units less actual production of 22 000 units) at £3 per unit.

(b)

	£000
Absorption costing net profit	77
Fixed production overheads included in the	10
stock decrease (2000 × £5)	—
Marginal costing profit	87

(c) Marginal costing is likely to be more relevant for short-term decision-making since it requires the segregation of costs into their fixed and variable elements. For short-term decisions fixed costs are likely to be irrelevant so a costing system that highlights such costs is required.

8.16

	(£)
Calculation of product cost	
Materials	10
Labour	2
Variable production cost	12
Variable distribution cost	1
Total variable cost	13
Fixed overhead (£10 000/1000 units)	10
Total costs	23

The product costs for stock valuation purposes are as follows:

Variable costing   £12 (variable production cost)
Absorption costing £22 (variable production cost + fixed manufacturing overhead)

It is assumed that all of the fixed overhead relates to production. Note that the distribution cost is per unit *sold* and not per unit *produced*.

(a)

(i) *Variable costing*

	t_1	t_2	t_3
Opening stock	1200	1200	1200
Production	12 000	12 000	12 000
	13 200	13 200	13 200
Closing stock	1200	1200	1200
Cost of sales	12 000	12 000	12 000
Sales at £25 per unit	25 000	25 000	25 000
Gross profit	13 000	13 000	13 000
Distribution costs	1000	1000	1000
Fixed labour costs	5000	5000	5000
Fixed overhead costs	5000	5000	5000
Net profit	£2000	£2000	£2000

Total profit £6 000

Absorption costing

	t_1 (£)	t_2 (£)	t_3 (£)
Opening stock	2200	2200	2200
Production	22 000	22 000	22 000
	24 200	24 200	24 200
Closing stock	2200	2200	2200
Cost of sales	22 000	22 000	22 000
Sales at £25 per unit	25 000	25 000	25 000
Gross profit	3000	3000	3000
Distribution cost	1000	1000	1000
Net profit	£2000	£2000	£2000

Total profit £6000

(ii) *Variable costing*

	t_1 (£)	t_2 (£)	t_3 (£)
Opening stock	1200	7200	4800
Production	18 000	9600	8400
	19 200	16 800	13 200
Closing stock	7200	4800	1200
Cost of sales	12 000	12 000	12 000
Sales at £25 per unit	25 000	25 000	25 000
Gross profit	13 000	13 000	13 000
Distribution costs	1000	1000	1000
Fixed labour costs	5000	5000	5000
Fixed overhead costs	5000	5000	5000
Net profit	£2000	£2000	£2000

Total profit £6000

Absorption costing	t_1 (£)	t_2 (£)	t_3 (£)
Opening stock	2200	13 200	8800
Production	33 000	17 600	15 400
	35 200	30 800	24 200
Under/(over) recovery	(5 000)	2000	3000
	30 200	32 800	27 200
Closing stock	13 200	8800	2200
Cost of sales	17 000	24 000	25 000
Sales at £25 per unit	25 000	25 000	25 000
Gross profit	8000	1000	—
Distribution cost	1000	1000	1000
Net profit	£7000	—	£(1000)

Total profit £6 000

(iii) *Variable costing*

	t_1 (£)	t_2 (£)	t_3 (£)
Opening stock	1200	7200	4800
Production	12 000	12 000	12 000
	13 200	19 200	16 800
Closing stock	7200	4800	1200
Cost of sales	6000	14 400	15 600
Sales at £25 per unit	12 500	30 000	32 500
Gross profit	6500	15 600	16 900
Distribution costs	500	1200	1300
Fixed labour costs	5000	5000	5000
Fixed overhead costs	5000	5000	5000
Net profit	£(4000)	£4400	£5600

Total profit £6000

Absorption costing

	t₁ (£)	t₂ (£)	t₃ (£)
Opening stock	2200	13 200	8800
Production	22 000	22 000	22 000
	24 200	35 200	30 800
Closing stock	13 200	8800	2200
Cost of sales	11 000	26 400	28 600
Sales at £25 per unit	12 500	30 000	32 500
Gross profit	1500	3600	3900
Distribution cost	500	1200	1300
Net profit	£1000	£2400	£2600

Total profit £6000

(b) For the answer to this question see Chapter 8: Note that profits are identical for both systems in (i), since production equals sales. In (ii) and (iii) profits are higher with absorption costing when production exceeds sales, whereas profits are higher with variable costing when production is less than sales. Taking the three periods as a whole there is no change in the level of opening stock in t_x compared with the closing stock in t_3, so that the disclosed profit for the three periods is the same under both systems. Also note that the differences in profits disclosed in (a) (ii) and (a) (iii) is accounted for in the fixed overheads included in the stock valuation changes.

Chapter 9

9.10 Answer = (b)

9.11 **(a)** Answer = (a)

(b) The increase in fixed costs will result in an increase in the break-even point. The only correct alternative that is listed is item C. This indicates an increase in the break-even point sales value.

9.12 **(a)** An increase in fixed costs will result in a lower break-even point (i.e. the number of units sold to break even). Therefore t will decrease. Answer = (iii)

(b) The slope of the profit line is represented by the change in contribution per unit. The diagram indicates that sales are 800 units in excess of the break-even point (represented by t) and these 800 units generate a profit of $16 000 (represented by w). Profit is equal to contribution above the break-even point so the contribution per unit is $20 ($16 000/800 units). Additional sales can thus be expected to generate an additional contribution and profit of $28 000 (1400 units × $20). Answer = (iii)

9.13 At zero activity the loss of $60 000 will be equivalent to the fixed costs for the period. The profit when sales revenue is $500 000 is $140 000 and the contribution is $200 000 ($140 000 + $60 000). Therefore the contribution to sales ratio is 40% ($200 000/$500 000) so the answer is C.

9.14 BEP = Fixed costs/PV ratio
PV ratio = Contribution/Sales = £275 × 000/£500 000
$$= 0.55$$
BEP = £165 × 000/0.55 = £300 000

Answer = (d)

9.15 Required sales revenue =

$$\frac{\text{Fixed costs (£75 000)} + \text{Target profit (£75 000)}}{\text{PV ratio (0.75)}}$$

=£300 000
Units of output = £300 000/£10 unit selling price
$$= 30 000 \text{ units}$$

Answer = (d)

9.16 Break-even point in units = £18 000 sales/ unit selling price (£15) = 1200 units
Contribution per unit sold = £15 × 0.4 = £6
Profit when 1500 units are sold = (1500 − 1200) × £6 = £1800

Answer = (b)

9.17 Variable costs are 60% of the selling price and the variable cost per unit is £36 so the selling price per unit is £36/0.6 = £60
Contribution per unit = £24 (£60 × 0.4)
Break-even point = Fixed costs (£81 × 000)/ contribution per unit (£24) = 3375 units
Margin of safety = 1625 units (5000 weekly sales − 3375 units break-even point)

Answer = (a)

9.18 Variable costs are 60% of the selling price and the variable cost per unit is £24 so the selling price per unit is £24/0.6 = £40
Contribution per unit = £16 (£40 × 0.4)
Break-even point = Fixed costs (£720 000)/ contribution per unit (£16) = 45 000 units

Answer = (d)

9.19 Contribution/sales (%) = (0.33 × 40% Aye) + (0.33 × 50% Bee) + (0.33 × ? Cee) = 48% Cee = 54% (Balancing figure)
The total contribution/sales ratio for the revised sales mix is : (0.40 × 40% Aye) + (0.25 × 50% Bee) + (0.35 × 54% Cee) = 47.4%

Answer = (c)

9.20 (a)

Budgeted contribution per unit = $11.60 – $3.40 – (5% × $11.60) = $7.62
Break-even point (units)   = ($430 500 + 198 150)/$7.62 = 82 500 units
Break-even point (sales value) = 82 500 × $$11.60 = $957 000
Budgeted sales   = $1 044 000 (90 000 × $11.60)
Margin of safety ($)   = $1 044 000 – $957 000 = $87 000
Margin of safety (%)   = $87 000/$1 044 000 = 8.33%

Answer = (b)

(b)

Budgeted contribution per unit = $12.25 – $3.40 – (8% × $12.25) = $7.87
Break-even point (units) = ($430 500 + 198 150)/$7.87 = 79 879 units

Answer = (c)

9.21 *Preliminary calculations:*

	Sales (units)	Profit/(loss)
November	30 000	£40 000
December	35 000	£60 000
Increase	5000	£20 000

An increase in sales of 5000 units increases contribution (profits) by £20 000. Therefore contribution is £4 per unit. Selling price is £10 per unit (given) and variable cost per unit will be £6. At £30 000 unit sales:

Contribution minus Fixed costs = Profit
£120 000   minus ?   = £40 000
∴ Fixed costs = £80 000

The above information can now be plotted on a graph. A break-even chart or a profit-volume graph could be constructed. A profit-volume graph avoids the need to calculate the profits since the information can be read directly from the graph. (See Figure 1 for a break-even chart and Figure 2 for a profit-volume graph.)

(a) **(i)** Fixed costs = £80 000.
  (ii) Variable cost per unit = £6.
  (iii) Profit – volume =

$$\frac{\text{Contribution per unit (£4)}}{\text{Selling price per unit (£10)}} \times 100 = 40\%$$

  (iv) Break-even point = 20 000 units.
  (v) The margin of safety represents the difference between actual or expected sales volume and the break-even point. Therefore the margin of safety will be different for each month's sales. For example, the margin of safety in November is 10 000 units (30 000 units – 20 000 units). The margin of safety can be read from Figure 2 for various sales levels.

  (b) and **(c)** See the sections on curvi-linear and linear CVP relationships in Chapter 9 for the answers.

FIGURE 1 *Break-even chart*

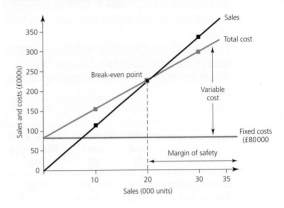

FIGURE 2 *Profit–volume graph*

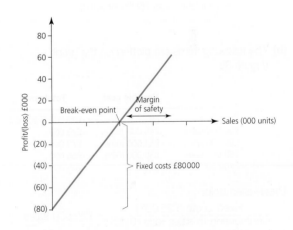

9.22 (a)

	August (£)	September (£)	Change (£)
Sales	80 000	90 000	10 000
Cost of sales	50 000	55 000	5000
Selling and distribution	8000	9000	1000
Administration	15 000	15 000	Nil

The only activity measure that is given is sales revenue. An increase in sales of £10 000 results in an increase in cost of sales of £5000 and an increase in selling and distribution costs of £1000. It is therefore assumed that the increase is attributable to variable costs and variable cost of sales is 50% of sales and variable selling and distribution costs are 10% of sales.

Fixed costs are derived by deducting variable costs from total costs for either month. The figures for August are used in the calculations below:

	Total cost (£)	Variable cost (£)	Fixed cost (Balance) (£)
Cost of sales	50 000	40 000	10 000
Selling and distribution	8000	8000	Nil
Administration	15 000	Nil	15 000
			25 000

Total cost = £25 000 fixed costs + variable costs (60% of sales)

(b) The following items are plotted on the graph (Figure 3):

	Variable cost	Total cost
Zero sales	Nil	£25 000 fixed cost
£80 000 sales	£48 000 (60%)	£73 000
£90 000 sales	£54 000 (60%)	£79 000
£50 000 sales	£30 000 (60%)	£55 000
£100 000 sales	£60 000	£85 000

Break-even point

$$= \frac{\text{Fixed costs (£25 000)}}{\text{Contribution to sales ratio (0.40)}} = £62\,500 \text{ sales}$$

FIGURE 3 *Contribution break-even graph*

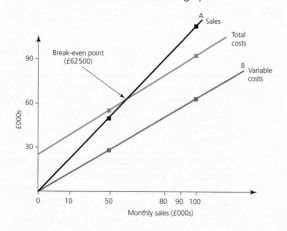

Area of contribution = Area AOB

(c)

		(£)
Actual sales = 1.3 × Break-even sales (£62 500)	=	81 250
Contribution (40% of sales)	=	32 500
Fixed costs	=	25 000
Monthly profit	=	7500
Annual profit	=	90 000

(d)

		(£)
Annual contribution from single outlet (£32 500 × 12)	=	390 000
Contribution to cover lost sales (10%)	=	39 000
Specific fixed costs	=	100 000
Total contribution required		529 000

Required sales = £529 000/0.4 = £1 322 500

(e) The answer should draw attention to the need for establishing a sound system of budgeting and performance reporting for each of the different outlets working in close conjunction with central office. The budgets should be merged together to establish a master budget for the whole company.

9.23 (a) Let x = number of units of output

Total cost for 30 000 units or less

= £50 000 + 5x (where 5 = variable cost per unit)

Total cost for more than 30 000 units = £100 000 + 5x

(b)

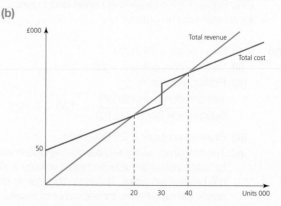

(c) There are two break-even points resulting in the production plan being profitable only between 20 000 and 30 000 units and above 40 000 units. The production plan should be set based on these considerations.

9.24 Break-even point $= \dfrac{\text{Fixed costs}}{\text{Contribution per unit}}$

Product X	25 000 units (£100 000/£4)
Product Y	25 000 units (£200 000/£8)
Company as a whole	57 692 units (£300 000/£5.20ᵃ)

Notes

ᵃAverage contribution per unit

$$= \frac{(70\,000 \times £4) + (30\,000 \times £8)}{100\,000 \text{ units}}$$
$$= £5.20$$

The sum of the product break-even points is less than the break-even point for the company as a whole. It is incorrect to add the product break-even points because the sales mix will be different from the planned sales mix. The sum of the product break-even points assumes a sales mix of 50% to X and 50% to Y. The break-even point for the company as a whole assumes a planned sales mix of 70% to X and 30% to Y. CVP analysis will yield correct results only if the planned sales mix is equal to the actual sales mix.

9.25

Workings:	**(000)**
Sales	1000
Variable costs	600
Contribution	400
Fixed costs	500
Profit/(loss)	(100)

Unit selling price $= £20$ (£1m/50 000)

Unit variable cost $= £12$ (£600 000/50 000)

Unit contribution $= £8$

(a) Sales commission will be £2 per unit, thus reducing the contribution per unit to £6. The break-even point will be 83 333 units (£500 000/£6) or £1 666 666 sales value. This requires an increase of 67% on previous sales and the company must assess whether or not sales can be increased by such a high percentage.

(b) A 10% decrease in selling price will decrease the selling price by £2 per unit and the revised unit contribution will be £6:

	(£)
Revised total contribution (65 000 × £6)	390 000
Less fixed costs	500 000
Profit/(loss)	(110 000)

The estimated loss is worse than last year and the proposal is therefore not recommended.

(c) Wages will increase by 25% – that is, from £200 000 to £250 000 – causing output to increase by 20%.

		(£)
Sales		1 200 000
Direct materials and variable overheads	480 000	
Direct wages	250 000	730 000
Contribution		470 000
Less fixed costs		550 000
Profit/(loss)		(80 000)

This represents an improvement of £20 000 on last year's loss of £100 000.

(d) Revised selling price = £24

Let X = Revised sales volume

Let X = Revised sales volume

∴ Sales revenue less (variable costs + *fixed costs*) = Profit

$$24X \text{ less } (12X + 800\,000) = 0.1(24X)$$
$$\therefore 9.6X = 800\,000$$
$$\therefore X = 83\,333 \text{ units}$$

Clearly this proposal is preferable since it is the only proposal to yield a profit. However, the probability of increasing sales volume by approximately 67% plus the risk involved from increasing fixed costs by £300 000 must be considered.

Chapter 10

10.10

Low	650 patients	$17 125
High	1260 patients	18 650
Difference	610 patients	1 525

Variable cost per patient = $1525/610 = $2.50

Total fixed cost using 650 patients = Total cost ($17 125) – variable cost (650 × $2.50) = $15 500

Estimated cost for 850 patients = Variable costs (850 × $2.50) + $15 500 = $17 625

Answer = (c)

10.11 The high low method is used to calculate the variable cost per unit but it is necessary to compare like with like by comparing the total costs at each level of activity without the increase in fixed costs:

Increase in total costs = (£470 000 – £18 000) – £380 000 = £72 000

Increase in activity = 9 000 units (24 000 – 15 000)

Variable cost per unit = £8 (£72 000/9 000)

Total fixed costs below 20 000 units = £380 000 – (15 000 × £8) = £260 000

Total costs for 18 000 units = £260 000 + (18 000 × £8) = £404 000

Answer = (a)

10.12 Given that unit variable costs are constant it is appropriate to compare the two activity levels that include the increase in fixed costs. An increase in production from 1200 to 1400 units results in an increase in total costs of £1600. Therefore the variable cost per unit is £8 (£1600/200 units). Total fixed costs at 1400 units = £68 200 – (1400 × £8) = £57 000

Total costs at 1000 units = £51 000

fixed costs (£57 000 – £6 000) + (1000 × £8)
= £59 000
Answer = (c)

10.13 The question paper included the formula provided in Chapter 10.

b = [(5 × 23 091) – (129 × 890)]/[(5 × 3 433)
– (129²)] = 1.231
a = (890/5) – [(1.231 × 129)/5] = 146.24
Answer = (a)

10.14 It is assumed that advertising generates sales. Therefore advertising is the independent variable and sales revenue the dependent variable. Applying the formula given in Chapter 10 which was also provided in the examination paper:

$$b = \frac{(6 \times 447\,250\,000) - (13\,500 \times 192\,000)}{(6 \times 32\,150\,000) - (13\,500)^2} = 8.714$$

Answer = (c)

10.15 (a) Advertising expenditure is the independent variable (x) and sales revenue the dependent variable (y).

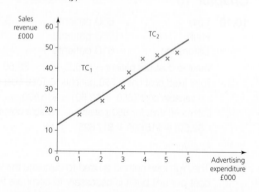

(b) Applying the formulae given in Chapter 10 (which was also provided in the examination paper):

$$b = \frac{(8 \times 1055.875) - (26.35 \times 289.5)}{(8 \times 101.2625) - (26.35)^2}$$

$$= 818.675/115.7775 = 7.07$$

$$a = (289.5/8) - (7.07 \times 26.35)/8 = 12.9$$

Therefore the regression line is y = 12.9 + 7.07x where x and y are expressed in £000s. The line of best fit is shown in the graph in (a)

10.16 (a) The dependent variable (y) is the maintenance cost (in £000) and the independent variable is production units (in 000).

$$\sum y = (265 + 302 + 222 + 240$$
$$+ 362 + 295 + 404 + 400) = 2490$$
$$\sum x = (20 + 24 + 16 + 18 + 26 + 22$$
$$+ 32 + 30) = 188$$
$$n = 8$$

Using formulae provided in Chapter 10 and also provided in the examination paper:

b = [(8 × 61 250) – (188 × 2490)]/
[(8 × 4 640) – (188 × 188)] = 12.32
a = (2490/8) – (12.32 × 188)/8 = 21.73

Therefore the linear equation is:
y = 21.73 + 12.32x where x and y are in 000's. This can be interpreted as fixed costs being equal to £21 730 and the variable cost per unit of production is £12.32.

(b) Predicted maintenance cost at 44 000 units = 21·730 + (12.320 × 44) = 563·81 or £563 810

The major reservation about this prediction is that 44 000 units of production is well outside the relevant range of data (16 000 to 32 000 units) that has been used to establish the linear regression equation. For example a step increase in fixed cost may apply outside the relevant range of output.

Chapter 11

11.13 The relevant cost of the skilled labour is the hourly wage rate of £8 per hour plus the lost contribution of £10 per hour (£25/2.5 hours) giving £18 per hour. The labour hours required to produce one unit of output is derived from dividing the labour cost (£25) by the hourly wage rate. The total relevant cost of labour is £1620 (90 hours × £18). Answer = (c)

11.14 The relevant cost of regularly used materials that will be replaced is the replacement cost (600 × £27) = £16 200
Answer = (c)

11.15 If the company uses the equipment on the contract it will lose its current sale value of £2000 and incur additional disposal costs of £800 giving a total relevant cost of £2800. Answer = (d)

11.16 The material is readily available and the use of the materials will necessitate their replacement. The relevant cost is therefore the replacement cost of £4050 (1250 kg at £3.24). Answer = (b)

11.17 The original purchase price is a sunk cost and therefore not a relevant cost. The relevant cost of the materials in stock is $1000 (100 reams at $10 net realizable value). An additional 150 reams must be purchased for $3900 (150 × $26) resulting in a relevant cost of $4900.
Answer = (b)

11.18

Component	Additional cost of buying in per unit £	Hours per unit to manufacture	Additional cost per hour £
A	48	4	12
B	60	6	10
C	45	5	9
D	39	3	13

Component C should be purchased because it has the lowest additional cost per hour saved.
Answer = (c)

11.19 (a)

	X	Y	Z	Total
Demand (units)	4000	5500	7000	
Materials (kg)	20 000	22 000	42 000	84 000
Labour (hours)	4000	4125	10 500	18 625

Labour is the limiting factor.
Answer = (i)

(b)

	X $	Y $	Z $
Selling price	28	22	30
Variable cost	17	13	24
Contribution	11	9	6
kg	5	4	6
Contribution per kg ($)	2.20	2.25	1
Ranking	2	1	3

Answer = (iv)

11.20 Apportioned fixed costs = £120 000 (0.6 × £200 000)
Fixed costs apportioned to Shop
 S = £40 000 (500/1500 × £120 000)
Specific avoidable fixed cost for Shop
 S = £30 000 (£70 000 – £30 000)

Shop S therefore provides a contribution of £30 000 (variable cost contribution of £60 000 less specific fixed costs of £30 000) to general apportioned fixed costs. The effect of closing down shop S is that total budgeted profit will decline by the lost contribution from S to £50 000.
Answer = (a)

11.21 (a) Marginal cost (MC) = £15 per unit
Profit is maximized when MC = MR giving:
 15 = 50 – 0.05Q
 Q = 700
 Price per unit (P) = 50 – (0.025 × 700) = £32.50
 Answer = (iv)

(b) When P = 20 :
 20 = 50 – 0.025Q
 Therefore Q = 1200
 Total contribution = 1200 × (£20 – £15) = £6000
 Answer = (iv)

11.22 (a) (i) The relevant cost of material in regular usage will be its replacement cost. Therefore the relevant cost of 2500 kg of material R is
£67 500 (2500 × 25 × 1.08)

(ii) The relevant cost of skilled labour in short supply is the hourly wage rate plus the lost contribution per labour hour. The alternative use of the skilled labour is the production of product T which makes a contribution of £30 per unit. The labour hours per unit of product T are 2.5 hours (£25 labour cost/£10 wage rate) giving a lost contribution per hour of £12 (£30/2.5). Therefore the relevant cost per skilled labour hour is £22 (£10 + £12).
Relevant cost of labour = £13 200 (600 × £22)

(b) Relevant costs are future costs that differ between alternatives. Variable overheads (e.g. power to operate machinery) will increase as a result of accepting the contract but fixed costs may remain unchanged with short-term changes in activity. However, it is possible for fixed cost to change when activity expands or declines. For example stepped increases in fixed costs can occur because of additional equipment rentals for undertaking the contract.

11.23 (a)

Machine hours required per unit of output for each product (5 + 6 + 7 + 8)	26
Required machine hours (2000 × 26)	52 000
Available machine hours	35 000
Shortfall	17 000

(b)

	E £/ unit	F £/ unit	G £/ unit	H £/ unit
Variable production cost	32	27	34	35
Buy-in price	48	51	55	63
Extra cost of buying in	16	24	21	28
Machine hours per unit	5	6	7	8
Extra cost per machine hour saved	3.2	4.0	3.0	3.5
Ranking for buying in	2nd	4th	1st	3rd

Optimal plan for buying in components:

Ranking	Component	Units	Machine hours saved	
1st	G	2000	14 000	
2nd	E	600	3000	(balancing figure)
Total shortfall of hours [as per (a)]			17 000	

(c) 1 The quality of components provided by the supplier;
2 Possible loss of control over the production and delivery of the components;
3 Exploration of alternative approaches to increasing capacity (e.g. rental of additional machinery or working overtime).

11.24 (a)

Relevant costs of the project

Material A	(1750)
Material B	8000
Direct labour	7000
Net cost of machinery	4750
Relevant cost	18 000
Contract price	30 000
Contribution	12 000

Notes:

(1) There is a saving in material costs of £1750 if material A is not used.
(2) The actual cost of material B represents the incremental cost.
(3) The hiring of the labour on the other contract represents the additional cash flows of undertaking this contract.
(4) The net cost of purchasing the machinery represents the additional cash flows associated with the contract.
(5) Supervision and overheads will still continue even if the contract is not accepted and are therefore irrelevant.

(b) The report should indicate that the costs given in the question do not represent incremental cash flows arising from undertaking the contract. As the company is operating at an activity level in excess of break-even point any sales revenue in excess of £18 000 incremental costs will provide an additional contribution which will result in an increase in profits. Assuming that the company has spare capacity, and that a competitor is prepared to accept the order at £30 000, then a tender price slightly below £30 000 would be appropriate.

(c) Before accepting the contract the following non-monetary factors should be considered.
  (i) Is there sufficient spare capacity to undertake the project?
  (ii) Is the overseas customer credit worthy?
  (iii) Has the workforce the necessary skills to undertake the project?
  (iv) Is the contract likely to result in repeat business with the customer?

(d) If the company were operating below the break-even point, acceptance of the order would provide a further contribution towards fixed costs and reduce the existing loss. In the short term it is better to accept the order and reduce the total loss but if, in the long run, there are not enough orders to generate sufficient contributions to cover total fixed costs, then the company will not survive.

11.25 (a)

	North East (£)	South coast (£)
Material X from stock (i)	19 440	
Material Y from stock (ii)		49 600
Firm orders of material X (iii)	27 360	
Material X not yet ordered (iv)	60 000	
Material Z not yet ordered (v)		71 200
Labour (vi)	86 000	110 000
Site management (vii)	—	—
Staff accommodation and travel for site management (viii)	6800	5600
Plant rental received (ix)	(6000)	—
Penalty clause (x)		28 000
	193 600	264 400
Contract price	288 000	352 000
Net benefit	94 400	87 600

(b) (i) If material X is not used on the North East contract the most beneficial use is to use it as a substitute material thus avoiding future purchases of £19 440 (0.9 × 21 600) Therefore by using the stock quantity of material X the company will have to spend £19 440 on the other materials.
  (ii) Material Y is in common use and the company should not dispose of it. Using the materials on the South coast contract will mean that they will have to be replaced at a cost of £49 600 (£24 800 × 2). Therefore the future cash flow impact of taking on the contract is £49 600.
  (iii) It is assumed that with firm orders for materials it is not possible to cancel the purchase. Therefore the cost will occur whatever future alternative is selected. The materials will be used as a substitute material if they are not used on the contract and therefore, based on the same reasoning as note (i) above, the relevant cost is the purchase price of the substitute material (0.9 × £30 400).
  (iv) The material has not been ordered and the cost will only be incurred if the contract is undertaken. Therefore additional cash

flows of £60 000 will be incurred if the company takes on the North East contract.

(v) The same principles apply here as were explained in note (iv) and additional cash flows of £71 200 will be incurred only if the company takes on the South coast contract.

(vi) It is assumed that labour is an incremental cost and therefore relevant.

(vii) The site management function is performed by staff at central headquarters. It is assumed that the total company costs in respect of site management will remain unchanged in the short term whatever contracts are taken on. Site management costs are therefore irrelevant.

(viii) The costs would be undertaken only if the contracts are undertaken. Therefore they are relevant costs.

(ix) If the North East contract is undertaken the company will be able to hire out surplus plant and obtain a £6000 cash inflow.

(x) If the South coast contract is undertaken the company will have to withdraw from the North East contract and incur a penalty cost of £28 000.

(xi) The headquarter costs will continue whichever alternative is selected and they are not relevant costs.

(xii) It is assumed that there will be no differential cash flows relating to notional interest. However, if the interest costs associated with the contract differ then they would be relevant and should be included in the analysis.

(xiii) Depreciation is a sunk cost and irrelevant for decision-making.

11.26 (a) (i)

Product	A (£)	B (£)	C (£)
Selling price	15	12	11
Less variable costs:			
Materials	(5)	(4)	(3)
Labour	(3)	(2)	(1.5)
Variable overhead (1)	(3.50)	(2)	(1.5)
Contribution	3.50	4	5

Note:
Fixed overheads are apportioned to products on the basis of sales volume and the remaining overheads are variable with output.

(ii)

Product	B (£)	C (£)
Selling price	12	9.50
Less variable costs:		
Materials	(4)	(3)
Labour	(2)	(1.80)
Variable overhead	(2)	(1.50)
Contribution	4	3.20

(b) (i)

Product	A	B	C	Total
Total contribution	350 000	480 000	400 000	1 230 000
Less fixed costs:				
Labour				(220 000)
Fixed administration				(900 000)
Profit				110 000

(ii)

Product	B	C	Total
Total contribution[a]	480 000	576 000	1 056 000
Less fixed costs:			
Labour[b]			(160 000)
Fixed administration[c]			(850 000)
Profit			46 000

Notes

[a] B = 120 000 units × £4 contribution,
C = 18 000 units × £3.20 contribution
[b] (25% × £320 000 for B) plus (25% × £160 000 × 2 for C)
[c] Fixed administration costs will decline by 1/6 of the amount apportioned to Product A (100/300 × £900 000). Therefore fixed overheads will decline from 900 000 to £850 000

(c) Product A should not be eliminated even though a loss is reported for this product. If Product A is eliminated the majority of fixed costs allocated to it will still continue and will be borne by the remaining products. Product A generates a contribution of £350 000 towards fixed costs but the capacity released can be used to obtain an additional contribution from Product C of £176 000 (£576 000 – £400 000). This will result in a net loss in contribution of £174 000. However, fixed cost savings of £110 000 (£50 000 administration apportioned to Product A plus £100 000 labour for A less an extra £40 000 labour for Product C) can be obtained if Product A is abandoned. Therefore there will be a net loss in contribution of £64 000 (£174 000 – £110 000) and profits will decline from £110 000 to £64 000.

11.27 (a) Initial selling price = [Variable cost (£4) + unit fixed cost (£18 000/3000)] × 1.40 = £14
Profit for the period = Contribution (3000 × £10) – fixed costs (£18 000) = £12 000

(b) Profits are maximized when marginal cost (MC) = marginal revenue (MR)

MC = variable cost = £4 and MR = 20 – 0.004Q
Therefore 4 = 20 – 0.004Q
Q = 4000 units
P = 20 – 0.002 (4000) = £12 = profit maximizing price.

(c) Cost information is only one of many variables that must be considered in the pricing decision. The final price that is selected will depend upon the pricing policy of the company.

A price-skimming policy is an attempt to exploit those sections of the market that are relatively insensitive to price changes. For example, high initial prices may be charged to take advantage of the novelty appeal of a new product when demand is not very sensitive to price changes. A skimming pricing policy offers a safeguard against unexpected future increases in costs, or a large fall in demand after the novelty appeal has declined. Once the market becomes saturated, the price can be reduced to attract that part of the market that has not yet been exploited. A skimming pricing policy should not be adopted when a number of close substitutes are already being marketed. Here demand is likely to be very sensitive to price changes, and any price in excess of that being charged for a substitute product by a competitor is likely to lead to a large reduction in sales. A penetration pricing policy is based on the concept of charging low prices initially with the intention of gaining rapid acceptance of the product. Such a policy is appropriate when close substitutes are available or when the market is easy to enter. The low price discourages potential competitors from entering the market and enables a company to establish a large share of the market. This can be achieved more easily when the product is new, than later on when buying habits have become established.

Chapter 12

12.14

	W (£000)	X (£000)	Y (£000)
Gross margin	1100	1750	1200
Less customer related costs:			
Sales visits at £500 per visit	55	50	85
Order processing at £100 per order placed	100	100	150
Despatch costs at £100 per order placed	100	100	150
Billing and collections at £175 per invoice raised	157	210	262
Profit/(loss)	688	1290	553
Ranking	2	1	3

Answer = (c)

12.15 Budgeted number of batches per product:

D = 1000 (100 000/100)
R = 2000 (100 000/50)
P = 2000 (50 000/25)
  5000

Budgeted machine set-ups:
D = 3000 (1000 × 3)
R = 8000 (2000 × 4)
P = 12 000 (2000 × 6)
  23 000

Budgeted cost per set-up = £150 000/23 000 = £6.52
Budgeted set-up cost per unit of R = (£6.52 × 4)/50 = £0.52
  Answer = (a)

12.16 Cost driver rates are as follows:

Receiving/inspection etc. = £1 400 000/5000 = £280 per requisition

Production scheduling/machine set-up = £1 200 000/800 = £1500 per set-up

	W (£)	X (£)	Y (£)
Direct costs	80.00	75.00	65.00
Receiving/inspection [a]	33.60	33.60	31.11
Production scheduling [a]	36.00	26.00	5.00
Total cost per unit	149.60	134.60	121.11
Selling price	200.00	183.00	175.00
Profit per unit	50.40	48.40	53.89

Notes

[a](Number of units of activity used by each product × Cost driver rate)/units produced
  e.g. Product W for receiving/inspection
  = (1200 × £280)/10 000 = £33.60

12.17 (a) (i) Service (or support) centres (see Chapter 4) exist to provide services of various kinds to other units within the organization. They provide essential services to support the production process, but they do not deal directly with the products produced. Examples include stores and maintenance departments.

(ii) A production centre is a centre where units of output are actually made. Examples include machining and assembly centres. Overheads are assigned to service centres and the total costs of the service centres are allocated to production centres resulting in all overheads being assigned only to production centres.

Overhead rates are established for each production centre and service centre costs are assigned to production within the production centre overhead rates.

(b) See 'A comparison of traditional and ABC systems' and 'Volume-based and non-volume-based cost drivers' in Chapter 12 for the answer to this question.

12.18 The answer to the question should describe the two-stage overhead allocation process and indicate that most cost systems use direct labour hours in the second stage. In today's production environment direct labour costs have fallen to about 10% of total costs for many firms and it is argued that direct labour is no longer a suitable base for assigning overheads to products. Using direct labour encourages managers to focus on reducing direct labour costs when they represent only a small percentage of total costs.

Approaches which are being adopted include:

(i) Changing from a direct labour overhead-recovery rate to recovery methods based on machine time. The justification for this is that overheads are caused by machine time rather than direct labour hours and cost.

(ii) Implementing activity-based costing systems that use many different cost drivers in the second stage of the two-stage overhead allocation procedure.

The answer should then go on to describe the benefits of ABC outlined in Chapter 12. Attention should also be drawn to the widespread use of direct labour hours by Japanese companies. According to Hiromoto[1] Japanese companies allocate overhead costs using the direct labour cost/hours to focus design engineers' attention on identifying opportunities to reduce the products' labour content. They use direct labour to encourage designers to make greater use of technology because this frequently improves long-term competitiveness by increasing quality, speed and flexibility of manufacturing.

Note
[1] Hiromoto, T. (1988) Another hidden edge – Japanese management accounting', *Harvard Business Review,* July/August, pp. 22–6.

12.19 **(a)** Total machine hours = (120 × 4 hrs) + (100 × 3 hrs) + (80 × 2 hrs) + (120 × 3 hrs) = (1300 hrs

Machine hour overhead rate

$$= \frac{£10430 + £5250 + £3600 + £2100 + £4620}{1300\ hrs}$$

= £20 per machine hour

Product	A (£)	B (£)	C (£)	D (£)
Direct material	40	50	30	60
Direct labour	28	21	14	21
Overheads at £20 per machine hour	80	60	40	60
	148	131	84	141
Units of output	120	100	80	120
Total cost	£17 760	£13 100	£6720	£16 920

(b)

Costs	(£)	Cost driver	Cost driver transactions	Cost per unit (£)
Machine department	10 430	Machine hours	1300 hours	8.02
Set-up costs	5250	Production runs	21	250
Stores receiving	3600	Requisitions raised	80 (4 × 20)	45
Inspection/ quality control	2100	Production runs	21	100
Materials handling	4620	Number of orders executed	42	110

Note

Number of production runs = Total output (420 units)/20 units per set-up.

Number of orders executed = Total output (420 units)/10 units per order.

The total costs for each product are computed by multiplying the cost driver rate per unit by the quantity of the cost driver consumed by each product.

	A	B	C	D
Prime costs	8 160 (£68 × 120)	7100	3520	9720
Set ups	1 500 (£250 × 6)	1 250 (£250 × 5)	1000	1500
Stores/receiving	900 (£45 × 20)	900	900	900
Inspection/quality	600 (£100 × 6)	500	400	600
Handling despatch	1 320 (£110 × 12)	1 100 (£110 × 10)	880	1320
Machine dept costs	3 851	2 407	1284	2888
Total costs	16 331	13 257	7984	16 928

Note
[a] A = 120 units × 4 hrs × £8.02 : B = 100 units × 3 hrs × £8.02

(c) Cost per unit

Costs from (a)	148.00	131.00	84.00	141.00
Costs from (b)	136.09	132.57	99.80	141.07
Difference	(11.91)	1.57	15.80	0.07

Product A is over-costed with the traditional system.

Products B and C are under-costed and similar costs are reported with Product D. It is claimed that ABC more accurately measures resources consumed by products. Where cost-plus pricing is used, the transfer to an ABC system will result in different product prices. If activity-based costs are used for stock valuations then stock valuations and reported profits will differ.

Chapter 13

13.10 Answer = (b)

13.11 Answer = (b)

13.12 Answer = (a)

13.13

	Kg
Materials required to meet production requirements (7200 × 3kg)	21 600
Add budgeted closing stock	500
Less opening stock	(400)
Budgeted purchases	21 700

Answer = (d)

13.14 (a) Cash received = Sales ($160 000) + Opening debtors ($27 500) − Closing debtors ($19 400) = $168 100

Answer = (iv)

(b)

Gross profit	= $88 000 (0.55 × $160 000)
Cost of sales	= $72 000 ($160 000 − $88 000)
Purchases	= Cost of sales ($72 000) + closing stock ($18 700) − opening stock ($16 600)
	= $74 100

Answer = (ii)

13.15 Total hours in cost centre X = 8000 × (3 + 2.5) = 44 000
Total hours in cost centre Y = 8000 × (1 + 2) = 24 000
Overhead rate (X) = £88 000/44 000 = £2 per hour
Overhead rate (X) = £88 000/44 000 = £2 per hour
Overhead rate (Y) = £96 000/24 000 = £4 per hour
Overhead cost per unit for P2 = (2.5 × 2) + (2.0 × 4) = £13

Answer = (d)

13.16 All figures are £000

Month	Sales	Cost of sales	Opening inventory	Closing inventory	Purchase	Paid
July	100	80	40	36	76	
August	90	72	36	50	86	**76**
September	125	100	50	56	106	**86**
October	140	112	56			**106**

13.17 (a) Raw materials:

(Units)	March	April	May	June
Opening stock	100	110	115	110
Add: Purchases	80	80	85	85
	180	190	200	195
Less: Used in production	70	75	90	90
Closing stock	110	115	110	105
(Units) *Finished production:*				
Opening stock	110	100	91	85
Add: Production	70	75	90	90
	180	175	181	175
Less:Sales	80	84	96	94
Closing stock	100	91	85	81

(b) *Sales:*

					Total
(at £219 per unit)	£17 520	£18 396	£21 024	£20 586	£77 526
Production cost:					
Raw materials (using FIFO)	3024 (1)	3321 (2)	4050	4050	14 445
Wages and variable Costs	4550	4875	5850	5850	21 125
	£7574	£8196	£9900	£9900	£35 570

Debtors:
Closing debtors = May + June sales = £41 610

Creditors:
June purchases 85 units × £45 = £3825

Notes:
70 units × £4320/100 units = £3024.
(30 units × £4320/100 units + (45 units × £45) = £3321.

Closing stocks:

Raw materials 105 units × £45	£4725
Finished goods 81 units × £110[1]	£8910

Notes
[1]Materials (£45) + Labour and Variable Overhead (£65). It is assumed that stocks are valued on a variable costing basis.

(c) *Cash budget:*

	March (£)	April (£)	May (£)	June (£)
Balance b/fwd	6790	4820	5545	132 415
Add: Receipts				
Debtors (two months' credit)	7680	10 400	17 520	18 396
Loan	—	—	120 000	—
(A)	14 470	15 220	143 065	150 811
Payments:				
Creditors (one month's credit)	3900	3600	3600	3825
			(80 × £45)	
Wages and variable overheads	4550	4875	5850	5850
Fixed overheads	1200	1200	1200	1200
Machinery	—	—	—	112 000
Interim dividend	—	—	—	12 500
(B)	9650	9675	10 650	135 375
Balance c/fwd (A) – (B)	4820	5545	132 415	£15 436

(d) *Master budget:*

Budgeted trading and profit and loss account for the four months to 30 June

	(£)	(£)
Sales		77 526
Cost of sales: Opening stock finished goods	10 450	
Add: Production cost	35 570	
	46 020	
Less: Closing stock finished goods	8910	37 110
		40 416
Less: Expense		
Fixed overheads (4 × £1200)	4800	
Depreciation		
Machinery and equipment	15 733	
Motor vehicles	3500	
Loan interest (2/12 × 7 1/2% of £120 000)	1500	25 533
		14 883
Less: Interim dividends		12 500
		2383
Add: Profit and loss account balance b/fwd		40 840
		£43 223

Budgeted balance sheet as at 30 June

	Cost (£)	Depreciation to date (£)	Net (£)
Fixed assets			
Land and buildings	500 000	—	500 000
Machinery and equipment	236 000	100 233	135 767
Motor vehicles	42 000	19 900	22 100
	778 000	120 133	657 867
Current assets			
Stock of raw materials		4725	
Stock of finished goods		8910	
Debtors		41 610	
Cash and bank balances		15 436	
		70 681	
Less: Current liabilities			
Creditors	3825		
Loan interest owing	1500	5325	65 356
			£723 223

	(£)
Capital employed	
Ordinary share capital £1 shares (fully paid)	500 000
Share premium	60 000
Profit and loss account	43 233
	603 223
Secured loan (71/2%)	120 000
	£723 223

(e) See the section of cash budgets in Chapter 13 for possible ways to improve cash management.

13.18 *Task 1*

Alderley Ltd Budget Statements 13 weeks to 4 April

(a) Production Budget

	Elgar units	Holst units
Budgeted sales volume	845	1235
Add closing stock[a]	78	1266
Less Opening stock	(163)	(361)
Units of production	760	1140

(b) Material Purchases Budget

	Elgar kg	Holst kg	Total kg
Material consumed	5320 (760×7)	9120 (1140×8)	14 440
Add raw material closing stock[b]			2888
Less raw material opening stock			(2328)
Purchases (kg)			15 000

(c) Purchases (£) ($1500 \times £12$) = £180 000

(d) Production Labour Budget

	Elgar hours	Holst hours	Total hours
Standard hours produced[c]	6080	5700	11 780
Productivity adjustment (5/95 × 11 780)			620
Total hours employed			12 400
Normal hours employed[d]			11 544
Overtime hours			856

Notes

[a]Number of days per period = 13 weeks × 5 days = 65
Stock : Elgar = (6/65) × 845 = 78,
Holst = (14/65) × 1235 = 266

[b](13/65) × (5320 + 9120) = 2888

[c]Elgar × 760 × 8 hours = 6080,
Holst × 1140 × 5 hours = 5700

[d]24 employees × 37 hours × 13 weeks = 11544

(e) Labour cost

	£
Normal hours (11 544 × £8)	92 352
Overtime (856 × £8 × 125%)	8560
Total	100 912

Task 2 (a) Four ways of forecasting future sales volume are: Where the number of customers is small it is

(i) possible to interview them to ascertain what their likely demand will be over the forecasting period.

(ii) Produce estimates based on the opinion of executives and sales personnel. For example, sales personnel may be asked to estimate the sales of each product to their customers, or regional sales managers may estimate the total sales for each of their regions.

(iii) Market research may be necessary where it is intended to develop new products or new markets. This may involve interviews with existing and potential customers in order to estimate potential demand.

(iv) Estimates involving statistical techniques that incorporate general business and market conditions and past growth in sales.

(b) Interviewing customers and basing estimates on the opinions of sales personnel are likely to be more appropriate for existing products and customers involving repeat sales.

Market research is appropriate for new products or markets and where the market is large and anticipated revenues are likely to be sufficient to justify the cost of undertaking the research.

Statistical estimates derived from past data are likely to be appropriate where conditions are likely to be stable and past demand patterns are likely to be repeated through time. This method is most suited to existing products or markets where sufficient data is available to establish a trend in demand.

(c) The major limitation of interviewing customers is that they may not be prepared to divulge the information if their future plans are commercially sensitive. There is also no guarantee that the orders will be placed with Alderley Ltd. They may place their orders with competitors.

Where estimates are derived from sales personnel there is a danger that they might produce over-optimistic estimates in order to obtain a favourable performance rating at the budget setting stage. Alternatively, if their future performance is judged by their ability to achieve the budgeted sales they may be motivated to underestimate sales demand.

Market research is expensive and may produce unreliable estimates if inexperienced researchers are used. Also small samples are often used which may not be indicative of the population and this can result in inaccurate estimates.

Statistical estimates will produce poor demand estimates where insufficient past data is available, demand is unstable over time and the future environment is likely to be significantly different from the past. Statistical estimates are likely to be inappropriate for new products and new markets where past data is unavailable.

13.19 (a) Production Budget in units

	Quarter 1	Quarter 2	Quarter 3	Quarter 4	Quarter 5
Required by sales	2250	2050	1650	2050	8000
Plus required closing inventory	615	495	615	375	375
Less opening inventory	−675	−615	−495	−615	−675
Production Budget	2190	1930	1770	1810	7700

Raw Materials purchases budget

Material B	Quarter 1	Quarter 2	Quarter 3	Quarter 4	Total
	kg	kg	kg	kg	kg
Required by production	6570	5790	5310	5430	23 100
Plus required closing inventory	2605.50	2389.50	2443.50	2011.50	2011.50
Less opening inventory	−2956.50	−2605.50	−2389.50	−2443.50	−2956.50
Material Purchases Budget	6219	5574	5364	4998	22 155
Value	£43 533	£39 018	£37 548	£34 986	£155 085

(b) If material A is in short supply the company will need to obtain an alternative source of supply or find a substitute material. If they are unable to do this they will need to use limiting factor analysis (see Chapter 11) to determine the optimum output level. In this situation sales will not be the limiting factor and the production budget will become the key budget factor in the budget preparation process.

(c) It is assumed that the flexible budget statement does not require the inclusion of direct materials. The statement is as follows:

Operating Statement

	Fixed Budget	Flexed Budget	Actual	Flexible Budget Variance
Activity	7700	7250	7250	
Overheads	£	£	£	£
Variable	168 000	158 182	185 000	26 818 Adv
Fixed	112 000	112 000	105 000	7000 Fav
Labour				
Skilled	462 000	435 000	568 750	133 750 Adv
Semi-skilled	415 800	391 500	332 400	59 100 Fav
	1 157 800	1 096 682	1 191 150	94 468 Adv

Note that the fixed and variable overheads for the fixed budget are respectively £112 000 (40% × £240 000) and £168 000 (60% × £240 000). The variable overhead rate per unit of output is £21.818 (£168 000/7700 units). This rate per unit is multiplied by 7250 units to obtain the flexible budget allowance for variable overheads.

(d) See 'The Budget Process' in Chapter 13 for the answer to this question. The answer should point out that rolling budgets are particularly useful when it is difficult to forecast future costs/activities accurately. Given that the company is experiencing an increase in competition and a shortage of raw materials it may need to react speedily to these factors in terms of competitive responses and sourcing alternative supplies. In these circumstances rolling budgets may be preferable.

Chapter 14

14.16 Answer = (a)

14.17 (a)

	Flexed budget		Actual results	Variances
Sales (units)	9750		9750	
Production (units)	11 000		11 000	
	£000		**£000**	**£000**
Sales revenue	292.5	= (30 × 9 750)	325	32.5 favourable
Cost of sales:				
Opening stock	0		0	
Production costs:				
Materials	55	= (5 × 11 000)	65	10 adverse
Labour	99	= (9 × 11 000)	100	1 adverse
Fixed production overheads	96 (1)	= (8 × 12 000)	95	1 favourable
	250		260	10 adverse
Closing stock	27.5	= (£22 × (11 000 − 9750))	27.5	
	222.5		232.5	
Profit	70		92.5	22.5 favourable

(b) The variance will have arisen because the actual selling price was greater than the budgeted price. The adverse materials variance may have resulted either because the number of kg used, or the amount paid per kg, was greater than expected.

14.18 (a) The assembly labour, furniture packs and other materials are assumed to vary with assembly labour hours. Therefore a cost per assembly labour hour is calculated for each of these items and the flexible budget allowance is derived by multiplying the cost per hour by 7140 hours for each element of cost. There is no change in step fixed costs when output is increased from 7500 to 10 000 hours so variable costs represent the increase in total costs. Therefore the variable cost per assembly hour is $5.40 (($90 000 − $76 500)

/2500 increase in assembly hours). The total variable cost at an output of 7500 units is $40 500 (7500 × $5.40) so the balance of $36 000 represents the fixed cost and stepped fixed cost. Given that the share of central fixed costs is $9000 the remaining $27 000 represent stepped fixed costs. The flexible budget allowance for variable overheads is $38 556 (7140 hours × $5.40 per hour). The following budget statement provides more meaningful information:

	Original Budget	Flexed Budget	Actual	Variance	
Assembly labour hours	6400	7140	7140		
Variable costs	$	$	$	$	
Assembly labour	49 920	55 692	56 177	485	Adv
Furniture packs	224 000	249 900	205 000	44 900	Fav
Other materials	23 040	25 704	24 100	1604	Fav
Variable overheads	34 560	38 556	76 340	37 784	Adv
Total variable costs	331 520	369 852	361 617	8235	Fav
Departmental fixed costs					
Manager	2.050	2050	2050	—	
Overheads	18 500	27 000	27 000	—	
Total departmental fixed costs	20 550	29 050	29 050	—	
Central costs	9000	9000	9000		
	361 070	407 902	399 667	8235	Fav

(b)

(i) The revised statement is more helpful to management because it:
- Compares 'like with like'. That is, it compares the manager's performance based on the actual activity level and not the level of activity anticipated when the budget was set. Thus it is more appropriate to compare a manager's performance with a flexed budget rather than a fixed budget;
- Distinguishes between controllable and non-controllable items;
- Distinguishes between fixed and variable costs.

(i) It is assumed that all variable costs vary in relation to assembly hours but some, or all costs, may vary with other factors. For example, assembly and fitting may vary with size, complexity and value. Therefore the company should investigate the extent to which costs vary with other cost drivers and flex the budget on the basis of what causes the variations in costs.

(c) The answer should describe the benefits and limitations of budgeting as outlined in the section in Chapter 14 titled 'Participation in the budgeting and target setting process'.

14.19 (a)

(i) Activity varies from month to month, but quarterly budgets are set by dividing total annual expenditure by 4.

(ii) The budget ought to be analyzed by shorter intervals (e.g. monthly) and costs estimated in relation to monthly activity.

(iii) For control purposes monthly comparisons and cumulative monthly comparisons of planned and actual expenditure to date should be made.

(iv) The budget holder does not participate in the setting of budgets.

(v) An incremental budget approach is adopted. A zero-based approach would be more appropriate.

(vi) The budget should distinguish between controllable and uncontrollable expenditure.

(b) The information that should flow from a comparison of the actual and budgeted expenditure would consist of the variances for the month and year to date analyzed into the following categories:

(i) controllable and uncontrollable items;

(ii) price and quantity variances with price variance analyzed by inflationary and non-inflationary effects.

(c) (i) Flexible budgets should be prepared on a monthly basis. Possible measures of activity are number of patient days or expected laundry weight.

(ii) The laundry manager should participate in the budgetary process.

(iii) Costs should be classified into controllable and non-controllable items.

(iv) Variances should be reported and analyzed by price and quantity on a monthly and cumulative basis.

(v) Comments should be added explaining possible reasons for the variances.

14.20 *Task 1:*

Performance Statement – Month to 31 October
Number of guest days = Original budget   9600
          Flexed budget   11 160

	Flexed budget (£)	Actual (£)	Variance (£)
Controllable expenses			
Food (1)	23 436	20 500	2936F
Cleaning materials (2)	2232	2232	0
Heat, light and power (3)	2790	2050	740F
Catering staff wages (4)	8370	8400	30A
	36 828	33 182	3646F
Non-controllable expenses			
Rent, rates, insurance and depreciation (5)	1860	1860	0

Notes:

(1) £20 160/9 600 × 11 160.

(2) £1920/9 600 × 11 160.

(3) £2400/9 600 × 11 160.

(4) £11 160/40 × £30.

(5) Original fixed budget based on 30 days but October is a 31-day month (£1 800/30 × 31).

Task 2:

(a) See the sections on the multiple functions of budgets (motivation) in Chapter 13, and 'Setting financial performance targets' in Chapter 14 for the answers to this question.

(b) Motivating managers ought to result in improved performance. However, besides motivation, improved performance is also dependent on managerial ability, training, education and the existence of a favourable environment. Therefore motivating managers is not guaranteed to lead to improved performance.

(c) The use of a fixed budget is unlikely to encourage managers to become more efficient where budgeted expenses are variable with activity. In the original performance report actual expenditure for 11.160 guest days is compared with budgeted expenditure for 9600 days. It is misleading to compare actual costs at one level of activity with budgeted costs at another level of activity. Where the actual level of activity is above the budgeted level adverse variances are likely to be reported for variable cost items. Managers will therefore be motivated to reduce activity so that favourable variances will be reported. Therefore it is not surprising that Susan Green has expressed concern that the performance statement does not reflect a valid reflection of her performance. In contrast, most of Brian Hilton's expenses are fixed and costs will not increase when volume increases. A failure to flex the budget will therefore not distort his performance.

To motivate, challenging budgets should be set and small adverse variances should normally be regarded as a healthy sign and not something to be avoided. If budgets are always achieved with no adverse variances this may indicate that undemanding budgets may have been set which are unlikely to motivate best possible performance. This situation could apply to Brian Hilton who always appears to report favourable variances.

Chapter 15

15.15 (a) Material price $= (SP - AP)AQ = (AQ \times SP)$
$$- (AQ \times AP)$$
$$= (53\ 000\ \text{kg} \times £2.50)$$
$$-£136\ 000 = £3500A$$

Answer = (ii)

(b) Material usage $= (SQ - AQ)SP = (27\ 000 \times 2\text{kg}$
$$= 54\ 000\text{kg} - 53\ 000)£2.5 = £2500F$$

Answer = (i)

15.16 Wage rate = (SP − AP)AH = (AH × SP) − (AH × AP)
  = (14 000 × £10 = £140 000) − £176 000
  = £36 000A

Labour efficiency = (SH − AH)SP = (5500 × 3 hours
= 16 500 hours − 14 000 hours) × £10 = £25 000F
Answer = (d)

15.17 Standard cost = 31 000 repairs × 24/60 hours × $10.60
  = $131 440

Actual cost = $134 540 (standard cost plus adverse *labour* variance of $3100)

Actual labour hours = 12 400 (31 000 repairs × 0.4 hours) given that actual hours are the same as the standard hours due to a zero labour efficiency variance

Actual wage rate = $10.85 ($134 540/12 400 hours)

Answer = (c)

15.18 Idle time variance = Unproductive hours(5500)
  × Standard wage rate (£540 000/60 000 hours)
  = £49 500 Adverse

Labour efficiency variance = (standard productive hours − actual productive hours) × standard wage rate
[(14 650 × 60 000 hours/15 000 units) − 56 000]
× £9 = £23 400 Favourable

15.19 The fixed production overhead capacity variance is the difference between the budgeted hours of input (25 000) and the actual hours worked (i.e. 24 000 actual hours of input) multiplied by the hourly standard fixed production overhead cost rate ($5). Therefore the variance is $5000 adverse. Assuming that the shortfall in hours would have been at the standard level of efficiency less fixed overheads are absorbed. Therefore the variance is adverse so the answer is A.

15.20 Budgeted overhead − actual overhead = £1250
Actual overhead = 0.98 × Budgeted overhead
Budgeted overhead − (0.98 × Budgeted overhead)
= £1250
Budgeted overhead = £1250/0.02 = £62 500
Actual overhead = £62 500 − £1250 = £61 250
Answer = (a)

15.21 Over-absorbed fixed overheads will result in a favourable total fixed overhead variance. Only item B results in a favourable total fixed overhead variance.
Answer = (b)

15.22 **(a)** Sales price variance = (Actual selling price
  − budgeted selling price) × actual sales volume
  (£31 − £26) × 8200 = £41 000 Favourable
  (Answer = (ii))
Note that fixed overhead rate per unit is £4
(£34 800/8700)

(b) Sales volume = (Actual sales volume
  − budgeted sales volume) × Standard margin
  (8200 − 8700) × £12 = 6000 Adverse
  (Answer = (i))

(c) Fixed overhead volume = (Actual production
  − budgeted production) × standard fixed overhead rate
  (8200 − 8700) × £4 = £2000 Adverse
  (Answer = (i))

15.23 The sales margin volume variance is the difference between the budgeted sales volume and the actual sales volume multiplied by the standard contribution margin of £10. Because actual sales exceeded budgeted sales by 200 units the variance is £2000 favourable.
Answer = (c)

15.24 The sales volume profit variance is the difference between the budgeted sales volume (1000) and the actual sales volume (900) multiplied by the standard profit margin of £11 (£50 − £39). Therefore the variance is £1100.
Answer = (b)

15.25 **(a)** Total materials cost variance = (actual production × standard material cost per unit of production) − actual materials cost
= (26 000 × £20) − £532 800
= £12 800A

Total variable overhead variance = (actual production × standard variable overhead rate per unit) − actual variable overhead cost
= (26 000 × £24) − £614 000
= £10 000F

Wage rate variance = (standard wage rate per hour − actual wage rate) × actual labour hours worked
= (£8 − £1 221 000/150 000) × 150 000
= £21 000A

Labour efficiency variance = (standard quantity of labour hours for actual production − actual labour hours) × standard wage rate
= [(26 000 × 6 hours) − 150 000] × £8
= £48 000F

(b)

	£	£
Budgeted contribution [25 000 × (£120 − £920]		700 000
Sales price variance (W1)		5000A
Direct materials		12 800A
Total variable overhead production		10 000F
Direct labour rate	21 000A	
Direct labour efficiency	48 000F	
Total direct labour		2700F
Actual contribution (W2)		719 200

Workings

W1 Sales margin = (actual selling price − standard
price variance   selling price) × actual sales
               volume
             = [(£2 995 000/25 000) − £120] ×
               25 000
             = £5000A

W2	£	£
Actual sales		2 995 000
Actual costs:		
Materials	532 800	
Labour	1 221 000	
Production overhead	614 000	
	2 367 800	
Less closing stock at		
standard cost (1000 × £92)	92 000	
Variable cost of sales		2 275 800
Actual contribution		719 200

(c) The two variances may be related if more
skilled labour, paid at a higher wage rate than
that planned, was used. Higher skilled labour
may have been more efficient resulting in a
favourable efficiency variance, but the higher
wage rate would also have resulted in an
adverse wage rate variance.

15.26 (a)

Sales margin = (actual selling price − standard
price variance selling price) × actual sales volume
           = [(£731 000/34 000) − £22] × 34 000
           = £17 000A

Sales margin   = (actual sales volume − budgeted
volume variance sales volume) × standard
                contribution margin
           = (34 000 − 32 000) × £13
           = £26 000F

(b) The actual selling price was £0.50 less than the
budgeted selling price resulting in an adverse
sales margin price variance, whereas the actual
sales volume was 2000 units in excess of the
budget resulting in a favourable volume
variance. The increase in sales volume may
have been due to the reduction in the selling
price. Therefore the two variances are
interrelated and should be considered together
rather than in isolation.

(c)

	£
Budgeted contribution (32 000 × £13)	416 000
Less budgeted variable/marginal costing profit	200 000
Budgeted fixed costs	216 000
Less budgeted non production fixed costs	96 000
(£1 152 000/12)	
Budgeted fixed production costs	120 000
Budgeted fixed production cost per unit	4
(£120 000/30 000)	
Variable costing budgeted profit	200 000
Less fixed overheads included in decrease in	8000
stocks (2000 × £4) with the absorption costing	
system	
Absorption costing profit	192 000

15.27 *Preliminary calculations*

The standard product cost and selling price are
calculated as follows:

	(£)
Direct materials	
X (10 kg at £1)	10
Y (5 kg at £5)	25
Direct wages (5 hours × £8)	40
Standard variable cost	75
Contribution margin	75
Selling price	150

The actual profit for the period is calculated as
follows:

	(£)	(£)
Sales (9500 at £160)		1 520 000
Direct materials: X	115 200	
Y	225 600	
Direct wages (46 000 × £8.20)	377 200	
Fixed overhead	290 000	1 008 000
Actual profit		512 000

The variances are analyzed as follows:

	(£)	(£)
Material price variance:		
(standard price − actual price) × actual		
quantity		
X: (£1 − £1.20) × 96 000	19 200 A	
Y: (£5 − £4.70) × 48 000	14 440 F	4800A
Material usage variance:		
(standard quantity − actual quantity) ×		
standard price		
X: (9500 × 10 = 95 000 − 96 000) × £1	1000 A	
Y: (9500 × 5 = 47 500 − 48 000) × £5	2500 A	3500 A

The actual materials used are in standard
proportions. Therefore there is no mix variance.

Wage rate variance:
  (standard rate – actual rate) × actual
  hours
  (£8 – £8.20) × 46 000   9200 A
Labour efficiency variance:
  (standard hours – actual hours) ×
  standard rate
  (9500 × 5 = 47 500 – 46 000) × £8   12 000 F   2800 F
Fixed overhead expenditure:
  budgeted fixed overheads – actual fixed
  overheads
  (£300 000 – £290 000)   10 000 F
Sales margin price variance:
  (actual selling price– standard selling
  price) × actual sales volume
  (£160 – £150) × 9500   95 000 F
Sales margin volume variance:
  (actual sales volume – budgeted sales
  volume)
  × Standard margin
  (9500 – 10 000) × £75   37 500 A 57 500 F
Total variance   62 000 F

	(£)
Budgeted profit (10 000 units at £75)	750 000
Less budgeted fixed overheads	300 000
Budgeted profit	450 000
Add favourable variances (see above)	62 000
Actual profit	512 000

15.28 *(a) Standard product cost for one unit of product XY*

	(£)
Direct materials (8 kg (W2) at £1.50 (WI) per kg)	12.00
Direct wages (2 hours (W4) at £8 (W3) per hour)	16.00
Variable overhead (2 hours (W4) at £1 (W5) per hour)	2.00
	30.00

Workings

(WI) Actual quantity of materials purchased at standard price is £225 000
    (i.e. actual cost plus favourable material price variance).
        Therefore standard price = £1.50 (£225 000/150 000 kg).

(W2) Material usage variance = 6000 kg Adverse (£9000/£1.50
      standard price).
        Therefore standard quantity for actual production
        = 144 000 kg (150 000 – 6000 kg).
        Therefore standard quantity per unit = 8 kg
        (144 000 kg/18 000 units).

(W3) Actual hours worked at standard rate = £256 000
      (£264 000 – £8000 being an adverse variance).
        Therefore standard rate per hour = £8(£256 000/32 000
        hours).

(W4) Labour efficiency variance = 4000 hours Favourable
      (£32 000/£8).
        Therefore standard hours for actual production
        = 36 000 hours (32 000 + 4000).
        Therefore standard hours per unit
        = 2 hours (36 000 hours/18 000 units).

(W5) Actual hours worked at the standard variable overhead rate
      is £32 000 (£38 000 actual variable overheads less £6000
      favourable expenditure variance).
        Therefore, standard variable overhead rate
        = £1(£32 000/32 000 hours).

15.29 **(a)** Material price:
  (standard price – actual price) × actual quantity
  (£3 – £4) × 22 000   = £22 000 A
Material usage:
  (standard quantity – actual quantity) × standard price
  ((1400 × 15 = 21 000) – 22 000) × £3 = 3000 A
Wage rate:
  (standard rate – actual rate) × actual hours
  (£10 – £11) × 6800   = £6800 A
Labour efficiency:
  ((1400 × 5 = 7 000) – 6800) × £10   = £2000F
Fixed overhead expenditure:
  (budgeted fixed overheads – actual fixed overheads)
  (1000 × £5 = £5000 – £6000) = £1000 A
Volume efficiency:
  (standard hrs – actual hrs) × FOAR
  (1400 × 5 = 7000 – 6800) × £1   = 200 F
Volume capacity:
  (actual hrs – budgeted hrs) × FOAR
  (6800 – 5000) × £1   = £1800 F
Variable overhead efficiency:
  (standard hrs – actual hrs) × VOAR
  (7000 – 6800) × £2   = £400 F
Variable overhead expenditure:
  (flexed budgeted variable overheads – actual
  variable overheads)
  (6800 × £2 – £11 000) = £2600 F
Sales margin price:
  (actual selling price – standard selling
  price) × actual sales volume
  (£132 – £130) × 1200
Sales margin volume:
  (actual sales volume – budgeted
  sales volume) × standard margin
  (1200 – 1000) × £20   = 4000 F

Reconciliation of budgeted and actual profit

		(£)
Budgeted profit		20 000

	Adverse (£)	Favourable (£)
Sales margin price		2400
Sales margin volume		4000
Material price	22 000	
Material usage	3000	
Wage rate	6800	
Labour efficiency		2000
Fixed overhead expenditure	1000	
Fixed overhead efficiency		200
Fixed overhead capacity		1800
Variable overhead expenditure		2600
Variable overhead efficiency		400
	32 800	13 400

	(£)
Net adverse variance	19 400
Actual profit (W1)	600

Workings (W1)
The actual profit is calculated as follows:

	£	£
Sales (1200 × £132)		158 400
Less: Materials (22 000 × £4)	88 000	
Direct wages (6800 × £11)	74 800	
Variable overheads	11 000	
Fixed overheads	6000	
	179 800	
Less closing stocks (200 × £110)	22 000	
Cost of sales		157 800
Profit		600

(b)

Stores ledger control account

Creditors	66 000	WIP	63 000
		Material usage variance	3000
	66 000		66 000

Variance accounts

Creditors	22 000	Wages control (labour efficiency)	2000
Stores ledger (material usage)	3000	Fixed overhead (volume)	2000
Wages control (wage rate)	6800	Variable overhead (expenditure)	2600
Fixed overhead (expenditure)	1000	Variable overhead (efficiency)	400
		Costing P + L a/c (balance)	25 800
	32 800		32 800

Costing P + L account

Cost of sales	132 000	Sales	158 400
Variance account (net variances)	25 800		
Profit for the period	600		
	158 400		158 400

WIP control account

Stores ledger	63 000	Finished goods stock	154 000
Wages control	70 000		
Fixed factory overhead	7000		
Variable factory overhead	14 000		
	154 000		154 000

Wages control account

Wages accrued account	74 800	WIP	70 000
Labour efficiency variance	2000	Wage rate variance	6800
	76 800		76 800

Fixed factory overhead account

Expense creditors	6000	WIP	7000
Volume variance	2000	Expenditure variance	1000
	8000		8000

Variable factory overhead account

Expense creditors	11 000	WIP	14 000
Expenditure variance	2600		
Efficiency variance	400		
	14 000		14 000

Finished goods stock

WIP	154 000	Cost of sales	132 000
		Closing stock c/fwd	22 000
	154 000		154 000

Cost of sales account

Finished goods stock	132 000	Costing P + L a/c	132 000

INDEX